THE OXFORD HANDBOOK OF

BLACK HORROR FILM

THE OXFORD HANDBOOK OF

BLACK HORROR

FILM

Edited by

ROBIN R. MEANS COLEMAN

and

NOVOTNY LAWRENCE

OXFORD

UNIVERSITY PRESS

OXFORD
UNIVERSITY PRESS

Oxford University Press is a department of the University of Oxford. It furthers
the University's objective of excellence in research, scholarship, and education
by publishing worldwide. Oxford is a registered trade mark of Oxford University
Press in the UK and certain other countries.

Published in the United States of America by Oxford University Press
198 Madison Avenue, New York, NY 10016, United States of America.

© Oxford University Press 2025

CIP data is on file at the Library of Congress

ISBN 978-0-19-762480-7

DOI: 10.1093/oxfordhb/9780197624807.001.0001

Printed by Integrated Books International, United States of America

MIX
Paper
FSC   FSC® C183721

CONTENTS

SECTION III: GENDERED BLACKNESS

SECTION IV: THE HORRORS OF
CONTEMPORARY BLACKNESS

Notes on Contributors

Tessa Adams is a PhD candidate in the School of Journalism and Mass Communication at the University of Iowa. Her research addresses race and representation in film and television. She is particularly interested in the intersections of racism, sexism, and classism in "woke" horror productions. Prior to her time at the University of Iowa, Adams worked professionally in videography and was an adjunct faculty member.

Jamie Alvey is an educator and writer with a passion for acting and filmmaking. Her horror works range from analytical to creative and are award winning (and award losing as well). She is best known for her intersectional feminist horror explications and the screenplay *Bystanders*. She can be found online at jamiealvey.com.

Tiffany A. Bryant, MA, is an independent scholar with literary and cultural studies degrees from William & Mary and James Madison University. She has worked as an arts education content producer at the John F. Kennedy Center for the Performing Arts for over a decade. Her research focuses on intersectional identity representation in contemporary horror across film and TV, literary arts, and interactive media and events; and she is co-chair of the Horror Studies area of the National Popular Culture Association. Her work appears in publications such as film journal *Offscreen* and *Reading Richard Matheson: A Critical Survey* (Lanham, MD: Rowman & Littlefield, 2014).

Rachal Burton is an assistant professor of African American Literature, Thought, and Cultural Studies at California State Polytechnic University, Pomona. Her research and teaching interests include Black film and literature, Afropessimist theory, and critical disability studies. She is currently working on a book about the precarity of Black life in the work of Toni Morrison.

Robin R. Means Coleman is professor of Media Studies and of African American and African Studies at the University of Virginia. She is the Director of the Black Fantastic Media Research Lab. She is the author of *Horror Noire: A History of Black American Horror from the 1890s to Present*, 2nd ed.; *Horror Noire: Blacks in American Horror Films from the 1890s to Present*; and *African-American Viewers and the Black Situation Comedy: Situating Racial Humor*. She is co-author of *The Black Guy Dies First: Black Horror from Fodder to Oscar* and *Intercultural Communication for Everyday Life*, editor of *Say It Loud!: African American Audiences, Media, and Identity*; and co-editor of *Fight the Power!: The Spike Lee Reader*.

Ayanni C. H. Cooper is a visual rhetoric scholar whose research focuses on multi-modal texts, particularly comics and animation. She works for the Modern Language Association as a program associate in the department of Academic Program Services & Professional Development. Dr. Cooper's wider interests include monster theory, gender and sexuality studies, erotica and pornography studies, and podcasting. Her work can be found in both public and scholarly forums, including the *Los Angeles Review of Books* and the forthcoming *Horror Comics and Religion: Essays on Framing the Monstrous and the Divine* from McFarland. She also produces and co-hosts the podcast *Sex. Love. Literature.*, which takes a "semi-scholarly" look at why and how media representations of sex, love, and desire matter.

Byron B Craig, PhD, is an assistant professor in the School of Communication at Illinois State University. His research focuses on race, racism, and citizenship in American democracy. His work has appeared in journals such as *Cultural Studies⇔Critical Methodologies, The Journal of Religion and Communication, Journal of the Scholarship of Teaching and Learning*, as well as edited volumes such as *The Gig Economy: Workers and Media in the Age of Convergence* (London: Routledge, 2021) and *Beyonce in the World: Making Meaning with Queen Bey in Troubled Times* (Middletown, CT: Wesleyan University Press, 2021). He is currently editing (along with Stephen E. Rahko and Patricia Davis) *Rupturing Post-Racial Fantasies: The Rhetorical Politics of Race and American Popular Culture since the Ferguson Uprisings* (Jackson: University Press of Mississippi). Dr. Craig is also a Fellow with the American Democracy Project and Faculty Fellow and chair of the Committee on LGBTQIA + Policies and Initiatives at Illinois State University.

Mark H. Harris is co-author of *The Black Guy Dies First: Black Horror Cinema from Fodder to Oscar* (New York: Saga Press, 2023) and has worked for more than 20 years as an entertainment journalist. He has written about cinema and pop culture for *New York Magazine*, Vulture.com, Rotten Tomatoes, About.com, PopMatters, Abertoir Horror Festival, Salem Horror Fest, and Napster, in addition to penning the liner notes for the vinyl reissue of the soundtrack to the film *Lord Shango* (Tidal Waves Music) and the U.K. Blu-ray release of the French horror movie *Frontier(s)* (Second Sight Films). In 2005, he created the website BlackHorrorMovies.com, the premier online source chronicling the history of Black representation and achievement in horror cinema, and he is a featured commentator in the acclaimed documentary *Horror Noire* and the Shudder series *Behind the Monsters*.

Estefanía Hermosilla Órdenes is a doctoral candidate in American Studies at the University of Santiago de Chile, Chile, and received a Master in Pedagogy at the National Autonomous University of Mexico and Professor of Philosophy at the University of Chile. Her research focuses on Latin American horror films directed by women and dissidents and analyzes terror from a gender perspective that makes visible how the marks of gender, race, class, gender identity, and sexuality define the ways in which fear is experienced and exercised. She has published in various academic journals on Latin

American horror literature and cinema with an emphasis on contemporary women writers and directors.

Jennessa Hester is a transgender scholar and poet working out of Lubbock, Texas. Her work focuses on the intersection of embodiment, personal identity, community identity, and various forms of classical and cutting-edge media. In addition to research, Hester is a managing editor for the *Iron Horse Literary Review*, assistant editor for the *Journal of Cinema and Media Studies*, and poetry editor for *Wrong Publishing*.

Colleen Karn is an associate professor of English and Humanities at Methodist College. Her scholarship focuses on monsters, horror, othering, and pedagogy. She is the recipient of the William M. Jones Award for her work "Cultural and Linguistic Misrepresentations in Disney's *The Princess and the Frog*." She also serves as Chair of the Popular Culture Association's Governing Board.

Novotny Lawrence is the Director of the Black Film Center & Archive and an associate professor of Cinema and Media Studies at Indiana University. His research focuses on Black cinematic/mediated experiences and popular culture, and he is the author of *Blaxploitation Films of the 1970s: Blackness and Genre* (New York: Routledge, 2008), the editor of *Documenting the Black Experience: Essays on African-American History, Culture, and Identity in Non-Fiction Films* (Jefferson, NC: McFarland, 2014), and the co-editor of *Beyond Blaxploitation* (Detroit, MI: Wayne State University Press, 2019). Lawrence has published book chapters and journal articles on a number of subjects, including, *C.S.A.: The Confederate States of America*, *Black Dynamite* (2009), and *Get Out* (2017), and he is the editor-in-chief of *The Journal of Popular Culture*.

Kristen Leer is a doctoral student specializing in media psychology in the Communication and Media graduate program at the University of Michigan–Ann Arbor. Leer's research investigates the intersectional relationship between trauma, media, and culture, specifically among the digital spaces of marginalized racial/ethnic communities. She has extended her research in trauma representations to the horror cinema, evaluating how the genre's narratives depict racially marginalized identities and trauma.

Adam Lowenstein is a professor of English and Film/Media Studies at the University of Pittsburgh, where he also directs the Horror Studies Working Group. He is the author of *Horror Film and Otherness* (New York: Columbia University Press, 2022), *Dreaming of Cinema: Spectatorship, Surrealism, and the Age of Digital Media* (New York: Columbia University Press, 2015), and *Shocking Representation: Historical Trauma, National Cinema, and the Modern Horror Film* (New York: Columbia University Press, 2005). His essays have appeared in *Cinema Journal*, *Representations*, *Film Quarterly*, *Critical Quarterly*, *Discourse*, and numerous anthologies. He serves on the board of directors for the George A. Romero Foundation.

Mia Mask is the Mary Riepma Ross Professor of Film at Vassar College, where she teaches African American cinema, documentary history, and genre courses. She is the author of *Divas on Screen: Black Women in American Film* (Urbana: University of Illinois Press, 2009). Mask edited the anthology *Contemporary Black American Cinema*, and she published the jointly edited collection *Poitier Revisited: Reconsidering a Black Icon in the Obama Age* (New York: Bloomsbury, 2015). She has written film reviews and covered festivals for IndieWire.com, *The Village Voice, Film Quarterly, Time Out New York, The Poughkeepsie Journal*, and *The Philadelphia Inquirer*. Her criticism was anthologized in *Best American Movie Writing*. Her cultural commentary has been featured on National Public Radio programs *Tell Me More, Marketplace*, and *Morning Edition*, as well as in documentaries for the Smithsonian Channel, the Criterion Channel, and CNN's *The Movies*. More recently, she published *Black Rodeo: A History of the African American Western*.

Tony Quick is a Black American scholar pursuing his PhD in Rhetoric and Professional Communication at Iowa State University. His research focuses on U.S. presidential rhetoric, popular culture, and social circulation theory. Quick received his Bachelor of Arts degree in English with a minor in African Diaspora Studies from St. Mary's College of Maryland. He earned his Master of Fine Arts in Creative Writing from North Carolina State University. He is currently on a self-imposed hiatus from social media.

Stephen E. Rahko, PhD, is an assistant professor in the School of Communication at Illinois State University. His research focuses on the challenges posed by the intersection of capitalism and race for American democracy. His work has appeared in journals such as *Cultural Studies⇔Critical Methodologies* as well as in edited volumes such as *The Gig Economy: Workers and Media in the Age of Convergence* (London: Routledge, 2021) and in *Beyoncé in the World: Making Meaning with Queen Bey in Troubled Times* (Middletown, CT: Wesleyan University Press, 2021). He is currently editing (along with Byron B Craig and Patricia Davis) *Rupturing Post-Racial Fantasies: The Rhetorical Politics of Race and American Popular Culture since the Ferguson Uprisings* with the University Press of Mississippi.

Maillim Santiago is a film scholar and cultural theorist. Her work focuses on using cinema as a cultural studies tool for underdeveloped film economies in the Caribbean. She holds a BFA in Film Production from the University of Central Florida. Santiago produced *Little Girls* (2013) as her undergraduate thesis film as part of a study of teen films and the effect they have on female teen societies. She earned her MFA in Digital Entrepreneurial Cinema from the University of Central Florida, where she created *Nightgaze* (2017), a "visual album" based in music video theory to depict a young woman's visceral experience with depression. She has contributed work to *MAI: Feminism & Visual Culture and Film Criticism*. Santiago currently hosts and writes the foreign horror–based podcast, *Horrorspiria*. She is pursuing a PhD in George Mason University's Cultural Studies program with a focus on Puerto Rico and the legitimization of its national cinema.

Dominique Shank is currently a PhD candidate in English at the University of California, Irvine. Her research areas include nineteenth- and twentieth-century gothic literature, Black Atlantic studies, television, and film. Her dissertation project, *Grotesque Realism: Gothic Genealogies of Black Horror*, traces the conversion of Black gothic horror through key historical stages. She turns to speculative fiction, epistolary novellas, legends, historical records, slave narratives, and visual texts that rely on the gothic mode to allegorize the horrors of gratuitous racialized violence, long-suffering, abjection, compulsory labor, and bodily dispossession. Further, she highlights the resistance, resiliency, and redress Black horror fabulates.

G. E. Subero is a researcher in Visual Cultures and Intersectional Studies at Imperial College London. His work focuses on queer citizenship, body politics, and gendered bodies in film, media, and the arts in Latin America, the Caribbean, and the Hispanic diaspora. More recently, his work has focused on the gender and sexual dynamics of horror cinema in these regions. He is currently working on a manuscript that investigates depictions of disability in cinema, television, and visual arts and how artists and creators explore health stigmas through their visual works. He is the author of *Queer Masculinities in Latin American Cinema* (London: I.B. Tauris, 2014), *Representations of HIV/AIDS in Contemporary Hispano-American and Caribbean Culture* (Surrey, UK: Ashgate, 2014), and *Gender and Sexuality in Latin American Horror Cinema* (London: Palgrave Macmillan, 2016).

Valeria Villegas Lindvall is a senior lecturer in Film Studies at the University of Gothenburg and specializes in Latin American horror film with a feminist and decolonial focus. She is also reviews editor for the journal *MAI: Feminism and Visual Culture* and member of the Advisory Board of MAI Imprint at Punctum Books. She has collaborated on several publications, most prominently as a co-editor, writer, and translator at *Rolling Stone Mexico*, as well as *Women Make Horror: Filmmaking, Feminism and Genre* (New Brunswick, NJ: Rutgers University Press, 2020), *The Body Onscreen in the Digital Age. Essays on Voyeurism, Violence and Power* (Jefferson, NC: McFarland, 2021), and *Folk Horror: New Global Pathways* (Cardiff, UK: University of Wales Press, 2023), among others.

James Wierzbicki is an essayist and cultural historian. Before embarking on an academic career (teaching musicology at the University of California, Irvine, the University of Michigan, and the University of Sydney), for more than 20 years, he served as chief classical music critic for the *St. Louis Post-Dispatch* and other U.S. newspapers. His books include *Film Music: A History* (New York: Routledge, 2009), *Elliott Carter* (Urbana: University of Illinois Press, 2012), *Music in the Age of Anxiety: American Music in the Fifties* (Urbana: University of Illinois Press, 2016), *Terrence Malick: Sonic Style* (New York: Routledge, 2019), and *When Music Mattered: American Music in the Sixties* (New York: Palgrave Macmillan, 2022).

INTRODUCTION

ROBIN R. MEANS COLEMAN AND
NOVOTNY LAWRENCE

ON February 24, 2017, Jordan Peele's *Get Out* opened in theaters to rave reviews. *Slate* critic Aisha Harris summarized: "In hitting that sweet spot between scary and hilarious, and laying bare the many layers of America's historic treatment of the black body, *Get Out* could soon land an enduring spot on the syllabi of many a college course, alongside both *Rosemary's Baby* and *Between the World and Me*."[1] In another review emblematic of *Get Out*'s nearly uniform, glowing, critical reception, NPR's Bob Mondello praised Peele's satirical and subversive prowess, before contending: "As a writer and a remarkably accomplished first-time director, Peele layers other notions on top as he's inverting those—about servitude, about social privilege, about law enforcement and *Guess Who's Coming To Dinner*–style liberals."[2]

As the critical reviews elucidate, *Get Out* is a multi-layered horror feature that taps into and articulates the United States' historic and 2017 racial zeitgeist. Consequently, after its release, many people thought Peele's film was a commentary on the 2016 presidential campaign, during which the Republican candidate, mediocre businessman and former reality TV star Donald Trump, disparaged women, Blacks, undocumented immigrants, and people with disabilities, among others. That he lost the popular vote but rode the Electoral College into the White House struck fear in the hearts of many U.S. citizens who fully recognized that Trump's brand of conservatism would have catastrophic sociopolitical and economic ramifications and potentially cost people their lives. To say the least, it was a *horrific* development for many people in the United States and around the world more broadly.

While *Get Out* certainly resonated more loudly than it may otherwise have in Trump's United States, Peele actually conceived of the film in 2008, after Barack Obama secured the White House. In the aftermath of his historic election, a segment of pundits, Republicans, news organizations, and everyday citizens cited his ascendance into the presidency as proof that the United States had transformed into a colorblind or post-racial utopia. Of course, those claims were ludicrous and proven false by numerous acts of anti-Black racism—Trayvon Martin, Rekia Boyd, Tamir Rice, Sandra Bland—that caused national outrage during Obama's presidency, as each victim's unwarranted death revealed that, at times, existing while Black is horrifying. Thus, *Get Out* is Peele's reverberating response to the post-racial fallacy. As he explained in an interview with NPR's Terry Gross, "It was very important to me to just get the entire audience in touch in some way with the fears inherent [in] being black in this country,"[3] an ambitious task for a film shot on a paltry $4.5 million budget.

Yet, in recounting the story of Chris (Daniel Kaluuya), a young Black man who finds himself in peril when he accompanies his white girlfriend, Rose (Allison Williams), on a weekend trip to meet her liberal parents at their country home, Peele accomplishes, and arguably exceeds, his cinematic and socio-political goals. In addition to the over-whelmingly positive reviews, *Get Out*'s box-office performance further demonstrates the extent to which it resonated with audiences. It opened as the number one film in the United States, grossing $33 million, and hauled in $28 million, $20 million, and $13 million over weeks two, three, and four, respectively.[4] It continued its impressive domestic run, remaining in the top 10 for 51 straight days, and it also defied Hollywood's racist, economic assumptions that Black films (read as Blackness) do not perform well with overseas audiences. In *The Hollywood Jim Crow*, Maryann Erigha highlights conversations between white industry executives who consistently rely on "sincere fictions" that allow them to blame outside parties—in this case, international audiences—to justify their discriminatory behaviors toward and lack of investment in Black films.[5] International moviegoers countered the execs' anti-Black economic logic, accounting for nearly $80 million, or over 30 percent of *Get Out*'s cumulative box office gross ($255,745,157 world-wide).[6] Hence, the film became an additional entry on the list of Black films that clearly illustrate that global audiences will flock to theaters to watch *good* movies, regardless of the lead actors' racial and ethnic backgrounds.

Clearly, *Get Out*'s critical reviews and worldwide box-office performance demonstrate that the modestly budgeted horror film, directed by a former member of a comedy duo, was a massive success. However, that the Academy of Motion Picture Arts and Sciences nominated it for three Oscars—Best Actor, Best Director, and Best Original Screenplay—is also noteworthy.[7] Even though horror, like other genres, addresses a range of important topics such as religious practices and beliefs, the importance of science, our treatment of "the foreign," gender and sexual identities, power and control, socio-political ideologies, good and evil, the monstrous, and (identity-based) violence, in the United States and abroad, the genre "has at times been marred by its 'B-movie,' low-budget, and/or exploitative reputation."[8] As a result, as Hutchings writes, it is easy to belittle horror consumers: "one way of denigrating the horror genre is to denigrate its audiences . . . by arguing that the only people who could actually enjoy this sort of thing are either sick or stupid (or sick and stupid)."[9]

Significantly, as Henry Jenkins writes, the "politics of race" in the horror genre has become a "hot topic."[10] Indeed, in the United States, Black horror or horror noire is increasingly visible in theaters, across streaming platforms, on television, and on websites such as Married to Horror, The Famuan, and Rotten Tomatoes that discuss or focus on the current "Black horror renaissance." With *Get Out* and his successful follow-ups, *Us* (2019) and *Nope* (2022), Peele, perhaps single-handedly, re-ignited mainstream interest in horror noire, a film genre that is (often) created by Black image-makers, stars Black actors, and features stories that emerge out of Blackness, not seen since the golden Blaxploitation age of horror that gave us cult classics such as *Blacula* (dir. William Crain, 1972), *Scream, Blacula, Scream* (dir. Bob Keljan, 1973), and *Sugar Hill* (dir. Paul Malansky, 1974). Peele's horror contributions are not limited to the films he has directed, as his production company, Monkey Paw, has gifted fans a racially infused incarnation of *The Twilight Zone* (2019–2020), the critically acclaimed and award-winning HBO series *Lovecraft Country* (creator, Misha Green, 2020), and the somewhat divisive *Candyman* (dir. Nia DaCosta, 2021), co-penned by Peele, Win Rosenfeld, and Nia DaCosta. Other film and media makers have also contributed to the Black horror boom, with projects such as *Sweetheart* (dir. J. D. Dillard, 2019), *Antebellum* (dirs. Gerard Bush and Christopher Renz, 2020), *Bad Hair* (dir. Justin Simien, 2020), *Them* (creator, Little Marvin, 2021), and *Kindred* (creator, Brandon Jacobs-Jenkins, 2022), among many others.

In the midst of what appears to be a Black horror renaissance, that is, the horror audience's renewed focus on race politics—identity, political discourses and policies, the social, and the cultural—it is imperative to note that horror noire has been relentlessly present, as horror fans and those interested in novel Black stories have always and continue to appreciate the genre.[11] The voluminous output of Black horror movies over the decades speaks to audiences' unquenchable appetites for the art form. For example, journalist and curator of the website BlackHorrorMovies.com, Mark Harris, presents a comprehensive catalog of Black horror, listing over 360 horror noire films made in the United States and the United Kingdom between 2010 and 2023 alone. Film scholars such as Novotny Lawrence, Brooks Hefner, and Chris Sieving focus on Blaxploitation-era horror noire, and Robin R. Means Coleman's *Horror Noire* body of scholarship (the 2011 and 2023 books, 2019 documentary, and 2019 *Horror Noire* syllabus) further illustrate the sustained production of and interest in horror noire. While the *Horror Noire* books focus on Blacks in U.S. horror, mentioning the U.K.'s *Attack the Block* (2011) and *The Girl with All the Gifts* (2016), and the *Horror Noire* documentary gestures toward Black horror from other countries, this output also indicates that much of what we know about horror noire emerges from Western discourses.

The United States looms large in defining the world's understandings of horror noire. For example, through the 1990s, "racial repackaging" of horror films for home video and international distribution (notably years after the original film was made) was not uncommon. To illustrate, the 1970s film *The Beast Must Die* (dir. Paul Annett, 1974) was later redistributed as *Black Werewolf*, and *Ganja & Hess* (dir. Bill Gunn, 1973) became *Black Vampire* and, still later, *Black Out*. Oddly, as Black characters in U.S. films are either erased or diminished in some international marketing campaigns, for their movies from other genres such as comedy, drama, and science fiction (e.g., *Couples Retreat* [dir. Peter Billingsly, 2009], *12 Years a Slave* [dir. Steve McQueen, 2013], *Star Wars: The Force Awakens* [dir. J. J. Abrams, 2015], *Black Panther* [dir. Ryan Coogler, 2018]), horror has been known to either "lean" into Blackness or even "blacken" non-Black movies. For instance, the poster for *Blacula* plays upon whites' fears of interracial intimacy by featuring the eponymous character biting a white woman on the neck, even though that does not happen in the film.[12] Further, the marketing team for *Nurse Sherri* (dir. Al Adamson, 1978), a low-budget, white-nurse-is-possessed film, changed the poster to center a Black star and renamed it *Black Voodoo*.[13]

It is unsurprising that studios rebranded *Nurse Sherri* as a Black voodoo horror movie, as films from around the globe consistently use religion to portray Blackness. As Coleman and Harris cheekily observe of Caribbean-themed films: "When a horror movie takes place in the Caribbean, you can usually count on it featuring either: (a) Black people as Big Bads who menace/murder the mostly white characters through voodoo-y means or (b) ancillary and often anonymous Black people who themselves fall prey to a Big Bad, be it a human killer or some such tropical creature, like a mutant mahi-mahi."[14] The Italian film *Il Dio Serpente* (*The Snake God*, dir. Piero Vivarelli, 1970), the U.S.-made and filmed-in-Jamaica *Zombie Island Massacre* (dir. John N. Carter, 1984), the U.S.-made and filmed-in-Santo Domingo, Dominican Republic *The Serpent and the Rainbow* (dir. Wes Craven, 1988), and *Ritual* (dir. Michael Evanichko, 2001), a U.S. production filmed in Jamaica but made for foreign release beginning with the Philippines and Japan in 2003 and 2006, respectively, exemplify the cinematic evil voodoo tradition.[15]

The issue is not merely the ways in which interconnected narratives emerge, such as the United States' view of Black countries which are then distributed back to them and to other countries around the world. More confounding is the way in which such practices may also spark the appropriation and stripping bare of non-Western cinema. Left out of the conversation, then, are the horror narratives and tropes that have been created for or by the Black diaspora.

The overdetermination of Western Black horror and the neglect of Black horror from across the diaspora mean that there is still much to be learned about how Blackness shows up in horror films from other parts of the globe. In *Horror International*, Schneider and Williams (2005) put a finer point on the implications of the prominence of the United States in film criticism and scholarship:

> The dominance of American film production and the ready availability of U.S. films from all periods may have gone a long way toward engendering the disproportionate critical focus on this nation's cinematic horror. But at the levels of style, technique, and narrative form, the influence of U.S. horror filmmaking practices, formulas, and (sub) generic conventions has by no means been unidirectional.[16]

It is the disruption of the "disproportionate" attention to the United States and other parts of the West (e.g., Hammer films of the United Kingdom and Bava and Argento films of Italy), the study of a "cross-cultural exchange" of filmmaking, and the centering Blackness from around the globe that drives this book.

North America and Europe produce numerous horror films that center Blackness. The book *Horror Noire: A History of Black American Horror from the 1890s to Present* catalogs hundreds of U.S. films (and a few U.K. entries) that reflect on Blackness. Likewise, European horror is abundant and has the honor of producing some of the most acclaimed horror films, from the influential *Nosferatu* (Germany, dir. F. W. Murnau, 1922) to classics *Les Diaboliques* (France, dir. Henri-Georges Clouzot, 1955), *Suspiria* (Italy, dir. Dario Argento, 1977), and *Let the Right One In* (Sweden, dir. Tomas Alfredson, 2008), to name a very few. Nonetheless, as Hudson argues in *Vampires, Race, and Transnational Hollywood*, even in the absence of Blackness, "making race" strange through "multicultural" whiteness prevails.[17]

Some U.K. horror films, however, have worked to avoid immediately centering whiteness through its Black characters or their histories. Namely, *Attack the Block* (dir. Joe Cornish, 2011), with its Black teen-hero Moses, and *The Girl with All the Gifts* (dir. Colm McCarthy, 2016), with its inquisitive, smart, bloodthirsty tween Melanie, are evidence that Black people can carry a film while bringing with them signifiers of their racial and cultural histories and mores.

By contrast, Canadian offerings are at the precipice of figuring out the role of Blackness in its films. Black characters often appear confined to recognizable tropes in a range of films in which Blackness is invoked through references to Haiti and voodoo (e.g., *Zombie Nightmare*, dir. Jack Bravman, 1987). Still, films like *Cube* (dir. Vincenzo Natali, 1997) provide meaty roles for Black performers while prompting questions about how horrific behaviors are perceived when performed by Black people. Canada has also benefited from cross-cultural influences. For example, the U.S. film *Night of the Living Dead* (dir. George A. Romero, 1968), with its Black hero, Ben, continues to inspire, as seen in Canada's lacking, copycat offering *Zombie Night* (dir. David J. Francis, 2003). *Zombie Night*, however, not only increases the number of Black humans and zombies but overtly hails Black culture, thereby rejecting notions of colorblind casting.

Rivaling the United States in its attention to Blackness in horror are those films emanating from the continent of Africa. "Nollywood," a portmanteau of "Nigerian" and "Hollywood," represents an industry of movies across genres that is so prolific that at one time the now-defunct U.K. network Nollywoodmovies.tv aired 30 new films per night! Nollywood horror films are noted for their Christian religiosity, amalgamated with the supernatural, which opens the door for tales about good and evil, with the devil, spirits, and practices such as black magic all being the wellspring of horror. Notable titles include *Karishika* (dir. Christian Onu, 1996), *Blood Sister* (dir. Tchidi Chikere, 2003), *Oracle* (dir. Andy Amenechi, 1998), *Sakobi: The Snake Girl* (dir. Zeb Ejiro, 1998), *Secret Room* (dir. Chris Eneaji Eneng, 2013), *Trip to Hell* (dir. Leila Djansi, 2014), and *Nneka: The Pretty Serpent* (dir. Tosin Igho, 2020), among many others. Nigeria's industry is one of the most lucrative businesses on the continent: "The Nigerian film industry is indisputably diversifying its economy by creating jobs in a country that depends principally on oil and agriculture. Nollywood is the most popular on the African continent and it produces an estimated $590ml in annual revenue."[18] South Africa, Egypt, Burkina Faso, Algeria, Morocco, and Somalia, to name a few countries, are also receiving international acclaim for their productions.

Further, South and Latin American filmmakers have made a number of horror films that push the traditional boundaries of the genre while upholding many of its standardized conventions. For instance, *Cronos* (dir. Guillermo del Toro, Mexico, 1993) and *Eterna Sangre* (dir. Jorge Olguín, Chile, 2002) approach vampire mythology differently, attributing the characters' bloodlust to an ancient artifact and a role-playing game, respectively. Other South and Latin American horror films include *Esta Noite Encarnarei no Teu Cadáver* (dir. José Mojica Morins, Brazil, 1967), *Al final del espectro* (dir. Jaun Filipe Orozco, Colombia, 2006), *La casa muda* (dir. Gustavo Hernández, Uruguay, 2010), and *Aterrados* (dir. Demián Rigna, Buenos Aires, 2017), among others. Yet, questions abound: Do these films center Blackness? Do the filmmakers engage in Black erasure and tokenism? Or, are representations of Blackness in South and Latin American horror films a complex mixture of representational practices?

While Australian industry execs, at times, "believe that horror is best done by Americans and Europeans," the country has not shied away from venturing into the genre. Like the remote landscapes of the Antarctic and some of Canada's provinces, the Australian bush and its Aboriginal people are deployed to heighten anxieties in which sparseness and people of color are united to form eerie, if not racist, excess, akin to the global obsession with jungles, Blacks, and voodoo. Nonetheless, the landscape is changing, as Indigenous filmmakers inspired by the success of *Get Out* are celebrating that films featuring people of color can be successful no matter where they originate:

> Jordan Peele is such an inspiration because he's hit the mainstream, but also because he's an amazing writer. And it just goes to show that people of colour—our stories are important and are resonating in the mainstream but can also sell in the mainstream. . . . The Djaru woman from the Halls Creek area in the East Kimberley is one of five Indigenous directors behind the 75-minute *Dark Place* horror anthology that will screen as part of Freak Me Out at the Sydney Film Festival. Her short film, *Scout*, is a revenge tale about a young woman who was kidnapped and held prisoner, seen through the lens of horror.[19]

The point is, the study of Blackness in horror, then, is neither merely about representations nor the presence or absence of stereotypes. As writer and cultural critic Sezin Koehler (e.g., *Huffington Post, Al Jazeera, Black Girl Nerds*) advised regarding this project, Blackness in this context is not only specific to "folks of the African diaspora and their descendants around the world, [but also, for example] Indigenous Australian perspectives and Desis in the UK . . . since they are often labeled/called Black even when not of African descent."[20]

Enter *The Oxford Handbook of the Black Horror Film*, which presents carefully curated, sophisticated, innovative, argument-driven research that brings to bear the most enlightened reflections upon Black horror's place in the world. Black creators and characters and Black stories have featured prominently in the genre globally and across cultures, and at the same time, we fully recognize that as a construct, "Blackness" is interpreted, exists, manifests, and means very different things depending on the locations from which it is addressed. With that in mind, the contributors explore, globally, Black horror cinema, across media platforms (e.g., theatrical releases, streaming services, etc.), interrogating Blackness in films from four continents—North America, South America, Europe, and Australia. The scholars here think expansively about

Blackness as a subject, pushing its boundaries and our understandings of the ways in which Blackness in horror is produced, seen, and shapes meanings. The questions that the authors take up are as pressing as they are illuminating. How are taxonomies of race presented? Who is considered Black? How is Blackness constructed in the culture(s) in which it is produced and/or distributed? What textual role does Blackness play in horror? They work to answer these queries and more through explorations of the most powerful themes, which include transgression, liberation, and subversion. Such inclusiveness invites more obvious sources of Black horror and also disrupts privileging cultural and sociopolitical geographic orientations.

Rather than country or continent, this volume is divided into four sections by themes that intersect, given that across the globe Blackness is bound up in nations' histories, colonialism, oppression, power, politics, economics, social norms, and resistance, among other factors. The first section, "Black Visual Culture Power," focuses on the cinema's profound influence in constructing sustained Black images, be they authentic, distorted, or metaphoric manifestations thereof. Novotny Lawrence and Robin R. Means Coleman's "Historicized Traumas: Black Art in Nia DaCosta's *Candyman*" centers on a personal interview with Trinidadian-born interdisciplinary artist and Northwestern professor Sherwin Ovid, who painted six of the pieces featured in DaCosta's sequel. Their chapter examines the ways in which artists and filmmakers use their agency to harness visual culture to meaningfully memorialize, meditate on, and recoup the Black traumatic.

In "The Politics of Black: Women's Identity as Monstrous Fetishism in Early Hollywood Horror Cinema," Gus Subero continues this robust examination, highlighting the ways in which early cinema employs Blackness to portray monstrosity and justify (post)colonial domination of people of African descent across the African-Caribbean diaspora. He focuses on George Terwilliger's *Ouanga* (1936) and *The Devil's Daughter* (1939), and Roy William Neill's *Black Moon* (1934), demonstrating how the directors conflate white femininity (portrayed as victimized damsels) and Black masculinity (portrayed as erotically raw, untamed and monstrous). In doing so, Subero argues that the films' ambivalent representations of race, gender, and monstrosity are attempts to reaffirm (post)colonial subjugation of the West over the "monstrous" other.

Estefanía Hermosilla Órdenes shifts to Latin America in "Colonial Terrors in *Trabalhar Cansa* and *As Boas Maneiras* by Juliana Rojas-Marcos Dutra: The Negritude as the Stain That Corrodes It All," providing insight into constructions of Blackness in Brazilian horror films. She focuses on Juliana Rojas and Marcos Dutra's, *Trabalhar Cansa* (*Hard Labor*, 2011) and *As Boas Maneiras* (*Good Manners*, 2017), both of which position horror as an experience profoundly entrenched with Brazil's colonial past. Using Mabel Moraña's scholarship about the monster in Latin America and the Caribbean and María Lugones's and Rita Segato's research on decolonial feminism, Hermosilla Órdenes sheds light on how the women characters' fears illustrate different expressions and intensity of the horror between the Black women and the white women as well as how they connect to Brazil's patriarchal, white, capitalist regime.

Mark Harris lends further insight into Latin American cinema in "Visible Blackness in Twenty-First-Century Brazilian Horror Cinema." As he explains, Brazil has a long and tumultuous history with race that extends from slavery to sanctioned prejudicial policies to informal discrimination that resulted in vast and enduring racial wealth and income gaps. While its citizens dispute the many designations within Brazil's multi-tiered racial caste system, it is indisputable that the inequity among the races consistently finds white Brazilians at the top and Black Brazilians at the bottom. Harris elucidates the ways in which this disparity has found its way into the nation's horror cinema, particularly within the past decade. He analyzes a selection of Brazilian horror movies—*O Anjo da Noite* (*The Angel of the Night*, dir. Walter Hugo Khouri, 1974), *Los Inocentes* (*The Innocents*, dir. Mauricio Brunetti, 2015), *O Diablo Mora Aqui* (*The Devil Lives Here*, dirs. Rodrigo Gasparini and Dante Vescio, 2016), *As Boas Maneiras* (*Good Manners*), and *O Nó do Diabo* (*The Devil's Knot*, dirs. Ramon Porto Mota, Jhésus Tribuzi, Ian Abé, Gabriel Martins, 2018)—laying bare the plight of Black Brazilians' struggles for social and economic equality, their increasing prominence in the country's horror films reflective of the rise of twenty-first-century Afrocentrism and movements against systemic racism that have taken root within Black populations around the world.

In "*Get*(ting) *Out* of the American Dream/Nightmare," Mia Mask uses abjection, post-colonial, and psychoanalytic theories to examine Jordan Peele's *Get Out*. Particularly, she illustrates how Peele's multi-layered horror movie spoofs Stanley Kramer's interracial-romance-social problem film, *Guess Who's Coming to Dinner* (1967), privileging Black masculinity in the process. Mask contends that by doing so, Peele subverts the horror genre's proclivity to center vulnerable, white women protagonists, a move that forces multi-racial audiences to grapple with the very real horrors of existing while Black in the United States and abroad.

The second section of this book, "Which Way the Black People?" interrogates Black representations, otherness, and racial anxieties. In "Horrific Indigeneity," James Wierzbicki continues the discussion of Blackness or "Aboriginal scariness" and Aboriginal people's limited visibility in Australian Gothic films such as *Walkabout* (dir. Nicolas Roeg, 1971), *Until the End of the World* (dir. Wim Wenders, 1991), and *Primal* (dir. Josh Reed, 2010), among others. Additionally, he discusses *The Last Wave* (dir. Peter Weir, 1977), demonstrating its visual, verbal, and sonic approaches to conveying the nature of fear that white Australians often exhibit when encountering certain aspects of the nation's Indigenous Black culture.

Adam Lowenstein also examines Australian cinema in "Dreaming of Blackness: Horror and Aboriginal Australia in *The Last Wave*," a chapter that positions Peter Weir's film as a much-needed cinematic intervention that disrupts the suffering of and othering of Aboriginal people as monstrous. This chapter works as an intellectual counterpoint of sorts to the previous chapter, as Lowenstein argues that the conceptual frame of "Blackness" helps refigure *The Last Wave*'s cinematic achievements, as the film cuts against notions of "Aboriginal people as others," transforming them from horrifying figures to sources of knowledge. Further, he illustrates that the horror stems from *The*

Last Wave's white Australian protagonist's inability to recognize his own *need* for the Aboriginal people, a point Weir hammers home through cinematic devices that simulate a nightmarishly dream-like state that encompasses viewers as well as the protagonist.

Dominique Shank forays into zombie horror, focusing on the creatures as representations of Blackness in "Zombie Roar: Slow Horror, Banal Supernaturalism, and Colonial Memory." Generally born from human irresponsibility, science gone awry, or radioactive meteorites, among other elements, zombies as often presented in films are mindless, flesh-eating monsters that thrust the world into chaos. However, Shank, relying on the scholarship of historians who remind us that zombies originated from "old African religious beliefs and the pain of slavery," examines *Atlantiques* (dir. Mati Diop, 2019) and *Zombie Child* (dir. Bertrand Bonello, 2019). She asserts that both films remove the zombie from its supernatural trappings and instead feature them as brutally ordinary. Hence, the zombies are doubly horrifying in that they resemble the millions of hyper-exploited people upon whose labor capitalist wealth now depends rather than the vampires, ghosts, and ghouls with which they have long been lumped.

In "Afro-Latinx Identity within Latin American Horror Cinema," Maillim Santiago explores Black manifestations in a corpus of contemporary Afro-Latinx horror films made between 2010 and 2021. She grapples with complexities that are both similar and dissimilar to Blackness in Western cinema and addresses the complicated racial discourses that construct Latin America as a monolith. In doing so, Santiago explores a range of films such as *El Hoyo del Diablo* (Dominican Republic, dir. Francisco Disla Ferreira, 2012), *Saudó, Laberinto de Almas* (Colombia, dirs. Jhonny Hendrix Hinestroza and Henry Rincon, 2016), *As Boas Maneiras*, and others, illustrating the discursive ways that narratives about Blackness spread through the distribution of films to global audiences.

Jennessa Hester moves from representations of Blackness to Black absence in "Havana's Living Dead: Curation, Colonization, and the Erasure of an Afro-Cuban Horror Cinema." She discusses Alejandro Brugués' *Juan de los Muertos* (*Jaun of the Dead*, 2011), illustrating that Cuba's Institute of Cinema Arts and Industry (and subsequently exhibitors across the world) disregarded its own cinematic horror tradition when it incorrectly advertised it as "Cuba's first horror film." Hester then explores important questions about contemporary conceptions of the island's cinema—Why have global cinephiles erased remnants of the Cuban horror tradition?; What terrors did they wipe away in the process?—by reexamining Cuba's Third Cinema with emphases on the historical race and enslavement dramas of non-Black filmmakers such as Tomás Gutiérrez Alea (*La Última Cena*, 1976) and Humberto Solás (*Cecilia*, 1982).

Significantly, Tony Quick opens the third section of this book, "Gendered Blackness," in "The Inauguration of Black Horror: Duane Jones's Racial Revision of *Night of the Living Dead*," investigating Black masculine agency and racial politics in George A. Romero's zombie classic. Particularly, he examines the efforts of the Black lead actor (Duane Jones) during production to shape the representation of his character and, by extension, other Black characterizations in the horror genre. Quick then connects Jones's efforts to his Black acting predecessors' cautious attempts to push the constraints of their scripted roles while also operating as a marginalized group within an entertainment ecosystem dependent on the majority's continued patronage.

Valeria Villegas Lindvall focuses on representations of Black women with emphases on sexuality, colonialism, and labor in "*Sem Medo de Lobisomem*: Subversion, Intimacy, and Animality in *As Boas Maneiras*." She contends that *As Boas Maneiras* challenges staunch heterosexism by underscoring the possibilities of queer intimacy and flipping the colonial hypersexualization of the Black body by projecting animality on to the white woman character. Further, Villegas Lindvall demonstrates how the film updates and subverts a figure derived from Brazilian colonial history—the Black nanny as the embodiment of racialized, unremunerated work.

In "La Llorona's Blackness in Latin American Horror Films *La Llorona* (Mexico, 1960) and *La Llorona* (Guatemala, 2019)," Kristen Leer continues the examination of identity and gender politics via the supernatural. She centers Afro-Latinx communities, which Latin America does not fully recognize as a distinct ethnic group, and Indigenous people, populations that experience similar forms of racial and institutional discrimination. Leer argues that in many Latin American horror films, the mythical ghost La Llorona unveils the functions of Blackness as a form of social prejudice informed by colorism. As a result, Blackness is both gendered and racialized through women's bodies (skin and clothes), indicating who is monstrous or othered.

Jamie Alvey takes readers back Down Under in "'They Trusted Me Even When I Didn't Particularly Trust Myself': The Complex Black Heroine in *Little Monsters*." She demonstrates the ways in which *Little Monsters* (dir. Abe Forsythe, 2019) depicts a multidimensional, Black woman character. In stark contrast to cinematic depictions around the globe that circumscribe Black femininity as ugly, loud, and overbearing, among other characteristics, Alvey elucidates how *Little Monsters* cuts against longstanding distorted myths by centering a strong, capable, beautiful Black woman hell-bent on saving the day.

The fourth section of this volume, "The Horrors of Contemporary Blackness," interrogates films that address issues that continue to plague Black populations around the globe. In doing so, the authors focus on past and recent films, illustrating that when it comes to Black struggle, yesterday's problems are still today's problems. In "Freddie vs. Michael: Horror Reality and the Spectacle of Black Surveillance in *Halloween: Resurrection*," Tiffany A. Bryant examines Black representations in *Halloween: Resurrection* (dir. Rick Rosenthal, 2002), in which a Black-owned production company's simulated horror experience turns deadly when infamous killer Michael Myers (The Shape) makes a surprise guest appearance. She interrogates the performances and constructions of Black perspectives situated within the combined, white-dominated genre expectations of the *Halloween* franchise (1978–2022) and the simulated horror reality format, which blur thematic ideas of authenticity, identity performance inspired by an active audience, and spectacles of fear.

In "'Time . . . Never Stops': The Power of 'Sonic Anachronism' in Misha Green's *Lovecraft Country*," Rachal Burton and Ayanni Cooper delve into television, exploring sound and Blackness in the eponymous, critically acclaimed, award-winning HBO drama. An amalgamation of horror and other speculative fiction genres, filled with ghosts, aliens, and vampiric monsters, *Lovecraft Country* deploys elements of the Black diasporic soundscape to chilling and powerful effect. Burton and Cooper contend that the series' creative team disrupts narrative temporalities by relishing in both seamless and jagged "sonic anachronisms," gesturing to the horror and potentiality of Black pasts, presents, and futures through nondiegetic sound. In this way, they demonstrate that *Lovecraft Country* unites sound and horror to highlight the pervasiveness of anti-Blackness globally, as well as the continuing importance and endurance of Black histories.

Drawing on horror scholarship that traces the relationship between the genre's rhetorical conventions and cultural trauma, theorists of Afro-pessimism, and postmodern adaptation theories, Byron B. Craig and Stephen Rahko expand the academic discourse surrounding the 2021 iteration of *Candyman* in "(Re)Summoning Candyman for a 'Post-Racial' Era: Black Horror, Allegorical Adaptation, and the Traumatic Racial Violence of American Capitalism." They examine DaCosta's film through an Afro-pessimistic lens, arguing that it advances an "allegorical adaptation" that does not posit a narrative redress of the violence of American structural racism.

In "The Allegory of the *Tickle Monster*," Tessa Adams examines constructions of Blackness in a short film from the United Kingdom. She employs critical race theory to analyze *Tickle Monster*'s (dir. Remi Weekes, 2016) main characters, arguing that the film functions as a response to historic constructions of Blackness in U.K. culture as well as oppression, microaggressions, and ideologies associated with post-racialism. In other words, Adams illustrates that *Tickle Monster* functions as an important reminder to "stay woke."

Significantly, both Means Coleman and I believe it would be insufficient to provide readers such complex examinations of global cinematic Blackness only to leave scholars, students, and horror aficionados interested in using this volume asking, "What now?" Hence, in "From *Tales from the Hood* to *Candyman*: Teaching Trauma Studies with Black Horror Cinema," Colleen Karn outlines an effective strategy via Black horror cinema that educators can employ to teach trauma studies in undergraduate general education courses. More specifically, she demonstrates how pairing trauma theories with Jeffrey Jerome Cohen's "Seven Monster Theses," screenings of *Tales from the Hood* (dir. Rusty Cundieff, 1995) and the original and reimagined *Candyman* (dir. Bernard Rose 1992; dir. Nia DaCosta, 2021) helps make the films and concepts accessible to students. Consequently, the students examine various types of trauma via Black experiences, the historic and institutional oppressions that cause trauma, and engage in dialogues and assignments informed by anti-racist pedagogical practices.

Notes

1. Aisha Harris, "Get Out," *Slate*, February 23, 2017, https://slate.com/culture/2017/02/get-out-jordan-peeles-horror-movie-reviewed.html.

2. Bob Mondello, "'Get Out' Offers Sharp Satire Along with Scares," *NPR*, February 23, 2017, https://www.npr.org/2017/02/23/516869364/get-out-offers-sharp-satire-along-with-the-scares.

3. "'Get Out' Sprang from an Effort to 'Master Fear,' Says Director, Jordan Peele," *Fresh Air*, NPR Radio, March 15, 2017. http://www.npr.org/sections/codeswitch/2017/03/15/520130162/get-out-sprung-from-an-effort-to-master-fear-says-director-jordan-peele.

4. Boxofficemojo.com. "Get Out," accessed January 27, 2023.

5. Maryann Erigha, *The Hollywood Jim Crow: The Racial Politics of the Movie Industry* (New York: New York University Press, 2019), 54.

6. Boxofficemojo.com, accessed January 2, 2023.

7. To be clear, *Get Out* did not need the Academy to validate its significance, as the themes that it addressed, its critical reception, and audiences around the globe signified that it is a special film.

8. Robin R. Means Coleman, *Horror Noire* (New York: Routledge, 2011).

9. Peter Hutchings, *The Horror Film* (Pearson: London, 2004), 83.

10. Henry Jenkins, "Cult Conversations: Interview with Robin R. Means Coleman (Pt. 1)," *Pop Junctions*, January 29, 2019

11. Robin R. Means Coleman, *Horror Noire: Blacks in American Horror Films from 1890's to Present* (New York: Routledge, 2011).

12. Novotny Lawrence, *Blaxploitation Films of the 1970s: Blackness and Genre* (New York: Routledge, 2007), 56.

13. Robin R. Means Coleman and Mark Harris, *The Black Guy Dies First: Black Horror Cinema from Fodder to Oscar* (New York: Saga Press, 2023).

14. Ibid.

15. Ibid.

16. Kevin Heffernan, "Risen from the Vaults," in *Merchants of Menace: The Business of Horror Cinema*, ed. Richard Nowell (New York: Bloomsbury, 2014), 1–2. https://books.google.com/books?hl=en&lr=&id=HGv4BgAAQBAJ&oi=fnd&pg=PA61&dq=u.s.+remakes+of+international+horror&ots=5LPii4Cxp_&sig=p6KK02_MzpMZLPaEe1wEnqEyOYY#v=onepage&q=u.s.%20remakes%20of%20international%20horror&f=false

17. Dale Hudson, *Vampires, Race, and Transnational Hollywood* (Edinburgh, UK: Edinburgh University Press, 2017).

18. "History of African Film Industry: An Introduction," Experience Africa, Institute for Cultural Diplomacy Inc., accessed February 4, 2023, https://www.experience-africa.de/index.php?en_annual-african-film-festival-2013_african-film-industry#:~:text=The%20Nigerian%20film%20industry%20is,of%20Nollywood%20is%20%24590mn.

19. Mowunyo Gbogbo, "Indigenous Filmmakers Give Us Something to Scream about at Sydney Film Festival," *ABC News*, February 4, 2023, https://www.abc.net.au/news/2019-05-25/horror-is-the-new-black-at-sydney-film-festival/11148010.

20. Sezin Koehler, "Eclectic Writings on Social Justice, Popular Culture, Horror, Flash Fiction, and More," February 4, 2023, https://www.sezin.org/.

SECTION I

BLACK VISUAL
CULTURE POWER

....

CHAPTER 1

HISTORICIZED TRAUMAS

Black Art in Nia DaCosta's Candyman

....

NOVOTNY LAWRENCE AND
ROBIN R. MEANS COLEMAN

It comes as a great shock around the age of five, or six, or seven, to discover that the country to which you have pledged allegiance along with everyone else has not pledged allegiance to you.

—James Baldwin, 1965

. . . in aesthetic theory: blackness has been associated with a certain sense of decay, even when that decay is invoked in the name of a certain (fetishization of) vitality

—Fred Moten, 2008

WHAT does it mean when trauma moves across Black lived experiences? What does it mean for film and art to address trauma—particularly the physical, emotional, and social trauma born out of racism's pasts and present—across the temporal plane? How does horror contribute to cinematic and artistic aesthetics to foreground Black experiences and illustrate how Black creative agency helps recuperate traumatic-turned-revolutionary visual culture? This chapter considers these questions using *Candyman* (2021) to illustrate the vital role that visual culture plays in memorializing Black traumas. This examination into the role visual culture, specifically art, plays in (de)constructing Black trauma is enriched by an interview with Trinidadian-born artist and Northwestern University professor Sherwin Ovid, who created six paintings for Nia DaCosta's *Candyman*. Particularly, his work on the film, and beyond, operates in conjunction with DaCosta's iteration of the Candyman to illustrate the power of Black arts traditions in mediating on and preserving Black trauma born out of racism.

EXIT THAT CANDYMAN?

During a 2023 interview for this chapter, we asked Sherwin Ovid a simple question: "What did Blackness look like in horror films that you are familiar with?" In response, Ovid described their understanding of the visual construction of Blackness, a construction that they would have to reckon with in their art and, ultimately, for its cinematic presentation: ". . . inclusion by negation in some ways because it was this sort of fatalist circumstance that usually would be part of the expectation of what would actually happen. Or, it would be Blackness as a kind of support, as a kind of flat support for more well-rounded, more defined characters in some way."[1]

Ovid is reflecting upon, and articulates, the ways that U.S. (horror) cinema has presented Black people and Black spaces, particularly at the time when the original *Candyman* (dir. Bernard Rose, 1992) opened in theaters. In the 2023 book *Horror Noire: A History of Black American Horror from the 1890s to Present*, I (Coleman) explain that in the 1990s, "The horror film genre celebrated its first century in high cinematic style by offering what can only be described as 'prestige' horror films."[2] Indeed, Hollywood's foray into horror was highbrow, as it included films such as *The Silence of the Lambs* (dir. Jonathan Demme, 1991), and *Interview with the Vampire: The Vampire Chronicles* (dir. Neil Jordan, 1994). These films, which featured A-list actors the likes of Jodie Foster, Tom Cruise, and Brad Pitt, performed well at the box office[3] and earned Academy Award recognition.

Lambs' and *Vampire's* success and critical acclaim demonstrated U.S. horror's national and international viability, and for the remainder of the 1990s, studios attempted to cash in on cinephiles' love for the monstrous. For instance, prominent directors such as Francis Ford Coppola, Kenneth Branagh, and Mike Nichols helmed new incarnations of classic horror boogeymen, *Dracula* (1992, $40 million budget) *Frankenstein* (1994, $45 million budget), and *Wolf* (1994, $70 million budget), respectively.[4] Later in the decade, relative newcomer M. Night Shyamalan dazzled audiences with his runaway hit *The Sixth Sense* (1999, $40 million budget), while the truly independent and enormously successful *The Blair Witch Project* (dirs. Daniel Myrick and Eduardo Sanchez, 1999, $60,000 budget) further satisfied horror movie fans' appetites.[5]

Significantly, Blacks did not feature prominently in Hollywood's prestige pictures. Instead, Hollywood relegated them to lowbrow horror movies with budgets that further illustrated their second-class film industry status. Notable examples include the critically acclaimed *Def by Temptation* (dir. James Bond III, 1990, budget unknown),[6] as well as *Candyman* (1992, $8 million budget), *Tales from the Hood* (dir. Rusty Cundieff, 1995, $6 million budget), *Tales from the Crypt: Demon Knight* (dir. Ernest Dickerson, 1995, $12 million budget), and *Eve's Bayou* (dir. Kasi Lemmons, 1997, $5 million budget). With its white, Oscar-winning director, Jonathan Demme, and a cast including then-world-renowned talk show host and sometime actor, Oprah Winfrey, and Danny Glover, *Beloved* (1998, $53 million budget) was the exception to the Black horror film low-budget rule.

Candyman is arguably the most notable "Blacks in horror film" from the 1990s. Based on British writer Clive Barker's 1985 short story "The Forbidden," it was initially set in an impoverished community in Liverpool and featured an iteration of the Candyman with "waxy jaundiced skin, rouged cheeks, blue lips, eyes like rubies, and a patchwork coat."[7] Comic artist John Stewart later reconceptualized the character as a non-Black ogre-type monster (figure 1.1).[8]

However, the setting and monster were changed when British director Bernard Rose became interested in making a film that depicted an impoverished, predominantly Black Chicago neighborhood after hearing about the murder of Ruthie Mae McCoy. A Black resident of the Chicago Housing Authority's ABLA projects, McCoy struggled with untreated mental health issues, and consequently, when she phoned the 911 police dispatcher on April 22, 1987, she was unable to clearly articulate the very real events that were transpiring around her. "I'm a resident at 1440 W. 13th St. and some people next door are totally tearing this down, you know—," she frantically explained.[9] When the dispatcher asked for additional information, McCoy continued, "Yeah, they throwed the cabinet down. I'm in the projects, I'm on the other side. You can reach—can reach my bathroom, they want to come through the bathroom."[10] In response to the calls, the police performed several welfare checks over the next two days but left when McCoy did not answer her door. When one of McCoy's neighbors called the apartment's management team to enter the apartment, the disturbance she had been trying to report became strikingly clear. Perpetrators had entered the apartment next door to McCoy's and were

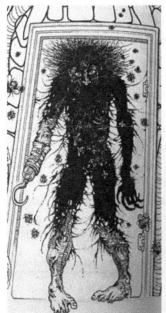

FIGURE 1.1 John Stewart's rendering of Clive Barker's Candyman and Tony Todd as the title character in Bernard Rose's 1992 film.

breaking into her home through the adjoining bathroom medicine cabinets. They even-tually made their way into her unit, where they robbed and murdered her.[11]

While McCoy's horrific demise inspired Rose's screenplay and direction of *Candyman*, the film engages in the Black negation that Ovid observes is present in filmic treatments of Blackness. Although the film draws on McCoy's death and the inequi-table systemic circumstances that enabled the violent perpetrators to take her life—a shoddily government-built high-rise housing project, medicine cabinets instead of walls separating apartments, and health-care system failures—the narrative ultimately negates McCoy's tragic experiences to center whiteness as heroic.

Candyman chronicles white graduate student Helen Lyle's (Virginia Madsen) foray into Chicago's Cabrini-Green housing project to study urban myths for her thesis. She quickly discovers that the legendary, mythic Candyman (Tony Todd) is a very real specter born from anti-Black violence. For in his previous life, he was the handsome Daniel Robitaille, an intelligent, sophisticated artist whose race, class, talents, and love interest spark the ire of whites, leading to his doom. In 1890, a wealthy white man hires Robitaille to paint a portrait of his daughter. He and the young woman defy segrega-tion and anti-miscegenation laws, falling in love. Outraged, the young woman's father assembles a lynch mob that captures Robitaille, saws off his right hand, replaces it with a metal hook, smears honey from a beehive over his body, and lets bees sting him to death—all before burning his body to a char. The remainder of *Candyman* follows Helen as she works to document the mythology surrounding Candyman, all while he pines for her and preys upon the disenfranchised Black Cabrini-Green housing project residents.

Bernard Rose's *Candyman* features a racialized narrative that presents as its protago-nist a "virtuous," albeit misguided, white woman seeking to exploit Black pain, trauma, and mythology in the name of her education. In addition to negating Ruthie Mae McCoy's experiences, the story fails to meaningfully examine the fact that Candyman was the victim of detestable racial violence, to construct him as menacing and justify his obsession with Helen. As Coleman notes, "the film strays from the monster-with-a-heart-of-gold theme by playing on fears of the big Black boogeyman coming in, King Kong–style, to take away the white woman."[12] Consequently, when *Candyman* began its theatrical run, notable Black directors expressed dissatisfaction with and concern for its racist undertones. Carl Franklin (dir. *Devil in a Blue Dress*, 1995) was among *Candyman*'s most vocal critics and was particularly offended by the eponymous character's preoccu-pation with Helen. "It smacked of 'King Kong.' Remember, Kong had all those Black is-land women for the taking but he gave his life for a blonde one, which is what Candyman does. Black women are again a non-entity in this film."[13] Reginald Hudlin (dir. *Sidney*, 2022) also found *Candyman* disturbing, noting, "Whatever's going on in 'Candyman' certainly isn't new. The first image recorded on film was of a Black midget tap dancer, and 'Birth of a Nation' (with its romanticized depiction of the Ku Klux Klan) is still being taught in film school."[14] Hence, Franklin and Hudlin position *Candyman* along-side other films that exemplify whites' historic fascination with as well as their inherent, longstanding fears of Blackness. It is these fears and confining representations that Ovid finds themself now navigating.

Even with the obviously (especially over three decades later) problematic representations of Black life, culture, and identities, Candyman and the prospect of summoning him (just look into the mirror and say his name five times), Ovid brought to his viewing of the film an additional attention to the physical iconography—that is, built environment and natural elements—of the Chicago setting. Ovid shared in our interview:

> The original *Candyman* was like really, really impactful, and I remember vividly being an art student at the School of the Art Institute when I was an undergrad when I first moved to Chicago. And, the skyline all over the South side and also the near North side had all these high-rises. They were things that were very visual and markedly different from where I was coming from around Houston, Texas, which was, you know, also a kind of suburban metropolis . . . there weren't as many high-rises that had that very similar look in terms of its architectural structure, and the confrontation with the history of public housing was something that was like very vivid.[15]

Rose introduces the Cabrini-Green setting via a sequence accompanied by acclaimed composer Phillip Glass's haunting song, "Cabrini Green." Helen and her classmate, Bernadette (Kasi Lemmons), travel from their safe (read, white) environs into the predominantly Black unsafe space that is Cabrini-Green. Shots of deteriorating towers and row homes, graffiti, trash, and the gang members awaiting them when they arrive function as one-dimensional signifiers of Blackness run amuck. *Candyman* evidences Moten's (2008) observation, ". . . in aesthetic theory: blackness has been associated with a certain sense of decay. . . ."[16] Further, the use of graffiti-as-vandalism visually distinguishes the behavioral, racial, and class divides between the poor, Black Cabrini-Green residents and the educated and "cultured" white, middle-class Chicagoans (as represented by Helen).

Ironically, though deployed as a signifier of decay and dysfunction in the film, graffiti art has become yet another exemplar of whites' historic tendencies to co-opt Black aesthetic culture. Although graffiti dates back centuries, Darryl McCray, a.k.a. Cornbread, is widely regarded as the first contemporary tagger. As a youth growing up in Philadelphia, he spray-painted his nickname on "bus stops, benches, even on the side of an elephant at the Philadelphia Zoo."[17] In the ensuing decades, graffiti artists and their work became more prevalent in Black Latinx urban neighborhoods in the United States and around the world where, as in *Candyman*, people initially considered their tags vandalism. Today, perceptions have changed, as museum curators, educators, and critics, and even consumers, now embrace graffiti as artwork. Cornbread succinctly describes his, and other graffiti practitioners by extension, transformation from a tagger often arrested for "vandalism" to a talented and respected virtuoso: "Today, I'm a street artist."[18] Indeed, Cornbread, often referred to as a "graffiti pioneer," has worked with the Philadelphia Mural Arts Program and even served as the inspiration for a mural arts tour. Thus, graffiti no longer symbolizes Black poverty and danger; instead, it is an influential art form that features prominently in the United States and around the globe.

Examples include Eduardo Kobra (Sao Paulo), Shamsia Hassani (Afghanistan), Vajo (Tunisia), and Lady Pink (Ecuador–New York).

The mural depicting Rose's Candyman, his brown skin creating a contrast with the whites of his eyes, and his wide-open mouth serving as the entrance into his lair, is a frightfully powerful visual of exploitation, distortion, and, per Ovid, even enslavement (figure 1.2).

Discussing conceptions of Blackness, Ovid related:

> . . . there's a range of things that I think come up and many of those things get heaped on to Black people in the way that we could think of . . . the way that the Atlantic becomes this kind of portal, you know, where there's, obviously . . . the tragedy and the catastrophe of all of those moments . . . where Africans are being trafficked, people are coming across that particular place, and then they end up on the other side as being Black, being turned into being Black, and Blackened."[19]

After Africans arrived in the United States, white slave traders and owners racialized them, exploiting their labor. The exploitation did not stop there. The ensuing centuries witnessed the commodified, distorted images of Blacks, enslaved and subsequently free, for white social, economic, and political gain. Like horror cinema's classic monsters and slasher killers, those images have continually haunted Blacks and serve as reminders of the ways in which anti-Black visual culture often negates and flattens out their existences to reaffirm whiteness symbolically and literally.

To illustrate, in North America's inaugural sound film, *The Jazz Singer* (dir. Alan Crossland, 1927), Al Jolson plays Jack Rubin, an aspiring singer who performs in black-face "to assimilate himself into jazz."[20] Further, "Blackface also gives Jack access to

FIGURE 1.2 Helen (Virginia Madsen) looks at the mural of the Candyman, 1992. Image captured from DVD. Sony Pictures Home Entertainment.

FIGURE 1.3 Al Jolson in blackface in *The Jazz Singer*, 1927. Image captured from Google images.

FIGURE 1.4 "Watch on De Rind" boardgame, circa 1931. Image captured from Google images.

allegedly black qualities, intense emotionality and its form of musical expression," and as such, his performance allegedly signifies Black "authenticity" (figure 1.3).[21]

Four years later, All-Fair Games featured wide-eyed, wide-mouthed pickaninnies on its board game, Watch on De Rind (figure 1.4). "The box was set up on a tabletop and the object was to throw a ball into the mouth or hats of a number of Black caricatures who

FIGURE 1.5 The Coon Chicken Inn. Image capture from Jim Crow Museum, Ferris State University.

are seen eating and standing around a large watermelon. Points were scored for landing in the targets."[22] Thus, for those at the earliest of age, this game helped make the Black grotesque fun.

Maxon Lester Graham repurposed similar imagery for the Coon Chicken Inn, a popular restaurant chain that thrived in the Pacific Northwest from the 1920s through the 1950s. He added the wide-mouthed, eye-bulging "coon" figure to the restaurant's doorway as a gimmick to attract children, and ultimately their parents, who would have to escort them to the restaurants, making Coon Chicken Inns family establishments (figure 1.5).[23] Families walked through a giant, grotesquely caricatured Black man's mouth, found a table, and ordered the "Coon Chicken" and "Baby Coon Specials."[24] Helen, in Rose's *Candyman*, walked through a similarly grotesquely caricatured Black man's mouth to play upon the audience's anxieties and dread regarding Blackness. In either instance, restaurant or dilapidated housing project, racist iconography of Blackness was deployed to assure white suzerainty and Black deficiency.

ENTER *THE* CANDYMAN

Discussing Black representations in cinema, Ovid explained:

> It's fascinating in terms of thinking about my introduction to film in terms of film history and film theory classes and even the way that it was taught also. Also, with that kind of negation or in the way people would talk about, well, the deficiency in a lot of those films, even films made by Black directors. . . . Their standards would

often be compared to . . . the film projects of white artists that had the capital and the connections and had all of the resources to be able to make these kinds of things that were . . . obviously full of all of these resources and time and the ability to even allow them to fail. There's a way that I think they even negated the importance of Blackness from the actual invention of the medium. . . .[25]

Here, Ovid correctly alludes to the invention and evolution of photography and cinema, mediums largely created by whites with the intention of memorializing whiteness. As Richard Dyer explains in *White*:

Stocks, cameras, and lighting were developed taking the white face as the touchstone. The resultant apparatus came to be seen as fixed and inevitable, existing independently of the fact that it was humanly constructed. It may be—certainly was—true that photo and film apparatuses have seemed to work better with light-skinned peoples, but that is because they were made that way, not because they could be no other way.[26]

In spite of an early technological privileging of whiteness, Black filmmakers and artists have seized the mechanics of cultural production, showcasing their abilities to use photography, film, paint, and other media to thoughtfully articulate Black histories and trauma. As art historian and museum curator Janet Dees elaborates, "From the horrors of slavery and lynching to the violent suppression of civil rights struggles and recent acts of police brutality, violence targeting Black lives has been an ever-present fact in American history. Images of African American suffering and death have constituted an enduring part of the nation's cultural landscape, and the development of creative counter points to these images has been an ongoing concern for American artists."[27]

In September 2018, horror fans, and cinephiles more broadly, responded enthusiastically when news broke that Nia DaCosta, through Jordan Peele's Monkey Paw Productions, planned to resurrect the iconic Candyman character. Peele, who had ascended to the status of A-list director for his poignant, racially infused, Academy Award–winning Black horror film *Get Out* (2017), co-wrote *Candyman* alongside Monkey Paw Productions president Win Rosenfeld and Nia DaCosta, who also directed the film. Speaking about the sequel, DaCosta explained:

I think stories in a community are really useful because they pass on lessons to learn, to remember people. And as it relates to racial violence, a warning. Like, this happened to so-and-so, so don't do that. I also think stories help us grieve and process as a collective—even if stories aren't perfect or they're wrong or made up. [Laughs] I think that's a lot of what "Candyman" is about. To pass along the story is also to change it and retool it for your community, generation, family, immediate surroundings. That's what's really fun and interesting about how "Candyman" works and how legends work in general. They change because they have to. But at their core, they're trying to give you the same message.[28]

DaCosta's *Candyman* is a sequel to the 1992 film that ignores the events of the follow-ups, *Candyman: Farwell to the Flesh* (1995) and the direct-to-video entry *Candyman 3: Day of the Dead* (1999), a strategy that allowed her to more firmly center Blackness in the mythology. The film chronicles Anthony McCoy (Yahya Abdul-Mateen II), a talented painter chasing recognition and approval through gallery exhibitions. Anthony and his art curator girlfriend Brianna Cartwright (Teyonah Parris) recently moved into a swanky, luxury apartment built on the former site of the Cabrini-Green housing projects. As he conceives his next, hopefully powerful, series of paintings, Anthony has a seemingly chance encounter with local resident William Burk (Colman Domingo), who tells him about the legendary Candyman. Anthony becomes consumed with translating Candyman's legend into his series of paintings-turned-art gallery exhibit. His motivation, however, is not merely hubris. Rather, Anthony is driven, in part, by panic, as white people control his career. First, there is his white benefactor, Clive, who describes Anthony's most recent work as "so two years ago" while questioning whether Anthony can deliver as the "great Black hope" of the Chicago art scene. Clive goes on to position himself as far more expert and culturally conscious about Blackness than Anthony when he dismisses Anthony's interest in the South Side of Chicago as "kinda played [out]." Grasping for ideas to serve as his artistic muse and, thereby, maintain Clive's sponsorship, Anthony suggests the destruction of Cabrini-Green. This idea is met with giddy approval by Clive, who views gentrification as the next hip subject. Anthony's exploration into Cabrini-Green leads to his fixation on Candyman lore, which, in turn, deeply informs his art. However, this time he is deflated by a white art critic, Finley (Rebecca Spence). Finley sneers as she delivers her brutal review directly to Anthony: his work is "didactic," playing around with "knee jerk cliches about the ambient violence of the gentrification cycle." Then she adds another blow, saying that people like Anthony (middle-class Black artists) are, in fact, responsible for gentrification and the demise of Black communities. Later still, when Candyman deaths are associated with Anthony's work, Finley delights in the macabre, promising a favorable review in the wake of renewed death and violence associated with Cabrini-Green. Anthony's own obsession with, as well as others' fetishization of, Candyman ultimately leads to still more gruesome deaths that are also presented as necessary to fuel lasting memories and the memorialization of Black trauma born out of racism.

Black art takes center stage in *Candyman*, beginning with an animated puppet-show teaser trailer, which DaCosta shared in June 2021. The teaser does not feature scenes from the then-upcoming film, yet it still serves as a haunting promotion that highlights racism and anti-Black violence. The Emmy-winning Chicago-based shadow puppet theater company Manual Cinema created the teaser, which features four vignettes composed of cut-out Black shadow puppets against white and sepia-toned backgrounds. In his interview, Ovid shared: ". . . there's something also interesting in terms of just not thinking about Blackness in terms of the way that maybe I'm sticking to it in regards to the racial and a cultural significance. But, even the way that I think about artists like Glenn Ligon and how even . . . the color black, you know, has this significance too. That's very central to the way that . . . we think about lightness and darkness in certain ways."[29]

Set to Black sound artist and composer Robert Aiki Aubrey Lowe's more haunting reworking of acclaimed composer Philip Glass's subtle song "Music Box" from the original film's soundtrack, the shadow-puppets teaser toys with conceptions of lightness and darkness as the white background accentuates the Black figures. The acts of anti-Black violence portrayed delineate whites from Blacks and, in that way, represent the darkness that consumes racists. With that in mind, the vignettes detail events from the film's diegesis, including the Candyman's origins and the fate of a friendly Black man named Sherman, who passes out candy to the neighborhood children. After a white child finds a razor blade in their Halloween candy, Sherman is wrongfully accused and beaten to death by the white police officers who find him.

Importantly, the other two vignettes highlight actual instances of state-sanctioned and extralegal anti-Black violence. The trailer recounts the tale of 14-year-old George Stinney Jr., who the state of South Carolina wrongfully convicted of murdering two white girls, Betty June Bickner and Mary Emma Thames, in 1944, and subsequently executed for the crimes (figure 1.6).[30]

The teaser also re-creates the 1998 lynching of James Byrd Jr., whom a group of white supremacists (one of whom Byrd Jr. had known most of his life) targeted as he was "walking while Black." The men offered Byrd Jr. a ride, drove him to a remote location, brutalized him, tied him to the back of their pickup truck, and dragged him along a road for three miles.[31] The film's teaser recounts real-life instances of Black trauma, and these vignettes are powerful not only for their work of reminding but, too, for the ways in which they seamlessly connect with the events in the film, exemplifying the eerie similarities between the reel and the real. Consequently, the trailer is key to understanding *Candyman*'s pervasive themes about Black experiences, which, though characterized by progress, joy, and accomplishment, are also painful and traumatic.

In an interview with *New York Times* writer Candice Frederick, DaCosta explained her decision to use shadow puppets to recount the atrocities Blacks endured both in the film and in real life.

FIGURE 1.6 Shadow-puppets trailer re-creation of George Stinney Jr.'s execution, 2021. Image captured from trailer. Monkeypaw Productions.

Shadow puppetry came out of the desire to not do flashbacks that were scenes from the original film cut into our film or recreated with different actors. [Laughs] We were like, "That's terrible." We realized that shadow puppetry is good not just for the flashbacks, but codifying the storytelling, the legend. Shadow puppets are much cruder, much more over-the-top. It's illustrating this isn't real life and the way we think of real life. This is a story, even though it's based on real life. We also got to tell the story of Candyman without showing that violence. So, it could still be evocative and sad, but we could not create more disturbing imagery of Black people being brutalized by race violence.[32]

DaCosta is part of a long history of political commentators and artists who used the visual to speak to anti-Black violence. For example, in her book, *Art in Crisis: W.E.B. DuBois and the Struggle for African American Identity and Memory*, Amy Helene Kirschke (2007) describes how DuBois gave visual/artistic space in *The Crisis* magazine, the organ of the National Association for the Advancement of Colored People (NAACP), for sociopolitical issues plaguing Black communities. Kirschke asserts that by DuBois asking the question in his famed "Criteria of Negro Art" speech, "Suppose the only Negro who survived some centuries hence was the Negro painted by White Americans in the novels and essays they have written. What would people in a hundred years say of black Americans?" He is asking us to consider "where would Black history, identity, and memory have gone?" She describes DuBois's relentless pursuit of documenting Black identity and, subsequently, Black history, giving space to the likes of artist John Henry Adams, who "addressed police brutality and the unfair judicial system. His January 1919 cartoon shows a small Black child, perhaps aged two or three, his wrists handcuffed together, in chains. He is presented to a White judge, who slumps over in his chair, showing no interest in the defendant, while an all-White jury listens. The caption, 'Disturbing the Peace, Your Honor!' says it all. The fate of the toddler symbolizes the way in which the vague charge 'disturbing the peace' was used to harass and oppress Black communities."[33]

Similarly, and importantly, throughout *Candyman*, Black art and examinations of Black trauma are pertinent themes that advance the narrative and illustrate the ways in which the arts traditions play a prominent role in struggles for social justice. With that in mind, DaCosta personally selected artists Cameron Spratley and, of course, Sherwin Ovid to create Anthony's work in the film. When DaCosta hired Ovid to work on the sequel, he was enthused and overjoyed, emotions that "mixed with a lot of uncertainty about how to actually live up to that kind of cinematic history."[34] At the same time, he was also intrigued by the issues (e.g., police violence, anti-Blackness, whiteness) that DaCosta planned to address in her iteration of the *Candyman* that the original film did not. He was particularly excited about the film's examination of the gentrification of the space on which Cabrini-Green once stood.[35]

In myriad ways, DaCosta's *Candyman* functions as a corrective of the 1992 film, as it indicts the system that created public housing and the ways in which gentrification erases Blackness. In *How the Streets Were Made: Housing Segregation and Black Life in America*, Yelena Bailey explains that public housing was initially built as transitory spaces for working and middle-class white Americans. Consequently, Black veterans returning to cities after World War I and Blacks already living in metropolises, as well as Blacks migrating from the South to the North, initially had to fight to live in government projects. "However, when public housing was finally opened up to Black Americans, not only did its racialization shift, but so did its very design and infrastructure. As the projects became increasingly associated with Blackness, they became decreasingly associated with family life. Rather than sheltering families in transition, the projects became a means of warehousing urban Black Americans."[36] As audiences learn in DaCosta's *Candyman*, real estate developers have torn down the Cabrini-Green high-rises and replaced them with luxury condos that neither former project residents nor those of lower socioeconomic statuses can afford. In that way, gentrification has erased Blacks' initial struggles to secure the right to live in public housing. Further, the government allowed the projects to fall into disrepair once they became synonymous with poor Black people.

Yet, *Candyman* and Ovid's artwork memorialize Cabrini-Green via the William Burk (Colman Domingo) character, who functions as a West African griot of sorts who passes the history of the projects and the Candyman along to Anthony. Through Burk, DaCosta reestablishes Cabrini-Green as a space that, while imperfect, once served as a community for Black families. When Burk recounts his childhood experience with Sherman—who was for him the Candyman—he recalls their meeting in the laundry room in the projects. Here, DaCosta uses a point-of-view shot to reverse the meanings of the grotesque, wide-mouthed mural that serves as the entrance into the Candyman's lair in Rose's film. Instead, audiences see young William from Sherman's vantage point, from inside the wall where he is hiding from white police officers (figure 1.7).

FIGURE 1.7 Sherman's (Michael Hargrove) watches William Burk from his hiding place inside the wall, 2021. Image captured from DVD. Universal Pictures.

FIGURE 1.8 Sherman (Michael Hargrove) prepares to step out of his hiding place, 2021. Image captured from DVD. Universal Pictures.

FIGURE 1.9 Sherman (Michael Hargrove) emerges from the wall offering William Burk sweets, 2021. Image captured from DVD. Universal Pictures.

When Sherman tosses a piece of candy to William from inside the hole, the youth is initially taken aback and screams (figure 1.8). However, when Sherman emerges from the wall extending his candy-filled hand to William, the youth soon realizes that he is only offering him sweets (figure 1.9). He takes the candy but soon realizes that his shriek alerted the white police officers on the prowl for Sherman. The officers rush into the laundry room, and it is there that they murder Sherman. Here, DaCosta engages in a visual reversal by redefining the building, making the dark hole in the wall a safe haven for an innocent Black man, while the whiteness on the outside poses the real danger.

DaCosta's is not the first reclamation of the gaping mouth in a gesture toward visual culture activism. As detailed by T.V. Reed in his book, *The Art of Protest: Culture and Activism from the Civil Rights Movement to the Streets of Seattle*, in 1973, Chicano muralists Willie Herrón and Gronk created "Black and White Moratorium Wall" at the Estrada Courts housing project in East Los Angeles. Intentionally playing with a monochromatic palette of black and white rather than the "common rainbow of bright colors"[37] defining murals, the artists adopted colors fitting the mural's subjects: the Vietnam War abroad and the war on Brown people at home. The mural commemorates a 1970 antiwar march that turned violent: "the mural vividly depicts the police unleashed against the demonstrators at the end of the rally, capturing the screams of victims."[38] One scream image, which appears on the far-right side of the mural, is a close-up of a person yelling, mouth wide (figure 1.10).

The mural rescripts anxiety and terror, shifting it away from racism-fueled disdain for impoverished people of color (as seen in Rose's *Candyman*). Instead, the terror spills

FIGURE 1.10 Willie Herrón and Gronk's "Black and White Moratorium Wall," 1973. Image captured from Google images.

outward, indicting those who are inciting the scream and inducing pain. The agape mouth in this "revolutionary wall," as Reed calls such works, invites empathy while imputing police violence.

Candyman also details the challenges Blacks experience as they work to break into and ascend in the arts. As DaCosta explained, "I think it's a really great way to show this Black man trying to navigate a very White world, someone who is also being asked to exploit his community in order to make art. He's trying to write a thesis, trying to get inspiration for his work and get out of the slump he's in. Almost all Black artists, no matter what industry they're in, deal with this."[39] In our interview, Ovid shared that he is indeed familiar with that art world, and that creating art for *Candyman* that articulates Black experiences instead of exploiting them was constantly on his mind.[40] Thus, he works to recuperate a history of racial iconography in which, as Cobb explains, "a changing Black presence in the North inspired anxieties about the meaning of U.S. citizenship, even as many people of African descent contemplated emigration to other locales, such as Mexico and Liberia."[41]

Ovid's work helps decenter whiteness and, in that way, reemphasizes that the Candyman lore is a result of the types of historic anti-Black violence and trauma that have circumscribed Blacks' experiences around the world. Perhaps William best articulates this notion when he tells Anthony, "Candyman is how we deal with the fact that these things happened. That they're still happening." Ovid created images of such happenings in paintings of Stinney Jr. and Sherman, artwork that further extends their presence and stories from the shadow-puppets teaser into the film's diegesis. In that way, Stinney Jr. and Sherman are ever-present reminders that the government-sanctioned assaults on Tamir Rice, Rekia Boyd, George Floyd, Breonna Taylor, and countless other Blacks are not a new phenomenon. Ovid also creates one of the most significant and prominently featured paintings in the film, that of Anthony as he becomes consumed by the traumatic memory of the many Black men—the Candymen (plural)—who are felled by anti-Black violence. Ovid renders Anthony in the process of him too becoming a Candyman.

The union between Black trauma and change represented through art is intentional, as Nia DaCosta explains: "The art within *Candyman* is about devolution, to mirror [Anthony's] psychological descent. I really wanted to show his early work, and then the work that he makes in the film, and how he's being changed not only through his own search and journey, but also by, maybe, a demon ghost."[42] In taking on the challenge of painting Anthony in transformation, Ovid started, perhaps surprisingly, by using a vibrant color palette comprising yellows and purples to paint the portrait, an approach that captures Anthony's likeness while, too, serving as a jarring visual manifestation of his confounding mental state. Ovid explains: "Everything revolved around that violet, with pops of yellow and blue, and I muddied it up a bit. It comes at this phase where he's transitioning and losing his sanity and his career is starting to nosedive."[43] Ovid's use of muted and light tones contrasts with the dark and rejects concerns about respectability, palatability, or an identification with the other. Instead, he plays with the ideals of citizenship by ensconcing them in the grotesque. "Picturing freedom," to borrow from

Cobb (2015), means a stare, scream, and contortion that is unrelenting in its demand to gaze upon it—to see what unfettered, rage-filled Black freedom looks like.

CONCLUSION

The horror noir renaissance brings with it an interrogation of the visual representation of the global slave trade and its ongoing aftermath. In one instance, there are critiques of an overdetermination of Black trauma porn, as reflected in Black horror such as *Antebellum* (2020) and *Them* (2021). In the case of the former, *New York* and *Vulture* critic Angelica Jade Bastién wrote: "I am tired. I am tired of pop-cultural artifacts that render Black people as merely Black bodies onto which the sins of this ragged country are violently mapped. I am tired of suffering being the primary lens through which we understand Black identity. . . . I am tired of thin characterization and milquetoast social messaging being the kind of representation Black folks receive. I am tired of films like *Antebellum*."[44] Similarly, Aisha Harris of *NPR* summarized: "*Them* suffers from the same predicament that has arisen in the wake of Black people becoming hashtags in death—the public knows far more about their last moments on Earth than all the moments that made up their life before. Viewers who make it through all 10 episodes will know plenty about how the Emorys have suffered and been traumatized, but they won't come away with much else."[45]

These critical reviews represent overwhelming sentiments regarding *Antebellum*, *Them*, and other works, and they also illustrate the challenges of recounting painful Black histories and experiences. When filmmakers and artists do not approach the material with sensitivity, or when those stories continually exist in the absence of a dynamic range of representations of Black life and culture, they are perceived as wounding not only for their graphic visuality but also for extending the persistent narrative around a "life-or-death struggle for recognition," with "the original traumatic experience of slavery and colonization" relentlessly inhabiting the Black story—historically and in the contemporary.[46]

Certainly, these are very real concerns, and at the same time, it is important to remember that the goal of horror cinema, Black or otherwise, is to horrify. Ovid fully recognized that when working on *Candyman*. As he explained in our interview, he was "thinking about the demands of cinema in a sense, in regard to the actual framework of attempting to make something that's a hit, and what that can mean."[47] For DaCosta, Ovid, Spratley, Lowe, and the other artists who collaborated on *Candyman*, that meant traversing the fine line between using the Black visual and aural to examine and uplift rather than exploit. Arguably, Ovid perfectly summarized what it looks like to achieve that difficult balance when we asked him what he wanted audiences to take from his paintings in the film:

> . . . I would hope that there's some both revolutionary potential for us to think about our ability to all use images, some kind of emancipatory potential in a high way. But,

I also hope that it would like, also offer a respite for people to have some kind of place to escape also. I would hope that it was very, you know, thought-provoking, but also on another level, like true to the form of horror and fulfill some satisfaction in terms of living up to that, in terms of its ability to actually be really amazing in terms of its visual, spectacularity.[48]

Indeed, that is the power of Black visual art and Black horror cinema.

NOTES

1. Sherwin Ovid (artist and Northwestern professor), in discussion with Novotny Lawrence, February 1, 2023.
2. Robin R. Means Coleman, *Horror Noire: A History of Black American Horror from the 1890s to Present* (New York: Routledge, 2023), 235.
3. *The Silence of the Lambs* was originally released in 1991, earning $130,742,922 worldwide. It saw two additional international releases in 2017 and 2021. In all, it has earned $272,742,922 worldwide (https://www.boxofficemojo.com/title/tt0102926/). The film (screenplay, picture, director, lead performers) earned five Academy Awards. *Interview with the Vampire* earned $223,664,608 worldwide (https://www.boxofficemojo.com/title/tt0110148/?ref_= bo_se_r_1) and was nominated for two Academy Awards (art, music).
4. Ibid.
5. Ibid.
6. The budget for *Def by Temptation* is unknown. However, it is certainly a low-budget effort. Distributed by Troma, it opened on only 11 screens, earning just over $50,000 in its original release. Its all-time earnings are $2.2 million.
7. Rob Ridenour, "Rare Depiction of Candyman Revealed," *The Clive Barker Podcast*, January 12, 2019, https://clivebarkercast.com/2019/01/12/rare-depiction-of-candyman-revealed/.
8. Ibid.
9. Steve Bogira, "They Came in Through the Bathroom: A Murder in the Projects," *Chicago Reader*, September 3, 1987, https://chicagoreader.com/news-politics/they-came-in-thro ugh-the-bathroom-mirror/.
10. Ibid.
11. Ibid.
12. Means Coleman, *Horror Noire*, 262.
13. Glenn Lovell and Knight-Ridder/Tribune, "Black Slasher 'Candyman' Draws Fire Over 'Racist' Depictions," *Chicago Tribune*, October 29, 1992, https://www.chicagotribune.com/ news/ct-xpm-1992-10-29-9204080203-story.html.
14. Ibid.
15. Ovid, in discussion with Novotny Lawrence, February 1, 2023.
16. Fred Moten, "The Case of Blackness," *Criticism* 50, no. 2 (Spring 2008): 177–218.
17. Peter Crimmins, "The First Graffiti Artist Shows New Work at Philadelphia Gallery," *WHYY PBS*, NPR, July 29, 2019, https://whyy.org/articles/cornbread-the-first-graffiti-art ist-shows-new-work-at-philadelphia-gallery/.
18. Ibid.
19. Ovid, in discussion with Novotny Lawrence, February 1, 2023.

20. Loree Seitz, "*The Jazz Singer* and Blackface: How Hollywood's Origins Will Always Be Entwined with Racism," *Moviemaker*, August 6, 2020, https://www.moviemaker.com/jazz-singer-blackface-birth-of-a-nation/.

21. Michael Rogin, quoted in Seitz, "*The Jazz Singer* and Blackface," https://www.moviemaker.com/jazz-singer-blackface-birth-of-a-nation/.

22. "Watch On De Rind," *Boardgames.com*, accessed March 10, 2023, https://boardgames.com/boardgame/watch-on-de-rind.

23. "The History of the Coon Chicken Inn," *The Jim Crow Museum*, Ferris State University, accessed March 10, 2023, https://www.ferris.edu/HTMLS/news/jimcrow/links/essays/chicken.htm.

24. Dale M. Brumfield, "The Story of the 'Coon Chicken Inn,'" *Medium*, January 3, 2020, https://medium.com/lessons-from-history/the-story-of-the-coon-chicken-inn-226fe444089c.

25. Ovid, in discussion with Novotny Lawrence, February 1, 2023.

26. Richard Dyer, *White* (London: Routledge, 1997), 90.

27. "A Site of Struggle: American Art Against Anti-Black Violence," *The Block of Museum Art*, Northwestern University, accessed March 11, 2023.

28. Candice Frederick, "Nia DaCosta on 'Candyman' and the Power of Terrifying Legends," *New York Times*, August 30, 2021, https://www.nytimes.com/2021/08/30/movies/nia-dacosta-candyman.html.

29. Ovid, in discussion with Novotny Lawrence, February 1, 2023.

30. On the day they went missing, Bickner and Thames approached Stinney Jr. and his sister while they were playing in their own front yard and asked them if they knew where they might find some flowers. The girls then left and went missing. While helping search for them, Stinney Jr. shared that he had seen them the previous day and was accused and subsequently convicted of murder when the girls' bodies were found in a ditch. In 2014, a South Carolina judge vacated Stinney Jr.'s conviction, noting that the Black youth did not receive a fair trial. For more on Stinney Jr. see: Kendell Bell, *Triple Tragedy in Alcolu: The Execution of 14-Year-Old George Stinney, Jr. Accused of the Murders of Betty June Bickner and May Emma Thames* (Rock Hill, SC: Bella Rosa Books, 2020).

31. Wade Goodwin, "Texas Executes Man Convicted in 1998 Murder of James Byrd, Jr.," *NPR*, April 24, 2019, https://www.npr.org/2019/04/24/716647585/texas-to-execute-man-convicted-in-dragging-death-of-james-byrd-jr.

32. Candice Frederick, "Nia DaCosta on 'Candyman' and the Power of Terrifying Legends," *New York Times*, August 30, 2021, https://www.nytimes.com/2021/08/30/movies/nia-dacosta-candyman.html.

33. Amy Helene Kirschke, *Art in Crisis: W.E.B. DuBois and the Struggle for African American Identity and Memory* (Bloomington, IN: Indiana University Press, 2007), 170.

34. Ibid.

35. Ovid, in discussion with Novotny Lawrence, February 1, 2023.

36. Yelena Bailey, *How the Streets Were Made: Housing Segregation and Black Life in America* (Chapel Hill: University of North Carolina University Press, 2020), 20.

37. T.V. Reed, *The Art of Protest: Culture and Activism from the Civil Rights Movement to the Streets of Seattle* (Minneapolis: University of Minnesota Press, 2005), 118.

38. Ibid, 119.

39. Frederick, "Nia DaCosta on 'Candyman' and the Power of Terrifying Legends," *New York Times*, August 30, 2021,.

40. Ovid, in discussion with Novotny Lawrence, February 1, 2023.

41. Jasmine Nichole Cobb, *Picture Freedom: Remaking Black Visuality in the Early Nineteenth Century* (New York: New York University Press, 2015), 148.

42. John Squires, "'Candyman' Featurette Spotlights the Arts and Artists Featured in Nia DaCosta's Sequel," *Bloody Disgusting*, August 19, 2021, https://bloody-disgusting.com/movie/3679171/candyman-featurette-spotlights-art-artists-featured-nia-dacostas-sequel-video/.

43. Quoted in Jazz Tangcay, "Meet the Artists Who Contributed to the Art of 'Candyman,'" *Variety*, August 27, 2021, https://variety.com/2021/artisans/news/artists-of-candyman-nia-da-costa-1235050543/.

44. Angelica Jade Bastién, "I am Tired of Films Like *Antebellum*," *Vulture*, September 14, 2020, https://www.vulture.com/2020/09/antebellum-movie-review-i-am-tired-of-films-like-this.html.

45. Aisha Harris, "'Them': The Trauma, the Trauma," *NPR*, April 8, 2021, https://www.npr.org/2021/04/08/984614649/them-the-trauma-the-trauma.

46. Kara Keeling, *The Witch's Flight: The Cinematic, the Black Femme, and the Image of Common Sense* (Durham, NC: Duke University Press, 2007), 139, 140.

47. Ovid, in discussion with Novotny Lawrence, February 1, 2023.

48. Ibid.

CHAPTER 2

THE POLITICS OF BLACK WOMEN'S IDENTITY AS MONSTROUS FETISHISM IN EARLY HOLLYWOOD HORROR CINEMA

G. E. SUBERO

In "The Spectacle of the 'Other,'" Stuart Hall explores the ways in which the racial other is represented as people and places that do not follow the categorization of sameness that has been paramount to popular culture discourses in Anglo-European film and media. Hall argues that the racial other becomes a figure of "secret fascination" and goes on to explore the different strategies through which the representation of the racial other becomes a conduit for the emergence of cultural and racial stereotypes in wider (assumed as white) culture.[1] Hall offers an in-depth look at the representational practices that foment the emergence of racial stereotypes (although this could be extended to several different types of stereotyping practices as well). Finally, he offers some alternatives and strategies designed to counter (mis)representation and "to contest 'negative' images and transform representational practices around 'race' in a more 'positive' direction."[2]

Importantly, critics of Hall's work explain that it is not intersectional in its approach, and as such, his analysis of racial otherness may inadvertently suggest that racial stereotypes operate similarly in regard to men and women. In fact, most of the case studies on which Hall relies are about images of Black men that represent or reaffirm racial stereotypes. Similarly, Jessica Baker Kee examines the racial tropes in postmodern horror cinema that characterize male bodies as monstrous and position Black men as either abject victims or hypersexual monsters. She claims that Black otherness is an artifice created through tropes and visual imagery that highlight difference and provoke a rejection of the racial other because their presence disrupts the paradigms that construct sameness and that locate certain cultural images in a safe space where their cultural power does not threaten normative societal beliefs.

In *Horror Noire: Blacks in American Horror Films from 1890s to Present*, Robin Means Coleman studies what "horror films can reveal, through representations, about our understanding of Black and Black cultural tropes, or Blackness, as well as what kinds of socio-political discourses these films contribute, and what meanings they might provoke."[3] The contribution of this book to understanding horror cinema as a vehicle to highlight and delve into the racialized imageries and narratives that construct Blackness as other is indisputable. Means Coleman is clear that the use of Black tropes and narratives speaks to differences, and even though most films Hall analyzed are/ were created with white audiences (Hollywood and European mostly) in mind, Black horror films illustrate the ways in which otherness can be used as a tool for demarcating difference and, in many cases, justifying racial discrimination toward people of color. One of the most important distinctions of the book is that it highlights how Blackness is constructed as monolithic (from the point of view of the white audiences such films were originally intended for) inasmuch as the ethnic origin of different Black groups, their ancestry or background, becomes homogenized for the "benefit" of such audiences in ways that disregard cultural or national/regional differences. This is clearly evidenced in the way that different religious or belief practices are amalgamated and conflated as one and the same in many horror films. This aligns with bell hooks assertion of the usefulness of the commodification of otherness, asserting that in "commodity culture, ethnicity becomes spice, seasoning that can liven up the dull dish that is mainstream white culture."[4] The homogenized version of Blackness that horror cinema offers via uniform culture, religious beliefs and practices, and customs also ease and reaffirm the consumption of certain cultural taboos around sexuality and desire that are viewed as transgressive when they occur via racialized bodies.

Following this line of argument, this chapter looks at the ways Black femininity is used as a horror trope in early Hollywood cinema to portray monstrosity and justify (post)colonial domination of people of color in the Afro-Caribbean diaspora. Since, as Stephen Spencer suggests, "social divisions are often intrinsically linked, forming a shifting lantern show of oppressions triggered by social economic and political realities of the time," it could be argued that early Hollywood horror movies set in the Caribbean (usually in plantation settings) operate as cultural texts that seek to justify the (post)colonization of racial others while fetishizing Black culture through the exoticization of Afro-Caribbean belief practices and rituals seen as intrinsically evil and transgressive toward white heteronormativity.[5] Black women's bodies are stereotyped in such films to demonstrate that racism does not reside outside the realm of the ordinary and that the colonial enterprise was necessary to ensure racial harmony among people whose cultural and religious practices were regarded as backward and, in most cases, lethal to those who fell prey to such primitivity and monstrosity. To that end, this chapter focuses on George Terwilliger's *Ouanga* (1936), Arthur H. Leonard's *The Devil's Daughter* (1939), and Roy William Neil's *Black Moon* (1934), demonstrating how these films show a conflation between white femininity (portrayed as victimized heroines) and Black femininity (portrayed as erotically raw, untamed, and embodied through monstrous figures). The chapter demonstrates the ambivalent representations of race, gender, and monstrosity in an attempt to reaffirm (post)colonial subjugation of the West over a "monstrous" other.[6] By utilizing film as a tool to justify foreign interference (in this case mainly from the United States) in national and regional politics, these films establish a relationship between Afro-Caribbean cultural practices and monstrosity in ways that sustain racial discourses of Black people as the inferior and uncivilized other. In short, the films both demonize and eroticize Black women's bodies as both luring and threatening to white femininity by supporting the notion that "slavery and the colonial subject undoubtedly developed an eroticised power relation between colonial master and subject."[7]

BLACK WOMEN'S BODIES AND HORROR CINEMA

To the contemporary viewer, the films chosen for analysis in this chapter may not easily be considered horror, since they do not necessarily follow the conventions and tropes of recent horror cinema. However, as Means Coleman suggests, horror cinema is a resistant genre that is both simultaneously stable (using fear and violence as key leitmotif in their narratives) and flexible (through a variety of aesthetic and taste choices made by directors to influence audiences' reactions).[8] Thus, the films analyzed here all investigate how race operates as a catalyst to expose audiences' understandings of the process of identity formation, through mediated messages that go beyond the desire for explicit on-screen terror or violence (the real-life psychology or bloodlust of the audience as manifested within a film's narrative). In the following analysis, the context in which violence occurs (even when such violence is more implied than explicit) is key to understanding how the horror of Blackness as a threat to stability (toward whiteness) feeds into the dimensions of Blackness that Fanon has famously discussed in his work, whereby Blackness has historically been associated with primitiveness and backwardness.[9] The three films were all directed by whites and responded to the needs of the Hollywood and British film industries. For instance, films such as *Ouanga* were only made to fill quotas that were necessary in order to export American films into the United Kingdom. Made with a shoestring budget and filmed in just 18 days, its storyline clearly reaffirmed existing cultural anxieties about people of color. Similarly, the other films studied here align with Fanon's assertion that "every colonized people—in other words, every people in whose soul an inferiority complex has been created by the death and burial of its local cultural originality—finds itself face to face with the language of the civilizing nation."[10] Therefore, these films operate as vehicles to examine cultural concerns that existed with regard to Black people and Black culture among white audiences.

If horror cinema was regarded as a means to (visually) externalize cultural fears, such fears became even more worrying when they were embodied by and through female protagonists. Barbara Creed has famously argued that what she terms the "monstrous feminine" constitutes a feminist and liberated archetype of horror villainess that holds power by her female abject position.[11] However, such female monsters are unquestionably white and represent a type of agency that disregards the complexities of women who hold multiple identities. Creed correctly asserts that the female body has traditionally been seen as deviant in most horror cinema while claiming that "the concept of the border is central to the construction of the monstrous in horror film, that which crosses or threatens to cross the 'border' is abject . . . the function of the monstrous remains the same—to bring about an encounter between the symbolic order and that which threatens its stability."[12] However, she fails to acknowledge that the issue of the border is further complicated when it is depicted on a female, Black monstrous body (or any colored body). In the three films under analysis, the Black, female protagonists spend most of the narrative struggling at the border of white and Black identities, whereby the full assumption of Black agency offers the demise of their social statuses, their class positions, and their own femininity. In these films, the white heroine (whether part of the film's narrative or just a phantasmatic cultural presence) occupies a key role in ensuring that Black, female otherness is read through every aspect of the protagonists' actions and their bodies. Rhona J. Berenstein sees a similar tension between Black, female monsters and white heroines in jungle cinema of the 1930s. She argues that,

> although threats of a male/female binary opposition are invoked via the heroine's exchanges with black men and monkeys, those encounters cannot be reduced to sexual difference. They are also inflected by racial liminality and species transgression, by the figuration of the heroine as a discursive vehicle through which the conventional physical and psychological distances between white/black, animal/human, and fear/desire are bridged.[13]

Although Berenstein's work does not focus on the Black characters, it would be impossible to disregard the Black monstrous figures as essential to the formation and articulation of white femininity in the films she studied. As such, whiteness is defined and articulated for what it is not. Thus, the presence of Black, female monstrous figures in the narrative provides audiences with ways to understand historic racial tensions, as well as social relations shaped by ethnic and racial identity. The four Black, female protagonists analyzed here (three of whom are depicted as villainous, monstrous-feminine) are defined either by the race they will never be able to embrace, or by racial codes they have rejected despite their own ethnic origins. As will be shown the in the following section, these monstrous women are less monstrous because of their desire to cause harm or engage in voodoo, witchcraft, or other ritual practices; rather, it is because they all reject the civilizing aspects of white culture that would place them, at the very least, as acceptable women of color in societies that openly reject non-white subjects.

BLACK IDENTITY AND FEMALE AGENCY IN THE PLANTATION FILM

Tommy L. Lott argues that Black cinema, as well as its directorial, narrative, and aesthetic considerations, seem to be exclusively orientated toward a cinema that focuses entirely on the experiences that are created by Black filmmakers centered on Black life.[14] However, as he rightly points out, this usually excludes a body of cinema created by white filmmakers and, many times, mainstream film studios. Although these films do not necessarily focus on the lived experience of Black communities, their reception and consumption among white and Black audiences alike play a pivotal role in identity formation and in responding to sociocultural concerns deriving from existing racial tensions. bell hooks claims that in her experience, regardless of whether filmmakers and studios embrace the lived experiences of Black individuals, there is a clear tendency to exclude the female experience on screen via a "cinematic racism—[and] its violent erasure of black womanhood."[15] She goes even further, arguing, "even when representations of black women were present in film, our bodies and being were to serve—to enhance and maintain white womanhood as object of the phallocentric gaze."[16] This idea seems even more pertinent in the context of horror cinema, where, as Creed asserts, "most horror films also construct a border between what Kristeva refers to as the 'clean and proper body' and the abject body, or the body which has lost its form and integrity."[17] Accordingly, the Black female body is abject because it cannot be both an object of desire due to its skin color (it operates outside the libidinal strategies permitted to film audiences in mainstream cinema), and because Black female agency is limited to servile positions in which other female experiences are erased. Although the films for analysis here show the demise of Black femininity by the end of the narrative, they operate in ways that provide a space of reckoning around the racial and sexual tensions operating toward Black, female subjects.

Black Moon tells the story of Juanita Perez Lane (Dorothy Burges), who returns from New York to the Haitian plantation where she spent her childhood. Now married, Juanita feels that the island is her true home and takes her five-year-old daughter with her. Her uncle, Dr. Raymond Perez (Arnold Korff), oversees the plantation and hopes that Juanita will not stay long, as he fears for his niece. Influenced by her old nanny—who planted the seed of voodoo in her—and lured by the sound of drums, Juanita becomes a white priestess who engages in the natives' rites and sacrifices. Her husband, Stephen Lane (Jack Holt), arrives on the island with the intention of taking her back to New York, to no avail. Juanita's internalization of voodoo practices is such that she kills an adolescent girl in a sacrifice and, finally, will try and sacrifice her own daughter (which her husband only avoids by shooting Juanita dead at the last minute).

This film clearly supports colonialist tropes and justifies the need for colonial oppression. Juanita shows that Black identity is rather porous and that what is considered Black—in other words primitive, savage, uneducated, etc.—does not only operate through the Black skin, but can also filter into other non-Black bodies by means of appropriation or assimilation. As Patrick Johnson already suggests, the appropriation of Blackness indicates that "individuals or groups appropriate this complex and nuanced racial signifier to circumscribe its boundaries or to exclude other individuals or groups. When blackness is appropriated to the exclusion of others, identity becomes political."[18] This politicization of Blackness as an identity does not guarantee, as it is clear in this film, that there is a desire to improve one's status or social standing (as documented in cases of white passing). Instead, the film sees Blackness almost as an identity that has the potential to contaminate white people and one that must be repressed and contained. It is not surprising, then, that even the press release for the film highlighted the dangers that Black identity and Black people (as a community) pose for the white colonizers. As reported by the *New York Times* at the time of the film's release (June 28, 1934), the film's narrative is described as one in which Juanita sends "2000 crazed natives to exterminate all the white folk on the imaginary West Indian island of San Christopher."

Despite her whiteness, Juanita is coded as a racial other from the very beginning of the film. The opening sequence is stressed by the sound of drums and shows her in a chiaroscuro close-up that pans down her face and body to show her hands drumming against a table while her daughter, Nancy (Cora Sue Lewis), looks entranced. Despite the close-up highlighting Burges' delicate and striking features (and her whiteness), the audience is asked to place her as an outsider, as someone who does not conform to and who rejects her own white identity. Her whiteness is not sufficient to guarantee a safe space of acceptance and the social/cultural mobility afforded to those who fully embrace whiteness as a marker of superiority. As Melissa L. Cooper observes, *Black Moon* "depicted and commodified the horrors and dangers whites encountered when confronted with African-born black savagery and sold this story to American audiences."[19] Juanita's is a cautionary tale that clearly reinforces the idea that whiteness is the only accepted form of cultural and racial identity, and that embracing whiteness should be regarded as a key enterprise for those individuals lucky enough to be or pass as white.

Importantly, this is further problematized by Juanita's family surname: Perez. The clearly Hispanic name has little to do with Black culture; however, the filmmakers seem happy to conflate all non-white cultural traits as a homogenous identity. Yet, the surname itself is not strong enough to demarcate all people who bear it as non-white. For instance, Dr. Perez does not seem to problematize his whiteness, despite sharing the same family name. In fact, he becomes an archetype of colonialist discourse that sees the subjugation of Blackness as a natural response in the natural world order. That the National Rifle Association (NRA) appears in the opening credits as a producing company justifies the film's elevation of gun use as the best and most natural defense against the savagery of the Black islanders. This is evident when Dr. Perez tells Stephen—while displaying his secret stash of rifles used to keep the plantation's servants controlled—"We've been prepared for the last 100 years [to contain the Black islanders]. Six times the blacks have tried to wipe us down . . . our family has been in the saddle in St. Christopher for the last 200 years. Many have died, but none has ever run away." For the doctor, whiteness is the only signifier of his identity, and no surname or other artifice will convince him otherwise. This idea of whiteness chimes with what Richard Dyer asserts in his work on white as a social construct, where he claims that "as long as race is something only applied to non-white peoples, as long as white people are not racially seen and named, they/we function as a human norm. Other people are raced, we are just people."[20]

On the other hand, Juanita is othered because she dares to embrace a part of her racial ancestry that is regarded as nonnormative. Her decision to assume the characteristics and customs inherent to a non-white identity trump her own "visible" white identity and make her a threat to the stability of the normative and patriarchal order. By embracing all aspects of the Black population and becoming their spiritual leader, she bridges the gap between the depiction of Black people as slaves (docile and servile) and those who have not been colonized and live "free," roaming around the island. Juanita evidences the mixing of these two visions inasmuch as the people of St. Christopher appear always subdued, but they, nonetheless, constitute a constant threat to the white people in the island.

Ultimately, Juanita's fate and the film's moral outcome use well-known colonialist tropes in order to justify the then continuous exploitation of the Caribbean islands at the hands of the United States. As Emiel Martens asserts, "most 1930s horror adventure films contained . . . scenes of romantic bliss and plantation wealth, yet with the notable difference that the overseas colonial setting found itself under constant threat of black invasion. As such, these movies offered a modern frontier variation of the southern plantation drama, one that negotiated the desires and anxieties of America's presence in the Caribbean."[21] By the time the film arrives at its narrative climax, Juanita has turned full "native" in both appearance and behavior. Yet, she is not fully depicted in the very same costumes as the other Black, female islanders. Instead, she is presented in a white chiffon dress that drapes her body very sensually while her white headscarf (trying to emulate those worn by the native, Black women) seems more in tune with an orientalist vision of the other. Thus, she is othered even among Black others to further stress her dislocation from all possible identities and to justify her extermination from the film. Her presence operates as a reminder that identity is fluid and complex and that skin color cannot be regarded as the only marker for identity formation. This type of double othering responds to Patrick Johnson, who argues that "when white Americans essentialize blackness, for example, they often do so in ways that maintain 'whiteness' as the master trope of purity, supremacy, and entitlement, as a ubiquitous, fixed, unifying signifier that seems invisible."[22]

Similarly, *The Devil's Daughter* plays out the anxieties and tribulations of identity formation through the tensions between the two Black, female protagonists. In the film, Sylvia Walton (Ida James), of Harlem, inherits her late father's Jamaican banana plantation and returns to manage it. This angers her disinherited half-sister, Isabelle Walton (Nina Mae McKinney), who wishes to own the plantation herself and who is also jealous of the love that John Lowden (Emmet "Babe" Wallace) professes for Sylvia. Isabelle plots with the plantation supervisor, Philip Ramsey (Jack Carter), and between the two they drug Sylvia and take her to the hill country, where the Black natives, led by their voodoo priest, perform a Blood Dance as a preliminary act to sacrificing Sylvia on a burning altar. The film was produced by Sack Attractions, a company formed in the 1920s in San Antonio, Texas, by Alfred Nathaniel, for what they considered their "specialty market." According to GLC Wiki, the "company was created for the production, distribution and exhibition of 'all black' or 'race' films (films made by black directors for black audiences and containing black actors)" (2020). Such films were made with low budgets and without the technical and commercial expertise of the big, mainstream film studios. Despite raving reviews for McKinney's acting, the story was ultimately regarded as poor. As one critic put it at the time, "Miss McKinney's work as an actress was flawless. She received able support from the rest of the cast. But excellent acting is not enough to make a great play out of a poor story, and *The Devil's Daughter* is lacking" (1943).

However, what makes this film unique regarding the depiction of racialized relations among non-white people is the fact that it uses its two female protagonists to show a duality in terms of identity formation attained through identity markers beyond skin color. The film reaffirms tired stereotypes of femininity, whereby Sylvia is portrayed as the demure and well-educated (soft- and well-spoken) Harlem native who has assimilated the mannerisms and the jargon of her white counterparts (despite the fact that her wealth would still not afford her entry in white-only spaces). On the other hand, Isabelle is portrayed as less educated, untamed, and less delicate in her mannerism and speech. She is an islander and not a city girl like her sister. The film heavily relies on the diasporic traffic of identity to distinguish between the two sisters as part of a binary opposite.

Although the film contends that Blackness is not as monolithic as suggested elsewhere (a departure from the type of racial discourse in the other two films studied here), *Devil's Daughter* continues to rely heavily on imperialist power structures to conflate the difference between the experience of Blackness within developed societies such as America and the experience of Blackness in the Black Caribbean diaspora. As Stephanie Leigh Batiste claims, "the position of cultural power inherent in this representational structure reified national differences between American blacks and the subjects they performed, but the form and its implications also permitted the appropriation of the film for antiracist expression that sought to bridge and recuperate difference."[23] However, where Leigh Batiste sees the film as an expression of a "transnational black sisterhood," it would be possible to counterargue that the film juxtaposes, or at least heavily implies, that these different experiences of Black identity are both part of aspirational narratives that are impossible to fulfil.[24] That both female protagonists have set their eyes on the only white person in the narrative further suggests that the ideals of whiteness must be sought and embraced in order to regain a level of agency that is regarded as normative. This explain why, as Martens explains, "the British Board of Censors [used the film] to show black populations in Jamaica and elsewhere in the colonial world that African-Caribbean religions were both fraudulent and dangerous."[25]

While *Black Moon* depicted voodoo practices as a supernatural evil force, *Devil's Daughter* portrays the practice solely as a fraudulent superstition. In this manner all of Isabelle's actions throughout the film are framed within the idea of a deceitful identity. Isabelle makes it very clear that she is aware that obeah and voodoo practices are scams and that they are only followed by gullible individuals. As a result, she pretends to be an obeah priestess to psychologically manipulate her sister into abandoning the island, by drugging her so she thinks that she is under a voodoo spell. Despite the excessive use of diegetic drum sounds and the many scenes with natives dancing (indicating Black savagery), the film posits Isabelle more as a cunning, evil Black woman who knowingly uses deceit and trickery to get ahead in life. The contrast between the two sisters permits audiences to economically understand the subject position of the filmmakers, who are, at all times, reinforcing the notion that the Blackness experienced in the Caribbean is twice as perverse, backward, and savage as elsewhere (or at least the one experienced in America).

This is further demonstrated through Sylvia's lighter skin color, which presents her as a rather civilized individual when compared to her sister. However, the film also infers that Sylvia can only attain a place of real social standing in the Jamaican planta-tion and that she would not be afforded such standing in New York. Sylvia's internalized whiteness becomes an artifice within the narrative, as it is not enough to conceal her Blackness. The fetishization of Blackness is evident from the lengthy opening sequence of the film, in which a group of shabbily dressed Caribbean islanders are seen singing and dancing in the plantation. This quickly moves to scenes of cockfighting and then to scenes of voodoo and ritual practices. To add to the didacticism of the film, this opening sequence uses footage that follows more the conventions of newsreels and ethnographic cinema than fiction cinema itself. The camerawork and the lighting are all natural, with an abundance of wide takes.

Even though the film has been praised for being the first feature film with a mainly Black cast, the fact that this film was scripted, directed, and produced by white filmmakers shows that it was never meant to reaffirm Black identity as a valid subject position. As Means Coleman indicates, "the divide between the sisters is at the line of the urban and urbane versus the rural and unsophisticated. However, even this contrast is recast through a caution about the dangers of leaving home, becoming uppity, and losing touch with one's own people."[26] In other words, for the Black individual, there is no winning situation, there is no subject position that would rid them of the baggage that is bestowed on such people as a result of their skin color and their ethnic origin. Sylvia and Isabelle are two sides of the same coin: a backward, nativist, gullible, unintel-ligent, savage coin. Continuing with Means Coleman, this reifies that "while the planta-tion work is seen as rudimentary and inelegant, being cultured and well-read is cast as rather useless."[27]

Further, the issues of colorism and of ethnic origin (a rather veiled and superficial comment on the ethnic differences of Black peoples from different territories) are brought upon in the film. On the one hand, Isabelle's half-Haitian heritage (through her mother) means that she is not Haitian enough to be able to engage "properly" in voodoo practices. Since both girls share the same Jamaican father, the idea here is that she is nei-ther fully Haitian nor Jamaican, placing her at an interstitial space where her Blackness is not pure enough. On the other hand, Sylvia's time in Harlem has stripped her of an es-sential part of her Black heritage, to the extent that by the end of the narrative she comes to the realization that "I don't belong."

Although colorism is vaguely addressed in *Devil's Daughter*, it is fully fleshed out in *Ouanga: A Story of Voodooism*. The film has been decried (both at the time of its release and in subsequent reviews) for its lack of technical and directorial prowess. However, it is undeniable that of all the films analyzed here, this explicitly questions and challenges audiences' perceptions of colorism, the politics of biracialism, and racial passing as a strategy of survival in the context of horror cinema. In *Ouanga* (aka *The Love Wanga*), Fredi Washington plays Clelie (or Klilie), a fair-skinned Black Haitian woman and plantation owner who is also secretly a voodoo priestess. Her unrequited love for Adam Maynard (Philip Brandon) drives her to use voodoo against Adam's fiancé, Eve Langley (Marie Paxton). In the meantime, the plantation's foreman, LeStrange (Sheldon Leonard), declares his undying love for Clelie, only to be rejected because she can only see herself with Adam (with whom she had previously maintained a two-year relationship).

From the outset, the film's dialogue directly deals with the politics of race and Blackness. For instance, in the opening sequence, which sees the love triangle sailing back to Haiti, Clelie declares her love for Adam, only to be told that "the barrier of blood that separates us can't be overcome." As Means Coleman rightly asserts, "Klili, who is phenotypically as light as Adam, cannot ever be White enough as somewhere in her bloodline there is African ancestry. Hence, she is tainted by the one-drop rule, in which just a bit of Black blood makes one instantly and forever Black."[28] When she retorts that "I'm white too. As white as she [Eve] is," only to be told that she could never be as white as a "real" white person such as the film's alleged heroine, she is quick to switch gears and claim, "Black, am I? Alright, I'm black. I'll show him what a black girl can do!"[29] In no other film is the dialogue so explicit in terms of race relations and the paradigms of the colonizer/colonized dichotomy, and the stereotyping of peoples of the diaspora in ways that resonate with Means Coleman, who asserts, "the tragedy of skin color and blood is textbook tragic mulatto stereotype, in which her [Klilie's] proximity to Whiteness makes her beautiful while the irreconcilability of her situation makes her a danger to herself or others, and ultimately leads to insanity."[30] The film operates as a cautionary tale, warning Black people with light skin of the dangers of passing as white.

In the films discussed here, as well as in many other similar genre films that emerged at the time, color (as a marker of ethnic and racial identity) plays a key role not only in the casting process but also as part of the narrative and the manifestation of the racial and gendered tensions prevailing at the time. In his work on race and space, David Delaney argues that passing is a process very much defined by the spacialization of race and the racialization of space.[31]

Although Delaney writes about passing as a survival strategy, it extends to horror cinema. Passing operates as a monstrous and evil transformation that fetishizes Blackness as a primitive, backward, and inescapable identity (even for those people whose skin color may afford them the possibility of embracing/faking a different ethnic or racial identity). *Ouanga's* mixed-race protagonist comes to manifest issues associated with being biracial that are equally close to the real-life experience of the actress interpreting such a role. As Cheryl Black argues, "in a white-supremacist culture that depended on fixed racial identities and essential racial 'difference' to maintain hierarchy, Washington's light complexion, blue-grey eyes, and unaccented speech did not signify 'Negro'. In such a context, Fredi Washington was an unintelligible sign."[32]

The in-betweenness experienced by Clelie already suggests that whiteness is monolithic and that any transgression from such identity (whether in the form of the cultural appropriation that occurs in *Black Moon* or the dichotomist experiences of race seen in *Devil's Daughter*) can only merit the disavowal of binary identities or the extermination (within the film narrative) of such ambivalent figures. This idea follows Kelli Weston's assertion that "by the time Washington played the role, she already had a history of appearing in films where her racial ambiguity promised her either misery or death, if not both."[33] Although the purpose of this analysis is to see the film beyond its clearly racist tonality and its caricaturization and fetishization of Blackness as a monolithic identity, it would be reductionist not to see a parallel between such characterizations and Washington's own acting career. This is a point further developed by Charlene Regester, who argues that the actress spent most of her theater and film career having to masquerade her biracial identity and being forced to play Black or white-passing roles despite her clear multiracial background.[34]

> A segment of people who shared similar phenotypical traits such as Washington's saw passing as a valuable shift in racial positionality. The individual was capable to move from a minority subject position to a majority one in ways that, undoubtedly, forced them to erase their biracial or multiracial identity. For passing to be successful, the mixed-race person had to completely reject any non-white traits or background that could potentially be read through their skin colour, behaviour, mannerism, speech, or any other cultural manifestation that had the potential to denunciate a black subject position. Thus, Clelie has to die by the end of the film (ironically at the hands of the one white actor passing as black) because her racial ambivalence and her overt desire to shift from white to black spaces without issue, was deemed too transgressive for audiences and the filmmakers. The real horror of the story is the realisation that race operates as a social construct that is fallible and people like Clelie have the power to transform and infiltrate white spaces. Clelie's monstrosity derives from her desire to proclaim and assume a white identity that should be denied to her at all costs.

Although *Ouanga* has not achieved the cult status of other similar films in which race can be seen as one of the drivers of the story (in fairness, none of the films discussed here really has achieved such a status outside academic circles), it is impossible to deny that the film was ahead of its time for the overt inclusion in the narrative of the anxieties experienced by the biracial subject in their search for a valid subject positionality. As Weston rightly writes,

> for all the racialised anxieties the film reinforces, amid all the blatant anti-miscegenation messaging, it is Clelie who displays the fullest interiority . . . There is no mistaking Clelie for the film's protagonist, at least in the sense of identifying with

her plight, given the story's monstrous view of her. Yet, above all else, the audience is forced to reckon with the emotional toil of her social bifurcation.[35]

This is further enunciated through the character's costumes as she navigates the racially interstitial spaces in which her whiteness and Blackness operate as markers of identity categorization. For instance, the film's preface, which is a parallel story recounted in a flashback, shows Clelie scantily dressed, dancing to the rhythm of drums in front of a fire in what appears to be a ritual ceremony. This depiction of Clelie as sexually alluring and monstrous conflates Caribbean, exotic eroticism and the primitiveness and backwardness of Caribbean ritual practices such as voodoo. However, the stark contrast between Clelie's costume and those worn by the rest of the islander women at the ritual also helps mark her as a fetishized commodity. Her sequined leotard is grandiose, and at the same time, it marks her as an exotic other in ways that align with those famously theorized by Shohat and Stam in relation to the trope strategies used by imperial texts to demarcate otherness.[36]

This scene swiftly moves onto the actual narrative, in which Clelie is found on the same ship as Adam as he returns to his Haitian plantation. Once again, the first person seen on the ship is Clelie, who this time is framed through a medium close-up, dressed in a sumptuous black gown while wearing a pale fur shawl over her shoulders. The lightness of her skin makes her practically indistinguishable from the other white passengers on the ship. However, her otherness is marked by the ouanga amulet that she is wearing underneath her luxurious dress. (It was conferred on her during the ritual ceremony previously described.) Since her skin color cannot be a definite marker of her racial otherness, the amulet is used in lieu to explain how she cannot be regarded as a "real" white subject.

As the sequence progresses, the love triangle at the center of the narrative is framed through a long shot that shows Clelie on the center left-hand side of the frame, while Adam and his fiancé are pictured on the right-hand side. The dresses that both female characters wear bear great resemblance; yet, while Clelie's dress is black, Eve's is white (perhaps an economic way to enunciate race through costume). Race and class are further conflated later in the film when Clelie is shown alongside her faithful maid, Susie (Babe Joyce), who is dressed in a typical maid outfit. Once again, Clelie is placed at an interstitial space where she is not white enough to be accepted as Adam's equal, but she is not Black enough to be confined to subservient roles. This corroborates Elle Scott's assertion that Clelie/Washington's "self-possession is of a piece with her high fashion and the film's glamour photography, the latter of which divulges Clelie in the repose, luxury, and haute opulence that white women naturally get and that black girls are typically doomed to support."[37]

As has been discussed before, the rest of the narrative positions Clelie as someone who struggles to make full sense of her racialized self because she is constantly reminded that her biracial identity opens up too many avenues of identity formation that problematize the monolithic view of race as identity that circulated in popular culture. In a similar manner, this also goes on to explain the reasons why Washington herself was not more prolific as an actress in the cinema of the 1930s and '40s. Soon after starring in a few more similar films, her political commitment to fight racial segregation and racial discrimination saw her engage with activism in ways that could not separate her activist from her star persona.

CONCLUSION

In *Divas on Screen: Black Women in American Film*, Mia Mask provides an insightful analysis of the ways in which many Black actresses have struggled to enjoy success in their acting careers in ways that their white counterparts have not because their skin color does not threaten the stability of the social and cultural order.[38] She goes on to analyze what it means to have a Black, female star system in Hollywood and the social and cultural impact that such a system has on people of color when they see people who share their own ethnicity or race on the screen. She acknowledges that Black actresses in previous generations (such as the ones analyzed in this study demonstrate) "possessed untapped talents they were never given opportunity to cultivate or regularly exhibit."[39] Indeed, most depictions of Black female identity in Hollywood cinema for most of the twentieth century were produced to reinforce prevalent stereotypes around race and sexuality, in which Black actresses portrayed lustful and primitive characters who were in need of the civilizing help of their white counterparts or of white culture at large.

Other scholars also examine Black actresses' experiences in Hollywood. For instance, in *Fatal Beauties: Black Women in Hollywood*, Karen Alexander discusses the number of Black actresses who could not negotiate the intricacies of being a Black actress in a studio system that favored white people.[40] However, it could be argued that horror cinema afforded many Black actresses a space in which the negotiations of their racial identities could be more easily brought to the forefront of the narrative, because such films relied on shock value as part of the genre's expectations. This is not to say that such films can be regarded as texts seeking to balance the racial inequalities operating in the societies at the time, but they, at the very least, allowed for the enunciation of certain aspects of inequality, which could be brought in as part of the storyline or the narrative discourse.

The fetishization of Black, female identity in these three films reaffirms racial stereotypes that have continually haunted Black actresses. Such films depended on the relationship between the sexuality of the Black woman (depicted as evil, monstrous, lustful, and primitive) and the asexualized white woman (depicted as tame, demure, and virginal). This is not to say that despite playing stereotypically racialized roles, actresses were unable to bring nuance to their performance and use their onscreen persona as a tool to contest and challenge such stereotypes (however subtle this may have been, so that filmmakers would still be pleased with such performances).

This coincides with Ingrid Banks's writing, as she suggests that "in moments of 'subversive' resistance, several black actresses were able to bring their own interpretations to stereotypical characters."[41] Despite the obvious attempt to depict Black identity as monolithic and to avoid any conversations about ethnic identity, these films have shown that Black identity is more nuanced and complex than originally envisioned through the films' narratives and storylines. When looking beyond the surface, these films, which in many cases had to walk a fine line between parodic stereotypes and lived identities and experiences, offer complex studies of identity formation for people of color. Although the narratives may seem rather reductionist, it is the interpretations of Black characters that allow audiences to peek into the more multi-faceted aspects of Black female agency that these films can illustrate. In *Black Moon*, Juanita is never fully fleshed out as a well-rounded character, because the narrative is too concerned with her transgression (and necessary punishment) at embracing a Black identity despite being a white subject. Since the film seems concerned only with the monstrous aspect of the female protagonist for rejecting the values and norms established by her racialized body (and the society in which it operates), the audience is never allowed to understand how she developed such strong links to Black culture and the native islanders in the first place. Blackness is, therefore, fetishized and commodified to the point of suggesting it is an effect rather than an innate identity. The elements of voodoo found in the film only serve to portray Afro-Caribbean cultures as backward and primitive without engaging in the complexities of diasporic cultural discourses around belief systems. In short, the film, and its female protagonist, are depicted as too dismissive and aloof to elicit any kind of sympathy (or at least understanding) by the film's audience as to the reasons for Juanita's actions.

In *The Devil's Daughter*, the racial tensions experienced by people of color in urban and rural settings is put forward by the narrative in the form of the feud between the two Black sisters, Isabelle and Sylvia. Since its release, the film has divided audiences and critics alike. Whereas some people see the film as a candid exploration of belief systems in the Black Caribbean, others have panned it for its lack of production values and poor script. Regardless of such positions, the film shows how Black women must constantly engage with structures of power in ways that construct them within the normative parameters of their gendered and racial selves. Race is further problematized in this film by the fact that it is very much subjected to class difference and upbringing. For instance, Sylvia is depicted as too gullible, because she has been away from the island for too long and has forgotten the "native" ways. In other words, that voodoo is trickery and that such beliefs are backward and uncivilized. On the other hand, Isabelle is cunning and lascivious, because she has not had the opportunity to experience societies that are more "civilised," as her sister has in Harlem. If one adds that, by mention, it is suggested that Isabelle's mother was Haitian (not Jamaican, as are the rest of the Black people in this film), the film further problematizes ethnic origin by separating different types of Blackness but continuing to insist that all experiences of Blackness remain monolithic in their savagery and primitiveness. The tepid ending of the film, in which the two sisters make peace and decide to run the plantation together, only serves to further fetishize Blackness and female agency as a lack (both gendered and racial).

Arguably, *Ouanga* was more successful in denouncing issues centered on colorism through the politics of biracial identity. Clelie's ability to move from white to Black spaces without suspicion shows that she is masterful, albeit monstrous, at masquerading race. As Scott suggests, "Clelie straddles the line between modernity and primitivism, showing herself able to fashion and wield either to perfection when the occasion calls— and in the process defying the power of their binary opposition."[42] Although the film still relies on old stereotypes centered on the image of the tragic mulatta, her ability to pass can be regarded as a progressive action, because not many films at the time dared to speak out about the racial tensions experienced by biracial subject in spaces of cultural and social in-betweenness. This idea chimes with Black, who poses the question, "what, finally, could be a more persuasive argument against the ideology of racial essentialism and its correlative, white supremacy, than the ability to successfully 'pass' from one racial identity to another?"[43] The film recognizes that biracial identity is complex when played out in bodies that cannot be easily racially codified. That Clelie needs to be killed by the end of the film comes as no surprise, because such ambivalence exposes the fragility of the power structures on which racial supremacy are built. Furthermore, the fact that she is killed at the hands of a white actor who is playing a Black character operates as an ironic enunciation of the power structures that are sustained through racial stereotyping. In short, these films demonstrate the fetishization of Black identity as a necessary tool to maintain separate subjects' positions in relation to race in early Hollywood horror cinema.

NOTES

1. Stuart Hall, "The Spectacle of the Other," in *Representation: Cultural Representations and Signifying Practices*, ed. Stuart Hall (London: SAGE, 1997), 225.
2. Ibid., 225–226.
3. Robin R. Means Coleman, *Horror Noire: Blacks in American Horror Films from 1890 to Present* (New York: Routledge, 2011), 2.
4. bell hooks, *Black Looks: Race and Representation* (New York: Routledge, 2015), 21.
5. Stephen Spencer, *Race and Ethnicity: Culture, Identity and Representation* (New York: Routledge, 2014), 105.
6. Ella Shohat and Robert Stam, *Unthinking Eurocentrism: Multiculturalism and the Media* (New York: Routledge, 2014).
7. Spencer, *Race and Ethnicity*, 105.
8. Means Coleman, *Horror Noire*.
9. Frantz Fanon, *Black Skin, White Masks* (London: Pluto, 1986).
10. Ibid., 18.
11. Barbara Creed, *The Monstrous-feminine: Film, Feminism, Psychoanalysis* (New York: Routledge, 2015).

12. Ibid., 10–11.
13. Rhona J. Berenstein, "White Heroines and Hearts of Darkness: Race, Gender, and Disguise in 1930s Jungle Films," *Film History* 6, no. 3 (1994): 319.
14. Tommy L. Lott, "A No-Theory Theory of Contemporary Black Cinema," *American Literature Forum* 25, no. 2 (1991): 221–236.
15. hooks, *Black Looks*, 119.
16. Ibid.
17. Creed, *The Monstrous-feminine*, 11.
18. Patrick Johnson, *Appropriating Blackness* (New York: Duke University Press, 2003), 3.
19. Melissa L. Cooper, "Selling Voodoo in Migration Metropolises," in *Race and Retail*, ed. Mia Bay and Ann Fabian (New Jersey: Rutgers University Press, 2015) 22.
20. Richard Dyer, *White: Twentieth Anniversary Edition* (London: Routledge, 2017), 1.
21. Emiel Martens, "The 1930s Horror Adventure Film on Location in Jamaica: 'Jungle Gods,' 'Voodoo Drums,' and 'Mumbo Jumbo' in the 'Secret Places of Paradise Island,'" *Humanities* 10, no. 2 (2021): 9.
22. Johnson, *Appropriating Blackness*, 4.
23. Stephanie Leigh Batiste, *Darkening Mirrors: Imperial Representation in Depression-Era African American Performance* (Durham, NC: Duke University Press, 2011), 203.
24. Ibid.
25. Martens, "The 1930s Horror Adventure Film on Location in Jamaica," 1.
26. Means Coleman, *Horror Noire*, 60.
27. Ibid.
28. Ibid., 58.
29. Ibid.
30. Ibid., 58–59.
31. David Delaney, "The Space that Race Makes," *The Professional Geographer* 54, no.1 (2022): 6–14.
32. Cheryl Black, "Looking White, Acting Black: Cast(e)ing Fredi Washington," *Theatre Survey* 45, no. 1 (2004): 19.
33. Kelli Weston, "Body and Soul," *Film Comment* 55, no. 2 (March–April, 2019): 18.
34. Charlene Regester, *African American Actresses: The Struggle for Visibility, 1900–1960* (Bloomington, IN: Indiana University Press, 2010).
35. Weston, "Body and Soul," 19.
36. Shohat and Stam, *Unthinking Eurocentrism*.
37. Ellen Scott, "More than a 'Passing' Sophistication: Dress. Film Regulation, and the Color Line in 1930s American Films," *WSQ: Women's Studies Quarterly* 41, nos. 1–2 (2013): 76.
38. Mia Mask, *Divas on Screen: Black Women in American Film* (Champaign: University of Illinois Press, 2009).
39. Ibid., 2.
40. Karen Alexander, "Fatal Beauties: Black Women in Hollywood," in *Stardom: Industry of Desire*, ed. Christine Gledhill (New York: Routledge, 1991).
41. Ingrid Banks, "Women in Film," in *African Americans and Popular Culture*, vol. 1, ed. Todd Boyd (Westport, CT: Praeger, 2008), 67.
42. Scott, "More than a 'Passing' Sophistication," 76.
43. Black, "Looking White, Acting Black," 29.

References

Spencer, Stephen (2014). *Race and Ethnicity: Culture, Identity and Representation.* New York and London: Routledge.

Shohat, Ella, and Robert Stam (2014). *Unthinking Eurocentrism: Multiculturalism and the Media.* London and New York: Routledge.

Berenstein, Rhona J. (1994). White Heroines and Hearts of Darkness: Race, Gender and Disguise in 1930s Jungle Films. *Film History.* 6: 314–339.

CHAPTER 3

COLONIAL TERRORS IN *TRABALHAR CANSA* AND *AS BOAS MANEIRAS* BY JULIANA ROJAS-MARCOS DUTRA

The Negritude as the Stain That Corrodes It All

ESTEFANÍA HERMOSILLA ÓRDENES

Escucha mundo blanco
Los salves de nuestros muertos
Escucha mi voz de zonbi
En honor a nuestros muertos
Escucha mundo blanco
Mi tifón de bestias salvajes
Mi sangre quebrando mi tristeza
Sobre todos los caminos del mundo
Escucha mundo blanco [. . .]
Mi rugido de zonbi

Soy el Capitán *Zonbi*, René Depestre

Yo no pertenezco a la civilización del Libro y del Odio. Los míos guardarán mi recuerdo en sus corazones sin necesidad de grafías.

Yo Tituba, la bruja negra de Salem, Marysé Conde

THE MONSTER USES: *ZONBIS*, WITCHES, AND WEREWOLVES

IN literature and fiction films, the ability to go unnoticed in visual or auditive terms is generally introduced as a sort of power that allows both heroes and heroines, and villains and despicable, evil women to defeat their rivals and even rule the world. Nonetheless, when the ability of not being visible or audible is embodied by the Black and Indigenous population, it is presented as a terrible sentence, a curse that silences and makes their identity invisible, therefore preventing them from having their own image and voice.

Since the European colonization of America, which, on the one hand, caused the deaths of millions of Indigenous peoples due to illnesses, hunger, forced displacement, and the inhuman exploitation they endured, and, on the other hand, the slave trade[1] to replace the native workforce, the white colonizing gaze has prevailed. This look has promoted an irrational and violent image of Black and Indigenous people. Thus, counting on the complicity of the European crowns and the Catholic Church in the sixteenth century, racism laid its first roots in Latin America by establishing a macabre hierarchy among inhabitants which determines the degree of humanity that each person possesses.

> Latin American racism has its roots in the conquest, the colony, and slavery. The war in the overseas territories, initiated by the European empires, along with the company of the Christian churches (mainly the Catholic one), entailed the need of legitimizing the subordination and transformation of the Indians and black people into slaves through speeches on the religious, civilizing mission and the natural superiority of Europeans.[2]

The violent discrimination toward and segregation of the Black and Indigenous communities reveal how "from the beginning, America is produced based on a 'teratological theology' from whose parameters any difference was interpreted as a deviation from the human that required the rigorous application of the civilizing project."[3] It is precisely for Mabel Moraña that such a project carried out during the conquest and colonization involved in stipulating the primitive and monstrous condition of all the non-white population that lives and arrives in America. This is especially patent in the Black population's situation in the Caribbean, mainly in Haiti under French control. Given this context, the figure of the *houngan*,[4] the *zonbi*,[5] and the *vodou*, all of which are part of complex rites and religious ceremonies held by Haitian slaves, suffered from a series of misrepresentations by the settlers. The latter, as Hoermann points out, considered such events demonic and the product of a savage religion[6] chaired by diabolical priests who turned slaves into cannibals.

This view was widely spread, particularly after the rebellion by the slaves under the leadership of Jean Jacques Dessalines, Toussaint L'Ouverture, and Jean-François.

The rebellion culminated in the liberation and independence of Haiti in 1804. However, instead of being seen as heroes and agents of their own freedom, the former slaves were portrayed as savage cannibals who mercilessly murdered and ousted the French settlers and their families from the island. Such representations are reflected in the words of the president of the United States, Thomas Jefferson, who described the government of Toussaint in Santo Domingo as "cannibals of the terrible republic."[7] Generally, the phrase summarizes the way in which European settlers demonized the revolution and independence of Haiti. The aim was to discourage other colonies from rebelling, while also justifying the perpetuation of slavery.

The negative and harsh reactions to the revolution and independence of the slaves in Haiti and the reinforcement of the savage and primitive mythology of the Black population in all of America are part of the colonial terrors, a term that refers to the settlers' persistent fear of losing the privileges they were granted by their race and the social class. Because even though they exerted control through a political, economic, and social regime which allowed them not only to accumulate wealth and power, but also to justify the horrors committed based on an alleged intellectual superiority of white people, settlers are permanently terrified of being subjugated by slaves. Settlers fear that the savage, furious, and unpredictable force that they attribute to Black people will be used against them, causing them to lose their wealth and, more importantly, their societal privilege.

In this regard, the colonial terrors refer to the historical and cultural fears that white settlers and their heirs have of, on the one hand, ending up in the same situation of submission and slavery to which Black and Indigenous people were forced and, on the other hand, witnessing the racial walls they have built to differentiate themselves and oppose Black population collapsing before their eyes.

However, unlike the monsters that the colonial terrors erect that demonize the culture, knowledge, and forms of resistance developed by the Afro-Caribbean population, as Mabel Moraña highlights, the very concept of "monster" is an open and plastic term that is susceptible to continuous cultural mutations, altering both its appearance and action, since "the monster is, first and foremost, a story. As such, it is language, discursive development, a picture, and a narrative."[8] This is evident in the works created by diverse artists challenging colonialism. For instance, the Haitian René Depestre, in his poem "Soy el capitán Zonbi," makes the *zonbi* a creature that condemned the thousands of deaths that slavery caused, as well as the resilience and organizational spirit which led slaves to obtain their freedom and independence in Haiti. We also see it in the novel *Yo, Tituba, la bruja negra de Salem* by Guadeloupean Maryse Condé. There, she brings the witch/healer of the Antilles back by rewriting the story of Tituba, the only Black woman accused of witchcraft in the Salem witch trials, who recounts in the first person her own story. Thus, she recounts the richness and complexity of the knowledge, wishes, and resistance of an Afro-Caribbean woman amid slavery on the island of Barbados.

Similar to how diverse authors reappropriate figures such as the *zonbi* or the witch to give a voice and draw attention to Black populations, the werewolf in Brazil is a key creature that shows the true place from which horror sprouts. Werewolves also allude to some of the most dreadful aspects of the colonial past and the way some of the colonial terrors conceived in the past still live on.

Originally from Greece, werewolf mythology has several variants, but it broadly alludes to the story of Lycaon, king of Arcadia—a town known for making human sacrifices—who, after finding out that Zeus raped his daughter Calisto and is the father of his grandson Arcade, hosts Zeus at his home and offers him Arcade's meat as a banquet. Upon discovering this, Zeus punishes Lycaon by transforming him into a wolf.[9] The werewolf myth has since spread and diversified across the different regions of Europe. Certain aspects of the story vary, but the transformation from a man or woman into a wolf and the need to consume human flesh remains in most of the popular tales.

However, the recognition of the werewolf as among the most notable monsters is mainly due to the popularity it reached through the film industry. Among others, Universal Studios produced a series of films around this creature, such as *Werewolf of London* (1935) by Stuart Walker, *The Wolf Man* (1941) by Georges Waggner, and *Frankenstein Meets the Wolf Man* (1943), films which would be followed up by Hammer productions such as *The Curse of the Werewolf* (1961) by Terence Fisher, among other films. The werewolf's film-originated fame extends to Latin America, where Mexico stands out, because a mythical werewolf shares scenes with famous characters from wrestling in films such as *Santo y Blue Demon contra los monstruos* (1970) by Gilberto Martinez Solaris and *El Santo y Blue Demon versus el vampiro y el hombre lobo* (1973) by Miguel M. Delgado. In Mexico, we can also find one of the first films in which a woman werewolf is the leading role, *La loba* (1966) by Rafael Baledón. Argentina's *Nazareno cruz y el lobo* (1975) by Leonardo Favio and *Mujer lobo* (2013) by Tamae Garateguy are also notable werewolf entries.

Even so, it is in Brazil that the werewolf myth has developed on television and cinema in a unique way. Its popularity in the media starts in the soap opera world. Among the highlights are *Saramandaia* (1976), *Roque Santeiro* (1985–1986), and *Pedra sobre pedra* (1992), whose fantastic characters include male werewolves who must cope with the curse that afflicts them and suffer the consequences of their appetites. Based on such productions, the films *Um Lobisomem na Amazônia* (2005) by Ivan Cardoso, *Trabalhar Cansa* (2011 and *As Boas Maneiras* (2019) by Juliana Rojas and Marco Dutra were released.

Although to a lesser degree than in the United States and Europe, the Latin American film industry undoubtedly shows sustained interest and fascination that the werewolf has galvanized across the various countries of the continent. This stems from the broad range of legends recounting how women and men transform into different animals that we find in both the various Indigenous cultures and the Afrodescendant population. From the Guarani culture of Northeastern Argentina telling stories about the *yaguareté-abá*—men who turn into jaguars—to stories about the successive transformations into birds and insects that the runaway slaves and Mackandal *houngan*[10] go through to escape death, the metamorphosis of humans into animals in the Latin American and Caribbean context displays, on the one hand, the complex ways of understanding nature and the connection between the human and the animal

domains and, on the other hand, how the metamorphosis is an act that unveils the colonial roots of racism.

In regard to the latter, the werewolf is a phenomenon that can be traced back to the
colonization process in South America with the arrival of Spanish and Portuguese
settlers.

> When Europeans immigrated to the American continent, they obviously brought
> their magical-religious cultural background as in the case of the male werewolf,
> who was well received in some Amerindian cultures in which the theriomorphic
> metamorphosis was not unknown: what is more, it belonged to the native magical-
> religious world: . . . In the Guarani culture territories, the myth of the *yaguareté-
> abá* —the jaguar-man—in the collective imagination of the new populations that
> settled in its territory laid the foundations for another immigrant: the *lobisome /
> lobizón / lobisón: lupus-homo*, the werewolf.[11]

Because of the myths and legends about human transformations into animals that
existed in the collective imagination of the Indigenous peoples, the werewolf myth
brought by settlers was incorporated relatively quickly. It was called *lobizón* or *lobisomen*
in Argentina and Brazil, countries where the Amazon rainforest is presented as one of
the regions in which stories about encounters with this creature are plentiful. That is
precisely why Portuguese settlers stand out as one of the main werewolf sources, since
both their male and female werewolves have particular features that were subsequently
exported to Brazil.

> In Portugal, on the other hand, the male werewolf restructures and rebuilds essen-
> tial points for Roman tradition: . . . Keeping structural points like the enchantment
> process, the animal transformation will not exclusively be into a wolf, but also into
> the last animal that has settled down in the place, with a strong tendency to trans-
> mutation in typical country animals such as the donkey, the pig, the goat, the dog,
> the horse, etc. The purpose of the enchantment was therefore an eventuality in the
> Portuguese culture: according to the local customs, the last brother to be born would
> turn into the werewolf man after the birth of seven women. Later on, the myth would
> be reformulated based on the Christian and moral vision, becoming also a fatal fruit
> of incest.[12]

In accordance with Maximiliano Ruste's study, there are several noticeable elements of
the werewolf in Portuguese popular culture that, although preserving general aspects
about the werewolf—for instance, as a punishment or curse cast at a person—also
modify some essential elements. Firstly, lycanthropy will not only be about the wolf.
After the myth is spread among rural villages, the transformation to which men are subject includes different characteristic animals of the countryside such as pigs, donkeys,
goats, and horses, among others. Secondly, the transformation of a man into a wolf
is from a father or mother curse which either of the parents bequeath to their son or
daughter who was born after seven brothers or sisters. This is an explanation that,

following the influence of the Catholic religion on the popular beliefs in Portugal, became understood as a punishment resulting from incest within the family.

Such elements were part of the tradition of the werewolf that made its way to Brazil,
especially in the northeastern cities.

> In Brazil, the human figure of the werewolf is not so different from the one which
> Portuguese popular culture suggests, although his paleness is frequently associ-
> ated to hemophiliac illnesses. This would explain its disposition to become a beast:
> according to some versions prevailing in the northeast and the north, once he has
> transformed, the werewolf would go out in search of blood to drink, hence staying
> alive in spite of his illness.[13]

From this point of view, and as evidenced by the stories spread in Brazil, lycanthropy is
described as a blood-related type of illness—hemophilia or anemia—transmitted by the
father or the mother, which causes a pale and weak appearance in those who suffer from
it. The person's appearance will only be corrected after they transform into a werewolf
and satisfying their need for blood.

The interesting thing about stories built around werewolves in Brazil is their constant associations with incest, which underscores sexual activity not only among blood
relatives, but also among in-laws, such as godfathers and godmothers.

> They said that they were men who, having had impure sexual intercourse with their
> godmothers, they lost weight. Every Friday night, at midday, they would leave their
> houses transformed into dogs or pigs, and bite people they came across. These people
> in turn were subject to be transformed into werewolves.[14]

The link between lycanthropy and incest is key to understanding the singularity of the
werewolf man and werewolf woman in Brazil, since it is an element we can connect to
inbreeding and the construction of the white, heterosexual, and bourgeois family on
which Brazilian society is built. Moreover, such an element can be linked to slavery,
which promoted a colonial economy and that remains, albeit differently. In the films
Trabalhar Cansa (2011) and *As Boas Maneiras* (2019) by Juliana Rojas and Marco Dutra,
the werewolf (whether man or woman) affords an opportunity to raise awareness about
reality of the Afro-descendant population in Brazil.

TRABALHAR CANSA: THE ABSENCE
OF A CLEAN BUSINESS

Trabalhar Cansa (2011) and *As Boas Maneiras* (2019) by Juliana Rojas and Marco Dutra
are movies that, unlike *Um Lobisomem na Amazônia* (2005), move the werewolf figure
from a rural space to the city. This change infuses the werewolf film with new meanings,

because it brings the racial and social class tensions that mark people—particularly women—in daily life in Brazil's capital to the center of the plot. This allows us to see, on the one hand, how fears of a historical experience with race defines and distributes the dangers threatening Afro-Brazilian and white women in different ways, while, on the other hand, it shows that the werewolf man and werewolf woman are essential to projecting the persistence of the colonial terrors built around the Afro-Brazilian population.

Trabalhar Cansa is the first full-length film codirected by Juliana Rojas and Marco Dutra to be selected for a Certain Regard at Festival de Cannes (2011), and it also received various awards from specialized critics. Against the backdrop of the economic crisis affecting Brazil, the movie tells the story of Helena, a relatively well-off middle-class white woman who, after years of being a housewife, decides to start a small local supermarket, just as her husband, Otavio, after years working as a company executive, is dismissed from his job and replaced by someone younger. These events turn Helena into the primary breadwinner at home.

Undoubtedly, *Trabalhar Cansa* is a movie focused on exploring the fears of a middle-class family. However, more precisely, it is centered on showing the terrors experienced by a middle-class white woman, Helena, who, as shown in the film, enjoys certain privileges. She has a beautiful, spacious apartment; a daughter in a private school; she has had the chance to save money to start her own business and to hire an employee—Paula—to take care of the household and her daughter. The tense relationship between Helena and Paula displays the economic and social inequalities between white and Black women in Brazil in relation to the opportunities to gain access to better living conditions.

> *Trabalhar Cansa* seems to be the echo of a slavery past. In this regard, the film appears to be haunted by the ghosts of Brazil, those who were exploited, murdered, and decimated, and, therefore, and by traumas from the past returning to the present moment. These are marks of a historical inequality which has not been definitively overcome yet, and that remains in the present through the current personal and social class relationships.[15]

Such slavery, as well as the ongoing contemporary racial and social class tensions, are expressed in the domestic setting and in the supermarket, where the ill-fated atmosphere surrounding Helena and her family and their many flaws serve as signs of a truth they try to hide and repress. This is evidenced from the moment Helena meets with Paula, since that is when the radical social difference between the two becomes visible, which the main character further emphasizes.

Paula is the opposite of Helena. She is an Afro-descendant young lady from the rural area of Brazil who, without previous work experience, arrives in São Paulo to work as a maid. Because she does not have a contract, she receives less than the minimum wage. Helena justifies this treatment because Paula has no work experience and, moreover, points out that by employing her, she is doing her a "favor." Thus, after forcing Paula to wear worker's clothes and providing her with a small, windowless, TV-less room next to the kitchen, Helena uses her privilege as a white, bourgeois woman to exploit Paula. It is even clearer when she forces Paula to work for the same salary she received at the supermarket and during Carnival times, which is usually a public holiday and a celebration day for everyone.

Despite all Helena's attempts to preserve her privileged status, *Trabalhar Cansa* shows how the terror of losing the rights she was afforded due to her race and social class is a constant concern, through diverse signs in the film. In the domestic environment, it expressed the untimely bleeding, first when Helena's nose bleeds and subsequently, inside an egg.

Blood stains are important symbols that display both Helena's hidden fears and the terrible truth underlying the supermarket's walls. A byproduct of decomposition, stains refer to a way of life that insists on coming back, in spite of the main character's efforts to erase and ignore them. This is not only about the bloodstains bursting out of Helena's body, but also about those invading the supermarket. It is precisely the supermarket that acts as a microcosm of Brazilian society, where the persistent and dark stain that appears on the wall serves as a metaphor. On the one hand, it is a metaphor for the terrors of losing the privileges that people like Helena have and, on the other hand, of the horrible lengths they are willing to go to preserve those rights. Their behaviors include firing their employees in the middle of the Christmas season when the merchandise starts disappearing, and checking their bags after their workdays.

However, such authoritarian and controlling behavior is useless for ending the ill-fated atmosphere in the supermarket and the continual suspicion of the evil threatening its foundations. This becomes apparent through a series of elements, such as the strong and unpleasant smell throughout the supermarket, black liquid emerging from the floor, hairs clogging the drain, emerging strange claw that Paula finds, and the persistent water stains bursting behind a wall, which Helena tries unsuccessfully to get rid of. All of these clues allude to the existence of a terrible truth and finally lead a distressed Helena to break the wall and find the corpse of a strange creature buried behind it.

Although the creature is never identified as a werewolf, stories about the "lunatic" and unstable behavior of one of the previous property owners, the constant barking of dogs at the supermarket, as well as the corpse's skull and the remaining hairs covering it, suggest that this creature is indeed a werewolf. Furthermore, that Helena and Otavio refuse to name the creature is indicative of the symbolic meaning of the werewolf in *Trabalhar Cansa*, because it is a reference to Brazil's slave past.

As stated above, lycanthropy is a mother or father's curse associated with incest. In other words, it is an evil affecting the family organization caused by transgressing the prohibition of sexual contact among direct family members or in-laws. Nevertheless, that incest is taboo and forbidden legally and socially did not prevent the promotion of inbreeding in Brazilian society; that is to say, marriages among members of the same family: cousins, stepbrothers and stepsisters, uncles or aunts and nephews or nieces, and relatives to a different degree. It was a common practice among men and women in the high social class in Brazil, where "marriage in the colonial period and in the nineteenth century was endogamic in terms of social class and skin color."[16]

With the support of the Church and secular institutions, endogamy or the recognition of sexual contact among members of a family clan when it leads to marriage allowed white bourgeois women and men in the same family to accumulate, keep, and reproduce the wealth and privileges they were granted due to their race and social class. In this way, we can understand endogamy as a "legal" form of incest which, since the colonial period in Brazil, has defined the ways in which people relate and forge links with each other by establishing who can or cannot be part of a family according to the race and social class they belong to.

Bearing this in mind, we can recognize that the incest and lycanthropy in *Trabalhar Cansa* is linked to the phenomenon of endogamy, which continues in Brazilian society today. Because Helena and Otavio, the previous tenants, and the supermarket owner and the real estate broker are white people, they get married, work or do business with white people with purchasing power. On the other hand, considering the diverse scientific and historical studies[17] connecting endogamy with the proliferation of genetic diseases within a family and even whole communities, the presence of a werewolf—historically linked to a sick, pale appearance that is only healed when going out to hunt—emerges as a sickness/curse caused by endogamy in white, bourgeois families, because it is a reproduction of wealth, through which anyone who does not fit within the racial and social hierarchies established during colonial times in Brazil is excluded.

Thus, lycanthropy in *Trabalhar Cansa* is an evil linked to endogamy in Brazilian society, which preserves forms of family organization that exclude contact with Indigenous and Afro-descendant people. The latter are left out of the white, bourgeois family construct spread throughout literature and in the film and television industries. In media, they are only represented in employee roles, like Paula. The former is a matter that in turn directly links the werewolf figure to the slavery regime. In the film, it is visible in the way Helena treats Paula, and in a direct way through the picture of the chains she finds in the supermarket. Here, the insinuation is that the previous tenants used them to chain their relative when they transformed into a wolf.

As Mabel Moraña explains, the werewolf is a monster that affects more than just the individual. Hence, as Hobbes contends the "man is a wolf for the man" (*homo homini lupus*), his figure refers to the "monstrification of the social,"[18] the permanent danger for society of being affected and dissolved by the savage violence nesting in individuals.

> The wolf transformation of a man does not only show the instability of that being we call "man," but also the constitutive monstrosity living within him and the fear this causes. The werewolf can no longer be found on the margins of the men community,

but within. It lives in the city . . . the man that becomes a wolf is no other than the internal enemy, who can affect the social order.[19]

In *Trabalhar Cansa*, the werewolf is presented as a threat to the social order, but as Andrea Torrano points out, lycanthropy is not an external threat to society. On the contrary, it is an inner element, which, as mentioned above, is a product of the endogamy established since colonial times that acts as a genetic curse/illness, attacking the well-off members of Brazilian society. Additionally, as an internal evil of a society based on labor exploitation, the werewolf serves as a reminder of the slavery upon which the colonial economy has sustained *Trabalhar Cansa*, through the chains that Helena finds in the cellar, shows us how slavery still remains through women like Paula who work without a contract—that is to say, without benefits, a defined work schedule, or delimited tasks, and whose dismissal places them in a constant precarious situation.

By studying *Trabalhar Cansa*, we can understand lycanthropy as an evil caused by endogamy, just as slavery was a result of colonialism. With that in mind, the werewolf that is materialized as an indelible stain on the wall represents the return of the colonial terrors and of the historic fear of the settlers and their heirs, as well as of the white, bourgeois class, of losing the social, political, and economic power they have over the society's most impoverished groups.

AS BOAS MANEIRAS: THE CONTAGION OF THE FEMALE MONSTER

As Boas Maneiras (2019), the second feature film produced by Juliana Rojas and Marco Dutra, can be understood along similar lines as *Trabalhar Cansa*. Its plot is focused on gay, interracial relationship between Clara, an Afro-descendant and working woman, and Ana, a white, bourgeois pregnant woman. The film is a singular Latin American version of the classic fairy tale centered on a princess exiled from home and punished with a curse. Specifically, Ana, the *Olim pulchra filis regis* ("The once king's beautiful daughter"), as her carpet reads, who is the modern version of a princess and the daughter of a powerful landowner. She shoulders a double curse: on the one hand, she is expelled from home for having had an affair with another man while engaged and, on the other hand, she is pregnant by a creature that carries the lycanthropic evil.

Importantly, Clara starts working for Ana and, just like Paula, she has many duties, including keeping the house clean, cooking, and taking care of Ana, whose preganancy is high-risk. From the beginning, it is explicitly stated that their lives are diametrically opposed. Clara is an unemployed, Black woman and a nursing student who desperately needs to find a job to pay her rent, while Ana is a white, rich woman who lives in a luxurious apartment in downtown São Paulo.

Their differences notwithstanding, if Helena and Paula maintainted a distant, subordinate relationship in *Trabalhar Cansa*, in *As Boas Maneiras*, the racial- and social-class tensions are attenuated by the loving relationship between Ana and Clara, who, while socially and economically different, are both consumed with loneliness. Neither have a family nor friends to support them. Consequently, they share empathy, solidarity, and love instead of rivalry. Significantly, their gradual loving relationship reveals the lycanthropy that lives with them, which once again acts as a reference to the colonial past of Brazil.

Ana belongs to the landowner, a stock middle-class figure in Brazil. As such, she is a direct heiress of the Portuguese settlers. Her arranged marriage with another member of her own race and social class reproduces endogamy in the white, bourgeois family. Undoubtedly, going out for a drink and having sex with a stranger breaks with the ideals of a conservative woman devoted to her husband and children. However, Ana satisfies her lust with a man who turns out to be the town's priest that carries and subsequently infects her with lycanthropic evil.

It is a key fact that the werewolf and the one who infects Ana with lycanthropy is a priest, because, on the one hand, as a Church member, he is part of one of the institutions that contributed to the promotion of endogamic relationships within the bourgeois society. At the same time, he is also a figure who is called "father" in both symbolic and historic terms by his parishioners. Thus, when Ana tries to escape from the oppressive endogamic family relationships, she falls back on them by interacting with a "father" who, as a figure of the Catholic, white family, represents another type of endogamic bond that infects her with lycanthropic evil after getting her pregnant.

This links the lycanthropy myth to endogamy again, illustrating this form of "legal incest" promoted by settlers and their heirs that remains today. However, what is new in *As Boas Maneiras* is that, despite Ana carrying lycanthropy, It does not manifest until the moment she connects with Clara.

As pointed out by María Lugones following Aníbal Quijano's analysis of "power coloniality" and Kimberlé Crenshaw's theory on the intersectionality, the process of colonization of Latin America and the Caribbean involved a "gender coloniality." It imposed a binary construction of sexes and established that the concept of "woman" proliferated to heterosexual white settlers, casting Indigenous and Black women aside. In their minds, "the non-white females were considered to be animals in the profound meaning of being 'genderless beings,' and sexually marked as females, but without the femininity characteristics."[20] This is reflected during slavery when Black women were treated as monstrous beings who were part animal and part human.

With that in mind, Clara, as an Afro-descendant, openly gay, hardworking woman whose body defined all the "registrations" historically considered part of the monstrous savagery that differentiates her from "civilized" white men, and white, bourgeois, heterosexual women. These foundations circumscribe Clara with a latent monstrosity that is a product of her race, social class, and sexual orientation, forged in colonial racism, and serves as a trigger of the monstrosity living inside Ana. Through their friendship and loving relationship, there is a sort of contagion, in which Clara's monstrosity feeds Ana's monstrosity via her blood and sexual desire.

Therefore, if Ana was the "black sheep expelled from the family, the unfaithful woman, and the single, pregnant mother who drinks alcohol and devotes herself to a stranger's care,"[21] after starting a loving relationship with Clara, the werewolf woman in her side is now free. This gesture, in contrast to *Trabalhar Cansa*, shows lycanthropy not only as an evil caused by endogamy, which refers to slavery—Ana literally feeds on Clara's body—but also as an act that makes it possible to establish an alliance with Clara's monstrosity. This is another way of reviving colonial terrors, since the link between both main characters leads to a questioning and blurring of the limits imposed by the settler between the civilization and the savagery, and between white and Black women.

CONCLUSION

In Latin America and the Caribbean, the monster is an important theoretical construct that allows us to think through the processes of conquest and colonization of the continent, and to claim the resistance and adopt the strategies of the Indigenous and Black community against the white settlers. In this context, the werewolf that arrives in Brazil is a creature that opens the possibility of reviewing the ways in which the narrations brought by the Portuguese settlers are rebuilt and re-adapted, as well as how the werewolf man and the werewolf woman who move from the countryside to the city are metaphors. There are sites where some of the most sinister practices shaped during colonial times are incarnated, such as the endogamy among white people and the enslavement of Black people.

Trabalhar Cansa and *As Boas Maneiras* by Juliana Rojas and Marcos Dutra reclaim the fascination and interest in the lycanthropy deeply rooted in Brazilian popular culture and explore the permanence of colonial terrors, the persistent fear of white settlers and their heirs of losing the privileges provided by their race and social class. This gives us the chance to understand how the werewolf man and the werewolf woman are creatures whose monstrosity reveals Brazilian society's endogamy, through which the white, bourgeois population preserves and accumulates its privileges, and ensures that the Afro-descendant community is denied those privileges, by means of precarious, abusive jobs that represent modern slavery.

Thus, the terror and fascination that lycanthropy generates demonstrates that it is part of Brazilian culture that reflects the country's taste for narrations about the multiple possibilities for human metamorphosis. Further, it is, also a metaphor that highlights some of the most sinister acts and events of colonial history in Latin America and the Caribbean. They show us once more that the terror caused by monsters is deeply rooted in reality.

NOTES

1. Between the sixteenth and nineteenth centuries, approximately 40 million slaves were forcibly transferred from Africa. "Afroamérica-crisol centenario," *Revista de Cesla* 7 (2005): 9.
2. María Dolores París Pombo, "Estudios sobre el racismo en América Latina," *Revista Política y Cultura* 17 (2002): 295.
3. Mabel Moraña, *El Monstruo como Máquina de Guerra* (Madrid: Iberoamericana, 2017), 63.
4. Mabel Moraña, "Priests Who Preside Over the Rites and Dances Typical of Vodoo Ceremonies," *El monstruo como máquina de guerra* (Madrid: Iberoamericana, 2017), 353–354.
5. Zombie in creole.
6. Raphael Hoermann, "Figures of Terror: The 'Zombie' and the Haitian Revolution," *Revista Atlantic Studies* 14 (2016): 152–173.
7. Ibid, 54.
8. Moraña, *El monstruo como máquina de guerra*, 24.
9. Aitor Freán Campo, "El Mito del Hombre Lobo en la Antigüedad," *Revista Florentia Iliberritana* 30 (2019): 50.
10. Based on the real character of Mackandal, Alejo Carpentier narrates in his novel *The Kingdom of This World* the various transformations that Mackandal undergoes, which will make him a legend and will inspire the rebellion between slaves and runaways.
11. Fabiola Y. Chávez, "Lupu Mannaru, Panaro y Lobizón: El Hombre-lobo, un Inmigrante Transoceánico," *Revista Folklore* 374 (2013): 5.
12. Maximiliano Ruste Paulino, "O Mito Lusitano do Licántropo e sus Herança no Brasil Contemporâno," in *Campos de Saberes da História da Educação no Brasil 2*, ed. Denise Pereira (Paraná: Atena, 2019), 104.
13. Ibid., 105.
14. João Simões Lopes Neto, *Lendas do Sul* (Pelotas: Echenique & C. Editores, 1913), 91.
15. Mariana Souta, "O Que Teme a Classe Média? *Trabalhar Cansa* e o Horror no Cinema Brasileiro Contemporâneo," *Revista Contracampo* 25 (2012): 54.
16. Alida C. Metcalf, "El Matrimonio en Brasil Durante la Colonia, ¿estaba Configurado por la Clase o por el Color?," in *Familia y Vida Privada en la Historia de Iberoamérica: Seminario de Historia de la Familia*, ed. Pilar Gonzalbo Aizpuru and Cecilia Rabell Romero (México, DF: Instituto de Investigaciones Sociales de la Universidad Nacional Autónoma de México,1996), 60.
17. Daysi Mesa Trujillo and Araceli Lantigua, "Impacto de la Consanguinidad en la Descendencia de Matrimonios Monsanguíneos," *Revista Cubana de Medicina General Integral* 35 (2019); A. Bittles, "Consanguinity and Its Relevance to Clinical Genetics," *Clinical*

Genetics 60 (2001): 89–98; Francisco C. Ceballos and Gonzalo Álvarez, "La genética de los Matrimonios Consanguíneos," *Revista de Humanidades Dendra Médica* 10 (2011).

18. Moraña, *El Monstruo como Máquina de Guerra*, 246.
19. Andrea Torrano, "El Monstruo en la Política: Defender la Sociedad del Hombre-lobo," *Revista Contemporânea* 3, no. 2 (2013): 433.
20. María Lugones, "La Colonialidad y el Género," *Revista Tábula Rasa* 9 (2008): 94.
21. Matías Marra and Yexalen Aquino, "La Monstruosidad en lo Propio: El Fantástico como Estrategia Expansiva," *Revista En la Otra Isla* 3 (2021): 94.

CHAPTER 4

VISIBLE BLACKNESS IN TWENTY-FIRST-CENTURY BRAZILIAN HORROR CINEMA

MARK H. HARRIS

WHEN considering the history of Blackness in Brazilian horror cinema, the overriding theme has been that of invisibility.[1] The struggle for Afro-Brazilian representation in horror has been an uphill battle facing two lines of resistance: to horror as a genre and to Blacks in on-screen starring roles, regardless of genre. The latter resistance is reflective of Brazil's history of societal attempts to "whiten" the populace in terms of both biology (i.e., encouraging miscegenation) and subjective racial classification. However, as the twenty-first century has progressed, a new wave of Brazilian horror cinema has rejuvenated the genre, channeling Afro-Brazilians' increasingly successful push for rights with overt socio-political statements and high-profile depictions of Blackness.

BLACKNESS IN BRAZILIAN HORROR HISTORY

Brazil does not boast as long and storied a history of horror cinema as nations like the United States, Great Britain, Italy, Germany, or Japan, in part because of media censorship enforced under the authoritarian regime of 1964–1985, whose military coup d'état was supported by the U.S. government as a preferable alternative to Communist-sympathizing President João Goulart. Even before the dictatorial suppression, however, horror had trouble penetrating the country, because Brazil's widespread religiosity tended to view spirits and the supernatural as altruistic rather than malevolent.[2] As "the most religious country in Latin America,"[3] with the most Roman Catholics of any country in the world,[4] Brazil has long found faith to be a driving force, and the often graphic, gory, occult nature of horror has had difficulty finding its footing.

As such, it was not until 1964 (coincidentally, the same year that the military dictatorship took control) that the film widely acknowledged as the first Brazilian horror movie was released: À Meia-Noite Levarei Sua Alma (At Midnight I'll Take Your Soul). In Midnight, writer-director José Mojica Marins introduced his alter ego: the villainous, sacrilegious undertaker Zé do Caixão (Coffin Joe), who murders and rapes his way through a small village in an effort to find the "perfect" woman to continue his bloodline. The violent, profane, counterculture nature of the movie and its 1967 sequel Esta Noite Encarnarei no Teu Cadáver (This Night I'll Possess Your Corpse) made Marins not only the father of Brazilian horror, but also the most censored filmmaker in the nation. By one estimate, more than 60 percent of his footage was banned by the government by 1970, including the entirety of 1970's O Despertar da Besta (Awakening of the Beast).[5]

Marins's lurid and subversive content, along with his recurring theme of the working class tormented by the rich and powerful (embodied by Coffin Joe), might have earned the ire of censors, but it appealed to a proletariat audience that found itself under the thumb of an oppressive dictatorship. His "Cinema do Lixo" ("Trash Cinema") was admired even by leaders of the high-brow, critically acclaimed Cinema Novo ("New Cinema") movement that valued "aesthetics of hunger" and strove to give a voice to the underprivileged by raising awareness of their social, political, and economic struggles.[6] As an untrained filmmaker who dropped out of school at age 13, Marins was able to connect with the masses—even casting working-class volunteers in his films—and achieve the popular appeal that eluded the elitist Cinema Novo filmmakers.[7]

However, while Marins made movies for and about the common man, his highly influential work features predominantly white casts, despite the fact that Black Brazilians have made up the bulk of the nation's lower socio-economic classes since the abolition of slavery in the late nineteenth century. Brazil provided little to former slaves in the way of compensation or opportunities for employment, education, or land ownership at the time of emancipation, relegating them to the bottom of the social hierarchy, with many Blacks returning to their former masters to work for minimal pay.[8] In fact, the high number of domestic workers in Brazil (with nearly triple that of the United States, despite Brazil having two-thirds the population) has been described as "a legacy of slavery."[9] Afro-Brazilians disproportionately fall into the lower wealth brackets, with a poverty rate twice that of white Brazilians and with even college-educated Blacks earning between 41 percent (for women) to 70 percent (for men) of white counterparts with similar education.[10] Until 2019, Brazil ranked among the 10 nations worldwide with the highest level of income inequality (figure 4.1).[11]

Marins's two most famous films, At Midnight I'll Take Your Soul and This Night I'll Possess Your Corpse, scarcely include any characters of observable African descent, and the few that are present are little more than background extras. Likewise, anonymous Black characters make brief appearances in Awakening of the Beast, Trilogia de Terror (Trilogy of Terror) (1968), Exorcismo Negro (The Bloody Exorcism of Coffin Joe) (1974), Estranha Hospedaria dos Prazeres (The Strange Hostel of Naked Pleasures) (1976), Delírios de um Anormal (Hallucinations of a Deranged Mind) (1978), and Coffin Joe's 2008 comeback, Encarnação do Demônio (Embodiment of Evil).

FIGURE 4.1 José Mojica Marins as Coffin Joe in *At Midnight I'll Take Your Soul.*

The Black representation, or lack thereof, in Marins's movies is typical of Brazilian horror of his era. Works like Raffaele Rossi's *Seduzidas Pelo Demonio* (*Seduced by the Devil*) (1978) and Ivan Cardoso's horror comedies *O Segredo da Múmia* (*The Secret of the Mummy*) (1982) and *As Sete Vampiras* (*The Seven Vampires*) (1986) contain the standard Black bit parts in the genre: slaves, domestic servants, blue-collar workers, and practitioners of Candomblé or a similar religion from the African diaspora. All are nameless characters who serve as little more than props to further the story, not fully formed humans. The invisibility of Black characters in horror has been compounded by the fact that horror itself, despite Marins's contributions, was a sparsely represented genre in Brazil during the Cinema Novo era of the late 1950s through the mid-1970s, when "the intellectual projects of these decades favored descriptions of 'the realities of life' to the detriment of 'the figments of the imagination.' "[12]

The deficiency of Black representation in Brazilian horror cinema is not unique to the genre; it is emblematic of Brazilian show business as a whole. The adherence to white-ness as a template for stardom was established from the onset of the Brazilian film industry around the turn of the twentieth century, when "a domestic film industry and a national audience of consumers were seen as central aspirations in the construction of modernity in Brazil, and the new republic used cinema to promote an ideal of Brazil that was cosmopolitan, urban and white."[13] In that sense, Brazilian cinema fell in line with American films, which came to dominate Brazilian theaters by the 1910s and did little to showcase non-white faces on camera. Like the output coming from Hollywood, Brazilian productions through the 1950s rarely featured Black performers, and when they did, they characteristically played minor roles and extras, particularly in musical comedies known as *chanchadas*—the one major exception being Afro-Brazilian comedian Grande Otelo, "King of the Chanchadas."

In the late 1950s and early 1960s, Cinema Novo, inspired by the neo-realistic film-making of Italy and France and in retaliation against the popularity of frivolous *chanchadas* and American imports, aimed to showcase the lower classes of society and their social, economic, and political hardships. In the process, these filmmakers created "what might be called a symbolically 'black' cinema, in which black Brazilians had a crucial role."[14] However, efforts to exhibit Black militancy have historically been subject to government censorship, even before the heavy-handed tactics of the military dictatorship began in the 1960s. In fact, the very first officially censored Brazilian film was 1910's *A Vida do Cabo João Candido* (*The Life of Commander Joao Candido*), about the leader of the "Revolt of the Lash," in which Black sailors in the Brazilian navy rebelled against corporal punishment at the hands of their white superiors.[15] Glauber Rocha's Cinema Novo landmark *Barravento* (*The Turning Wind*) (1962), about the economic exploitation of Black fishermen by the white owner of a fishing net that he loans them in exchange for a hefty portion of their catch, was banned for its revolutionary message, the censor commenting, "I don't understand the creole urging the coloreds to revolt, claiming that blacks are considered a sub-race living exploited by whites, who don't give them a minimal opportunity to survive, living totally at their cost."[16]

This statement is indicative of the Brazilian attitude toward racism that had taken shape by this time: that of incomprehension, if not complete denial. The 1933 book *Casa-Grande & Senzala* (*The Masters and the Slaves*) by sociologist-anthropologist Gilberto Freyre established the concept of Brazil as a "racial democracy," in which racism was a nonfactor because, unlike America's segregationist approach, Brazil (out of necessity, due to the large number of former slaves and the relatively small number of white women) engaged in sanctioned, widespread miscegenation between whites and Blacks. The book mined national pride from Brazil's mixed-race heritage, but in doing so, it (1) helped legitimize the widespread belief that miscegenation was a solution to the "Negro problem" by "whitening" the Black population, and (2) pushed the notion of racism and the concept of racial diversity to the background of national import. Indeed, simply raising the prospect of being a victim of racism was long dismissed in Brazil as improbable and contrary to Brazilian culture, with social inequity and prejudice explained away as a consequence of class differences, not race. Meanwhile, assertions of Blackness were downplayed in favor of a nonracial "Brazilianness," even when dealing with Afro-Brazilian cultural touchstones like samba music and the *Baiana* turban-and-dress look of Black women from the state of Bahia, both of which were appropriated on a global scale by the light-skinned, Portugal-born singer Carmen Miranda.

As such, Blackness was rendered invisible, and a climate of "cultural censorship" arose regarding race and racism, a collective, implicit understanding to not discuss the racial unpleasantries of the past and present.[17] A scene from Marins's entry in the anthology *Trilogy of Terror*, "Pesadelo Macabro" ("Macabre Nightmare"), epitomizes this mindset. In it, an engaged couple explores an old barn, and when the fiancée observes a set of antique chains, she exclaims, "This must be from when there were slaves. They probably tied them here to torture them." Her fiancé replies, "You told me not to speak of sad things. Mine must be the only slavery left: slave to your beauty." They kiss and brush off such "sad things," engaging in the Brazilian practice of "willful forgetting" of slavery and its legacy, up to and including the incidence of Blackness in one's own family tree.[18] Indeed, the "whitening" of the Brazilian population through a combination of miscegenation, encouragement of European immigration, and arbitrary racial self-identification succeeded in increasing the official white population of Brazil from 38 percent in 1872 to 63 percent in 1940.[19]

The erasure of Blackness in Brazilian society has been reinforced in show business with a "lingering national preference for white skin, with which, ever since *embranquecimento* or 'Whitening' first appeared as a political agenda, cinema and later television have been complicit."[20] Film and TV, the latter of which came to outstrip the former in popularity due to its affordability and ease of access, are conspicuous showcases for Brazilian culture that have been resistant to displays of Blackness. When Blackness is allowed a spotlight, it tends to be under strict conditions, as explained by Abdias do Nascimento and Elisa Larkin Nascimento: "The generally pejorative notion of Africanity is carefully weeded out of Brazilian national identity except in very specific instances such as music, cuisine, religion, and sports. In these cases, it is defined largely by those who did not create it and then displayed as 'proof' of racial harmony and tolerance of diversity."[21] The use of Blacks as props in this manner was seen by some as a downside to the increased representation of the Cinema Novo efforts of the 1950s and 1960s, which faced accusations of inauthenticity. That is, the white creatives behind the scenes were actually "talking about themselves, projecting onto black characters."[22]

Paralleling the Blaxploitation era of American film and reflecting a growing Black consciousness movement among the Afro-Brazilian populace, the 1970s witnessed a blossoming of Black filmmaking, as the first significant Black Brazilian directors addressing Black topics emerged.[23] However, that burgeoning movement was stymied by the takeover of Brazilian film production and distribution by the state-owned company Embrafilme in 1969. Embrafilme's efforts to subsidize and promote Brazilian cinema resulted in quotas requiring theaters to show a certain number of homegrown movies, triggering an influx of cheap *pornochanchada* sex comedies that proved easier and cheaper to make and more popular than statement dramas with racial import. Horror movies during the Embrafilme era of the 1970s and 1980s tended to fall into the harmless *pornochanchada* mold—sex-filled horror comedies—and Marins, defeated by his battles with censors, ended up as a director for hire for more conventional genre fare. He even directed several pornographic movies, which were less objectionable to censors than his earlier subversions of government and religious authority.

As what was perceived to be a frivolous genre, horror rarely touched upon social issues like race, and when it did, it had to do so in a subtle, often allegorical manner to avoid censorship.[24] In the 1984 slasher *Shock*, for instance, director Jair Correia outfitted the killer with military boots as a commentary on the brutality of military rule.[25] Perhaps the best example from this era, however, is the modern gothic tale *O Anjo da Noite* (*The Angel of the Night*) (1974), from writer-director Walter Hugo Khouri. On its surface, *Angel* presents the standard horror scenario of a babysitter menaced by threatening phone calls, but beneath the surface, it hints at veiled commentary on Brazil's troubled history with race and class. The story follows a white college student from Rio named Ana (Selma Egrei), who is assigned by her babysitting agency to look after two young children, Carolina (Rejane Saliamis) and Marcelo (Pedro Coelho), over a weekend in the nearby town of Petrópolis. Brazil's racial imbalance of power is subtly established early on when the camera glances at the letter from the children's physician father, Rodrigo (Fernando Amaral), specifying to the agency that the babysitter should have "good looks," coded language for whiteness.[26] The alignment of race with class is further solidified when Ana arrives at the remote mansion to find that all of the white family's servants are Black except for the governess, Beatriz (Isabel Montes), who clearly holds rank over the "help." This is in line with reality in Brazil, where to this day, nearly two-thirds of domestic workers are Black.[27]

The racially coded class schism in the film does not paint the wealthy white family in a positive light, consistent with the recurring theme in Khouri's work of "the malaise of the Brazilian bourgeoisie."[28] Rodrigo and his socialite wife, Raquel (Lilian Lemmertz), are elitist and cold toward the domestics. Raquel complains freely to Ana about the unreliability and irresponsibility of the servants, relegating their worth to the extent to which they can perform the duties she requires. The stoic Rodrigo, meanwhile, leers at Ana and is curt with his interaction, cutting her off when she tries to introduce herself. The children are coddled and require special attention; Marcelo sleepwalks, and Carolina needs medicine for an unnamed ailment. They are what Beatriz terms "fragile." Marcelo is particularly precocious, using profanity, refusing to go to sleep, and forming an unhealthy obsession with Ana.

When Rodrigo, Raquel, and Beatriz all leave, the only person left with Ana and the kids is Augusto (Eliezer Gomes), the Black, middle-aged night watchman who patrols outside the home. As the night progresses, Ana begins to receive anonymous phone calls from a craggy voice threatening to kill her. Eventually, she finds Marcelo on the other end of the line and scolds him for the prank before putting him to bed. However, with the boy asleep, she receives another harassing call, and this time, she discovers that Augusto is the culprit. Upon this reveal, the night watchman pulls out his revolver and shoots both Ana and the two children dead.

The murder comes as a shock, because up until this point, Augusto was the most genial character in the movie, frequently checking on Ana's well-being—offering her food, drink, and protection—showing affection to the children, and conveying his sympathetic back story about being a longtime worker on the grounds who had to switch from gardener to watchman due to an unspecified illness. Upon closer viewing, it becomes apparent that he is possessed by an impulse, be it supernatural or psychological, that drives him to kill. During the film, he explains to Ana that he prefers to work outdoors because the house isn't "friendly." The implication is that there is something inherently wicked about the building. "My boss's grandfather built the wrong house in the right place," he explains to her. Augusto rarely steps inside voluntarily but is forced to do so when the calls begin, and as a result, something possesses him, propelling him into a murderous rampage. Only when he finds himself back outside at the end of the movie does he regain his senses and realize what he's done. He screams in terror.

There is no clear explanation of what mysterious force pushes Augusto over the edge, but there is compelling evidence that it is a reflection of the deep-seeded racial and economic schisms that have long plagued Brazil. In addition to the social divisions evident in the hierarchy of personnel inside the house, the building itself is a testament to the legacy of racial exploitation and violence born of slavery and colonization. Its sprawling opulence far exceeds the needs of a family of four, spurring Augusto to comment that, although he also has a wife and kids, he prefers his small, modest home. Despite its size and ornate decorations, the mansion is cold and foreboding, decorated with violent imagery like statues of sword-wielding angels and antique firearms, the type used to control Augusto's ancestors and to maintain the nation's racial status quo. In one powerful scene, as the force begins to overtake Augusto, we see him facing a wall of guns, all pointing toward him in a foreboding and symbolic fashion (figure 4.2).

Even the setting of Petrópolis is itself noteworthy in that it is renowned as a wealthy tourist destination. A mountain town situated about 40 miles north of Rio, it served as the summer home for the Brazilian monarchy and aristocracy during the nineteenth century and for Brazilian presidents in the twentieth century. Significantly, in the story, Raquel brags to Ana that the reason she and Rodrigo have to leave for the weekend is that they are attending three events for "the Queen" in Rio and Brasilia. The weight of the historical subjugation of Afro-Brazilians, embodied by this elitist house in this elitist town, seems to imbue the building with an intangible malevolence that envelopes Augusto, who confesses to Ana that, in the past, he has been overcome with an enigmatic sensation during the night: "some kind of sadness I can't explain." This sadness, it seems, turns

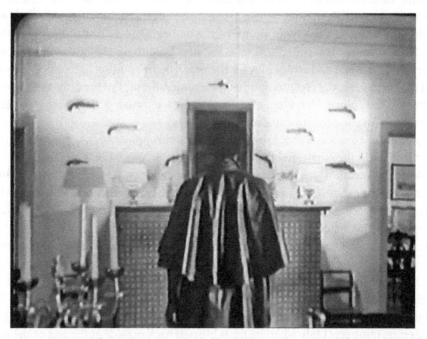

FIGURE 4.2 Augusto (Eliezer Gomes) menaced by decorative firearms in *The Angel of the Night*.

into rage, directed not only at the upper-class children, but also at the middle-class babysitter, presumably because her whiteness is enough to signify oppression.

According to Daniel Serravalle de Sá, "Khouri's film shows awareness of the possibilities that would strike fear in a bourgeois audience in relation to their domestic workers. . . . The night guard develops a gradual but unconscious perception of the mediocrity that he is doomed to watch and live. The indifference of the Brazilian bourgeoisie to the angst of those living on the margins of society erupts in this conclusion as a horrifying and threatening Gothic manifestation."[29] Augusto is possessed not by a traditional demon, but by a demon of society's making. The house is haunted not by a ghost, but by sins passed from one generation to the next. It is cursed not by the traditional trope of a murdered innocent, but by murdered innocence, hope decimated by systemic racism, inequality, and deprivation of human rights.

Cited by Laura Loguerchio Cánepa as "one of the most relevant films of this genre ever made in Brazil,"[30] *The Angel of the Night* is far and away an exception to the rule for Brazilian horror of the twentieth century, both in terms of commentary and racial inclusion. It was decades ahead of its time in mining horror from Brazil's class and racial inequity, from the fear of the haves of retribution from the have-nots, and from a general sense of societal comeuppance for past wrongs. Such themes would become a common thread through many Brazilian horror films of the twenty-first century, but until then, horror was largely a neglected genre, with output of the 1980s and 1990s characterized by low-budget, low-brow "Trash Cinema," including exploitation fare and parodies that by and large continued to exclude Blacks. The 1990s were further hampered by a near-complete shutdown of Brazilian film production in 1990, when Embrafilme was shuttered by Fernando Collor de Mello, the first democratically elected president after the end of military rule in 1985. Without Embrafilme's funding, the nation's cinematic output fell from 74 films in 1989 to a low of nine films in 1993.[31] However, in 1995, the government began to offer financial support through tax incentives, reinvigorating Brazilian film production and setting the stage for a new era of horror cinema that would finally begin to embrace the country's significant Black presence and more openly address socially relevant topics like race and class.

BLACKNESS IN TWENTY-FIRST CENTURY BRAZILIAN HORROR

The rebirth of Brazilian cinema in the late 1990s was not the only cultural shift in the nation during that time. It coincided with a pronounced shift in the government's response to campaigns from social activists and nongovernmental organizations (NGOs) for the rights of Afro-Brazilians and underprivileged segments of the population. Following the end of the military dictatorship in 1985, Brazil began "a period of re-democratization," during which the government displayed increased openness to the demands of the *movimento negro* ("Black movement") and other advocates for marginalized Brazilians along lines like gender, ethnicity, and class.[32] The fruit of the Black movement's labor was a stipulation in the new national Constitution of 1988 that made racism a crime punishable by imprisonment—although enforcement of the law was more the exception than the rule.[33]

While racial progress was slow during the Collor presidency and that of his successor, Itamar Franco, President Fernando Henrique Cardoso began implementing more concrete, actionable social programs in 1995. Most notable were efforts creating governmental offices devoted to tackling racial inequity, as well as quotas for Afro-Brazilians in public service and other affirmative action programs that had long been advocated by activists but "had to wait until the emergence of worldwide anti-racism and pro-human rights activism in order to be taken into consideration by Brazilian policy-makers."[34] Along the way, Cardoso readily admitted the fantasy of Brazil's supposed racial utopia, stating that the country "is not yet a perfect racial democracy."[35] Cardoso's successor, Luiz Inácio Lula da Silva, displayed even more commitment to correcting generations of racial inequality, implementing racial quotas in higher education, incorporating Afro-Brazilian history and culture into school curriculums, and creating the government agency the Special Ministry for the Promotion of Racial Equality.

Indeed, the increasing acknowledgment of Brazilian Blackness—that is, "Brazil's 'ethnic diversity' in opposition to the traditional celebration of its racial mixture"[36]— was part of a global push for social equality and political upheaval that began to gain momentum during the late 1990s and into the 2000s before exploding in the 2010s with the Arab Spring, the Occupy Movement, Black Lives Matter, #MeToo, and other protests, uprisings, and calls for social justice. Latin America in particular was subject to a number of left-leaning social and political movements throughout these decades that "emerged out of the resistance to neoliberal globalization of the 1990s and 2000s,"[37] throwing into flux traditional balances of power, social mores, and prevailing mindsets. Despite the majority of Brazil's population being *preto* (Black) or *pardo* (interracial), the Black movement has been relatively small, but the fact that three successive two-term presidents who adhered to its messaging were elected between 1994 and 2014 was an indication that the populace held sympathy for the movement's ideals.

The evolving attitude toward Black rights manifested itself in artistic output like horror movies. As a transgressive genre, horror has always tested the boundaries of social norms, triggering censorship in Brazil under military rule, but released from the yoke of such heavy-handed restrictions, Brazilian horror was free to flourish. Like all other genres, it slowed to a trickle in the 1990s after the government ceased its support for filmmaking, with micro-budget, shot-on-VHS, comedic *gorechanchada* efforts by cult director Petter Baiestorf—made independently outside of the traditional production system—keeping horror on life support. However, once government support returned, the genre picked up in the 2000s, inspired by foreign imports shown in theaters, on television, and eventually, on Netflix's video streaming service, which chose Brazil as its first market outside of North America in 2011.[38]

While modern Brazilian horror filmmakers have taken a cue from international fare, they have also imbued their movies with a cultural identity that touches on class and (more implicitly) race, with casts boasting a racial makeup more in line with the majority *preto* and *pardo* general population than what has typically been seen in Brazilian show business. Contrasting the approach of twenty-first-century Brazilian horror to that of more esteemed cinematic fare, Ana Maria Bahiana comments, "Unlike Oscar-ready films with sociological concerns, such as *City of God* and *Central Station*, these horror films aren't being made to capture foreign recognition and awards—these are films made for Brazilian viewers, who embrace the pop and pulp trappings on the surface while the movies smuggle in commentary on Brazilian politics and social issues underneath."[39] However, despite there being no threat of dictatorial censorship, the fact that film production is still largely dependent on public funding means that filmmakers are subject to the whims of the government, as well as businesses and individuals, who are allowed to invest a portion of their income taxes in approved film projects.[40] Thus, with horror being a divisive genre, it continually fights an uphill battle to receive funding over more respected genres, meaning that horror creatives frequently have to seek independent financing to get their movies made.

One film that set the tone for twenty-first-century Brazilian horror and is often credited with igniting the genre's revival is 2008's *Mangue Negro*—*Black Mangrove* in English, but released internationally as *Mud Zombies*. The debut of writer-director Rodrigo Aragão, who would become a driving force in Brazilian horror of this era, *Mud Zombies* features a low-budget, light-hearted "splatstick" style reminiscent of early Sam Raimi or Peter Jackson. Despite its comedic inclination, it touches upon issues such as environmentalism and economic exploitation in the story of a zombie outbreak that strikes a rural community situated alongside a mangrove forest. The cause of the outbreak appears to be man-made contamination—with one character observing that "the mangrove is a garbage disposal; all that's worthless is thrown here"—killing off or mutating wildlife in the area that the locals use for food.

The designation of this area as a dumping ground raises the issue of class, as the commoners in the movie reside on the front lines, bearing the brunt of the environmental deterioration. Like Aragão's follow-up films—*A Noite do Chupacabras* (*Night of the Chupacabras*) (2011), *Mar Negro* (*Dark Sea*) (2013), *El Bosque Negro* (*The Black Forest*) (2018), and *O Cemitério das Almas Perdidas* (*Cemetery of Lost Souls*) (2020)—*Mud Zombies* revolves around lower-class protagonists, a sympathetic portrait that runs through many Brazilian horror efforts of the twenty-first century. These backwoods residents are portrayed as struggling to earn a living—even struggling to find enough to eat—with some subsisting under the thumb of one of the few people with an appreciable amount of disposable income: the villainous Júlio (Júlio Tigre). Júlio is an outsider who complains about "coming to this shithole," and because he exerts economic control over the elderly Antônio (Antônio Lâmego) by buying his crabs, he feels entitled to act in a boorish, demanding manner, even sexually harassing Antônio's daughter, Rachel (Kika Oliveira).

Much like the disintegration of the myth of racial democracy, *Mud Zombies*, according to Serravalle de Sá, "articulates critiques of the underbelly of Brazil's stereotypically cheerful surface."[41] While *Mud Zombies* does not mention race specifically, in Brazil, it is inextricably tied to class, and several of the working-class characters in the film appear to have Afro-Brazilian heritage. As Serravalle de Sá comments, "Brazilian mangrove communities are usually populated by people of indigenous African descent, many of whom found refuge in this remote environment during slavery. In this sense, the film gestures back to the Brazilian history of subjugation, genocide and colonisation."[42] Undoubtedly, race colors everything in societies like Brazil and the United States that are built upon racial inequity. Aragão himself acknowledges that his works hold a mirror up to society, stating, "All movies reflect the social fears from their time, and present-day Brazil is full of fears, uncertainty, and hate" (figure 4.3).[43]

The two identifiably *preto* characters in *Mud Zombies*, Agenor (Markus Konká) and Dona Benedita (André Lobo), are old, wise founts of knowledge who help young protagonists Rachel and Luis (Walderrama Dos Santos) survive the ordeal. The portrayals of the *pretos* are not unproblematic, however, and reflect a sense of colorism that, even within Blackness, is a natural residual effect of white supremacy. The darker characters are clear subordinates to the lighter-skinned Rachel and Luis. Agenor ultimately embodies the horror cliché of the Black sidekick sacrificing himself to save the lead couple at the end of the movie, while Benedita is played by a lighter-skinned male actor disguised in blackface makeup to resemble a mammy-type figure who, aligning with the "magical Negro" trope, is skilled in the mystical practices of the Afro-Brazilian Candomblé religion.

FIGURE 4.3 (L–R) Agenor (Markus Konká), Luis (Walderrama Dos Santos), and Dona Benedita (André Lobo) in *Mud Zombies*.

Mud Zombies was an underground success, but in 2008, the new wave of Brazilian horror was still in its infancy. That year, there were only three horror movies released in the country, but that number mushroomed to 37 in 2019.[44] Horror was still not widely accepted in 2008, as evidenced by the box office failure of Coffin Joe's return in *Embodiment of Evil*, but even in José Mojica Marins's failed effort to revive his legendary character, the increased diversity in Brazilian genre filmmaking is evident. It is subtle, to be sure, but *Embodiment of Evil* features several Black characters—none of them the leads, but it is a notable increase from previous Coffin Joe films. In a sign of progress, one of the many women Coffin Joe kidnaps in his eternal quest to find the "perfect" one to continue his bloodline is Black. She even appears at the end of the film as one of the half dozen women impregnated by Coffin Joe, meaning her race did not disqualify her from biological perfection.

That said, the quality of the majority of Black roles in *Embodiment of Evil* is dubious, as their presence can be attributed to the fact that the film's setting has been moved to a *favela* in São Paulo. Early scenes establish a sense of societal decline in the 40 years that Coffin Joe has been incarcerated in a mental institution, including a shot of Black addicts huffing fumes from a paper bag on the street. Coffin Joe is portrayed as a champion of the underclass, saving a Black street urchin from being exterminated by corrupt police. Later, after other boys are killed by cops, several local Black residents attend their funeral. Similar to American "hood cinema" like *Boyz n the Hood* (1991) and *Menace II Society* (1993), Blackness here is associated with urban poverty and crime. It follows in the footsteps of one of the most acclaimed Brazilian films of all time, 2002's *Cidade de Deus* (*City of God*), which was nominated for four Oscars and "presented for the first time in a big-budget home-grown production a cast made up almost entirely of Afro-Brazilian actors."[45] The story of competing drug dealers, gangs, murderers, and rapists highlights the potential shortcomings of increasing the spotlight on Black characters, receiving criticism from some as "an update on the stereotype of the black man as a criminal,"[46] an issue that becomes increasingly problematic when orchestrated by white directors, as was the case with *City of God*.

More polished than *Mud Zombies* and *Embodiment of Evil* but still focused on a sympathetic portrayal of the underclass is the dark fairy tale *As Boas Maneiras* (*Good Manners*) (2018). Like *The Angel of the Night*, it portrays a blasé upper class that is subjected, perhaps karmically, to a supernatural curse. Class and color are correlated from the first scene in the movie, in which dark-skinned Clara (Isabél Zuaa) is buzzed into a luxury apartment building and instructed via intercom to take the service elevator. She is there to interview for a nanny position with the pregnant, light-skinned Ana (Marjorie Estiano), a selfie-taking, bourgeois woman of leisure who was shipped off to São Paulo by her wealthy family to abort the baby, a love child conceived when she cheated on her fiancé during a drunken one-night stand. When she refused to terminate the pregnancy, Ana's parents disowned her, and her fiancé broke off their engagement. Undaunted by the cessation of her parents' financial support, Ana hires Clara as a live-in domestic, a position that serves as the largest form of employment for Afro-Brazilian women.[47]

The two women share a loneliness that draws them together, and Ana makes sexual advances toward the reserved Clara. While Clara seems to reciprocate willingly, the imbalance of power in the relationship raises questions of appropriateness and serves as a reminder that domestics in Brazil have routinely been exploited by employers for generations. In fact, it wasn't until a 2013 constitutional amendment and subsequent related legislation that they were granted labor rights allotted to other job sectors, including stipulations regarding minimum wages, work hour limitations, unemployment benefits, overtime pay, compensation for unjust dismissal, and workplace injury insurance.

The true horror of the scenario, however, comes into play when it is revealed that the father of Ana's child is a werewolf. Clara finds herself trying to keep Ana safe during her full moon sleepwalking excursions and ends up as the child's guardian after Ana dies during childbirth. The second half of the movie jumps seven years into the future, with Clara caring for young lycanthrope Joel (Miguel Lobo), who, like his ostracized mother, is an outcast, restricted by Clara from eating meat and from attending nighttime events for fear of his increasingly uncontrollable nature. She is seen by Paula Halperin as embodying the traditional figure of the *mãe preta* (Black mammy), "an emblem of devotion and subordination to the elites especially present in 1930s childhood memoirs and the visual arts and recurrently recycled in mass media through today."[48] However, Clara is not defined by subservience. She interacts with Ana more like a partner, admonishing her for not taking proper care of herself and offering emotional support during the difficult pregnancy. She is portrayed as intelligent and resourceful; having trained to be a nurse, she deduces and tracks Ana's symptoms and takes carefully plotted safety precautions when acting as a surrogate parent for Joel. Clara is a more loving and responsible mother than the emotionally unbalanced, alcohol-chugging Ana would have been, making for a well-rounded, sympathetic Black lead character rarely seen in Brazilian horror (figure 4.4).

Labor roles and class conflict is a running theme in the works of *Good Manners* filmmakers Juliana Rojas and Marco Dutra, most notably in their previous feature together, *Trabalhar Cansa* (*Hard Labor*) (2011), which has been cited along with *Mud Zombies* as kicking off Brazil's twenty-first-century horror renaissance.[49] Just as *Hard Labor* undermines the character and conduct of the bourgeoisie, the title *Good Manners* can be interpreted as a tongue-in-cheek repudiation of Brazilian class values. In the movie, Ana relates a story to Clara about being forced by her wealthy family to attend a course on etiquette, a family that would later coldly disown her with the sort of superficial, appearance-conscious mindset that has driven Brazil's approach to race and national identity. The country's long-held belief in the inferiority of the Black race raised concerns about its international reputation as a largely African-descended nation, prompting Brazil to reinvent itself as genteel, tolerant, and increasingly white, willfully forgetting its Blackness just as Ana's family willfully forgets her.

Lacking the structured, state-sponsored segregation and the highly publicized lynchings and race massacres of the United States, Brazil's approach to racial subjugation has been by comparison more polite and gentlemanly. As Lúcio Reis Filho and Sheila Schvarzman point out, the title *Good Manners* "reveal(s) the contradictions of

FIGURE 4.4 (L–R) Clara (Isabél Zuaa) and Ana (Marjorie Estiano) in *Good Manners*.

a society organized under the guise of cordiality . . . the hierarchy of social relations . . . characterized by obedience tinged as 'docility.' "[50] The term "cordiality" is an allusion to the 1936 essay "Raízes do Brasil" ("Roots of Brazil") by sociologist and historian Sérgio Buarque de Holanda. It was a key document in the early twentieth-century reformation of Brazil's identity, along with Gilberto Freyre's racial democracy-touting *Casa-Grande & Senzala*, and included the concept of the prototypical Brazilian as a "cordial man." The nature of this cordiality would be called into question in 1995 by a national survey called *Racismo Cordial* (*Cordial Racism*), conducted by Brazil's largest newspaper, the *Folha de São Paulo*. When asked if whites are prejudiced against Blacks, 90 percent of survey respondents said yes, but 90 percent of whites and "Browns" paradoxically claimed that they personally held no such prejudice, and even 75 percent of Blacks and Browns said that they had never experienced racism. For a long time in Brazil, racism has been like a rumor, a legend, a story that happened to someone who knows someone who knows someone. Black and white Brazilians alike have turned a blind eye to it, seeming to wish a racial democracy into existence. The result is, as described by Florestan Fernandes, "a precarious form of accommodation obtained through obedience to these rules of racial etiquette, proceeding in accordance with good tone, *good manners* and courtesy, as is fitting 'among gentlemen' " (italics added).[51]

But the country's legacy of slavery is not so easily erased. Brazil imported more African slaves than any other nation, a number exceeding that of the United States in part because the brutality of Brazilian slave masters led to such a high a mortality rate that, while the slave population in the United States grew through reproduction, it flatlined in Brazil.[52] The slave masters' reign of terror lasted longer in Brazil than elsewhere in the Americas, as it was the last country to abolish slavery, in 1888, two decades after the United States did so. A new generation of Brazilian horror filmmakers has not been willing to sweep this past under the rug and has in fact used it as fuel for stories that explore the country's inconvenient history.

In *O Diabo Mora Aqui* (*The Devil Lives Here*) (2016), the literal ghost of slavery's past comes back to haunt a group of white teens who, with typical horror movie hubris, gather at a remote farm to conjure the spirit of a slave rumored to haunt the location. The ghost is that of a baby born to a slave woman raped by her notoriously violent master (Ivo Müller), referred to as the Honey Baron because of his beekeeping livelihood. When the baby was born, the mother murdered it as payback for the Baron killing her older son, and ever since, the slaves and their descendants—most recently, modern-day brothers Luciano (Felipe Frazão) and Tião (Pedro Caetano)—have kept watch over the site of the death, performing a ritual every nine months to prevent the escape of the ghosts of the baby and the Baron. The slave bloodline has ensured that the spirits remain trapped in their basement dwelling for over a century—until the four white adolescents, intrigued by the legend, decide to intervene.

The Devil Lives Here does not shy away from the atrocities of slavery, both those committed by slave masters and those—like filicide—committed by slaves who felt they had no other choice. The Baron's beekeeping provides him not only honey, but also a template for the perfect slave. The insects know their place in the colonies. "They don't fight. They don't ask questions. They just work," he expounds to one of his chattel, "but you Blacks only respect fear." Just as much of the Brazilian population has not taken seriously the enduring legacy of slavery—racism, limited educational and career options for Blacks, underdeveloped and crime-ridden *favela* living, a wide racial wealth gap—so too do the white youngsters in the movie fail to take seriously the legend born out of the horrors of slavery. They conduct a ceremony to free the baby ghost as part of a drunken getaway, unaware that they are awakening evil. The story in many ways parallels the American horror classic *Candyman* (1992), even beyond the shared apian imagery. Both involve middle-class whites investigating an urban legend from the Black community and, not taking it seriously, conjuring the malevolent spirit of a victim of a nineteenth-century incident of racialized violence. Like the kids in *The Devil Lives Here*, Helen (Virginia Madsen) in *Candyman* pays a violent price for her cockiness and ends up a spirit herself, intertwined in the generational cycle of violence for an eternity.

While *The Devil Lives Here* features a prototypical white "Final Girl" who serves as the primary protagonist, it elevates its Black characters to something approaching co-star status. When Tião expresses concern that Luciano does not understand their role, Luciano replies, "Of course I understand. We are the heroes." Such is the shift in emphasis from white to Black leads in horror cinema, a trend that isn't particular to Brazil. American horror movies have also made drastic shifts in the twenty-first century to become more inclusive with their starring roles (highlighted by the award-winning work of Jordan Peele) and to not relegate Blacks to expendable supporting cast members who, according to the clichéd trope, always die first. Even other Latin American countries' horror cinema has begun displaying an openness to Black-focused stories, like Argentina's *Los Inocentes* (*The Innocents*) (2015) and Colombia's *Saudó, Laberinto de Almas* (*Saudó, Labyrinth of Souls*) (2016).

The multi-generational *O Nó do Diabo* (*The Devil's Knot*) (2018) takes the Brazilian legacy of slavery to an epic level in a sprawling narrative spread over 200 years. Originally conceived as a miniseries, the horror anthology from four different directors (including Afro-Brazilian Gabriel Martins, a rare Black Brazilian horror filmmaker) consists of five tales told in reverse chronological order from 2018 to 1818. The stories illustrate the enduring impact of race on the functions of society and the way in which slavery has set up a racialized power dynamic that continues to have residual influence in generation after generation, even a century after abolition. According to co-director/writer Ramon Porto Mota, the film operates as a wake-up call to a nation that is still mired in outdated concepts of race and racism and that still feels a need to coat itself in a fabricated veneer of perfection: "We need to overcome this idea of the myth of racial democracy and the cordial man that [was] constructed in the 1930s with Gilberto Freyre and Sérgio Buarque de Holanda, and this necessity of constructing a peaceful Brazilian society. *Nó do Diabo* reflects this society constructed upon conflicts and that tries to throw the problems under the rug."[53]

Each tale is centered on a sugar plantation run by the vicious, vehemently racist Vieira family, whose hatred and inhumane abuse has seemingly damned the property with a curse of pain, despair, and violence. The head of the household for each generation is played by the same actor, Fernando Teixeira, as an acknowledgment of the continuity of present and past. The first story, set in 2018, equates modern-day conservatives with the racialized violence of the slave masters of yesteryear, as a watchman, Cristian (Tavinho Teixeira), who is hired to guard the derelict plantation from the dark-skinned residents of an encroaching *favela*, guns down unarmed residents in a maniacal killing spree. Ironically, the migration of *favela* residents toward land like this on the outskirts of town is due to the fact that they were already victims of "state-sponsored racism and violence toward blacks," pushed out of urban neighborhoods onto the edges of the city in urban renewal efforts benefiting the rich.[54] Such "spatial exclusion" pulls the poor away from jobs and resources, furthering the cycle of poverty, crime, and desperation.

Cristian's rage is fueled not only by the insistence of his boss, Vieira, that "these niggers know this place is mine," but also by the ravings of right-wing talk radio that complain about the crime that *favelas* bring, that celebrate the success of "removing the lefties" from office by way of the 2016 impeachment of social democratic President Dilma Rousseff, and, mirroring American politics, that cite "fake votes" and "programmed ballot boxes" in dismissing the legitimacy of any unfavorable election results. Eventually, the watchman finds himself haunted by the spirits of not only those he's killed, but also those who have died on the land over the past centuries over petty prejudices like those he harbors.

The next tale draws even closer parallels to slavery in its portrayal of the exploitive, abusive relationship between domestic workers and their bosses. In it, Black husband and wife Sebastiao (Alexandre De Sena) and Joana (Clebia Sousa) approach the Vieira plantation in 1987 seeking work. As they perform their new duties in and around the property, the couple encounters remnants from the slave past: Sebastiao comes across antique torture devices and restraints ("for the stubborn, the ones that don't know their place," explains Mr. Vieira), and Joana has visions of a bloody female ghost. When Sebastiao begins to suffer physical injuries, Joana insists they leave, but he has become possessed by a sense of servitude ingrained within the fabric of the farm and feels that, like Jack Torrance (Jack Nicholson) in *The Shining* (1980), he has always been there and always will be.

The third story shifts back to 1921, a time when, despite being more than 30 years removed from the abolition of slavery, Vieira kept the yoke of forced servitude on Blacks working on his plantation. Choosing to defy the emancipation of slaves, his philosophy is: "If the chain is broken, what follows is disorder. That's why on my farm, things are done my way. I don't like these laws from outside." The perils of females in particular are highlighted when Vieira offers Cissa (Yurie Felipe da Silva) to one of his guests as a sexual slave. Known as "stubborn" and "bad-tempered," Cissa reacts violently, killing the guest and is herself murdered in retaliation. Incensed, her "meek" sister Maria (Miuly Felipe da Silva) snaps, enacting violent retribution via her covert ability: pyrokinesis.

The fourth tale involves a similar act of vengeance, this time a male slave (Edilson Silva) killing a white man in 1871 after the deaths of his wife and infant child. He goes on the run, pursued by Vieira, and finds himself mystically drawn toward the supposed location of a *quilombo*, a settlement of escaped slaves, but on the way, he gets more than he bargained for. The *quilombo* is a key symbol of Afro-Brazilian pride, embodying the strength, bravery, resilience, and resourcefulness of those who managed to break the chains of captivity and form functional societies—some boasting thousands of residents. The 1988 Constitution legitimized these settlements by granting the residents and their descendents—*quilombolas*—"final title" to their lands—appropriately, exactly 100 years after the abolition of slavery.[55]

The fifth and final story in *The Devil's Knot* addresses this issue of land ownership, which has become controversial in modern-day Brazil as *quilombolas* have sought to assert their constitutional rights, to the chagrin of others with interests in those lands. *The Devil's Knot* meaningfully begins and ends with this topic. The first vignette involves Vieira's efforts in modern times to keep *favela* interlopers off of his property, while the last vignette presents Vieira and his ilk as the interlopers who must be warded off. Set in 1818, the tale follows a small group of *quilombolas* fleeing from a mob of whites who have destroyed their *quilombo*. In *Night of the Living Dead* (1968) fashion, the ex-slaves barricade themselves on the Vieira property as the whites surround them, breaking through the walls like marauding zombies. The attackers are purposefully portrayed as monstrous, unfeeling, and ravenous. "These animals will kill everyone," comments one of the *quilombolas*. Another replies, "They follow their instincts. We are just playthings for them." As their time runs short, elder Afi (Zezé Motta) reflects to her granddaughter, Tete (Cíntia Lima), on the Vieira family's treatment of the land:

> This used to be full of jurema trees. Then, the Vieiras came like weeds and destroyed it all. They decided to make a garden in the farm as a wedding gift to the old man's wife. The plants grew no more, all withered. Then, the son decided to turn it into a slave's graveyard, but we couldn't take care of it, nor have our rituals. When he got

tired of it, he just abandoned it but wouldn't let us come here. . . . This land belongs to the *quilombo*, Tete. It doesn't belong to the Vieiras. It belongs to you, me, the others, the living and the dead.

Her reference to "the dead" is apt, not just as an indication of the perennial nature of the land rights passing down from one generation to the next, but also because sole survivor Tete is ultimately saved by raising the actual dead. She conjures the corpses of slaves killed by the Vieiras—the *real* zombies—to rise from the ground and defend their land against the attackers (figure 4.5).

Such cinematic portrayals of rebellion and upheaval of authority would have been a prime target for censorship under the decades-long dictatorship, but Brazilians' new-found freedom after the end of military rule presented a blank slate upon which they could reshape their national identity, which had long been defined by spoken and un-spoken white supremacy. Although it took 20 years from the 1988 Constitution, which granted land rights to *quilombolas* and criminalized racism, for Brazilian horror cinema to reflect the nation's more pronounced celebration of Blackness, the 1980s were still, as described by Kjersti Thorkildsen and Randi Kaarhus, "a critical decade, not only through the making of a new democratic constitution in Brazil but also in setting the stage for the identity-based movements that would shape the new politics of representa-tion and cultural recognition from the 1990s onwards."[56]

Even without the overt, racialized social and political commentary of a film like *The Devil's Knot*, other Brazilian horror films have made statements by casting Black protagonists, from *Good Manners* to *A Gruta* (*The Grotto*) (2020), in which a Black woman (Nayara Justino) trapped in a cave is possessed by a murderous spirit that causes the deaths of her fellow hikers, to Rodrigo Aragão's *Cemetery of Lost Souls*, whose

FIGURE 4.5 Tete (Cíntia Lima) and her ancestors in *The Devil's Knot*.

Black leading man (Diego Garcias) is a traveling carnival worker who saves the day by defeating a horde of demonically possessed undead Jesuits.

There have been a host of other horror films that, lacking Black leads, have nonetheless prominently featured Brazilian class inequity and social issues that carry racial implications. The ghost story *O Rastro* (*The Trace We Leave Behind*) (2017) is set in and around a hospital that is closed due to a strike by healthcare workers, a rebuke of the Brazilian healthcare system that turns into an indictment of political corruption when it is revealed that the governor is involved in illegal organ harvesting. The restaurant setting of *O Animal Cordial* (*Friendly Beast*) (2018) allows for a scathing portrayal of the abusive and exploitative circumstances under which blue-collar workers frequently toil—taken to the extreme when the restaurant owner takes his employees hostage. *Morto Não Fala* (*The Nightshifter*) (2018) revolves around a São Paulo morgue worker who can talk to the dead—including a Black gangster murdered by corrupt cops—and includes sympathetic portrayals of Afro-Brazilian criminals who abide by a moral code. "I'm a thug, man," one comments, "but I'm no psycho." In the satirical *O Clube dos Canibais* (*The Cannibal Club*) (2019), meanwhile, the (noticeably white) rich literally eat the poor, but one wealthy couple who plans to have their caretaker for dinner ends up having the tables turned on them.

Horror-adjacent fare from this time period similarly touches on class schisms, frequently with racial undertones. The drama *O Som ao Redor* (*Neighboring Sounds*) (2012) is an example of what Jack A. Draper III terms "materialist horror," or "a dramatic narrative emphasizing not fantastical characters . . . but the everyday, material reality of class, race and/or gender violence and unequal social relations."[57] The film paints a portrait of the daily life of the (mostly light-skinned) residents of a middle-class neighborhood and the (largely darker-skinned) domestic and security workers they employ. The implication that this racialized power structure is a legacy of slavery is established in the film's opening, a montage of vintage black-and-white photos of plantation laborers. The horror elements in the film are of an elusive, symbolic nature: fleeting imagery like a waterfall on a plantation turning into the blood of those who have died there, or a nightmare about intruders breaking into an upscale apartment building as a reflection of "the collective middle-class affect of fear."[58] Like *The Devil's Knot*, the haves are paranoid about intrusion on their property by the have-nots, even if the property—from the plantation to the urban neighborhood—seems tainted by the sins of the past. Those sins ultimately return with deadly vengeance when it turns out that the security guards hired to protect the block have ulterior motives: to retaliate against the richest man in the neighborhood, Francisco (W.J. Solha), who years earlier killed their father.

Meanwhile, *Bacurau* (2019) and *Carro Rei* (*King Car*) (2022) celebrate the struggle of the working class against the elites and the government with unorthodox style and subject matter. In the quasi-Western thriller *Bacurau*, a corrupt mayor attempts to strong-arm the residents of a small rural settlement into signing their water rights over to him, even hiring racist white American hitmen to do his bidding. In the allegorical fantasy *King Car*, an Afro-Brazilian teen with the ability to telepathically communicate with cars leads an army of older models into a revolution when the government outlaws vehicles more than 15 years old (i.e., those belonging to the poor). Both movies present David-and-Goliath stories of small, self-reliant, largely Black communities triumphing over attempts of the powerful to impose their will on the seemingly powerless.

Anita Rocha da Silveira's feminist satire *Medusa* (2022) champions the rebellion of another type of underclass—women—in a biting condemnation of traditional gender roles, sexual mores, and religious repression. The film follows a group of adolescent girls and young women who, by day, are active in a youth-oriented church, singing Christian pop songs that advocate conservative values with lyrics like, "I shall be a modest and pretty housewife." At night, however, they become vigilantes, donning masks and seeking out women they deem to have loose morals, physically assaulting them and coercing promises to atone for their sins. When one of the vigilantes, Mari (Mari Oliveira)—notably, Afro-Brazilian—receives a scar on her face from an attack, her eyes are opened to the superficiality of those around her—including the notably white, blond group leader, Michele (Lara Tremouroux)—who pity and shun her because of her disfigurement. Mari gradually breaks away from the control of the church and its followers, whose actions Rocha da Silveira cites as inspired by the recent "rise of the ultra-right in Brazilian society."[59] Mari gains further liberation through sexual exploration and ultimately spreads that sense of freedom to the other women in the church, triggering a climactic uprising in which they take on the rigid male hierarchy and flee into the streets, screaming in a unified catharsis.

Conclusion

Proclamations of the visibility of Blackness in modern Brazilian horror cinema should be tempered by the reality that Afro-Brazilian characters are still underrepresented compared to the population at large. In a survey of 34 Brazilian horror movies from 2008 to 2022 conducted for this study, only eight feature observably Black major characters.[60] This amounts to less than 25 percent of the films, compared to a population that is more than 50 percent *preto* and *pardo*. Still, this is a marked improvement in representation over previous decades of Brazilian horror traced back to José Mojica Marins's genre debut in the 1960s.

The twenty-first-century movement in Brazilian horror cinema toward increased Blackness reflects, according to Draper, "a clear trend in the region . . . to reshape this generic influence into a tool to represent everyday class-, race- and gender-based violence."[61] Racial identity came to the forefront of Brazilian culture with the 1988 Constitution and then continued to rise through a series of left-wing administrations in the 2000s and 2010s that passed social programs like affirmative action quotas for higher education and civil service jobs, plus employment benefits for domestic workers and the teaching of Afro-Brazilian history in schools. This celebration of racial diversity paralleled the growth of social justice movements on a global level, from the political upheaval of the Arab Spring to the class-based protests of the Occupy Movement to the women's rights focus of #MeToo and the Women's March to the race-based Black Lives Matter, as nations began to come to terms with their legacies of oppression of marginalized segments of society.

However, Brazil, as with the United States and many other countries around the world, experienced right-wing backlash against what conservatives viewed as an overly sharp correction for sins of the distant past. The Brazilian right wing used the easy target of social welfare policies benefiting poor and Black residents to channel the frustrations of a populace disenchanted by inflation, infrastructure deficiencies, and political corruption. The massive Brazilian protests of 2013 began as a rally against a rise in bus fare pricing, but when a police crackdown resulted in young, attractive, white female journalist Giuliana Vallone getting shot in the eye by a rubber bullet, her bloody image sparked nationwide outrage, fueling millions to take to the streets in more than 300 cities over the course of several weeks. The source of anger immediately shifted; "instead of seeing the police as targeting a radical student group, many now perceived the June 13 protest as a brutal crackdown on the middle class as a whole."[62] Poor and Black citizens were largely excluded—sometimes intentionally, as, in a familiar refrain of Black invisibility, "mass media emphasized white women and erased black Brazilians."[63] The topics that fueled the middle-class protests ranged widely, from the cost of hosting the World Cup and the Olympics to the quality of healthcare and education to "freedom of speech, the right to protest, and generalized anger with police and elected officials," plus crucially, "backlash to the affirmative action and welfare policies that were improving the living standards and social positions of many black Brazilians."[64]

The erosion of belief in established politicians—and, from Brazilians who yearned for the days of the dictatorship, in democracy as a whole—fed into the 2018 election of the anti-establishment, despot-like Jair Bolsonaro, who rode racism, sexism, and homophobia to victory in much the same way that Donald Trump channeled the subtext-laden desire to "Make America Great Again." Bolsonaro's anti-Black campaigning was more than just rhetoric. Within his first two days in office, he pushed for legislation aimed at ending racial quotas and removing the land rights of *quilombolas* and the Indigenous.[65] The attack on Black rights has a longstanding base in Brazilian culture, with its "racial democracy" ideal that demonizes any insinuation that racism is a major issue, just as conservatives in America have launched an anti–critical race theory campaign to erase from history books teachings that highlight racism, that imply the existence of white privilege, that cause anyone "discomfort, guilt or anguish on account of their race," or even more broadly, "any doctrine or theory promoting a negative account or representation of the founding and history of the United States of America."[66]

As has been shown, such erasure of the Black perspective is not new to Brazil, and there is legitimate fear that it can happen again. While there has not been the outright censorship of cinema that took place during the dictatorship, there are reports that making horror movies has become more difficult, and certainly Bolsonaro-era Brazil has not shown itself to be receptive to progressiveness or social commentary. With film funding subject to the whims of financiers, it is conceivable that money could not be available to projects deemed to be out of step with current values and beliefs, which would make it difficult to fund movies promoting Black rights—or even featuring Blackness at all, with a vocal contingent ready to declare any semblance of diversity as "woke." Longtime Brazilian horror filmmaker Petter Baiestorf cites "the growth of the extreme right and evangelicals in Brazil, two groups linked to agribusiness and the militias, which are essentially against the arts, cinema, and books," as stifling current horror cinema.[67] "The film industry itself is practically extinct," he declares, "so in the last few years, while we had been experiencing fantastic growth within the fantastic cinema genres, it has practically been undermined, giving hints that in the next decade there could only be leftover independent filmmakers who raise the money in a non-traditional way."[68]

It remains to be seen if Brazilian horror can overcome the coercive powers of conservative interests and continue to feature racial diversity and social criticism. Who appears on screen should reflect who appears in real life, and for a nation that has, since the 2010 census, acknowledged that the majority of its population is non-white, the erasure of Blackness would be a disservice to the heritage of a diverse and continuously evolving populace.

Notes

1. For the purposes of this study, "Black" refers to those of African descent, categorized in Brazil's racial classification system as either *preto* (Black) or *pardo* (mixed white and Black), although it should be noted that a minority of *pardos* are of mixed white and Indigenous descent.
2. Laura Loguercio Cánepa, "José Mojica Marins Versus Coffin Joe: Auteurism and Stardom in Brazilian Cinema," in *Stars and Stardom in Brazilian Cinema*, ed. Tim Bergfelder, Lisa Shaw, and João Luiz Vieira (New York: Berghahn Books, 2017), 182.
3. Sarah Brown, "Everything You Need to Know About Brazil's Diverse Religious Beliefs," *Culture Trip*, April 8, 2017, https://theculturetrip.com/south-america/brazil/articles/eve rything-you-need-to-know-about-brazils-diverse-religious-beliefs.
4. Joseph Liu, "Brazil's Changing Religious Landscape," *Pew Research Center*, July 18, 2013, https://www.pewresearch.org/religion/2013/07/18/brazils-changing-religious-landscape.
5. André Barcinski, "Coffin Joe and José Mojica Marins: Strange Men for Strange Times," in *Fear Without Frontiers: Horror Cinema Across the Globe*, ed. Steven Jay Schneider (Godalming, England: FAB Press, 2003), 33.
6. Sean Lindsay, "Coleção Zé do Caixão—50 Anos do Cinema de Jose Mojica Marins," *Offscreen*, June 2005, https://offscreen.com/view/coleo_caixo.
7. Dolores Tierney, "José Mojica Marins and the Cultural Politics of Marginality in Third World Film Criticism," *Journal of Latin American Cultural Studies* 13, no. 1 (March 2004): 70, https://doi.org/10.1080/1356932042000186497.
8. Robert Stam and Ella Shohat, *Race in Translation: Culture Wars around the Postcolonial Atlantic* (New York: New York University Press, 2012), 29; André Salata, "Race, Class and Income Inequality in Brazil: A Social Trajectory Analysis," *Dados: Revista de Ciências Sociais* 63, no. 3 (October 2, 2020), https://doi.org/10.1590/dados.2020.63.3.213.

9. Louisa Acciari, "Practicing Intersectionality: Brazilian Domestic Workers' Strategies of Building Alliances and Mobilizing Identity," *Latin American Research Review* 56, no. 1 (January 2022): 68, http://doi.org/10.25222/larr.594.

10. Claudiney Pereira, "Ethno-Racial Poverty and Income Inequality in Brazil," in *Commitment to Equity Handbook: Estimating the Impact of Fiscal Policy on Inequality and Poverty*, ed. Nora Lustig (New Orleans, LA: CEQ Institute at Tulane University and Brookings Institution Press, 2018), 555.

11. By 2020, Brazil had fallen to the fifteenth highest, per the "Gini Index," The World Bank, https://data.worldbank.org/indicator/SI.POV.GINI?end=2020&most_recent_value_d esc=true&start=2020.

12. Daniel Serravalle de Sá, "The Strange Case of Brazilian Gothic Cinema," in *Tropical Gothic in Literature and Culture: The Americas*, ed. Justin D. Edwards and Sandra Guardini Vasconcelos (New York: Routledge, 2016), 241.

13. Lisa Shaw and Tim Bergfelder, "Introduction," in *Stars and Stardom in Brazilian Cinema*, ed. Tim Bergfelder, Lisa Shaw, and João Luiz Vieira (New York: Berghahn Books, 2017), 4.

14. Robert Stam, "Slow Fade to Afro: The Black Presence in Brazilian Cinema," *Film Quarterly* 36, no. 2 (1982): 21, https://doi.org/10.2307/3696991.

15. Ibid., 16.

16. Frederick Schiff, "Brazilian Film and Military Censorship: Cinema Novo, 1964–1974," *Historical Journal of Film, Radio and Television* 13, no. 4 (1993): 477.

17. Robin E. Sheriff, "Exposing Silence as Cultural Censorship: A Brazilian Case," *American Anthropologist* 102, no. 1 (2000): 114, http://www.jstor.org/stable/683542.

18. France Winddance Twine, *Racism in a Racial Democracy: The Maintenance of White Supremacy in Brazil* (New Brunswick, NJ: Rutgers University Press, 1998), 13.

19. Brian Owensby. "Toward a History of Brazil's 'Cordial Racism': Race beyond Liberalism," *Comparative Studies in Society and History* 47, no. 2 (2005): 329, http://www.jstor.org/sta ble/3879307.

20. Ben Hoff, "The Black Body Reframed: Lázaro Ramos and the Performance of Interracial Love," in *Stars and Stardom in Brazilian Cinema*, ed. Tim Bergfelder, Lisa Shaw, and João Luiz Vieira (New York: Berghahn Books, 2017), 227.

21. Abdias do Nascimento and Elisa Larkin Nascimento, "Dance of Deception: A Reading of Race Relations in Brazil," in *Beyond Racism: Race and Inequality in Brazil, South Africa, and the United States*, ed. Charles V. Hamilton et al. (Boulder, CO: Lynne Rienner Publishers, 2001), 125.

22. Stam, "Slow Fade to Afro," 28.

23. Ibid., 25.

24. Schiff, "Brazilian Film and Military Censorship," 469.

25. Felipe M. Guerra, "Brazilian Outlaw Cinema, pt. 3—Felipe M. Guerra," interview by Sean Leonard, *Nervousmaker*, August 23, 2021, https://www.nervousmaker.com/words/brazil ian-outlaw-cinema-pt3-felipe-m-guerra.

26. Laura Loguercio Cánepa, "*The Angel of the Night*, Gothic Horror and the Brazilian Social Tensions in the 1970s," *Chasqui: Latin American Journal of Communication* no. 134 (April 2017): 291, https://doi.org/10.16921/chasqui.v0i134.2599.

27. Acciari, "Practicing Intersectionality," 68.

28. Serravalle de Sá, "Brazilian Gothic Cinema," 244.

29. Ibid., 246.

30. Cánepa, "*The Angel of the Night*," 280.
31. Cacilda M. Rêgo, "Brazilian Cinema: Its Fall, Fise, and Renewal (1990–2003)," *New Cinemas: Journal of Contemporary Film* 3, no. 2 (September 2005): 86, https://doi.org/10.1386/ncin.3.2.85/1.
32. Rebecca Lemos Igreja and Gianmarco Loures Ferreira, "The Brazilian Law of Racial Quotas Put to the Test of Labor Justice: A Legal Case Against Banco do Brasil," *Latin American and Caribbean Ethnic Studies* 14, no.3 (October 2019): 294, https://doi.org/10.1080/17442222.2019.1667635.
33. Marta Rodriguez de Assis Machado, Márcia Lima, and Natália Neris da Silva Santos, "Anti-racism Legislation in Brazil: The Role of the Courts in the Reproduction of the Myth of Racial Democracy," *Revista de Investigações Constitucionais* 6, no. 2 (May/August 2019): 291, http://dx.doi.org/10.5380/rinc.v6i2.70080.
34. Leone Campos de Sousa and Paulo Nascimento, "Brazilian National Identity at a Crossroads: The Myth of Racial Democracy and the Development of Black Identity," *International Journal of Politics, Culture, and Society* 19 (2008): 133, https://doi.org/10.1007/s10767-008-9023-y.
35. Ibid., 134.
36. Ibid.
37. Richard Stahler-Sholk, Harry E. Vanden, and Marc Becker, "Introduction: New Directions in Latin American Social Movements," in *Rethinking Latin American Social Movements: Radical Action from Below*, ed. Richard Stahler-Sholk, Harry E. Vanden, and Marc Becker (Lanham, MD: Rowman & Littlefield, 2014), 1.
38. As of 2021, Brazil had the highest number of Netflix subscribers outside of the United States, per Rebeccah Moody, "Netflix Subscribers and Revenue by Country," *Comparitech*, September 10, 2021, https://www.comparitech.com/tv-streaming/netflix-subscribers.
39. Ana Maria Bahiana, "The Blair Witches of Brazil," BBC, July 6, 2017, https://www.bbc.com/culture/article/20170701-the-blair-witches-of-brazil.
40. Stephanie Dennison, *Remapping Brazilian Film Culture in the Twenty-First Century* (New York: Routledge, 2020), 12.
41. Daniel Serravalle de Sá, "Gothic Forests and Mangroves: Environmental Disasters in *Zombio* and *Mangue Negro*," in *B-Movie Gothic: International Perspectives*, ed. Justin D. Edwards and Johan Höglund (Edinburgh: Edinburgh University Press, 2018), 76.
42. Ibid., 76.
43. Rodrigo Aragão, "Brazilian Outlaw Cinema, pt. 2—Rodrigo Aragão," interview by Sean Leonard, *Nervousmaker*, August 20, 2021, https://www.nervousmaker.com/words/brazilian-outlaw-cinema-pt-2-rodrigo-arago.
44. Nick Story, "Brazil's Horror Genre Is Having a Revival," Little Black Book, October 28, 2021, https://www.lbbonline.com/news/brazils-horror-genre-is-having-a-revival.
45. Dennison, *Remapping*, 99.
46. Ibid.
47. Acciari, "Practicing Intersectionality," 68.
48. Paula Halperin, "Horror, Motherhood, and Brazilian Manners in *As Boas Maneiras*," *The Mantle*, June 5, 2018, https://www.themantle.com/arts-and-culture/horror-motherhood-and-brazilian-manners-boas-maneiras.
49. Jon Towlson, *Global Horror Cinema Today* (Jefferson, NC: McFarland & Company, 2021), 53.

50. Lúcio Reis Filho and Sheila Schvarzman, "An Uncanny Absence: Lovecraft in Brazilian Cinema, 1975–2016," in *Lovecraft in the 21st Century: Dead, But Still Dreaming*, ed. Antonio Alcala Gonzalez and Carl H. Sederholm (New York: Routledge, 2022), 48.

51. Teun A. van Dijk, *Antiracist Discourse in Brazil: From Abolition to Affirmative Action* (Lanham, MD: Lexington Books, 2020), 107.

52. João José Reis, "Slavery in Nineteenth-Century Brazil," in *The Cambridge World History of Slavery*, ed. David Eltis et al. (Cambridge, UK: Cambridge University Press, 2017), 129, https://doi.org/10.1017/9781139046176.007; *Brazil: An Inconvenient History*, directed by Phil Grabsky (Seventh Art Productions, 2000), 46:33, https://www.kanopy.com/en/lapl/video/47288.

53. Marques Travae, "Is 'Nó do Diabo' (Devil's Knot) Brazil's 'Get Out'?", *Black Brazil Today*, July 29, 2018, https://blackbraziltoday.com/is-no-do-diabo-devils-knot.

54. Keisha-Khan Y. Perry, *Black Women Against the Land Grab: The Fight for Racial Justice in Brazil* (Minneapolis: University of Minnesota Press, 2013), xv.

55. Constitution of Brazil 1988, The Transitional Constitutional Provisions Act 1988, Article 68, translated by Keith S. Rosenn, Constitute Project, https://constituteproject.org/constitution/Brazil_2017?lang=en.

56. Kjersti Thorkildsen and Randi Kaarhus, "The Contested Nature of Afro-descendant *Quilombo* Land Claims in Brazil," *The Journal of Peasant Studies* 46, no. 4 (2017): 793, https://doi.org/10.1080/03066150.2017.140053.

57. Jack A. Draper III, "'Materialist Horror' and the Portrayal of Middle-Class Fear in Recent Brazilian Film Drama: *Adrift* (2009) and *Neighbouring Sounds* (2012)," *Studies in Spanish & Latin American Cinemas* 13, no. 2 (2016): 122, https://doi.org/10.1386/slac.13.2.119_1.

58. Draper, "'Materialist Horror,'" 121.

59. Anita Rocha da Silveira, "Dream We All Scream: Interview with *Medusa* Director Anita Rocha da Silveira," interview by Michael Talbot-Haynes, *Film Threat*, July 28, 2022, https://filmthreat.com/interviews/dream-we-all-scream-interview-with-medusa-director-anita-rocha-da-silveira/.

60. *Mud Zombies, The Devil Lives Here, Good Manners, The Devil's Knot, Friendly Beast, The Nightshifter, Cemetery of Lost Souls*, and *The Grotto*.

61. Draper, "'Materialist Horror,'" 120.

62. Brian Winter, "Revisiting Brazil's 2013 Protests: What Did They Really Mean?," *Americas Quarterly*, March 1, 2017, https://www.americasquarterly.org/article/revisiting-brazils-2013-protests-what-did-they-really-mean/.

63. Katherine Jensen, "Black Brazil Never Slept," *Contexts* 13, no. 2 (Spring 2014): 45, https://doi.org/10.1177/1536504214533499.

64. Winter, "Revisiting"; Joseph Jay Sosa, "Choreographing Exclusion: Protest, Race, and Place in São Paulo," *Latin American and Caribbean Ethnic Studies* 15, no. 3 (2020): 325–326, https://doi.org/10.1080/17442222.2020.1785616.

65. Antonio Jose Bacelar and Erika Robb Larkins, "The Bolsonaro Election, Antiblackness, and Changing Race Relations in Brazil," *The Journal of Latin American and Caribbean Anthropology* 24, no. 4 (2019): 893, https://doi.org/10.1111/jlca.1243.

66. Greg Allen, "Fla. Bill Bans Businesses and Schools from Making Anyone Feel Guilt About Race," NPR, February 8, 2022, https://www.npr.org/2022/02/08/1079112803/fla-bill-bans-businesses-and-schools-from-making-anyone-feel-guilt-about-race; Sarah Schwartz, "Map: Where Critical Race Theory Is Under Attack," *Education Week*, June 11, 2021

(updated April 28, 2022), https://www.edweek.org/policy-politics/map-where-critical-race-theory-is-under-attack/2021/06.

67. Petter Baiestorf, "Brazilian Outlaw Cinema, pt. 1—Petter Baiestorf," interview by Sean Leonard, *Nervousmaker*, August 15, 2021, https://www.nervousmaker.com/words/brazil ian-outlaw-cinema.

68. Ibid.

CHAPTER 5

···

GET(TING) OUT OF THE AMERICAN DREAM/ NIGHTMARE

···

MIA MASK

GET Out will be remembered as one of the most significant films of the twenty-first century for its subversion of the racial contract to which most American movies—and certainly *all* U.S. horror pictures—blithely conform. For decades, American movies rendered Black characters expendable. Black bodies have historically been semiotically coded (and constructed in the collective consciousness) as abject.[1] Abjection in this context has theoretical implications and real-world resonance. While abjection theory has been applied in the social sciences and humanities, it emerges from the psychoanalytic work of Julia Kristeva. Drawing on Mary Douglas's *Purity and Danger*, Kristeva's foundational book, *The Powers of Horror*, develops the theory of abjection through literary, psychoanalytic, and anthropological works. It describes the social and psychological processes by which objects like garbage, sewage, corpses, and rotting food elicit powerful emotional responses such as horror and disgust.[2] Kristeva draws on Sigmund Freud's and Jacques Lacan's psychoanalytic theories to examine horror, marginalization, castration, the phallic signifier, the Oedipal complex, exile, and other concepts. Her theories of abjection dovetail with Frantz Fanon's postcolonial psychoanalytic theory and with the theories of critical race scholars such as Cheryl I. Harris. Taken collectively, theories of abjection, postcoloniality, psychoanalysis, and critical race illuminate the cultural and political implications of a self-reflexive, revisionist text like *Get Out*.

Frantz Fanon was one of the first scholars to examine the complex signifiers informing the European reactions to Black bodies in the public sphere and to place these interracial interactions within a psychoanalytic framework. When Fanon published *Black Skin, White Masks* in 1952, the U.S. South was still segregated by Jim Crow laws. From the 1860s until the 1960s, segregation in the United States meant the legally sanctioned, physical separation of facilities, services, and economic opportunities (i.e., housing, medical care, education, employment, and transportation) along racial lines. "The color line" was the colloquial expression commonly used to refer to the legally and socially enforced separation of human beings into distinct racial groups.[3] The color line was the legally enforced boundary used to demarcate African Americans (and other people of color) in the public sphere via statutes, codes, and regulations.[4] To varying degrees, other people of color have also experienced dreadful forms of racial segregation and mistreatment, including the annihilation of Indigenous communities, Japanese internment camps, anti-immigrant xenophobia, and Islamophobia.

With some exceptions, African experiences in the New World began with the Middle Passage—a stage of the transatlantic slave trade in which millions of enslaved Africans were transported to the Americas as part of the triangular slave trade in *abject* African bodies.[5] These Black bodies were situated at the interstices between subject and object, human and inhuman, valuable and disposable, African and American. They stood outside of the symbolic order as taboo entities whose bodies were placed into liminal subhuman spaces. African Americans' liminal status as not fully human beings—in fact as three-fifths of a human being—was written into the U.S. constitution.[6]

The Three-fifths Compromise was an agreement reached during the 1787 U.S. Constitutional Convention, wherein politicians discussed whether to include slaves in a state's total population (for apportioning voting representation). This was critically important, as the number of citizens in each state would determine the number of seats it would have in the House of Representatives; the states' numbers of electoral college votes; and the amount of money states would pay in taxes. The compromise counted three-fifths of each state's slave population toward that state's total population for the purpose of apportioning the House of Representatives. Even though slaves were denied voting rights, this gave Southern states more representatives and more presidential electoral votes than if they had excluded slaves from the count. The "Three-Fifths Clause" rendered Black people as less than human and at the same time, increased the political power of free (read: white) persons in slaveholding states.

Southern states profited tremendously from Black abjection and, along with Northern states, continued implementing de facto regulations that informed American race relations well into the twentieth century. From Black Codes to convict labor-leasing programs, to sundown towns, to lynching, to racial profiling and mass incarceration in an era of carceral capitalism, there is an enduring legacy of rendering African American bodies as abject grist for the American capitalist mill.

In 1951, a class action suit filed against the Board of Education in Topeka, Kansas, led to a change in the Jim Crow laws that kept educational facilities segregated, and therefore, unequal. On behalf of their children, 13 Topeka parents filed the lawsuit, calling for the school district to reverse its policy of racial segregation.[7] However, racial desegregation was threatening—potentially destabilizing—to those who identified as "white" Americans, because they believed that any social integration between the races, particularly between African Americans and white people, potentially threatened white manufacturers' control over Black, working-class laborers. Perhaps more importantly, desegregation posed a threat to white supremacy and the exclusive neighborhoods, civic centers, municipal/religious facilities, and job opportunities that it afforded whites.

On May 17, 1954, the U.S. Supreme Court handed down its unanimous decision: segregated educational facilities were inherently *un*equal.

One reason the *Brown* decision was so critical (and is relevant to any discussion of race in popular culture or to a film such as *Get Out*) is because the governing state apparatus, and most of mainstream America, also fiercely opposed integration. Maintaining a racial state, an arguably apartheid state, was constitutive of institutional and epistemological norms. Apartheid was part of the normal protections deemed necessary to prevent white women and girls from socially interacting with African American men and boys. Many devout white Christians—particularly in the Southern United States—believed these interactions were an offense to religious tenets and principles.

Ironically, upholding religious tenets and principles meant that an African American man or boy could be abducted, tortured, or lynched for "violating" the racial order, even an offense as trivial as whistling at a white woman. In 1955, this is precisely what happened to one Black teenager. Roy Bryant and his brother-in-law, J. D. Milam, abducted 14-year-old Emmett Till from his uncle's home in Money, Mississippi, and murdered him for whistling at Carolyn Bryant-Donham. Till had supposedly violated the anti-miscegenation "codes of conduct" set forth by the racial state when he allegedly made a pass at Miss Donham. Although witnesses positively identified Bryant and Milam as Till's kidnappers, in September 1955 an all-white jury found them not guilty of the teenager's murder. Protected by the Double Jeopardy Clause, the perpetrators could not be tried twice on the same charges. Aware of the double jeopardy protections, in a 1956 confessional interview with *Look* magazine, the two men bragged that they had tortured and murdered Emmett Till. The magazine paid Bryant and Milam $4,000 (equivalent to $40,000 in 2021) for their story (figure 5.1).

U.S.

Woman Linked to 1955 Emmett Till Murder Tells Historian Her Claims Were False

By RICHARD PÉREZ-PEÑA JAN. 27, 2017

Carolyn Bryant Donham in 1955.
Gene Herrick/Associated Press

For six decades, she has been the silent woman linked to one of the most notorious crimes in the nation's history, the lynching of Emmett Till, a 14-year-old black boy, keeping her thoughts and memories to herself as millions of strangers idealized or vilified her.

But all these years later, a historian says that the woman has broken her silence, and acknowledged that the most incendiary parts of the story she and others told about Emmett — claims that seem tame today but were more than enough to get a black person killed in Jim Crow-era Mississippi — were false.

RELATED COVERAGE

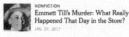

NONFICTION
Emmett Till's Murder: What Really Happened That Day in the Store?
JAN. 27, 2017

FIGURE 5.1 2017 *New York Times* article in which Carolyn Bryant admits to falsely accusing Emmett Till of inappropriately touching and harassing her.

South African critical race scholar David Theo Goldberg notes that racial states (like the United States or apartheid-era South Africa) "employ physical force, violence, coercion, manipulation, deceit, laws, taxes, penalties, surveillance, military force, repressive apparatuses (i.e., prisons), ideological mechanisms and *media* . . . to represent the interests of the racial ruling class."[8] Young Emmett Till was the victim of racial vigilantism that the racial state's policies and practices (its ruling class and the statutes on miscegenation) supported.

The term "miscegenation" had been utilized in the United States since the nineteenth century to refer to interracial marriage, any interracial socializing or contact, and more generally to genetic mixture. In the 1890s, the word was legitimized by the growing, worldwide eugenics movement. Eugenics was a pseudo-science with the goal of improving human populations through selective breeding.[9] Proponents of eugenics believed in the genetic superiority of Nordic, Germanic, and Anglo-Saxon peoples and supported strict immigration policies and anti-miscegenation laws banning interracial marriage and sex. Although advocates held that Black people were intellectually inferior to whites, they thought *some* Black people were physically *superior* (i.e., stronger, more athletic, built for hard labor, and capable of great endurance).

The twin epistemologies of racism—eugenics and miscegenation—emerge conterminously in Jordan Peele's revisionist horror film *Get Out*, in which Black bodies are liminal, abject repositories for white people's taboo desires. Outdated concepts though they are, discourses of racial inferiority and superiority continue to inform everyday actions (discrimination), interactions (police profiling), juridical practice (Rockefeller drug laws), public policies (mass incarceration), and individual behaviors, particularly in light of Donald Trump's politics. In pairing discourses of racial segregation, director Jordan Peele is, to paraphrase philosopher Dan Flory, "provoking us to examine fundamental questions such as what it is to be a 'human being' and how do we acknowledge the humanity of others?"

Importantly, anti-miscegenation statutes in the United States were finally struck down as a result of the Supreme Court decision *Loving v. Virginia* in 1967.[10] After the *Loving* case, the number of interracial marriages increased in the United States. In December of the same year, Stanley Kramer treated moviegoers to *Guess Who's Coming to Dinner* (1967), his once celebrated but now widely contested dramedy. Whereas earlier films had suggested interracial couplings (i.e., *Princess Tam Tam* [1935]; *Duel in the Sun* [1946]; *Pinky* [1949]; *Island in the Sun* [1957]; *Shadows* [1959]; *A Patch of Blue* [1965]), none explicitly examined the proverbial question looming for mainstream white America: "What would you do if your daughter married a Black man?"

The *Loving v. Virginia* case and the Stanley Kramer social-problem picture were groundbreaking events that marked a shift in national culture. Until that point, there existed a national obsession with the *putative* sexual threat Black men posed to civil society in general and to white women in particular. Ever since the eighteenth century, the construction of whiteness in America required the reproduction of white bodies to maintain the colonial racial order. As Richard Dyer notes in his book *White*, "interracial heterosexuality threatened the dominance of whiteness."[11] David Theo

Goldberg supports Dyer's assertion, noting that the anti-miscegenation laws were one key mechanism by which the racial state regulated social interaction with the goal of sculpting demographic definition.[12] Ann Laura Stoler corroborates both Dyer's and Goldberg's analyses. She offers a Foucauldian interpretation of the construction of desire throughout the colonial era of empire by drawing on Foucault's little-known 1976 College de France lectures to address his treatment of the relationship between biopower, bourgeois sexuality, and what he identified as "racisms of the state."[13] These laws and practices made the message clear: phenotypically white-passing subjects were socialized—in the mother countries and colonies—to avoid interracial sexuality because phenotypic whiteness/Europeanness had (by the seventeenth century) become a global signifier of racial privilege.

In her essay "Whiteness as Property," legal historian Cheryl Harris, explains the link between concepts of race and concepts of property. According to Harris, "following slavery, whiteness became the basis of racialized privilege—a type of status in which racial categories provided the foundation for the allocation of societal benefits."[14] The exploitation of Black labor was accomplished by treating African Americans as *objects of property*.[15] Race and property were conflated by establishing a form of possession and ownership contingent on whiteness. Black people could not own property. They did not even have ownership of *themselves*. The "color line" became a line of protection from the potential threat of exploitation and commodification for whites.[16] It was also the demarcation of subjugation for African Americans.

After slavery, during Reconstruction, and well into the post–World War II era, a "concept of a protectable property interest in whiteness" endured.[17] This *protectable property interest* (and the associated biopower and privilege of being able to commodify, exploit, capture, and possess Black bodies as abject objects of property) is what Jordan Peele addresses in his movie *Get Out*.

Get Out simultaneously accomplishes three tasks. First, *Get Out* spoofs the prototypical interracial romantic comedy, *Guess Who's Coming to Dinner*, restaging the film, and the narration, by telling an analogous story from the perspective of the Black male character rather than the white female ingenue. In doing so, *Get Out* jettisons conventional notions of spectator identification and situates moviegoers as active yet resisting spectators. Second, *Get Out* re-imagines and reconfigures the horror film as a transgressive cult picture in which familiar conventions of the horror genre are carefully but comically subverted. Third, by closely reading the protagonist's experience, we see how *Get Out* reactivates Frantz Fanon's critique of race and racial categories. A close textual reading renders visible the invisible (or normalized) white supremacist logic informing modes of cognition and epistemologies of race, not to mention the implementations of disciplines such as psychology and psychiatry.

Get Out is a horror-satire spin on *Guess Who's Coming to Dinner* rendered for the post-Obama age. To fully appreciate it as a parody, one must be familiar with *Guess Who's Coming to Dinner*. Starring Sidney Poitier, Katharine Hepburn, Spencer Tracy, and Katharine Houghton, *Guess Who's Coming to Dinner* tells the story of a newly betrothed interracial couple. Sidney Poitier portrays Dr. John Wade Prentice, a sophisticated doctor who, fresh on the heels of their engagement, travels home with his white fiancée, Joey (Katherine Houghton), to meet her upper-class parents. Unbeknown to his fiancee's parents (Matt and Christina Drayton), John is African American. Because they are a mixed couple, the film is essentially an interracial couple "coming out" story.

Importantly, Joey's parents initially attempt to conceal their shock and discomfort over the relationship, yet their efforts prove futile as their astonishment is beyond both their and Joey's control. The film devotes little attention to John's African American parents. The Prentices' reaction to their son's bethrothal plays out as an afterthought of sorts. Therefore, the film focuses on whiteness as property. It focuses on The Drayton's *protectable property interest* in their daughter and in her white privilege. Joey's parents function as a metonymic stand-in for the mainstream white audience and for middle America's anxiety about interracial marriage (given the threat such unions pose to the biopower of white bourgeois privilege). The amount of screen time devoted to Joey and her family as they "come to terms" with the engagement makes it clear that *Guess Who's Coming to Dinner* is intended for mainstream white audiences.[18]

In contrast, *Get Out* is a tongue-in-cheek horror thriller that tells its coming-out-of-the-miscegenation-closet story from the perspective of the Black male character with resistant African American spectators in mind (figure 5.2). Capturing African American subjects and spectators is literally (and figuratively) a theme within the film from its very first images. When the film opens, spectators first see a young African American man named Andre Logan King (Lakeith Stanfield), walking through an un-marked, unnamed, but expensively landscaped, suburb en route to meet a friend. These initial images bring *Get Out* into intertextual relationship with horror franchises such

Get Out (Jordan, Peele, 2017)

Guess Who's Coming to Dinner (Stanley Kramer, 1967)

FIGURE 5.2 The interracial couples in Stanley Kramer's *Guess Who's Coming to Dinner* (1967) and Jordan Peele's *Get Out* (2017).

as *Halloween* (1978–2022), *Friday the 13th* (1980–2009), and *Nightmare on Elm Street* (1984–1990), in which serial killers stalk teenagers through manicured, middle-class suburbs and campgrounds.

Because the film privileges Andre's point of view, spectators are alarmed when it becomes apparent that he is being followed and is forcibly abducted. Whereas most films, including classic horror movies (i.e., everything from *Dracula* [1931] and *Frankenstein* [1931] to slasher film of the 1970s), usually feature a fragile, vulnerable, white female protagonist imperiled by "the monster," the alien, or the threat, *Get Out* privileges African American subjects—most notably Black men—(and by extension Black spectators) as vulnerable, subverting audiences' expectations of horror films. The following scene will subvert audience expectations that the plot will revolve solely around Chris and Rose's relationship. Spectators eventually realize that while eugenics remains central to the plot, interracial relationships function as *Get Out*'s MacGuffin.[19]

The central story does not revolve around Andre King's abduction either; rather, it begins with Chris Washington (Daniel Kaluuya), a talented, young, New York–based photographer who epitomizes the expression "young, gifted and Black." His girlfriend, Rose Armitage (Allison Williams), is taking Chris home "to meet the parents"—her dad, Dean (Bradley Whitford), a neurosurgeon, and her mother, Missy (Catherine Keener), a psychiatrist-hypnotherapist. Initially, Chris is apprehensive and sensitive about her parents' potential reactions to their interracial relationship. Eventually, he/we learn that Chris's apprehensions and micro-aggressions radar might *not* be in his head. In fact, the entire movie might be best summed up via a riff on the ironic Joseph Heller quip: "Just because you're paranoid, doesn't mean they're *not* out to get you."[20]

As Chris and Rose plan for their weekend trip, Rose repeatedly tries to reassure him that her parents are progressive: "My dad would have voted for Obama three times if he could have," she teasingly insists. By invoking Obama, Rose tries to put Chris at ease; however, her dialogue is painfully awkward, ringing hollow with neoliberal insincerity. Their road trip to her parents' home features a few spooky jump-scares, but none are as profoundly moving or haptically impressive as the music that plays in the background. The music evokes the spirits of African ancestors much like the soundtracks of landmark L.A. Rebellion school films *Diary of an African Nun* (Julie Dash, 1977) and *Sankofa* (Haile Gerima, 1993).

Upon the couple's arrival in the country, Rose's parents are very welcoming, yet things seem slightly askew and soon begin to slowly spiral downward. After initial introductions, Dean gives Chris a tour of the house, during which red flags start appearing via Dean's passive-aggressive, racially charged conversation. First, he laments his father's loss to Jesse Owens in a 1936 Olympic qualifying track meet. Dean explains that his father never recovered from this devastating loss, and then, sounding much like a colonial anthropologist, he tells Chris how much he enjoys collecting artifacts from other cultures. Next, Chris meets the family's housekeeping servants—Georgina (Betty Gabriel) and Walter (Marcus Henderson)—who "just happen" to be African American. Dean awkwardly tries to explain their Blackness as incidental rather than an intentional display of racial and class privilege. Ironically, Dean's explanation, like all of his microaggressive and faintly hostile introductory remarks, accentuates the existence of the Racial Contract,[21] that historic imbalance of access to opportunity between racial groups. While Dean's behavior is perceptible to the extra-diegetic viewing audience as a departure from conventional (read: bourgeois) norms of hospitality and friendliness, it is not clear whether these comments are racially motivated or merely the antics of an overprotective, underexposed, neoliberal father toward his daughter's suitor.

The film's tone shifts dramatically in the next scene. At dinner, Rose's brother, Jeremy (Caleb Landry Jones), makes several overtly racist remarks about Chris's physical prowess, muscularity, and potentially bestial strength when he challenges Chris to wrestle. By literally comparing Chris to a "beast," referencing his genetic makeup, and assuming Chris's penchant for aggression, Jeremy's comments animate pseudo-scientific, eugenics-based discourses and stereotypes about Black masculinity as physically brutal, inherently savage, animalistic, and sexually aggressive. Jeremy proceeds, suggesting that Black masculinity might be a commodity worth exploiting.

Later that night, Chris rouses from sleep and steps outside for a cigarette. When he returns inside, he encounters Rose's mother, Missy, drinking tea in her office. She invites him to sit down and talk. Suddenly, a seemingly innocent invitation turns into a coerced, therapeutic nightmare. Missy questions Chris about his mother's sudden, accidental death, his failure to help her, and his feelings of profound guilt. During their conversation, she furtively drugs and hypnotizes Chris into complete paralysis. Entrapped in the "sunken place," Chris experiences "locked-in syndrome," a pseudo-coma in which he's conscious but selectively "de-aff-e-rented" (having no means of producing speech, limb, or facial movements).[22] In acute "locked-in syndrome," eye-coded communication and cognitive emotional function are limited, because alertness fluctuates. Eye movements may be inconsistent and very small, and a person is easily exhausted. The film's use of this Cartesian mind/body split, or cognitive condition, is literal and figurative. Within the film's narrative, Chris is literally physically paralyzed but fully cognizant of his surroundings. For the extra-diegetic (particularly the African American) audience, being "locked-in" is a recurring motif and an apt metaphor for the sociopolitical experience and "Fact of Blackness" within white America (i.e., lacking socioeconomic mobility, feeling voter disenfranchisement, unable to control one's environs).

The next morning, Chris awakens hoping his nonconsensual hypnosis was a spine-chilling nightmare. Later in the film, the audience realizes this "locked-in syndrome" is the reason Georgina, the maid, Walter, the groundskeeper, and party-guest Andre (Dre) King have limited communication skills, severe speech impediments, watery eyes indicating conflicted emotions, and a "look" or countenance suggesting profound cognitive dissonance. The latter could be read by spectators as a metaphor for DuBois's concept of double-consciousness as described in *The Souls of Black Folk* (1903). Within the film's diegesis, it's clear that, like Chris, they were also hypnotized or fell asleep, and were "locked-in."

The importance of staying awake or staying WOKE (as a form of vigilance against violence) is foreshadowed by *Get Out*'s opening credits and soundtrack. Childish Gambino's soulful song "Redbone" plays over the scene, and its chorus repeatedly tells audiences/listeners to "stay woke," *not* to close their eyes, *not* to get caught sleeping, because niggas is creeping. It is no accident that the concept of staying woke became synonymous with political awareness in the first few years after *Get Out* was released.

Chris endures another bizarre day of socially inappropriate comments and explicitly tone-deaf (read: racist) remarks during a party sequence that begs comparison with a scene from Roman Polanski's 1968 horror classic *Rosemary's Baby*. In Polanski's celebrated film, a devil-worshiping cult of aging witches uses Rosemary's body as the abject liminal object to procreate with the devil. Similarly, and unbeknown to Chris, the Armitages' party guests are examining and assessing him in a process that harkens back to slave auctions. Director Jordan Peele, who is well aware of cinema history, uses the mise-en-scène in a manner similar to Polanski. The witches who "covet" Rosemary gaze upon her much like the Order of the Coagula holds Chris in their sights. Even some of the characters' names are similar (i.e., Roman Castevet of *Rosemary's Baby* has a doppelganger in Roman Armitage [Richard Herd] of *Get Out*). Peele is clearly inviting these comparisons with his intertextual references.

Additionally, the allusion to forms of slavery (i.e., sexual for Rosemary and chattel for Chris) is unmistakable. The viewing audience later learns that Dean will auction (read: commodify) Chris, much the same way Guy sacrificed (read: sold or pimped) Rosemary to a coven of witchy believers. Hence, in both films, an aging, affluent clientele initially conceals their capitalist consumption of younger bodies while they inspect, exploit, and commodify the abject object of their choice. As an aside, it is worth noting that both *Rosemary's Baby* and *Get Out* are based on Ira Levin's novels that evoke *The Stepford Wives*, which chronicles a young mother who believes the submissive housewives in her new, idyllic neighborhood are being controlled by their husbands.

To size Chris up, the guests ask him subtly and overtly racist questions. For instance, Gordon and Emily Greene (John Wilmot and Carin Larkey) insist he demonstrate his golf technique, even though he does not play the sport, while Lisa Deets (Ashley LeConte Campbell) and wheelchair-bound husband Nelson (Lory Tom Thompson Sr.) delve into myths about Black male sexuality as she seductively gazes at Chris, asking: "Is it true . . . it's better?" (figure 5.3). Parker (Rutherford Cravens) and April Dray (Julie Ann Jones) make off-color comments about Chris's complexion, and finally, Mr. Hiroki Tanaka (Yasuhiko Oyama) boldly asks Chris if being African American is an advantage or disadvantage (figure 5.4). This loaded question implies that it is indeed easier to be African American than white or Asian.

The inclusion of Mr. Tanaka is another brilliant, if not-so-subtle, maneuver by Jordan Peele, in which he signifies on post–civil rights American race relations. Tanaka's question alludes to specific, albeit hotly contested, judicial policies and reparations for historically disadvantaged minority groups (i.e., affirmative action). Tanaka exposes the tensions between African Americans and Asian Americans. Asian Americans are the so-called model minorities, that have thrived socioeconomically in the United States despite institutional and systemic racism (figure 5.5). Peele knew he need not explicitly rehash the socioeconomic tensions between African Americans and Asian American immigrant groups (i.e., Koreans or Southeast Asians and Afro-Caribbeans), because

The Party

Mr. and Mrs. Greene – on Tiger Woods

Parker & April Dray – "Black is in fashion!"

Nelson & Lisa – wondering if sex is better?

Lisa sizes up Chris

FIGURE 5.3 The Armitage's white party guests show a perverse fascination with Chris (Daniel Kaluuya), while making racist remarks and sizing him up.

FIGURE 5.4 Dean (Bradley Whitford), Mr. Tanaka (Yasuhiko Oyama), and other party guests excitedly greet Chris (Daniel Kaluuya) as he exits the Armitages' home.

Spike Lee's *Do the Right Thing* inscribed that conversation on the modern American cinematic landscape.

After meeting these guests, Chris eventually encounters Andrew/Andre—the only other African American party guest. Not only does Andrew fail to recognize Chris as a "brotha," or their shared identity and experience as Black men in this bizarre white

FIGURE 5.5 The cover for the August 31, 1987, issue of *Time* magazine, which features a story that details Asian American kids' success in the U.S. educational system.

milieu (as symbolized by the missed fist-bump), he also seems to lack any sense of Black pride, racial solidarity, or cultural identity. Even more curious is Andrew's choice of partner: an overweight, matronly white woman, twice his age. When Chris grabs his camera and snaps a picture, it triggers Andrew's inert, or dormant, eyes, and for an instant, he becomes woke. The flash momentarily retrieves Andre from the sunken place, at which point he turns to Chris and screams to him to "get out!"

Andrew's sudden arousal, and switch back to Andre, as well as his warning to Chris recalls another influential classic horror film. In William Friedkin's enormously successful movie *The Exorcist* (1973), a disturbed teenage girl gains momentary reprieves from the demon inhabiting her body. Her mother, an actress, also named Chris, is repeatedly told to "get out" of her room when the girl screams in agony. By flipping the script and positioning the Black male character, rather than white female character, as vulnerable, liminal, and desirable, Jordan Peele's *Get Out* completely upends decades of conventions within the horror genre. It is not the white female body that must be protected and rescued, but the Black male body that is endangered.

In some ways, *Get Out* is what we might call a *programmatic cult film*, which appeals to spectators in terms of altering (even violating) shared generic values. These films extend beyond mainstream ideology to present disruptive, rather than conservative, concepts. As cinema scholar Bruce Kawin observes: "When cult films have a political subject, they may use style to transfigure the subject or genre to rethink it. Cult films also offer extreme spectacles of rebellion. They offer unifying visions for an alienated"[23] audience. Jordan Peele goes outside of mainstream ideology to present a disruptive vision of American cinema (i.e., a retelling of *Guess Who's Coming to Dinner*) and to offer an extreme spectacle of rebellion against diegetic traditions (narrative fiction) and nondiegetic traditions (American race relations).

Known for his self-conscious sketch comedy, director Jordan Peele is also aware of horror movie conventions and that African American audiences have historically been underrepresented, stereotyped, and alienated. The "inside joke" within the African American community is that in horror movies Black characters either are excluded completely or die first—usually while saving their white counterparts. This trope has been a cinematic convention since the World War II combat films of the 1940s, as demonstrated by Jeanine Basinger in *The World War II Combat Film: Anatomy of Genre* (1985). Robin R. Means Coleman also addresses this trope in her books and documentary, *Horror Noire: Blacks in American Horror Films from the 1890s to Present* and *The Black Guy Dies First: Black Horror Cinema*. The pattern is so entrenched and familiar to American audiences that it has been lampooned and referenced in multiple films, including the 1997 horror sendup *Scream 2* (Wes Craven, 1997) (figure 5.6).

As a programmatic cult film, *Get Out* carries its rebellion through to the end. After the cocktail party, Chris and Rose retreat. Unbeknown to Chris, Dean holds a silent auction back at the Armitage house. The camera slowly pulls back, revealing that Chris is the item on auction. His buyer is Jim Hudson (Stephen Root), a blind, middle-aged art dealer who covets Chris's brilliant "vision" as a photographer.

Vision has multiple meanings in this context. Once again, Peele revisits eyesight, artistic vision, and the gaze as motifs layered with significance. The themes of eyes, vision, "staying woke," and vigilance are like the return of the repressed that cannot be suppressed. Therefore, just as *Scream* films constituted a self-reflexive horror franchise referencing other horror films, *Get Out* is also a self-reflexive horror film using the recurring motifs of eyes, sight, images, photography, film, and the subconscious to subvert generic conventions and notions of abjection.

The bizarre, off-color, racially loaded questions Chris faces at the party resonate with the experiences of African American spectators watching the film who can relate to the surreal tenor of the party. Peele is creating a surreal "spectacle of rebellion" (for an

When the hell you get
your Ph.D. in Black Cinema,
Sister Souljah ?

FIGURE 5.6 Phil (Omar Epps) and Maureen (Jada Pinkett-Smith) discuss Black film characters'
fates in horror cinema shortly before they meet similar ends in the opening of Wes Craven's
Scream 2 (1997).

already resisting and skeptical audience) by making visible the invisible humiliations,
slights, indignities, embarrassments, and inappropriate questions Black people encounter regularly in their interactions with the socially and racially tone-deaf.

The party scene resonates with Frantz Fanon's treatise on the phenomenon of
Blackness in his book *Black Skin, White Masks*. A psychiatrist and an intellectual, Fanon
was interested in the impact of racism on the psyche. His book is written in the style
of auto-theory, in which Fanon shares his own experiences in addition to presenting
a historical critique of the effects of racism and dehumanization inherent in colonial
situations. Moreover, he articulated the way Black people become hyper-aware of
how they are "seen" by non-Blacks. For Fanon, "Consciousness of the body is solely a
negating activity. It is a consciousness in which the body is surrounded by a [surreal]
atmosphere of certain uncertainty." In his encounters with white French people, Fanon
could not dismiss racist comments, because he knew that his Blackness signified various stereotypes of African cannibalism, intellectual deficiency, sexual fetishism, racial defects, slave ships, and even media caricatures—all simultaneously.[24] Peele evokes
the stereotypes of Black identity, what Fanon terms "the fact of Blackness," by having
Chris navigate the certain-uncertainty that surrounds him at the Armitage's surreal
household.

Much later that evening, the protagonist and the audience discover that Chris has
entered the "terrible house," the house of unspeakable, barbaric evil. The terrible house
is a familiar convention recognizable to horror movie fans. Whether it is the decaying
mansion in *Mandingo* (Richard Fleischer, 1975), the chop shop in *The Texas Chainsaw
Massacre* (Tobe Hooper, 1974), the teenager's bedroom in *The Exorcist* (William

Friedkin, 1973) or the homes in *Last House on the Left* (Wes Craven, 1972), *Amityville Horror* (Stuart Rosenberg, 1979), or *Poltergeist* (Tobe Hooper, Spielberg, 1982), the "terrible house" is the place where the protagonist confronts, or comes into "mano-a-mano" combat with, the monster and face-to-face with abjection.

In *Get Out*, Peele uniquely recasts the monster and the house of horrors. Monstrosity here is not in the form of cannibals or hillbillies, angry ghosts, or egg-laying extraterrestrials. It is not in devil worship or a witches' coven. Neither is the monster a threatening Black rapist or a creature from the Black Lagoon, or a racially coded other. Instead, the attractive, well-educated, upper-class, all-American white family inhabits the surreal and abject house of horrors. Indeed, in the era of carceral capitalism (including human and organ trafficking), these entitled people who engage in human trafficking are the monsters we should fear.

Like the inhabitants of the "terrible house" in *Texas Chainsaw Massacre*, Missy and Dean run a chop shop in which they only carve up dark meat. Instead of organ transplantation, neurosurgeon Dean has perfected the "Coagula Procedure"—the final phase of which is brain transplantation that fuses the Black host's brain and nervous system (to allow for limited consciousness) with the white occupant's motor control functionality. Thus, the Black body is rendered an abject liminal vessel in which a white person's consciousness can lodge and remain vibrantly alive. Younger, stronger, healthier bodies are made available to white people who have aged, are ill or infirm, or who are simply ready for a newer, superior corporeal model. Wedding sardonic humor and racial horror, Peele's extreme spectacle of rebellion also poses real-world questions about the intersections of biomedical ethics (i.e., neurosurgery, psychiatry, cognitive science) and black-market organ trafficking.

Jim Hudson's desire to steal Chris Washington's eyes and brain signifies more than organ trafficking. On one level, Jim envies Chris's vision because Jim is going blind. He seeks to gain the renewed sight of youthful eyes. But Jim also confesses to being an admirer of Chris's artistic vision and emerging talent in the highly competitive commercial art world. Therefore, at another level, in buying/appropriating Chris's eyes and brain stem, Jim seeks to steal Chris's artistic gift. He stands to gain physical, monetary, and cultural capital by transplanting Chris's eyes, brain, and identity. This reel diegetic thread evokes the real nondiegetic actions of several ill-fated mature artists who have tried to remake themselves and preserve cultural relevance by adopting, appropriating, and stealing the aesthetics of younger Black artists in rap music, art, tap dance, and cinema.[25]

DuBoisian, Fanonian, Kristevian, and Foucauldian methodologies (not to mention Mills's, Goldberg's, and Dyer's) have already provided the answer to Chris's haunting question: "But why use Black people?" The Armitages use Black bodies because ethnic notions[26] of, and beliefs about, Black primitivism and inferiority undergird the racial contract in which abject or subpersons are thought to have inferior rights but superior physical capabilities.

When Chris is finally ready to leave, he makes a startling discovery. But his escape is thwarted; first by Rose, then by Jeremy, and finally secured by Missy, who pulls the psychotropic trigger that locks Chris into paralysis once again. He awakens in the basement in a scene that plays like a cross between David Croneneberg's *Videodrome* and Tobe Hooper's *Chainsaw Massacre*.

At this point in the dénouement, *Get Out* speaks loudest. In the final moments, horror fans want to know: Will the protagonist survive? A character's survival at the end of a horror film (particularly a Black character's survival) is never inconsequential, because horror is so self-referential. These movies establish expectations, patterns, and parameters that fans understand and rely on. Carol Clover made this point emphatically clear in her seminal book *Men, Women & Chainsaws* when she talks about "The Final Girl." We hope Chris survives, but his survival is not guaranteed—even in light of the "spectacle of rebellion" that a programmatic cult film like *Get Out* offers. For instance, take *Night of the Living Dead* (George Romero, 1968) as an example of a cult film in which the lone Black male character survives the undead zombies, only to be shot down by the white police officers, thereby subverting the subversion presented by the conclusion.

CONCLUSION

Jordan Peele constructs a film that philosophizes about what it means to be a human being endowed with inalienable rights. He invites contemplation of our very constitution and its supposition that all men are created equal. His film recalls how Black filmmakers often deconstruct white racial privilege and its deforming impact on Black lives, making us think critically about whether Black lives do matter. Or, to use Jackie Wang's term, the way abject Black lives are literally consumed to become *matter* for the lives of others in an era of carceral capitalism.

Get Out was a critical and commercial success, partially because its themes touched a nerve in the Black Lives Matter movement and U.S. zeitgeist. In addition to anti-Black police brutality and racial profiling occurring today, *Get Out* alludes to past and present tragedies, like the infamous Tuskegee syphilis experiment (1932–1972), the Atlanta child murders (1979–1981),[27] the Jeffrey Dahmer serial killings (1978–1991), and the profitmaking privatization of prisons in an age of mass incarceration. The film evokes bioethics and current questions for philosophers of medicine regarding informed consent on clinical trials, the definition of death, and the ethics of behavior control.

More prosaically, however, *Get Out* calls upon horror movie audiences to rethink three genres: (1) the social-problem picture as romantic comedy, such as *Guess Who's Coming to Dinner*; (2) the self-reflexive horror film (like *Night of the Living Dead, Halloween, Nightmare on Elm Street,* or *Scream* franchises); and (3) the transgressive cult movie (i.e., *The Rocky Horror Picture Show, Myra Breckinridge,* or *Casablanca*).[28]

Get Out is a movie for moviegoers, cinema for cineastes, a film for those who are conversant with, appreciative of, and in on the generic conventions, intertextual jokes, double entendres, and baroque flourishes movies can provide their loyal patrons. Whereas many horror movies engage some aspect of the fantastic, the supernatural, or otherworldly, *Get Out* is thoroughly entrenched in realism and modes of realist film-making, right down to self-reflexive details like assigning its protagonist the occupation of photographer.

NOTES

1. Julia Kristeva, *Powers of Horror: An Essay on Abjection*. Translated by Leon S. Roudiez (New York: Columbia University Press, 1982). Originally published in French as *Pouvoirs de l'horreur. Essai sur l'abjection* in 1980.

2. While abjection theory has been used in various ways across the social sciences and humanities, it emerges from the psychoanalytic work of Julia Kristeva. Drawing on Mary Douglas's *Purity and Danger* (1966), Kristeva's foundational book *The Powers of Horror* (1982) develops the theory of abjection through literary, psychoanalytic, and anthropological works. See Mohammad Rafi Arefin's introduction at: https://discardstudies.com/2015/02/27/abjection-a-definition-for-discard-studies/.

3. See Larry Adelman's documentary *Race: The Power of an Illusion*, produced by California Newsreel. As evolutionary biologists have shown: "Not a single characteristic, trait, or gene distinguishes all the members of one so-called race from all the members of another so-called race, no matter how we divide people. Nevertheless, the idea that race corresponds to biological differences (e.g., traits such as IQ, behavior, propensity for disease, physical appearance) has long shaped public policy and social discourse—and can even lead to biological consequences."

4. Black Codes were laws passed by Democrat-controlled Southern states in 1865 and 1866, after the Civil War. These laws had the intent and the effect of restricting African Americans' freedom and of compelling them to work in a labor economy based on low wages or debt. In the first two years after the Civil War, white-dominated Southern legislatures passed Black Codes modeled after the earlier slave codes. They were particularly concerned with controlling movement and labor, as slavery had given way to a free labor system.

5. This is excluding the African experience in ancient America as documented by Ivan Van Sertima in *They Came Before Columbus* (New York: Random House, 1977). Sertima addresses pre-Columbian contact between Africans and the Americas.

6. Article One, Section Two of the Constitution of the United States declared that any person who was not free would be counted as three-fifths of a free individual for the purposes of determining congressional representation. The "Three-Fifths Clause" thus increased the political power of slaveholding states.

7. In December 1952, the Justice Department filed a friend of the court brief in the case. The brief was unusual in its heavy emphasis on foreign-policy considerations of the Truman administration in a case ostensibly about domestic issues. Of the seven pages covering "the interest of the United States," five focused on the way school segregation hurt the United States in the Cold War competition for the friendship and allegiance of non-white peoples in countries then gaining independence from colonial rule.

8. David Theo Goldberg, *The Racial State* (Hoboken, NJ and Oxford: Wiley, 2002), 112.

9. Madison Grant, a lawyer known more as a conservationist and eugenicist, created the "racialist movement" in America advocating the extermination of "undesirables" and certain "race types" from the human gene pool. He played a critical role in restrictive U.S. immigration policy and anti-miscegenation laws. His work provided the justification for

Nazi policies of forced sterilization and euthanasia. He wrote two of the seminal works of American racialism: *The Passing of the Great Race* (1916) and *The Conquest of a Continent* (1933). *The Passing of the Great Race* gained immediate popular success and established Grant as an authority in anthropology and laid the groundwork for his research in eugenics.

10. The case was brought by Mildred Loving, a Black woman, and Richard Loving, a white man, who had been sentenced to a year in prison in Virginia for marrying each other. Their marriage violated the state's anti-miscegenation statute, the Racial Integrity Act of 1924, which prohibited marriage between people classified as "white" and people classified as "colored." The Supreme Court's unanimous decision determined that this prohibition was unconstitutional, overruling *Pace v. Alabama* (1883) and ending all race-based legal restrictions on marriage in the United States.

11. Richard Dyer, *White* (London and New York: Routledge, 1997).

12. Goldberg, *The Racial State*, 102.

13. Ann Laura Stoler, *Race and the Education of Desire: Foucault's History of Sexuality and the Colonial Order of Things* (Durham, NC: Duke University Press, 1995).

14. Cheryl Harris, "Whiteness as Property," *Harvard Law Review* 106, no. 8 (June 1993): 1707–1791.

15. The Western-European and American notion that Black people were property was metaphysical. It was rooted in cosmology, epistemology, and ontology.

16. Harris, "Whiteness as Property," 1716–1719.

17. Ibid.

18. Writing about the film, Donald Bogle quipped: "By concentrating on nice decent people entangled in personal heartaches, director Kramer diverted the audience from real issues. There stood Poitier, charming, good-looking, mannerly, and brilliant. Who could refuse him for a son-in-law? That was part of Kramer's point of course. But it was far too simplistic." Donald Bogle, *Toms, Coons, Mulattoes, Mammies, and Bucks: An Interpretive History of Black in American Films* (New York and London: Bloomsbury, 2016), 195.

19. In a fiction film, a MacGuffin is a plot device in the form of an object, event, goal, or character that serves to set and keep the plot in motion despite usually lacking intrinsic importance. The most common type of MacGuffin is a person, place, or thing (such as money or an object of value). Other more abstract types include victory, glory, survival, power, love, or some unexplained driving force. The MacGuffin's importance to the plot is not the object itself, but rather its effect on the characters and their motivations. It is a convention used and popularized by Alfred Hitchcock.

20. Joseph Heller, *Catch-22* (New York: Simon & Schuster, 1961). American author Joseph Heller began writing the satirical war novel *Catch-22* in 1953 and it was first published in 1961. Often cited as one of the most significant novels of the twentieth century, it uses a distinctive nonchronological third-person omniscient narration, describing events from the points of view of different characters. The separate storylines are out of sequence, so the timeline develops along with the plot.

21. Charles Mills, *The Racial Contract* (Ithaca, NY, and London: Cornell University Press, 1997), 11.

22. De-afferentation is the loss of sensory input from portions of the body caused by interruption of nerve fibers. People with brain stem lesions often remain comatose for days or weeks, but often remain paralyzed and voiceless, superficially resembling patients in a vegetative state or akinetic mutism.

23. Bruce Kawin, "After Midnight," *The Cult Film Experience: Beyond All Reason* (Austin: University of Texas Press, 1991), 19.

24. Frantz Fanon, *Black Skin, White Masks* (Paris: Editions de Seuil), 112.

25. Examples include Tom Jones in covering Prince's *Kiss*; Madonna and her work with many artists including Missy Elliot, Pharrell Williams, and Timbaland. And then there's Justin Timberlake's covers.

26. See Marlon Riggs's 1987 documentary *Ethnic Notions*.

27. The abduction of the Black bodies (mostly male) in *Get Out* recalls the the Atlanta murders of 1979–1981, sometimes called the "Atlanta child murders" (although several of the victims were adults). This was a series of murders committed in Atlanta, Georgia, from the middle of 1979 until May 1981. Over the two-year period, at least 28 African American children, adolescents, and adults were killed. Police subsequently attributed several of the child murders to Wayne Williams and closed the cases, although he has not been tried or convicted in any of those cases. Between August and November 1980, five more killings took place. All the victims were African American children between the ages of 7 and 14, and most were asphyxiated.

28. A cult film transgresses the boundaries we usually associate with the idea of genre. It is a film marked by both its highly specified and limited audience, as well as the pleasure this audience finds in the film's transgressions. The cult work speaks meaningfully to a specific group of people. Many works gain a cult aura because of anti-canonical and extra-industrial forces. Just as rising gay consciousness and feminism helped the resurrection of films like *The Women* or *Rocky Horror*, resisting Black spectators appreciate a violation of certain classical narrative formulations (like in the World War II combat film, horror film, Black characters die saving White characters). For Bruce Kawin, there's the inadvertent cult film and the programmatic cult film. The programmatic cult film such as *The Texas Chainsaw Massacre 2* sets out to be a cult film and makes its appeal in terms of violating shared values. In the case of *Get Out*, that shared value is to see the Black character survive to the end of the film and survive whiteness.

SECTION II

WHICH WAY THE BLACK PEOPLE?

....

CHAPTER 6

HORRIFIC INDIGENEITY

....

JAMES WIERZBICKI

PETER Weir's 1977 *The Last Wave* is not a "horror film" in the conventional sense; it features no monsters or mayhem, no ghosts or ghouls, and the acts of violence that frame the story are depicted only vaguely. Yet for many viewers, *The Last Wave* was and remains terrifying, not so much because of the apocalyptic visions that fill the dreams of the protagonist but because of its confrontation—unresolved within the narrative, and likely unresolvable in the real world—between modern attitudes and certain traditional ways of life. For persons of European persuasion, surely the most unnerving thing about *The Last Wave* is its portrayal of Indigenous Australians. In the context of the film, what is most troubling about these characters is not anything they say or do but, rather, how they look; their dark complexion is obvious, and that trait is symbolic of the idea that, in terms of their potential powers, they are utterly unknowable.

The actual word "black" is spoken only a few times in the course of *The Last Wave*. It comes up casually in the final reels, as a radio newscaster makes a joke about the petroleum-filled "black rain" that lately has plagued Sydney and as the central character—a very white tax attorney (played by Richard Chamberlain) who to his surprise finds himself serving as defending barrister in the case of several young Aborigines accused of murder—comments either to a listener or to himself about what he has been, or still is, seeing. (Weir's film was in fact titled *Black Rain* when it was first released in the United States.) More tellingly, both because it pertains to skin color and because it marks the point midway through the 101-minute film where a combination of camera techniques and music make it perfectly clear—in case anyone thus far had wondered that this *is* a horror film—the word figures into a conversation between the lawyer's wife and young daughter as both get ready for costume parties.

Dressed as a fairy princess, the daughter stands at an upstairs window and says, "I don't like that man, Mommy." "What man?" the mother asks. Using the adjective merely as a descriptor, without a hint of racial implication, the daughter says: "That Black man." Distracted with her own preparations, the mother asks: "What Black man?" With a giggle in her voice, and with prescience of which she is surely unaware, the daughter turns from the window and says, "I think he's a witch!" Now very much paying attention, the mother rushes to the window, and the precise moment of her fear is marked by the accompanying score's abrupt change from a high-pitched drone to a full-bodied "shock" chord; the mother's fear grows, and the dire music thickens, as an instant later a point-of-view shot reveals that standing outside the house and staring straight up at her—*glaring* at her—is Charlie, the thickly bearded elderly Aboriginal man who earlier in the story had surprised both her and her husband by showing up as an unannounced dinner guest. She is clearly terrified, and likely so are members of the audience, when her frantic attempt to telephone her husband is interrupted by increasingly urgent rappings on the glass panel of the front door; holding to one of the horror genre's well-worn tropes, the severe tension is relieved when it turns out that at the door is only the babysitter, yet an ominous mood persists through the next two scenes, which show the parents at a posh cocktail party where the dull conversation focuses only on the strange weather and then back at home, where, after tucking in the two children, the still distraught woman at last starts to tell her husband about what is bothering her. In barely held-back tears, she says: "He was here. The old man. He was out there, on the street, watching." And then, after breaking down completely, she asks: "Why, in the name of God, are you *helping* them? Why are they so *important*?"

Answering that simple question—why?—requires unfolding the whole of *The Last Wave*'s complex and not entirely logical plot. To make a long story short: Charlie is not merely an elder but a shaman of a supposedly nonexistent Sydney-based Aboriginal tribe whose sacred sites are located in caves deep beneath the city's Central Business District. The man whose death is shown at the start of the film is a would-be initiate who violated tribal law by removing an artifact from one of the sites, and his death is caused not by any violence committed against him by the five men accused of murder but simply by Charlie pointing a "death bone" at him and muttering a curse.[1] The tax lawyer who is assigned to the defendants' case eventually figures this out, but only after experiencing a series of visions that include not just persons and objects connected with the tribe but also scenes of cataclysmic flooding. After consulting with an anthropologist, the South American–born lawyer is convinced (and this is where the story starts to get really preposterous!) that he in fact is a *mulkrul*, a member of what the anthropologist describes as "a race of spirits who came from the rising sun" and who had "incredible premonitory dreams." After the lawyer loses the court case, one of the convicted defendants shows up at his house and offers to take him down to the sacred sites. In the caves, the lawyer finds not just a mask whose features are remarkably similar to his own but also "a calendar" that seems to predict the coming of a catastrophic wave. He also finds Charlie, very angry and wielding an axe. After a brief struggle that is shown only in torchlit shadows, the lawyer, with blood on his hands, starts to make his way out of the cave. After first thinking that he is doomed to be trapped forever in the underground tunnels, eventually he finds a drainage pipe that leads him to a beach some distance south of the city. Kneeling in the gentle surf, he looks up and sees, or imagines that he sees, a tremendous tsunami.

There is much in Weir's film that, when subjected even to the gentlest analysis, makes little sense. But the telling of this far-fetched and purely fanciful story is nonetheless effective. Notwithstanding its clichés, the above-described sequence during which the lawyer's wife discovers "the old man" lurking about the house is, in terms of timing and nuance, and in terms of affective impact, very well done. Likewise the brief moment near the end of the film when the voice of the enraged Charlie is made to sound like a barking didgeridoo.[2] So long as one willingly goes with its flow, *The Last Wave* holds the audience members' attention and provides them with a rich supply of disturbing memories. And its most enduringly haunting images—at least for this viewer, and I suspect for many others as well—have to do with the Aborigines' characteristic Blackness.

* * *

To interrogate Blackness within the context of Weir's *The Last Wave* for the most part involves, as noted above, consideration of the Aborigines' skin color as symbolic of their impenetrable and thus perhaps fearsome mystique. But it also involves, for the sake of putting things into perspective, recounting Australia's troubled history of race relations.

Working uncomfortably toward a conclusion of an otherwise breezy book on Australia, the American travel writer Bill Bryson observes that:

> you don't have to be a genius to work out that Aborigines are Australia's greatest social failing. For virtually every indicator of prosperity and well-being—hospitalisation rates, suicide rates, childhood mortality, imprisonment, employment, you name it—the figures for Aborigines range from twice as bad to up to twenty times worse than the general population. . . . Overall, the life expectancy of the average indigenous Australian is twenty years—*twenty years*—less than that of the average white Australian.[3]

Earlier in his antepenultimate chapter, Bryson recounts an experience in Alice Springs, a small city in the heart of Australia's Northern Territory, famous for its role in a novel by Nevil Shute and for being near the United States National Security Agency's ultrasecret surveillance facility at Pine Gap:[4]

> I bought a newspaper and took it to an open-air café on Todd Street, a pedestrian mall. I read for a minute or two, but then found myself watching the passing scene. It was quite busy with Saturday shoppers. The people on the street were overwhelmingly white Australians, but there were Aborigines about, too—not great numbers of them, but always there, on the edge of the frame, unobtrusive, nearly always silent, peripheral. The white people never looked at the Aborigines, and the Aborigines never looked at the white people. The two races seemed to inhabit separate but parallel universes. I felt as if I was the only person who could see both groups at once. It was very strange.[5]

Strange, for sure, is the relationship not just between Aborigines and white Australians but also between Aborigines and "persons of color" who, since the 1950s, have immigrated to Australia from all over the world.[6] One hesitates to comment on the situation, for almost anything one says about it nowadays opens the speaker to charges of racism. Still, it is impossible to ignore the apparent fact that Aborigines have not mixed well with the rest of Australian society. Possibly for reasons of "political correctness," persons of Indigenous heritage are today very much welcomed into television journalism, university administration, and other professions whose members are highly visible. But always, it seems, these persons whose "indigeneity" is advertised at least by their employers do not *look* Indigenous. In some cases, their skin color is a bit darker than that of their colleagues, but their facial features typically bear little resemblance to those of the Aboriginal characters in *The Last Wave*. Some of them may indeed be "token" figures, and some of them may indeed have used a long-lost but recently discovered Indigenous ancestry as a career booster. But none of them is what might be termed, probably without fear of attack even by the fiercest "social justice" warriors, a *full-blooded* Aborigine.

British historian Kenneth Morgan suggests that full-blooded Aborigines have chosen not to assimilate largely for reasons of pride. "Many Aboriginal people resist the notion of multiculturalism because they resent being considered just one ethnic group among many in Australian society," Morgan writes in his contribution to Oxford University Press's "Short Introduction" series.[7] But this is arguably a romantic notion, and one not-too-distantly related to the attitude of benevolent patronization whose manifestations range from the once common forced removal of Aboriginal children from their families[8] to the still-current practice of grant-supported scholars, mostly in the fields of linguistics and ethnomusicology, spending time in remote Aboriginal communities and in effect "nursing" whatever might be left of those communities' traditional stories and songs.

A more blunt notion would have it that full-blooded Aborigines remain unassimilated not by their own choice but for reasons of centuries-old race-based discrimination. This is a simple enough explanation, but it fails to take into account certain anthropological details that are often ignored by international campaigners for civil rights. To be sure, although modern Australia has a relatively small population (just 25.7 million according to the 2020 census), it boasts as much racial prejudice as many a larger Western nation. But it did not start out that way. Subjugating natives was not on the agenda of the British who sailed into what eventually would be known as Sydney Harbour on January 26, 1788 (a date celebrated as "Australia Day," but one which some Australians, including many of strictly European descent, prefer to call "Invasion Day"). First and foremost on the minds of Captain James Cook and the other naval officers who led the First Fleet was the setting up of a secure repository for convicts, but it also included the making possible of a safe haven for future "free settlers" and, mostly with the forced labor of the convicts, exploiting whatever natural resources the newfound land had to offer. As had been the case throughout as much of the British Empire that by that time had been established—as had been the case with successful colonizers since time immemorial—the newcomers had enormous technological advantages over the natives. If the natives cooperated with the colonists' plans, all was well; if the natives resisted, well, that was too bad for the natives. The British received both cooperation and resistance from the Australian natives, and, as was to have been expected, the resistance was countered not just with violence but with residual ill will. Also as expected, the persons who made their homes in Australia, regardless of their economic status, eventually started to act as though they owned the place, and thus each fresh crop of immigrants has been met with suspicion if not downright hostility. In terms of antisocial behavior toward persons who are both in the minority and in some obvious way "other," contemporary race relations in Australia compared to elsewhere in the world are not much different.

But there *was* something different about the situation in Australia, noticed straightaway by the early governors and still noticed, although not much commented on, today. Robert Hughes, best known for his long tenure as art critic for *Time* magazine, was also a historian of considerable heft, and he pulled no punches in his monumental study of his homeland's early years. Hughes explains:

> The legal status of Aborigines—and of their "claims," as white officials interestingly put it, to the territory they had occupied for some eighteen millennia before the arrival of the whites—seemed almost insoluble to the whites. Everywhere else in the historical experience of the British Empire, colonies had been planted where the "natives" and "Indians" understood and defended the idea of property. In Virginia as in Africa, in New Zealand as in the East Indies, British colonists encountered cultures of farming people who had houses, villages and plots of cultivated land. These proofs of prior ownership might be violated by the whites (and often were); but they could not be denied or ignored. Even Charles II's instructions to the Council of Foreign Plantations on the conduct of the English colony in Virginia had recognised that as the new settlement would "border upon" the lands of the Indians, their territory had to be respected, for "peace is not to be expected without . . . justice to them."[9]

The various Australian tribes encountered by the British certainly had territories that they defended against other tribes and, with less success, the colonists. But they did not so much "own" these territories as simply occupy them. In fact, they "owned" virtually nothing at all. They were "hunter-gatherers who roamed over the land without marking out boundaries or making fixed settlements. They had no idea of farming or stock-raising. They saved nothing, lived entirely in the present and were, in the whites' eyes, so ignorant of property as to be [regarded as] little more than intelligent animals."[10] Although some of the early Australian governors hoped that Aborigines might be recruited to work on plantations, this soon proved to be mere wishful thinking. As Hughes puts it: "The convicts might [have been] scum, but they had an economic value. The blacks clearly had none; therefore, they were less than scum."[11] So dismissive did the British grow of the natives that, especially "on the expanding limits of settlement, the Aborigine was seen as a mere native pest, like a dingo or a kangaroo. . . . He could be killed without hesitation."[12] As late as 1841, Hughes writes, "one observer heard 'a large proprietor of sheep and cattle' maintain 'that there was no more harm in shooting a native, than in shooting a dog.'"[13]

That the typical nomadic Aboriginal tribe did not "own" the lands it occupied, and was not led by a king or a chieftain, made it easy enough for New South Wales governor Richard Bourke to declare, in 1835—sixty-five years after Captain Cook first sailed into

Botany Bay for a quick look, and almost a half-century after the landing of the convict-laden First Fleet—that the vast entirety of Australia was *terra nullius* and thus legally ripe for occupation.[14] By 1835, of course, Australia had already long been occupied. Opinions differ as to the length of that occupation; it may well be that "archaeological evidence indicates that Aborigines have lived in Australia for at least 60,000–70,000 years, and possibly for over 100,000 years,"[15] but credible commentary, based on the study of changes in sea level, has it that their residence dates only from the so-called Pleistocene period and that they arrived only between 45,000 and 30,000 years ago, more or less the same time that Asians began to move into North America across what was once a land bridge between Siberia and Alaska.[16]

However one splits the hairs, it remains that Aborigines had resided in Australia for quite a while before the British first set foot on the continent's soil, and thus there is some justification for claims by Indigenous rights activists that Australia hosts the world's "oldest surviving (or living) culture."[17] That culture—especially in terms of attitudes toward personal property and what pioneering sociologist Max Weber called the "work ethic"[18]—seems to have changed hardly at all over the millennia. As a result, rightly or wrongly, Aboriginal culture has come to be thought of not just by "white city-dwellers" but also by "persons of color" more or less recently arrived in Australia from Africa, India, and elsewhere as "a static culture, frozen by its immemorial primitivism, unchanged in an unchanging landscape."[19] As a result, too, representatives of this culture—that is to say, unassimilated Aborigines of the sort that Bryson describes, of the sort who appear throughout a much celebrated travelogue by Bruce Chatwin,[20] and of the sort who figure fictitiously in *The Last Wave*—are often characterized as belonging to "a backward, static race."[21] Especially in the outback communities, where they tend to be more visible,[22] Aborigines on the lower end of the socioeconomic scale tend to be regarded by their fellow Australians as well as by visitors from abroad not so much with sympathy as with suspicion. The stereotype may be without foundation, but it nonetheless exists. For many, full-blooded Aborigines *seem* to belong not to the modern era but to the Stone Age,[23] and perhaps that is what makes them suitable as "mysterious figures" in horror films.

* * *

So suitable for horror films is the full-blooded Aborigine that at first it is a wonder that he in fact is not much included in the genre. In the wake of *The Last Wave* there were indeed a number of Australian horror films whose plots had to do with Aboriginal legends, and in recent years there has been a veritable spate of horror films that feature Aboriginal characters.[24] But, for obvious political reasons, none of these has gone so far as to cast Aborigines as boogeymen.

Aborigines make up a very small percentage of the Australian population,[25] but they loom increasingly large in the public conversation. In recent years, newscasters on public as well as commercial stations have taken to introducing themselves first with their names and then a statement to the effect that they are "coming to you" not just from Melbourne or Sydney but from the lands of the Wurundjeri or the Cadigal people.

University officials nowadays dare not begin an address without first paying respect to the elders—past, present, and emerging—of whatever tribe traditionally occupied the property on which they stand. As recently as January 2022, the library of the University of Sydney added to its searchable website a pop-up warning that the "collection may contain culturally sensitive materials."[26] Flagrant racism exists in modern-day Australia as much as in many another country;[27] Australia is hardly innocent of racism directed toward its Indigenous people, but regarding expressions of such racism, Australians in the spotlight perforce are very, very careful.

Peter Weir was certainly careful as he worked on *The Last Wave*. The idea for a story about "tribal" Aborigines who live secretly in modern Sydney was entirely his own, yet once he found the Aboriginal persons who would play two of the film's major characters (David Gulpilil and Nandjiwarra Amagula[28]), he not only gently pumped them for suggestions for details but cleared with them all of the film's dialogue and references, visual as well as verbal, to Aboriginal culture. In 1985, Weir told an interviewer that "certain scenes in the film were all [Gulpilil's], such as those about getting messages from his family through a twitch in his arm," and that "Nandji changed quite a bit of dialogue and asked for certain things [such as the lines, spoken in the dinner scene, "about the law and the law being more important than the man"] to be put in."[29] Weir's concern was not that he get "right" his totally made-up and admittedly "too complex"[30] tale about an aboriginal tribe living secretly in the depths of Sydney and cultivating a relationship with a descendent of a South American "super race" of mystic seers; rather, his concern was that, vis-à-vis genuine aboriginal concepts, he not get anything "wrong." In that, he seems to have succeeded, but nevertheless he came in for criticism.

Mild complaints had it that *The Last Wave* was simply one of a number of films that fit in neatly not just with Australia's new policy of what historian/anthropologist Timothy Rowse called "liberalising the frontier"[31] but also with an aggressive campaign on the part of the Australian government to promote tourism. Along with the sudden appearance in airport gift shops of didgeridoos and boomerangs, and the emergence of a style of painting that involved the placement of many small dots on relatively large canvases,[32] films such as Henri Safran's 1976 *Storm Boy*, Weir's 1977 *The Last Wave*, Fred Schepisi's 1978 *The Chant of Jimmie Blacksmith*, and John Honey's 1980 *Manganinnie* (aka *Darkening Flame*)—all of which feature aboriginal characters, and all of which benefited from funding from various of Australia's recently established state film boards—were seen to collectively "produce a set of conceptions which, rather than delineating the specific characteristics of a given group in a specific situation, construct Aborigines and their lifestyles as unitary in relation to some essential (and unknowable) principle such as the 'spirituality of the dreaming' or 'closeness to nature' which ultimately engenders all action."[33]

Harsher opinions had it that in *The Last Wave* a fanciful concept of "mysticism replaces any depiction of [what] the Aboriginal male" might really be, making him no longer "a man" but simply something "chthonic—a natural earth force without humanity,"[34] that for all its supposed good intentions the film "obscured the issues that real Aboriginal people faced,"[35] and that "the respect [the white lawyer] appeared to pay to Aboriginal culture" resulted only in "a fictionalizing appropriation of that culture."[36] Indeed, it is charges of "cultural appropriation" that over the years have most often beset *The Last Wave*. One of the most blistering attacks came from Graeme Turner in a 1988 article, prompted by the bicentennial of the arrival of the First Fleet, that surveyed more than a dozen cinematic depictions of Aborigines. *The Last Wave* in particular "unashamedly exploits a white mythology of blackness," Turner wrote, and one of the things about it that is especially offensive is its occasional horror-triggering focus on certain characters' faces. The film "continually infers rather than depicts the supernatural, the uncanny, and the mystical," and in it,

> the lingering close-up on the black face is a central strategy for sustaining the threat of disruption. Here all the old assumptions about the difference of the black race are mobilized as motivational agents for a supernatural thriller. Weir's detribalized Aborigines may be living in the city, but they retain a race memory from centuries ago. Their memories are, as it were, in their blood—even the diluted blood of the white lawyer, David, who shares a fraction of their ancestry. Biological determinism at its most uncomplicated provides the narrative justification for the Aborigines' premonition of a tidal wave destroying Sydney; for David's sharing of that premonition; and even for the capacity to register and recognize such a premonition. The whole farrago of supernatural goings-on is given a specific material location: a lost underworld of darkness, ritual, and contagion in the sewers emptying onto Bondi beach. Admittedly, the film has a limited interest in or need for realistic plot-lines or a liberal politics, but its unthinking recycling of Darwinian racial myths is implicitly reactionary.[37]

To sustain old racial myths was clearly not Weir's intention as he set out to make what one American reviewer aptly described as "a fascinating psychological thriller" with "apocalyptic undercurrents"[38] and what another called "a movingly moody shock-film, composed entirely of the kind of variations on mundane behavior and events that are most scary and disorienting because they so closely parallel the normal."[39] Weir seems to have appreciated praise of that sort, and in his various interviews he gives little indication that he was personally stung by accusations, from critics international as well as Australian, that in *The Last Wave* he was being culturally insensitive. Nevertheless, after *The Last Wave* he made only one more Australian-set film that features "an uncanny subversion of bourgeois values,"[40] and he moved forward in a career that showed him to be, as both writer and director, anything but typecast.[41]

* * *

Weir's fourth film, made for television on commission from the South Australian Film Corporation, was the 1979 *The Plumber*, about a married couple (one of them an anthropologist writing her thesis on shamans in New Guinea) who are "bothered" by their apartment building's psychologically disturbed maintenance man. His first and second feature-length films were the 1974 *The Cars That Ate Paris*, a horror-comedy about a small town in remote New South Wales that earns a gruesome living by salvaging from automobile crashes that it causes, and the now-classic 1975 *Picnic at Hanging Rock*, an eerie treatment of Joan Lindsay's same-titled 1967 "true story" novel about girls from a finishing school in rural Victoria who simply vanish, apparently into thin air, while on a Valentine's Day outing.

Both *The Cars* and *Picnic* arguably fall into the category of "Australian Gothic," a genre easily enough recognized by international critics but one that, so it seems, is rarely acknowledged by Australians themselves. Whether manifest in film or novels, the essential ingredient in Australian Gothic is the idea of isolation. Scholars have attempted to trace modern Australians' apparently widespread nervousness about "enclosure and entrapment,"[42] their worries about being somehow "stuck" in the middle of some god-forsaken nowhere, back to "fears and themes that [were] endemic in the colonial experience,"[43] but that runs counter to the simple fact that most modern Australians are *not* directly descended from colonists, or from convicts. A more realistic analysis would have it that Australia, probably in the minds of locals more than tourists, is a scary place.

Like television news everywhere, the television news in Australia reports dutifully on rapes, murders, and the like. But it also reports, so regularly that it seems predictable, on devastating floods and bushfires, on infestations by poisonous jellyfish and disease-ridden mice, on the drownings of rock fishermen taken by waves or beachgoers caught by rip currents, on attacks by sharks and saltwater crocodiles, on the activities of venomous spiders and snakes, and wild dogs. Most Australians, of course, live in the major cities, and among the educated classes most of them are relatively well-traveled. But their travels take them far more often to Europe or the United States than to anywhere in their own very expansive backyard. Some Australians do have an ongoing physical relationship with the landscape that inspired the 1906 poem by Dorothea Mackellar whose second stanza provided Bill Bryson with the title for his book on Australia, but most, I think, prefer the relative safety of cities. Mackellar's poem has a beautiful resonance: "I love a sunburnt country, / A land of sweeping plains, / Of ragged mountain ranges, / Of drought and flooding rains. / I love her far horizons, / I love her jewel-sea, / Her beauty and her terror— / The wide brown land for me!" It was not for nothing that Mackellar included that particular word at the end of the stanza's penultimate line.

The British critic Jonathan Rayner, whose scholarly output has focused much on matters Australian, writes that "the most conspicuous elements at work with Australian Gothic, which register most forcefully through cinematography and *mise-en-scène*, are the horrors associated with the natural landscape. The immensity and difference of the land, from an Anglo Saxon perspective, is inseparable from its inhospitableness and latent menace."[44] Because its setting is urban, and because its main character is so meticulously urbane, *The Last Wave* does not really fit into the Australian Gothic pigeonhole. Yet Rayner gives the impression that he would *like* Weir's film to qualify. In *The Last Wave*, he writes, "the remoteness of the country is replaced by an existential isolation engendered by the complacency and disappointment of middle-class, urban life." He links *The Last Wave* with such other Australian urban mysteries as Phillip Noyce's 1981 *Heatwave* and Ben Lewin's 1988 *Georgia*, and he argues that "what unites these stories and justifies their Gothic classification is their scathing scrutiny of the establishment (in legal, political, capitalist and class-based terms) and their insistence on a return of repressed history and memory."[45]

That seems a bit of a stretch for the standard definition of Australian Gothic. Still, there is no denying that *The Last Wave* is a chiller, and a thriller. The essence of its plot is the central character's nightmare visions of an impending apocalypse, and perhaps that basic idea might indeed translate to a setting other than that of a modern Australian city. It is difficult to imagine the story, though, without the ominousness that comes—tacitly, by visual means alone—from the very white dreamer's contact with other dreamers whose faces are impenetrably Black.

Notes

1. Until early in the twentieth century, the practice of death-inducing "bone pointing" by a shaman known as a "kurdaitcha man" was common among tribes in central Australia. See Spencer Baldwin and F. J. Gillen, *Native Tribes of Central Australia* (Cambridge, UK: Cambridge University Press, 2010), 476–477.

2. The sound is, in fact, that of a didgeridoo, played by David Gulpilil, the actor who portrayed one of the young men accused of murder and, significantly, the one who appears to the lawyer in his dreams. The music for *The Last Wave* was nominated for the Australian Academy of Cinema and Television Arts award for "best original score," yet much about it remains shrouded in mystery, at least in part because the name of the credited composer— Charles Wain—is alleged to have been a pseudonym for someone who at the time of the making of the film worked as a producer of music for television advertisements. Writing casually in an online publication called *Neighbourhood*, Michael Dwyer attests that "Charles Wain, aka Groove Myers," was a real person who "was in a lot of beat bands in Sydney in the '60s, then he started working in advertising. You know that CCs ad, 'You can't say no'? Or those KFC ads with Hugo and Holly?" (Michael Dwyer, "Raiders of a Lost Art," *Neighbourhood*, n.d., https://neighbourhoodpaper.com/culture/raiders-of-a-lost-ark/). Writing more officially, Philip Hayward notes that "Charles Wain was an experienced TV advertisement composer who lived on an ashram as a devotee of esoteric Hindu Sidda Yoga guru Baba'Muktananda." Quoting from an anonymous article that appeared in the autumn 1978 issue of the magazine *Metro*, Hayward writes that "Wain has stated that his inspiration [for the score] was 'the element of spirituality in both the concept of the film and in many of the locations.'" Drawing from the same source, Hayward adds that "Wain has identified that the synthesizer was appropriate for the film due to what he has described as the tendency for early-mid 1970s synthesizer music (of the style typified by German artists Tangerine Dream and Klaus Schulze) to resemble 'chant-like tribal music'" in its use of "drones, slow modulations and gradual crescendos and diminuendos." Hayward points out that "these elements are strongly in evidence in the film's soundtrack and are also associated with the iconic cinematic sound of Aboriginality: the didjeridu." Wain has characterized the decision to use didgeridoo sounds in the score as Weir's idea, but his approach was to blend the instrument with his score, retaining its signature sound but infusing it as an ambient element, rather than a foregrounded one. The didgeridoo sounds derived from tracks performed by David Gulpilil, and these were subsequently slowed down to half-speed to "embellish" the instrument's "eeriness and to make it a much thicker and fatter sound without destroying

its natural qualities." Philip Hayward, "Numinous Ambience: Spirituality, Dreamtimes and Fantastic Aboriginality," *Screen Sound* 1 (2010): 30–31. The quotations are from "Who the Hell Are You?," *Metro* (43) (1978): 14–16.

3. Bill Bryson, *In a Sunburned Country* (New York: Random House, 2000), 270. Emphasis in original.

4. Shute's 1950 novel, about a British woman who moves to Australia after surviving a Japanese prison camp in Malaysia, is *A Town Like Alice*; the NSA's surveillance facility figures obliquely in numerous film and television productions, most notable among them the six-part Netflix miniseries *Pine Gap*, that was aired by the Australian Broadcasting Corporation in 2018.

5. Bryson, *In a Sunburned Country*, 269.

6. Unofficially but commonly known as the "White Australia Policy," Australia's Immigration Restriction Act and Pacific Island Labourers Act, both of which severely limited movement into the country by non-white people, went into effect almost simultaneous with Australia's federation in 1901. Both policies began to relax in the years immediately following World War II, but not until 1973 did the government pass a Racial Discrimination Act that made it illegal to restrict visas for reasons of race or ethnicity. For details on the original legislation, see Myra Willard, *History of the White Australian Policy to 1920* (London: Routledge, 1967). Originally published in 1923. For an account of the policy's background, see N. B. Nairn, "A Survey of the History of the White Australia Policy in the 19th Century," *The Australian Quarterly* 28, no. 3 (1956): 16–31. For a controversial argument to the effect that the 1901 legislation had to do with economic rather than racist concerns, see Keith Windschuttle, *The White Australia Policy* (Sydney: Macleay Press, 2004).

7. Kenneth Morgan, *Australia: A Very Short Introduction* (Oxford: Oxford University Press, 2012), 27.

8. Australia's so-called Stolen Generation resulted from practices by which Aboriginal children were removed from their families and sent to white-run boarding schools or placed as domestic servants in white households. Most of the removals took place between 1905 and 1967, but a euphemistically titled Aboriginal Protection Act in the state of Victoria dates back to as early as 1869. The term stolen generation was coined in 1981 by historian Peter Read, who used it in the title of a short paper commissioned by the New South Wales Department of Aboriginal Affairs ("The Stolen Generations: The Removal of Aboriginal Children in New South Wales 1883–1969"); later, with a more nationwide focus, he used it in the subtitle of his book *A Rape of the Soul So Profound: The Return of the Stolen Generation* (London: Routledge, 1999). The effects of the Australian government's policy of relocating Indigenous children "for their own good" are poignantly depicted in Phillip Noyce's 2002 film *Rabbit-Proof Fence*, which is based on Doris Pilkington's 1996 autobiographical novel *Follow the Rabbit-Proof Fence*.

9. Robert Hughes, *The Fatal Shore: The Epic of Australia's Founding* (New York: Alfred A. Knopf, 1986), 273. The quotation in the final sentence is from C. D. Rowley's *Aboriginal Policy and Practice: The Destruction of Aboriginal Society* (Canberra: Australian National University Press, 1970).

10. Ibid.

11. Ibid., 274.

12. Ibid., 277.

13. Ibid. Usually meticulous in his citations, on this one Hughes is vague. The quoted words *seem* to come from a letter that the agriculturalist Benjamin Hurst wrote in 1841 to Charles

La Trobe, then superintendent of the Port Phillip District of New South Wales and later lieutenant-governor of the state of Victoria, that is quoted in Jean Woolmington, ed., *Aborigines in Colonial Society, 1788–1850: From "Noble Savage" to "Rural Pest"* (Melbourne: Cassell Australia, 1973).

Some activists for Indigenous rights have claimed that Aborigines were officially classified as less than human under a "Flora and Fauna Act" that supposedly was not repealed until 1967. In 2008, an investigation by the ABC (Australian Broadcasting Corporation) showed that no such "act" ever existed. For details, see Samuel Byrnand, "Reconfiguring History: The "Flora and Fauna Act" and Other Myths of Australian Legislation," PhD thesis, University of Canberra, 2015.

14. Only in 1976 did so-called land rights—not ownership per se but financial rights to certain mineral and water resources—start to be granted to Aboriginal tribespeople. For discussions of the complex and still highly contentious issues surrounding Aboriginal land rights, see, for example, David Mercer, "*Terra Nullius*, Aboriginal Sovereignty and Land Rights in Australia: The Debate Continues," *Political Geography* 12, no. 4 (1993): 299–318; Stuart Banner, "Why *Terra Nullius*? Anthropology and Property Law in Early Australia," *Law and History Review* 23, no. 1 (2005): 95–131; Gary Foley and Tim Anderson, "Land Rights and Aboriginal Voices," *Australian Journal of Human Rights* 12, no. 1 (2006): 83–108; and Shane Chalmers, "*Terra Nullius*? Temporal Legal Pluralism in an Australian Colony," *Social & Legal Studies* 29, no. 4 (2020): 463–485.

15. Morgan, *Australia: A Very Short Introduction*, 4.

For reports on recently discovered evidence, see Helen Davidson and Calla Wahlquist, "Australia Dig Finds Evidence of Aboriginal Habitation up to 80,000 Years Ago," *The Guardian*, July 20, 2017, https://www.theguardian.com/australia-news/2017/jul/19/dig-finds-evidence-of-aboriginal-habitation-up-to-80000-years-ago; and Tony Wright, "Aboriginal Archaeological Discovery in Kakadu Rewrites the History of Australia," *Sydney Morning Herald*, July 20, 2017, https://www.smh.com.au/technology/aboriginal-archaeological-discovery-in-kakadu-rewrites-the-history-of-australia-20170719-gxe 3qy.html.

16. Hughes, *The Fatal Shore*, 8; Yuval Noah Harari, *Sapiens: A Brief History of Humankind* (New York: Vintage, 2015), 21, 67–68.

17. The origins of the phrase are lost in the mists of media babble, but nowadays the phrase—almost always in those exact words—is ubiquitous, and probably spoken far more often by white politicians than by persons of Aboriginal heritage.

18. Weber coined the phrase, and perhaps with it the idea, in his 1905 *The Protestant Work Ethic and the Spirit of Capitalism* ("Die Protestantische Ethik und der Geist des Kapitalismus").

19. Hughes, *The Fatal Shore*, 7.

20. Bruce Chatwin, *The Songlines* (London: Franklin Press, 1987).

21. Morgan, *Australia: A Very Short Introduction*, 24.

22. According to census data compiled in 2016 by the Australian Bureau of Statistics, persons self-identifying as being of Indigenous descent numbered 798,400, or 3.3 percent of Australia's total population. Of these, the vast majority (81 percent) lived in cities, most of which are located on Australia's eastern or southern coasts. Only 12 percent of the Indigenous population lived in areas described as "very remote," and only 7 percent lived in communities—i.e., towns and small cities—described as "remote." Australian Bureau of Statistics, "Estimates of Aboriginal and Torres Strait Islander Australians," August 2018, https://www.abs.gov.au/statistics/people/aboriginal-and-torres-strait-islander-peoples/

estimates-aboriginal-and-torres-strait-islander-australians/latest-release. In comparison, persons identifying as wholly or partly Native American—a total of almost 10 million according to the 2020 census—number 2.9 percent of the population in the United States; in Canada, persons identifying as being of "First Nations" descent—1.6 million according to the 2016 census—represent 4.9 percent of the population.

23. It was only recently that the term Stone Age as a descriptor not of modern-day but of historical Aboriginal culture fell into discredit. See Alice Gorman, "Australian Archaeologists Dropped the Term 'Stone Age' Decades Ago, and So Should You," *The Conversation*, August 27, 2018. Gorman, a senior lecturer in archaeology at Flinders University in Adelaide, points out that the term has long been equated with "backward" or "primitive," and that "in Australia, 'Stone Age' was seen not as a technology practised by Aboriginal people, but rather the essence of what they were."

24. The early round included such unabashed potboilers as *Howling III: The Marsupials* (1987; dir. Phillippe Mora), *Kadaicha: Stones of Death* (1988; dir. James Bogle), and *The Dreaming* (1988; dir. Mario Andreacchio). Later efforts more or less in the same genre were *BeDevil* (1993; dir. Tracey Moffatt) and *Primal* (2010; dir. Josh Reed). Along with the five short films that constitute *Dark Place* (2019; dir. Kodie Bedford, Perun Bonser, Rob Braslin, Liam Phillips, and Bjorn Stewart), the recent crop includes the television series *Shadow Trackers* (2016; dir. Dena Curtis) and *Firebite* (2021; dir. Warwick Thornton).

25. Morgan, *Australia: A Very Short Introduction*, 24.

26. The warning reads: "The Library collection may contain culturally sensitive materials. Aboriginal and Torres Strait Islander peoples are advised our collection may contain images, voices and names of people who have died. The Library recognises the significance of the traditional cultural knowledges contained within its collection. However, some material may be considered insensitive, outdated, or inappropriate in today's context. These materials reflect the views of the authors and/or the period in which they were produced and don't represent the views of the Library."

27. For recent discussions of the situation, see, for example, Alice Pung, "Living with Racism in Australia," *New York Times*, December 7, 2016, https://www.nytimes.com/2016/12/07/opinion/living-with-racism-in-australia.html; Jenna Price, "Yes, We Can 'Do Better': The Ugly Truth about Racism in Australia," *Sydney Morning Herald*, February 14, 2021, https://www.smh.com.au/national/yes-we-can-do-better-the-ugly-truth-about-racism-in-australia-20210204-p56zqq.html; Annabel Crabb, "'Australia Talks' Shows We Agree There's a Lot of Racism Here, But Less than Half Say White Supremacy Is Ingrained in Our Society," *ABC News*, May 31, 2021, https://www.abc.net.au/news/2021-05-31/annabel-crabb-analysis-racism-australia-talks/100172288; and Cameron Gooley, "Unheard No More: Australia's Racism Problem on Global Display," *The Age*, October 25, 2021, https://www.theage.com.au/culture/tv-and-radio/unheard-no-more-australia-s-racism-problem-on-global-display-20211021-p591xc.html.

28. David Gulpilil, 24 years old at the time of *The Last Wave*, played Chris, one of the young men accused of murder. A native of the Arnhem Land in the northeastern corner of the Northern Territory, Gulpilil in 1971 had made his debut as the "black boy" in Nicolas Roeg's *Walkabout* and then, after appearing in various television shows and *The Last Wave*, had minor or major starring roles in such internationally successful films as Philip Kaufman's 1983 *The Right Stuff*, Peter Faiman's 1986 *Crocodile Dundee*, Wim Wenders's 1991 *Until the End of the World*, Rolf de Heer's 2002 *The Tracker*, Baz Luhrmann's 2008 *Australia*, and Shawn Seet's 2019 *Storm Boy*.

Thomas Nandjiwarra Amagula, who played Charlie, was a then 51-year-old man who at the time of meeting Weir ran a dance troupe and served as a magistrate on the Northern Territory's Groote Island. As chairperson of Groote Island's Angurugu Council, he helped develop legislation that protected the island's traditional sites from mining operations; in 1981, he chaired the Aboriginal Cultural Foundation, and four years later he chaired the Groote Eylandt Aboriginal Task Force. His role in Weir's *The Last Wave* would be Nandjiwarra's only on-screen appearance.

29. Peter Weir (interviewed by Susan Mathews), "Years of Living Dangerously: *The Last Wave, The Plumber, Gallipoli, The Year of Living Dangerously*," in *Peter Weir: Interviews*, ed. John C. Tibbetts (Jackson: University Press of Mississippi, 2014), 90–91. Mathews's interview with Weir is excerpted from *35mm Dreams: Five Directors* (Sydney: Penguin, 1985). Much of what Weir has to say about working with Gulpilil and Nandjiwarra is more or less repeated in "Peter Weir on *The Last Wave*," an eleven-minute monologue that is included on the 2001 Criterion Collection edition of the DVD. Weir's commentary is available on YouTube at https://www.youtube.com/watch?v=D_7BYTf95Vc.

30. Weir, "Years of Living Dangerously," 92.

31. Timothy Rowse, "Liberalising the Frontier: Aborigines and Australian Pluralism," *Meanjin* 42, no. 1 (1983): 71–84.

    The "liberalisation" process, according to Rowse and many other observers, included the opening of an Aboriginal Embassy in Canberra in 1972 and the next year the establishment of the National Aboriginal Conference.

32. Commonly touted as a traditional art form, so-called dot painting in fact was invented in 1971 by the Sydney-born art educator Geoffrey Bardon when he was teaching in Papunya, a small Aboriginal community located about 150 miles northwest of Alice Springs. For details on Bardon's work, see John Rennie Short, "Representing Country in the Creative Postcolonial City," Annals of the Association of American Geographers 102, no. 1 (2012): 129–150. For an anecdote about how London art critic Peter Conrad in 2013 called attention to the origin of this style, hitherto "consecrated as a new form of Aboriginal high art, with a significant presence in both national and international art markets," see Tony Bennet, "Adjusting Field Theory: The Dynamics of Settler-Colonial Art Fields," in *The Routledge International Handbook of the Sociology of Art and Culture*, ed. Laurie Hanquinet and Mike Savage (London: Routledge, 2016), 247.

33. Catriona Moore and Stephen Muecke, "Racism and the Representation of Aborigines in Film," *Australian Journal of Cultural Studies* 2, no. 1 (1984): 41.

34. Colin Johnson, "Chauvel and the Centring of the Aboriginal Male in Australian Film," *Continuum: The Australian Journal of Media & Culture* 1, no. 1 (1987): 49.

    The surname in the article's title belongs to Charles Chauvel, whose 1955 *Jedda* is a landmark in Australian cinema not only because it was the first Australian film to be made in color and the first to be exhibited at the Cannes Film Festival but also the first to feature Indigenous actors in leading roles. The main character in *Jedda* is a thief and a rapist, but according to Johnson he is nevertheless "in full control of his being," and "the only dignified Aboriginal male lead that has [ever] been allowed to exist in films made by white directors in Australia" (49).

    For more recent commentary on the still-controversial *Jedda*, see, for example, Barbara Creed, "Breeding out the Black: *Jedda* and the Stolen Generations in Australia," in *Body Trade: Captivity, Cannibalism and Colonialism in the Pacific*, ed. Barbara Creed, Jeanette Hoorn, and Peter Hulme (London: Routledge, 2002), 208–230; Ben Miller, "The Mirror of

Whiteness: Blackface in Charles Chauvel's *Jedda*," *Journal of the Association for the Study of Australian Literature* (2007): 140–156; Suneeti Rekhari, "The 'Other' in Film: Exclusions of Aboriginal Identity from Australian Cinema," *Visual Anthropology* 21, no. 2 (2008): 125–35; and Chelsea Barnett, "'They Don't Tame, Only on the Surface': Masculinity, Race and the Project of Assimilation in *Jedda* (1955)," *History Australia* 15, no. 1 (2018): 36–61.

35. Andrew W. Hurley, "From Aboriginal Australia to German Autumn: On the West German Reception of Thirteen 'Films from Black Australia,'" *Studies in Australasian Cinema* 3, no. 3 (2009): 253. Paraphrasing, Hurley attributes the comment to Karena Niehoff, "Die Letzte Welle," *Tagesspiegel*, February 26, 1978.

36. Ibid. Hurley attributes the comment to Rudolf Thome, "Blick auf den Leinwand: Die letzte Flut," *Der Tagesspiegel* (West Berlin), August 31, 1979.

37. Graeme Turner, "Breaking the Frame: The Representation of Aborigines in Australian Film," *Kunapipi* 10, no. 1 (1988): 142.

38. Gary Arnold, "Peter Weir Catching The Last Wave from Down Under," *Washington Post*, February 4, 1979, H8.

39. Vincent Canby, "Film: 'Last Wave,' Storm of Occultism," *New York Times*, December 19, 1978, C7.

40. Jonathan Rayner, *The Films of Peter Weir* (London: Bloomsbury Academic, 2003), 89.

41. Weir's list of internationally successful post-1980 films, as diverse in genre as they are in their settings, include *Gallipoli* (1981), *The Year of Living Dangerously* (1982), *Witness* (1985), *The Mosquito Coast* (1986), *Dead Poets Society* (1989), *Green Card* (1990), *Fearless* (1993), *The Truman Show* (1998), *Master and Commander: The Far Side of the World* (2003), and *The Way Back* (2011).

42. Ken Gelder, "Australian Gothic," in *The Routledge Companion to Gothic*, ed. Catherine Spooner and Emma McEvoy (London and New York: Routledge, 2007), 119.

43. Gerry Turcotte, "Australian Gothic," in *The Handbook of Gothic Literature*, ed. Mulvey Roberts (Basingstoke, UK: Macmillan, 1998), 18.

44. Jonathan Rayner, "Gothic Definitions: The New Australian 'Cinema of Horrors,'" *Antipodes* 25, no. 1 (2011): 92.

45. Ibid., 95.

CHAPTER 7

DREAMING OF BLACKNESS

Horror and Aboriginal Australia in The Last Wave

ADAM LOWENSTEIN

FEW films have haunted me in a deeper and more sustained way than *The Last Wave* (Peter Weir, 1977). Encountering it initially on cable television during my childhood introduced me to many layers of fascinating strangeness: my first Australian film; my first Peter Weir film; my first introduction to the people of Aboriginal Australia. All of this was very new to me as a child growing up during the 1970s in suburban New Jersey, USA. As I returned to the film again and again over the years, I learned that its blending of horror and Aboriginal spiritual beliefs such as "Dreamtime" have some- times earned the film an uneasy or even potentially exploitative reputation with re- gard to debates concerning colonialism, Aboriginal representation, and Australian film history. Weir himself has spoken of *The Last Wave* as a "failure," a flawed tes- tament to his personal encounter with Aboriginal culture that he was perhaps not "meant to put in a film."[1] But even as I gained a more critically informed sense of *The Last Wave*'s cultural contexts, the power of the film's horror remained undiminished for me; *The Last Wave* is as mysterious, spellbinding, and unnerving to me now as it was all those years ago.

In this essay, I will argue that the conceptual frame of "Blackness" helps us to refigure the cinematic achievements of *The Last Wave*. The Indigenous Aboriginal people, as the "Blacks" of Australia, have often suffered from the othering lens of monstrousness that has been associated with the horror film by critics from Robin Wood onward.[2] It would be difficult to divorce *The Last Wave* from such questions of othering, since the history of dispossession, racism, and genocide endured by the Aboriginal people at the hands of white European settlers in Australia is a foundational fact with inescapably traumatic implications that continue to unfold today.[3] What I want to contend is that *The Last Wave*'s horror should not be interpreted simply as Aboriginal othering aligned with ex- ploitation or racism, but rather as an invitation to acknowledge what I have described elsewhere as "transformative otherness": the horror film's ability to present the categories of self and other not as dichotomized opposites, but as always metamorphosing, always intertwined identities that resist binaries such as "normality vs. monstrosity" or "progressive vs. reactionary."[4]

The Last Wave refuses to present us with a normal, white Australian self that is opposed to a monstrous, Black Aboriginal other. The film's Aboriginal people are ultimately a source of knowledge, not horror. The film's horror stems from its white Australian protagonist's inability to recognize his own *need* for the Aboriginal people he becomes increasingly obsessed with. It is the white man's own missing identity that he seeks to discover among Aboriginal people that is the true source of the film's horror, and Weir hammers this home through cinematic devices that simulate a nightmarishly dreamlike state that encompasses the viewer as well as the protagonist. It is in this spectatorial space where "dreaming of Blackness" occurs, and this is where I want to situate *The Last Wave*: a space enabled by theories of Black spectatorship, Aboriginal presence, and horror cinema's modes of viewer confrontation.

Dreaming between Shadow and Act

David Burton (Richard Chamberlain), the white Australian protagonist of *The Last Wave*, is a successful corporate lawyer in Sydney who is asked to serve as the public defender for a group of Aboriginal men accused of murdering one of their own. As David dives deeper into the case, he becomes convinced that the murder was a tribal matter and that the Aboriginal men he is defending hold secret, ancient answers to the threateningly strange weather events occurring in Australia and to his own ominous dreams and visions that seem to concern an oncoming apocalyptic event. Even though the Aboriginal men, who live in Sydney, profess again and again that they are not tribal people, David insists on investigating the case and pursuing their defense from a tribal angle.

Two of the Aboriginal men, the younger Chris Lee (David Gulpilil) and the older Charlie (Nandjiwarra Amagula), have interactions with David that lead him to believe not only that they are tribal people, but that he himself is connected to an Aboriginal spirit force that gives him access to the sorts of prophetic dreams associated with tribal Aboriginal knowledge. David's reality becomes increasingly anxious and hallucinatory, to the point where he sends his wife and children away for fear of some impending catastrophe. He loses the legal case, but in the aftermath, Chris breaks tribal law and leads David to a sacred Aboriginal site underground, hidden beneath Sydney's sewer system. There David finds evidence for his dreams, with the prophecy of an apocalyptic tidal wave foretold in paintings at the site. Chris disappears, while David steals relics from the site to prove its existence. David kills Charlie when the Aboriginal elder intercepts him at the sacred site and nearly becomes entombed himself when he cannot find his way back out. He accidentally drops the relics during his panicked flight, but he eventually finds a sewer passage that empties out onto a beach. Kneeling in the surf, he sees one last vision: a massive tidal wave approaching, threatening to drown everything in its path.

Is David's final vision a dream? A reality? A hallucination? A warning sign of things to come? A wish fulfilled? A nightmare realized? A projection of Aboriginal otherness onto himself? A recognition of Aboriginal knowledge beyond himself? Weir offers no easy answers to such questions, and part of the masterful achievement of *The Last Wave* is its suggestion that such questions must pass through a redefinition of "dreaming" itself.

In a crucial scene earlier in the film, Chris and Charlie come to visit David and his wife, Annie (Olivia Hamnett), at their home. At one point during their conversation, David asks Chris what dreams are. Chris replies that dreaming is "like seeing, hearing, speaking; the way of knowing things." As Chris explains, he gestures toward his own eyes, ears, and lips, underlining how Aboriginal dreaming is a sensory, bodily experience rather than just the mental activity denoted by Western notions of dreaming. When David looks puzzled, Chris highlights this point by giving an example: if Chris's family is in trouble, they will contact him through dreams and his body will register their message. Chris illustrates this example on his own body by reaching for a muscle in his forearm and making it move. Again, the bodily dimension of dreaming is emphasized, and again, David seems uncomprehending.

So Chris provides another example. "I will show you a dream," he tells David, as he grabs the lamp hanging above the table at which they are seated. He points the light directly at David's face, then passes his hand through the light's glare to create a shadow. "A dream is a shadow of something real," Chris intones.

Chris's striking gesture not only educates David on the nature of Aboriginal dreaming, but also reminds the audience of *The Last Wave* about the proximity of dreaming to cinema. By manipulating light and shadow and positioning David as a spectator, Chris stages dreaming and cinema as experiences that mirror each other.[5] If Chris defines Aboriginal dreaming as a bodily experience, then Weir's emphasis on Chris's physical gestures and especially Chris's manipulation of light and shadow suggest that cinematic spectatorship can entail a sort of embodied dreaming as well. If a dream is the shadow of something real, then cinema's play with light and shadow may also generate images, sounds, and bodily experiences that provide access to something real for the spectator.[6]

Weir confirms that Aboriginal dreaming was fundamental to his cinematic concerns in *The Last Wave* and that he devoted considerable personal study to the subject as well as extensive conversation about it with his two lead Aboriginal actors, Gulpilil and Amagula.[7] Indeed, Weir's collaboration with Gulpilil and Amagula on the film was unusually close, with the actors given the power to approve each of their lines of dialogue and the ability to suggest changes and additions of their own. Weir, like most Western commentators, admits that Aboriginal Dreamtime is a topic that he finds very hard to grasp fully and define successfully.[8] But he also confesses to being deeply compelled and moved by it: "I think the aspect of Dreamtime that most interested me was that it was a totally different way of seeing things; it's another perception. It's not obviously purely to do with dreams in the Western sense. It's to do with [Aboriginal] culture, their mythology, their stories. . . . But I never got what I thought was a full understanding of it, and that's because it's terribly hard to *see* in this way, to really *see*."[9] Weir's emphasis here on Dreamtime as an alternate form of perception, a new way of seeing things, as well as the difficulty in attaining this mode of vision, helps to frame *The Last Wave* as an experiment forged at the intersection of Aboriginal dreaming and cinematic dreaming.

In other words, I wish to pair Chris's Aboriginal formulation of embodied dreaming as the shadow of something real with Weir's gestural corollary ("I will show you a dream") that cinema can be a conduit for a kind of embodied dreaming that reveals the real for its viewers. Together, the Aboriginal formulation and the cinematic gesture produce a complex series of suggestions that lead us inward to the heart of *The Last Wave* as well as outward to what "dreaming of Blackness" might encompass. To approach the latter first as a means of returning eventually to the former, I want to note how Chris's formulation echoes the African American novelist and critic Ralph Ellison's reflections on race and cinema in his seminal 1949 essay "The Shadow and the Act."[10]

For Ellison, Hollywood's contemporary social-problem films dealing with questions of race, such as *Home of the Brave* (Mark Robson, 1949), *Lost Boundaries* (Alfred L. Werker, 1949), and *Pinky* (Elia Kazan, 1949), are often ridiculous at best and offensive at worst if they are understood as attempts at accurate representations of lived Black experience. But Ellison is not interested in condemning such films for their inaccuracies. On the contrary, he wishes to open a critical space where these films can be appreciated as significant for the ways that they choose to speak about race at all. So Ellison draws a distinction between "the shadow" and "the act." Film is the shadow, the realm of the image, and the act is history, the realm of action. For Ellison, the act precedes the shadow and cuts a sharp divide between the two; to treat the shadow as if it were the act would be to "confuse portrayal with action, image with reality."[11] Distinguishing shadow from act allows Ellison to find symptomatic value and emotional power in Hollywood's social-problem films that address race, no matter how blinkered or even absurd they might be in their imagining of actual Black experience and subjectivity. Their value stems from the opportunity they provide, especially for white viewers, to connect to "the deep centers of American emotion" touched by the films. As Ellison observes, "One of the most interesting experiences connected with viewing [these films] in predominantly white audiences is the profuse flow of tears and the sighs of profound emotional catharsis heard on all sides. It is as though there were some deep relief to be gained merely from seeing these subjects projected upon a screen."[12]

What Ellison draws our attention to so productively is how cinema's power around race must not be delimited by simply equating shadow with act, image with reality. For Ellison, the shadow can catalyze real emotion in spectators regarding race, even if the shadow's relation to the acts of history is inaccurate or unreal. In other words, the dreaming of Blackness enabled by these films for their spectators is valuable in its own right, quite apart from the question of whether the dream is an accurate representation of reality. For Ellison, the shadow is not the same as the act; dreams are not real. But dreams can certainly capture the shadow of something real, especially in terms of the embodied reactions of white viewers indicated by the tears and sighs he describes.

Ellison, as a Black spectator himself, is not solely concerned with white viewers and their emotional reactions of catharsis and relief. He also notes that seeing these same films with Black audiences produces quite a different reaction: "when the action goes phony, one will hear derisive laughter, not sobs."[13] By contrasting Black laughter with white sobs, Ellison reminds us that even though these 1940s films represent a major leap forward for Hollywood's engagement with race by attempting to imagine Black persons as human, they are still rooted (with the exception of *Intruder in the Dust* [Clarence Brown, 1949]) in earlier models such as *The Birth of a Nation* (D. W. Griffith, 1915) that denied humanity to African Americans. As Ellison puts it so eloquently: "If [*The Birth of a Nation*] became the main manipulator of the American dream, for Negroes that dream contained a strong dose of such stuff as nightmares are made of."[14]

Ellison's formulation, with its juxtaposition of dream and nightmare alongside the delineation of shadow and act, helps us to return to Chris's notion of dreaming in *The Last Wave* with greater nuance. When Chris states, in a language that is not only verbal but also gestural and cinematic, that "a dream is a shadow of something real," he does so in the context of a horror film. The dreamlike images and sounds that Weir assembles so meticulously in *The Last Wave* almost always veer toward nightmare, even when their manifest content appears harmless or mundane.

For example, a sequence early in the film depicts a trail of water spilling slowly down the stairs of the Burtons' home while the family converses over dinner. By cross-cutting between the falling water and a shot that tracks slowly inward on the Burton family, accompanied by a single, eerie synthesizer note on the soundtrack that repeats like the ping heard on a submerged submarine, Weir creates an atmosphere of dread using decidedly unfrightening raw material. There is nothing inherently threatening about a trickle of water or a family eating dinner. Even when Weir reveals the source of the water—an overflowing bathtub upstairs—there is nothing beyond the everyday behind it. Indeed, David's two young daughters play in the shower of falling water with delight.

And yet the dread remains. This is because Weir has already established a rich set of connected images revolving around water and weather that suggest imbalance and disorder, images that multiply and mutate relentlessly across the film as a whole: a violent summer hailstorm in Australia's interior; black rain in Sydney; a torrential downpour that becomes a vision of the passersby drowned underwater, their bodies now floating corpses. The culmination of these images is David's climactic vision of the last wave: an image of water as overwhelmingly horrific as the earlier trickle of water on the stairs is underwhelmingly mundane, but conjoined nonetheless in their shared sense of disturbance, of dream logic turned nightmarish. The last wave is also an Aboriginal prophecy made real, or at least cinematically tangible—an eruption of Aboriginal Dreamtime into the everyday reality of white Australia. If the Aboriginal people have endured apocalyptic forms of genocidal dispossession inflicted by the European settlers of Australia, then the last wave promises a dispossession on a similarly apocalyptic scale for white Australia: an entire civilization lost, buried beneath the water.

Given the connective cinematic tissue binding these images in *The Last Wave*, and recalling Ellison's insights on shadow and act in filmic dreams and nightmares of race, it might be possible now to paraphrase Chris's formulation "a dream is a shadow of something real" in a somewhat different way: something closer to "a cinematic dream of

Blackness is an invitation to encounter the real Aboriginal nightmare of lived history." In this new formulation, horror is the bridge that traverses dream and nightmare, shadow and act.

As the Indigenous scholars Eve Tuck and C. Ree remind us, "Colonization is as horrific as humanity gets: genocide, desecration, poxed-blankets, rape, humiliation. Settler colonialism, then, because it is a structure and not just the nefarious way nations are born, is an ongoing horror made invisible by its persistence." Tuck and Ree turn to the horror genre's capacity for haunting as a corrective to settler colonialism's invisibility: "Haunting, by contrast, is the relentless remembering and reminding that will not be appeased by settler society's assurances of innocence and reconciliation."[15] This sort of haunting is precisely the sort of power activated by the horror genre when it bridges fictional dream and historical nightmare, or representation's shadow and history's act. Indeed, Tuck and Ree mention Toni Morrison's novel *Beloved* (1987) as an example of how horror's hauntings can make visible the sort of racialized historical anguish that too often remains invisible. In *Beloved*, according to Tuck and Ree, "the violent past and the haunted present seep into the narrative until it is slavery itself in its multiplying psychic forms that haunts the family and readers, the horror and haunting of today."[16] Just as Morrison's use of horror through the ghostly, haunting figure of Beloved makes slavery's hidden pain visible, so too does *The Last Wave* harness horror to dream of Blackness so that the hidden experience of settler colonialism becomes visible experience.

This does not mean that the Aboriginal characters of *The Last Wave* stand on the same footing as the white characters, for they are not imagined in the same ways nor given the same sorts of psychological interiority. In a certain sense, Weir never permits us to really know his Aboriginal characters. But what he does invite is an opportunity for viewers to dream of Blackness, to feel the significance of Aboriginal experience made visible through horror rather than remaining cloaked in the invisibility generated by everyday habits of denial and forgetting. Still, the question of what exactly comprises the relations between horror and dreaming in *The Last Wave* requires further exploration.

"WHO ARE YOU?"

Later in *The Last Wave*, a fascinating analogue to the visit of Chris and Charlie to David's home occurs. In this sequence, one of many "doubled" moments in the film that enhance its dreamlike texture (such as the water trickle/tidal wave described above), David visits Charlie's home. Charlie lives in a small, spartan urban apartment that differs dramatically from David's large, comfortably appointed suburban house. An Aboriginal woman answers the door and leads David to Charlie's room. David asks her to stay and translate, since Charlie spoke only in an Aboriginal dialect at David's house and Chris explained then that Charlie does not speak English. But before the woman can reply, Charlie addresses David himself: "Sometime I speak English, sometime I don't."

Charlie's utterance carries the charge of an electric shock. It is yet one more indicator, among several others in the film, that David's impulse to force a confession of tribalism from the Aboriginal people he is responsible for defending legally is a flawed, incomplete, and ultimately self-serving desire. Charlie's words express not some pure, untouched Aboriginal tribal essence, but rather a complex sense of hybridized Aboriginal identity that is entwined with that of modern white Australia. We can hear the echoes of Charlie's words both earlier and later in the film, when David is reminded by his fellow lawyer Michael Zeadler (Peter Carroll)—who specializes in legal cases involving Aboriginal people—that David's notions of tribal Aboriginal people living in today's Sydney is a "romantic" idea both empirically unfounded and legally dangerous. When David insists on pursuing the tribal defense against Zeadler's advice, Zeadler accuses David of harboring a "middle-class patronizing attitude . . . towards the Blacks" that "revolts" him. Zeadler continues, "For the best part of ten years I've worked with these people, while you sat making a fortune on tax dodgers and corporations. And you come in here with this idiotic, romantic crap about tribal people. . . ." At this point, David leaves Zeadler and tells him to send the paperwork involving the case to his office.

David's refusal to listen to Zeadler is prefigured by his inability to listen to Charlie. After Charlie reveals that sometimes he chooses to speak English and sometimes he doesn't, David tells Charlie that his wife has seen him outside their house and that he has frightened her. David asks, "What do you want? Who are you?" Charlie, who has insisted that David join him in sitting on the floor of his apartment for their conversation, immediately fires David's question back at him, but in a hypnotic, repetitive murmur that becomes a kind of chant: "Who are you? Who are you? Who are you?" David, who seems to fall into a trance, cannot answer the question. When Charlie asks him if he is a fish, or a snake, or a man, David shakes his head no. Finally, Charlie asks him if he is Mulkurul, an ancient race endowed with special powers according to Aboriginal spiritual beliefs. David says yes. Charlie then unveils an Aboriginal ritual axe that has been lying covered by cloth in the space between them on the floor. Charlie gets up to leave, directing these parting words toward David: "Don't speak in the court."

David does not follow Charlie's advice, nor Zeadler's, nor that of the anthropologist who tells David that Aboriginal beliefs exclude the possibility that Mulkurul's powers can be manifested in non-Aboriginal people such as himself. The fact that *The Last Wave* appears to prove David "correct" in the sense of showing us the sacred site and artifacts that "prove" Chris and Charlie are members of a tribal Aboriginal group based in Sydney and suggest that David may be Mulkurul after all, does not silence these other voices. Instead, these voices demand that we recognize how David being "correct" is not equivalent to David being "right." David cannot be exonerated from coercing a confession of tribal Aboriginal identity from Chris in the white Australian courtroom, nor stealing sacred Aboriginal artifacts, nor killing Charlie. David may have "reasons" for doing all of these things, but these reasons do not add up to a position we can call "right."

In fact, David loses his way so thoroughly by the end of the film that he not only fails to defend the Aboriginal men he is representing legally, but he becomes the killer of an Aboriginal man himself. He also becomes a sort of double for Billy Corman (Athol

Compton), the Aboriginal man murdered by Charlie for breaking Aboriginal law. Like Billy, David steals artifacts from the sacred site and breaks the trust he has built with the Aboriginal people. The two even wear similar trench coats as they navigate the same passages through the sewer system, and David's murder weapon is a sacred stone that Billy stole from the site originally. Again, the fact that we see the murder of Billy early in the film accomplished using Aboriginal magic practiced by Charlie (who points an Aboriginal death bone at Billy) is not enough to exonerate David. Instead, we are faced with two laws and two realities—one Black, one white—so that there can be no such thing as absolute guilt or innocence in one through the lens of the other.[17]

Weir visualizes this notion of two laws brilliantly during the courtroom sequence. As Chris and his Aboriginal compatriots face murder charges before an all-white jury, in a white courtroom staffed solely by white lawyers in white wigs and presided over by a white-wigged judge, the absurdity and unfairness of Chris being forced to take an oath by placing his hand on the Holy Bible and swearing to tell "the whole truth and nothing but the truth" is driven home through the mise-en-scène. Everything about the setting speaks of whiteness, white law, and the whiteness of the law, not the law's universal impartiality that is purported to apply equally to "all Australians." When David forces Chris to admit his tribal Aboriginal identity while under oath, he forces Chris to speak about his Blackness in the language of whiteness. But before David can proceed much further, Charlie intervenes: he appears to Chris (and to us) as a fleeting visual presence in the courtroom, frightening Chris and causing him to recant his admission. When he recants, Chris explains to the courtroom that David got him confused, that tribal times were long ago, not in the present. And in the eyes of white law, what Chris says now is true—there is no such thing anymore as tribal Aboriginal people in Sydney, even if they did once exist in the distant past. In other words, Chris now tells the white courtroom what it wants to hear about Aboriginal people (they get drunk and kill each other) as well as Black law (it no longer exists, it has been superseded by white law). Yet Charlie's visage in the courtroom suggests another law outside of white law, another reality outside of white reality. These two laws and two realities prove irreconcilable in the legal context of the courtroom, but in the cinematic contexts of dreaming and horror offered by *The Last Wave*, there is an opportunity for imagining forms of conflicted coexistence.

For example, if the courtroom is ill-equipped to tell the story of Aboriginal death in any language other than white law, Weir offers a cinematic alternative by staging the events of Billy's death through forms of dreamlike perception. We witness Billy fleeing the sacred Aboriginal site with the artifacts he has stolen, then his pursuit by Chris and four of his Aboriginal compatriots. They catch up with Billy in a bar, then chase him out. Billy runs through the rain to a nearby construction site, and suddenly this conventional reality becomes something quite different. One of the Aboriginal men calls out to Billy, and instantly the drenching rainfall ceases completely. All diegetic sound vanishes, replaced with the haunting tones of a didgeridoo, a traditional Aboriginal musical instrument. And it is not only the rain and sound that transform suddenly; movement itself now thickens with slowness, as the sequence switches abruptly to slow-motion cinematography. Slow motion allows us to see the raindrops dripping from the bodies of the Aboriginal men, heightening our awareness of how strange it is that the rain has simply disappeared instantaneously. We also see Billy's terrified face in all of its contorted fear, as he turns away from the men and their threateningly hulking shadows only to encounter Charlie, who watches him unblinkingly from a nearby car. Billy clutches his heart as Charlie continues to stare him down. As Billy's body crumples with the Aboriginal men in the background, we hear Charlie's voice whispering in an Aboriginal dialect and see him pointing the death bone at Billy. Then with a cut, we are returned to the conventional reality we just left: rainfall, police sirens, radio dispatches, Billy's corpse inspected by police officers bearing a flashlight. Charlie and the Aboriginal men are nowhere to be seen, although we hear through the radio dispatch that five men have been taken into custody.

What Weir constructs in this sequence is an alternate reality around Billy's death that the white courtroom will never understand. But rather than downgrade this alternate reality for its lack of white rationality, Weir lends it unforgettably intense cinematic impact by investing it fully with the powers of horror. This is a dream far more real for spectators in its embodied, nightmarish power than any courtroom explanation ever could be. Indeed, we will remember Billy's death the way this sequence has presented it to us, long after we have forgotten the courtroom statement that narrates his death in terms of white law. When we dream of Billy's death, and of Billy's Blackness, we will dream of it cinematically. We will have gained a dreamer's opening, however partial and fleeting, to a cinematic version of Aboriginal perception, Aboriginal law, Aboriginal reality. To be clear, I am not claiming that *The Last Wave* is an Aboriginal film in the same way we could speak about the films of an Aboriginal artist like Tracey Moffatt, or the horror-tinged television series *Cleverman* (2016–2017) and *Firebite* (2021–2022) created by Aboriginal Australians, or the Indigenous media productions by a variety of Aboriginal Australian communities.[18] But the fact that *The Last Wave* offers us a dreamer's opening to Aboriginal reality while surrounded by white reality, and that this opening comes laced with nightmare and horror, serves as an important reminder that the stakes attached to the coexistence of these two realities is not some easily achieved balancing of equals in multicultural harmony. It is the painful reckoning with the inordinately severe social and historical price paid by Aboriginal people for not being seen as human or present by whites. If the cinematic dream is the historical shadow of something real, then *The Last Wave* insists through its horror that any cinematic dreaming the film enables for its spectators must travel through the terrain of real nightmare.

Indeed, Weir frustrates temptations to interpret Aboriginal reality as somehow mystically separate from white reality by incorporating disturbing images that emphasize the bleed between Aboriginal reality and white reality. What follows immediately after the dreamlike scene that shows us Billy's death according to Aboriginal law are two scenes that show us the consequences of that death for Aboriginal people who are subjected to white law. First, we witness Chris and his brother escorted by white guards to a prison cell. Chris's brother recoils and screams on the threshold of the cell, clearly horrified by this forced confinement that will remove him from his land and his people in ways that are specifically traumatic for Aboriginal Australians. Chris, too, must be physically restrained as he resists entering the cell. In the next scene, a white detective and a white coroner discuss Billy's autopsy in a lab as faceless and coldly institutionalized as the prison cell. The coroner observes that there was a small amount of water in Billy's lungs, but not enough to cause his death. The detective quips that the coroner once told him that a cup of water was enough to drown a sheep, so surely half that amount would be enough to "drown an Abo." The casual racism of the detective's statement, which the coroner does not contest, hinges on an assumption of Aboriginal identity as less than human. Weir underlines the impact of this racism visually by having Billy's body present but mostly invisible during their conversation. Aside from a brief glimpse of Billy's foot, these men speak about a body that has already effectively disappeared, just as the confinement of Chris and his brother treats the needs of their bodies as immaterial and absent.

The cumulative effect of scenes such as these, with their emphasis on how Aboriginal bodies and subjectivity vanish in the face of white law and white reality, comes back to inform later scenes in *The Last Wave*, including Charlie's repeated question to David: "Who are you?" Who is David without the Aboriginal people who give his life meaning and purpose? What is white Australian culture without the Aboriginal culture that predates it and has been present from its very foundation but is still so often imagined as absent?

Aboriginal Presence and Absence

Weir illuminates a significant aspect of *The Last Wave*'s approach to Aboriginal presence and absence when he speaks of the relation between Aboriginal culture and white Australian culture: "The Aborigines use the same word, *culture*, to mean something far richer than what we have come to mean by it. Here was a most interesting case where *we* had lost something since contact with the Aborigines—something *they* still had."[19] Weir's insistence that Australian culture must be imagined as an intermixing of Aboriginal culture and white European culture, and that this intermixing cannot be simplified using only the conventional tropes of Aboriginal loss and white gain, resonates with more recent attempts to theorize Aboriginal presence in Australian culture. For example, the Australian cultural studies scholar Chris Healy introduces the term "Aboriginality" as a way to reframe contact between Indigenous and non-Indigenous Australians as a cultural matter rather than solely a historical one. For Healy, "Aboriginality" is an "intercultural activity" that "figures indigenous and non-indigenous as coming into existence for each other at points of intersection," through cultural phenomena such as television programs, art, and museum exhibitions.[20]

By recognizing the value of a cultural space for "Aboriginality" that is not identical to the historical space of actual Aboriginal experience, Healy helps make room for the significance of cultural objects such as *The Last Wave*. Even though he does not discuss Weir's film, Healy aids us in seeing how *The Last Wave* combats the recurring problem of Aboriginal absence in Australian culture. As Healy explains: "The pre-eminent mode in which indigenous people are remembered in Australia is as absent. The evidence of this trope and its dominance is ubiquitous. We can find it in continental metaphors— the silent country with a dead heart—more broadly in the poetic and visual imagining of Australian space; and most powerfully in the founding faith of colonization in Australia, that land was there for the taking."[21] Healy refers here to *terra nullius*, the infamous Australian legal concept that asserts the continent was officially uninhab- ited when white European settlers first arrived in 1788. *Terra nullius* was not subject to serious legal revision until 1992, with the *Mabo* decision that recognized the possi- bility of Aboriginal title in Australian land rights claims. Even post-*Mabo*, Aboriginal land rights continue to be a point of painful contention in Australian politics.[22] But pre-*Mabo*, which includes the period of *The Last Wave*'s production, Aboriginal people were legally erased from Australian law's definition of the country's origins—an ab- sence of horrific proportions.

The Last Wave mobilizes cinematic horror to contest this horrific absence of Aboriginal people from Australian legal, cultural, and physical presence. The film's cen- tral premise, that ancient, traditional Aboriginal culture still exists within the modern, white metropolis of Sydney, is completely fictional. But Weir gives that fictional premise stunning cinematic presence through his commitment to fostering spectator opportunities to dream of Blackness, to convert Aboriginal absence into embodied presence through the language of cinema. *The Last Wave* accomplishes this goal through a variety of methods, as demonstrated above, but another significant method not yet mentioned is point of view.

Point of view (POV) in the cinema, conventionally understood as moments when the camera adopts a particular character's perceptual or psychological subjectivity, has been a topic of great debate in film theory in general and in horror film criticism in par- ticular.[23] While the arguments about the nature and effects of POV may differ, there is much consensus around the notion that it is a remarkably powerful cinematic device. POV is usually understood, by virtue of its relative rarity and formal flamboyance, as bestowing a striking significance on its bearer. For the character whose POV is adopted, an abundance of cinematic power is invested, even if only temporarily, in their perspec- tive. We see through their eyes, or think through their thoughts, or remember through their memories. In other words, POV grants a vivid cinematic presence to its bearer.

So it is no small thing that *The Last Wave* provides POV shots for its Aboriginal characters. If Aboriginal people are routinely relegated to positions of absence in Australian culture, then their presence through POV in *The Last Wave* is all the more important. *The Last Wave* was lonely yet not alone in Australian cinema of the time in terms of featuring Aboriginal people in major roles, but its emphasis on Aboriginal presence through unusual formal strategies such as POV makes it even more unique.[24] For example, after Charlie and Chris leave David's home we see Charlie conferring with the other Aboriginal men. We do not hear what they say, but then Weir grants Charlie a striking POV sequence that appears to explain what they are discussing—the Aboriginal men want more information about David, and Charlie provides it.

Charlie closes his eyes, and we are transported back inside David's house. Only now we see the house through Charlie's perspective rather than David's. Where Charlie was led during his visit from room to room by David and his wife as the dinner's hosts, now Charlie explores the house on his own terms, without any interference from others. Using a roving camera that simulates human movement through a mostly unbroken tracking shot, Charlie peruses the house's exterior, then enters the home through the closed front door (with the aid of an unobtrusive cut). He returns to the dining room and reexamines the photographs of David's ancestors that interested him earlier, then moves up the stairs toward David and Annie's bedroom. Charlie pauses to note the decorative artworks that line the walls of the house along the way, another subtle assertion of his own agency because it contrasts with Annie's guided tour of the art during his earlier visit. Then, Charlie was led by Annie to observe an Aboriginal-style painting she made herself. Charlie, who we know is also a painter because we see him at work in the film's opening scene, compliments her politely (through Chris's translation) rather than questioning this white appropriation of Aboriginal art. Now, Charlie casts his own gaze on the Western art that adorns the home. The fact that Charlie's gaze is accompanied here not by diegetic sound but by the same haunting didgeridoo tones that characterize Billy's murder scene lends his POV a sense of Aboriginal presence as well as dread. This is no longer a polite Aboriginal gaze complimenting a white imitation of Aboriginal art, but a potentially deadly Aboriginal gaze with looks that can kill. When Charlie reaches the bedroom to observe the sleeping bodies of David and Annie, the POV sequence ends suddenly with a cut to a close-up of Charlie's face painted with traditional Aboriginal markings and illuminated by torchlight.

It is at this moment that the POV shifts from Charlie to David. It is no longer Charlie looking at David but David looking at Charlie, causing David to awake abruptly and shout out in fear. But Charlie is no longer there. The face is gone, the doorway is empty, and now it seems that David was just having another one of his nightmares. What prevents this moment of POV-driven Aboriginal presence based on Charlie's perspective from converting into a moment of POV-driven Aboriginal absence based on David's perspective is the syntax of horror, where "it was only a dream" is never an adequate explanation. Chris has already taught us that a dream is a shadow of something real, and indeed David's "dream" image of Charlie in face paint is later revealed as a flashforward to the film's conclusion, when David kills Charlie. By fusing Charlie's POV and David's POV around shadows of murder that prove all too real eventually (encompassing both Charlie's killing of Billy and David's killing of Charlie), *The Last Wave* insists on a reckoning with horror that is not just about potential Aboriginal threat to whites, but real white threat to Aboriginal people as well.

The Last Wave predates John Carpenter's American horror landmark *Halloween* (1978) by one year, but viewers familiar with both films will recognize the formal similarities between Charlie's POV sequence and the famous opening of *Halloween*. In Carpenter's film, an extended POV sequence from an unknown killer's perspective stalks outside and then inside a suburban house, climaxing in the brutal murder of a young woman. The POV is ultimately revealed to belong to Michael Myers, a young boy in a clown costume wielding a bloody knife. The rest of the film takes place years later, with an adult Michael returning to kill again. The American film critic Vincent Canby, writing in the *New York Times* in 1979, discusses *The Last Wave* and *Halloween* together as two films he admires for their ability to achieve Hitchcockian scare effects. He praises *The Last Wave* as a "first-rate scare-picture," singling out the skills of Weir as he "manipulates our fears by gently distorting the commonplace."[25] Canby does not focus on POV specifically, but his sense of *The Last Wave*'s effectiveness as a horror film is worth noting, precisely because it occurs quite apart from the Australian cultural context and through favorable comparisons to a film that would become one of the most influential in the genre's history.

But by returning to the Australian cultural context, *The Last Wave*'s evocation of horror through POV becomes even more striking for the ways it differs from *Halloween* rather than resembles it. *Halloween*'s POV sequence reveals a killer who remains an inhuman psychotic threat throughout the entirety of the film. *The Last Wave*'s POV sequence reveals not an inhuman killer, but instead thorny questions about the human nature of killing, dreaming, and even of POV itself, stretched across Aboriginal and white subjectivities that always mix. In fact, when we juxtapose Charlie's POV sequence with other POV moments in the film, *The Last Wave*'s ability to complicate horror's conventional mechanics of looking becomes even more pronounced.

In another notable POV moment, Annie, alerted by her daughter, who looks outside to see the "Black man" the young girl thinks is a "witch," goes to an upper-story window of her house to witness Charlie standing in the street below. We observe Charlie through Annie's POV, in a high-angle long shot with Charlie staring up at her. Weir then cuts to a medium shot of Charlie after Annie has left the window, inserting a visual suggestion that Annie's POV is not only perceptual, but also psychological—she sees Charlie as a threat even when she is not looking at him directly. This suggestion is made explicit as the sequence continues, when Annie shrinks from the knock on her front door. "Go away," Annie whispers to herself fearfully, withdrawing from what she assumes to be Charlie's presence as her perceptual POV is reestablished (she sees a blurred figure outside, rapping on the door's thick glass). But then the knock is revealed to belong to her babysitter, not Charlie. Annie, overwhelmed with relief, finally opens the door and admits the babysitter. Charlie is nowhere to be seen.

In this scene, Annie's POV is activated so that we perceive Charlie through her eyes, as a fearful threat. But we are also made aware of how she has projected fear onto Charlie's presence in ways that are not substantiated by his physical actions. In other words, Charlie's presence is not a matter of purely objective threat, but subjective threat as constructed through Annie's gaze. The scene recalls Annie's nervous reaction to the earlier presence of Chris and Charlie in her home. Before their arrival, she confides shakily to David, "I'm a fourth-generation Australian; I've never met an Aboriginal before." When Chris raps on the door, the shot is identical to the one that will be repeated later when Annie believes Charlie is stalking her. So Annie's fear of Aboriginal presence is expressed cinematically, through POV, as a matter involving subjective fear of the unknown at least as much as any sort of objective threat.

The Last Wave also grants Chris a pivotal POV moment, during the courtroom sequence described above. While David is questioning Chris on the stand, we see, through Chris's POV, the sudden appearance and disappearance of Charlie in the audience. Charlie stares at Chris, his presence unseen by anyone else. With this embodied reminder of Aboriginal law inserting itself into the all-white setting of the courtroom, Chris abruptly changes course in his answers to David's questions about Billy's murder. Chris retracts his initial admission that he is a tribal Aboriginal person, asserting instead that David got him "confused." But through Chris's POV, we know that he is not confused at all—he has seen Charlie, and, whether through fear of his power or respect for his status as an Aboriginal elder (or some combination of the two), has decided to uphold Aboriginal law rather than white law.

As in Annie's POV sequence, the activation of Chris's POV returns us to an earlier moment in the film. During the dinner scene, Charlie challenges David's statement that men are more important than laws by maintaining that the law, in Aboriginal tradition, is more important than men. Charlie's distinction gains added significance when Weir reveals that it originated with Amagula rather than himself; Amagula served as a magistrate in his own Aboriginal community, and Weir studied law briefly before becoming a filmmaker.[26] So both within and outside the film, Charlie's Aboriginal presence in the white courtroom enhances Chris's POV as testimony to the existence of Aboriginal law in a space founded on the assumption of that law's absence. By investing Chris's POV with cinematic power, *The Last Wave* invites us once again to dream of Blackness, to see Aboriginal presence where there is usually only Aboriginal absence.

The net effect of *The Last Wave*'s network of POVs distributed among Charlie, Annie, and Chris is a decentering of David's own POV moments. There is no doubt that David's visions throughout the film, up to and including the last wave itself, provide the film with much of its most fascinating imagery. But by embedding David's POV within a network of POVs belonging to others, we come to realize that seeing through David's eyes alone is not adequate. We cannot fully trust his perceptions, nor can we assume that he (or we) understands fully what his perceptions might mean. When David reminds Chris that he is facing dire legal consequences for his actions, Chris warns David that he faces more trouble than Chris does. "You don't know what the dreams mean anymore," Chris tells him. What *The Last Wave* insists upon is viewer participation in the film's dreams of Blackness beyond David's guidance. If a dream is a shadow of something real, then David alone cannot perform the translation between dream and reality, shadow and act. We must attempt to fill in the gaps ourselves.

THE LEGACIES OF *THE LAST WAVE*

By way of conclusion, I wish to speculate briefly on how reframing the achievements of *The Last Wave*, as this chapter has strived to do, might alter our understanding of the nexus between the horror film, Australian cinema, and Blackness. In other words, what are the legacies of *The Last Wave*, and how might those legacies grow in the future?

Following its initial release in 1977, *The Last Wave* was attacked in the Australian press along with another Aboriginal-focused film, *The Chant of Jimmie Blacksmith* (Fred Schepisi, 1978), for leading Australian cinema "away from commercial values and genre filmmaking." Another Australian commentator, referring to *The Chant of Jimmie Blacksmith* in particular, said the film's director "should have known that films about Aborigines are box-office poison."[27] These sorts of claims, paired with *The Last Wave*'s underwhelming box-office performance and Weir's own reflections on the film as a "failure," have hindered the film from taking its rightful place as a pioneering achievement in Weir's career and in Australian cinema writ large.

In fact, the current limbo of Weir's critical reputation, stranded somewhere between art films and genre films, Australian films and American films, commercial successes and commercial failures, could be reframed usefully by placing *The Last Wave* at the center of his career rather than at its margins.[28] *The Last Wave*, which is connected as intimately to Weir's art films *Picnic at Hanging Rock* (1975) and *Gallipoli* (1981) as it is to his horror films *The Cars That Ate Paris* (1974) and *The Plumber* (1979), disrupts the entire conventional narrative of Australian film history as divided between celebrated art films with national significance and lowbrow genre films without national substance. Even more recent attempts to challenge this narrative, such as the documentary *Not Quite Hollywood: The Wild, Untold Story of Ozploitation!* (Mark Hartley, 2008), that proudly praises the achievements of Australian genre and exploitation cinema (or "Ozploitation"), does so by setting it against the art films of the Australian New Wave. The pantheon of the Australian New Wave includes directors such as Gillian Armstrong, Bruce Beresford, Phillip Noyce, Fred Schepisi, and Weir. The result? *The Last Wave* is as illegible to the project of *Not Quite Hollywood* (where it is not featured) as it is marginalized in many accounts of the Australian New Wave.[29] So *The Last Wave* is left homeless: too much horror for art, too much art for horror, and perhaps too much Aboriginal focus for easy critical or commercial success in the 1970s. But it is time for *The Last Wave* to come home.

Shortly after I began writing this chapter, David Gulpilil died. His death on November 29, 2021, inspired tributes from a wide variety of voices across the Australian cultural spectrum, as befits a man who was one of Australia's most nationally and internationally recognized actors. He was also in many ways the most iconic cinematic face of Aboriginal Australia, with a career spanning more than 50 years and appearances in everything from *Walkabout* (Nicolas Roeg, 1971) to *Crocodile Dundee* (Peter Faiman, 1986), from *Mad Dog Morgan* (Philippe Mora, 1976) to *The Tracker* (Rolf de Heer, 2002), from *Rabbit-Proof Fence* (Phillip Noyce, 2002) to *Cargo* (Yolanda Ramke and Ben Howling, 2017). But for me, *The Last Wave* will always be the first and most vivid memory of Gulpilil that I carry.

Apparently, I am not alone in this sentiment. On the critically and popularly acclaimed American dystopian television series *The Leftovers* (2014–2017), Gulpilil appears as an Aboriginal man named Christopher Sunday who could be an extension of Chris Lee, or at least a warm homage to the film in which Gulpilil starred as Chris. As in *The Last Wave*, Gulpilil's presence in *The Leftovers* suggests special access to mysterious prophecies about the end of the world. Gulpilil's role in *The Leftovers* is more tongue-in-cheek and self-referential than in *The Last Wave*—when a white character assumes that Sunday's ancestral song is the key to stopping an apocalyptic flood, Sunday corrects him and explains that his song brings the rain rather than halts it. Yet when Gulpilil reappears later in *The Leftovers* as Australia's prime minister, the effect feels less comedic than poetically just. The moment is brief and lodged within a complicated, hallucinatory series of plot twists, but still, the image exists. David Gulpilil appears here in a role that Australian history would never permit him to play, but in another sense, precisely the sort of role he had always been playing as the cinematic face of Aboriginal Australia. Through film, Gulpilil became a cultural ambassador of Aboriginal Australia to the world and in the process, became an ambassador of Australian cinema to the world. Without the films in which Gulpilil appeared, our sense of Australian cinema would be radically diminished. And without Gulpilil's ability to embody Aboriginal presence in those films, our images of the Aboriginal-European encounter that has always been at the heart of Australian culture (whether that encounter is embraced or denied) would also be much more impoverished.

While researching this chapter, I learned that Gulpilil was even more than an iconic actor. He was also a celebrated dancer, singer, and author. In fact, he published a book for children (based on an Australian television series in which he appears) not long after he starred in *The Last Wave*, entitled *Gulpilil's Stories of the Dreamtime* (1979). The traditional Aboriginal stories Gulpilil tells contain joy, wonder, and laughter, but also pain, loss, and, yes, horror.[30] I wish I had discovered this wonderful book in my childhood (I have now shared it with my own daughter), but perhaps I was even luckier to discover *The Last Wave*. When I hear Gulpilil's words in the documentary *Guplilil: One Red Blood* (Darlene Johnson, 2002), I am returned to everything he has helped to teach me about horror, Blackness, and Aboriginal Australia by keeping *The Last Wave* so thrillingly alive for me over so many years: "We are the brothers and sisters of the world. It doesn't matter if you're bird, snake, fish, or kangaroo. One red blood."

In Gulpilil's vision of one red blood, beyond distinctions between Black and white or even human and animal, I see a dream that is a shadow of something real.

Notes

1. Peter Weir, quoted in Pat McGilligan, "Under Weir . . . and Theroux," *Film Comment* 22, no. 6 (November–December 1986): 28.
2. Robin Wood, "An Introduction to the American Horror Film," in *Robin Wood on the Horror Film: Collected Essays and Reviews*, ed. Barry Keith Grant (Detroit, MI: Wayne State University Press, 2018), 73–110. On horror films in the Black American context, see Robin R. Means Coleman, *Horror Noire: Blacks in American Horror Films from the 1890s to Present* (New York: Routledge, 2011).

3. See Elizabeth A. Povinelli, *The Cunning of Recognition: Indigenous Alterities and the Making of Australian Multiculturalism* (Durham, NC: Duke University Press, 2002).

4. See Adam Lowenstein, *Horror Film and Otherness* (New York: Columbia University Press, 2022).

5. Much has been written on the relationship between dreaming and cinema. For an example that focuses on horror and mentions *The Last Wave* specifically, see Bruce Kawin, "The Mummy's Pool," in *Planks of Reason: Essays on the Horror Film*, rev. ed., ed. Barry Keith Grant and Christopher Sharrett (Lanham, MD: Scarecrow, 2004), 3–19.

6. My claims here and below are informed by ongoing critical discussions of embodied cinematic spectatorship. For a few landmarks in the vast literature on this subject, see Scott C. Richmond, *Cinema's Bodily Illusions: Flying, Floating, and Hallucinating* (Minneapolis: University of Minnesota Press, 2016); Steven Shaviro, *The Cinematic Body* (Minneapolis: University of Minnesota Press, 1993); Vivian Sobchack, *Carnal Thoughts: Embodiment and Moving Image Culture* (Berkeley: University of California Press, 2004); Alanna Thain, *Bodies in Suspense: Time and Affect in Cinema* (Minneapolis: University of Minnesota Press, 2017); Linda Williams, "Film Bodies: Gender, Genre, and Excess," *Film Quarterly* 44, no. 4 (Summer 1991): 2–13.

7. On Weir and Gulpilil, see McGilligan, "Under Weir," 28. On Weir and Amagula, see "Peter Weir on *The Last Wave*," interview on *The Last Wave* DVD (New York: Criterion Collection, 2001).

8. See Cliff Goddard and Anna Wierzbicka, "What Does Jukurrpa ('Dreamtime,' 'the Dreaming') Mean? A Semantic and Conceptual Journey of Discovery," *Australian Aboriginal Studies* no. 1 (2015): 43–65.

9. Weir, quoted in "Peter Weir on *The Last Wave*."

10. Ralph Ellison, "The Shadow and the Act," in *American Movie Critics: An Anthology from the Silents Until Now*, expanded ed., ed. Phillip Lopate (New York: Library of America, 2008), 192–197. My discussion of Ellison is informed by a rich critical tradition concerned with Black spectatorship. See, for example, Manthia Diawara, "Black Spectatorship: Problems of Identification and Resistance," in *Black American Cinema*, ed. Diawara (New York: Routledge, 1993), 211–220; bell hooks, "The Oppositional Gaze: Black Female Spectators," in *Black Looks: Race and Representation*, 2nd ed. (New York: Routledge, 2015), 115–131; James Snead, "Spectatorship and Capture in *King Kong*: The Guilty Look," *White Screens/Black Images: Hollywood from the Dark Side*, ed. Colin MacCabe and Cornel West (New York: Routledge, 1994), 1–27; Jacqueline Stewart, "Negroes Laughing at Themselves? Black Spectatorship and the Performance of Urban Modernity," *Critical Inquiry* 29 (Summer 2003): 650–677. I build here on my earlier discussion of Ellison in Adam Lowenstein, "Jordan Peele and Ira Levin Go to the Movies: The Black/Jewish Genealogy of Modern Horror's Minority Vocabulary," in *Jordan Peele's Get Out: Political Horror*, ed. Dawn Keetley (Columbus: Ohio State University Press, 2020), 101–113.

11. Ellison, "The Shadow and the Act," 194.

12. Ibid., 197.

13. Ibid.

14. Ibid., 194.

15. Eve Tuck and C. Ree, "A Glossary of Haunting," in *Handbook of Autoethnography*, ed. Stacey Holman Jones, Tony E. Adams, and Carolyn Ellis (Walnut Creek, CA: Left Coast Press, 2013), 642.

16. Tuck and Ree, "A Glossary of Haunting," 643.

17. Here and below, I draw on *Two Laws* (Alessandro Cavadini and Carolyn Strachan, 1982), an important documentary on Aboriginal Australian land rights. See James Roy MacBean, "*Two Laws* from Australia, One White, One Black," in *New Challenges for Documentary*, ed. Alan Rosenthal (Berkeley: University of California Press, 1988), 210–226.

18. On different forms of Aboriginal Australian media production, see Faye Ginsburg, "Screen Memories and Entangled Technologies: Resignifying Indigenous Lives," in *Multiculturalism, Postcoloniality, and Transnational Media*, ed. Ella Shohat and Robert Stam (New Brunswick, NJ: Rutgers University Press, 2003), 77–98; Meaghan Morris, "Beyond Assimilation: Aboriginality, Media History, and Public Memory," in *Identity Anecdotes: Translation and Media Culture* (London: SAGE, 2006), 105–123.

19. Weir, quoted in McGilligan, "Under Weir," 28.

20. Chris Healy, *Forgetting Aborigines* (Sydney: University of New South Wales Press, 2008), 7.

21. Ibid., 11.

22. See Povinelli, *The Cunning of Recognition*, 157–185.

23. See, for example, Edward Branigan, *Point of View in the Cinema: A Theory of Narration and Subjectivity in Classical Film* (New York: Mouton, 1984); Carol J. Clover, *Men, Women, and Chain Saws: Gender in the Modern Horror Film* (Princeton, NJ: Princeton University Press, 1992).

24. For further contextualization of *The Last Wave* beside other Australian films that feature Aboriginal people, see Colin Johnson [Mudrooroo], "Chauvel and the Aboriginal Male in Australian Film," *Continuum* 1, no. 1 (1987): 47–56; Tom O'Regan, *Australian National Cinema* (New York: Routledge, 1996), 57–59.

25. Vincent Canby, "Chilling Truths about Scaring," *New York Times*, January 21, 1979, 13.

26. See "Peter Weir on *The Last Wave*"; Diane Jacobs, "His Subject—Mysteries of Different Cultures," *New York Times*, January 14, 1979, 26.

27. See O'Regan, *Australian National Cinema*, 59.

28. For studies of Weir's career, see Michael Bliss, *Dreams within a Dream: The Films of Peter Weir* (Carbondale: Southern Illinois University Press, 2000); Serena Formica, *Peter Weir: A Creative Journey from Australia to Hollywood* (Bristol, UK: Intellect, 2012); Marek Haltof, *Peter Weir: When Cultures Collide* (New York: Twayne, 1996); Richard Leonard, *The Mystical Gaze of the Cinema: The Films of Peter Weir* (Melbourne: Melbourne University Press, 2009); Jonathan Rayner, *The Films of Peter Weir*, 2nd ed. (New York: Continuum, 2003); Don Shiach, *The Films of Peter Weir: Visions of Alternative Realities* (London: C. Letts, 1993).

29. See, for example, David Stratton, *The Last New Wave: The Australian Film Revival* (Sydney: Angus and Robertson, 1980). Even though Stratton's important book riffs on *The Last Wave* in its title and devotes a chapter to Weir (57–82), the film itself is not focused on as particularly significant in terms of the Australian New Wave nor Weir's career.

30. See Gulpilil, *Gulpilil's Stories of the Dreamtime*, compiled by Hugh Rule and Stuart Goodman (Sydney: William Collins, 1979).

CHAPTER 8

···

ZOMBIE ROAR

Slow Horror, Banal Supernaturalism,
and Colonial Memory

···

DOMINIQUE SHANK

The social geography of black life in the Atlantic arena was demarcated by
the blurred and bloodied boundaries between captivity, commodification,
and diaspora. Slaves did not so much leave one behind and enter another as
proceed involuntarily, propelled always by agendas and agents other than
themselves. With no itinerary and no directional control over their move-
ment, captives had no clear cognitive map to guide them through the transi-
tion from land to water, the shift from smaller to larger ships, or the passage
from coastal waters to open sea. The migration of the black captives was an
unforgiving journey into the Atlantic market that never drew to full closure.

Stephanie E. Smallwood, *Saltwater Slavery*[1]

A labor dispute between Senegalese migrant workers and their contracting company
spurs supernatural intervention in Mati Diop's *Atlantique* (2019). The film opens on a
construction site for a lavish coastal skyscraper. A group of shouting men congregate at
the site's office. Inside, the workers demand their wages, having worked without compensation for four months. The employees managing the office insist they neither have
control over nor access to the company's finances. The man heading the operation, Mr.
N'Diaye (Diankou Sembeme), rarely deals with the site directly and evades account-
ability for his exploitative labor practices. To no avail, one young worker, Souleiman
(Traore), speaks on everyone's behalf and pleads with the agents to pay them the wages
they have earned. With the dispute still unsettled, the men pile into the bed of a truck
and return home to Dakar.

The mise-en-scène creates an unnerving stillness and establishes the mood of the
film. The workers' unrest penetrates through the general languor, contrasting with the
shots of deserted, half-constructed buildings. Chiefly, *Atlantique* is preoccupied with
the stillness of the ocean, which serves as an objective correlative for interior feelings,

and ultimately, a repository for past and present Black pain. Each shot of the sea lingers, deploying time as a means to compel viewers to contemplate what it holds, encodes, and reflects. Slavery and its stain on contemporary Black life serve as the unstated yet familiar subject haunting the film. Zombies, whose deprived consciousness mirrors the subjecthood of the slave, figure centrally in the film and drive the plot forward; however, the most significant supernatural effects in *Atlantique* arise from the listless sea.[2] It stands as a receptacle for countless dead and a medium through which they are able to communicate within the living. The supernatural force of the ocean manifests in the ordinary, everyday lives of Black people who continue to endure losses and slow deaths in Senegal.

In terms of genre, *Atlantique*'s banal supernaturalism distinguishes it from straightforward drama or fiction classifications. Despite a lack of scares and general torpidity, it manages to achieve horror through its exploration of supernatural possession. In the context of scholarship related to the horror film genre, banality means more than stillness or mundaneness. Though this study will not venture into the realm of horror criticism rooted in psychoanalysis, Sigmund Freud's articulation of banality proves foundational for understanding the film's general approaches to horror. In his reflections on the uncanny, Freud provides a useful explanation of banality, which, for him, indicates a painful impression that is suppressed, and subsequently, replaced by another: "Since it was the *significant* components of the impression that made it objectionable, these must be absent from the memory that replaces it, and so it may well seem banal. We find it unintelligible because we would like to see the reason for its retention in its intrinsic content, when in fact it resides in the relation between this content and another, which has been suppressed."[3]

Although Freud theorizes about the psychoanalytic and individual trauma, his formulation might also apply to collective, historical memory. In Senegal, the content of a suppressed memory—in this case, the extraction of labor achieved through a system of slavery—is revisited through stories of the banal, everyday adversity and labor troubles experienced by countries formerly held under French occupation. Bertrand Bonello's 2019 film *Zombi Child* deploys a similar kind of banal supernaturalism to confront the fraught nature of Haiti and France's (post)colonial entanglements. In *Atlantique*, the sudden disappearance of Senegalese workers undoubtedly haunts Dakar, but it also brings to mind the devastating yet displaced memory of the thousands lost during the Middle Passage. Both films carefully negotiate the supernaturalism they deploy, always resisting a full return of slavery's suppressed memory in favor of telling a messier, though perhaps truer, narrative about the postcolony's contemporary labor relations. The authors of *Beyond Slavery* call attention to the gaps in scholarship looking at labor relations in the post-emancipation and postcolonial eras:

> The question of what free labor meant, in the very different contexts of independent versus colonial regimes, of contestations over who was included and excluded from the realm of citizenship, has proven an elusive one. All too often students of slavery treated its aftermath—freedom—as an undifferentiated unexamined conceptual foil

to bondage. Slave labor could be analyzed in economic, social, and political terms, but free labor was often defined as simply the ending of coercion, not as a structure of labor control that needed to be analyzed in its own way.[4]

Frederick Cooper specifically focuses on labor tensions pervading African countries from Congo to Zanzibar in the centuries following the official abolition of slavery on the continent.[5] He highlights Dakar—a major port in Atlantic trading history—as the site of a months-long strike in 1945 that represented an "overlapping and coordinated set of movements" involving "ordinary laborers seeking a livable wage, commercial workers a minimum wage equivalent to that of European workers, and civil servants full equality of benefits for all categories of workers."[6] Both films offer contemporary accounts of the postcolony as a site of labor trouble and economic gloom, contiguous to past moments in a longer timeline of history, and seek to preserve the distinctness of place and time in their representations. Through use of banal supernaturalism, *Atlantique* and *Zombi Child* attempt to bridge the gaps between contemporary, post-colonial labor conditions and the haunting memory of Atlantic slave labor. At the same time that the horrific is situated within the banal, the zombie elements of the film decrypt the violence and desperation registered in its representations of the migrant workers' everyday lives.

Like *Atlantique*, *Zombi Child* embraces banality as a mode of disturbance and re-membrance. It follows the mundane lives of French schoolgirls while telling a grim tale about Haitian vodou and zombie labor, all at a hyperbolically slow speed. The narra-tive centers on Mélissa (Wislanda Louimat), a Haitian exchange student who struggles to navigate the racial and cultural barriers between herself and her peers. Through her story, *Zombi Child* explores the lasting effects of French colonialism and Mélissa's per-sonal struggle to make her culture and experiences legible to others. By rendering the passage of time tedious, each film strips the supernatural of its sensational effects and forces viewers to confront a kind of slow horror. Evacuating the familiar and attention-grabbing aspects of horror that account for its broad appeal (e.g., vengeful monsters, gratuitous violence, suspense, or surprise) affords *Zombi Child* room to consider what else constitutes horror, particularly in the postcolonial Atlantic World. The film gestures toward the 2010 earthquake, commercialization of vodou, and modern labor extraction practices achieved through zombification; in other words, reflections of present-day horrors faced by Haitian people that fail to capture the attention of those who readily consume genre horror, like Mélissa's classmates.

Further, *Zombi Child* and *Atlantique* ask two questions: What counts as Black horror? and What does it mean to revisit the legacy of slavery with an everyday, prosaic super-naturalism? With films like Harold Holscher's *The Soul Collector* (2019) feign critique post-apartheid race relations in South Africa while indulging in racist stereotypes about possession, Bonello and Diop's films disrupt a layered cinematic and historical feed-back loop. By stretching time and slowing the pace of film, in contrast to horror films' typical formulas, they force viewers to reckon with moments that, once placed in con-text, are deeply unsettling. The waiting involved in experiencing each film simulates the experience of Black laborers, but never without disaggregating the specific violence endured by slaves along the Middle Passage, zombies compelled to toil beyond the point of death, or migrant workers braving unknown horrors in the hopes of earning a living. At the same time, *Zombi Child* and *Atlantique* appraise the postcolony through interrogations of national myths and the aftereffects of colonial exploitation on Senegal and Haiti. Achille Mbembe says the postcolony figures "an age" and "an entanglement" that "encloses multiple durées made up of discontinuities, reversals, inertias, and swings that overlay one another, interpenetrate one another, and envelope one another."[7] The postcolony holds a convoluted temporal position by expressing the past, present, and future all at once. Mbembe's description of the postcolony provides a useful framework for understanding the systemic horrors underlying *Zombi Child* and *Atlantique*.

Once the site workers in *Atlantique* leave their posts, the film gathers momentum, though at an unhurried pace. The site workers sing to lift their spirits during the ride back to Dakar, but Souleiman, the primary dissenter, remains visibly distressed and fixates on the ocean. The high-exposure shot renders the water and sky nearly indecipherable, uncanny, and fiercely white. In this moment, the frustration and despair that Souleiman feels distorts his perception—his single-mindedness causes him to see the world almost monochromatically, a view that the cinematography literalizes. He cannot conceive of any escape from his current situation besides sailing to Spain in search of opportunity. His demeanor during the journey to town, as well as his hesitancy to part with his lover, Ada (Mame Bineta Sane), during their rendezvous in the following scene, suggests that Souleiman is in the middle of making a life-altering decision, but one that offers only the illusion of choice.

Ada, however, does not understand the extent of Souleiman's precarity. She initially resents his fixation on the sea, which seems to leave him distracted and unable to be present. Her displeasure with his distant behavior stems from her desire to imagine their future together. Their respective preoccupations are more aligned than might initially appear: the difficulty they find in forging a stable and socially acceptable relationship is underpinned by deeper forms of adversity. Their community—like others that bear the scars of past colonial conditions—struggles economically. As a result, dysfunctional social practices, including unhappy arranged marriages and migrant contract labor, persist. Ada fails to acknowledge that their affair distracts them from two otherwise bruising realities: Souleiman does not have the means to support a wife or family, and Ada has been pledged to marry another man, Omar, to secure herself and her family. The sea holds the history they are trying to move past as well as a potential escape from present circumstances.

Ada and Souleiman's individual situations exemplify the hardships their community faces daily. The town to which they return, Dakar, houses the families for which they are expected to provide. However, as the opening labor dispute makes clear, they cannot do so. This collective incapacity to provide for others or achieve upward socioeconomic mobility compels the men, including Souleiman, to board a ship bound for Spain in search of opportunity. Rather than confide in Ada and face her supplications to remain, Souleiman lets her believe that she will reunite with him later on. Unfortunately, as the film's title suggests, the Atlantic determines how Souleiman and Ada's story unfolds. The men tragically disappear at sea, never to return, leaving behind the young women who love them.

Once Ada heads to the local club expecting to see Souleiman, she finds that he and the others have departed. Young women huddle in small groups, comforting one another and exchanging scant details about the men's departure. At this moment, the ocean becomes more than an emblem of opportunity, escape, or disappearance. As if embarking on her own journey, Ada wanders along the shoreline, turning to the sea for answers about Souleiman's fate. The ensuing shot captures only the horizon and the ocean within the field of vision. The sensation of seeing only the sky and water in every direction, without having a clear sense of direction or focus, simulates the experience of the men who went to sea. These shots are reproduced throughout the film, visually capturing not only Ada's attempts to see through her lover's eyes but also depicting passage through the Atlantic generally. Further, it seems that Ada's compulsive looking—and yearning—potentially exposes the generational wound caused by the slave trade in Senegal, which occasioned disappearance and communal rupture on a massive scale. The water holds the answer to what transpired once the workers left Senegalese shores but, without the force of the supernatural, would never reveal what happened or make closure possible for the loved ones they left behind.

Supernaturalism turns the tide of the film when Dakar's young women are possessed by the spirits of the recently deceased men—brothers, friends, and lovers—whose living likenesses appear only in mirror reflections. Shortly after the men's exodus, an unknown illness passes through Dakar, infecting Ada's friends and the young man investigating Souleiman, Detective Diop. The symptoms appear to include weakness, profuse sweating, and fever; after nightfall, the infected become possessed and take to the streets. Although possession is typically believed to transform hosts into mindless zombies, the film departs from familiar Hollywood tropes and opts to maintain the agency of the living and dead. According to Mbembe, through necropolitics comes "the creation of *death-worlds*, new and unique forms of social existence in which vast populations are subjected to conditions of life conferring upon them the status of *living dead*."[8] Thus, *Atlantique* uses the zombie figure to clarify its critique of current conditions in Dakar, where people are compelled to work despite earning unlivable wages and facing challenging circumstances. In this framework, the parallels that run between the possessed zombie women and the site workers are clear.

In the dead of night, the possessed slip away from their bedrooms and congregate at the home of Mr. N'Diaye, the contractor leading the Muejiza Tower construction project that galvanized the men's departure from Dakar. He is startled by the dozens of girls sprawled throughout the living room, all of whom stare in silence with glowing, frosty-white eyes—they are literally inhabited and ventriloquized by the deceased men. The color of their eyes invokes the images of the white waters that consumed the men as well as a longer history of African labor migrating overseas. They demand the $32 million in wages he owes "them" for the construction of the tower. Through the women, they voice their demands and warn N'Diaye against cheating them again. Here,

the living dead speak to N'Diaye, proving that the necessity for reparations extends beyond the grave and cannot be evaded. As their return proves, "[death] in the present is
the mediator of redemption. Far from being an encounter with a limit, boundary, or
barrier, it is experienced as 'a release from terror and bondage.' "[9] Like their enslaved
ancestors, the workers and the women are displaced to perform labor in service of
others. Construction on the tower places pressure on the Senegalese workforce to mi-
grate in search of work for wages. Whereas Black slaves' displacement in and around
West Africa during the colonial period was completely involuntary, Dakar's contract
construction workers were lured in under the false pretenses of earning a living wage.
The parallels between current and past conditions extend to labor management itself:
whether multinational corporations and investment firms, or slaving companies, foreign agents propel production forward at the expense of the local labor force and their
communities.

Women of the domestic space become the interlocutors who finally deliver justice
by compelling N'Diaye to acknowledge the site workers, pay their wages, and dig their
graves. With the invocation of supernaturalism in the form of the zombie figure, one
might expect horror conventions to follow. However, the film refuses to indulge in
features or stereotypes that might render its women violent or monstrous. The men inhabit women's bodies to communicate their own demands, and nothing more. Rather
than seek revenge, they simply request their unpaid wages. Their stillness, while not
sensational or particularly thrilling, terrifies N'Diaye enough to pay the deceased.
Through these women, the men who perished at sea are able to deliver a message directly to him.

The possessed also deliver important information to Ada, who desperately needs closure over Souleiman's death. One woman who is inhabited by Souleiman's friend tells
Ada what transpired on their voyage:

> It was quiet in the boat. As the sun was rising, the guys were quiet. I thought we were
> nearly there because I could see the mountain in the distance. I thought we'd reached
> Spain. . . . Then it all happened so quickly. A strong wind whipped up the sea. We
> were terrified by the power of the waves. Some were shivering with fear. Others were
> sobbing with distress. What I'd thought was a mountain was a wave. Immense. It
> lifted up our boat, which collapsed like a building. We were cast into the depths.[10]

The passage from Dakar—one of the westernmost points of the African coast—to Spain
conjures a distant reflection of the Middle Passage.[11] The sheer power of the massive
wave mirrors the depth and crushing weight of the colonial history that attends it (i.e.,
exploitation, displacement, disappearance). This description evokes imagery eerily
reminiscent of J. M. W. Turner's famous painting *The Slave Ship*.[12] Outside of a survivor's
account, the pandemonium and terror of slaves' final moments would not be told. Here,
Atlantique compensates for this silence through supernatural, if displaced, means,
through which the migrant workers' experiences are disclosed and recognized, indexing
the longer history by association. Without supernatural intervention, the men would

have been swiftly forgotten by their community; except for Ada, who never doubts that Souleiman is alive, and accordingly, never becomes possessed. The strange, abrupt, and unexplainable onset of the illness that overtakes Dakar's young women marks the introduction of the zombie conceit. Yet what produces a deeply unsettling mood is the nonchalance with which the community responds to the sudden disappearance of its young men. In fact, only the young women seem concerned about the incident. Everyone else seems preoccupied with preparations for Ada's approaching wedding. Additionally, the unfinished tower, dilapidated buildings, and distressingly calm waters give the setting its unhomely effect. During the daytime when they are not possessed, the young women also encourage Ada to forget Souleiman and embrace the lifestyle that Omar can provide her. The possessions not only redirect attention back to the fallen men but also furnish the collective memory of the living, driving forth the eerily reminiscent circumstances surrounding their absence. Put another way, the uncanniness that characterizes *Atlantique* is not contingent upon a set of personal traumas, but rather, determined by a collective history of slavery and postcolonial conditions of economic struggle, corruption, invisibility, and inertia.

The uncanny tension between martyrdom and state power is embodied through Souleiman's possession of Detective Diop. Diop has a responsibility to enforce the law—during his conscious hours, Diop works to locate Souleiman, whom he suspects of setting fire to Ada and Omar's marriage bed. Souleiman becomes a nuisance to Diop because he constantly evades capture and disrupts the union between Ada and Omar. Once night falls, however, Diop transforms into a conduit for Souleiman's spirit and is able to return to Ada to consummate their love. Through Diop, one body represents both containment through policing and rebellion through re-embodiment. In connection with Senegal's past, historical accounts of the colonies suggest that officials discouraged or outright prohibited the practice of African healing, protection, and spellcasting. Commonly, people who disappeared from, or rebelled against, the plantation were hailed as martyrs by the slave population. Martyrdom, in turn, inspired more resistance. It was difficult for European settlers to police African spiritual practices that eluded understanding. Diop similarly runs into dead ends during his investigation and ultimately fails to catch Souleiman. By leading the worksite dispute in life, dying for a cause, and fighting for his relationship with Ada in death, Souleiman emerges as a kind of martyr. Turning again to "Necropolitics," Mbembe thinks through the forms of resistance or escape available to those subjected to what he terms "necro-power," or the power to decide who lives and dies. In the case of martyrdom, he proposes that rather than becoming inert in death, "the [besieged] body duplicates itself and, in death, literally and metaphorically escapes the state of siege."[13] As the film suggests, totalizing power dissipates through possession. Beyond that, the empowerment long deferred and denied to the workers is finally realized. In making a state agent into a martyr's human vessel, *Atlantique* evacuates the state's authority, hindering its ability to restrict its subjects. Ironically, it is through Detective Diop that Ada finally learns how Souleiman's spirit came to be re-embodied: "I saw you in the enormous wave that consumed us. All I saw was your eyes and your tears. I felt your weeping dragging me to the shore. Your eyes never left me. They were there, within me. Pouring their light into the depths."[14] Here, the depth of Ada's love overcomes the depth of the ocean that separates them and the pain its waters bear. Unlike the story Ada is initially told about the terrifying moments leading up to the shipwreck, Souleiman describes how the thought of Ada brought him peace.

In moving beyond zombification and considering the ocean a body capable of holding supernatural properties, *Atlantique* achieves another level of resistance. By ushering the supernatural into the labor dispute, the workers' struggle functions on historical and formal levels, as if the spirits have hijacked the camera and drawn attention to the exploitation they suffered in life. Supernatural elements supplement realist elements, telling a story that cannot be fully articulated otherwise, at least not without disavowing the zombie myth or the resistive valences of local Black spiritualism. The belief systems of the enslaved, and those living under colonial occupation in Senegal, add complexity to the rigid and recursive capitalist narrative framework that threatens to subsume the specificity of Black subjects working within a postcolonial global labor context. This point is underscored when the possessed women employ N'Diaye in what they call the "real work" of digging their graves, suggesting that the labor involved in constructing his tower pales in comparison to the work of providing recompense for the disappearances, deaths, and debts he has caused. Nevertheless, N'Diaye seems more unprepared for the encounter with the zombies than shocked by it. His reaction gives the impression that he has swindled his countrymen before. Despite being an African man himself, N'Diaye perpetuates capitalist practices that date back to the colonial siege of the continent. Yet rather than simply designate N'Diaye as a villain—which he undoubtedly is to some degree—the film implicates larger forces responsible for the workers' deaths in a historical and generational sense. While the institution of slavery haunts this and other stories about Black labor, reductively labeling *Atlantique* as a film about labor threatens to obscure the colonial history of Senegal that the film continually gestures toward. In short, the uniquely supernatural elements of the film allow the Senegalese workers' stories to be seen and heard. Time and again, the frame is fixed on the ocean as if the camera insists upon conjuring some distant memory. The Atlantic was always more than a final, dispersed resting place—the ocean is the site of events and histories that lead directly to moments captured by the film. *Atlantique* takes a situation that was rendered unremarkable, and nearly inconsequential to daily life in Dakar, and places it in context, affirming its significance to, and continuity within, a protracted Atlantic struggle.

More affecting than the film's ambivalence toward oversimplification or overreliance on horror conventions is its practice of measured restraint. At the levels of both narrative and form, *Atlantique* emphasizes recognition rather than revenge as its focal point. While vengeance against a corrupt capitalist could throw the tension of the film into relief, that kind of resolution threatens to overshadow the particularity of the workers' condition by cluttering the narrative with a set of predictable horror tropes. Foregrounded by the disturbing circumstances surrounding their deaths, the reappearance of the workers instills a profound sense of alarm. Nothing makes their situation legible until they possess their female peers and the sea mediates their voices.

In a film that thinks about (in)perceptibility in relation to Black suffering and the specter of slavery, the labor dispute connotes *Atlantique*'s economic critique: in the wake of centuries-long extractive labor practices borne out of French colonial conquest, Dakar continues to struggle with economic conditions that compel workers to turn back to European power, risking their lives for imagined opportunity and perishing en route in a hauntingly similar fashion to slaves along the Middle Passage.

The zombie figure simultaneously exposes the scope of France's economic control, particularly over Black subjects, and the potential to escape the bounds of state power. Through ethnographic and historical work, Colin Dayan observes the social ambivalences associated with Haitian vodou, a tradition that unites African rituals with European witches, vampires, and devils. Dayan finds that the ultimate power of vodou comes through "possession," which is a far richer concept than is typically understood. Possession creates reciprocal relations between humans and gods that are ideally balanced in a single body, similar to the kind of seamless and agential union between the spirits and hosts in *Atlantique*. If an imbalance occurs and the spirit becomes dislocated, the individual is susceptible to becoming a zombie. Dayan explains that "[whereas] the zombi is the husk of the human emptied of substance—nothing more than a thing—the human 'possessed' can satisfy needs and impulses, can open up to a plentitude possible only because of the ultimate nonidentity of the spirit and the spirit-possessed."[15] Dayan distinguishes zombification from possession on the basis of mental fortitude, clarifying that successful possession is neither a matter of weakness nor imposition of despotism but rather a form of liberation. This distinction punctuates *Zombi Child* and begs the question of how the juxtaposition of zombification and possession might clarify the relationship between Blackness, horror, and bondage. The zombie's slippage between states of life, death, rebellion, and submission makes it apt for exploring the fraught relationship between postcolonial Haiti and its French inheritances.

Like *Atlantique*, *Zombi Child* is interested in linking the contemporary genre category of zombie horror to a longer history of transatlantic slave trade. France's detached and apathetic treatment of its former colonies finds its roots in the abolitionary period, especially in the middle of negotiations with Black Jacobin leadership, carrying through the reign of François Duvalier and into the present. For Christopher Taylor, Jeremy Bentham's treatise titled, *Emancipate Your Colonies!* set the stage for rapid decolonization and disassociation in the West Indies. Taylor notes that revolutionary France abandoned the idea of empire to save itself, hardly considering the ripple effects such a withdrawal would have on Saint-Domingue. Bentham proposes that "[so] long as France does 'not direct the raising' of sugar, French people 'need not trouble' themselves about how sugar is raised."[16] Bentham makes this proclamation knowing that the condition of slavery will not change for thousands living outside mainland France. In other words, the country made an active decision to abandon and ignore the source of its opulence. Taylor argues that Bentham's policy of indifference "casts into relief the violence of neglect that haunted the many emancipation programs floated by abolitionists," unburdening them, and pro-slavery advocates alike, from responsibility for the slave

colonies. The physical and racial divides between the French metropole and its periphery manifests in both *Zombi Child* and *Atlantique*.

Zombi Child seizes time and stretches it to unsettling lengths, leading some to
question whether it should be considered a horror film.[17] The film moves languidly,
subjecting viewers to its primarily white characters' experiences of time. Temporally, the
film's presentation of events is nonlinear, jumping between the present life of a young
Haitian girl attending a French boarding school and the reawakening of her zombified
grandfather in the 1980s. Clairvius Narcisse is exhumed, abducted, and forced to work
in Haiti's sugarcane fields. His Black overseers push him and other zombies to work with
increasing efficiency, regardless of their lethargic and semiconscious states. The sunny
landscape appears dusky and underexposed through Clairvius's eyes, suggesting that he
is animated by rather than fully aware of his surroundings. While he initially appears
mentally vacant, he has a tendency to wander. An unknown gravitational pull lures him
away from the fields and eventually entices him to escape to the hills. There, he recollects
images from his living past, including the wife he left behind. Slowly but surely, he
rebuilds his consciousness by recalling memories, locating his excavated grave, and returning to his hometown. After regaining consciousness, he reveals himself to his wife,
assuring her that "[it's] over. I'm no longer a slave. I will never be one again."[18]

By referring to himself this way, Clairvius gestures toward the overlapping, entwined
origins of slaves and zombies. The horrifying and haunting reproduction of bondage
labor in *Zombi Child* reunites the lived experiences of Haitians with the regularly co-
opted and decontextualized zombie figure. Throughout the film, white francophone
characters deny the existence of zombies, even as they fetishize them. Instruction in history at the boarding school centers on the French Revolution while omitting conflicts
that culminated in the Haitian Revolution. At one level, the film thinks critically about
transcoded colonial dynamics, particularly as Haiti continues to supplement mundane, bourgeois life in France through its continued production of sugarcane and textile
clothing. At another level, the film reclaims the zombie figure by ridding it of sensational
effects, thus challenging dominant narratives that seek to bury it.

The task of tracing the zombie figure in history, apart from the ghouls, vampires, and
ghosts with which it is routinely and wrongfully grouped, poses several challenges. Amy
Wilentz claims that the zombie's specter "sprung from the colonial slave economy" because it is "devoid of consciousness and therefore unable to critique the system that
has entrapped [it]."[19] She critiques the defunct yet recognizable explanation of the
zombie's prevalence in Western screen culture, and more recently, economic and political discourses—one reliant on the belief that zombies are inherently un-agential. In *The
Transatlantic Zombie*, Sarah Juliet Lauro finds that as the zombie myth is routinely co-
opted, transposed, and instrumentalized in Western contexts, each reproduction inevitably sublimates the figure's African roots. Lauro notes the figure's broad and expanding
recognition in popular media and critical discourses, particularly in recent years. From
the big and small screens (e.g., *World War Z*, *I Am Legend*, AMC's *The Walking Dead*)
to the streets during the Occupy movements of the early 2010s in the United States, the
zombie has been used as a universal symbol of sorts. With each evolution of the zombie

myth, Lauro suggests, its origins reemerge. "The zombie," she claims, "signifies . . . the positive, resistive return of the revenant and the specter enslaved, doomed to repeat."[20] For Lauro, the zombie has two constitutive components: the first as a specter of the colonial slave and the second as the slave's ever-present potential for rebellion. They acknowledge that the generic myth of individuals or beings who defy death appears far back in time and in many different cultures, but that the zombie figure is tethered to a specific historical context that defies both generalization and sublimation. Lauro also emphasizes the power of cultural myths and metaphors, especially those that emerge in colonial contexts:

> metaphors have weight and myths have real-world power: Have not accusations of cannibalism, the practice of dark magic, and even rumors of the raising of the dead justified various interventions and occupations of foreign lands, including the "birthplace" of the zombie, the island colony of Saint Domingue that became Haiti? In the figure of the living dead, as with most of its boundaries, the lines between history and myth, fiction and nonfiction, reality and the imaginary, blur.[21]

The problem Lauro identifies is how the United States—a nation with a long and ugly history of slavery—has exploited the zombie myth to critique a wide array of issues. The zombie "has come to be legible as a global mythology and interpolated in society nearly as a symbol, a kind of icon of disempowerment that can be made to signify everything from distrust of the government to fears of terrorist attack or viral pandemic to suspicion of science or a critique of consumerism."[22] This proliferation of meanings signifies a concerted effort to make the zombie myth about capitalism without acknowledging how slavery shaped capitalism's history. At the time the myth was formed, it helped African people to rationalize mass disappearances, captivity, and European invasion:

> This was seventeenth century West Central Africa, prime hunting grounds for Dutch and Portuguese slave traders. The myth serves as an attempt to explain life's cruel mysteries: Why were people disappearing? Where were they going? They were bewitched by sorcerers, their souls forced to labor in a desert land far away. Zombies at first explained slavery as an act of sorcery that steals the person's soul. Just as myths reconcile an unexplained natural occurrence (such as a solar eclipse) as having a supernatural cause, the application of this type of mythologization to a human phenomenon like slavery only further underlines the peculiarity of the "peculiar institution" as distinctly non-natural.[23]

For Lauro, the zombie myth not only reflects the state of enslaved Africans and transmutes history into folklore, "but also itself intervenes in, messes up, and resists 'history.' In a manner similar to the way all monsters trouble taxonomy, the zombie myth flouts the empirical impulses that seek, in labeling, categorizing, and defining, to conquer intellectual territories."[24] Considering the plight and experiences of people during the colonial conquest of Africa during the eighteenth and nineteenth centuries and onward, buys the zombie incorporation into the discourses of empire while, importantly, resisting efforts to sever its ties to colonial ancestry. In her 2013 book, *Farewell, Fred Voodoo*, Wilentz suggests the zombie figure "is the very purest form of the slave, deadened, soulless, egoless, empty-eyed."[25] Critical conversations around the zombie promulgate a similar refrain, especially in Western contexts. After all, rationalizing the constant appropriation, denigration, and refashioning of the zombie depends upon the assumption that zombies are mere cultural puppets, devoid of specificity, and available to imbue with meaning. While some have identified the linkage between the zombie myth and Atlantic slavery, few have speculated about how bringing the origins of the zombie into film sheds light on everyday, slow horror.

Time becomes a central source of tension in *Zombi Child* and demonstrates the disparities between life in France and Haiti. Mélissa, the film's Haitian protagonist, experiences culture shock in her new French boarding school. Although she does befriend her white peers, the latent antagonism between Haiti and France accentuates Mélissa and the girls' casual interactions. As the girls repeatedly express ignorance about Haiti, the film turns a critical eye toward white fetishizations of Haitian spiritual practices, which are appropriated for white consumption. Mélissa relocates to France after being displaced by a major earthquake and the subsequent death of her parents. As the only Black girl in the school, Mélissa navigates the tokenization, ignorance, and cultural insensitivity of her classmates, struggles that are exacerbated by her Haitian identity and family history. She befriends members of the school's literary sorority, who utterly disregard the details she shares about her past—like the fact that her mother won the Legion of Honor medal for fighting dictatorship and injustice in Haiti—and only become intrigued when she reveals that her aunt is a mambo (i.e., vodou practitioner). They call her history "fake" and imagine zombification as a form of living hell. Despite their refusals to understand or respect Mélissa, the juxtaposition of life on both sides of the Atlantic, and power, functions to bring two disparate realities into productive conversation. From the time of Clairvius's reawakening in the 1980s to the present captured by the film, the cushy lifestyle of white francophone elites and their children is made possible by the labor and inequality experienced by others dwelling within France's former colonies. *Zombi Child* intercuts scenes depicting zombie slave labor with scenes of the schoolgirls' chronic boredom. On one side of the Atlantic, the undead groan and toil under the pressure to produce sugarcane expediently. On the other side, the privileged whine incessantly, demonstrating their apathy and inertness.

The film dramatizes its critique of cultural commercialization and confirms several premises put forth in Wilentz's and Lauro's scholarship. Fanny (Louise Labeque), with whom Mélissa becomes the closest, and the others romanticize quotidian life using gothic clichés. They identify nearly everything as "freaky" or "gross" and call themselves corpses to pass the time. They gossip about Mélissa and watch zombie slashers, such as one titled, "Voodoo Possession," that turn the tragic history of the zombie into a farce. Regardless of their fancies, Fanny's storyline affirms the awfully real consequences of misusing and misunderstanding Haitian vodou. Fanny indulges in blissful ignorance, obsessing over Pablo, her proclaimed distant lover who is causing her to feel possessed. During an exchange early on, Mélissa and Fanny discuss their interest in horror films.

While Mélissa is able to see the distinctions between genre horror and horror verité, and distinguish the creations of Stephen King from the lyrics of her favorite rapper, Damso, Fanny fails to make such distinctions and conflates fantasy with reality.[26] Just as the girls begin identifying some of their favorite horror films, voiceover narration infiltrates and overtakes the scene. Hearing Fanny's voice at the precise moment when the girls discuss horror demonstrates not only that what proceeds in the film should be considered horrific but also how distorted the framework becomes when mediated via Fanny's experience. Beginning with this dialogue, she interrupts various scenes to reminisce about her summer love affair with Pablo and romanticize her pain from being separated from him. She finds the slow passage of time away from him particularly agonizing and describes the sensation in a letter:

> I count the days to half-term. I count the hours. Time passes so slowly here. We live in such isolation. We just work and wait. I try to take an interest here, in classes, in the others, I've met a new girl here named Mélissa. She's Haitian. She seemed as lonely as me. . . . She's odd, but we like the same horror movies and books, the same clothes and music. . . . I'd like her in the sorority, but we haven't decided yet.[27]

Mélissa becomes a sort of a distraction or a pastime for Fanny, used to alleviate her boredom and longing. Fanny minimizes the differences between herself and Mélissa, collapsing them into superficial shared interests. Fanny rapidly becomes obsessed with Mélissa's personal life, especially the parts that stimulate her interest in spells and possession. Still, her understanding of Mélissa amounts to a mere illusion situated in fantasy and fetishization. Notably, the terms upon which she relates to Mélissa—their clothing, musical taste, and interest in horror—all align with France's material and cultural appropriations from Haiti.

As Fanny spends time with Mélissa, her frivolous projections of horror into daily life intensify. She makes herself Pablo's zombie, saying that without him, she is "like a soulless body at night." When Pablo allegedly responds to her letters, informing her that he will not visit, she interprets her feelings of disappointment and heartache as possession. Rather than give herself time to accept the news and overcome her sorrow, she tracks down Mélissa's aunt, Katy, and asks her to perform "black magic." In exchange for money, she wants to reconnect with Pablo on the spirit plane. Katy is a Haitian immigrant and works as a tutor, dogwalker, and mambo to make ends meet. She initially denies Fanny's request but agrees to contact two spirits to restore Fanny—Feray for healing and Ogou for strength—after being offered a large sum of money. Fanny ignores several of Katy's warnings about the dangers of the séance, and subsequently, becomes possessed by a dangerous spirit because of both her and Katy's irreverence. The sequence becomes unstable and jumps between scenes: one, of the ceremony celebrating Clairvius, and another of Katy attempting to regain control over Fanny's disorderly possession. The juxtaposition demonstrates the spectrum of vodou spiritualism and the range of experiences possible within it. At the same time, Fanny's actual possession is far more disturbing than any fantasy or stereotype promulgated earlier in the film. Instead of experiencing the ecstasy she imagined, Fanny writhes and struggles against the spirit taking over her. The whites of her eyes turn black when Baron Samedi seizes control over her body and mind. After the botched possession, Fanny becomes a shell of her former self, losing all of her thoughts and memories. Rather than receive healing for her pain, she becomes a chwal (servant) used to punish Katy for her transgressions as a practitioner. He moves from Katy's body to Fanny's, and when Katy pleads with Baron to switch bodies, he asks her why she is "trying to please little bitches who are upset over little things . . . the day of your father's ceremony. So disrespectful!"[28] Baron confronts Katy for acting in service of, and putting Haitian gods in service of, an outsider for a frivolous matter, despite the significance of the day to Katy's own life and ancestry. The concurrence between Clairvius's anniversary of resurrection and Fanny's dispossession not only point to the force of vodou but also the desire of white French subjects to benefit from the very power France sought to quell in the past. Without the energy of vodou generated through Mélissa's personal accounts, Katy's spiritual practices, and Clairvius's reawakening, *Zombi Child* would not amount to a film, let alone a story, to any degree. The film, then, is a product of the Black culture and labor put forth to make it available for consumption. Fanny's story becomes the avenue through which this painstaking message finally arrives.

After spending the entire film following Fanny through her misguided quest to feel anything beyond emptiness and indifference, Mélissa finally intervenes in the story. As if relinquishing the narrative from Fanny's grip, Mélissa challenges her classmates, who still deny the legitimacy of vodou, saying "It isn't fake. Every word is true. My grandfather's real. My aunt too. And all the spirits, they're there. [Vodou] is beautiful, it's powerful. It shows that life and death are inseparable."[29] Not only does Mélissa set the record straight about her cultural practices according to her own mediated experiences, she also defends the legitimacy of Black life beyond the bounds of believability established by Eurocentric frameworks. Mélissa strives to make sense of her position straddling two worlds, neither of which she is entirely part of, and faces the kind of existential crisis that her friends only pretend to. The extent to which Mélissa's peers are merely products of an elite if myopic French education becomes clear. *Zombi Child* takes an interest in how formal education—specifically knowledge about language and history—imparts dominant narratives that seek to sanitize Western colonial histories. Mélissa's school exalts Napoleon Bonaparte's philosophies, and according to their literature lesson, the Balzacian notion of "neither a novel nor fiction. Everything is true."[30] During a history class lecture, the instructor discusses the French Revolution as an emblematic moment in time.[31] He identifies Napoleon as the man who "stops" the revolution, claiming that history from that period is incomplete and that true liberty was never achieved. He insists that what remains over time is a residual, subterranean ideal of liberty that never quite reaches actualization. He further suggests that the nineteenth century was a period unlike any other because people could imagine democracy, even if it did not come to fruition. The lesson is noteworthy for its total omission of the liberty brought forth by the Haitian Revolution. The instructor also fails to acknowledge how the destruction of French planting and trading strongholds in Haiti marked the beginning of the end of the French Revolution. Unwittingly, the instructor admits that France created its own account of revolutionary history; however, without any instruction about the Haitian revolution, the French students are unable to detect the historical dissonance.

As described by the authors of *Beyond Slavery*, "Haiti is often represented as a kind of black mischief, an entity taking the form of a modern nation-state but without its contents, the site of brutal tyranny and strange religious beliefs, its poverty as much a marker of its alleged primitiveness as of its exploitation by European nations and the United States."[32] This perception of Haiti is reflected in the film through the schoolgirls' interest in commercialized forms of vodou, and the history teacher's elision of Haiti from his account of the French Revolution. These misrepresentations of Haiti and its part in history shape Mélissa's opposition to Western teachings and foster her belief in the axiom that "everything is true." In her lived experience, history does not account for certain truths, especially the history taught by her teachers in France. For her, history is more fantastical and constructed than zombies, gods, and transcendental forces. Shortly after Mélissa first appears in the film, her voiceover prefaces the ensuing events, identifying them as an "announcement to the white world." During her induction into the school's literary sorority, she is pressured to share something deeply personal and important with the other girls. As she recites her poem, "Captain Zombie," it immediately resonates as a counter to the earlier history lesson:

> Listen white world, to the voice of our dead. Listen to my zombie voice. Honoring our dead. Listen white world. To my typhoon of beasts. To my blood rending my sorrow, on the world's paths. Listen white world. Negro blood runs. The slave ships' hold pours into the sea. The foam of our suffering. The fields of cotton, coffee, and sugarcane. The Chicago abattoirs, the cornfields of Indigo. The sugar factories, your ships' holds. The mining companies, your empires' constructions. Factories and mines are hell for our muscles on this earth. The foam of black sweat descends to the sea tonight. Listen white world. Listen to my zombie roar.[33]

Mélissa imagines the zombie as a being that demands recognition and accentuates Atlantic slavery's historical consequences. The horrifying and haunting legacy of slavery lives on through the zombie figure, but Western popular culture often recommissions the figure's subversive potentiality. This enables the continued sublimation of slavery within historical frameworks and the continued extraction of cultural value from the zombie. Susan Buck-Morss insists that while the "abolition of slavery was the only possible logical outcome of the ideal of universal freedom," liberty "did not come about through the revolutionary ideas or even the revolutionary actions of France; it came about through the actions of the slaves themselves."[34] The reality of a self-liberated, Black democracy does not support France's revolutionary narrative, so it is subsumed in French history. I posit that not unlike ghost value, which Diana Ramey Berry describes as the value placed on slave cadavers used to redeem insurance policy payouts or aid in scientific discovery, zombie value reflects the usage of the zombie, whether a subject or a concept, to perform labor.[35] Both forms of value stretch bondage so that it endures beyond physical death. The resistive valences of the afterlife collapse under the time-less and boundless reach of enslavement. However, as Mélissa's story proves, the zombie possesses the power to respond to, disrupt, and break cycles of oppression or erasure.

Zombi Child and Atlantique emphasize the slow horror constitutive of African and Caribbean life cast in the shadow of French colonialism and the ensuing labor trouble it occasioned. Given Dakar's or Haiti's histories of exploitation within the Atlantic trading system, the banality and supernatural haunting depicted in each film translates as pedestrian. Consequently, something as seemingly banal as the relationship be-tween Souleiman and Ada appears fantastical and at odds with the realities that de-termine their lives. Similarly, the most terrifying aspect of Zombi Child is not Fanny's botched possession but rather the realization that the French schoolgirls do not know of, let alone believe in, the inhumane labor conditions that Black people endure in places such as Haiti or Senegal. Atlantique and Zombi Child engage in the current fascination with the zombie figure as a kind of catch-all signifier of late capitalist harm and work to synthesize the contemporary discourse with its origins in the transatlantic slave trade, which is an origin point for the figure of the zombie and the global capitalist economy for which recent zombie iterations are a belated expression. They begin the long overdue conversation about the zombie's roots in Black diasporic culture and the role the figure should play in confronting the living past.

NOTES

1. Stephanie E. Smallwood. *Saltwater Slavery: A Middle Passage from Africa to American Diaspora* (Cambridge, MA, and London: Harvard University Press, 2008), 8.
2. For continuity, I will henceforth use the general term "zombie" to refer to the Haitian zombi as well as the gothic, Westernized figure, who I suggest are entangled and are pro-ductively appraised together.
3. Sigmund Freud, *The Uncanny*. Translated by David McLintock (London: Penguin UK, 2003), 63 (emphasis in original).
4. Thomas C. Holt et al. *Beyond Slavery: Explorations of Race, Labor, and Citizenship in Postemancipation Societies* (Chapel Hill: University of North Carolina Press, 2000), 3.
5. Cooper describes the trouble colonial regimes had in abolishing slavery, and representing themselves as agents of morality or progress, while they remained reliant on coercive labor practices. To maintain the flow of goods being produced on the continent, and hide the contradictions of such a system, European powers promoted the narrative that Africans were "peculiar" in nature since they presumably had little inclination to work and, there-fore, needed guidance through coercion until they could form their own systems of pro-duction and exchange.
6. Holt et al, *Beyond Slavery*, 144.
7. Mbembe Achille, *On the Postcolony* (Johannesburg, South Africa: University of Wits Press, 2015), 14.
8. Mbembe Achille, "Necropolitics," *Public Culture* 15, no. 1 (Winter 2003): 40 (emphasis in original).
9. Ibid., 39.

10. *Atlantique* (Atlantics) directed by Mati Diop (2020; The Criterion Collection).

11. According to contributors at Atlas Obscura, there is an ongoing debate among historians over whether slaves were held, bought, sold, and transported in Dakar or not. Nonetheless, the House of Slaves monument at Gorée Island, situated near Dakar, is a symbol of Senegal's historical relationship to the trade. As for Dakar itself, the city became a major industrial port following the abolition of slavery in the nineteenth century and is known for its "somber" and "graveyard-like" ambiance.

12. J. M. W. Turner, 1840, *The Slave Ship*, originally appeared in the Royal Academy of Arts.

13. Mbembe, "Necropolitics," 37.

14. *Atlantique* (Atlantics).

15. Joan Dayan and Colin Dayan, *Haiti, History, and the Gods* (Oakland: University of California Press, 1998), 72.

16. Christopher Taylor, *Empire of Neglect: The West Indies in the Wake of British Liberalism* (Durham, NC: Duke University Press, 2018), 78.

17. Andrew Lapin discusses how *Zombi Child* bridges the gap between Haiti and France by revealing their interlaced colonial histories. For Lapin, the shortage of terror or ardent tension in the film suggests that *Zombi Child* is not quite a horror film. While Lapin acknowledges that the film returns the zombie figure to its revolutionary Haitian origins, he criticizes Bonello for failing to engage with the colonial past the film evokes with adequate depth and attention. Further, Bonello does not examine the context that shapes the film alongside the gothic conventions, or lack thereof, within it. Despite the legitimacy of Lapin's critique, Bonello succeeds in complicating horror conventions to reveal disconcerting truths about the persisting, uneven power dynamics between France and Haiti. Indeed, Bonello's film calls for further critical engagement.

18. Bertrand Bonello et al., 2020. *Zombi Child*.

19. Amy Wilentz, "A Zombie Is a Slave Forever," *New York Times*, https://www.nytimes.com/2012/10/31/opinion/a-zombie-is-a-slave-forever.html.

20. Sarah J. Lauro, *The Transatlantic Zombie: Slavery, Rebellion, and Living Death* (New Brunswick, NJ: Rutgers University Press, 2015), 2.

21. Ibid., 14.

22. Ibid., 10.

23. Ibid., 16.

24. Ibid., 24.

25. Amy Wilentz, *Farewell, Fred Voodoo: A Letter from Haiti* (New York: Simon & Schuster, 2013), 97.

26. Alison Landsberg, "Horror Vérité: Politics and History in Jordan Peele's *Get Out* (2017)," *Continuum* 32, no. 5 (2018): 629–642, DOI: 10.1080/10304312.2018.1500522.

27. Bonello et al., *Zombi Child*.

28. Ibid.

29. Ibid.

30. Ibid.

31. Ibid.

32. Holt et al., *Beyond Slavery*, 11.

33. Bonello et al., *Zombi Child*.

34. Susan Buck-Morss, "Hegel and Haiti," *Critical Inquiry* (2000): 833.

35. Diana R. Berry, *The Price for Their Pound of Flesh: The Value of the Enslaved, from Womb to Grave, in the Building of a Nation* (Boston, MA: Beacon Press, 2017).

CHAPTER 9

....

AFRO-LATINX IDENTITY WITHIN LATIN AMERICAN HORROR CINEMA

....

MAILLIM SANTIAGO

SINCE their inception in the late nineteenth century, films have captured fragments of "reality" from the Lumière brothers' actualities to military footage of colonial invasions. It would take postwar economic and social depression for the development of one of the most enduring and influential genres to arise in cinematic history. Tony Magistrale claims it is likely that the "first" motion picture was a horror film, citing *The Devil's Manor* (1896, Georges Méliès) as the first vampire film. Magistrale states: "The art of terror, whether literary or celluloid, has always addressed our most pressing fears as a society and as individuals. Like any other art form, horror cannot and should not be viewed as separate from its social and historical context; it is nothing less than a barometer for measuring an era's cultural anxieties."[1] This was demonstrated for the first time in film history with German Expressionist films which featured geometric, abysmal, and shadowy sets that mirrored their dark subject matter. *The Cabinet of Dr. Caligari* (1919, Robert Wiene), considered the earliest surviving German Expressionist film, is enhanced by mise en scène that distorts physics with acute camera angles and impossible architecture, and a diegesis that reflects the perspective of its protagonist, a hypnotized serial killer. The film, written by Hans Janowitz and Carl Mayer, was inspired by postwar malaise and village legends recounted to both scribes during their time as soldiers roaming the German countryside during World War I. This transformation of postwar trauma into fantastical celluloid terror invigorated the depressive yet prolific creative circle in Germany. They mimicked the Expressionist style of the country's popular painters via cinematic codes that would spawn the horror genre and become immensely popular in Latin American industries throughout the twentieth century.

The purpose of this chapter is to examine the corpus of contemporary Afro-Latinx horror films made between 2010 and 2021—a time when discourses of Blackness in Latin American media rose to the mainstream. To look at this body of work in a range of national contexts is to tackle a complexity both similar and dissimilar to discourses of Blackness in Western cinema, particularly in Hollywood. Further complicating racial discourses is the idea of a monolithic Latin America. When "Latin America" is typically discussed, the term encompasses three distinct geographical regions across 21 countries: Argentina, Bolivia, Brazil, Chile, Colombia, Costa Rica, Cuba, the Dominican Republic, Ecuador, El Salvador, Guatemala, Haiti, Honduras, Mexico, Nicaragua, Panama, Paraguay, Peru, Puerto Rico, Uruguay, and Venezuela. The racial makeup of each of these individual countries is heterogenous, each with its own distinctive and historically specific narratives of race. Yet, the idea of Latin America and a Latinx diaspora is ubiquitous, especially in Western media-making centers, where these identities are treated as a monolithic, subaltern subject. It is vital to examine the presentations of Blackness in contemporary Latin American horror to reveal anxieties and narratives each country has about its racial politics in order to note how similar and dissimilar it is across not only "Latin America," but also in relation to the hegemonic Hollywood horror industry and the Afro-Latinx diaspora. As Rosana Díaz-Zambrana contends:

> [Through the] diverse repertoire of "the monstrous" in Latin American horror cinema, the subject is revealed in their fragile and conflictive humanity, in their debate against adverse forces and the unknown. . . . If fear "is not only a way of speaking about the world, it is also a way of acting," the visual image and the filmic discourse of horror provide us with an unfailing key to address ontological, political, racial, cultural, ethical conjectures, socioeconomic and/or gender-related to those unfathomable and overwhelming experiences in Latin America and the Caribbean that other genres are not capable of articulating.[2]

While horror cinema has been theorized as a political cinema in Western scholarship, such examinations throughout Latin America are complicated by the decolonial efforts in filmmaking of many Third Cinema movements across the region. Horror cinema in Latin America, particularly prior to the twenty-first century, has often been considered a form of exploitation cinema that has low cultural capital and is not essential to national culture. Also, because most of the countries in Latin America have some version of a film law or film fund that economically supports national productions, the horror film genre has suffered, as it is not prioritized for funding.

While Díaz-Zambrana's framework is important to this consideration of contemporary Afro-Latinx horror, there are other helpful frameworks within genre and horror that illuminate differences between representations and presentations of Blackness. Robin Means Coleman makes a distinction between Blacks-in-horror films and Black horror films. Blacks-in-horror films "present Blacks and Blackness in the context of horror . . . [that] possess a particular discursive power in their treatment of Blackness."[3] In addition, these films have typically been produced by non-Black filmmakers and are more often produced in mainstream film economies. On the other hand, Black horror films "are informed by many of the same indicators of horror films, such as disruption, monstrosities, and fear . . . they have an added narrative focus that calls attention to racial identity, in this case Blackness—Black culture, history, ideologies, experiences, politics, language, humor, aesthetics, style, music, and the like."[4] It is necessary to keep this distinction in mind.

In choosing the material, I was concerned with films that were distributed outside of each respective country's borders, particularly films that were exported to the United States or Europe where a Latinx diaspora is most prominent. This is important, because such films intend to disseminate narratives across the world rather than keep them within their countries' borders. Once those narratives are presented to the world, ideas of "Latin American horror" are discussed across media forums and genre-specific trade websites and animate the symbiotic Latin America–to-West media-making machine, where remakes of Latin American titles happen frequently across U.S. and European production. Each of the films discussed in this chapter has at least one Black main character who identifies with the Latin American country, is set partially in Latin America or Latinx-specific neighborhoods in the diaspora, and was distributed in some form outside of their respective country's borders. *El hoyo del diablo* (2012, Dominican Republic, Francisco "El Indio" Disla), *Saudó, laberinto de almas* (2016, Colombia, Jhonny Hendrix Hinestroza), *As Boas Maneiras* (2017, Brazil, Juliana Rojas and Marco Dutra), *Bacurau* (2019, Brazil, Kleber Mendonça Filho and Juliano Dornelles), *Diablo Rojo (PTY)* (2019, Panama, Sol Moreno), *Zombi Child* (2019, France, Betrand Bonello), and *Vampires vs. the Bronx* (2020, United States, Oz Rodriguez) meet the aforementioned criteria in discursive ways that reveal narratives of race spread through the distribution of the films to global audiences. Keeping Means Coleman's definitions in mind, *El hoyo del diablo*, *Saudó, laberinto de almas*, and *Vampires vs. the Bronx* are the only Black horror films in this examination. However, it is important to understand Afro-Latinx positionality at large when it comes to Latin American cinema.

BLACKNESS IN LATIN AMERICAN CINEMA

Salomé Aguilera Skvirsky once posed the question: "How do questions of race modify the specificity of Latin American history?"[5] When looking through the lens of horror, this question becomes even more specific: How do Latin American filmmakers construct presentations of race in horror films predicated on the notion of cultural anxieties? Where is the anxiety emerge from in these narratives? Is it within racial subject-object creation, as it is so often in U.S. Black horror films, or is race not articulated clearly within a certain country's genre filmic narratives? These questions reveal a distinction between U.S. and Latin American ideologies of racial identification. Aguilera Skvirsky explains:

> In Latin America, perhaps the most notable aspect of the conception of race is the prevalence of *mestizaje* throughout the region and, along with it, the development of national ideologies of *mestizaje* from the time of independence. . . . Despite the high level of miscegenation in the region, it was not until the time of independence in the

early nineteenth century that the *criollo* elite began to integrate the indigenous and Afro-descendant populations—almost always subordinating them—within the incipient national imaginaries.[6]

The myths around *mestizaje* are different in each national context, but predominantly alludes to the racial mixing of three "races" that create *la raza*—the Latin American race. These identities include the European settlers from their respective countries, their native populations, and the imported African slave population from colonial rule. The concept of *mestizaje* is not present in U.S. narratives of race, particularly as North American settlers were concerned with whitening the population and condemned mixing between races. Racial boundaries are much more fluid throughout Latin America than in North America. This does not mean there is genuine racial harmony throughout Latin America; rather, it indicates a different plight for racialized Latin Americans depending on the country and the geographic region. For example, in Argentina, there is a dominant national discourse emphasizing European ancestry within national identity, particularly due to post–World War II migrations. In the Caribbean, *mestizaje* is not commonly evoked, as racial fluidity in national identity is more widely accepted, especially given the migration waves from Black-majority non-Hispanophile Caribbean countries to Hispanophile Caribbean countries. In the continental United States, the civil rights movement of the 1960s saw Black Americans fight for rights, property, and cultural agency across a country built by their ancestors' labor and the systemic subjugation embedded in the state since the beginnings of the transatlantic slave trade. Similar movements have occurred throughout Latin American countries such as Argentina and Mexico since colonial times, but the hegemonic racial narrative of *mestizaje* complicates the visibility of the fight across borders. Latin Americans who advocate for the rights of racialized groups are often accused of importing North American discourses of racism, which are seen as an attack on both the cultural dialogues born out of decolonization movements and advocating for North American cultural colonialism. While some Latin American countries have amended their constitutions to protect racialized populations, the dominant response to racialized civil rights movements is a redirection to *la raza*— we are not white, black, or brown; we are the Latin American race.

Yet, what is conspicuously absent in various *la raza* discourses is the emphasis on whiteness as the most desirable of the three-pronged mixture, which is reflected in cinematic representations across Latin America from Chile to Puerto Rico. Additionally, each geographic region—the Caribbean, Central America, and South America—does not have the same racial makeup, which has led to a racialized hierarchy within Latin America itself. Certain national cultures prioritize formal Spanish grammar and countries like Venezuela or Uruguay are more strictly segregated than even some areas of the United States. The Caribbean countries contain the highest percentage of Black and Brown Latin Americans in their populations and dialects that exhibit a transnational influence due to their lucrative trade positions in the eighteenth and nineteenth century, often featuring words that borrow from Arabic and English. As a result, many continental Latin American narratives include perspectives that delegate *los caribeños*—an area of the world with many *negros* and bastardized Spanish—as the bottom tier of the Latin American hierarchy. The Latin American framework is useful to understand in how it operates outside of the region, but is also a framework that must be problematized. Throughout this chapter, I will speak to the national ideologies of race specific to each country, rather than to the region as a whole, with the hope that by the end of the chapter, the similarities and differences present in filmic representations and social constructions of race can be compared and contrasted to reveal what it means to discuss an "Afro-Latinx" identities in national narratives and in diaspora-specific narratives. If horror cinema is political cinema, what are the stories of most politicized people in Latin America?

SAUDÓ, LABERINTO DE ALMAS

In the early 2010s, Natalie Adorno wrote one of the first essays examining representations of Afro-Colombian identity in its national cinema. At the time of the essay, Adorno claimed that Colombia had been experiencing a "new wave" of cinema, largely due to the presence of filmmakers from the Pacific Coast of Colombia, a region with a large Afro-Colombian population. A lot of these films also were set in and cast actors from that geographical area. Yet, Adorno identified one of the main issues plaguing cinema from Colombia, a problem that could easily be transposed onto most of Latin America: Even if films are made, how can they travel outside the country given their stiff global competition?

One of the filmmakers profiled in the piece is Jhonny Hendrix Hinestroza, an Afro-Colombian filmmaker from Chocó on the Pacific Coast. His debut feature, *Chocó* (2012), a story about the rural environment in which he grew up, launched him to national fame. He cast non-actors, and the film was striking in its authentic portrayals of a different Colombia seldom depicted in media. Hendrix Hinestroza illustrates another Afro-Colombian experience in *Saudó, laberinto de almas*, which was released four years after *Chocó*. He directed the film and wrote the script alongside Alfonso Acosta and Alonso Torres. Hendrix Hinestroza explains that the script was written over six years, which included multiple in-depth interviews with communities living on the Pacific Coast of Colombia who practice Santería. During one interview, Hendrix Hinestroza claims a matriarch of one of the villages rolled her eyes into the back of her head and started to speak in "a strange language." She recounted a story about a *palenque*, a town in the jungle on the Pacific Coast that slaves would escape to when fleeing plantations. The groups of runaway slaves would perform rituals meant to make them invisible so that they were not captured again. This tale is relayed nearly word-for-word in the film's opening sequence: the screed ending with the town's name, Saudó.

Saudó is about an Afro-Colombian doctor, Elias, who lives in a residential city area that is never named explicitly in the film, but could easily stand in for Bogotá or other "white" cities in Colombia. He is a successful doctor-in-residency with a non-Black, Colombian wife, Sofía, and a Black son, Francisco. Throughout the film, Black patients arrive at the hospital who have an unexplained connection to Elias. The film ultimately culminates in a surreal journey Elias and Francisco take together to Saudó in order to resolve the ghostly spirits haunting both father and son. The visual and aural motifs to Saudó linger" throughout Elias's conscious and subconscious as the film weaves scenes set in the present day, hallucinatory flashbacks, flash-forwards, and sublime cinematography of the Colombian coasts and jungles.

The film never explicitly details how Elias knows where Saudó is, or what exactly happened to Elias in his past. The film is meandering and lyrical, full of hazy transitions to people-less jungle landscapes juxtaposed with extreme close-ups to the physicalities of Afro-Colombian bodies—past, present, and future in a cyclical filmic timeline. The sounds include disembodied voices calling father and son "home" until their arrival in Saudó and is as uncanny as their flashbacks to a past both or neither of the characters lived. The rich visual language of the film explores the landscape of Saudó as if existence in the runaway village is the birthright of Afro-Colombians like Elias and Francisco. In the washed-out, muted colors of the nameless metropolis, Elias and Francisco struggle to conform to the classist expectations of a white and mestizo Colombian society. In Saudó, the grotesque and eerily familiar specters are vibrant, curative in their horror, and protective of land and history. The racial politics of the film are never explicit, but they do not need to be. Saudó breathes life into its stitches, transposes timelines and narratives alongside each other with little transition or explanation, instead preferring to roam a cinematic landscape through cultural and visual motifs that recall the real-life legends of runaway towns during Colombia's colonial era. The film speaks its political truth through its design, not through its narrative. A fatalistic car crash is what sends Elias and Francisco to Saudó, and also what sends Francisco back to his mother as the visual representation of the event is intercut with the elegiac, slow exploration of Saudó, both in its first iteration and again toward the end of the film. This truth may appear as a refraction of Elias's mortality and sanity as image and character devolve into poetic wide shots of the untethered, coastal world of Saudó juxtaposed with Black bodies in a river. Hendrix Hinestroza probes a conundrum through the meditation of image and ritual: how do the stitches of past, present, and future reveal an Afro-Colombian history that is threatened with the cultural assimilation instigated by migration from ancestral homes?

The final frames of Saudó feature Francisco returning to the muted world of Sofia's care in the hospital where his father worked. The film fades to black with one final intertitle: "Life is a succession of cycles that rotate like circles among themselves, a labyrinth of hell." Throughout the very cycle present in Saudó—from disaffected, filial crisis to spectral hauntings to ethereal transportation to ancestral homes and back to filial disaffection—there is a reflection of this denial and realization of ancestry in Colombian history. Just as there is never any explanation of Elias's past, there is no explanation for his absence in the end; there is instead a juxtaposition of inherited realities. Elias's metaphorical and literal death transformed him into the cyclical benefactor of Saudó, whereas Francisco's survival condemns him to the cyclical disaffection in his struggle to assimilate to life under his mother's care. The film's meditation on ritual, image, and history problematizes the racial dialogue of *mestizaje* in Colombia by revealing various traumas inherent in Afro-Colombian culture. In *Saudó*, Elias is called to protect the ancestral home and goaded into murdering his son in order to be the sole heir of the land. This is revealed through vague imagery and incorporeal whispers until the montage breaks into stillness and Francisco's desaturated fate. Francisco remains alive, escaping the wrath of Saudó, but he is now fatherless, in a wheelchair, and tethered to the care of his mother. There is no harmony in the film's resolution or politics. In *Saudó, laberinto de almas*, Afro-Colombians embody the struggle between identity and ancestry as a labyrinthine hell. However, could this story be comprehended in all of its racial and historical nuance outside of Colombia's borders?

BRAZILIAN GENRE CINEMA AND AFRO-LATINX IDENTITIES

In Brazil, narratives of *mestizaje* are more foregrounded than in most other countries on the South American continent. Aguilera Skvirsky explains:

> In the Brazilian context, African cultural forms not only survived the Atlantic crossing and the period of slavery more intact than in the United States, but these forms in Brazil have also been more integrated by other groups beyond the black population. A large number of brown and white Brazilians practice African-derived religions such as Candomble and, in particular, Umbanda (Telles, Race). . . . Furthermore, the Brazilian government facilitated this state of affairs by not implementing legalized segregation and by actively promoting Afro-Brazilian cultural practices, sanctioning them during the 1930s and 1940s as distinctive elements of national identity.[7]

The distinction in how race is handled differently in contemporary Brazilian horror is demonstrated in the examples of *As Boas Maneiras* and *Bacurau*. *As Boas Maneiras* is a Brazilian werewolf film directed by Juliana Rojas and Marco Dutra. The film follows a Black domestic worker, Clara, who is hired to be a nanny for a white pregnant woman, Ana, who lives in São Paulo. After Clara moves in, Ana asks for more help around the house than detailed in her interview, which creates a racial tension reminiscent of *Black Girl* (1966, Ousmane Sembene). Rojas said of the film's inspiration:

> In most of our films, the story takes place in São Paulo. Thus we are very interested in showing São Paulo's social aspects, because that's part of the characters' lives. What kind of society do we live in? How does society treat us? It's part of our lives so we should portray it in our films. We always saw this film as a fairy tale in São Paulo, but we wanted to create a São Paulo that was both at the same time magical and realistic. So then it was important to have conflicts and political aspects present in the narrative. I think that the tensions we try to portray in the film come also from the idea of

duality and contrast that you have in every werewolf tale. The social difference and tension are also related to the city geography: the center that is richer and the periphery that is poor. This relates to racial issues as well: you have a character that is black from humble origins and a white rich woman.[8]

Further heightening the tension Rojas speaks of is Ana's increasingly bizarre behavior as the full moon nears. Incidents include sleepwalking, kissing Clara in one of these stupors and biting through to break skin, and a craving for raw meat and blood. The film focuses on Clara's perspective of these events, highlighting her alarmist reactions and covert remedies, which range from tracking the moon on her personal calendar to sneaking blood into Ana's daily meals. Instead of being repulsed by the violation of boundaries, Clara develops an affection for Ana that leads them to consummate their relationship in a night of passion that establishes their romantic bond. Only a few days after their tryst, Ana goes into labor with her son literally crawling his way through her stomach, killing her during the gruesome act. With half the runtime left, the film changes from a fantastical tale of strange desires and racialized love to a werewolf fable for temperamental children.

With this shift in narrative also comes a change in the humanity for Clara. In the first half of the film, Clara's narrative is central to the spectator. The viewer experiences all interactions with Ana through her perspective. In this first half, their lives are juxtaposed—Clara struggles to find a job to scrape by in one of São Paulo's peripheral slums while Ana oversteps boundaries by kindly, but obliviously reinforcing class hierarchies when ordering Clara around a large, impeccably decorated house. Clara does not initiate a sexual relationship with Ana and is instead literally cornered into the refrigerator by Ana. Continually in the first half, the viewer identifies with Clara in her moments of stress and desire. As Ana bleeds out on the mattress, Clara is devastated, kissing her lips and crying over the shell of her corpse until the reality of the situation becomes clear and the film flashes forward.

In the second half of the film, the simmering social critique and racial nuance of the narrative is relinquished for a self-sacrificing Clara raising her ex-lover's white son, Joel, whose werewolf condition she must keep secret. In the first half of the film, Clara is the image of resilience. She could have disappeared into the narrative if Ana's perspective was centered, but all information and decision-making around Ana's condition is filtered through Clara's perspective. While this prioritization may be subtle to the spectator, the identification is vital in understanding the critique of class in the first half of the film. It is not Ana's story that unfurls in a paradoxical tale of love gained and lost; it is Clara's story of emotional gain through resilience and love. However, in the second half of the film, Clara becomes the self-sacrificing Blacks-in-horror character as the film "replicates images of violence against Black Brazilians (a part of a larger cultural debate that has been reverberating in Brazil these past few years)."[9]

Instead of Clara reclaiming any agency lost through Ana's microaggressions and her biological child, she loses all sense of herself to raise this werewolf offspring. She ultimately fails, as Joel goes rogue in search of his father and victims. Her story could at best be read as compulsory love, or at worst, feral white violence. Her identity is subsumed by everything Ana left behind—a situation created due to social and economic inequality and underscored by racialized casting—which she chooses to take up as her burden for reasons that seem impulsive and nebulous. To the end, Clara remains faithful to Joel in spite of her best failed attempts to domesticate his lycanthropy, her all-consuming love revealing his humanity. Thus, by the end of the film, the narrative or triumph is not directly about Clara. She is a means to end Ana's arc.

In *Bacurau*, by contrast, the threat to racialized groups is treated differently. *Bacurau* takes place in a fictional village set in Brazil's *sertão* (backcountry). After the death of the town's matriarch, strange events occur, culminating in a third act that explodes with blood, resistance, and a different approach to racial politics than *As Boas Maneiras*. Dornelles explains the film's inspiration:

> We come from the big city, not from [the *sertão*]. We're from the northeast region, which is a huge region. So, the culture is very different there. We were always concerned about not making a film of people that we don't really know. So, I think this contact, this wish to use archive images and history, it kind of gives us more safety to walk into this terrain.[10]

There is a careful intentionality to *Bacurau* that also makes it a film with two halves—the first a rumination on grief and sacred cultural rites in a racialized geographical area of Brazil, and the second a genre implosion where race, class, and status intersect across horrors in spades. *Bacurau* is not often labeled as straightforward because it includes genre codes, from the Western and science fiction; however, it is a film that calls back a useful maxim: horror is in the eye of the beholder. Additionally, the film reflects Aguilera Skvirsky's postulation of a blended Brazilian culture more effectively than *As Boas Maneiras'* atonal racial contrasts. Religion is sacred to the townspeople—a mixture of *pardo*[11] and Black Brazilians—recalling scenes of Afro-descendant funeral rites and mourning rituals. The threat in *Bacurau* comes from the industrial world—the white Brazilian city elite who sells out racialized communities in the *sertão* for wealthy Americans who travel to the remote area to kill Black and brown Brazilians indiscriminately for sport. Thanks to the villagers' ancestral practices, a psychotropic drug native to their land allows the town to fight back victoriously against such barbarism. As effectively explained by Marcelo Ikeda: "*Bacurau* concerns several characters who complement each other and contribute different skills in their efforts towards a common goal: the very idea of community, and its salvation."[12]

Bacurau and *As Boas Maneiras* work differently, but both operate in the service of narrativizing racial differences in Brazil. *As Boas Maneiras* attempts to tell a tale of love overcoming all, including racial and social inequality, grief, and undisclosed illnesses, in Brazil's largest metropolis. *Bacurau*, on the other hand, depicts a struggle for native populations to remain on their own lands, salvaged by their connection to the earth amid the threat of outside forces, which include the city elite symbolically present in *As Boas Maneiras*. What saves the racialized community are their customs heavily structured around Afro-Brazilian religious and musical blends, and their sense of community, something that is both morally and culturally bankrupt in the elite who are outsmarted by the people of Bacurau in nearly every stitch of the third act. While narratives of Blackness are not explicit in either film, aside from the stark contrast that there are no non-white murderers in *Bacurau*, both features relish in narratives of divergence through social and genre codes. Each film ends up with a distinct solution to the problems of racial mixture, particularly as it pertains to social class more than it does to the color of people's skin. In *Saudó*, a split discourse surfaces as to the cultural rites of Afro-Colombians; the narrative is very specific to the singular experience of its Black main character and his ties to land. In these Brazilian films, singularity in the Black experience is not as clear, due in large part to the blended nature of Brazilian ideologies with its Afro-descendant past.

DIABLO ROJO (PTY)

Diablo Rojo (PTY) is a Panamanian horror film directed by Sol Moreno. It is also considered to be the first Panamanian horror feature film. The premise revolves around a controversial Panamanian symbol, *diablos rojos*, which are school buses retrofitted as expressive public transportation that travel up and down Panama's villages, jungles, coasts, and mountains for work and leisure. These buses were also one of the only methods of public transportation in Panama for decades. Michelle Watts and Kimberly Dannels Ruff further contextualize the vehicles:

> Diablos Rojos were introduced under General Omar Torrijos in a populist gesture. He wanted to take away control, and the resulting profit from transportation, from the elite. He intended to democratize transportation by allowing independent drivers to run buses (Upegui, 2010). These buses were essential in providing employment and transporting slum dwellers in the interior of Panama to the city, where employment opportunities are abundant, but the buses were not regulated, the drivers were not trained, and safety standards were not enforced (Müller-Schwarze, 2009).[13]

The symbol of the *diablos rojos* is essential to the various nuances present in *Diablo Rojo (PTY)*, especially 10 years after the buses were outlawed due to the various incidents reported by Panamanians. The film takes place in modern-day Panama in the Chiriquí province, known for its sprawling jungles. One of the drivers of the infamous *diablos rojos* (Miguel) and his assistant (Junito) get lost one night as they come across priests, police officers, ghosts, and witches in a bombastic tale reminiscent of Sam Raimi's early works, such as *The Evil Dead* (1981) and *Darkman* (1990). Moreno says of the inspiration behind the choice of centering *diablos rojos*: "Many times these buses were driven recklessly, causing several deaths on different occasions, especially due to the races that were held between Red Devils, to see who would arrive first at a designated bus stop. The drivers and helpers were quirky, so the movie is also about a Red Devil's chauffeur and helper. The Red Devil is the only shelter from the terrors of the night."[14] Additionally, Moreno's frequent collaborator, J. Oskura Nájera, wrote the script based on the *horror vacui* (fear of empty spaces) associated with the *diablos rojos*, while Moreno was interested in blending the symbol with the Panamanian folklore surrounding witchcraft. She continues: "The truth is, the popular stories of the Panamanian imaginary are very rich and can serve to feed the arguments of a few films, however the most popular stories arise from the syncretism between Catholicism, indigenous beliefs and other Afro-descendant religions. Most of the stories were instructive for good customs, they were also used to evangelize."[15] This blending is a thread throughout the film's outlandish scenarios, such as ghost-administered fellatio, demon cryptids, Indigenous warriors, and vengeful specters. Furthermore, the film does not demarcate racial lines subtly or explicitly unlike *Saudó*, *As Boas Maneiras*, or *Bacurau*. The main characters are both Black, while the rest of the cast could fall between *mestizo*, Indigenous, and Afro-Panamanian.

In Panama, ideologies of race are more complex than in continental Latin American countries due to a large West Indian population. This population migrated during the building of the Panama Canal in the 1950s, with numbers increasing throughout the century as construction continued. Throughout most of the Hispanophile countries in Latin America, the Black population refers to Afro-Hispanics, descendants of slaves in each respective country. In Panama, the Black population is not homogenous, as it includes this Black West Indian population and Afro-Hispanics. As a result, the Black population is fractured across cultural lines and "older generations of West Indians . . . continue to assert their black consciousness over their Panamanian nationality. . . . Thus, the articulation of race, language, and nation is problematic within Panamanian literary discourse because it is tied to a national imaginary that emphasizes *panameñidad*, or Panamanianness, and, by extension, *hispanidad*, or Spanish nationality."[16] The Panama Canal was a multicultural project that sets the country apart and further complicates in its racial discourse. Cultural coherence supersedes national discourses of race, leading to a marginalization within its own Black community, complicating the idea of what is Afro-Panamanian identity.

When Moreno speaks of syncretism, she refers to the idea of *panameñidad*, emphasizing Afro-Hispanic representation in her own film through its cast. There are neither social nor racial emphases among the groups represented in the film which focuses on somewhat standard dead versus the living, good versus evil conflicts. The film is a twist on the Indigenous tale of La Tulivieja, the soundtrack and musical cues recall Afro-descendant rhythms specific to Panama like *cumbia*, while there are witches more specific to pagan Christianity fighting monsters modeled after 1980s U.S. creature-feature films in a movie with two Black leads. *Diablo Rojo (PTY)* thus becomes one of the few films in Latin American horror in which racial diversity is present while absolving its racialized leads of the responsibility to represent those differences. Violence is endured on the basis of bad luck and folkloric wrath. Furthermore, there is no class-related subtext across racial lines; the film pays homage to *panameñidad* and its syncretic culture by embodying it in its narrative. *Diablo Rojo (PTY)* puts all Panamanians on the same metaphysical playing field, though the elisions of another dimension of

Panamanian identity complicate deeper readings of racial politics in the film. Yet, it is difficult to assign responsibility to address the myriad complexities surrounding Panamanian identity to its sole horror film with global distribution, particularly for a country established through direct colonial intervention by the United States. After all, the United States commissioned the project "specifically to enable the construction of travel infrastructures that would support strategic and military agendas and facilitate economic growth and influence."[17] Furthermore, a Panamanian national cinema is impossible to define clearly when the earliest films made in and about the country were by U.S. filmmakers for government interests. Lee Grieveson explains: "The celebration of newly created transportation networks was a central trope in government filmmaking, including in a series of films about the Panama Canal and the related expansion of economic and infrastructural connections with Latin America."[18]

In the present day, there have been many efforts by the Panamanian government and Panamanian filmmakers to establish a prolific national cinema. In 2011, the International Film Festival Panama was founded by local governments with the help of Toronto International Film Festival co-founder Henk van der Kolk. Since its inception, "IFF Panama is the only high-profile, high-capacity festival in the region that also focuses on the development of film industries in Panama and Central America. Only the Festival of New Latin American Cinema in Havana reaches more people, with over twenty participating theaters and screenings that accommodate thousands of people at a time."[19] Moreno is also active in establishing local opportunities for genre filmmakers, as she founded the Panama Horror Film Festival, one of the few genre-specific film festivals in Latin America and the only one in Central America. It may be too early to understand racial differences and nuance within a country that has a thriving but very young film industry, especially when racial groups in the country are marked by cultural difference. Nevertheless, *Diablo Rojo (PTY)* is a bold first step into the possibilities of representing the transnational influences and consequences of centuries of colonial and neo-colonial intervention. It is a horror film that seeks to represent all three prongs of *panameñidad* across its protagonists, villains, and folklore.

AFRO-LATINX IDENTITY IN DIASPORIC FILMMAKING

The construct of "Latin America" seems predominantly useful to address the diaspora of Western countries, such as the United States and France. Latinx populations are regarded as a subaltern, "minority" in countries with predominantly white populations, which is often where the catch-all monolithic assumptions of a "Latin American" identity are established. Furthermore, to be Afro-Latinx in France implies different racial assumptions than being Afro-Latinx in a U.S. metropolis. Two films can reveal these differences—both in method and reception through genre and folklore.

Zombi Child is a French film directed by Bertrand Bonnello that leans heavily on the Haitian practice of voodoo and the real-life story of Clairvius Narcisse. A Haitian teenager, Mélissa, is recruited into a group of popular white teenage girls, led by Fanny, at a private school in France. As Mélissa gets to know the teenagers, she reveals that she is an orphan due to the 2010 Haiti earthquake. As a result, she lives with her aunt (Katy), who is a *mambo*, a Voudou high priestess. While Mélissa does not detail her aunt's profession further, the white teenagers research Voudou behind Mélissa's back, with Fanny taking a particular interest in what *mambos* do. Plagued by an unrequited relationship, Fanny seeks out Katy for a Voudou ritual to unite her with her lover. Interspersed with this teenage tale are frequent flashbacks to 1962 Haiti, where Mélissa's relative is buried alive by white colonists, then brought back as an undead "zombi." Bonnello states that his influences for the film were *I Walked with a Zombie* (1943, Jacques Tourneur), *Les maîtres fous* (1955, Jean Rouch), and *Divine Horsemen: The Living Gods of Haiti* (1985, Maya Deren). He details this further:

> *I Walked with a Zombie* because, of course, it deals with zombies, and I wanted to see again how Tourneur shot the sugar cane plantations. With the Maya Deren, even though the text is a little dated, the images are fantastic. I was talking this morning about trying to find the right distance when you are filming something in a country that is not yours, especially a country like Haiti and that kind of culture. And I wanted to know how far and how close Deren was from the people she was filming. And of course Jean Rouch, always, because he was really close to the possession ceremonies he was filming and I wanted to see what kinds of distances he created.[20]

Here, Bonnello reveals a colonial gaze that permeates the film as Fanny appropriates Voudou culture, even going so far as to accuse Katy of racial prejudice over her reluctance to perform a ritual for Fanny. The protagonist is the white savior utilizing a traumatized character and her culture to serve her romantic means, a message that is never problematized, even by the end of the film, when Fanny is assumed to be possessed by one of the *loa* of Voudou culture, Baron Samedi. *Zombi Child* repeats many of the cultural appropriations and ignorance present in *I Walked with a Zombie*, a Blacks-in-horror film. Means Coleman explains *I Walked with a Zombie* further: "Though the film works to assert that slavery's history and effects remain at the fore for Blacks and their existence on the island, [the film] works to illustrate how filmmakers could not help but to dilute such messages with a postcolonial fantasy of primitive exoticism and beauty."[21] Years later, this is echoed in *Zombi Child* with the centering of Fanny's narrative, a fact that is glossed over in many Western appraisals of the film. Yet, in Latin America, the reception was much more critical: "*Zombi Child* is an *I Walked with a Zombie* version 2.0. There is not the crude racism of a 1940s Hollywood B-movie, but the age-old fascination of the North with the 'hot tropics,' a symbolic—and invented— space on which colonial fantasies are projected. . . . *Zombi Child* is divided between the world above and the world below."[22] Similar to the way images of sacrificial Black bodies in *As Boas Maneiras* served white characters' means, there is a comparable violence in the appropriation of Haitian customs, especially as Mélissa exists in the film for expository means. She rarely gets a scene to herself and blooms in the narrative in proximity to her white counterparts. The film is about Fanny and all her obsessions. The exoticism is insidious in its appropriation, especially when done under the directorial guise of being "sensitive" to the culture being appropriated. This filmic fascination seems all the more egregious when the Haitian film industry struggles to exist, yet French directors, cast, and crew are afforded the privilege of shooting a postcolonial story on its land, appropriating its customs, for a film that is often the singular result when contemporary spectators search for "Haitian horror films."

On the other hand, there are Black horror films like *Vampires vs. the Bronx*, directed by Oz Rodriguez, that emphasize the sense of community in Latin American subaltern communities in the United States, in this case, Dominican populations in the Bronx. Rodriguez describes the inspiration behind the film:

> It was December 2016, so it was a month after the election, so I felt really inspired to write a story that represented me and that had people who looked like me on the screen because of that event. . . . [Dominicans] kept saying [gentrifiers are] sucking the culture out of the neighborhood. You know, it's easy to make that connection to vampires. The Bronx has a big Dominican community too, and it felt like it's the last frontier as far as gentrification. . . . I wanted to show the community before [gentrification] happens just to showcase that this community is worth looking at and could be interesting and they could be heroes for their community.[23]

The relationship between the Dominican Republic and New York City has been depicted in film before, though not within horror. Currently, the local film economy of the Dominican Republic has been experiencing a production boom due to a film production law established in 2011. Yet, the cinematic relationship between the Caribbean countries and the United States dates back to the Spanish-American War, and has contributed to artistic migration, particularly due to the colonized economies of nations like the Dominican Republic and Puerto Rico:

> As the many films made and exhibited in the U.S. with the Spanish-American War theme evidence, the Caribbean entered into U.S. popular culture very early in the development of cinema. . . . Further, throughout the twentieth and into the twenty-first century, Puerto Rican and Dominican filmmakers have relied on transnational Caribbean communities to make productions cost-effective.[24]

Due to this proximity with the United States and more recent colonial interventions, transnational cultural flows between Caribbean countries like Puerto Rico and the Dominican Republic and the United States are more fluid than in other Latin American countries. This fluidity is reflected in dialogues of national identity, particularly as the racial makeup of the Dominican Republic tends to be darker-skinned than that in most of Latin America. In this tension are competing national discourses of race—a white hegemonic dialogue in the United States and a national identity dialogue in the Dominican Republic reliant on the equalization narrative of *la raza*. In an interview with Tamara Katayama, a Dominican immigrant based in New York City stated: "I have friends that [in the Dominican Republic] considered themselves white. When they came to this country they realized that they were not white. So, for many of our people the contact here has made them discover themselves a bit and begin to concern themselves with who they are."[25] This distinction contrasts discourses of *mestizaje*, Latinidad, Blackness in the United States, and a diasporic subaltern with a film like *Vampires vs. the Bronx*. Afro-Latinx people—from the child protagonists to their families to owners of bodegas—in the film are the heroes against a white, hegemonic capitalist blood-and-soul-sucking class. The film centers a blend of Black U.S. culture, Dominican culture, and the struggle against gentrifiers masked as vampires, a triumph of a narrative rarely seen in U.S. horror cinema.

However, this racialized distinction that reads clear to U.S. audiences and follows a racial discourse associated with the region is not as easily translated to the Dominican context. In *El hoyo del diablo*, also directed by a Black Dominican, Francisco Disla, a group of friends encounter a "devil's hole," a house where Haitians were brutally murdered during the dictatorship of Rafael Trujillo. The film focuses on a light-skinned, *mestiza* woman whose grandfather is revealed to be a part of the military regime that tortured Haitians. One by one, her friends—ranging from *mestizos* to Black Dominicans—are murdered mercilessly by spirits of the military regime for disturbing the devil's hole until a third-act showdown between Christian iconography figures (angels and witches) and the woman. At the last minute, there is a revelation that the woman's grandfather never took part in murdering Haitians, which is the reason for the vengeful, vicious haunting. In this instance, a Dominican filmmaker reappropriates the pain from Haitian bodies caused by a murdering regime for a horror film to stray closer to ideologies of *mestizaje* and the prioritization of Dominican life over Haitian pain. The fact that Haitians were murdered and tortured in the house becomes a superficial detail, an excuse for the film's bloodiest scenes that focus on the brutalization of Haitian bodies to emphasize the cruelty of these officer-spirits. This prioritization recalls the critique of *panameñidad* assimilating Afro-Hispanics over a West Indian Black population in Panama. National identity supersedes racial identification.

These three examples illustrate a problem that arises when reading Afro-Latinx films across the diaspora and across the geographic region. Even within identities stemming from the same country of origin, racial discourse in cinematic representation cannot be read in the same way. Furthermore, ex-colonial relationships within the diaspora often lend to a racist appropriation by non-Black filmmakers, as in the case of *Zombi Child*, that intends to be more sensitive and realistic to the subject matter and instead colonizes cultural tradition for whiteness and white audiences.

CONCLUSION

Across these examples from different geographic regions, variances in national ideologies about race can be compared. A commonality about the understanding of what it is to be "Latin American" is the three-pronged racial mixture of Indigenous, white settler, and African descendancy. To varying degrees, *la raza* discourse is utilized to cohere national identity for respective Latin American countries as well as in the diaspora, where to be Latinx is to belong to a subaltern ordained by hegemonic narratives. However, there have been growing movements led by Afro-Latinx and Indigenous populations to highlight inequality in media representations, both in the diaspora and within national borders. To be Latin American in a country of origin or to the perspective of outsiders often ties back to racial presentation, particularly as it is an assumption that often leaves out Afro-Latinx populations and has systematically erased their contributions to national cultures. When it comes to horror cinema—a transgressive cinema, a cinema of cultural fears and anxieties—the most politicized stories in Latin America are just as easily excluded. Furthermore, *who* has access to make films, and the experiences put to film, has excluded Afro-Latinx people behind the camera as much as it has in front of the camera.

However, there have been growing movements led by Afro-Latinx and Indigenous populations to highlight inequality in media representations, both in the diaspora and within national borders. Who is afforded the right to be Latin American within their country of origin or to the perspective of outsiders often ties back to racial presentation, particularly as it is an assumption that often leaves out Afro-Latinx populations and has systematically erased their contributions to national culture by eliding them within *la raza* discourse or excluding their contributions altogether. When it comes to horror cinema—as a transgressive cinema of cultural fears and anxieties—the stories of those most politicized in Latin America are just as easily elided or excluded.

Latin American horror is often lumped together to represent a heterogeneous region, which can lead to confusing and inconsistent interpretations of racial and national discourses that complicate homogenous readings of cultural anxieties. The land-dependent Afro-Colombian ideologies embedded in a film like *Saudó, laberinto de almas* is not comparable to the syncretic stitches of *Diablo Rojo (PTY)*, which presents an equalizing take on *panameñidad* and its folkloric horror. In Brazil, race can be as heavily problematized as in Hispanophile countries, though there is a strong bent toward Afro-Brazilian cultural traditions that have naturally melded into national culture, unlike in regions of the Caribbean where Black cultural rites remain siloed in Afro-descendant communities. When it comes to the diaspora and the stories exported there, as well as the stories made within its spaces, horror films aimed at foreign audiences reveal familiar racial dynamics, while those aimed at national audiences are fundamentally different and more racially ambiguous.

Thus, it is up to a responsible spectator to pull apart these differences per country and region, which can lead to rich experiences and nuances in how anxieties specific to racialized peoples present themselves in Afro-Latinx horror. Latin American horror faces distribution and exhibition challenges versus a global Hollywood hegemony that prioritizes filmmakers and creatives of the United States and Europe to inform cinematic representations of subaltern populations. Furthermore, the national cinemas of

Latin America struggle against a prioritization of a Spanish-language European cinema in global markets. Yet, if spectatorship prioritizes nuance and cultural difference in its engagement, the problematization of Latin American horror can lead to a recognition of diverse and marginalized voices in the region.

If Western audiences continue to project a monolithic Latin American identity onto foreign horror output, they reinforce the elision of differences in a cultural construct that spans several countries and geographic regions. If *Zombi Child* is to be read on the same level as *Saudó, laberinto de almas*, ideas of Blackness within Latin American regions become nonsensical. Furthermore, racial identity in Latin American regions often adheres to cultural-specific markers rather than to racial-specific markers. It would be counterproductive to detach generations of cultural identification to be specific to race, particularly as the racial makeup of Latin American countries is heterogeneous. Yet, a sensitivity to these differences, and understanding that national cinemas include *all* filmmakers within the nation and not a certain subset, can make Latin American horror cinema one of the most racially diverse, folklorically rich, and narratively complex in the world. The idea is not to impose racial discourses necessary to Western countries on to Latin America, but rather to understand the nuances of *la raza*, the problematizations of the ideology, and the ways that the blending of identities create a distinct genre cinema that could only be specific to Latin America, and how such a political cinema can uplift its most marginalized populations, filmmakers, and spectators.

NOTES

1. Tony Magistrale, *Abject Terrors: Surveying the Modern and Postmodern Horror Film* (New York: Peter Lang Publishing, 2007), xi.
2. Rosana Díaz-Zambrana, "Horrografías: Rutas transcontinentales del miedo," in *HORROfílmico: Aproximaciones al cine de terror en Latinoamérica y el Caribe*, ed. Rosana Díaz-Zambrana and Patricia Tomé (San Juan, Puerto Rico: Editorial Isla Negra, 2012), 5–6.
3. Robin R. Means Coleman, *Horror Noire: Blacks in American Horror Films from the 1890s to Present* (New York: Routledge, 2011), 6, ProQuest Ebrary.
4. Ibid., 7.
5. Salomé Aguilera Skvirsky, "Las cargas de la representación: Notas sobre la raza y la representación en el cine latinoamericano," *Hispanófila* 177, no. 1 (2016): 137, https://link.gale.com/apps/doc/A502652775/LitRC.
6. Ibid., 138.
7. Ibid., 140.
8. Juliana Rojas and Marco Dutra, "A Socially Conscious Fantasy Tale in São Paulo," interview by Guillermo Severiche, Cinema Tropical, July 26, 2018, text, https://www.cinematropical.com/cinema-tropical/a-socially-conscious-fantasy-tale-in-so-paulo-an-interview-with-brazilian-filmmakers-juliana-rojas-and-marco-dutra-on-good-manners.
9. Ela Bittencourt, "Black Brazilian Cinema: Directors and Actors to Watch," *Sounds and Colours*, August 4, 2020, https://soundsandcolours.com/articles/brazil/black-brazilian-cinema-directors-and-actors-to-watch-52852/.

10. Marshall Shafer, "Interview: Kleber Mendonça Filho and Juliano Dornelles on Bacurau's Politics," *Slant Magazine*, March 12, 2020, https://www.slantmagazine.com/features/interview-kleber-mendonca-filho-and-juliano-dornelles-on-the-politics-of-bacurau/.

11. *Pardo* is the Brazilian Portuguese equivalent ideology to the Hispanic-specific *mestizaje*.

12. Marcelo Ikeda, "The Ambiguities of *Bacurau*," *Film Quarterly* 74, no. 2 (December 1, 2020): 82, https://doi.org/10.1525/fq.2020.74.2.81.

13. Michelle Watts and Kimberly Dannels Ruff, "Drugs, Thugs, and the Diablos Rojos: Perils and Progress in Panama," *Latin American Policy* 3, no. 2 (December 2012): 202, https://search.ebscohost.com/login.aspx?direct=true&db=poh&AN=83148171&site=ehost-live.

14. Sol Moreno, "Q&A with Sol Moreno, Director of *Diablo Rojo (PTY)*," interview by Cult Projections, September 10, 2020, text, http://www.cultprojections.com/interviews/qa-with-sol-moreno-director-of-diablo-rojo-pty.

15. Moreno, interview.

16. Sonja Stephenson Watson, *The Politics of Race in Panama: Afro-Hispanic and West Indian Literary Discourses of Contention* (Gainesville: University Press of Florida, 2014), 2, ProQuest Ebrary.

17. Lee Grieveson, *Cinema and the Wealth of Nations: Media, Capital, and the Liberal World System* (Berkeley: University of California Press, 2018), 27, JSTOR.

18. Ibid., 33.

19. Jasper Vanhaelemeesch, "Starpower, Industry-Building and Regional Cinema: IFF Panama 2019," *Film Criticism* 43, no. 3 (June 3, 2019): https://www-proquest-com.mutex.gmu.edu/scholarly-journals/starpower-industry-building-regional-cinema-iff/docview/2509660677/se-2.

20. Joe McElhaney and David A. Gerstner, "Zombi Child and the Spaces of Cinema," *Cineaste*, Spring 2020, https://www.cineaste.com/spring2020/zombi-child-spaces-of-cinema-bertrand-bonello.

21. Means Coleman, *Horror Noire*, 67.

22. Heitor Augusto, "Zombi Child: Bonello, largue esse tambor," Urso de Lata, September 7, 2019, https://ursodelata.com/2019/09/07/zombi-child-bonello-largue-esse-tambor/.

23. Oz Rodriguez, "LAFS Theatre Rewind: Vampire vs. The Bronx with Oz Rodriguez," interview by The Los Angeles Film School, October 15, 2021, video, 3:52, https://vimeo.com/630224571.

24. Naida García-Crespo, "Caribbean Transnational Films and National Culture, or How Puerto Rican or Dominican Can You Be in 'Nueba Yol'?," *Centro Journal* 28, no. 1 (Spring 2016): 150, https://search.ebscohost.com/login.aspx?direct=true&db=zbh&AN=115648641&site=ehost-live.

25. Tamara Katayama, *The Racial and Ethnic Identities of Dominicans in New York City* (Scarborough, ME: National Association of African American Studies, 2000). https://www-proquest-com.mutex.gmu.edu/conference-papers-proceedings/racial-ethnic-identities-dominicans-new-york-city/docview/192411638/se-2?accountid=14541.

CHAPTER 10

HAVANA'S LIVING DEAD

Curation, Colonization, and the Erasure
of an Afro-Cuban Horror Cinema

JENNESSA HESTER

THE MYTH OF *JUAN*

CONVERSATIONS about Cuban horror cinema begin, and typically end, with the mythic *Juan de los muertos (Juan of the Dead)*.[1] Even before entering the international festival circuit in 2011, Alejandro Brugués's comedy of the undead was already making a name for itself as the nation's very first foray into the genre. While the exact origin point of this reputation remains somewhat murky, it first found footing with the public by way of pop entertainment website LatinoReview, which secured initial exclusivity rights to the film's teaser. "Check this out," the trailer's debut post implored: "This crazy filmmaker [Brugués] got some coin in Spain, got a Red Camera, some adventurous crew members, went to friggin' communist Cuba, smuggled bodyparts in suitcases through customs and made that country's FIRST HORROR FILM! That takes some serious cojones folks! My mind is still blown how they managed to pull this off."[2]

The declaration spread like wildfire through the blogosphere, and by the time *Juan* reached foreign shores, horror fans were ready and waiting to treat the movie as a "sort of homecoming" for Havana cinema within the rest of the world. *Juan* found itself met by choruses of "uproarious applause" wherever it went, its praises sung by an international family bound not by any common bloodline, but by a common interest in blood spilt—and in this case, spilt by the latest gruesome messiah of the silver screen, that brave director Brugués who defied Cuban norms to come home, at long last, to his terror-loving flock.[3] These praises echoed into the filmophile mainstream, with *Juan* ascending in status to become a slayer of "Cuban sacred cows" and a reflection of "growing cinematic freedom in a country where open criticism of the political system is barely tolerated"—defiance only possible because the movie was "embedded in the constructs of a popular action genre," that of the contemporary zombie flick.[4] As Cuba's very first horror film, *Juan* signified a liberation of the nation through on-screen degradation, a real-world revolution by way of celluloid bloodletting. By all accounts, Brugués's "serious cojones" had paid off tremendously, both for himself as an up-and-coming independent movie maker, as well as for global cinema as an institution of aesthetic freedom.

The only problem with this story is that *Juan de los muertos* is not, in fact, Cuba's first horror film. Even on its surface, this statement is a rather ridiculous one, as viewers need only watch a movie like 1985's ¡*Vampiros en La Habana!* (*Vampires in Havana*) for proof of a historic generic movement within the island, albeit an admittedly small one.[5] However, these sorts of mix-ups happen all the time—both intentionally to hide traces of derivation in marketing and unintentionally as a general social consequence of the flow of time. To this end, merely debunking the myth of *Juan* is not particularly noteworthy. Rather, what makes this fable of reception so interesting—and so *concerning*— is the ease with which it found global acceptance. Cuban cinema is nearly as old as its more famous counterparts in countries like the United States, and it is doubtless as storied as other national film movements. How, then, does a myth take hold that horror somehow never penetrated the island's movie theaters until 2011? Why has it been so easy for people to accept the idea that the entire country of Cuba, despite fostering an exceedingly diverse range of filmmakers whose work spans over a hundred years of imperial, revolutionary, and post-revolutionary social and aesthetic discourse, somehow never managed to produce a single frightening film? Most importantly, what terrors were subtly wiped away in this process of historical erasure, and what expressions of horror were obscured by treating the myth of *Juan* as a decisive origin point for Cuban horror cinema?

To answer these questions, this chapter introduces the concept of *curatorial colonization* to argue that genre labels function as a subjective (and in many cases, subjecting) aesthetic lexicon by which we determine what forms of expression qualify as "genuine"—in this case study, what counts as true horror, and what does not. This process of classification has perniciously inflected global understandings of Cuban cinema with imperial conceptions of whiteness, resulting in the erasure of Afro-Cuban subjection as constitutive of actual horror. Through a rereading, or more accurately a *re-curation*, of Tomás Gutiérrez Alea's 1976 film *La última cena* (*The Last Supper*) as a horror text, this chapter demonstrates how the genre and its fans have unassumingly swept away narratives of Black marginalization and terror. In doing so, this essay also provides a potential pathway toward resurrecting Afro-Cuban experiences from the graveyards of Havana cinema.[6]

CURATORIAL COLONIZATION

Scholars long ago disavowed film studies of the notion that genre in some way exceeds or is exempt from political ideology. Rather, genre pictures "are intimately imbricated within larger cultural discourses as well as political ones," functioning as part of a socio-industrial system founded on the interplay between primary cinematic texts, secondary paratextual materials, and acculturated audience expectations.[7] Yet despite this overwhelming acceptance of genre as an inherently loaded aspect of the cinema—acceptance both academically as well as popularly, as seen in the widespread adoption of scholastic terms like Carol Clover's *Final Girl* within slasher fandoms and even noncinematic publics[8]—most still treat the process of generic classification as largely divorced from questions of ideology, as something only tangentially related to the issues of audience conditioning mentioned above. In this way, while one might shudder (in fear or delight) at what horror films choose to depict and subsequently ponder the deeper social motivations for such inclusions, the decision of whether something actually falls into this classificatory category tends to revolve around surface aesthetics to the exclusion of anything else. When one critiques a zombie flick, for example, their analysis typically revolves around the nature of the zombies depicted on screen or adjacent elements of narrative, thematic, or formal concern. The analyst takes for granted that the feature in question is clearly and indelibly linked with horror as a genre; they do not feel a need to break down why elements like revived corpses are constitutive of horror, and instead focus their critique on a particular textual representation of said elements. After all, it goes without saying that stories of the living dead are also tales of terror, so why even bring that fact up (let alone interrogate it)?[9]

Though this impulse against definitional introspection makes sense on a case-by-case basis—for instance, little to no immediate harm is done by simply slapping the horror label on *Juan de los muertos* and moving on—the overwhelming systematization of such an evasive critical methodology carries with it serious consequences. Specifically, the silences surrounding questions of generic classification have laid the groundwork for a subtle form of ideological pollution here called *curatorial colonization*. Pulling upon Kenneth Coutts-Smith's similarly phrased notion of cultural colonialism, this new term shares the scholar's belief that "the dynamics of culture . . . tend towards the freezing of concepts supportive to the interests of a dominant minority within that society." This process transforms ideas that arose to solve legitimate concerns, such as the need to delineate between types of films, into ideological nodes "cited in justification of attempts . . . to maintain the status quo."[10] In other words, through the repeated use of common genre labels, critics perpetuate a system by which an oppressive order reinforces itself.

Curatorial colonization further builds upon this concept by looking beyond what vestiges of culture include within themselves. In the context of cinematic taxonomy, this means that the critical point of departure is not (to return to the previous example) the problem of whether calling zombies *horrific* may function as a form of subjection; scholars have amply covered such concerns, and continue to do so, through their close readings of specific texts. Rather, curatorial colonization provides an additional interpretive lens through which we might determine how the process of excluding certain things from a label—as is the nature of curation, an act which communalizes by way of segregation—upholds the same absolutes noted by Coutts-Smith, but in an even more insidious way. Within this framework, the question shifts from "why is X a zombie movie?," an interrogation of why a cultural object was represented as terrifying, to "why *isn't* Y a zombie movie?," an interrogation of that cultural object's exclusion from horror representation. This important change makes clear the forces through which the myth of *Juan* gained discursive power, and through which Cuban Blackness found itself whitewashed away.

CURATING A (WHITE) CUBAN CINEMA

Discourses on Cuban filmmaking locate it almost entirely within the context of revolutionary struggle. At its broadest, many of the island's movies find inclusion within the grand aesthetic movement known as New Latin American Cinema, which encompasses a majority of Central and South American nations.[11] As leading scholar in the field Ana López describes, this semi-organized collective proved distinct from both Hollywood and other "New" forms of moving image art precisely for its insurgent aims; the fact that it was "political cinema committed to praxis and to the socio-political investigation and transformation of the underdevelopment that characterizes Latin America" was the entire point, therefore it "cannot be properly understood in isolation from political, social, economic, cultural, and aesthetic forces."[12]

Narrowing in, Cuban movies also find themselves defined by the term Third Cinema, originally proposed by Fernando Solonas and Octavio Getino in 1969. Following the rise of both a "new historical situation and a new man born in the process of the anti-imperialist struggle," the duo argued that the fresh filmmaking practices they saw gaining traction in nations like Cuba—practices structured in opposition, they believed, to a first wave of movie production erected by the Hollywood studio system, and a second wave grounded in French theories of auteurism—constituted at long last a true "*cinema of subversion.*"[13] From this perspective, the island had finally combined silver screen aesthetics with a revolutionary proletariat ideology. Its cinematic output now necessarily functioned as an extension of "[t]he anti-imperialist struggles of the peoples of the Third World and of their equivalents inside the imperialist countries," with the central aim of each picture always the "[construction] of a liberated personality with each people as the starting point."[14] The word *always* is important here, as the popularization of Third Cinema as a concept within academic and filmophile circles has ensured its continued use to this day and, in the same way, its continued application to Cuban movies.

For one more important example, we can zoom in even further to the *cine imperfecto* dreamed up by Julio García Espinosa. A Cuban director himself, Espinosa's understanding of his own work at first seems less totalizing than those mentioned above, as he centralizes form and aesthetics as being of extreme importance. However, it quickly becomes clear that these elements matter only inasmuch as they provide a barometer by which filmmakers might measure their defiance of bourgeois structural norms. Indeed, Cuban cinema is imperfect precisely because it "is no longer interested in quality or

technique ... no longer interested in predetermined taste, and much less in 'good taste.'"
In line with the definitions of New Latin American Cinema and Third Cinema above, all
cine imperfecto cares about is "how an artist responds to the following question: What
are you doing in order to overcome the barrier of the 'cultured' elite audience which up
to now has conditioned the form of your work?" Though couched in the language of
aesthetics, Espinosa makes it crystal clear that each of the island's creatives "should put
his role as revolutionary or aspiring revolutionary above all else," and intimates just as
strongly that the world needs to judge those individuals and their work on the grounds
of insurgency.[15] Put another way, the *cine es imperfecto*, because it resists the imperial
mainstream, and the aesthetics only matter when they make the movement legible as an
Imperfect Cinema even when confronted with anglicization.

The lines of liberation spiral on further from here. While different terms flow in
and out of conversation, each one ends up reinforcing the same idea—as far as Cuban
cinema is concerned, it's revolutions all the way down, and it will remain that way until
the end of time. And to be clear, this chapter levies no challenge to the idea that many
of the nation's pictures, perhaps even a majority of them, deal to some degree with anti-
imperialist struggle. After all, the trouble for curatorial colonization stems not from
simply applying labels like New Latin, Third, and Imperfect to select movies or makers,
given that these actions work perfectly fine and yield no negative consequences on a
case-by-case basis.

Rather, the issue here regards the absolutism of said application. In so strictly curating
what Cuban films can be, what they *must* be, critics have frozen discourse in such a way
that it endlessly re-inscribes the aims of the island at its most revolutionary point. While
the nation itself and its people may ebb and flow in terms of political, personal, and aesthetic aims, genre conventions ensure that the only expression possible in Cuba's moving
image arts—or more accurately, the only expression broader audiences can be easily and
consistently receptive to on a community level, as it is in line with their existing ideological conditioning—are those which function as upholstery to the socialist revolutions
of Karl Marx and Che Guevera. There is a reason that the definitions above borrow so
liberally from the two figures, as with the framing of New Latin American Cinema as an
endpoint of particular historical processes à la Marx's conception of socialism, as well
as the clear reference to Guevera's *new man* by Solanas and Getino. Through excluding
the possibility of supplementary or contrary interpretations, the generic structures that
envelop the Cuban cinema in its past and present states serve to either segregate and
make illegible any aspects of a work that do not constitute political subversion, or to forcibly re-inscribe those aspects so that they are seen to function solely within the mode
of imperial subversion. This is in spite of claims by many of the island's creatives that
their movies can, and in fact do, fulfill other functions beyond those or instead of those
demanded by whatever regime(s) they personally produced their art under. Take director Tomás Gutiérrez Alea and his proclamation that while he understands and agrees
with the notion that "cinema's social function should be in Cuba" to "contribute in the
most effective way possible to elevating the viewer's revolutionary consciousness and
to arming them for the ideological struggle which they have to wage against all kinds of

reactionary tendencies," it must also and at the same time "contribute to their enjoyment of life."[16]

Given his comment, it is not surprising that Alea's own work provides the best example of how curatorial colonization serves to erase important aspects of a text in service of dominant forces—perhaps the most egregious instance of which involves the crushing of Afro-Cuban subjectivity by white ideological power structures in *La última cena*. Released in 1976, the feature follows an eighteenth-century Spanish plantation owner caught up in the throes of imperial Catholicism. Envisioning his status as equivalent to that of a messianic figure, the man decides he wants to recreate the mythic Last Supper (as recorded in the Bible and aestheticized by Leonardo Da Vinci's famous painting), and he does so by placing himself at the center of the story and forcing the Afro-Cubans he has enslaved to fill the roles of the disciples. The dinner comes and goes, during which a wine-drunk Count makes myriad Christ-like promises that would better the lives of those under his whips. However, his failure to fulfill any of them leads to a rebellion across the plantation, resulting in a massacre that annihilates all but one of those twelve disciples.

From even such a cursory glance as the one proffered above, the average contemporary moviegoer should be able to recognize that *La última cena* is at least in part a film about Black subjection at the hands of white oppressors. After all, the story quite literally revolves around Afro-Cubans bound within the system of chattel slavery, and the narrative conflicts resolve in their deaths at the hands of the white man who enslaved them. And yet, standard readings of this film do not seem to care much about the plight of the Black characters, and only manage to do so when those figures serve a figurative function within the broader Cuban revolutionary struggle. As fellow director from the island Pastor Vega argued, *La última cena* "is one in a series of films attempting to reevaluate the role of the blacks in Cuba's national development."[17] Or, more directly, the Afro-Cuban only matters if they further understandings of how the socialist revolution came to be.

Similar interpretations abound, and nearly all tie back to those generic liberatory modes outlined above. For Nadine Smith, the movie "express[es] the rich possibilities of cinema freed from the demands of empire and industry."[18] For Julia Levin, the film exists as part of Cuba's "'grey' years," when the "political atmosphere acquired distinctive oppressive undertones" and the nation's "art lost its vitality" as a direct consequence.[19] Even Paul Schroeder, despite acknowledging that *La última cena* attempted "to construct an Afro-Cuban subaltern perspective on slavery," still binds that perspective to "the formation of the current national consciousness" and intimates that "the African element" gains importance when located within broader "Cuban consciousness."[20] As expected, it's revolutions all the way down, and genuine Black subjectivity is nowhere to be found. In its place is nothing but a whitewashed conception of socialist liberation, one which only recognizes the existence of Afro-Cubans when said existence supports the dominant (white) histories and ideologies of the nation.

Perhaps most troubling of all is that this has happened in spite of the film's own stark and quite explicit narrative condemnations of just such a scenario. Early in the picture, the plantation overseer gives the Count and his associates a tour of the sugar mill. The overseer has implemented a new initiative designed to increase sugar production, and Alea uses this as an opportunity to explain these processes to the audience. Of particular emphasis is a special powder which enslaved workers mix into heated cauldrons, resulting in the transformation of liquified sugar cane from a saturated green to an undefined "dark" color. In a stilted comparison to the process of transubstantiation,[21] the overseer states that the "green juice turns dark because what will be white must first be black." The imagery here is direct and damning: Cuba got where it is today by grinding down Blackness in pursuit of a whiter (and to their mind holier, à la transubstantiation) island. Unfortunately, curatorial colonization has ensured that those very same historic systems inflected and continue to impact global reception of the island's cinema.

Curating a (White) Horror Cinema

In a similar way, and as this chapter previously gestured toward, conversations on horror cinema have found themselves just as constrained by common conditioned understandings about what the genre actually is. However, while curatorial colonization impacted Cuban movies in the sense that it forced each of them to deal with socialist revolutionary ideals to be considered genuine and worthwhile, the process impacted horror pictures by demanding they each incorporate specific frightening elements into the narrative should they hope to receive validation as to their classificatory status. While tales of terror are undeniably diverse and cover a lot of disparate ground; the general logic is that each story needs to contain at least one uniquely fearful or monstrous element to justify its presence within the space. To qualify as horror, a movie must depict zombies, or werewolves, or demons, or psycho-killers, or ghosts, or vampires, or witches, or evil aliens, or some type of creature (either a physical body or ethereal force) which clearly deviates from human normalcy and wreaks havoc on our world. Films that break this trend yet still find broad acceptance as *horror* are exceedingly rare and often either become known as the exception that proves the rule or meet with eventual suspicion about whether the work should actually be grouped with adjacent genres, such as that of the thriller.

We see this trend most obviously in the ways that film fans and video distribution companies subclassify horror movies. For example, streaming service Shudder deals exclusively with tales of terror, and its categorization methods regularly sort content by way of those same terms listed above. As viewers navigate through the site, they are encouraged to pick, and by extension interpret, specific pictures primarily as examples of psycho-killer cinema, supernatural cinema, and so on. However, the trend also manifests within academic spaces, indicating once more the pervasive lack of categorical introspection even among audiences known for ruthlessly interrogating media. To note but two useful examples here, we can look to the work of disciplinarily dominant horror critics Carol Clover and Robin Wood. In her seminal text *Men, Women, and Chainsaws*, Clover avoids creating a deep taxonomy of what the genre as a whole consists of. Instead, she simply relies on those popular subclassification methodologies listed above. As she states in a footnote: "It has not been my concern to define horror.... I have been guided for the most part by video rental store categorizations, which, despite some variation from store to store, seem to capture better than any definition I know what the public senses to be 'horror.' "[22]

The chapters of the book play this statement out, covering in order the slasher, occult, rape revenge, and self-reflexive pictures one might commonly see grouped together on those video store shelves or in Shudder's streaming catalog. Meanwhile, Robin Wood gets more specific, introducing the genre (and specifically, its Americanized form) as being defined by the five categories of beasts that horror pictures of the time were most likely to include: "The monster as human psychotic or schizophrenic," or movies that contain a proto-psycho-killer; "The revenge of nature," or movies that contain deadly animals; "Satanism, diabolic possession, the Antichrist," or movies that contain de-monic creatures; "The terrible child," or movies that contain kid beasts or demons; and "Cannibalism," or movies that contain flesh-eaters.[23] We need not repeat the video-store and streaming comparison, for as above, so below, and even more obviously in this instance.

After even a surface reading of this remarkably rigid framework, indicative as it is of the constant and continuing curatorial colonization of horror as a genre, it should be easy to see why *La última cena* would find itself excluded from such a family of films. After all, the picture does not feature terrifying aliens touching down from space, am-phibious creeps crawling out of the local lagoon, or ghosts whirling their way through creaking wooden floors and ceilings. The Count does not turn into a wolf at night, nor does he summon vengeful vermin to sic on his enemies, nor does he suck blood from the necks of his victims. No, as described in the previous section, the film deals squarely with the all-too-human concerns of racism and chattel slavery. It spotlights Black object-bodies impressed by white subject-bodies and exposes to audiences a cruel man who slaughters others without any uniquely psychotic or supernatural cause. *La última cena* cannot be a horror film, for realistic and humanistic suffering are incompatible with the definition of the genre as constructed. Terror is zombies, not atrocities, so nothing be-fore *Juan de los muertos* actually fits.

The result of this categorical delimitation is the same as it was for Cuban-specific labels like *cine imperfecto*: the erasure of Afro-Cuban subjectivity. In her book *Horror Noire*, Robin R. Means Coleman describes the ways in which certain pictures, even if they do not fit within the common understandings of the genre outlined above, none-theless constitute tales of terror for Black audiences. The example she gives of this is D.W. Griffith's *The Birth of a Nation* (1915), which "[t]o be sure . . . is not part of the horror genre. Nevertheless, it introduced, and secured in the American popular imag-ination, a character of quintessential horror that would become a recurring, popular narrative device for instilling fear."[24] In the documentary companion to the book, guest speaker Tananarive Due gets even more explicit, doing away with any classificatory am-biguity by stating bluntly, "*The Birth of a Nation* was a horror film, especially if you were a Black person."[25] This idea, that non-white audiences might find terror in stories that white audiences cannot, is by no means limited to clearly and aggressively hateful works like Griffith's. Rather, as Paul Lehman describes, it persists anywhere that racism does:

> Racism is likened unto the evil monster that lives under the children's bed. That monster was invented for the sole purpose of controlling the children's behavior with fear and intimidation. As long as the children believe the monster is real, the inventors have control of them. The monster's power resides in the minds of both the children and the inventors, but for the children, it is real; for the inventors, it is power to control and manipulate.[26]

In this way, Black subjection is not just reminiscent of terror or viewable through a fearful interpretive lens, but in fact constitutes horror in and of itself. Racism *is* the beast, *is* the demonic force, and it is all too real for those caught within the snare of its terrible teeth. However, because those inventors of racism—which we can understand in this context as meaning those who participate, even unwittingly, in curatorial colonization—cannot conceive of or describe terror through a Black perspective, it means that any monsters fitting the descriptions proffered by Coleman, Due, and Lehman above are denied the label of horror proper.

By extension, this means they are also denied respect as genuine fears on the level of those represented on screen time and time again by white creatives, upholding an ideological system whereby the terror of Black subjection gets treated not as a deviation from human normalcy that wreaks havoc on our world, but simply as the normal world. Within this colonized curatorial system, it does not matter if Afro-Cuban viewers might approach *La última cena* similarly to the way Due approaches *The Birth of a Nation*, as I will argue is a possibility in the following section. It does not even matter if the film depicts clear moments of violence designed to shock and terrify viewers in the same way as a slasher death—and indeed, such is the case when the enslaved character Sebastian has his ear cut off by the plantation overseer, an action so shocking and gruesome that even the Count is taken away retching in total bodily shock. None of this matters, because curatorial colonization has produced an aesthetic lexicon which dictates that terror is zombies, not atrocities, so nothing in Alea's humanistically grounded picture could ever match that prescribed by white generic structures.

RE-CURATORIAL PRACTICES

The previous sections described both the processes of terminological exclusion by which the myth of *Juan* came to be, as well as why said processes do real ideological harm—in this specific case, to Afro-Cubans. As a solution, this chapter proposes that scholars adopt a form of analytical practice designed to fix the issue at its source, a methodology which we might call *re-curation*. Since curatorial colonization functions not by changing the representation of material on screen, but by limiting the labels one can apply to said representations, it is not something resolvable by shifting or deepening existing habits of close reading; shot-level, scene-level, and even sequence-level interrogation may work great in certain situations, but here amount to little more than putting a bandage on a broken bone, as it treats a symptom as opposed to a sickness. By contrast, re-curation demands we interrogate the generic definitions that a film has already been saddled with, backgrounding textual material to instead inspect the tools of inspection. For *La última cena*, this means changing our conceptions of horror, as well as the particular amalgamation of New Latin American/Third/Imperfect Cinema relevant to Cuban pictures.

Starting with the former, we can re-curate the horror genre so that it includes a broader range of Black experiences. One useful way of doing so might be by severing the label's connection to the specific characters or tropes a picture utilizes and tying it instead to the uniquely terrifying feelings it engenders within viewers. Sigmund Freud provides a foundation for this in his conceptualization of the *uncanny*. Though the scholar (in true psychoanalytic fashion) provides a remarkably complex breakdown of the idea that complicates and expands it in ways potentially incompatible with the content of this chapter, his opening definition is very much of use. In it, Freud explains that the uncanny "undoubtedly belongs to all that is terrible—to all that arouses dread and creeping horror." Moreover, since "the word is not always used in a clearly definable sense . . . it tends to coincide with whatever excites dread. Yet we may expect that it implies some intrinsic quality which justifies the use of a special name."[27] We find in this concept of the uncanny a new approach to horror, one that retains all the elements of the existing label—traditional monsters like zombies are, for most people, *creeping* figures that possess the ability to *arouse dread*—but also admits fears that manifest in forms not reliant on dominant (white) ideology.

However, since we know the particular problem that we hope to employ methods of re-curation to solve—the lack of Black subjectivity within the horror genre and specifically as it may exist in a Cuban picture about slavery—we can use Freud's observations as a launching point to get even more precise. Sticking with psychoanalytic theory, Julia Kristeva offers another explanation of terror based in the uncanny but dealing more directly with subject and object relationships. Her conception of *abjection* denotes any type of terror that possesses "only one quality of the object—that of being opposed to I."[28] Encountering the abject results in a "massive and sudden emergence of uncanniness" positioned "as radically separate, loathsome," an assailant who "disturbs identity, system, order" through methods that are "immoral, sinister, scheming, and shady: a terror that dissembles, a hatred that smiles."[29] This more particular definition fits well within the context of enslavement terrors, and with it, we gain a precise theoretical label to explain why *La última cena* constitutes a horror film. The next step simply involves connecting the dots. The *I* of the Afro-Cubans depicted on screen (with which viewers, both Black and otherwise, are encouraged to empathize and identify) are directly opposed to the film's central perpetrator of atrocity, the Count. The subjected Afro-Cuban characters, and by extension any empathetic-identificatory audience members, thus experience a fear founded in the loathsome whiteness of the enslaver, a monstrous figure who has punctured the natural system of human relations in order to dominate others on the basis of race. And of course, he does this with a smile, painting his actions through religious imagery and ideology.

As demonstrated above, by simply shifting our generic expectations (and without providing any interpretation beyond that intuitable from a basic plot summary), we suddenly possess the ability to approach *La última cena* as a genuine horror movie. Yet abjection need not be the only definitional factor at play. Whereas curatorial colonization relies on fixed classifications, re-curatorial practice allows us to expand in whatever direction is necessary for a particular situation. Additionally, constantly inspecting our classification standards ensures that we do not ensnare ourselves within another sunken place, that we do not merely replace one troublesome ideology for another. To model this, consider Japanese director Kiyoshi Kurosawa's approach to his own horror movies, which he views as belonging "to that family of films that take as their subject matter *the fear that follows one throughout one's life*."[30] In this case, the addition to classical Freudian uncanniness is inescapability, the idea, as so often intimated at the end of tales of terror, that *evil never dies*. The application to enslavement narratives, and to *La última cena* specifically, is obvious. Considering the film narrowly, we see the omni-oppressiveness of the Count vis-à-vis his slaughter of the disciples, a massacre so successful that only the previously mutilated Sebastian manages to flee. Falling perfectly in line in all ways but gender with the slasher's Final Girl archetype—Sebastian exists alongside a terrible place in the form of a plantation-turned-slaughterhouse; a phallic weapon in the form of a cane knife; and a Count-turned-psycho-killer rampaging through the sugar cane fields, leaving scores of bloody Black bodies in his wake[31]—this victim's escape simply means that there is someone left to terrorize later, that the cruelty of the Count has not ceased permanently, but just for a moment. Thinking more broadly, chattel slavery was an inescapable system for those in shackles, given that they could not physically get away from the slaveholder, as well as for the descendants of the enslaved, since the psychological and systemic traumas rooted in the system have been continually passed down from generation to generation. Through Kurosawa's perspective, slavery becomes the ultimate cinematic bogeyman, a monster under the bed that contains far greater stakes because it is actually real. Unlike with *Juan*, the monsters of this story are not just myths.

RE-CURATION, REPARATIVITY, RESURRECTION

At this point, only one question remains: Should scholars re-curate Cuban cinema as a whole so that it is compatible with these notions of an abject and/or inescapable Black terror, in turn granting cinema studies the ability to treat the island's enslavement narratives as horror films instead of exclusively revolutionary texts? There are at least a few arguments against it, such as those leveraged by Saidiya Hartman and Stephen Best. For Hartman, the issue revolves around the ethical indeterminability of the enslavement archive, the fact that for any good searching for identity within that past might do, it also deals inevitably with "the reproduction of [originating] scenes of violence, which define the state of blackness and the life of the ex-slave" in ways that may be harmful.[32] Similarly, Best feels it is unwise to uphold any ties between enslavement and Blackness, to "understand slavery as the scene of the crime and that scene of the crime as a scene of origin," thereby creating a constricting and impossible-to-sustain "black selfhood that is grounded in a kind of lost black sociality, in black sociality's groundedness in horror."[33]

These scholars' concerns are more than warranted, and re-curation does provide an answer to them. In the examples above, it is easy to think that the employed method- ology injects horror into enslavement, that it reinforces the already-strong bands of historical racism and, by consequence, actively creates the inescapability it purports to merely label. In actuality, what this practice does is transform enslavement into a tale of terror, thereby providing a new point of sociocultural origination for Afro-Cuban viewers. When conceived of as a revolutionary, nonhorror text, *La última cena* either prohibits meaningful Black fabulation and identity formation altogether, crushed as it is under the weight of white socialism, or forces a conception of Blackness that is tied without question to very real precedents of subjection. However, when audiences treat *La última cena* as a horror picture, suddenly it gains the benefits built into the genre. As slasher director Wes Craven argues, films like his are a "boot camp for the psyche," using narrative techniques to organize our "fears into a manageable series of events" that we can learn to overcome.[34] While a moving picture cannot, of course, directly fix the fears it examines, it provides audience members a space in which they can learn how those fears impact them psychologically and, over time, learn to overcome them. In the case of *La última cena*, while Alea's work cannot heal the very literal wounds of slavery, it can help Afro-Cuban viewers disconnect themselves from the enduring trauma of the system and overcome its lasting holds on their psyche. Indeed, re-curation is a system whereby ideologically harmful pictures can start to function reparatively, providing communities of viewers with the tools necessary to "[extract] sustenance from the objects of culture—even of a culture whose avowed desire has often been not to sustain them."[35]

Through this reparative gaze, one can begin to see the outlines of a potential path forward for Afro-Cuban horror cinema as an aesthetic, critical, and global movement. Returning one final time to Sebastian, the concluding sequence of *La última cena* shows the man sprinting through the woods and hills of the plantation, fleeing for his life from the Count and his killing squad. As he runs, the camera slowly tilts down until the lens is entirely obscured. Cut to black, and "FIN" fades onto the screen. Per the prior passages on re-curatorial practice, this moment falls neatly into the pattern of classic horror endings, providing a temporary reprieve from a seemingly escaped but inevitably recur- ring evil. However, that same definitional legibility also permits the possibility of using genre to wage war against racist monsters like the Count, those all-too-real bogeymen sustained for so long by a cinema perniciously infected by curatorial colonization. Just as Final Girls like Laurie Strode and Sidney Prescott have returned in film after film to defend others from unstoppable beasts, so too might a character like Sebastian recur to protect and resist on behalf of fellow subjected persons. Just as Black moviemakers like Jordan Peele have placed their chilling pictures in conversation with, and framed them as corrections of, the cinemas they grew up with, so too might Afro-Cuban horror filmmakers do the same with their island's distinct filmic history. And just as the horror label attracts the genre's sizable family of fans to so many lost and forgotten narratives around the globe, so too might it bring international viewers together to witness the true terrors impressed upon the bodies and souls of the island nation's racial subaltern.

To re-curate Cuban cinema so that it includes Black terror is to correct the errors spread by the myth of *Juan*, to proclaim to the world that it is not just those fictional zombies that matter, but also the corpses of atrocity and enslavement still walking the streets of Havana to this very day. Through horror, scholars can begin the process of resurrecting those narratives of subjection buried beneath the island's plantations and other terrible places—and, with time, breathe life once more into the stories for so long hidden by the master's genres.

NOTES

1. *Juan de los muertos*, directed by Alejandro Brugués (2011; Seville, ES: Canal Sur).
2. El Mayimbe, "Exclusive: Debut Trailer of JUAN OF THE DEAD! Cuba's 1st Horror Film!," *LatinoReview.com*, July 7, 2011, https://web.archive.org/web/20110709182453/http://www.latinoreview.com/news/exclusive-debut-trailer-of-juan-of-the-dead-cuba-s-1st-horror-film-14094.
3. Richard Whittaker, "FF2011: 'Juan of the Dead' Premiere," *Austin Chronicle*, September 24, 2011, https://www.austinchronicle.com/daily/screens/2011-09-24/ff2011-juan-of-the-dead-premiere/.
4. Victoria Burnett, "Socialism's Sacred Cows Suffer Zombie Attack in Popular Cuban Film," *New York Times*, December 10, 2011, https://www.nytimes.com/2011/12/11/world/americas/zombies-in-juan-of-the-dead-chomp-on-cubas-sacred-cows.html.
5. *¡Vampiros en La Habana!*, directed by Juan Padrón (1985; Havana, CU: Instituto Cubano del Arte e Industria Cinematográficos).
6. *La última cena*, directed by Tomás Gutiérrez Alea (1976; Havana, CU: Instituto Cubano del Arte e Industria Cinematográficos).
7. Barry Keith Grant, *Film Genre: From Iconography to Ideology* (London: Wallflower, 2007), 6.
8. As example, look to recent novels *The Last Final Girl* by Stephen Graham Jones, *Final Girls* by Riley Sager, and *The Final Girl Support Group* by Grady Hendrix.
9. For further clarity, the popular zombie film receives constant scrutiny for the ways it uses monstrosity to represent broader cultural forces, as with critical race readings of *The Night of the Living Dead* (1968) and Marxist readings of *Dawn of the Dead* (1978). However, only when a picture intentionally places zombies within a seemingly incompatible genre does their status as horror signifiers come into question—and even then, this typically serves nothing more than narrative or comedic ends, as with romantic comedy *Warm Bodies* (2013) and slapstick romp *Shaun of the Dead* (2004). To be sure, it is no accident that the latter directly inspired *Juan de los muertos*.

10. Kenneth Coutts-Smith, "Cultural Colonialism," *Third Text 16*, no. 1 (2002): 2.
11. For further context and critical approaches to New Latin American Cinema, see John King's *Magical Reels* and Zuzana Pick's *The New Latin American Cinema: A Continental Project*.
12. Ana M. López, "An 'Other' History: The New Latin American Cinema," in *New Latin American Cinema*, vol. 1, ed. Michael T. Martin (Detroit, MI: Wayne State University Press, 1997), 137.
13. Fernando Solanas and Octavio Getino, "Towards a Third Cinema: Notes and Experiences for the Development of a Cinema of Liberation in the Third World," in *New Latin American Cinema*, vol. 1, ed. Michael T. Martin (Detroit, MI: Wayne State University Press, 1997), 34–35.
14. Ibid., 37.
15. Julio García Espinosa, "For an Imperfect Cinema," in *New Latin American Cinema*, vol. 1, ed. Michael T. Martin (Detroit, MI: Wayne State University Press, 1997), 82.
16. Tomás Gutiérrez Alea, "The Viewer's Dialectic," in *New Latin American Cinema*, vol. 1, ed. Michael T. Martin (Detroit, MI: Wayne State University Press, 1997), 110.
17. Karen Jaehne, "The Last Supper," *Film Quarterly* 33, no. 1 (1979): 48.
18. Nadine Smith, "A Cuban Filmmaker's Brutal Satire of Religion and Colonialism," *Hyperallergic*, June 4, 2019, https://hyperallergic.com/503548/decolonizing-cinema-film-forum-the-last-supper/.
19. Julia Levin, "Alea, Tomás Gutiérrez," *Senses of Cinema*, October 2003, https://www.senseso fcinema.com/2003/great-directors/alea/.
20. Paul A. Schroeder, *Tomas Gutierrez Alea: The Dialectics of a Filmmaker* (New York: Routledge, 2002), 69.
21. In Catholicism, transubstantiation is the process by which the sacrament transforms from bread and wine into the body and blood of Jesus Christ. This comparison sets up the central premise of the film, that being the Count's staging of "master and slave" as messiah and disciple.
22. Carol J. Clover, *Men, Women, and Chainsaws: Gender in the Modern Horror Film* (Princeton, NJ: Princeton University Press, 2015), 5.
23. Robin Wood, *Robin Wood On the Horror Film: Collected Essays and Reviews*, ed. Barry Keith Grant (Detroit, MI: Wayne State University Press, 2018), 89.
24. Robin R. Means Coleman, *Horror Noire: Blacks in American Horror Films from the 1890s to Present* (New York: Routledge, 2013), 28.
25. *Horror Noire: A History of Black Horror*, directed by Xavier Burgin (2019; Brooklyn, NY: Icarus Films).
26. Paul R. Lehman, *The System of European American (White) Supremacy and African American (Black) Inferiority* (Bloomington, IN: Xlibris, 2016), vii.
27. Sigmund Freud, *The Uncanny*. Translated by David McLintock (London: Penguin, 2003), 1.
28. Julia Kristeva, *Powers of Horror: An Essay on Abjection*. Translated by Leon S. Roudiez (New York: Columbia University Press, 1982), 1.
29. Ibid., 2–4.
30. Kiyoshi Kurosawa, *Eiga wa osoroshii [Film is Scary]*. Translated by Kendall Heitzman, Seidosha, 2001 (emphasis in original).
31. Clover, *Men, Women, and Chainsaws*, 26–42.

32. Saidiya Hartman, "Venus in Two Acts," *Small Axe* 12, no. 2 (2008): 7.

33. Stephen Best, *None Like Us: Blackness, Belonging, Aesthetic Life* (Durham, NC: Duke University Press, 2018), 22.

34. *The American Nightmare*, directed by Adam Simon (2000; Rome, IT: Minerva Pictures).

35. Eve Kosofsky Sedgwick, *Touching Feeling: Affect, Pedagogy, Performativity* (Durham, NC: Duke University Press, 2003), 150–151.

SECTION III

GENDERED BLACKNESS

CHAPTER 11

....

THE INAUGURATION OF
BLACK HORROR

Duane Jones's Racial Revision of
Night of the Living Dead

....

TONY QUICK

INTRODUCTION

....

In 1999, the United States Library of Congress inducted *Night of the Living Dead* into the National Film Registry alongside other motion pictures deemed "culturally, historically, or aesthetically significant" to American culture.[1] This chapter argues that the film's lead actor, Duane Jones, transformed *Night of the Living Dead* from a mono-racial independent film into a historically significant cultural artifact that interrogates the racial climate of the 1960s through a combination of Jones's on-screen performance, intentional revisions to his pre-scripted role, and numerous negotiations with director George A. Romero. John Russo and George A. Romero's script, written for a white lead but unedited after casting a Black lead actor, was never intended to serve as a racial commentary. However, Jones's performance and subversive intervention during the filming process imbued the film with deeper meanings.[2]

The original script, which focused on the metaphoric class revolt on the farmhouse's exterior, is supplanted by an alternate parable focused on the racial revolution. As his capable protagonist attempts to assert leadership over his white counterparts in an emergency scenario that disrupts the racial status quo, Jones offered audiences an unprecedented glimpse into the struggle to survive as a Black man in 1960s America, only to find his efforts futile in the face of an armed militia incapable of recognizing his humanity.

Duane Jones's negotiation of his character depiction fits within a subversive tradition among twentieth-century Black actors who engaged in similar representative bargaining to infuse some degrees of authenticity and nuance to roles that were, in many cases, burdened with their white counterparts' preconceived notions of Blackness.[3] Russo and Romero wrote their script with a white protagonist in mind—curtailing some risks of racially stereotyping their contemporaries, but their experiment in race-blind casting also required Jones to account for unintentional cultural cues that emerged as a result of a Black actor occupying the lead role.[4] This chapter surveys three instances during the film's creation process in which Jones attempted to revise his character— some successful, others unsuccessful—in an attempt to improve the representations of Blacks on screen. By scrutinizing the negotiations between Jones and Romero as an interracial compromise in Black representation, we can better appreciate the invisible, subversive efforts of Black actors in the twentieth century. We can also interrogate the dynamics that transmuted a low-budget experiment in horror into a culturally relevant snapshot of a nation in the middle of a radical, racial transformation.

ORIGINS OF THE *LIVING DEAD*

By all accounts, Romero and Russo never intended for *Night of the Living Dead* to serve as a racial commentary, but as scriptwriters and filmmakers, neither man was immune to the cultural climate and conversations taking place in the late 1960s.[5] McFarland argues that the U.S. military occupation of Haiti from 1915 to 1934 introduced a U.S. interpretation of Haitian Vodou traditions into the American public's psyche.[6] These anachronistic tropes of voodoo priests and re-animated corpses were "soon reflected in magazine stories, stage plays, and films that featured 'zombies' as servile and un-canny revenants."[7] This Haitian appropriation carried over into art and media produced in later decades, providing inspiration for early Cold War tropes present in films that depicted an alien, organized other such as 1964's *The Last Man on Earth*, and even 1968's *Night of the Living Dead*. In fact, both films draw their inspiration from Richard Matheson's 1954 novel *I Am Legend*, an early narrative about Cold War anxieties written amid the Second Red Scare and McCarthyism.[8] Romero and Russo may not have in-tended to draw on either the Haitian Vodou tradition or voodoo tropes more broadly, but by drawing inspiration from Matheson's novel, the scriptwriters indirectly tapped into an Americanized version of traditions steeped in the African diaspora. The United States' ongoing dialogue between diaspora and colonization manifests, improbably, as a social parable about survivors barricaded in a Pennsylvania farmhouse as cannibalistic "ghouls" rise from the dead.

Romero and Russo have argued that their original intention was to create a meta-phoric depiction of societal chaos and dysfunction that could make a profit on a shoestring budget.[9] Their attempts to dramatize post–World War II American life's insecurities became more significant due to their preexisting inspirations, future interpretations influenced by the sociopolitical climate, and the auspicious casting of Duane Jones as *Night of the Living Dead*'s starring lead. Romero insists that Jones's casting was a colorblind process that did not focus on the actor's race, and as such, he did not revise the script to account for a Black protagonist.[10] Importantly, Jones's race inherently changes the context of the lead character and the subtext surrounding his on-screen interactions with the film's white cast. Though Ben's race is never explicitly mentioned in the film, audiences in a segregated United States entrenched in discourses about integration and racial justice would have been keenly aware of the social transgression at work in *Night of the Living Dead*. Historical hindsight brings an even more nuanced appreciation for the unique relevance of this countercultural subversion of the late 1960s status quo.

Duane Jones served as much more than a passive vessel for Ben's character. *Night of the Living Dead* was an experimental, low-budget project that relied on support from charitable contributions, volunteer labor, and actors who took on multiple roles.[11] Jones often intervened on his character's behalf and suggested changes to dialogue, specific narrative details, and major plot points to ensure *Night of the Living Dead* would better represent Black Americans to the film's audiences. His success varied, with some suggestions incorporated and other requests rejected, and yet, his efforts cemented *Dead*'s unimpeachable status as a Black film. Jones's efforts also connected him to a storied tradition of Black actors who attempted to bring nuance to Black characters and narratives written, directed, or distributed by those outside their ethnic background.[12]

LITERATURE REVIEW

The United States has a fraught history at the intersection of race and entertainment. Beyond better-known phenomena such as minstrel shows, scholar Ersula Ore describes how photographs of lynchings were circulated as postcards in the nineteenth and twentieth centuries.[13] Ore notes that while "most of these images of lynching were sent as commemorative mementos among supporters of and sympathizers with white supremacy, others were sent as threats to those who challenged it."[14] Just as film can communicate cultural information, these postcards "imparted crucial knowledge about civil life and functioned epideictically for citizens as lessons in civics."[15] They were a grotesque form of entertainment among white supremacists that also carried an instructive purpose for white and Black Americans alike. Like nineteenth- and twentieth-century minstrel shows, these postcards entertained white audiences and reinforced perceptions of Black inferiority across the national populace. Pioneers in early twentieth-century film carried their prejudices into their creative works and recycled minstrel show tropes, ensuring these racial degradations migrated into early cinema.[16]

Just over a half century before *Night of the Living Dead*, cinema saw the creation of the racist propaganda film *Birth of a Nation*. D. W. Griffith's 1915 adaptation of Thomas Dixon Jr.'s 1905 novel, *The Clansman*, was said to have "altered the entire course and concept of American moviemaking, developing the close-up, cross-cutting, rapid-fire editing, the iris, the split-screen shot, and realistic and impressionistic lighting," but those technological innovations were used to produce "the most slanderous anti-Negro movie ever released."[17] Griffith's Confederate sympathies, commitment to white supremacy, and zealous insistence on the myth of Black inferiority also inaugurated a collection of racial archetypes that caught on with general audiences that were "cinematically untutored" but equally conditioned to accept *Birth of a Nation's* depiction of such racial archetypes as "brutes, the bucks, and the tragic mulatto," to name a few.[18] Many of Griffith's white contemporaries recycled and repeated the distorted, racist tropes in cinema for the next century.

This context is necessary to appreciate Duane Jones's unique role as the first Black lead in an independent horror film and how his intervention on his character's behalf connects to a greater legacy of Black performers. Though cinema has become a multi-billion-dollar industry with global distribution and significant cultural cachet, the industry's early acceptance of segregation, engagement and reinforcement of Jim Crow practices, and continued reluctance to engage in substantial top-to-bottom systematic reform has created a hierarchy that mimics the United States' racial caste system.[19] Prior generations of Black performers had to compete for the right to perform Black characters against white performers who adopted blackface and acted out offensive, exaggerated racial caricatures.[20] That early filmmakers accepted these white actors' performances is not only a testament to their ingrained prejudices but also speaks volumes to the lack of depth or substance within their scripted roles for Black characters. As Donald Bogle notes, "[w]ithout scripts to aid them and generally without even sympathetic directors or important roles, black actors in American films were compelled to rely on their own ingenuity to create memorable characters."[21] Thus, Black performers in the 1930s and beyond had to improvise humanizing qualities and charming characteristics that would resonate with their audiences, increase their chances of recurring roles, and prove that they belonged on stages and silver screens alongside their white counterparts.

Even today, Black creatives have limited opportunities to present characters written, directed, and portrayed by members of their own background compared to their white counterparts.[22] Erigha cites a 2014 study that found, in instances where a director is Black, on-screen representation rises significantly compared to when a Black director is not at the helm of a film.[23] Similarly, Black directors lead to more representation in roles such as "set designers, gaffers, office workers, lab technicians, visual artists, colorists, and carpenters," which means Black directors' underrepresentation in the field extends across Black involvement in all film-related careers.[24] Given the absence of representative directorial discretion and scripts written by culturally careless—if not racially hostile—screenwriters, Black actors have traditionally exercised a subtle agency over their performances. Black thespians such as Lincoln Perry, Hattie McDaniel, Bill Robinson, Clarence Muse, Louise Beavers, and Fredi Washington worked within the constraints of degrading stereotypes, yet worked to humanize their renditions of Blackness for general audiences. Duane Jones, as an actor working amid the civil rights movement, continued that tradition in his performance as Ben with his proactive negotiations over the character.

DISCUSSION

Jones's contributions to *Night of the Living Dead* defy simple summary but this chapter singles out three specific negotiations between the actor and director that influenced the independent film's racial tenor. First, Jones entirely re-imagined his character's dialogue, converting the dialect of a working-class, everyman truck driver into a measured but confident cadence that better matched the actor's own academic background.[25] Given the racial archetypes that informed fictional depictions of Blackness in film at the time, Jones likely understood that the white single-syllabic everyman might read differently performed by a Black man. Second, Jones negotiated to remove an act of intergender violence from the film by arguing against the scene in which Ben physically strikes a hysterical Barbra, played by white actress Judith O'Dea. Jones would have understood the deeper implications of his Black male character physically harming a white woman. Though the scene still appears in the film, his intervention shows his awareness of the negative perceptions this might cause for audiences across the racial spectrum.

Finally, when Romero considered revising the film's iconic ending, Jones again intervened and persuaded him to maintain the original ending. Though disturbing, Ben's death at the hand of a roaming militia reminiscent of a lynch mob, paired with the high-profile assassinations of the 1960s, is most likely the reason the film has been elevated from regional cult classic to an American classic, formally recognized as a "culturally, historically, or aesthetically significant" contribution to the nation's collective cinema.[26] Together, these rhetorical negotiations between director and actor led to a much more nuanced film that culturally resonates with audiences generations after its release. Duane Jones rarely spoke about his experience with *Night of the Living Dead*, but a 1987 interview with Tim Ferrante conducted seven months prior to the actor's premature death is a rare exception. During their conversation, Jones explains his reluctance to speak about the film both publicly and privately:

> I wouldn't want anyone to think that I'm so arrogant as not to be grateful for the acclaim they have given me and the film and it should never be misconstrued that my enigmatic, mysterious persona that I have—in some instances deliberately created just to have the space in which to have a private life—is a lack of gratitude. It's not. But it is my absolute insistence that I be seen as a total human being and not Ben.[27]

Jones's statement explains why scholarship surrounding him is supplemented by so many external voices and also speaks directly to the actor's understanding of how representation, identity, and image can affect people's lived experiences. His revisions to Ben's character were neither uninformed nor capricious whims. They were byproducts of careful consideration of representation that Jones practiced in his personal life as well as in his professional roles.

Though many amateur actors and filmmakers were involved in *Night of the Living Dead*, Jones was a professional actor who performed alongside actors in the Negro Ensemble Company and the National Black Theater.[28] Jones also served as executive director of an association of theater companies known as the Black Theater Alliance from 1976 to 1981.[29] Romero's long-running assertion that Jones was hired to play Ben solely on account of his being the best actor who auditioned is substantiated by the actor's biography.[30] In addition to acting and theater administration, Jones had an accomplished academic career. He had taught literature courses at Long Island University, served as head of Antioch College's literature department, instructed on literature at Long Island University, headed the English department at Harlem Preparatory School, and developed instructional programs.[31] His resume reflects an actor and academic capable of balancing the responsibilities of his on-screen performance with negotiating the literary dimensions of his character.

During his 1987 interview, Jones speaks about the limitations of his role, wryly observing, "Ben didn't even really have a biography. Where was he coming from? Really ... Ben was just passing through."[32] Prior generations of Black actors infused humanity into flat, stereotyped roles that otherwise degraded Blacks. In an ironic inversion, Jones adjusted his character's dialogue and mannerisms to add depth to a generic character the script's authors intended to serve as a nondescript everyman who would appeal to general audiences.

That Ben was underdeveloped was not lost on the script's coauthors. Regarding their original draft, Romero has written, "Ben was ill-defined. He had to be young, fit, powerful, and cunning."[33] John Russo repeats this observation, describing their first incarnation of Ben as "a crude, uneducated, but intelligent and resourceful truck driver" that contrasted with Duane Jones, "an intelligent, refined young man whose power was tempered by subtlety and restraint."[34] Judith O'Dea described a loose commitment to the written script and an on-set environment that gave the actors freedom to pitch changes to characters and scenes.[35] Jones "upgraded the character's dialogue" to better suit his personal speech and avoid any connotations between lack of education and Blackness.[36] Though *Night of the Living Dead* was written and filmed in a collaborative environment that invited feedback from a cast and crew that considered themselves friends as well as coworkers, Jones's academic and creative biography made him ideal for the role.

Though Jones successfully appealed revisions to his character's dialogue and dialect, he was unable to alter every aspect of his character. Romero insisted on keeping a scene where Barbra succumbs to a sudden bout of madness and tries to leave the farmhouse. To calm her down, Ben strikes her with a close-fisted punch. Romero has reflected on the conversation and his own naiveté about the nation's racial climate: "Duane was aware of it and he was concerned about it. There was a scene where he has to slug the white [character] Barbra ... and he said, 'You know what's going to happen to me when I walk outside the theater if I slug this woman?' He was concerned about all of that. I kept saying, 'Come on, man. It's 1968!'"[37]

Despite Romero's insistence on following the script, whether out of artistic principle or a misguided commitment to colorblindness, Jones's attempts to revise the scene are worthy of commemoration and reflection. Romero came to understand the lead actor's concerns, but his flippant reaction as a younger man also exposes a surprising gap in his knowledge of film history. For D. W. Griffith's racist, propagandistic *Birth of a Nation*, which helped inaugurate cinema as a medium, explicitly trafficked in racial tropes that positioned Black men as "brutes" in opposition to "virginal, innocent" white women.[38]

Ersula Ore addresses what was referred to as miscegenation, a pervasive fear among white men horrified by the thought of interracial sexual relationships between Black men and white women. She argues that "white women's bodies were 'marked territory' in lynching discourse. Rhetorically constructed as 'no-trespass-zones,' white women's bodies 'symbolized the plenitude of white supremacy.'"[39] Ore describes vigilante lynchings as rhetorical acts of communication, much like films, that present white women as "'the most precious form' of white space and white property."[40] Duane Jones performed his role before published scholarship could properly engage the nuanced pathologies of white supremacy, but the circulation of this "lynching discourse" throughout the nineteenth and twentieth centuries had informed his experience enough to make him wary.

In his 1987 interview with Tim Ferrante, Duane Jones also recounts receiving a ride to his mother's home from his friend and colleague, Betty Ellen Haughey, and being followed through Pittsburgh by teenagers wielding a tire iron.[41] He describes the horrific irony of the incident, after similarly wielding a tire iron on the set, and said the "total surrealism of the racial nightmare of America being worse than whatever we were doing as a metaphor in that film lives with me to this moment."[42] Jones's life experiences laid bare the illusion of the colorblind philosophy, and he would have recognized the potential reaction to his now-Black character physically punching his white costar on the silver screen.

Romero has recounted conversations with the actor in which Jones, faced with the director's colorblind vision, replied, "Ben *is* Black now. So you have to *think* about that."[43] In the interview, Romero refers to Jones's "sensitivity" about any scenes involving violence but cites the scene in which Ben strikes Barbra as a specific source of tension and remembers Jones saying, "I'm going to be in trouble."[44] His costar Judith O'Dea recalled that Jones had multiple objections to the original scene, which also called for Barbra to strike Ben multiple times.[45] Russo and Romero revised the scene so that Ben is slapped once, but they refused to remove his retaliatory punch.

For over a century, anti-miscegenation laws, vigilante lynch mobs, and societal segregation reinforced that message, and cinema assisted in distributing decades of scenes, subplots, and entire narratives that positioned the Black "buck" stereotype as an inherent threat to white women and, by extension, white civilization.[46] For nearly a century, cinema has continued to adopt this lynching discourse, and as a result, "juxtapositions such as 'pure lovely girl' and 'wonton brute' [sic] recast the epic struggle between good and evil as the ongoing battle to protect white purity from the taint of black wickedness."[47] Romero, either unaware or unconcerned, refused to heed Jones's advice.[48]

Judith O'Dea noted in subsequent interviews, "Clearly, it was something on Duane's radar, even if it wasn't with the rest of the cast. . . . I never once stopped to consider that Duane could fall into danger because of it."[49] Though Jones was unsuccessful in this particular negotiation, his attempts demonstrate the lead actor's consideration of racial representation as he navigated playing Ben on-screen. Whether Jones did this for the cause of Black representation at large, or for his personal safety as a Black man, he showed an explicit consideration for this aspect of the film and his portrayal of Ben.

Duane Jones's most significant intervention was his advocacy for George A. Romero to keep *Night of the Living Dead*'s iconic ending. At first glance, Ben's death at the film's conclusion may seem to fit trends seen in the science fiction-horror genre for decades. Afrofuturist scholar Ytasha Womack has written about this racial narrative trope that has seen Black characters in fiction, but cinema in particular, as a perpetual source of victimhood:

> It was an age-old joke that blacks in sci-fi movies from the '50s through the '90s typically had a dour fate. The black man who saved the day in the original *Night of the Living Dead* was killed by trigger happy cops. The black man who landed with Charlton Heston in the original Planet of the Apes was quickly captured and stuffed in a museum.[50]

However, it is a mistake to dismiss Ben's death as yet another instance of expendable Blackness. For one, Black characters in science fiction rarely received as much screen time or focus as Ben and were often dispatched as these films' first victims. These characters' deaths were often dismissive, seldom designed to create the same emotional impact as Ben's. The ending, written prior to any casting decision, was also negotiated throughout filming.[51] The script was changed so that everyone died at the end, and the production's creative team argued over Ben's fate until they all agreed it was the most likely scenario under the circumstances.[52] Jones co-signed the decision on cultural and artistic grounds:

> I convinced George that the Black community would rather see me dead than saved, after all that had gone on, in a corny and symbolically and confusing way. . . . The heroes never die in American movies. The jolt of that and the double jolt of the hero figure being black seemed like a double-barreled whammy.[53]

Dead's ending transformed what might have been a unique footnote in horror cinema history into a racially resonate film that encapsulates inherent paradoxes of Black American life. For all Ben's versatility and resourcefulness in the face of an emergency, he meets his end at the hands of sanctioned vigilantes who fail to recognize his humanity and execute him. Romero has recounted hearing about King's assassination soon after the film's completion, and the ending's resonance is often connected to its 1968 release. However, in citing Black Americans, Jones would have been aware of the race-related shootings of Medgar Evers, Malcolm X, and numerous other high-profile figures; cognizant of lynch mobs used to enforce the color line; and informed of the numerous instances of gun violence that led to "race riots" in the late 1960s.[54] Ben's death in the original script speaks to a self-cannibalistic impulse within human society, but with Duane Jones playing the role, those cultural connotations became focused on a more specific manifestation of that societal violence.

Dead concludes with multiple still-shots of the armed militia retrieving Ben's corpse with meat hooks and heaping it onto a pyre—a mass grave. These images are reminiscent of graphic photos of nineteenth- and twentieth-century lynchings, and of anti-Black violence and domestic terrorism circulating in the media over the past decade.[55] The film's monochrome footage was a budgetary decision to cut costs, since filming in color is more expensive, but the black-and-white imagery worked to the film's advantage.[56] At the time, 75 percent of homes still had black-and-white television sets, and since these devices also acted as a source of information for most families, "[t]o audiences in 1968, the on-screen actions would have visually evoked the newscasts they were seeing at home."[57] This visceral epilogue to Ben's journey would seem familiar to Black American audiences who became an important early audience for *Night of the Living Dead*.

Scholar James McFarland notes that the early marketing and distribution strategy for the film, "paired it with explicitly race-centered movies . . . in urban venues patronized by African American audiences."[58] Jones's intervention did not lead to this particular decision, but the actor's advocacy for the ending likely carried weight with Romero, who refused film distributors' late requests to change the ending on artistic grounds.[59] Above all, Duane Jones's preceding performance and careful consideration of representation lent invaluable weight to his death scene and the grim epilogue.

Duane Jones's interventions in these three instances—rhetorical negotiations between director, scriptwriters, and actor—shifted his character's dialogue and dialect, revealed underlying tensions about how race should be presented on-screen, and imbued the collectively created artifact with enhanced cultural meanings that extended the film's longevity in global public memory. Further, Jones's contributions influenced the future of Black representations in the horror genre, with specific successors in the competent, resourceful Black heroes and heroines of the zombie subgenre that *Night of the Living Dead* inaugurated in 1968.

CONCLUSION

Duane Jones's performance and rhetorical negotiations during *Dead*'s production had a cultural impact on the horror genre that dwarfs Russo's and Romero's original script, transforming the work into an unimpeachably Black film. The greatest proof may be in Jones's unintentional successors—the Black thespians who went on to play roles in zombie subgenre films. In the twenty-first century, the zombie subgenre experienced a revival, and Jones's groundwork in 1968 ensured that Black performers were included in this renaissance. Romero's 1978 follow-up to *Night of the Living Dead*, the appropriately titled *Dawn of the Dawn*, included Ken Foree as the capable Peter Washington, while in the 2002 film *28 Days Later*, Naomie Harris costars as a member of a small band of survivors navigating a zombie outbreak in London. Five years later, Will Smith played the resourceful survivor and scientist Robert Neville in *I Am Legend* (2007), a modernized retelling of the 1954 novel that inspired *Night of Living Dead*. In 2016, child actor Sennia Nanua starred as the protagonist in *The Girl with All the Gifts*.

Kinitra D. Brooks has written about Naomie Harris's Selena in *28 Days Later* and Danai Gurira's Michonne on the comic-inspired television series *The Walking Dead* (2010–2022). Brooks argues that both "contain complex constructions of black female characters, Selena and Michonne, respectively,"[60] and that their creators effectively use "the dynamics of zombie horror to broach the stereotypes that riddle the constructions of the strong black woman, stereotypes of black female sexuality, and the powerful race and gender dynamics that influence the systematic rape of black women."[61] Hence, *Night of the Living Dead*'s reputation made room for creatives working within the zombie subgenre to explore unacknowledged and suppressed societal issues that are brought to the surface in the crucible of a crisis.

The Walking Dead franchise also includes a series of interactive choice-based games, the first of which features a Black protagonist named Lee Everett. Voiced by Dave Fennoy, Lee is a former University of Georgia history professor tried and convicted for murder before the zombie crisis delayed his imprisonment. These circumstances could have easily relied on aged tropes of Black criminality, but instead, the game's narrative focuses on the character's resourcefulness, leadership potential, and parenting skills as Lee finds himself charged with protecting an orphaned child. His crime is an important element of the story that the character conceals, contemplates, and confronts as surrounding characters discover his past. Though the narrative engages his past and the game examines racialized assumptions of criminality, Lee's past is used to interrogate the extreme actions characters are pushed to take in a survival-based emergency.

These high-profile examples omit a number of resourceful Black protagonists across lesser-renown comics, films, television series, video games, and other media. Duane Jones's contribution grants a twofold benefit to the global Black community—one pragmatic; one representational. From a practical standpoint, Black actors have found a comfortable home within the zombie genre, not as the undead's first victims but as enduring survivors. For film actors, this means more exposure that might lead to more work in the future. For actors on television series, a resourceful character suited to survival directly translates into increased profits, future employment on subsequent seasons, and numerous additional benefits that come with re-occurring roles.

The second, representational benefit manifests in the repeated images of resourceful Black survivors that circulate throughout our cultural ecosystem. As Erigha notes, "Hollywood exerts a widespread domination of mass dissemination, production, distribution, and exhibition of popular culture in both American and global markets."[62] Cinema has proven "powerful tools for shaping consciousness" that can "influence people's views about ideas, social issues, and groups in society."[63] Cinema's early embrace of segregation and white supremacist doctrines in the late nineteenth and twentieth centuries has resulted in quantifiably limited Black participation even in the twenty-first century.[64]

Jones's effect on future actors' careers, paired with the surrounding cinema ecosystem, proves that films "can be a vehicle for both racist and antiracist ideologies . . . cinema can serve to counteract racist ideologies."[65] Despite the numerous distorted stereotypes disseminated by the media, the horror zombie subgenre is a reprieve of sorts in that it introduces more nuanced depictions of Blackness. Today, Duane Jones's contribution to racial representation circulates within our individual imaginations and collective popular culture discourses as subsequent generations use genre films to portray Black excellence and expertise to our wider world.

NOTES

1. Library of Congress, "Frequently Asked Questions, Film Registry," https://www.loc.gov/programs/national-film-preservation-board/film-registry/frequently-asked-questions/; Library of Congress, "Preserving the Silver Screen, Library of Congress Information Bulletin," https://www.loc.gov/loc/lcib/9912/nfb.html.
2. George Romero, et al., *Birth of the Living Dead,* directed by Rob Kuhns (2013: First Run Features).
3. Donald Bogle, *Toms, Coons, Mulattoes, Mammies, and Bucks: An Interpretive History of Blacks in American Films* (New York: Bloomsbury Publishing Inc., 2016).
4. John Russo, *The Complete Night of the Living Dead Filmbook* (Pittsburgh, PA: Movie Emporium Inc., 2012); Romero, et al., *Birth of the Living Dead.*
5. Russo, *The Complete Night.*
6. James McFarland, "Philosophy of the Living Dead: At the Origin of the Zombie-Image," *Cultural Critique* 90, no. 1 (2015): 22–63.
7. Ibid., 22.
8. Russo, *The Complete Night*; McFarland, "Philosophy of the Living Dead"; Mathias Clasen, "Vampire Apocalypse: A Biocultural Critique of Richard Matheson's *I Am Legend*," *Philosophy and Literature* 34, no. 2 (2010); Kevin Heffernan, "Inner-City Exhibition and the Genre Film: Distributing *Night of the Living Dead* (1968)," *Cinema Journal* 41, no. 3 (2002).
9. Russo, *The Complete Night*; McFarland, "Philosophy of the Living Dead"; Aaron Pinnix, "*Night of the Living Dead* Dissects the News: Race, the 1967 Riots, and 'Dead Neighbors,'" *Journal of Cinema and Media Studies* 60, no. 4 (2021).
10. Romero et al., *Birth of the Living Dead,* 00:27:20.
11. Russo, *The Complete Night.*
12. Bogle, *Interpretive History of Blacks in American Films.*
13. Ersula Ore, *Lynching: Violence, Rhetoric, and American Identity,* (Oxford: University Press of Mississippi, 2019), 55–64.
14. Ibid., 60.
15. Ibid., 56.
16. Bogle, *Interpretive History of Blacks in American Films.*
17. Ibid., 7.
18. Ibid., 13–14.

19. Maryann Erigha, *The Hollywood Jim Crow: The Racial Politics of the Movie Industry* (New York: New York University Press, 2019).
20. Bogle, *Interpretive History of Blacks in American Films*, 19–20.
21. Ibid., 30.
22. Erigha, *The Hollywood Jim Crow*.
23. Ibid., 33.
24. Ibid., 33–34.
25. Russo, *The Complete Night*; Pinnix, "*Night of the Living Dead* Dissects the News."
26. Library of Congress, "Preserving the Silver Screen."
27. Ben Jones, Duane Jones on *Night of the Living Dead*, Interview by Tim Ferrante, *The Criterion Channel*, December 13, 1987, https://criterionchannel.vhx.tv/videos/duane-jones-on-night-of-the-living-dead, 00:01:40.
28. C. Gerald Fraser, "Duane L. Jones, 51, Actor and Director of Stage Works, Dies," *New York Times*, July 28, 1988, https://www.nytimes.com/1988/07/28/obituaries/duane-l-jones-51-actor-and-director-of-stage-works-dies.html.
29. Fraser, "Duane L. Jones . . . Dies."
30. Romero, et al., *Birth of the Living Dead*.
31. Fraser, "Duane L. Jones . . . Dies."
32. Jones, Duane Jones on *Night of the Living Dead*, 00:01:07.
33. Russo, *The Complete Night*, 7.
34. Ibid., 34.
35. Richard Eldredge, "Q&A with *Night of the Living Dead*'s Judith O'Dea," *Atlanta Magazine*, October 20, 2013, https://www.atlantamagazine.com/news-culture-articles/qa-with-night-of-the-living-deads-judith-odea/.
36. Pinnix, "*Night of the Living Dead* Dissects the News," 121.
37. Arun Rath, "The Secret behind Romero's Scary Zombies: 'I Made Them the Neighbors,'" Weekend Edition, NPR, Sunday, June 20, 2014, https://www.npr.org/2014/07/20/332644099/the-secret-behind-romeros-scary-zombies-i-made-them-the-neighbors, 00:03:50.
38. Bogle, *An Interpretative History of Blacks in American Film*; Ore, *Lynching*.
39. Ore, *Lynching*, 48.
40. Ibid.
41. Jones, *Duane Jones on* Night of the Living Dead, 00:18:00.
42. Ibid.
43. Romero et al., *Birth of the Living Dead*, 00:34:30.
44. Ibid.
45. Eldredge, "Q&A with Judith O'Dea."
46. Bogle, *An Interpretative History of Blacks in American Film*; Ore, *Lynching*.
47. Ore, *Lynching*, 49.
48. Romero et al., *Birth of the Living Dead*.
49. Eldredge, "Q&A with Judith O'Dea."
50. Ytasha Womack, *Afrofuturism: The World of Black Sci-Fi and Fantasy Culture* (Chicago: Chicago Review Press, 2013).
51. Eldredge, "Q&A with Judith O'Dea"; Romero, et al., *Birth of the Living Dead*.
52. Russo, *The Complete Night*, 38.
53. Pinnix, "*Night of the Living Dead* Dissects the News," 121.
54. Henry Hampton and Steve Fayer, *Voices of Freedom: An Oral History of the Civil Rights Movement from the 1950s through the 1980s* (New York: Batham Books, 1990); Rath, "The

Secret Behind Romero"; Romero, et al., *Birth of the Living Dead*; Pinnix, "*Night of the Living Dead* Dissects the News."

55. Hampton and Fayer, *Voices of Freedom*.
56. Russo, *The Complete Night*, 7.
57. Pinnix, "*Night of the Living Dead* Dissects the News," 117.
58. McFarland, "Philosophy of the Living Dead, 24.
59. Romero et al., *Birth of the Living Dead*.
60. Kinitra Brooks, "The Importance of Neglected Intersections: Race and Gender in Contemporary Zombie Texts and Theories," *African American Review* 47, no. 4 (2014): 468–469.
61. Brooks, "Race and Gender in Contemporary Zombie Texts," 469.
62. Erigha, *The Hollywood Jim Crow*, 34.
63. Ibid., 14.
64. Bogle, *An Interpretive History of Blacks in American Films*; Erigha, *The Hollywood Jim Crow*.
65. Erigha, *The Hollywood Jim Crow*, 29.

CHAPTER 12

SEM MEDO DE LOBISOMEM

Subversion, Intimacy, and Animality
in As Boas Maneiras

VALERIA VILLEGAS LINDVALL

As Boas Maneiras (*Good Manners*, Juliana Rojas and Marco Dutra, 2017) focuses on Clara (Isabél Zuaa), a Black nurse hired as a caretaker by Ana (Marjorie Estiano), a white, single, pregnant woman cut off by her wealthy family. The characters eventually develop an intimate relationship, and it is revealed that Ana bears the child of a werewolf, as she displays voracious inclinations to consume blood and raw meat. When Ana dies in childbirth, Clara raises the baby (Joel, intimated to be a *lobisomem*: in English, were-wolf), embracing his animality with tenderness until the final moment of reckoning. This chapter takes a cue from decolonial thought and explores the possibilities of subversion that *As Boas Maneiras* brings about, which I suggest facilitates a critique of the coloniality of gender and Being as discussed by María Lugones and Nelson Maldonado-Torres, re-spectively. I posit that Clara's character re-imagines the Black *babá* (nanny/caretaker) as a paramount figure originated in Brazilian colonial history, subverting her role in il-lustration of what Aph Ko denominates *afro-zoological resistance*. I contend that such subversion is done via the vindication of Clara's subjectivity, which I broach by drawing from bell hooks's meditations on the oppositional gaze and love. In order to articulate this argument, I contextualize the film in relation to Brazilian horror to then explore the significance of the Black *babá* as a representational trope. Lastly, I offer instances that illustrate the subversion of the figure and the film's imagination of an alliance between Clara and Joel as a figurative mend between human and nonhuman animal.

CONTEXTUALIZING *AS BOAS MANEIRAS*

As Boas Maneiras was released after Rojas and Dutra's acclaimed first feature film, *Trabalhar Cansa* (*Hard Labor*, 2011), and after Rojas's well-regarded fantasy musical

Sinfonía da Necrópole (*Symphony of Necropolis*, 2014). *Trabalhar Cansa* was co-directed and co-written by Dutra and Rojas; existing between the realms of the fantastic and the horrific, it offers a grim allegory of the thinning of the middle-class in contemporary Brazil. The film tells the story of Helena (Helena Albergaria) and Otávio (Marat Descartes), a middle-class couple experiencing economic hardship who buy a failing supermarket, hoping to find a way out from their increasingly difficult situation. The supermarket houses a sinister presence that first manifests as an ominous stain, which seems to allegorize the rapid decay of their economic and emotional stability. Importantly, Helena hires Paula (Naloana Lima), a racialized domestic worker whom she underpays and treats with prepotency. In the process, the film suggests the complicity that female liberation and economic autonomy conceal in neoliberal discourses, for this independence often comes at the oppression of the impoverished and/or racialized domestic worker. Such preoccupation is anything but ancillary to the horrific tone of the film, and I would suggest that it effectively predates the relevance of Clara's characterization as a racialized caretaker in *As Boas Maneiras*.

After *Trabalhar Cansa*, the directorial duo's work was quickly incorporated to a canon of features acknowledged for their poignant social critiques articulated through horror and fantasy, alongside works like *Mormaço* (Marina Meliande, 2017) and *O Animal Cordial* (Gabriela Amaral, 2017).[1] Providing valuable contextualization, Alfredo Suppia offers that the filmmakers' work is embedded in a juncture that is progressively departing from what critics and academics have called *Novíssimo Cinema Brasileiro*, a label attributed to Brazilian filmmaking post-2010 and differentiated from the period that preceded it, *Cinema da Retomada* (beginning in the early 1990s). In *very* broad strokes, the *Retomada* period alludes to the resurgence of film production in the country, facilitated by state resources and fiscal exemption, which translated into a steady increase in national productions.[2] On its part, *Novíssimo Cinema Brasileiro* builds on the contributions of the *Retomada* period, but is also complicated with the expansion of streaming and the opportunities for funding, distribution, and production that derive from this practice. *As Boas Maneiras*, like other critically acclaimed, contemporary pieces of fiction––chief among them the exceptional genre-bending *Bacurau* (Juliano Dornelles and Kleber Mendoça Filho, 2019)–– is embedded in a distinct context of industrial and political turmoil precipitated by the multitudinous demonstrations in the country during 2013, the impeachment of Dilma Rousseff in 2016, and the later rise of the extreme-right political establishment led by Jair Bolsonaro.[3] As Suppia underlines, inequality, capitalist exploitation, and systematic violence against Indigenous peoples, Afro-Brazilians, women, and dissidents from gender and sexuality norms have been fundamental preoccupations for the latest genre filmmaking in the country.[4]

It is worth mentioning that contemporary independent and low-budget genre productions have also thrived, enabled by home video distribution and digital technologies. This is no minor detail, for such features come to reflect the ways in which consumers have become active producers able to bypass budget constraints and limited amounts of institutional support.[5] This tendency has resulted in a variegated output, enlisting contributions such as Rodrigo Aragão's *O Cemitério das Almas Perdidas*,

Mavi Simão's *Terminal Praia Grande*, and Glenda Nicácio and Ary Rosa's *Voltei!*––all of them released during 2020, in the face of a challenging panorama aggravated by the COVID-19 pandemic. The shift in production dynamics for genre film and its resilience in the face of budget constraints or political unrest demonstrates that, as Laura Cánepa writes, horror filmmaking in Brazil at large has been an occurrence traversed by discontinuities.[6] The author posits that the country's media intimates a continuous development of horror, but the fact was seldom acknowledged until the 1960s.[7] Cánepa attributes this historiographical silence to the construction of a discernible cinematic national canon, an observation that Suppia seconds by stating that Latin American sci-fi and fantasy media continue to be subject to academic prejudice.[8] In addition, the colonial registry of English written academic work, as Dolores Tierney and Victoria Ruétalo argue, has often contributed to the pigeonholing of Latin American genre film production to the realm of "bad film" appeal.[9] However, the work of specialized critics and academics like Cánepa, Suppia, Carlos Primati, and Eugênio Puppo, among others, establishes valuable coordinates to re-create a history of Brazilian genre filmmaking able to account for the unique ridges and marginal practices that have characterized it.[10]

Ultimately, the discussions that these authors uplift shed light on the difficulty of looking at Brazilian genre filmmaking through the lens of U.S. American and European genre theory. Such historical and methodological discussions also make a strong case to regard *As Boas Maneiras* against a backdrop marked by coloniality, crisis, and governmental neglect of racialized and impoverished peoples to address the ways in which representation has responded to these circumstances. Crucially, *As Boas Maneiras* could be said to be a *rara avis* in the country's production. Its narrative allows for Clara, a Black, queer, female character, to become an embodiment of care and intimacy, resisting her portrayal as a unidimensional figure and championing her unfolding as a subject. As we will see, the relevance of this emphasis on Black, queer, female subjectivity is greater when placed in the genealogy of the representation of the Black body in Brazilian film at large.

BLACK REPRESENTATION IN BRAZILIAN VISUAL CULTURE

The representation of the Black body in Brazilian cinema—and in horror filmmaking, in particular—is a complex matter across mainstream, independent, and exploitation practices. Early observations by Robert Stam tell us that while it came into prominence during the 1960s and '70s, Black representation in Brazilian visual culture has often been contentious. Stam attributes this to the *foundational* colonial gaze that dominated national filmmaking from early on and eventually advanced a vision of Brazil "as a merely tropical appendage of European civilization," as it later saw its visions transform into paternalistic renditions of slavery during the 1940s and '50s. These were productively

challenged during the subsequent decades by way of stylistically innovative and politically engaged strategies of the likes of Cinema Novo and *tropicalismo*, which illustrate
cultural alternatives to Western *and* Westernizing modes of seeing.[11] By way of example,
films like the tropicalista *Macunaíma* (Joaquim Pedro de Andrade, 1969) put the finger
on the discursive and figurative whitening of Brazilian identity via a story that trades in
the absurd to deliver critical sharpness. The decades that followed saw the nuancing of
Black characters and advanced the gaze of Black filmmakers, presenting different takes
on easily recognizable tropes and eventually facilitating their subversion.

Consequently, the colonial implications of the gaze that Stam traces can be said to
linger across decades of horror in written and audiovisual form. For instance, Cánepa
notes that Brazilian folklore is also traversed by colonial history and its modes of representation of historical trauma. By way of illustration, she introduces *O negrinho
do pastoreio*, a tale, collected by folklorist Luis da Câmara Cascudo in 1945, about an
enslaved Black boy fed to the ants by his enslaver, who is later assailed by the boy's spirit.
The representation of the Black body in relation to horror visual culture also appears
informed by racial hierarchies that heavily code the gaze. A case in point is *Macumba
Love* (Douglas Fowley, 1960), a B film that Cánepa denominates a "racist prodigy." The
writer aptly denounces that the U.S. American production shot in Brazil hinges on
the exoticization of the sexual and spiritual lives of Afro-Brazilians, casting the onus of
the monster on the racialized body by alluding to voodun as a malignant practice. The
complex relation of the image to the Black body, Cánepa intimates, also carries on to
other representations in Brazilian horror film proper.

The author makes related observations about later films and suggests the potential political and racial implications of *O anjo da noite* (Walter Hugo Khouri, 1974), in
which a babysitter is harassed by mysterious phone calls in a mansion in Petrópolis.
For Cánepa, it is telling that the groundskeeper (the only Black character in the film)
is accosted by sinister forces that emanate from the luxurious mansion, potentially
narrativizing the tensions between the aristocratic Brazilian family and the racialized
working class. Further, the representation of the Black body as a subject of desire was
substantially transformed in narratives that traded in horror, comedy, and pornography
during the 1980s: chief among them are those starring Chumbinho, a Black performer
with dwarfism—such as *Fuk fuk à la Brasileira* (Jean Garret, 1986) and *As taras de um
mini-vampiro* (José Adalto Cardoso, 1987).[12]

The variegated portrayal of Black characters in horror that Cánepa offers illustrates
what João Carlos Rodrigues writes: the imagination of the Black body in Brazilian popular culture has been made intelligible by way of character types that tend to negotiate
Afro-diasporic imagination—molding their characteristics after certain *orishas* (broadly,
divinities) in the Candomblé and Umbanda spiritual traditions—and colonial ideation.
Therefore, reading these representations through U.S. American filters would be reductive and misleading, as Stam suggests.[13] Doing so, I would second, would also constitute
a neocolonial strategy that imposes vocabularies of the Global North onto Brazilian audiovisual production. Here, it is useful to turn to Rodrigues, who offers a taxonomy of
recurring representational tropes in national visual culture. Briefly: *pretos velhos* (older

figures that in origin convey ancestral knowledge, often depicted as superstitious, ig-norant, or servile); *mártir* (martyr, made intelligible through suffering and punish-ment, often in the context of slavery narratives); *negro de alma branca* (educated folks assimilated to a society that still alienates them, reminiscent of the forms of colonized subjectivity that Frantz Fanon discusses in his *Black Skins, White Masks*); *nobre selvagem* (the noble savage, taken to embody respectability and resilience); *negro revoltado* (often a belligerent Black, male figure associated with anti-colonial resistance set up to fail in his utopian enterprises of liberation); *negão* (as the manifestation of the objectified and hypersexualized Black man, portrayed as a figure dangerously close to animality); *malandro* (cunning figure turned bandit to varying degrees of sympathy); *favelado* (char-acter inhabiting peripheral or marginalized spaces associated with working-class or impoverished Brazilian folk); and the *crioulo doido* (comical figure that in Rodrigues's view collects European and local traditions to render an infantilized Black trickster).[14]

Rodrigues's taxonomy also reflects the ways in which gendering traverses these tropes. Black female characters are predominantly represented in terms of the function of their sexual appeal—or lack thereof: as objectified, hypersexual figurations (*mulata boazuda*, often portrayed by light-skinned performers); as an idealized figure that contests the conception of the Black female body as only destined to satiate sexual desire (*musa*) and the *mãe preta*, referring to the archetype of the Black wet nurse in service of white, wealthy families, a figure that originated in Brazilian colonial history. The *mãe preta* speaks to the lasting effects of colonial power in its organization of private and public spaces, and underlines the naturalization of the female, racialized body as an in-strument, rather than as a subject. Vitally, it is this trope that proves the most productive for this analysis, allowing us to think through its relevance and subversion in the figure of Clara.

CONSIDERING CLARA AS BABÁ

The significance of the *mãe preta/babá* as a representational trope conjures the historical relation between mother and wet nurse/nanny as a racialized occurrence and is relevant to the discussion of Clara as its challenging flipside. Crucially, the Black wet nurse is a paramount trope in the construction of national identity, as she appears in foundational discussions pertaining to the racial hierarchies that stem from colonial history. However, these matters are far from straightforward: as Lilia Moritz Schwarcz problematizes, "it is often said that Brazil is not for beginners."[15] To assert a precise view of the ways in which racial relations have amounted to the creation of a national identity is an ambi-tious enterprise. Key meditations on the matter, such as Gilberto Freyre's *Casa-grande & senzala* (1933) and Sérgio Buarque de Holanda's *Raízes do Brasil* (1936), take a keen look at the implications of racial mixture (*mestiçagem*) as impactful in the creation of a modern Brazilian nation-state—a discussion in which the Black wet nurse appears as a relevant presence.[16] As Tiago de Luca summarizes, Freyre's writing constituted the

spatial proximity of the *casa grande* (big manor) and the *senzala* (slave quarters) as a figurative relation of intimacy and thus, relationality between enslavers and enslaved in a
fashion that "[allegedly established] a more humane relationship than the ones observed
in other slave-holding societies."[17] In essence, such discussion pertains to the melding
of public and private spaces, literally and figuratively, in the construction of a national
character that grapples with the racial hierarchies inherited from a past of slavery by centering intimacy. On his part, Buarque de Holanda famously posits that Brazil would "give
the world a cordial man" (*o homem cordial*). This affirmation, note Schwarcz and Heloisa
Starling, has been widely misunderstood: far from complacency, they affirm, the author
alludes to the tendency of championing intimacy as a national trait and makes a critical
"reference to the difficulty in being proactive in establishing effective institutions."[18]

Both authors have been vastly critiqued. By way of illustration, Rachel Randall
asserts that the nostalgic rendition of the Afro-Brazilian wet nurse in colonial Brazil
is in Freyre also a yearning for intimacy that romanticizes a tense past and constitutes
these relationships as a quasi-mythical building block of national identity.[19] Rita Segato
seconds this contention, arguing that Freyre and Buarque de Holanda dim their focus
to accommodate a view that eventually occluded the multiple sites of enunciation from
which history can be told, written, and experienced.[20] Relatedly, Segato notes that the
nostalgically regarded bond of breastfeeding began fading by the second half of the
nineteenth century, as public-health discourses started characterizing the Black *babá*
as a transmitter of disease. These concerns, she writes, were related to the impulse of
keeping Black figures of care away from the jealously kept intimacy of the white home.

The reification of the *babá*'s motherly body that Segato notes could be said to persist
in the naturalization of poorly remunerated domestic labor as exercised by racialized
bodies.[21] Moreover, the author denounces the idea that the Black *babá* appears to be
a paradoxically hyper-visible and hyper-invisible presence, doubly obliterated: she
is negated in her undeniably relevant labor of care on account of her Blackness, and
yet appears to drive the narrative of a modern, integrated Brazil that gazes at its past
of slavery at a distance. Such discursive gesture carries on to the fashioning of visual
culture: giving an account of family photographs during the nineteenth century, Segato
intimates that Black *babás* appeared concealed in the crafting of the image, holding the
child of wealthy white families to keep them from fussing but standing beneath a layer
of fabric.[22] Nevertheless, the contours of their figures refused to disappear. This overt
visual separation between white motherhood and Black surrogate care illustrates bell
hooks's contention of the female Black body as traversed by a hegemonic, white, and
patriarchal gaze that fashions the image. As hooks writes with potency, Black female
bodies have become naturalized accoutrements "to enhance and maintain white womanhood as object of the phallocentric gaze."[23] In light of these reflections, the fashioning
of a national discourse in legitimation of colonial patriarchy appears undetachable from
the role that the Black *babá* has been historically granted in visual culture.

Consuelo Lins's film *Babás* (2010) aptly presents this correlation in the making. The
film opens with the portrait of a white child and a Black *babá* during the 1800s (figure
12.1). The voice-over that accompanies the image states that a historian once commented

FIGURE 12.1   Opening frame of Lins's *Babás* (2010). Screenshot by the author.

that "almost all of Brazil fits in that picture."[24] The voice's script gestures toward the intimate, yet hierarchical, relation between the two bodies, describing the following: as the
child leans over her shoulder, her confrontational gaze seems to evoke the pain of separation from her own children, inflicted so she could be "*his* wetnurse."[25] Importantly,
this stark visual resource is not lost on its relevance. Rather, I would posit that this image
fiercely suggests the possibility of resistance. I return to hooks's elaborations on the oppositional gaze, as she posits that "even in the worse circumstances of domination, the
ability to manipulate one's gaze in the face of structures of domination that would contain it, opens up the possibility of agency."[26] The image, I would contend, intimates a
gesture that defies resignation. Looking back, the woman in the frame reminds us that
visual culture can also entail the examination and indictment of colonial, patriarchal
modes of seeing and representing.

The depiction of the Black *babá*, the image tells us, is the product of national, historical circumstances that inform visual culture in a country that allowed slavery until
1888. As Schwarcz and Starling write, racial tensions stand at the core of national identity, and as a result, "the country defines itself on the basis of gradations of skin colour.
Whereas those who achieve success become 'whiter,' those who become impoverished
become 'darker.' "[27] The authors credit this phenomenon to the reception of 40 percent of
enslaved persons brought from Africa by Portuguese invaders to what today constitutes
the territory of Brazil, adding that the Indigenous population was decimated by 95 percent after the invasion.[28] By elucidating the significance of this process, Schwarcz and
Starling strike a chord: for them, the legacy of slavery informs all manners of structural
violence toward racialized bodies. Consequently, such violence also results in the naturalization of an ontological differentiation that takes whiteness as a point of departure
to understand humanity and subjectivity. In other words, the authors illuminate the
relevance of race as an impactful fiction: the gradation of color to which they allude

also becomes a gradation in the construction of subjectivity and, thus, permeates the construction of the image. Such dynamics evince the persistence of colonial hierarchies embodied in the relation between child and Black *babá*, and allude to what Aníbal Quijano conceptualizes as the coloniality of power.[29] The author elucidates a matrix of power facilitated by the invention of race and the colonial exploitation of labor that survives in the systematic oppression of the racialized body, exercising influence over the management of labor, authority, gender/sexuality, and knowledge/intersubjectivity in the fashioning of colonial modernity as a teleological process. María Lugones contests Quijano's elaborations by asserting that gender is in fact also traversed by the constitution of race, advancing that the gender binary is a colonial by-product. For Lugones, the racialization and gendering of bodies is also a violent, co-constitutive colonial gesture.[30]

Importantly, Lugones argues that the racialized body under coloniality becomes fashioned after its alleged animality. In her view, normative gender categories stem, in fact, from the foundational differentiation between human/nonhuman. Therefore, for the author there is no such thing as "Indigenous woman" or "Black woman," as the term "woman" in principle only recognized a full, ontologically valid point of departure on white womanhood.[31] Lugones sharply indicts the colonial logic, that intertwines race and gender as powerful, yet driving fictions, and has historically justified oppression and violence over the racialized body. As a result, she asserts, racialized, masculinized bodies are constituted as *machos*, and racialized, feminized bodies are constituted as *hembras*: as gendered animals.[32] Consequently, Lugones tells us, the understanding of "rational" and "human" became associated with the normative, white body of the colonizer, forcefully entitled to the exploitation of the racialized body. She denominates the arbitration of gender and sexuality molded after colonial ideation as the modern/colonial gender system. The author suggests that such a system is not only colonial in its conception, but also heterosexist in its formulation, for heterosexuality only operates as a hegemonic mode of relationality in the grander discourse of coloniality.

In summary, for Lugones race and gender are inextricably bound in the upkeeping of colonial hierarchies of power: here, racism, patriarchy, and capitalism appear as co-constitutive systems of oppression. Similarly, Aph Ko asserts that the very constitution of race and animality as co-related colonial notions is in fact a pervasive gesture of conceptual violence, positing that "animal is part of the vocabulary of white supremacist violence; it signifies the rhetorical and social branding of certain bodies, which white supremacy wants to *consume, exploit and eliminate* without question."[33] Lugones and Ko touch upon the foundational, colonial differentiation of the racialized, animalized, and feminized body as defined in its hierarchical relation to a white, male, universal subject as the measure of humanity.

Drawing from both authors, "woman," just like "animal," is revealed as a relational concept that only makes sense in a colonial, white supremacist frame of reference of reality and truth. Nelson Maldonado-Torres broaches the philosophical legitimization of this ontological differentiation, which he conceptualizes as the coloniality of Being. The author builds on the work of Enrique Dussel on colonial modernity and reformulates Fanon's writing to explain the historical constitution of the Black subject as a "non-subject," as if expelled to a zone of nonbeing.[34] Maldonado-Torres urges us to look at the effects of coloniality in the very fashioning of the subject, appealing to the naturalization of what Fanon conceptualizes as the *damné*: the colonized body made expendable, denied interiority, and understood in function of its suffering. By turning to these thinkers' contributions, it is possible to better understand the ways in which the racialized, feminized subject appears on the bottom rung of subjectivity within coloniality. Further, such formulations enable us to think through the Black *babá* as a figure that, stemming from colonial ideation, is subverted in *As Boas Maneiras*.

CLARA AND ANA: INTERIORITY AND LOVE AS RADICAL POSSIBILITIES

Consequently, I would argue that the portrayal of the *mãe preta/babá* as the embodiment of a hierarchical relation of domestic and emotional labor cannot be detached from the naturalized, colonial notion of the racialized body as close to animality and subservience. This figuration is provocatively turned on its head in *As Boas Maneiras*: the negation of colonized subjectivity that Maldonado-Torres, Lugones, and Ko indict is vindicated in the film by its underscoring of Clara's interiority. I posit that such vindication is conveyed, in first instance, through the portrayal of desire and agency in Clara's relationship to Ana. In the film, the Black *babá* is a recognizable figure and yet, the hierarchical relations at the core of its inception are contested through the portrayal of desire and pleasure, facilitated by the fantastic as a mode of telling.

By admission of the film's directors, this narrative mode of delivery originated from a dream that they turned into a fairytale.[35] The very first minute of the feature confirms the choice: as Clara stands in Ana's threshold, she is welcomed by a doormat that reads *Olim pulchra filia regia* (roughly, "once upon a time, a ruling girl"). Initially, the film delineates a relationship that hinges on hierarchy. This is effectively established in a distinctly tense opening scene, sobering in its tone after the promise of fairytale intimated by the doormat. In an awkward exchange, Ana expresses her hesitance about hiring Clara due to her lack of work references. Clara directs her gaze down, avoiding meeting Ana's eyeline—a gesture captured with impertinence in an over-the-shoulder shot. The exchange establishes a clear spatial and figurative distance between employer and prospective employee. Nevertheless, the distance is quickly broken as Ana seems to go into painful contractions. The camera remains fixed on her, and it is Clara who transgresses the spatial delimitation by quickly assisting her with an embrace from behind, urging her to breathe slowly. The physical gesture swiftly undoes their hierarchical relation, and intimacy is foregrounded with sudden efficacy: the decisive moment has Clara dwelling freely in a space otherwise reserved for Ana's disposition. Clara's movement in the frame breaks the visual stillness that reminds one of Lins's tableau, and she is hired on the spot.

As the film unfolds, the distance between both characters is abolished in full, and their emotional and sexual investment is showcased as an ultimate manifestation of intimacy. I would argue that the film presents an intimate relationship that not only challenges a colonial arrangement of labor, but also contests the heterosexist constitution of the colonized body—a gesture uplifted by Rui Poças's cinematography. An illustrative instance of this challenge is the depiction of Clara's and Ana's first kiss, which I would posit constitutes a negotiation. As Clara comes back from a night out, the camera spies on Ana enfolded in a blue hue, illuminated only by the refrigerator's intense white light as she rummages inside it. Clara urges her to go back to bed, as Ana plunges forward to reduce the space between their bodies: the camera takes their image in as she smells Clara, drawing her near in an embrace that develops into a kiss. She licks Clara's lips, grabbing her by the back of the neck and scratching her shoulder. The vibrancy of the scene's string music matches the sway of their bodies engaging in a passionate kiss, the camera closing in. Suddenly, the passage flirts with the expectation of the Black body as consumable *and* as animal. Ana violently bites Clara's lip. To Clara's shock, she has drawn blood. A close-up displays Ana savoring the blood, her vacant stare cutting through the cerulean darkness with its yellow hue. Immediately after, we see Clara crying before the bathroom mirror as she rinses the scratches on her shoulder, her breathe sinking into a contained sob—the reinforcement of a relation of dominion has come with a deceitful, abusive kiss that Ana does not remember the next morning.

Based on this instance, their desire appears complicated by racial hierarchies that gesture toward the prevalence of coloniality even in the encoding of desire and pleasure. Nevertheless, I would suggest, the passage that depicts their first sexual encounter challenges the seeming inescapability of heterosexist, colonial constraints on intimacy. The scene follows a moment in which Clara comes to Ana's room as she screams, seemingly prey to a nightmare. The private space of the room becomes a site where hierarchies dissolve by the intervention of pleasure: backlighting enfolds them in soft pink shades as if to gesture toward the shift that consent brings about in this instance, visually opposing the blue lighting that enfolded them during their first kiss. The blocking of the actors is starkly reminiscent of their first, awkward encounter during the interview. Clara sits behind Ana, comforting her in a similar embrace shown via a medium shot. However, the action's context shifts to develop into an erotically coded instance. As they kiss, Clara caresses Ana: reciprocity becomes the undertone to this interaction, and her gaze is no longer evasive.

As hooks reminds us, love is one of the ultimate manifestations of interiority. When she writes that "[w]e yearn for love—that we seek it—even when we lack hope that it can really be found," we are reassured that agency can be found in tenderness.[36] In *Clara*, the embodiment of love entails a bold claim to subjectivity in the face of coloniality, which has for long naturalized the idea that racialized existence can only be made intelligible through pain, trauma, and loss. Clara's look at Ana is one of recognition (figure 12.2), and with this, the frame in which Clara is centered reminds us of the interrogating gaze that hooks describes as oppositional, political, and subversive of hierarchies of power. As the characters embark in the knowledge of each other though desire, they are

FIGURE 12.2 The first intimate encounter: Ana (left) and Clara (right). Screenshot by the author.

imagined as unburdened by the employment relationship that brought them together in the first place.

The role of subservience and alterity recurrently associated with the Black *babá* in our historical overview appears contested in Clara's active search for pleasure. Moreover, it is significant that this defiance still gestures toward the recognition of the labor of care that the Black *babá* embodies: a close-up shows Ana's pregnant belly in the foreground as Clara kisses it gently, slowly tracing its curve to disappear between her lover's legs. This re-imagination of the Black *babá* vindicates the historical occlusion of the figure in the unapologetic centering of her pleasure and agency. Tight shots are championed throughout the scene, underlining the complicity of both women in giving *and* receiving pleasure. The camera remains close in its rendition of the encounter but pans sporadically and almost unnoticeably. The scene is devoid of music: the faint sighs and moans of the couple are afforded to the viewer for a few seconds, bookended by an overhead shot of both women next to each other, heads on pillows, again enfolded in blue hues. The encounter is short but intense, sparing the viewer from a voyeuristic, objectifying treatment of lesbian intimacy. The scene effectively reformulates their closeness as a chosen occurrence. However, the seeming limitations of this intimacy cannot elude the viewer: immediately after their passionate encounter, Clara notices Ana's supernatural transformation as a wandering automaton, as she cuts across an empty square to find a cat that she devours with vicious hunger. The next morning, an enthusiastic Ana is shown exercising before a televised Zumba class to João Bosco and Vinicius's tune "Chora, me liga," a song that suggests a veiled warning: *você sabia que eu era assim, paixão de uma noite que logo tem fim* (in reference to a one-night stand). As Clara stares, leaving the frame behind a wall, the events of the night prior cannot help but become suspect.

Once more, this tension is narrativized in the film, which returns to the consumption of the Black body in a gesture that evinces the historical burden of coloniality.

Immediately after finding out about Ana's flesh-eating desires, Clara sneaks some of her blood into the spaghetti sauce she cooks for lunch. As Ana devours with gusto, her literal consumption of Clara's blood illustrates what Ko denominates "zoological oppression," whereby the Black body is seen as a "consumable fleshy item to be ingested and/or materially repurposed by white supremacy."[37] Ko draws on Vincent Woodard's work on the figurative and literal consumption of the Black body in U.S. slave culture, which illuminates the pervasive, colonial politics of desire that have historically informed its hegemonic depiction.[38] The film's acknowledgement of this dynamic displays a negotiation that, with poignancy, reflects back on colonial vocabularies of desire, animality, and intimacy while confronting their influence in the depiction of erotic involvement. Moreover, with the death of Ana in childbirth, the radical potential of love and intimacy takes a different form, displaced to Joel (Miguel Lobo). In the second half of the film, I argue, the narrative imagines a future where the colonial schism between human and nonhuman animal can be mended.

CLARA AND JOEL: HUMAN AND NONHUMAN ANIMAL ALLIANCES

Another way in which the film confronts and subverts racial and labor hierarchies embodied in Clara is its portrayal of the bond she develops with Joel. While the first hour of the film builds up the intimacy between the two women, Ana's death prompts the narrative to uplift the relationship between Clara and the boy. Interestingly, Ana's death and Joel's birth occur the night of the Festa Junina, a celebration that dates back to the colonial introduction of Catholicism and over time became a melding of local, Afro-diasporic and European customs. In other words, birth and death appear marked by negotiation, and Joel's entering the world becomes a transformative event. Craving pine nuts during what resembles the onset of a panic attack, Ana convinces Clara to buy the food she longs for—a gesture of care that quickly turns into a traumatic passage. Upon returning to the apartment, Clara witnesses how, as a close-up reveals, Ana has her belly torn from the inside as Joel claws his way out. Blood welcomes him into life as his mother dies.

However, the distressing passage of Ana's death does not foreclose the radical possibilities of transformation that love and intimacy bring about in the film. I would argue that the scene contests what hooks notes as the distinctly white, patriarchal worshipping of death over love. In transmuting such nearness to Joel as he comes into the world embraced by a grieving Clara, the liberating potential of an ethics of love is underscored as a gateway to a graspable future.[39] In the face of a racialized subjectivity violently marked by colonial ideation, the continuity of love, death, and transformation in this chain of events becomes a powerful prospect. In its narrative disposition, the film allows Clara's character to be foregrounded in her interiority through desire, love, *and* grief, dispelling the animalization/de-subjectivation of the racialized body under coloniality. In the process, I would suggest, this gesture reminds us of Audre Lorde's indictment of the colonial philosophical project: "The white fathers told us: I think, therefore I am. The Black mother within each of us—the poet—whispers in our dreams: *I feel, therefore I can be free*."[40] The recuperation of love and care in the figure of the proverbial Black mother that Lorde alludes to is also a claim to interiority, an enterprise championed in the second half of the film. Further, hooks's discussion on love and loss potently resonates with the development of the narrative after Ana's death: the bond that Clara develops with Joel in the embrace of his animality becomes a radical possibility of mending the colonial, conceptual violence that conflates the racialized body with animality.

Crucially, the expectations of animality are not cast upon the Black body, but rather displaced to Joel's werewolf self. The relationship between Clara and him constitutes, I posit, a rupture of the colonial alterity forcefully inscribed on the racialized body: monstrosity resides outside of Clara's own body, and yet, is embraced by her through care and kinship. The first gesture that sets the tone to this tenderness is Joel's birth. As a shocked Clara comes home to discover Ana's corpse, belly clawed open, she also encounters the minuscule werewolf baby wrapped in the umbilical cord. As a close-up reveals, she detangles the baby with exceptional care, facilitating his harrowing entrance into the world. The film continues to establish visual kinship with the figure of Clara as a *babá*—the character is shown offering her breast to a sobbing Joel, who mercilessly latches on, drawing blood. As the camera remains in tight view of this instance of breastfeeding, Clara's hand wipes the baby's mouth, effectively establishing a connection with the significance of nurturing of the Black wet nurse's bosom and the newborn to reconceptualize it as an operation of voluntary engagement (figure 12.3).

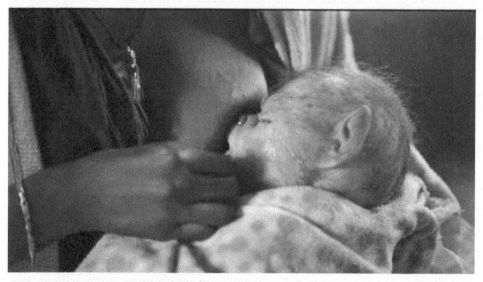

FIGURE 12.3 Clara breastfeeding Joel. Screenshot by the author.

The film reprises the gesture of alliance between human and nonhuman animal as it progresses. It is intimated that seven years have gone by, and Joel's werewolf nature is depicted as a part of the character's daily life. Clara has made a provision to have Joel sleep safe in a hidden, steel-reinforced room where nobody else will be the wiser about his night transformation into a *lobisomem*. The disposition of the space in which Joel is kept to ensure his safety mirrors the care implied in Clara's embrace of Joel's animality. As the camera pans around, the small space is shown as a room made homey with toys, a series of chalk marks to document Joel's height, and even a mattress atop of which the boy sits tucked in blankets, extending his arm as Clara shackles him to the wall.

Here, Joel's animalized body becomes the object of Clara's love, and their bond suggests a mode of relationality in which the human and the nonhuman animal become inextricably linked. Such a bond is aptly underlined in Clara's routine, tending to Joel with exceptional tenderness: the camera pays keen attention as she cuts his nails and shaves his body, as to allow for him to pass undetected and, thus, unharmed through life. Such kinship, I suggest, momentarily fulfills the possibility of "relocating the animal within the landscape of white supremacist domination but also learning to reclaim our senses and our experiences with nature as well as our natural selves," as Ko writes. The author conceptualizes this operation as Afro-zoological resistance: the mending of the relationship between Black/colonized body, nature, and animals, severed by coloniality.[41]

The closing sequence of the film sharply foregrounds the political potency of this alliance. After Joel starts acting out on account of his stirred animality after tasting beef for the first time—tellingly, while away from Clara's sight—he goes on several forays to find his origins. His rebelliousness precipitates a discovery of his own nature as a werewolf, and culminates with his escape to the Festa Junina despite Clara's vehement opposition. The occasion evokes the night of his birth: an evening crowned by a full moon in which transformation is impending. The boy is shown rehearsing with a girl from school for an upcoming musical number with his class. However, the joy is undercut as a close-up of his hands reveals long hair and nails sprouting suddenly and seemingly painfully: the boy is shown in his full *lobisomem* form. Panic-ridden screams from Joel's former dancing partner drown the music, stirring anger and outrage in the partygoers. Strikingly, the passage offers a defiant contrast, signaled by the incorporation of nondiegetic music: a lullaby takes over the lynch mob's raucous noise. The scene underscores the restless hunting of Joel and Clara by the mob, but offers solace and safety as the characters find shelter in the reinforced room that keeps the boy every night. As the tension increases and the lynch mob approaches, the recurrent depiction of touch as communion and comfort is reprised. The lullaby overflows and challenges the violent yells of their prosecutors. Clara undoes the shackles that keep Joel restrained, caressing his paw. A look of recognition is underlined in intercut close-ups of the characters staring at each other —-the power of the gaze as a means of communion and alliance is stressed one last time. The mend between both bodies, historically oppressed and put at the service of colonial patriarchy, is played out as the mend between mother and son. As a last act of resistance, the characters hold on to the agency in their gaze. Placed behind

FIGURE 12.4 Closing frame of the film. Screenshot by the author.

them, the camera aligns the spectator with their point of view, facing the door about to open to the violence of the lynch mob, to face it come what may (figure 12.4).

The last scene teases that they look back to stand their ground, fulfilling hooks's formulation about the radical potential of the gaze as a claim to subjectivity. Ultimately, hooks posits:

> the "gaze" has been and is a site of resistance of colonized black people globally. Subordinates in relations of power learn experientially that there is a critical gaze, one that "looks" to document, one that is oppositional. In resistance struggle, the power of the dominated to assert agency by claiming and cultivating "awareness" politicizes "looking" relations—one learns to look a certain way in order to resist.[42]

That such a stark scene brings the film to an open ending becomes a promise of subversion that embodies hooks's observations on love, the gaze, and resistance. The last frame teases a future in which historically oppressed racialized human and nonhuman animal bodies stand their ground, gazing back and visually aligning the viewer to a future sketched from Clara and Joel's vantage point. With this vindication, the film suggests a view of liberation and autonomy before the realities reified through the lens of coloniality and its forcefully universalized truths.

CONCLUSION

This chapter discusses the relevance of *As Boas Maneiras* as a piece of politically engaged horror/fantasy filmmaking. As I contend, the historical significance of the Black *babá* as a paramount figure of Brazilian visual culture is uplifted in the film's articulation of Clara, and foregrounds her interiority as a strategy of subversion that also functions as a gateway to the narrative. Moreover, the film's challenge to this trope speaks to the profound influence of racial hierarchies as the continued legacy of coloniality, aptly confronting its articulation of the racialized body as an animalized subjectivity of ontological alterity. As I demonstrate, the film employs the vocabularies of fantasy and horror to suggest an ethics of love by establishing explicit kinship between the racialized body and the body of the animal. This operation, I argue, gestures toward a future of resistance and contestation that reflects on the white supremacist construction of racialized and animal bodies, placing keen attention on bonds of intimacy and reparation that escape conceptualization. Dutra and Rojas propose a disobedient politics of representation that illuminates the currency of colonial notions of race, gender, and sexuality, delivering a different iteration of racialized subjectivity as vindicated in experiences of love, desire, and even grief. Ultimately, this re-imagination of the Black *babá* becomes a potentially powerful indictment: it gestures toward the creation of genre filmmaking firmly rooted in epistemologies that speak *about* and *from* the South, unruly and difficult to contain in the paradigms of Global Northern frameworks.

NOTES

1. See Giancarlo Backes Couto and Carlos Gerbase, "A Mancha no cinema de horror brasileiro da década de 2010: Uma análise de Trabalhar Cansa, Mormaço e O Animal Cordial," *Revista ECO-Pós* 24, no. 3 (2021).

2. Alfredo Suppia, "On the Present and Future of Brazilian Film Studies: Some Preliminary Notes," *Romance Quarterly* 67, no. 1 (2020): 37–40. An invaluable account of the *Cinema da Retomada* as a pivotal moment of Brazilian cinema is Lúcia Nagib's and Samuel Paiva's documentary *Passages* (2019).

3. At the time of writing, elections in the country have once again stirred political and civil unrest, for they are still to capitulate by means of a second round disputed between Bolsonaro and the country's former president, Luiz Inácio Lula da Silva. In the middle of this galvanizing scenario, *Bacurau* continues to posit a relevant statement by portraying the resistance of the periphery as propelled by racialized, impoverished, and insurgent bodies. The film has inspired manifold pieces on its implications as contemporary genre cinema that unapologetically showcases its political vein, and as a meaningful representation of the Brazilian Northeast. See Felipe Bastos and Eduardo Gonçalves, "Quem nasce em Bacurau é gente? Género e precariedade de vida no filme Bacurau," *Revista Digital do LAV* 13, no. 2 (2020); Bethania Assy and Vera Karam de Chueiri, "Lentes potentes e empoeiradas: violência e resistência em Bacurau," *Viso: Cadernos de estética aplicada* 14, no. 26 (2020).

4. Suppia, "On the Present and Future of Brazilian Film Studies," 43.

5. Alfredo Suppia, "The Quest for Latin American Science Fiction & Fantasy Film," *Frames Cinema Journal* 6 (2014), http://framescinemajournal.com/article/the-quest-for-latin-american-science-fiction-fantasy-film/.

6. Laura Loguercio Cánepa, "Medo de quê? Uma história do horror nos filmes brasileiros." PhD Universidade Estadual de Campinas, 2008; Laura Loguercio Cánepa, "Panorama

histórico en el cine brasileño," in *HORROfílmico. Aproximaciones al cine de terror en Latinoamérica y el Caribe*, ed. Rosana Díaz-Zambrana and Patricia Tomé. Translated by Jorge Cáceres (San Juan, PR: San Juan Editorial Isla Negra, 2012).

7. Several critics and academics suggest that the inception of Brazilian horror film can be dated back to José Mojica Marins's *À Meia-Noite Levarei sua Alma* (1964), though Cánepa skillfully demonstrates that proto-horror texts can be found as early as 1908 with the silent film *O Diablo* and, in terms of sound film, with Luis Barros's *O Jovem Tataravô* (1937). Cánepa, "Panorama histórico en el cine brasileño."

8. Suppia, "The Quest for Latin American Science Fiction & Fantasy Film."

9. The authors propose "latsploitation" as a methodological tool to approach manifold Latin American cinematic practices within production, reception, and distribution that are often decontextualized in academic and fan literature. See Victoria Ruétalo and Dolores Tierney, eds., *Latsploitation, Exploitation Cinemas and Latin America* (New York: Routledge 2009).

10. See Eugênio Puppo, *Horror no Cinema Brasileiro* (São Paulo: Centro Cultural Banco do Brasil, 2009); "Sangue, sexo e riso: Espectros do horror nos filmes brasileiros," http://www.portalbrasileirodecinema.com.br/horror/ensaio-sangue-sexo-riso-por-carlos-primati.php?indice=ensaios. Suppia also sheds light on Bernadette Lyra's and Gelson Santana's *Cinema de bordas* (2006) as a related discussion about fringe and genre practices. Suppia, "On the Present and Future of Brazilian Film Studies," 39; Suppia, "The Quest for Latin American Science Fiction & Fantasy Film."

11. Robert Stam, "Slow Fade to Afro: The Black Presence in Brazilian Cinema," *Film Quarterly* 36, no. 2 (Winter 1982–1983): 17. The author's later work on Brazilian Tropicalismo, popular, and visual culture is fundamental to the field, as evinced by his *Tropical Multiculturalism. A Comparative History of Race in Brazilian Cinema and Culture* (1997).

12. Loguercio Cánepa, "Medo de quê?," 74; 223; 302–303; 404–405.

13. Stam, "Slow Fade to Afro," 27–28.

14. João Carlos Rodrigues, *O negro brasileiro e o cinema* (Rio de Janeiro: Pallas, 2011), 20–40. The author offers a character type that stands in the middle: the *afro-baiano*, a figure that intently recuperates cultural traits and attires associated with, or taken to evoke, African traits at large. However, he notes this particular embodiment as a relatively recent occurrence, and asserts his caution by stating its ambiguous position as a trope that could become a caricature.

15. Lilia Moritz Schwarcz, "Sérgio Buarque de Holanda e essa tal de 'cordialidade,'" *Psicanálise e Cultura* 31, no. 46 (2008): 83.

16. Schwarcz in Rachel Randall, "Cordiality and Intimacy in Contemporary Brazilian Culture: Introduction," *Journal of Iberian and Latin-American Studies* 24, no. 3 (2018): 295–296.

17. Tiago de Luca, "'Casa Grande & Senzala': Domestic space and class conflict in Casa Grande and Que horas ela volta?," in *Space and Subjectivity in Contemporary Brazilian Cinema*, ed. Antônio Márcio da Silva and Mariana Cunha (2017), 207.

18. Lilia Moritz Schwarcz and Heloisa M. Starling, *Brazil. A Biography* (New York: Picador, 2020), xxiii.

19. Ibid., 297–298.

20. Rita Laura Segato, "El Edipo Negro: Colonialidad y Forclusión de Género y Raza," in *La Crítica de la Colonialidad en Ocho Ensayos y Una Antropología por Demanda* (Buenos Aires: Prometeo, 2013), 183.

21. Updated data on domestic work in Brazil reveals this overrepresentation. As per data for 2020, over 92 percent of the 4.9 million domestic workers accounted for are women, and over 65 percent are Black people. *Trabalho doméstico no Brasil*, Departamento Intersindical De Estadística e Estudos Socioeconômicos (2021), https://www.dieese.org.br/outraspublicacoes/2021/trabalhoDomestico.pdf.

22. Segato, "El Edipo Negro," 203.

23. bell hooks, "The Oppositional Gaze," in *Black Looks: Race and Representation* (Cambridge, MA: South End, 1992), 119.

24. Quote from Lins's film.

25. My emphasis from the film's voice-over. Lins's short film explores the historical commodification of domestic labor in the figure of the Black *babá* in wealthy and middle-class households.

26. hooks, "The Oppositional Gaze," 116.

27. Schwarcz and Starling, *Brazil: A Biography*, xix.

28. Ibid., xx.

29. Aníbal Quijano, "Coloniality of Power, Eurocentrism and Latin America," *Nepantla: Views from South* 1, no. 3 (2000); Aníbal Quijano, "Coloniality of Power and Eurocentrism in Latin America," *International Sociology* 15, no. 2 (2000).

30. The author develops the concept across María Lugones, "Heterosexualism and the Colonial/Modern Gender System," *Hypatia* 22, no. 1 (2007); María Lugones, "Colonialidad y Género: Hacia un Feminismo Descolonial," in *Género y Descolonialidad*, ed. Walter Mignolo (Buenos Aires: Ediciones del Signo, 2008); María Lugones, "Toward a Decolonial Feminism," *Hypatia* 25, no. 4 (2010); María Lugones, "Hacia un Feminismo Descolonial," *La Manzana de la Discordia* 6, no. 2 (2011).

31. María Lugones, "Subjetividad Esclava, Colonialidad de Género, Marginalidad y Opresiones Múltiples," in *Pensando los Feminismos en Bolivia*, Serie Foros 2 (La Paz: Conexión Fondo de Emancipación, 2012), 133.

32. Lugones stresses the use of these terms in Spanish, for they denominate "male" and "female" animals, respectively.

33. My emphasis. Aph Ko, *Racism as Zoological Witchcraft. A Guide to Getting Out* (Brooklyn, NY: Lantern Books, 2019), 53, 99.

34. Nelson Maldonado-Torres, "On the Coloniality of Being: Contributions to the Development of a Concept," *Cultural Studies* 21, nos. 2–3 (2007); Frantz Fanon, *Black Skins, White Masks*. Translated by Richard Philcox (London: Penguin Classics, 2021).

35. "Juliana Rojas and Marco Dutra talk about Good Manners BFI London Film Festival," (360 Magazine), YouTube, 2017.

36. bell hooks, *All about Love: New Visions* (New York: Harper Perennial, 2001), xvii.

37. Ko, *Racism as Zoological Witchcraft*, 99, 52.

38. Vincent Woodard, *The Delectable Negro: Human Consumption and Homoeroticism within US Slave Culture* (New York: New York University Press, 2014).

39. hooks, *All About Love*, 193–195.

40. My emphasis. Audre Lorde, "Poetry Is Not a Luxury," in *The Master's Tools Will Never Dismantle the Master's House (Selected Texts)* (London: Penguin Random House UK, 2018), 4.

41. Ko, *Racism as Zoological Witchcraft*, 108.

42. hooks, "The Oppositional Gaze," 116.

Selected reading

Fanon, Frantz (2021 [1952]). *Black Skins, White Masks*, trans. Richard Philcox (London: Penguin Classics).

Lugones, María (2007). "Heterosexualism and the Colonial/Modern Gender System." *Hypatia* 22 (1), 186–219.

Lugones, María (2012). "Subjetividad esclava, colonialidad de género, marginalidad y opresiones múltiples," *Pensando los feminismos en Bolivia* (Serie Foros 2; La Paz: Conexión Fondo de Emancipación), 129–137.

Maldonado-Torres, Nelson (2007). "On the Coloniality of Being: Contributions to the Development of a Concept." *Cultural Studies* 21 (2–3), 240–270.

Quijano, Aníbal (2000). "Coloniality of Power, Eurocentrism and Latin America." *Nepantla: Views from South* 1 (3), 533–580.

Segato, Rita Laura (2013). "El Edipo Negro: colonialidad y forclusión de género y raza." *La crítica de la colonialidad en ocho ensayos y una antropología por demanda* (Buenos Aires: Prometeo), 179–210.

CHAPTER 13

LA LLORONA'S BLACKNESS IN LATIN AMERICAN HORROR FILMS *LA LLORONA* (MEXICO, 1960) AND *LA LLORONA* (GUATEMALA, 2019)

KRISTEN LEER

LA Llorona is one of the most prominent feminine figures in Latin American folklore, and throughout the decades, many films have retold, re-adapted, and remonstrosized her story. Known as "The Weeping Woman" or "The Crying Woman," depictions of La Llorona in Latin American horror films have been analyzed by scholars through feminist, Chicano/a, cultural, folkloric, and sociological lenses. However, the evaluation of La Llorona's racialization in Latin American horror cinema has yet to be analyzed through an interdisciplinary lens emphasizing horror and Blackness. Given that the cultural attitude toward racial identification and classification is heavily (but not solely) based on physical appearance rather than ethnicity, this influences the way that race, and Blackness, is represented and positioned in certain marginalized Latin American communities, specifically, as is explored in this chapter, in Black and Indigenous communities.

When evaluating the relationship between Blackness[1] and horror, Robin R. Means Coleman's work takes center stage. In *Horror Noire: Blacks in American Horror Films from the 1890s to Present*, Coleman teases out the difference between *Black* Horror films and Black people *in* horror films: "Black horror films are informed by many of the same indicators of horror films . . . however, Black horror films are often 'race' films. That is, they have an added narrative focus that calls attention to racial identity, in this case Blackness."[2] Black Horror as a genre is presented as inherently rooted in Western film. Nevertheless, by examining Blackness in a global context, specifically within Latin American culture, we can begin to see how the boundaries and characteristics of Blackness are challenged and expanded not just outside of a Western, but specifically a U.S., cultural-historical context.

In Latin American culture, Afro-Latin American[3] communities are not readily seen as their own ethnic group. Afro-Latin American communities in Mexico represent only 1 percent of the total population, and it was not until 2015 that the Mexican government recognized its citizens of African descent.[4] The racial and social stratification, hierarchy, and classification in Latin American countries focus more on physical appearance than familial/ethnic heritage or other modes of race-thinking endemic to the United States, such as blood quantum.[5] Edward Telles and Tianna Paschel analyzed distinct patterns of racial identification in four Latin American countries (Brazil, Colombia, Panama, and the Dominican Republic) that include the highest percentage of people identifying as Black, Afro-Latin American, or in mixed-race categories and found that skin color was the most important predictor of racial identification in all four countries.[6] Given that the cultural attitude toward racial identification and classification is heavily (but not solely) based on physical appearance rather than ethnicity, this influences the way that race, and Blackness, is represented and positioned in certain marginalized Latin American communities, specifically, as is explored in this chapter, in Black and Indigenous communities. Therefore, I argue that Blackness in Latin American films functions not solely for those of African descent, but also among Latin American communities whose members are culturally understood to have darker skin tones, often attributed to Afro-Latin American and Indigenous communities.

To be clear, I am not trying to homogenize or monolithize Black and Indigenous communities, as both have their own varied experiences, histories, and cultures within Latin American countries. However, given that Latin American racial classification is largely based on skin tone, these two distinct communities often experience similar forms of racial and institutional discrimination and face similar barriers to accessing resources and recognition. In turn, representations of Black and Indigenous communities can be seen as a source or embodiment of cultural anxiety existing within the Latin American culture that horror films seek to expose.[7] The theoretical challenge of analyzing Blackness in a Latin American context is that the category of Blackness is expanded in comparison to the racial context of the United States, and is often viewed as not solely indicating Afro-Latin American communities but also encompassing Indigenous communities, given that the Latin American racial classification—the "othering"—is directed toward all of those with dark skin, regardless of ethnic or tribal heritage.

Taking into account the particularities of how racial formations emerge in the Latin American context, this chapter argues that La Llorona, as the subject of many Latin American horror films, unveils the functions of Blackness as a form of social prejudice. For the purposes of this analysis, colorism is defined as discrimination against individuals with darker skin tones. By emphasizing the expanded understanding of Blackness in the Latin American context, I suggest that the emphasis on Blackness in Latin American horror films illuminates the experiences and racial disparities of Latinos with dark skin or Indigenous roots. Latin American horror films featuring La Llorona often depict and associate those with darker skin with monstrous entities. This repeated semiotic coding shows that the function of Blackness in Latin America is limited not only to the experiences, culture, and life of those of African descent, but also to the experiences and belonging of communities associated with darker skin, particularly Latin American Indigenous communities.

This chapter expands explorations of Black identities and Blackness in Latin American popular culture, particularly horror films. Through textual analysis, I compare the function, presence, and cultural meaning of Blackness in two film adaptations of the La Llorona story from two different time periods and geographic locations: *La Llorona* (Mexico, 1960) and *La Llorona* (Guatemala, 2019). In these two adaptations, Blackness is both gendered and racialized through women's bodies (particularly through skin and clothes), indicating who is conceptualized as monstrous or "othered." Furthermore, Blackness in La Llorona film adaptations functions as a vehicle by which various cultural anxieties in Latin American culture are negotiated. These narratives in a Latin American context ultimately offer space to expand that unveiling of how the films themselves operate within a racist conception that associates Blackness with monstrosity but offers an oppositional narrative function that challenges prior definitions of Blackness.

BLACKNESS IN LATIN AMERICA

This chapter's examination of La Llorona and the representations of Blackness in Latin American horror films is informed by the following questions: How is race conceptualized in Latin America? How is Blackness, specifically, constructed in Latin America, and who is considered "Black"? What is the relationship between Blackness and horror in Latin American films? What is the historical, sociological, and cultural evidence that informs how Blackness functions in Latin American horror films? What cultural anxieties does Blackness represent in Latin American horror films? This section of the chapter specifically addresses the complexity of the representation of Black Latin American communities and the evocation of Blackness in contemporary Latin American film. This allows the historical, cultural, and social context to be prioritized for the analysis of La Llorona.

Analysis of Blackness in Western contexts is reduced to the Black American experience:[8] of culture, lives, history, ideologies, language, humor, and politics, among many other aspects.[9] In the United States, Blackness has been historically constructed through exclusionary practices (segregation, slavery, etc.). In contrast, in Latin America, Blackness was constructed through inclusionary practices that were deployed through colonization. In the twentieth century, post-revolutionary Mexican governments constructed and promoted *mestizaje*, a term for mixed-race peoples of Indigenous and Spanish origin. The term is derived from *mexicandidad*, the combining of terms for Indigenous and Spanish people and *indigenismo*, "a cultural thrust symbolically celebrating indigenous peoples through state-sponsored cultural production . . . and . . . as a set of government programs . . . which sought to both hispanize and modernize indigenous Mexicans."[10] While Mexico has adopted a discourse of inclusion and seemingly celebrates Indigenous ancestry, there is evidence of intolerance toward anything "mestizo and Indian[11] among the white Mexican elite."[12] Despite the presumed inclusion

of Indigeneity, there remains to this day a privileging of whiteness within Mexican culture and within Latin American cultures, more broadly.

Through the sociocultural deployment of terms like *mestizaje*, Latin American
countries informally abided by "whitening logic"—sociocultural practices, behaviors,
and pressures that position whiteness as the desired collective.[13] Black and Indigenous
groups were encouraged to "marry lighter," as economic and social mobility could be
achieved through marrying into lighter-skinned (and ultimately higher-status) families.
Whitening logic promotes the mindsets of "bettering the race," further stigmatizing
non-white folks.[14] While *mestizaje* serves a socio-ideological function, it has become
embedded in institutional structures that attempt to empirically capture racial representation. Racial and ethnic categories then become binaries, classifying people
into "'black' (or indigenous) and 'nonblack' (or nonindigenous)" categories,[15] further grouping Afro-Latin American and Indigenous Latin American populations and
rendering them as a collective non-white "other."[16] The ways that this problematic binary classification adheres to white idealism have been noted in scholarship, such as
that of Gabriel Estrada and others, focusing on representations of race in media and the
function of whiteness within those texts. Specifically, Estrada deploys the Indigenous
myth of the *el coyote* to discuss *Star Wars*' whiteness. During Spanish colonization of
Latin America, specifically Mexico, the Spanish term *el coyote* was imposed on those
who were considered lesser than white Spaniards but still granted more social capital
than "full blooded" Indians and Africans. In addressing the casting and treatment of
Latin American characters, Estrada asserts that "[George] Lucas also shuns the mixed-
race realities of Hispanic colonial life."[17] The absence of *el coyote* or mixed-race Latin
American groups in the case study of the film franchise *Star Wars* further establishes the
binaries enforced by colorism. According to Estrada, the absence of the mixed-bloods,
the *el coyote*, shows "that true difference really does separate white and tribal peoples.
Underlying the white fear of mixed-blooded peoples is the fear of dark tribal peoples
who must be shown as technologically and morally inferior."[18] Though depictions of La
Llorona are not set within a sci-fi setting, like *Star Wars*, La Llorona in the 1960 adaptation, and in folkloric narratives of her archetype, depicted her as mixed-blood, an
el coyote in her own right, representing the anxiety and hesitation of not maintaining
pureness or whiteness. This consistent colorism grouping of Blackness with Indigenous
identity, communities, and experiences raises the question of whether Indigeneity
and Blackness can respectfully be recognized as separate cultures, communities, and
ideological formations. Furthermore, given Latin America's racial context, can both
Blackness and Indigeneity truly be analyzed through the lens of Blackness?

To situate the consistent grouping of Black and Indigenous communities and
experiences in a broader context of representations of Blackness, we must first understand the absence of "Blacks *in* film." This notion echoes Coleman's model that, while
there might be Black people in horror films, "the films themselves may not be *Black*."[19]
Both *La Llorona* (2016) and *La Llorona* (2019) originate in areas of Latin America,
Mexico and Guatemala, that do not have large Black Latin American populations.
As stated above, Black communities in Mexico represent only 1 percent of the total

population and were not officially recognized until 2015.[20] Three years later, the film *La Negrada* (Mexico, 2018) was released. Though *La Negrada* is not the focus of this chapter, it is important to review the discourse surrounding its release given the nuance it provided of the Afro-Mexican experience that was neglected until then.

La Negrada was well received as the first Mexican feature film about the Afro-Mexican community that also had an all-Black cast, transitioning from "Blacks *in* film" to films themselves becoming "*Black*."[21] The film sought to tell the story of Mexican people "that nobody sees,"[22] a key phrase in the *La Negrada* promotional materials. Though the film was internationally acclaimed for portraying the Afro-Mexican experience, there were some concerns about how *La Negrada* reinforced negative stereotypes and problematic narratives of Black Latin American populations, such as hypersexualization, poor paternal figures, and the subordination of women. One could deploy an analysis of Blackness onto *La Negrada* given that it centers Afro-Latin American actors, experiences, and symbology. However, interestingly, this film unveils a complicated relationship, not only of Afro-Mexican but Indigenous Mexican communities as well. Ebony Marie Bailey, though primarily focused on the colonial aspect and codings of Blackness in Mexican cinema, particularly in *La Negrada*, notes that, "[the director's, Jorge Perez Solano] understanding of Blackness in Mexico is based on an exoticization of dark skin tones"[23] often imposed onto both Black and Indigenous Latin American populations. The director, in this moment, justifies the incorporation of a problematic stereotype in *La Negrada*, not to intentionally further harm but to unveil a core behavior that is imposed on both Black and Indigenous communities, as they both are discriminated against based on the darkness of their skin. Tiffany Lethabo King, in her book *The Black Shoals*, further suggests that the eroticization of both Black and Native[24] people together in film, and "the afterburn (or afterlife) of that encounter," can be seen as a condition of conquest.[25] Deploying eroticism onto Black and Indigenous bodies displays and reinforces the colonial desire and gaze, but at the same time, as King notes, in their reading of the erotic, can be acts of "decolonial worldmaking."[26] The Indigenous positionality of *La Negrada*'s director, a native Oaxacan,[27] informed his engagement, awareness, and reflection on the parallel experience of Black and Indigenous Mexican communities; how such experiences unveil historical and social discrimination is not completely recognized but also hold a place for liberation and revisioning.[28]

Despite the attention *La Negrada* gained for "starting a conversation" surrounding the historical, racial, and societal aspects imposed or ignored when situating Black Latin Americans at the center of film, the call for more Black Latin American representation is more heavily presented in Western contexts, like the United States, that are not as immediately apparent in Latin American culture. For instance, despite the international recognition of Alfonso Cuarón's 2018 film *Roma* and the success gained by actress Yalitza Aparicio, who is of Mixtec ancestry, "the fact that this 'Indian' [a pejorative way to refer to people who identify as Indigenous] was representing Mexico on the world stage . . . was, according to many Mexicans, a problem."[29]

Analyzing how Blackness functions within the *La Llorona* films (1960 and 2019), in a Latin American context, reveals that Blackness is not solely reducible to the experiences of people who identify racially as Black or of African origin (as constructed in the U.S. context), but is also a signifier of the utilization of darker skin in relation to the "other." In this way, we can begin to understand the complexity of Blackness within a Latin American cultural context, and especially in horror films. Blackness needs to be analyzed in Latin American horror films, especially to explore how it functions through colorism, which exposes cultural anxieties around "darkness" associated with the dark skin/appearance often, in turn, associated with Black and Indigenous Latin American people, who are seen as a threat, given their attempt to integrate into white culture.

Analyzing Latin American film through the lens of Blackness offers a new way to engage with colorism, racialization, and the stigmatization of Black and Indigenous groups in Latin America. Examining Blackness and Indigeneity expands previous discourses that primarily centered whiteness and Indigeneity. Mónica García Blizzard addresses the tension between whiteness and Indigeneity as a form of racial masquerade termed "whiteness-as-indigeneity"[30]—where the construction of white Indians of Mexican cinema manifested unresolved fissures.[31] García Blizzard contends that in Mexican constructions of race, whiteness "functions as the polar opposite of Indigeneity."[32] This Latin American framework illuminates similar tensions as in the relationship between whiteness and Blackness in the United States and beyond. The relationship between whiteness and Indigeneity not only mimics the polarization of whiteness and Blackness, it furthers both a historical polarization of whiteness as the opposite of "tainted" lineage and also racialized othering that includes both Indigenous and African heritage.[33] Not only do there seem to be mimicking tensions that unveil the polarization between whiteness and Indigeneity, and whiteness and Blackness, Garcia Blizzard relies on texts about the Black experience to support the anxiety, discrimination, and depiction of Indigeneity in cinematic contexts. For instance, García Blizzard relies on the term "racial masquerade," which was inspired by the work of Michael Rogin who used it to explain the function of blackface for Irish and Jewish immigrants as casting off the stigma of immigration so they would be seen as U.S. citizens. Frantz Fanon's *Black Skin, White Masks* is also utilized to explain the colonial tension of Spanish men (considered white) being with Indigenous women.[34] This showcases how scholars analyzing film continuously see and unveil the intersectionality of Black and Indigenous experiences.

As Latin American film continues to reinforce a binary between Indigeneity as the opposite of whiteness, we can see two truths existing simultaneously: first, Blackness in Latin America functions not solely based on African descent, but also based on dark skin tone, reinforcing colorist ideology that establishes racial, classed, and social distinctions; second, as a result of this, Blackness and Indigeneity are homogenized in social and entertainment practices. Situating Indigeneity as a placeholder for Blackness furthers the symbolic annihilation of Black and Afro-Latin American people within Latin American film. I believe that, though Blackness, othering, and racial tensions have been examined within Latin American films, they have been understudied with regard to the horror genre of Latin American films. Therefore, an exploration of the presence of skin color and blackness as signifiers of horror or monstrosity is required.

By unveiling the unique positionings of Blackness in horror films, we can understand further how Blackness might be operating in Latin American culture via the ways that it is represented in film.

LA LLORONA

The legend of La Llorona has been predominantly associated with Latin America for centuries. Her story can be traced to various areas outside of Mexico and even in southern parts of the United States.[35] However, her archetype has been memorialized and adapted for a multitude of communities globally. La Llorona holds similar attributes to other folkloric monstrous women around the world, like "The White Lady" in Germany[36] or "Pontianak" in Malaysia.[37] Many myth and folklore scholars[38] agree that a persisting archetype existing across a multitude of cultures for centuries indicates that La Llorona and these other similar folklore women hold similar cultural anxieties and are intended to convey a moral lesson for their communities. In this case, elements of motherhood/madness, purity/tainted, desirable/repulsive, and Blackness/whiteness are some of the binaries or borders that La Llorona challenges and threatens.

According to Latin American folklore, La Llorona was a young woman who fell in love with and married a man of higher social status. After her children are born, her partner chooses to be with another woman. In a violent act of anger and grief, La Llorona drowns her children. Shortly after, her own life is taken, either by herself or by others. She returns as a ghost, a vengeful entity who takes other women's children and kills corrupt men. The story of La Llorona is built upon racial, gender, and class dynamics. La Llorona is often depicted as a darker-skinned woman of a lower class falling in love with a lighter-skinned, privileged man. Often, this situates La Llorona as an Indigenous woman falling in love with a Spanish conquistador, which echoes the colonial tensions that the La Llorona story represents. In more recent accounts, La Llorona can represent the racial and geographic tensions between the U.S. and Mexican border, extending her threat to binaries to literal borders.[39] In this iteration, La Llorona is a beautiful but poor Mexican woman who falls in love with an American man. When she is crossing the river with their child to reunite with her American lover, the child accidentally drowns.[40] The core of La Llorona's story unveils race, gender, and class power dynamics and cultural anxieties, making the La Llorona story what Jeffery Cohen calls a "cultural vessel that appears at times of categorical crisis."[41] Therefore, La Llorona's monstrosity appears to reflect the current and ongoing categorical crises of colonialism, gender, borders, whiteness, and more. La Llorona appears so because, "the monster signifies something other than itself: it is always a displacement, always inhabits the gap between the time of upheaval that created it and the moment into which it is received, to be born again."[42] The La Llorona that this chapter is interested in is the revisiting folklore representations that position La Llorona as an Indigenous woman reborn again and again in different media texts throughout time.[43]

These crises are most evident in the relationship between La Llorona and her husband/lover. La Llorona's love affair illustrates a multitude of betrayals: La Llorona betrays her life and community for a higher-class status, and, in turn, her husband betrays La Llorona. Furthermore, La Llorona's failed relationship serves as a warning to women who desire a life outside of their race and class status. Her rage and heartbreak, when she learns that her husband has chosen another woman, incites La Llorona to betray her children by doing the most horrific thing a mother could do—kill them. La Llorona embodies the fear of "failed" ' motherhood and fails to adhere to patriarchal expectations of women. In this way, she also functions as a foil to the archetypal maternal Virgen de Guadalupe, the mother of Jesus, who sacrifices herself for her child. She is even used as a behavioral warning to children: *behave or La Llorona will come after you.* La Llorona's darkness is especially evident in the representations that position her as a threat to her children, and other women's children, as she "signifies malevolence and death in contrast to the children, who represent virtue and life."[44] The generational threat that La Llorona holds over children is a powerful anxiety: the extinction of innocence, lineage, and nurturing.

By deploying a comparative textual analysis of the two Latin American horror films *La Llorona* (Mexico, 1960) and *La Llorona* (Guatemala, 2019),[45] I begin to explicate the complexity of how Blackness operates within the context of Latin American popular culture, particularly horror film. These films were chosen because of their focus on themes of colorism in their construction of the La Llorona narrative. I focus on how the visual elements of the women's bodies are racialized as a function of Blackness, whereby darker skin, clothes, and their environment are the signifier of the other and the monstrous. Exploring how Blackness functions through the visual elements of these two films exposes the complex and deep-rooted cultural anxieties that La Llorona represents beyond the traditional monstrous feminine.

LA LLORONA (1960)

René Cardona's 1960 Mexican film *La Llorona* was released near the end of the "Mexican Golden Age of Horror" (1940–1960).[46] Gustavo Subero asserts that during this golden age the representation of the "Other" threatens "to destabilize society, [but] also narrates stories of Mexican identity that put in evidence the struggle between Mexico's aboriginal ancestry and its post-colonial past."[47] La Llorona explicitly represents this categorical crisis, as she is depicted as half Indigenous[48] and half Spaniard; her biracial status threatens to destabilize the desired white, colonial, or Spaniard familial structure that the family of focus in the film strives to maintain. Though La Llorona functions primarily as a monstrous woman who is an unfit mother and wife (killing her children and cursing her husband's bloodline) and represents the cultural anxiety of family disruption, she also brings forth discussions of racial identity in relation to Blackness. Borders of class, racial identity, and womanhood are imposed on the 1960 cinematic version of La Llorona.

La Llorona (1960) is set in twentieth-century Mexico, where a newlywed couple, Felipe and Margarita, are visited by Margarita's father, Don Montes. Don Montes tells them the folkloric story of La Llorona, which takes place in sixteenth-century Mexico. Before becoming La Llorona, she was known as Luisa, a half-Indigenous, half-Spanish woman who falls in love with an upper-class Spanish conquistador named Don Nuño. Luisa leaves her hometown to start a new life with him and conceives two children, a boy and a girl. During one of Don Nuño's missions, Luisa gets word that Don Nuño would not return home for longer than usual time. Growing suspicious, Luisa tracks down Don Nuño and finds out that he plans to marry another woman, because Luisa is not pure Spanish. Luisa places a curse on Don Nuño and his new bride: the firstborn of his bloodline will be murdered and die violently. Enraged by the betrayal, Luisa stabs her children and is sentenced to death for her crime. When Margarita's father finishes telling the story, Felipe dismisses it as a folktale, even though Margarita sees a connection to her brother, who was firstborn and murdered. Later in the film, Luisa, now La Llorona, arrives disguised as a nanny for Margarita's newborn baby boy, and plans to murder the child with the dagger she used to kill her children. Don Montes stops La Llorona by burning the dagger and a picture of her holding it, breaking the curse, vanquishing the monstrous woman, and reestablishing the privileged family structure.

La Llorona's story is rooted in colonial themes, as Luisa first abandons her Indigenous roots and is then abandoned because of her Indigeneity. She dismisses and subsequently betrays her Indigenous heritage when in search of a better life, she leaves home and falls in love with a conquistador who colonized and oppressed her people. Even though she successfully "whitened" herself and her children by marrying Don Nuño, this proves futile, because La Llorona is still "tainted" by her Indigenous heritage, which threatens her racial upward mobility. Further building upon its colonial and racial themes, La Llorona (1960) deploys visual elements that racialize the film's women, particularly utilizing Blackness to signify the other. Analyzing race, class, and gender allows for a deeper understanding of La Llorona's cultural function as a symbol of social anxiety and allows for an explanation of how race and class function in representations of Mexican women more broadly.

While La Llorona has a fair complexion, similar to other Spanish women in the film, her hair and clothing code her as dark, here meaning Indigenous, tainted, and, ultimately, other. La Llorona has very dark hair and wears dark clothing, which serves as a contrast to the lighter hair and clothing of the supposedly more desirable Spanish women. Further, other elements of the characters' appearances—jewelry, intricately designed clothing, white cleanliness—delineate their stark class differences. La Llorona's darker features and clothing, being of a simpler nature, mark her as a racialized and class status other. Figure 13.1 illustrates how La Llorona's appearance differs greatly from that of Don Nuño and the Spanish woman he intends to marry. The lighter attire represents a higher-class status as well as purity and femininity, which is similarly represented in figure 13.2. Nevertheless, in the scene with La Llorona and Don Nuño's new love interest, the clothing and the positioning of the women indicates who is monstrous and

FIGURE 13.1 La Llorona confronting Don Nuño and the new woman he intends to marry.

FIGURE 13.2 Margarita speaking with La Llorona on the staircase.

who is the victim. La Llorona faces the woman, dark brows furrowed, as the woman looks away, refusing to meet her gaze. La Llorona is depicted as the villain, a threat to Don Nuño's pure bloodline, and an outcast. The other woman's light hair and clothing characterize her as more desirable, replacing La Llorona and ultimately becoming the target of her rage. As the film continues, Blackness becomes a more prominent feature of La Llorona's characterization, as it extends from her clothes to her Indigenous heritage and skin.

Flustered after confronting Don Nuño, La Llorona flees to a town square, where she is surrounded by Indigenous people dressed in traditional clothing dancing around her. The camera passes back and forth between La Llorona's face and the male Indigenous dancers, reconstructing La Llorona as undesirable, not attractive to a white male gaze because of her Indigeneity, but recoding her into an Indigenous space.[49] Passing between her and the Indigenous men's faces contrasts and makes apparent the dark complexion of the dancers around her that she does not share. As the music intensifies, La Llorona begins grabbing at her skin, a physical, inescapable reminder of her Indigenous roots that she is unable to whiten (figure 13.3). As the music escalates, La Llorona is shown in a dark void, both a symbolic representation of the darkness, the evil that is overtaking her, and a representation of the dark skin of the Indigenous people surrounding her (figure 13.4), showing that La Llorona is enveloped in blackness and Blackness, physically and symbolically. This scene serves as a catalyst for La Llorona's monstrosity; after this encounter with other Indigenous people, she stabs her children to death. The positioning of La Llorona's crime as arising from an encounter with her Indigeneity illustrates her

FIGURE 13.3 La Llorona clutching her face, overwhelmed by the music of Indigenous dancers.

FIGURE 13.4 La Llorona is surrounded by a black void.

monstrous transformation, which the film attributes to her racial identity and represents the abandonment of her futile attempts at "whitening," motherhood, and upper-class femininity.

After murdering her children, La Llorona's physical appearance, particularly her skin, is coded to indicate monstrosity. As she walks toward her sentencing, additional physical signifiers are introduced that emphasize La Llorona's Blacknesss—her fair complexion is now covered in splatters of mud. This darkening arguably represents the transformation of her de-whitening furthered by murdering her children; de-whitening, as she failed to obtain and maintain a higher-class status, the dirt on her clothes reestablishes her lower status. The physical darkening of her complexion by mud smeared on her skin also shows her "darker" side surfacing, and her failed attempt to whiten herself and not extinguish her Indigenous identity. Furthermore, as the townspeople gather in the streets to condemn her, they not only tamper with her skin, but also grab at her hair, unraveling it, which positions her physical body as a site of transition. This all represents the destruction of La Llorona's supposed sanity, morality, and womanhood. It is a punishment for her crimes of failed whitening, motherhood, and class mobility (figure 13.5).

What solidifies the deployment of Blackness to signify La Llorona as monstrous in relation to her Indigenous roots is her interaction with Margarita and her son near the end of the film. After her legend is recounted, the ghostly entity appears and infiltrates Margarita's family by posing as a caretaker for her young son. As La Llorona first enters the home, despite being seen as a living being, the ghostly hidden entity holds a monstrous transformation imposed upon her since her death. Upon looking at a portrait of

FIGURE 13.5 Townspeople grabbing at La Llorona as she is sentenced to death.

Don Nuño, La Llorona's face transforms from a beautiful, fair-complexioned woman to a more masculine and shadowed face with disheveled hair. The masculine aspect of her transformation shows the abandonment of her femininity that occurred in her previous life and that fuels her monstrosity, making her a threat to women and motherhood. Given her betrayal and rejection of motherhood, she is no longer granted access to her femininity. Such a threat of absent femininity is contained in this stark transformation, indicating that La Llorona's femininity and the lightness of her skin are illusions that hide her monstrosity from Margarita and her family (figure 13.6).

Importantly, La Llorona's ghostly transformation reveals that her complexion, hair, and body also signify her Blackness. These elements make her a powerful representation of monstrosity. When Margarita's son wanders from his room unsupervised, La Llorona confronts him on the staircase in an attempt to harm him. La Llorona is shown in dark clothing, which is in contrast with Margarita's child, who has light skin, hair, and clothes (figure 13.7). This has been the traditional model that signifies La Llorona as monstrous: her dark hair and clothes. However, what becomes significant is that the color of her clothes and hair are repositioned to illuminate the darkness of her skin as a new signifier of her monstrosity. This becomes apparent when La Llorona's hands, which reach out to grab Margarita's son, appear much darker, are greatly exaggerated in contrast to the child, who is positioned visually between them (figure 13.8). This transformation shows that La Llorona's quest for revenge, by murdering the firstborn of Don Nuño's family, is

FIGURE 13.6 La Llorona's monstrous transformation when looking at Don Nuño's portrait.

FIGURE 13.7 La Llorona and Margarita's son on the staircase.

motivated by a feminized monstrosity and a seemingly racialized monstrosity. Meaning, her inability to whiten either herself as an "acceptable" white Spaniard or her children, motivates her to try to thwart Don Nuño's upward mobility by killing the firstborn son, who holds Don Nuño's name and racial position. The positioning of Blackness, alongside or as synonymous with Indigeneity in Latin America, as a racial monster in horror might seem odd. As noted, there are different attitudes toward relations with Blackness and Indigeneity in literature focusing on Blackness within a Western, U.S. context: "[while] some Americans who identify themselves as white will admit to, or even boast of, a Native American ancestor, [but] yet to meet a white person who acknowledged African ancestry, unless he or she had made a personal decision to identify racially as black."[50] The use of colorist imagery in *La Llorona* (1960) illuminates differing racial formations from the U.S. context, where ethnic ancestry and blood lineage determine monstrosity, compared to a Latin American context, where skin tone and Indigeneity

FIGURE 13.8 La Llorona reaches out to grab Margarita's son.

link people of African descent, Black people, and Indigenous Latin American people with Blackness.

La Llorona (1960) casts the folkloric woman as a monstrous entity seeking revenge on an elitist family whose ancestor, Don Nuño, wronged her. It is a typical tale of defeating the monster, to reestablish order in the environment it has invaded.[51] The scale of this defeat casts La Llorona as a monstrous woman who has abandoned her femininity and extends her legend to larger themes of racial, social, and economic threat that are signified through the film and fuel the monstrous representation of La Llorona. This early cinematic depiction of La Llorona confines her to a repetitive figure of defiance and a threat to the colonial ideal of whiteness. However, this is encouraging, as it motivates retellings of La Llorona that challenge and attempt to break free from stereotypical imprisonment. Thus, decades later we see La Llorona liberate her Indigenous community.

LA LLORONA (2019)

Given the problematic construction of La Llorona, filmmakers have re-envisioned her as a symbol of agency that takes revenge on those who have wronged her and her people. This alternative depiction of La Llorona characterizes her as a defender of citizens who have been wronged either by the government or by colonial elites. Miriam Fernandez analyzed two public performances (a 2017 protest and a yearly play in Xochimilco) that adapted the legend of La Llorona to represent painful cultural memories: a protest in reaction to the disappearance of 43 students while in police custody and a play focusing on colonial violence. Both public performances utilized La Llorona as a symbol of defiance, a vessel to evoke cultural memories, and a threat that will take revenge on those who committed these crimes. Interestingly, when speaking about the memories that La Llorona evokes, Fernandez discussed the concept of *critical memory*, a practice from the Black public sphere. Specifically, it is "a purposeful recollection of past events or people with the intent of challenging dominant institutions that suppress the histories of marginalized groups."[52] This positioning of Blackness and La Llorona's Indigeneity highlights continuing conversations about the dynamics of her representation and the embodiment of Indigenous experiences echoing Black experiences, and arguably Blackness, to further understand her role within Latin American culture and history. This reenvisioning of La Llorona as a liberating entity instead of a monstrosity is what *La Llorona* (2019) aims to successfully depict.

Jayro Bustamante's *La Llorona* (Guatemala, 2019) is a critically acclaimed film that was praised for its artistic visuals and political narrative, which fuels the horrific elements of the film. It was selected as the Guatemalan entry for the Best International Feature Film at the 93rd Academy Awards. Some contend the appraisal of this film was a stark contrast to the controversy and production of Warner Bros.' *The Curse of La Llorona*, released that same year.[53] The take on the folktale of La Llorona by the Conjuring Universe—an American franchise and shared universe that includes multiple supernatural horror films—grossly stereotypes her as a monstrous foreign entity from Mexico that terrorizes a Los Angeles family in the 1970s. *The Curse of La Llorona* (2019) received poor reviews and was criticized for misrepresenting the mythic figure of La Llorona, detaching her story from its Latin American context and cultural significance.[54] In contrast, Nobel laureate Rigoberta Menchu Tum viewed Bustamante's *La Llorona* (2019) as a starting point for Indigenous Latin American people to "harness filmmaking as a social catalyst."[55] Bustamante's adaptation of La Llorona simultaneously deploys similar tactics of Blackness to signify monstrosity in his film, but, in turn, shows the misidentification and unfairness of associating those with dark skin and Indigeneity with evil.

The film is set in modern-day Guatemala, where dictator Enrique Monteverde[56] is on trial for initiating the genocide of native Mayans between 1982 and 1983. The narrative focuses on Enrique's family, which is comprised of his wife, Carmen, their daughter, Natalia, and their granddaughter, Sara, who are all struggling to maintain their lives during Enrique's trial. Despite the raw testimonies of the Indigenous women, specifically Kaqchikel, detailing their experiences with the genocide, and providing evidence placing Enrique at the center of this horrific act, the verdict is overturned. In reaction to the verdict, the public's protesting traps Enrique and his family inside their house for days. During their isolation, a maid named Alma comes to help Valeriana, the only other maid in the house who hasn't been scared off by the trial. Both women are Kaqchikel, and are darker skinned than Enrique's family. Supernatural occurrences descend on the family upon Alma's arrival: the family is plagued by nightmares, whispers in the wind, visions of spirits, and other haunting illusions. Bustamante visually indicates that Alma is La Llorona by using natural elements (water faucets turning on by themselves, the strong wind coming through the windows) as cues that La Llorona's vengeance is near. The question is, What is La Llorona's motivation?

At the beginning of the film, the camera zooms in on Carmen's face, drawing attention to her light skin, pearl jewelry, and white hair—all of which illustrate her whiteness and higher social class. As she prays, the camera zooms out, showing her surrounded by her family members, illuminated by natural light, and praying for protection during Enrique's trial (figure 13.9). The next scene shows the staff of the house, all of whom are dark-skinned, blowing out candles as they walk down the hall, darkening both the house and themselves. These two contrasting scenes indicate a distinction in class and color by utilizing the polarizing skin tones and environments. The cinematographer use light to establish tone and darker environments, which are more associated with darker-skinned characters. This includes the quarters of the maids versus the quarters of Enrique's family.

When the trial begins, we see a similar positioning of an Indigenous woman, echoing the position in which Carmen was previously seen. A stark utilization of color shows the different situations in which the women in this film are positioned. In the trial scene, the camera mimics a person staring, as it is close to the Indigenous woman's face before slowly zooming out to reveal her environment. The Indigenous older woman has darker skin, and though she wears a colorful veil, it casts deep shadows across her face. Instead of praying like Carmen, she is testifying in front of the court, recounting the rapes, assaults, and genocide she witnessed inflicted on her community.[57] Moving from praying to testimony echoes La Llorona's Indigeneity being seen as a subject of God's punishment, praying leading to religious pressures on Indigenous communities,

FIGURE 13.9 Carmen surrounded by her family, praying.

and "allud[ing] to the devastating effects of Christianity on Native communities."[58] The camera zooms out, showing the woman's position in relation to the two sides of the court; to the left are dark-skinned Kaqchikel people wearing traditional colorful clothes/patterns, and to the right are people with lighter skin wearing contemporary, neutral-colored clothes. The Indigenous woman on trial is physically positioned between the racial binary that exists, which is signified through the use of color. *La Llorona* (1960 and 2019) does not echo "Black *in* film" nor film that is "*Black*." Seeing the signifiers of blackness and Blackness imposed on Indigenous communities and La Llorona in the films resituates us to integrate how Black and Blackness exist in such spaces (figure 13.10).[59]

After hearing the testimonies, Natalia, Enrique's daughter, begins to question her alliance with her father. Carmen is appalled that Natalia would trust the words of the Indigenous women, whom she calls them "savages" and "unkempt mothers." Carmen also blames the Indigenous women for the sexual violence they experienced at the hands of Guatemalan soldiers. This interaction between Carmen and Natalia further characterizes Carmen as an elitist and positions the dark-skinned women around her as lesser, hypersexual, and deserving of punishment. Carmen's attitude toward Indigenous women is representative of Guatemalan society's stigmatization of Indigenous and Afro-Latin American communities. Her problematic beliefs about Indigenous people are exacerbated when Alma arrives at Montverde's home.

Elements of this 2019 reenvisioning of La Llorona echo and differ from *La Llorona* (1960). The introduction of Alma as a caretaker to the family echoes the anxiety around invasion of the home and the trust that *La Llorona* (1960) took advantage of. However, the 2019 La Llorona's intentions seem to be different, just like her physical signifiers

FIGURE 13.10 An Indigenous woman testifying at Enrique's trial.

of Blackness, which have shifted. Alma's clothes are not signifiers of monstrosity, for La Llorona's Blackness and Indegenity are evident solely in her dark hair and skin. Ultimately, the white garb casts Alma's physical features in great contrast to her skin, which also brings attention to the largeness of her white eyes. Despite her stoic facial expression, she is physically attractive and unlike in the 1960 *La Llorona*, her face is unaltered. In addition to her physical alterations contrasting with the physical markers of monstrosity in *La Llorona* (1960), there are also narrative alterations that make the audience question what La Llorona's backstory will be.

Traditionally, La Llorona falls in love with a higher-class man. Audiences come to find out that Bustamante removed that element of La Llorona's story, once her backstory is revealed; however, this is played with, as Alma is hypersexualized by Enrique's gaze, which Carmen picks up on. Finding her swimming in the pool, Enrique's desires unravel when he is lured by La Llorona into her sleeping quarters. The room flooded with water, and there, he finds her naked body cast by dark shadows. These shadows testify to the Indigenous woman's darkening, signifying the blackness not only in the environment (at night, her dark hair clinging to her body) but in her Indigeneity. In the 1960 La Llorona, it is not her clothes that signify another layer of blackness with Blackness, but her skin (figure 13.11). This foregrounds Alma's Indigeneity, rather than making it a narrative turning point, as deployed on Luisa in *La Llorona* (1960).

Alma breaks Enrique's trance when she begins screaming at him. Consequently, all the other people in the house wake up and find Enrique in Alma's room. Carmen, Natalia, and Sara all huddle together on the staircase as Enrique goes back to bed, and Carmen says, "Enrique has always liked chasing women. Particularly native women...."

FIGURE 13.11 Alma waiting for security to let her pass into Enrique's house.

All women drive Enrique crazy. . . . I never thought that at this age I was still going to have to deal with this."[60] Often, La Llorona is constructed as a beautiful young woman, eroticized by the white colonial gaze, and she is often punished for her desirability. In this scene, it is the oppressor (Enrique) who is caught, met with disgust, and ultimately punished, not the oppressed (La Llorona).

Alma's body and darkness continue to be used to horrify and displace her environment. For instance, when Valeriana and Alma go to sleep in a bunk bed, Alma's long black hair quickly flips down, illuminating a sense of instability lurking around the corner. Additionally, the delusions Alma imposes on Enrique cast her in the shadow of the pool, which she has transformed into a dark, swampy pond inhabited by dark-green frogs. Alma's Blackness becomes more apparent during the nighttime, as she is surrounded by natural/supernatural elements often attributed to her archetype. For instance, Enrique, who has increasingly bad lung problems, discovers black mold under his bed and climbing up his walls, prompting Valeriana to say that it is dark/black magic at hand (figure 13.12).

The insensitivity and lack of empathy Carmen has for Indigenous women is addressed by La Llorona, who subjects Carmen to horrific nightmares surrounding the genocide. Importantly, which the audience finds out the nightmares are Alma's memories, or, a collection of her last mortal moments. Memories are a vital component in the construction of La Llorona in Bustamante's film, as she reminds Enrique of the horrible things he has done to her people and viciously imposes them on those who do not understand the things they experienced. Just as there was a contrast between La Llorona's Blackness (in clothes and body) and Margarita's son's whiteness in *La Llorona* (1960), when Carmen is shown experiencing Alma's memories, Carmen's whiteness (in clothes

FIGURE 13.12 Alma (La Llorona) bathed in moonlight, naked.

and body) contrasts with Alma's children, showing them with dark skin and tattered, muddy clothes. The cinematic representation of the physical state of the children "communicate[s] the class of the children and hints at an additional source of their vulnerability beyond age and innocence," in which their Indigeneity and dark skin makes them vulnerable to the violence to which they will fall victim.[61]

The children are a driving force to de-monstrosize La Llorona for the audience. Specifically, in Carmen's nightmares (Alma's memories), she is shown protecting her children, not harming them, a key action that often monstrosizes La Llorona.[62] In a climactic scene, Carmen is in a trance, reliving the moment Alma and her children were being captured and dragged by a river. Alma watches as her children are drowned, and she is executed by none other than Enrique. This shared memory that Carmen witnesses de-monstrosizes and justifies La Llorona's vengeance and shifts the character's attitudes about Indigeneity, colonialism, and class. Carmen, now having seen Alma's suffering and frustrated by Enrique's infidelity, strangles him to death. After he is dead, La Llorona does not seek further revenge on the remaining family, all of whom are women. Although she spares the remaining family members, at Enrique's funeral, Alma, revealed to be a spirit of La Llorona, continues to seek revenge upon other men involved in the genocide of her people. For instance, water begins to pool in the men's bathroom, and ultimately drowns another general who was a part of the genocide. The ending of the movie shows Alma regaining the elements and identities which previously made her monstrous. She regains motherhood, as she is shown protecting her children; her femininity, given that she spares the women from her revenge; and her Indigeneity, by not abandoning her people to either whitening or secure a man of a higher class who oppressed her people. Hence, La Llorona is reimagined as a liberator for Indigenous communities and women (figure 13.13).

FIGURE 13.13 Carmen runs with Alma's children to find safety.

There are contrasting folkloric aspects to this utilization of La Llorona that mirror and contrast *La Llorona* (1960). This film is not just rooted with colonial themes—oppressed versus oppressor—but highlights a categorical crisis about Indigeneity in Guatemala. As noted in an article focusing on Indigenous activist Rigoberta Menchú Tum, *La Llorona* (2019) shows that there was not just an attempted annihilation of Indigenous people in Guatemala, but also a symbolic monstrosizing via negative stories told by soldiers to warn the communities about "these people."[63] The monstrosizing historical narratives about the Indigenous communities in Guatemala mirror the telling of La Llorona's story, which functioned as a warning about an Indigenous woman's rage and thirst for vengeance.[64] Furthermore, the film utilizes natural elements often associated with La Llorona to illuminate her presence and intentions. Like the air, spirits are ever present, and thus, they are constant, invisible threats, as no one is able to see when or where they will inflict horrors on people.

La Llorona villainizes water by using it to drown children, and Alma often associates water with Enrique's young granddaughter Sara. Because Alma teaches her to hold her breath underwater, it seems that she intends on harming Sara. Therefore, both air and water are associated with the villainous intentions of La Llorona, which Bustamante teasingly deploys across all the family members to confuse audiences and make them question her intentions. The audience is left to question if La Llorona plans to only murder Enrique or punish his entire family, as she intends in the 1960 film. Nevertheless, the film still uses Blackness to make La Llorona and the Indigenous people she represents monstrous. However, Bustamante's deployment of Blackness, though teasing the expected monstrosity of La Llorona, ultimately attempts to displace monstrous acts associated with La Llorona to her white counterparts. Despite including more historical and cultural components that illustrate the Indigenous disparities that La Llorona represents, in *La Llorona* (2019) the color black racializes the women. In particular, the film associates Blackness with Indigenous communities, positioning them as racialized others. Blackness is not only a function of color but is racially associated with Indigenous communities. In this case, *La Llorona* (2019) attempts to utilize the traditional signifiers of Blackness previously imposed on La Llorona to show the misassociation of Blackness and monstrosity, which, as indicated by the film, should be attributed to whiteness, elites, and colonialists that hold darker intentions.

By focusing on genocide, the film deploys Western aspects of Blackness as an echo in the narrative, though Blackness is very rooted in Guatemala's history, culture, and racial politics. For instance, this film can be read as a post-racial haunting: a metaphor for how whiteness in the United States—the ideology, history, and modernization of the United States—is haunted by the "ghosts" of racial injustice, slavery, segregation, and genocide.[65] *La Llorona* shows the racial haunting of the native Mayans, who were victims of colonial genocide. Interestingly, the illusive justification Enrique provides at his hearing for approving and enacting the genocide on the Indigenous community is, "But you well know my intention was to create a national identity in this country." This quote illustrates that the alleged national identity Enrique, and colonialists by extension, envisioned does not include Indigenous communities. This is similar to the historic intentions of the United States in not seeing Black folks as either American or human, which as previously noted, goes against the notions of "inclusion" and shows a false or skewed proudness and progressiveness for having Indigenous roots and accepting Indigenous communities.

Ultimately, *La Llorona* (2019) attempts to alter the relationship of Blackness with monstrosity, recasting La Llorona as a woman of agency and as a liberator. *La Llorona* (2019) is one iteration of a common contemporary trend of re-imagining the narrative as representing the horror of colonialist nationalism. It is important to reinforce the racial dynamic that La Llorona represents, because there are still ongoing struggles to acknowledge and account for the harm done to Indigenous communities, especially in Latin America. Furthermore, by understanding how they are being constructed as other in cinema—in this case, through the deployment of Blackness—we can begin to understand the historical and social contexts that fuel this tactic.

FUTURE DIRECTIONS OF BLACKNESS IN LATIN AMERICAN HORROR FILMS

This chapter explores how Blackness functions differently within Latin American horror films by analyzing *La Llorona* (1960) and *La Llorona* (2019). In addition, it challenges how Blackness is viewed in a global context, specifically how it differs in meaning and function in Latin American horror films compared to typical U.S. horror films. By examining the visual and folkloric narrative of *La Llorona* (1960) and *La Llorona* (2019), it is evident that Blackness functions through color, which is apparent in the racialization of women within these films, particularly in their clothes, environment, and physical appearance. Though Blackness traditionally is associated with the lives, culture, experiences, and histories of those of African descent, these films suggest that Blackness seems to apply to Indigenous communities in Latin American contexts, as they are signified in these horror films as other and monstrous through the color black.

I want to emphasize that my analysis of the ways that Blackness functions in these two films does not capture the totality of how Blackness is represented within Latin American horror films. Given the limiting representations of Black communities in Latin American film, and understanding that the racial dynamics differ from Western culture, this analysis indicates that Blackness is functioning differently, motivated by colorism and desires rooted in colonialism, especially in Latin American horror films. Nevertheless, it would be negligent to not mention the film *El Regreso de La Llorona* (Honduras, 2021), as it represents a continuation of how La Llorona as a folkloric figure and the utilization of her body is still being associated with Blackness in a Latin American context as "Blacks in film."

While the film is not praiseworthy, it exemplifies the way another Latin American horror film approaches La Llorona. *El Regreso de La Llorona* begins with La Llorona's backstory, showing her as a victim of femicide: her presumed husband/lover kills her and their children on a nearby riverbank. This film monstrosizes and positions La Llorona as a victim of femicide, which coincides with consistent revisioning of her as a vengeful but liberating folkloric figure. La Llorona's liberating spirit is cemented as one of the main women characters is a reporter whose goal is to unveil the unfair and alarming femicide occurring in her local town. Immediately, La Llorona and her children are coded as racial "others" with dark skin and hair, which are emphasized in contrast to her white gown that mimics the appearance of *La Llorona* (2019). Having recounted La Llorona's backstory, the film follows a group of young kids who disrupt La Llorona's grave and engage in criminal activities, after which La Llorona seeks revenge upon them.

In addition to the stereotypical casting and positioning of Black characters in *El Regreso de La Llorona*, the functioning of Blackness as color coding the "other" in the appearance of clothes, hair, and skin remains apparent. Besides La Llorona, for instance, when the group of friends goes to a club, a darker-skinned woman catches the eyes of the men from the friend group, who, upon seeing her, immediately hypersexualize her. Seeing how the men react, the women members of the friend group see her as a romantic threat. The woman's dark skin is also starkly contrasted with her tight white dress, which continues to racially categorize her as "other." Both the men and women in the friend group call her a slut and claim she is "asking for it." This hypersexualization leads the men to eventually gang-rape her. Though she initially escapes from them, and despite La Llorona seemingly trying to save her, the men run her over in their car. They then attempt to bury her to cover up their crimes. This killing of the dark-skinned woman and the destruction of La Llorona and her children's graves are the catalysts for La Llorona's quest for vengeance against the friend group. The dark coding of La Llorona as "other" and monstrous is cemented when La Llorona appears to the last male perpetrator who she intends on killing. She appears behind him in the night, with dark hair, dark, soulless eyes, and dark decaying skin (figure 13.14).

FIGURE 13.14 La Llorona appears behind a boy.

El Regreso de La Llorona is poorly executed, uses Blackness to signify monstrosity, and reinforces the different ways Blackness functions in Latin American horror films about La Llorona as well as others. Importantly, globalization in the form of international filmmakers' exposure to Black stereotypes in Western horror films might partially explain why they reproduce these images and ideologies in their projects. All of the films examined in this chapter have small Black Latin American identifying populations: in Mexico's population, 1.2 percent identify as having African ancestry, while 1–2 percent of Guatemalans identify as of African descent and 2 percent of Honduras's population declare themselves Black. Given the relatively low number of Black people in these countries, it is safe to assume that they do not have much input into the ways in which their national cinemas develop and depict Afro/Black Latin American people. Examining the ways film employs Blackness as a signifier of monstrosity and Indigenous communities' otherness illustrates how deeply colorism negatively effects Afro-Latin Americans' cinematic representations and their experiences in the world.

To understand Blackness and its complex functions within non-U.S. global contexts in the horror genre, we must attend to the sociohistorically specific contexts in which different racial formations emerge. Though comparing formations of Blackness in U.S. contexts with other global contexts can be useful, Blackness in non-U.S. global contexts also deserves its own space and analysis. This analysis neither examines how non-Western horror films appropriate Blackness nor contends that non-Western films horror films should adhere to Western conceptualizations of Blackness; rather, all films need to aim for authentic representations of Black people across the globe. Filmmakers need to consistently and respectfully approach sensitive aspects of Blackness rooted in suffering, trauma, and marginalization of oppressed communities, to avoid stereotyping and othering members of historically marginalized populations. For us to understand aspects of Blackness thoroughly, we must allow space for such conversations to exist.

Though this chapter used retellings of the La Llorona narrative as a site of analysis for how Blackness functions within Latin American horror films rooted in colorism, colonial, and othering of dark-skinned populations, particularly Indigenous and Afro-Latin American communities, I hope this analysis fosters continuing evaluation, discussion, and interest in the complexity of Blackness and its function within Latin American horror films. By evaluating the constructions and functions of Blackness in Latin American cinema, we can aspire to situate marginalized voices at the forefront of media analysis research, in hopes of recognizing disparities that often are overlooked.

NOTES

1. The capitalization of Black from black is to show the difference when referring to racial categories (Black) to the use of color (black).
2. Robin Means Coleman, *Horror Noire: Blacks in American Horror Films from the 1890s to Present* (New York: Routledge, 2011), 7.

3. When speaking about Black and Indigenous communities in Latin America, I respectfully refrain from utilizing the term Latinx, as members of the Latin American community have expressed hesitation toward that label; its usage is controversial. I use Latinx when speaking specifically about communities in the United States with Latin American origins to adhere to the collegiate practice. Furthermore, Afro-Latin American and Black Latin American are interchangeable throughout the chapter.

4. Zayaan Jappie, "An Interview with the Filmmaker behind 'La Negrada,' the First Feature Film Starring an All Afro-Mexican Cast," last modified August 23, 2018, https://www.oka yafrica.com/an-interview-with-the-filmmaker-behind-la-negrada-the-first-feature-film-starring-an-all-afro-mexican-cast/.

5. Edward Telles and Tianna Paschel, "Who Is Black, White, or Mixed Race? How Skin Color, Status, and Nation Shape Racial Classification in Latin America," *American Journal of Sociology* (2014): 865, https://pubmed.ncbi.nlm.nih.gov/25848671/.

6. Ibid., 866. The strength of this predictor varied between the different countries, but skin color and appearance were still the most important indicators of racial identification.

7. Jeffery Jerome Cohen, *Monster Theory: Reading Culture* (Minneapolis: University of Minnesota Press, 1996).

8. Western Blackness also focuses on an African lineage that was moderated in either the historical colonization, slavery, or segregation that was forced upon African populations.

9. Means Coleman, *Horror Noire*, 7.

10. Mónica García Blizzard, "Whiteness Wars in Las Niñas Bien," *Latin American and Caribbean Ethnic Studies* (2021): 2, https://doi.org/10.1080/17442222.2021.1944483.

11. "Indian" is an old term used by European colonizers to refer to those who are Indigenous.

12. García Blizzard, "Whiteness Wars," 3.

13. Telles and Paschel, "Who Is Black," 870.

14. Ibid., 870.

15. Black is not capitalized, because it is a direct quote of the binary classification system.

16. Peter Wade, "Racism and Race Mixture in Latin America," *Latin American Research Review* 52, no. 3 (2017): 477–485, http://doi.org/10.25222/larr.124.

17. Daniel Bernardi, *The Persistence of Whiteness* (New York: Routledge, 2008), 76–77.

18. Ibid., 76–77.

19. Means Coleman, *Horror Noire*, 5–8.

20. Jappie, "An Interview with the Filmmaker," 2018.

21. Means Coleman, *Horror Noire*.

22. Carlos Aguilar, "'La Negrada' Is Mexico's First-Ever Fiction Film to Have an All-Black Cast," last modified August 18, 2018, https://remezcla.com/film/trailer-la-negrada-afro-mexican/.

23. Ebony Marie Bailey, "Codings of Blackness in Mexican Cinema: An Analysis of *La Negrada*" (*PALARA*, 2019), 5.

24. In *Black Shoals*, Tiffany King discusses Black peoples' experiences in the United States and in a Western context and Native experiences linked to the Indigenous Cherokee community. Tiffany King, *Black Shoals: Offshore Formations of Black and Native Studies* (Durham, NC: Duke University Press).

25. Ibid., 142.

26. Ibid., 143.

27. Being ethnically tied to the Indigenous people of Oaxaca, Mexico, who inhabited the area before the Spanish invasion.

28. Jappie, "An Interview with the Filmmaker," 2018.

29. Mónica García Blizzard, *The White Indians of Mexican Cinema: Racial Masquerade throughout the Golden Age* (Albany: State University of New York Press, 2022), 2.

30. Indigeneity is lowercase to reflect a direct quote from the text itself.

31. García Blizzard, *The White Indians*, 5.

32. Ibid., 7.

33. Ibid., 7, 10.

34. Ibid., 43–45.

35. Bacil F. Kirtley, "'La Llorona' and Related Themes," *Western Folklore* 19, no. 3 (1960): 155.

36. Ibid., 157–161.

37. Rosalind Galt, *Alluring Monsters: The Pontianak and Cinemas of Decolonization* (New York: Columbia University Press, 2021).

38. Joseph Campbell and Bill Moyers, The Power of Myth (New York: Doubleday, 1988); Claude Lévi-Strauss, "The Structural Study of Myth," *Journal of American Folklore* 68, no. 270 (1955): 428–444, https://doi.org/10.2307/536768; Roland Barthes, *Mythologies* (New York: Noonday Press, 1972).

39. Domino Renee Perez, *There Was a Woman: La Llorona from Folklore to Popular Culture* (Austin: University of Texas Press, 2008), x.

40. Orquidea Morales, "La Llorona and Horror: A Chicana Feminist Reading of the Films *The Wailer* and *The Wailer II.*" Dissertation, ProQuest, 2011, 1.

41. Cohen, *Monster Theory*, 4–7. Cohen associates the "Monster's Body," as a "Cultural Body," but I am using vessel as a synonym because it visually assists the reader in understanding how the monster's body hosts different cultural constructions.

42. Ibid., 4.

43. Michael Kearney, "La Llorona as a Social Symbol," *Western Folklore* 28, no. 3 (1969): 200.

44. Perez, *There Was a Woman*, 154.

45. This is not to be confused with the 2019 U.S. film release of their version of La Llorona, *The Curse of La Llorona*.

46. Gustavo Subero, *Gender and Sexuality in Latin American Horror Cinema Embodiments of Evil* (London: Palgrave Macmillan, 2016), 2.

47. Ibid., 4.

48. In the film, La Llorona is referred to as "Indian," but that is an old term used to describe those who are Indigenous, which is not regarded favorably today.

49. Laura Mulvey, "Visual Pleasure and Narrative Cinema," *Screen* 16, no. 4 (1975): 6–18.

50. Harryette Mullen, "Optic White: Blackness and the Production of Whiteness," *Diacritics* 24 (1994): 71–89.

51. Joseph Campbell, *The Hero with a Thousand Faces* (New York: Meridian Books, 1956).

52. Miriam L. Fernandez, "La Llorona and Rhetorical Haunting in Mexico's Public Sphere," *Journal for the History of Rhetoric* 24, no. 1 (2021): 56–57.

53. Katie Rife, "Slow-burn Chiller *La Llorona* Offers a More Intelligent Take on the Spooky Myth," AV Club, last edited August 6, 2020, https://www.avclub.com/slow-burn-chiller-la-llorona-offers-a-more-intelligent-1844622999.

54. Russell Contreras, "'La Llorona' Movie Promotion Draws Fire," Hispanic Outlook, last edited June 2019, https://www.hispanicoutlook.com/articles/la-llorona-movie-promotion-draws-fire; Noah Levine, "'The Curse of La Llorona' Scares with Its Recycled Horror Clichés," *Daily Texan*, 2019, https://doi.org/https://proxy.lib.umich.edu/login?url=https://www.proquest.com/wire-feeds/curse-la-llorona-scares-with-recycled-horror/docview/2191725121/se-2?accountid = 14667.

55. Carlos Aguilar, "How Horror Film 'La Llorona' Amplifies the Message of Indigenous Activist Rigoberta Menchú Tum," *Los Angeles Times*, last modified August 19, 2020, https://www.latimes.com/entertainment-arts/movies/story/2020-08-19/la-llorona-rigoberta-menchu-guatemala.

56. Enrique is loosely based on José Efraín Ríos Montt, who was also on trial in 2013 for committing and allowing genocide of Native Guatemalan communities. He died in 2018, a year before the movie was released.

57. Ibid., 2020. Maria Marcos, the Maya Ixil actress, shown in figure 13.10, asked Bustamante for permission to change the dialogue to her own personal story for the emotion to come across realistically. The testimonies in the film therefore are of actual experiences and accounts from the actress herself.

58. Perez, *There Was a Woman*, 156.

59. Means Coleman, *Horror Noire*, 7.

60. *La Llorona*, directed by Jayro Bustamante (Shudder, 2019; Guatemala), 0:51:53–0:52:37.

61. Perez, *There Was a Woman*, 155.

62. Ibid., 155.

63. Aguilar, "How Horror Film 'La Llorona' Amplifies," 2020.

64. Ibid.

65. Tammie M. Kennedy, Joyce Irene Middleton, and Krista Ratcliffe, *Rhetorics of Whiteness: Postracial Hauntings in Popular Culture, Social Media, and Education* (Carbondale: Southern Illinois University Press, 2017).

CHAPTER 14

"THEY TRUSTED ME EVEN WHEN I DIDN'T PARTICULARLY TRUST MYSELF"

The Complex Black Heroine in Little Monsters

JAMIE ALVEY

INTRODUCTION

IN January 2019, *Rotten Tomatoes* award editor Jacqueline Coley made an apt observation via *Twitter* regarding Black women's roles in Hollywood: "In the entire 90+ years of the Academy Awards, 34 Black women have been nominated for an acting Oscar (Lead/Supporting) 20 of 34 were slaves, maids or living in abject poverty. That's the current legacy of Black actress [sic] in Oscar-worthy cinema & it's beyond depressing."[1]

Coley highlights a problem in cinema that transcends countries and genres. Black women are denied depth in film and relegated to roles that primarily feature them as chattel, caregivers, impoverished, or a combination of these characteristics. The lack of variance in Black women's character types in that sample is inherently troubling. Unfortunately, the horror genre is not an exception, as many of the films feature a Black woman as the Black best friend who seems to have neither goals nor a life outside of aiding a white protagonist. Sometimes the characters are fodder for the monsters and maniacs, and as such, their ability to be killed is their greatest attribute. This lack of nuance is disconcerting and a prevalent issue; still, quality depictions do exist and deserve to be celebrated. These portrayals raise the standards of how Black women are depicted not only in horror, but in media as a whole.

The year 2019 was exceptional for Black-centered horror. Jordan Peele released his sophomore feature *Us*, starring Lupita Nyong'o as a woman pitted against her doppelganger. However, that was not Nyong'o's only 2019 horror film; she also starred as Miss Audrey Caroline in the Australian zombie horror comedy *Little Monsters*. In it, Nyong'o plays a beloved kindergarten teacher who is caught at the epicenter of a zombie virus outbreak while on a class trip to a petting zoo with her students. With only two other adults present, one a foulmouthed children's entertainer and the other a student's slacker uncle, Miss Caroline is tasked with keeping her class relatively safe, mostly unharmed, and untraumatized. What ensues is a grotesque and raucous chain of events that seamlessly melds horror and comedy into a uniquely heartwarming story.

For the uninitiated, horror comedy may seem like an oxymoron. In *The Horror Spoofs of Abbott and Costello: A Critical Assessment of the Comedy Team's Monster Films*, Jeffrey S. Miller effectively summarizes the subgenre: "The comedy and horror genres have always been close cousins to each other. Films from each are meant to provoke a physical reaction in the reviewer—comedy films make people laugh while horror films make people shiver and scream. Both reactions are uncontrollable reflexes."[2] Miller elaborates, adding, "Horror comedies are more than horror films with a few scenes of comedic relief; they are works where each genre is represented equally."[3] Thus, intrinsically, horror comedy is an equal hybrid of the two genres, delivering laughs without skimping on the integral horrific elements. Other entries in this unique canon include James Whale's *The Old Dark House* (1934), Roger Corman's *The Little Shop of Horrors* (1960), Mel Brooks's *Young Frankenstein* (1974), Stuart Gordon's *Re-Animator* (1985), Wes Craven's *Scream* (1996), Karyn Kusama's *Jennifer's Body* (2009), and Eli Craig's *Tucker and Dale vs. Evil* (2010).

It is worth noting that *Little Monsters* is *not* a Black horror film in the sense that it is created solely by Black horror creators. It was written and directed by Abe Forsythe, a white Australian man. However, it does center a Black character in horror who is not tokenized, an important point that warrants examination. She is not a one-dimensional Mammy figure, she is not evil, and she is not included in the film to reaffirm or support whiteness. Instead, she is presented as a multi-dimensional, self-actualized woman who is competent, flawed, frightened, and fearless. While it is important that Miss Caroline does not fall into long-standing racialized tropes, her humanistic traits make her a distinct and important rarity among other Black women characters in horror media. The overall eschewing of poorly wrought tropes in favor of a brilliantly multifaceted humanity allows Miss Caroline to evolve into a unique character.

Robin R. Means Coleman highlights the differences between Black characters in horror films and Black horror films in her book *Horror Noire: Blacks in American Horror Films from the 1890s to Present*. She explains, " 'Blacks in horror' films present Blacks and Blackness in the context of horror, even if the horror film is not wholly or substantially focused on either one. Nevertheless, these films possess a particular discursive power in their treatment of Blackness."[4] Black horror films are made specifically for Black audiences, whereas films that simply include Black characters are made for mainstream consumption. This categorization is crucial to studying Miss Caroline's depiction in *Little Monsters*.

It is important to note that, societally, Black women and the horror genre are both subject to unfair stigmatization and are thus relegated to reductive stereotypes. As previously mentioned, films often depict Black women as lower-class, uneducated, and impoverished, and the continual unremittent portrayals of these stereotypes reinforces racist paradigms. Media representation can perpetuate harmful stereotypical clichés about Black women. Additionally, horror is often considered low-brow, which is classist and inaccurate. Low-brow insinuates that the films are primarily made for unintelligent audiences that lack culture. The low-brow label denigrates both those who enjoy horror and its cultural significance by positing that it is unimportant. Thus, using horror as a space to explore Black women as distinctive people is rather apt. It flips the script, so to speak, creating an environment where historically disenfranchised people can see themselves represented clearly and truly. Horror has often pushed against societal conventions, challenging preconceived notions about humanity. Naturally, Black women's roles in horror should also push against societally conceived margins and expand audiences' worldviews about Black women in film and society more broadly.

Black women are becoming increasingly visible in horror as a result of films like J. D. Dillard's *Sweetheart* (2019), Mariama Diallo's *Master* (2022), and Jordan Peele's *Nope* (2022). However, they have yet to achieve the same visibility in the horror comedy subgenre. In horror comedies, Black women toe the line between trope and subversion. Many horror comedies—much like horror as a whole—fall victim to the dated Black best friend trope. Regina Hall's Brenda Meeks from the horror parody series *Scary Movie* (2000–2013) is the lead white character Cindy's (Anna Farris) Black best friend who dies and is resurrected several times over the series, poking fun at mainstream horror's tendencies to cast people of color in supporting roles and use them as fictional serial-killer fodder. Similarly, Wes Craven's meta-horror satire *Scream 2* (1997) opens with Maureen Evans (Jada Pinkett Smith) slaughtered in front of a theater full of moviegoers who assume the carnage is merely a publicity stunt promoting the fictional horror film they have paid to watch. Brenda and Maureen's characters are based in tropes as well as subversion, making Black women in horror comedy explorations of Black women's treatment in horror at large.

Even more modern and progressive examples of the subgenre, such as Nyla Chones (Celeste O'Connor) in Christopher Landon's *Freaky* (2020), cast Black women as supporting characters. Nyla is a more nuanced and less tokenized example of the Black best friend trope, but she is also an example of the subgenre's continued pattern of relegating Black women to supporting roles. She plays into and also subverts the stereotypical Black best friend. Sharai Bohannon of *Dread Central* notes just how integral Nyla is to the story. Bohannon writes, "If more horror movies had a Nyla in the central squad, then maybe more squads would survive to the end of these movies."[5]

In contrast, Miss Caroline is *Little Monsters'* central figure. Miss Caroline has all the charms of a Disney princess with her genteel beauty and versatile talents, but she proves to be ruthless and cunning when necessary. With her dazzling prodigious ability, she could easily be a one-note character, but beneath all of the positive and charming elements lies a woman who has experienced personal hardships and found her life's purpose—teaching, a calling that has brought her happiness and fulfillment. A well-rounded character, Miss Caroline feels like a real person caught in a bizarre situation. Her character development helps ground the film's more bombastic elements and creates a wholly human tale amid zombie chaos. Miss Caroline is undeniably the film's lifeblood.

While it may be easy to denigrate *Little Monsters* as either overly saccharine or simply emptily entertaining, Nyong'o's Miss Caroline proves otherwise. Nyong'o plays an adaptable hero who is intelligent and beautiful, a portrayal that actively decenters Eurocentric ideals about feminine attractiveness and intelligence. Her character is afforded depth, autonomy, and distinction that are usually reserved for white heroes in horror, and while many Black heroines in horror are often left with at best bittersweet endings, Miss Caroline's ending is joyful and affirming. It is a much-needed reprieve and a reminder that Black women are deserving of their own happy endings in the real world. The hard-hitting societally conscious narratives are important and will always be integral to encompassing the experience of Black women in horror, but *Little Monsters* adds variety to the stories that feature Black women as a focal point.

Nyong'o's role in the film was even more compelling because she was the only actor who the film's director, Abe Forsythe, wanted to play Miss Caroline. It is an entirely pleasant surprise, and in a way, the exact opposite of the casting of Duane Jones in George Romeo's classic zombie film *Night of the Living Dead* (1968). It was not a matter of a Black actor auditioning the best; rather, Nyong'o was selected for the role. In an interview with *The Hollywood Reporter*, Forsythe explains, "She was just the ultimate person for me. I knew that she would bring a certain amount of strength and truth to that character which was really important, and I was a massive fan of hers."[6] In another interview with *Vulture*, the director contends, "I wouldn't have been able to make the movie that we made with anyone else."[7]

Importantly, Audrey Caroline is a part of a small but powerful tradition of Black women featured in zombie media the world over. These characters include Selena from *28 Days Later* (2002), Michonne from *The Walking Dead* (2010–2022), and Melanie in *The Girl with All the Gifts*. *Little Monsters* stands as an Australian entry in this particular canon, helping further Black women's narratives within a subgenre to which many viewers continue to gravitate.

Little Monsters provides audiences with a distinctive Black heroine who is constructed in respectful, multi-layered, and fascinating ways that simultaneously reject deeply troubling hackneyed film tropes regarding Black women and work as a celebration of Black women's right to joyful experience. By centering a Black woman as a lead character instead of a supporting player, *Little Monsters* also delves into uncharted horror comedy territory. The film pulls Black women from the margins of genre and puts them in the spotlight in inventive and novel ways.

In her essay "Can We Have More Black Girl Rage in Slashers?," Sharai Bohannon explains the significance of films' unapologetic portrayals of Black women in the slasher subgenre, and all of horror by extension. Bohannon deftly writes, "I have a running list of Black final girls and the numbers are so low it's depressing. I feel like I'm screaming into the void as we get an onslaught of movies every year that refuses to fix this problem."[8] Miss Audrey Caroline is a deeply nuanced and unlikely heroine, a Black final girl for the ages, exploring the niches and worlds that have previously been denied to Black women in horror.

CENTERING BLACK MIGRANT NARRATIVES IN AUSTRALIAN FILM

Black people live all over the world and there is a wide and varied cultural diaspora. Each part of the Black diasporic experience is different, and as such, often dictated by the place a person lives. For example, the life of a Black person in London will differ from the life of a Black person in Kenya. There is a rich community of migrant Black people who have settled in Australia, an occurrence that Miss Caroline exemplifies in *Little Monsters*. She immigrated to the country on a whim after following the popular '90's boy group Hanson while they were on tour. During an encounter with Taylor Hanson, she gets injured and stuck in Australia—though she soon made it her home when she found that teaching was her life's calling. This is likely a reflexive commentary, one that was not wholly intended yet still manages to be impactful.

Victor Counted and Andre M. N. Renzaho from Western Sydney University note in their article, "Fitting In or Falling Out: How African Migrants Adapt to Life in Australia": "About 400,000 people of African origin were living in Australia in 2020. This represents 1.6% of the Australian population and 5.1% of Australia's overseas-born population. Most (58%) are white South Africans but 42% are black Africans from sub-Saharan countries. Not all adjust well to Australian society because of its predominantly Anglo-Saxon culture."[9]

That Australia is a "predominantly Anglo-Saxon culture" makes it all the more important to center Black narratives in the country's cinema. Dr. Yadira Hazel Perez observes, "Locally, 'Black Australians' acts as a continuously expanding umbrella category and includes various non-Aboriginal communities of which African migrant communities are the fastest growing."[10] *Little Monsters* slyly facilitates a way to depict a character who is a migrant Black woman in Australia, and horror comedy's accessibility gives the film broad appeal. Because the character's plotline does not explicitly deal with her migration to Australia, it would be facile to dismiss how the narrative subtly normalizes the reality of migrant Black people in Australia who come from diverse backgrounds.

Australia's history is connected to British colonialism, making humanized depictions of Black people in the national cinema radical. In "Blackness as Burden? The Lived Experience of Black Africans in Australia," Virginia Mapedzahama and Kwamena Kwansah-Aidoo note: "The black body in white space has always been constructed as a problematic difference to whiteness: an inferiority and an 'other.' Blackness is thus not merely about skin color but rather it is a social construct persistently conceived of as an opposition to whiteness: It is not only that which defines whiteness but is also inferiorized by it."[11] Importantly, Miss Caroline is never portrayed as inferior because of her skin color; instead, her character is the most competent character in the film, and her Blackness is not treated as a threat to the white characters or their identities. Her character is literally the most competent character in the film, and her Blackness is not treated as a threat to the white characters or their identities.

Importantly, Miss Caroline's Blackness is not aligned with the horror elements in the film. She is not the "other" that the characters fear. The other—the zombie outbreak—at hand is directly caused by an incident at a U.S. Army base in the vicinity. Too often in horror, Black characters are constructed as a menacing other, and subsequently, the fear of white protagonists. In *Little Monsters*, the other is presented as something wrong, unnatural, and threatening to the white characters and their inherent whiteness. Miss Caroline's character will in no way end racism in Australia, but she normalizes Black migrants' stories. It's a small act that aids in the larger decolonization of spaces in Australian film. It decenters purely white narratives and makes space for more Black characters—particularly Black women who are not merely props to aid whiteness and uphold the white social paradigm.

An Unapologetically Black Hero

In countries that have experienced colonization, many people are held to Eurocentric beauty standards that do not account for the inherent attractiveness of those who do not fit the narrow toxic paradigm of beauty. Darker skin, natural hair types, and body diversity, among other characteristics, are constantly denigrated. Black women often bear the brunt of this insidious institution and are encouraged to assimilate to white beauty standards. Writer Emily Richards discusses this struggle and how it has affected her in an editorial for *An Injustice*: "However, there's one benefit of being white that meant I learned to dislike the colour of my skin at a very young age (no older than 10, I believe). I would match the Eurocentric beauty standards. To be fair-skinned, tall, have light-coloured eyes, a small nose, and blonde or brunette hair, would be a dream."[12]

Mark E. Hill of Pennsylvania State University studied gender and colorism for his article "Skin Color and the Perception of Attractiveness among African Americans: Does Gender Make a Difference?" Hill references numerous studies, ranging from the '40s to the late '80s, that illustrate that colorism generally affects Black women more than men. People also question Black women's femininity, because fairer skin is equated with femininity in colonized spaces. "Throughout Europe and the West, fair skin tone has long been perceived as a particularly desirable feminine characteristic," writes Hill.[13]

These issues affect dark-skinned Black women's experiences and can have negative consequences on Black women's mental health. In "Beauty and Body Image: Concerns Among African American College Women," a participant in the study of Black women at an unidentified American university said, "People just couldn't see past the skin color my whole life you know even when it came to prom and homecoming queen. We had very pretty dark skinned girls at my school but the light skinned girls always won . . . it was just because they were pretty or just because they looked more like the white people."[14]

Little Monsters subtly and powerfully subverts Eurocentric beauty standards. Precocious student Felix (Diesel La Torraca) adores Miss Coraline, a point evidenced by the way he goes on about how talented she is, that she plays ukulele, and sings Taylor Swift songs for him and his classmates. Children are a notoriously tough crowd to win over, but the class looks up to Miss Caroline and adores her.

Miss Caroline's introduction further subverts Eurocentric beauty standards. The film prominently emphasizes her beauty. Still, she is not overly sexualized or objectified. While other characters may be attracted to Miss Caroline, the film's visual language does not translate this into needlessly eroticizing the character.

The lack of objectification by the filmmakers counteracts the gross oversexualization of Black women in media, refusing to erroneously conflate the ideas of attractiveness and desirability with the oversexualization of a person or character. It is well known that beginning at a young age, Black women are overtly objectified in their daily lives as well as in media (i.e., the hypersexualized Jezebel archetype). In a 2017 report from Georgetown Law School titled "Girlhood Interrupted: The Erasure of Black Girls' Childhood," researchers Rebecca Epstein, Jamilia J. Blake, and Thalia Gonzalez found that Black girls are perceived by others as having more knowledge about sex and are incorrectly regarded as more mature.[15] This often leads to the harmful phenomenon "adultification," which strips many Black girls of their childhoods.

Many characters throughout the film are taken by Miss Caroline's beauty. Dave (Alexander England), Felix's slacker uncle, becomes infatuated with Miss Caroline from the moment he meets her. At first, his attraction to her is admittedly shallow and driven by lust, but Dave falls more deeply for Miss Caroline and admires her for her bravery and honesty. Even the lecherous children's entertainer Teddy McGiggle (Josh Gad) comments on Miss Caroline's beauty. Sadly, Miss Caroline is no stranger to amorous advances, and it is revealed that she wears an engagement ring to keep her students' fathers at bay.

The film makes Miss Caroline a loveable character, constructing her as an archetypal beauty, a hero who is as capable as she is attractive. While it may not seem radical, these roles are often reserved only for women who fit the Eurocentric beauty paradigm. *Little Monsters* makes a statement that dark-skinned Black women are beautiful and desirable in their unabashed Blackness. This is important considering that Drs. Ninochka McTaggart, Vaness Cox, and Caroline Heldman, researchers at the Geena Davis Institute on Gender in Film, found that "Only one-in-five (19.0%) of Black leading ladies from the past decade have a dark skin tone."[16]

Miss Caroline is feminine and dainty, characteristics usually related via costuming. Yet, her colorful attire is subversive, as it is fit more for a damsel in distress than a kid-wrangling, zombie-killing teacher extraordinaire. Though she is quite capable of taking care of herself and her students, her womanhood is not in question, nor is she masculinized. Even when fighting zombies and threatening abhorrent children's show hosts, she remains a picture of womanly strength, going to war with shambling corpses while clad in a yellow dress.

"I STARTED TO BELIEVE IN MYSELF AGAIN, YOU KNOW?"

While the film positions Miss Caroline as the ideal beauty and a picture of grace, talent, and resilience, she is much more than just an attractive Black woman. Her entire character hinges on her imperfections, and that she had to fight to attain the life she leads. The Miss Caroline the audience meets at the beginning of the film is the woman who has experienced hardships and has had a transformative journey. Her backstory is admittedly a little silly, because the film is a horror-comedy hybrid. Nonetheless, it grounds and humanizes a character who is seemingly perfect, sending the message that Black women don't have to be paragons in order to be deserving of love and respect.

Miss Caroline also deals in extremity and dichotomies. Her feminine exterior could be used to discredit the character as weak, akin to ingenues, yet Miss Caroline has the capacity for brutality when it comes to the safety of the children left in her charge. When Teddy McGiggle is hysterical and out of line, Miss Caroline effortlessly threatens him. "This is not a negotiation," she says to the now terrified McGiggle.[17] In the world of *Little Monsters*, dainty and feminine are not equated with weakness. Miss Caroline embodies a space where women can be not wholly one facet or another. There are gray areas and spaces that touch on people's often frightening capacity for duality. Miss Caroline is characterized by softness and sharpness and violence and vulnerability in ways rarely afforded Black women. One moment she is fighting a horde of zombies, using only her wits and weaponry, and the next she's singing the children sweetly to sleep.

In addition, Miss Caroline embodies humanity, as she experiences many different emotions. She is not always darling and genteel or an all-out warrior. A character cannot be all radiant sunshine and pithy threats, and Miss Caroline encompasses far more. When she is afraid, the audience can see the terror in her eyes that she tries desperately to hide from her students. She openly tells Dave at one point, "I'm fucking terrified, too."[18] When her students are rowdy or annoying, she's reasonably frustrated. The film develops Miss Caroline's character even more and, in turn, wholly endears her further to viewers.

Miss Caroline is indicative of all the messy complexity of being a young woman. As previously mentioned, she landed in Australia as a result of her teenage obsession with the boy band Hanson. She had drained her college fund to support her Hanson habit.

When she naively broke into Taylor Hanson's hotel room, she sustained injuries trying to escape. The mistake left her with a hefty hospital bill and no way to return home, but it introduced Miss Caroline to a revelation that she desperately needed. In order to pay off her medical debt, Miss Caroline started a job helping out at a local school. It was at the school that Miss Caroline learned she was adept at handling children and loved teaching and interacting with children.

The character's passion for teaching and caring for children are her most charming features. The path that led her there is comical but earnest enough to speak to real women. Many people have accidentally "found themselves." It was through teaching that Miss Caroline found not only herself but also the strength she needed to create a life she loved living. When talking to Dave about her past and career, she says, "They trusted me even when I didn't particularly trust myself, I started to believe in myself again, you know? You know, learned to step up? Now I can't imagine myself doing anything else."[19]

It is worth noting that Miss Caroline upends the highly offensive Mammy figure, a well-known racist caricature of dark-skinned Black women. They are often portrayed as sexless, obese, ugly, and caretakers of white children and their families. In the documentary *Horror Noire: A History of Black Horror*, actor Rachel True shares her frustration surrounding the Mammy archetype's enduring presence in modern media: "I'm over that. I've seen that in almost every movie I grew up with as a child, where, you know, the desexualized Black woman Mammy figure gives her life so the little white girl can live."[20]

While Miss Caroline is definitely a caretaker, she is not a Mammy. Professionally speaking, she is first and foremost an educator. Her job is not merely to care for the children but to expand their minds. It is a powerful role in society that is often undermined. It is with gentle authority that Miss Caroline teaches and commands the respect of the children. The character has a backstory, wants, dreams, goals, and is far from being sexless. Miss Caroline is depicted as the most desirable character in the film without playing into fetishization of Black women. There is also an instance in which she briefly mentions her attraction to the Hanson brothers, the objects of her infamous affections.

More interestingly, Miss Caroline does not die to save the lives of her students. She is not the sacrificial lamb, and the film never puts her in the position to even contemplate self-sacrifice. It would not be wrong to say that Miss Caroline functions as an antithesis to the Mammy archetype that still permeates culture. When compared to recent Mammy figures in horror, such as Alfre Woodard's character in *Annabelle* (2014) and Octavia Spencer's title character in *Ma* (2019), Miss Caroline has little in common with these characters.

Miss Caroline's backstory and teaching vocation gave her the tools she needed to reach self-actualization. Her origin story illustrates that she has never been the perfect woman others perceive her as; rather, she is multifaceted. Broad audiences can aspire to be the character, as she demonstrates that complex Black women are deserving of admiration even if they have chaotic life stories. She doesn't have to be an exemplary person, some ultimate good for those around her to still view her as a role model and worthy of their respect. With whole genres dedicated to the artfully delineated humanity of chaotic white women, it is important for a film to portray the intricate and imperfect life of a Black woman with the same care and grace.

In *Horror Noire: The History of Black Horror*, acclaimed horror author Tananarive Due discusses Black characters' lack of development onscreen: "They don't have wants, needs, of their own. Their only concern is the welfare of the white protagonist, and that is where it becomes problematic."[21] *Little Monsters* combats that by giving Miss Caroline a backstory, ambitions, and a developed life and interests. Conversely, her character doesn't fall into the trap of simply being the Black best friend, a glorified supporting role that is notorious for portraying Black women as having no life outside of simply being a white character's friend and often advisor. She is a main character, not a buttress to the white characters or a person they can employ to help out to ensure their own success in the scheme of the film. While she does employ her own wisdom and imparts it to Dave, it is simply because she has been in a similarly difficult situation in her life. It comes across as a human moment, as commiseration and reassurance, than as a white character seeking magical sage wisdom from a Black character whose importance to the plot is sadly dubious. Her connection with Dave becomes one of kindred spirits and is more in line with mutual understanding of one another's humanity instead of using her as a source of unpaid emotional labor.

Miss Caroline's ending is happy and hopeful. The conclusion sees Miss Caroline, Dave, and the children escape to safety and Miss Caroline and Dave forming a romantic connection. Black women characters are often left with bittersweet endings at best, but *Little Monsters* leaves Miss Caroline making the best of an objectively horrid situation, singing with Dave to her beloved class as they wait out a mandatory quarantine. It is a proverbial silver lining that reminds audiences that even the strongest people are flawed and that everyone is a work in progress. It is an uplifting ending: Miss Caroline has accomplished her personal mission of keeping the kids safe, is trauma-free, and it is quite possible she has found her soulmate. In a time when hope is in short supply, the world needs stories in which Black women have happy endings. There is a place for harshly realistic endings, and there is also a space for filmic conclusions that tease the possibility of a happier future. *Little Monsters* is assuredly the latter.

Author Kinitra D. Brooks has extensively explored the role of Black women in zombie-centered horror media and expertly points out that often Black men are featured in zombie films and Black women are excluded from the narratives. Most of the women that are depicted are white women, and Brooks rightly finds this troubling, because it erases Black women and how their existence in these spaces could be used to comment on Black femininity and the intersections of gender and race. In her brilliant piece "The Importance of Neglected Intersections: Race and Gender in Contemporary Zombie Texts and Theories," she writes:

> Including multifaceted black women characters such as Michonne and Selena in horror texts not only expands the audience; it also increases the potentiality of

the horror genre itself. Their very existence strengthens contemporary zombie and horror theory by complicating the theory and making it flexible enough to encompass and demonstrate multiple intersections of identity even as it broadens the audiences of the genre, ensuring its survival and relevance. It is not enough to simply include black female characters; horror creators must also make them individuated figures woven into the main narrative. I insist that the demonstrated dangers of normativity in horror must be challenged by interrogating the theory with the multiplicity of racially gendered intersections that exist within and without Western hegemony.[22]

Miss Caroline is challenging, complicated, and undeniably holds space for the continued portrayal of Black women in zombie horror. She is an extension of Black women in zombie fare that came before her—Selena in *28 Days Later*, Michonne in *The Walking Dead*, and Melanie in *The Girl with All the Gifts*. Horror allows for room to explore characters of marginalized identities who do not receive attention within more traditional mainstream spaces. It allows for subversive and affirming portrayals that attempt to make viewers think more than about blood and guts. While there still might not be many portrayals of Black women in zombie horror films, Miss Caroline expands the representations, and the content of her character makes a wonderful argument for the continued representation of these headstrong Black heroes.

CONCLUSION

Coleman writes, "Horror has something to say about religion, science, foreigners, sexualities, power and control, class, gender roles, sources of evil, an ideal society, democracy, etc. These topics take a compelling turn when examined through the lens of Black culture."[23] *Little Monsters* is no different, and whether intentional or not, the film communicates a great deal about Black women characters and the need for Black women in horror. The film does not necessarily have to be groundbreaking, but the inclusion of Black women in movies that are simply fun and bombastic can be meaningful and worthwhile.

Miss Caroline's character embodies grace, which makes the film extraordinary. The character provides Nyong'o the opportunity to showcase her range, as she is funny, complex, talented, brave, brilliant, messy, and beautiful. Miss Caroline is multi-dimensional, and in that way she tells Black women that they should be their varied and lovely selves. It is refreshing to see a narrative that shies away from stereotyped constructions of Black womanhood and that offers the audience something to ponder and interrogate on deeper levels.

Lupita Nyong'o is *Little Monster*'s heart and soul, and without her performance and the charisma and depth she brings to Miss Caroline, the film would not be nearly as entertaining nor as heartfelt. The life that she and other Black actors breathe life into genres is invaluable. In the *Horror Noire* documentary, Rachel True discusses the frustrations she's experienced as a Black actress:

> reading script after script after script and wanting to read for the lead girl, but going "Oh no, okay, I'm the friend though. I'm going to say are you okay? Are you okay? Are you okay?" I mean six million different ways to Sunday, I have to figure out a million different line readings for this same line because whatever thing is going on it's not about the Black people or what we're going through, it's are you white person in peril okay.[24]

Jacqueline Coley's all-too-pertinent Twitter observation and Rachel True's maddening experiences prove that while *Little Monsters* might not be Oscar-worthy material, it offers much-needed variation in Black women's film roles. Even these seemingly silly roles are crucial and push back against white supremacist tropes and colonialism. *Little Monsters* provides a stunning depiction of a Black woman who is an exceptional person as well as a work in progress. The film sends a subtle yet powerful message for women akin to Miss Caroline. They are flawed, but they are no less deserving of love, respect, and honor. Miss Caroline is an unlikely complex Black heroine—a woman that films need more of.s

Notes

1. Jacqueline Coley, Twitter post, December 20, 2019, 10:57 a.m.
2. Jeffrey S. Miller, *The Horror Spoofs of Abbott and Costello: A Critical Assessment of the Comedy Team's Monster Films* (Jefferson, NC: McFarland, 2004), 1.
3. Ibid. .
4. Robin R. Means Coleman, *Horror Noire: Blacks in American Horror Films from the 1890s to Present* (New York: Routledge, 2011), 6.
5. Sharai Bohannon, "Black Final Femmes: 10 More Black Women Who Make It to the End," *Dread Central*, November 19, 2021.
6. Suzy Evans, Lupita Nyong'o, and Abe Forsythe, "Little Monsters Star Lupita Nyong'o on 'Why She Loves Melodrama,' 'Specific Rules' of Horror Movies," *Hollywood Reporter*, October 9, 2019.
7. Jordan Crucchiola and Abe Forsythe, "How on Earth Did Lupita Nyong'o End Up in the Same Zombie Movie as Josh Gad?," *Vulture*, October 16, 2019.
8. Sharai Bohannon, "Can We Have More Black Girl Rage in Slashers?," *Dread Central*, June 23, 2022.
9. Victor Counted and Andre M. N. Renzaho, "Fitting In or Falling Out: How African Migrants Adapt to Life in Australia," *The Conversation*, October 3, 2021.
10. Yadira Perez Hazel, "Bla(c)K Lives Matter in Australia" *Transition*, no. 126 (2018): 59–60.
11. Virginia Mapedzahama and Kwamena Kwansah-Aidoo, "Blackness as Burden? The Lived Experience of Black Africans in Australia," *Sage Open* 7, no. 3 (2017): 1.
12. Emily Richard, "Stop Imposing Eurocentric Beauty Standards," *An Injustice!*, November 9, 2021.

13. Mark E. Hill, "Skin Color and the Perception of Attractiveness among African Americans: Does Gender Make a Difference?," *Social Psychology Quarterly* 65, no. 1 (2002).

14. Germaine H. Awad et al., "Beauty and Body Image Concerns Among African American College Women," *The Journal of Black Psychology* 41, no. 6 (December 1, 2015).

15. Rebecca Epstein, Jamilia J. Blake, and Thalia Gonzalez, *Girlhood Interrupted: The Erasure of Black Girls' Childhood* (Washington, DC: Georgetown Law, 2017).

16. Ninochka McTaggart, Vaness Cox, and Caroline Heldman, *Representations of Black Women in Hollywood* (Rancho Cucamonga, CA: Geena Davis Institute on Gender in Media, 2021), 3.

17. *Little Monsters* (Australia: Neon, 2019).

18. Ibid.

19. Ibid.

20. *Horror Noire: A History of Black Horror* (United States of America: Shudder, 2019).

21. Ibid.

22. Kinitra D. Brooks, "The Importance of Neglected Intersections: Race and Gender in Contemporary Zombie Texts and Theories," *African American Review* 47, no. 4 (2014): 472–473.

23. Coleman, *Horror Noire*, xix.

24. *Horror Noire: A History of Black Horror*.

THE HORRORS OF CONTEMPORARY BLACKNESS

CHAPTER 15

··

FREDDIE VS. MICHAEL

Horror Reality and the Spectacle of Black Surveillance in Halloween: Resurrection

··

TIFFANY A. BRYANT

BEFORE the *Halloween* franchise rebooted in 2007, its then-final installment, *Halloween: Resurrection* (2002), was not particularly well received. Many viewers panned it as one of the weakest entries, mired by uninspired onscreen kills, storytelling choices both predictable and controversial (e.g. killing off Jamie Lee Curtis' Laurie Strode in the film's first 15 minutes), and questionable performances.[1] Yet bound within this *Halloween* sequel is a unique amalgamation of horror themes focused on the power and dangers of popularized surveillance cultures. It reflects topical concerns about the evolution and normalizing accessibility of the internet; the imprint of the new digital age changed the possibilities of creative, professional, and interpersonal trajectories for these young generations. *Resurrection* uses a reality TV live stream nestled within the larger slasher story to create its own meta-narration of watcher/watching relationships, playing off what Carol Clover refers to as the "killer's first person (I-camera)"[2] made famous by Michael Myers in the original *Halloween* (1978).

Horror scholarship often references Laura Mulvey's seminal essay "Visual Pleasure and the Narrative Cinema" to discuss Hollywood narrative identifications of a dominant, sadistic, and masculinized gaze upon a female object—we are encouraged to look at the feminine on display and gain pleasure (scopophilia) in watching. Inherent is a gendered power dynamic of the watcher, or the source of the gaze, inscribing symbolism onto the object, suggesting that the presumed status quo approach to looking and being looked at in Hollywood filmmaking is through the masculine as active and the feminine as passive. In *Black Looks: Race and Representation*, bell hooks re-interprets Mulvey's work to identify a racialized "power in looking"[3] rooted in the challenge for Black autonomy against the historically oppressive power of white supremacist surveillance. The position of watcher and/or possessor of the active gaze has traditionally been dominated by a white status quo. hooks argues "[t]hat all attempts to repress our/black people's rights to gaze had produced in us an overwhelming longing to look, a rebellious desire, an oppositional gaze"; we should (re)claim our gaze and manipulate it against "the structures of domination."[4] The discriminatory practice of surveillance as the gaze has had worldwide implications: "The 'gaze' has been and is a site of resistance for colonized black people globally. Subordinates in relations of power learn experientially that there is a critical gaze, one that 'looks' to document, one that is oppositional. In resistance struggle, the power of the dominated to assert agency by claiming and cultivating 'awareness' politicizes 'looking' relations—one learns to look a certain way in order to resist."[5] Intentional acts can resist a fraudulent white authority, including interrogations of the expressions or erasures of Black representation in media—especially if one believes that popular culture has power in producing impressionable images of identity and cultures that can have lasting detrimental effects if rooted in discrimination.

This chapter aims to magnify the significance of Freddie Harris, Nora Winston, and Rudy Grimes within *Resurrection*'s centralization of surveillance themes amid a slasher genre backdrop. As an installment within a mainstream franchise centered in whiteness, *Resurrection* includes multiple Black experiences, though not with equity to their character developments or screen time. Thus, this analysis will acknowledge and critique the offered performances of Blackness contextualized by their roles within a diegetic examination of celebrity culture, capitalism, and the tricky breadth of surveillance within the internet broadcast plot (with playful and problematic racialized surveillance on display). A cultural studies approach will help deconstruct how the representation of Blackness is treated within a film that blends the familiarity of an iconic slasher franchise with issues of surveillance culture intensified by reality TV programming.

In the main plot of the movie, six Haddonfield University students win a contest run by *Dangertainment* to participate in a live web show. As a slasher film using the paranormal reality TV process for its storytelling device, *Resurrection* frames a famous cultural place (what remains of Michael Myers's childhood home) as a televised space of historicized trauma. The participants will use cameras to document their findings and their subjective affectations. What the college students (including culinary student Rudy Grimes [Sean Patrick Thomas]), *Dangertainment* team members (Freddie Harris [Busta Rhymes] and Nora Winston [Tyra Banks]), and diegetic internet audience members think will be a uniquely interactive and fun Halloween event transforms into immediate terror as participants and crew are brutally murdered by the real Michael Myers. *Dangertainment* customizes the paranormal reality search for ghosts into a search for understanding the monstrous living by investigating Michael's childhood home for insight or evidence as to why "ordinary people turn to murder"[6] (Nora's interview question for Sara [Bianca Kajlich]).

In "The Liveness of Ghosts: Haunting and Reality TV," Karen Williams contextualizes the 2000s paranormal reality TV show as an extension of blurring, if not crossing, representational boundaries of the "real" for audience consumption. She describes general reality TV as having a propensity for publicizing private spaces in ways that "grant access to homes by sensationalizing the domestic lives within," which leads to a "documenting authority [that] mediates the intimate for public display."[7] Consider *Big*

Brother, a show in which casted "housemates" live together 24/7 and compete against each other to avoid "eviction" and win a large sum of money. The successful concept of the original Dutch program (1999–2006) led to international spinoffs in the United Kingdom, United States (both est. 2000), and countless other countries. Paranormal reality is an expansion of the format with two goals: "one of earnest authentication and the other of spectacle and effect"—authentication through proving the existence of supernatural entities by capturing photographic, video, or audio evidence; and sensationalism through the supernatural functioning as "manifest[ations of] the horrors of national histories," of "public spectacles of unspeakable historical trauma and unspoken family disputes."[8] Part of this authenticity and spectacle discussion incorporates an emphasis on temporality, or framing our concept of time as it relates to storytelling (what is happening here *now*) and understanding history (what happened in this place *then* to create this atmospheric affect). Such programming relies on an "ideology of liveness" by having participants make discoveries onscreen that create an "impression of immediate 'real time' . . . of a simultaneous present tense to our own and the inevitable unfolding of natural time."[9]

For *Resurrection*, the diegetic *Dangertainment* (both the company's and the web special's name) exemplifies "youth culture shows," which Williams specifies as "documented teens or young adults encountering and investigating haunted places" in a manner reminiscent of "a youth culture practice called 'legend trips,' in which teens . . . go to places with grisly pasts to 'defy superstition' and test their own capacity for fear, 'all in an effort to invoke—and then successfully escape—the wrath of the ghost.' "[10] Shows like MTV's *Fear* (2000–2002) encourage audience investment in watching the participants' experiences as they react in terror to their environments. The digital equipment used in these programs provides chances for perspective to play innovative roles in the storytelling experience, such as:

1. the subjectivity of raw-aesthetic first-person perspective (being able to see participants' facial reactions and their visceral responses at eye-level) through individual body or handheld cameras
2. the objectivity or observational mode of captured static footage, which offers credibility by being content from unmanned stationary equipment, increasing the chance that the recordings show the truth or real moments of a situation

Personal, user-generated surveillance cameras offer mobile, immersive viewpoints to make viewers feel involved (evocative of the "shaky" handheld camera style replicated in the found footage aesthetic). Offering multiple perspectives is a key feature in both actual paranormal reality shows and the *Dangertainment* broadcast, suggesting that, as Williams puts it, "the power of reality TV lies as much in its depiction of the *experience* of reality as it does in the depiction of reality itself."[11] The viewer both experiences and evaluates the authenticity of surveilled subjects' responses to their circumstances. In this way, "reality TV's emotional spectacle of subjects engaged in intense personal dramas is readily restaged as the paranormal reality show's display of terrified subjects confronting their ghosts."[12] With this consideration, our real-world perception of *Resurrection*'s reality show narrative includes three framing aspects: (1) the intentionally staged spatial boundaries of the reality show—the six participants' viewpoints and the production team's static cameras in the Myers house; (2) the Halloween party audience's operation of the microsite's curated points of view; and (3) filmic glimpses of Michael's perspective as the supernatural-coded threat.

In *Tales from the Haunted South*, Tiya Miles delves into the identity politics of representation within mainstream dark tourism and popular media's presentation of ghost hunting. Dark tourism frames sightseeing at locations at which tragic circumstances occurred, often involving death if not stories of suffering; it functions as an inclusive term under which ghost tours and the like fall. Miles explains: "At the turn of the twenty-first century and into the next decades, Americans became obsessed with spirits of the dead and joined that fascination with an equally intense appetite for traveling 'outside their usual environment.' The search for ghosts and a quest for novelty went hand in glove at a moment when tourism was steadily rising to become a multitrillion-dollar global industry."[13] Her work acknowledges that part of dark tourism's general allure is how it has become a more accessible means for learning about, if not confronting, concepts like death through measures of simulated reality and fiction. Says Miles:

> Televised ghost stories and visits to haunted sites have grown in frequency, density, and popularity in American culture since at least the early 2000s. Now what I have come to call "ghost fancy" is a cultural tsunami fed by new, mostly digital technology; reality and dramatic TV series about ghosts and other undead creatures (vampires, zombies, demons); local paranormal hobbyist groups; books; websites; social media spaces; and a plethora of ghost tours. Travel—touristic travel in particular—emerged as a central feature of the ghost hunting experience.[14]

About the topic of racial experiences in dark tourism, Miles suggests that it may appear that Black people are less likely to engage in ghost tours or supernatural hunt experiences, be that as investigator (the hunter or contestant participating in an event) or as client (a property-owner or employee at an alleged activity hot spot). This absence may relate to sociocultural and/or religious affiliations that tap into a spiritual sensitivity or spiritual reverence for the dead—a respect in recognizing that spirits and the supernatural, in whatever monstrous, demonic, or unnatural form, should not be provoked.

Miles notes that popular reality TV shows (like *Ghost Hunters* [2002–present]) and fictional texts (the CW's *Supernatural* [2005–2020]) about supernatural hunting partnerships center a very specific demographic as the go-to "leaders" who venture into spaces with dark histories: white men presented as heterosexual, cis-male, able-bodied, and predominantly from the working class. This specific intersectionality of who gets to tell whose histories may give additional insight as to why there may not be as many people of color present. The exclusivity leads scholars like Miles to read these media texts for white supremacist capitalist patriarchal trends of perspective, wherein white viewpoints surveil sites of traumatic notoriety wherein the historically oppressed are summoned by these white voices of authority. Instead of respect given to unfortunate histories, certain dark tourist experiences can seem like exploitations of tragedies.

For the *Resurrection* characters, exploring "the childhood home of our most brutal mass murderer, Michael Myers,"[15] remixes the real concept of dark tourism sites as a meta-narrative contextualization for the plot. Presumed abandoned, the old Myers house represents a location infused with an evil cultural memory to both Haddonfield locals and the larger world conscious of the true crime legend—the place where child Michael Myers committed his first murder by killing his big sister, Judith (as originally portrayed in the 1978 John Carpenter film). Michael's subsequent charge to a sanitarium remains consistent in the *Halloween* canon. Michael's escape and murder sprees across town caused unforgettable generational and community trauma, elevating him to a violent mythic status popular enough to centralize as the "mystery" for a web series decades later.

The adult character of Michael Myers is referred to as "The Shape" in the ending credits of the original two John Carpenter *Halloween* movies, a canonical nickname that alludes to his shifty presence looming in the peripheries of cinematic gazes. In *Playing in the Dark: Whiteness and the Literary Imagination*, Toni Morrison says, "These images of impenetrable whiteness need contextualizing to explain their extraordinary power, pattern, and consistency. Because they appear almost always in conjunction with representations of black or Africanist people who are dead, impotent, or under control, these images of blinding whiteness seem to function as both antidote for and meditation on the shadow that is companion to this whiteness."[16] Michael represents Morrison's "image," whose presence transforms others into collateral damage if they cross his path. Optics of racial inclusion in slasher movies have predicated tradition- ally on characters of color dying. In "Horrifying Whiteness," Tiffany A. Bryant notes, "The slasher does not operate as a direct representative of the patriarchy, yet his white- ness and disposal of deviants to patriarchal regulations of conduct makes him an ex- tended renegade member of the club. Michael trails from the visible aspect of whiteness through his constant vanishing acts from the viewer's perspective, an invisibility trick that I deem potentially symbolic of the omnipresent nature of patriarchy."[17] At least one white person—the Final Girl—usually survives the murderous mayhem. Meanwhile, people of color cast in supporting roles have a low-to-no life expectancy. Yet characters maintain an illusion of being in control of their circumstances until Michael cuts them down, functioning as both a whiteness that refuses visibility (per his constant smooth mobility, making it difficult for characters to notice him until it is too late for them) and a macabre shadow whose bursts of violence literally drive Haddonfield (and any other *Halloween* settings) into panic modes.

The ghost as a figure in paranormal reality situations becomes a complicated rep- resentation of the passage of time. Williams notes that the supernatural is challenged as representing the "material past"[18] in that "the liveness of television somehow dematerializes the ghost and the past it represents.... Liveness drains historical spaces of their objective reality and endows them with subjective affect instead. There is a reason no 'real' ghost is represented in these reality shows. Neither the medium of television nor its forms of reality TV could ever represent its 'reality': death and disconnection."[19]

Alissa Burger references Jacques Derrida's concept of hauntology to deconstruct the ghost's inability to be pinned down to a specific temporal condition. In this argument, "the ghost as always returning pulls the paranormal out of the past by instead emphasizing the immediate and future nature of such hauntings and investigations. Framed within the possibility of the imminent and inevitable return, the ghost becomes a preoccupation of the present and future, rather than remaining contained within the discourse of the past, its more traditional position."[20]

Resurrection transforms the ghost hunt aspect of paranormal reality TV and infuses symbolic representation of a place's haunting past with Michael as a corporeal "ghost" attacking intruders. The word "resurrection" in the title directly connects to Michael, who, yet again, defies what we assume was his death-by-decapitation in the previous movie (*Halloween H2o: 20 Years Later* [1998]). We might also interpret "resurrection" beyond Michael returning from the presumed grave and consider his shared characteristics with the supernatural. With the franchise's evolution, Michael possesses metaphorical and literal powers that seemingly deny him normal confinement to the parameters of time, place, and death—a characteristic shared by other slashers like Jason Vorhees of *Friday the 13th*. Michael only gets stronger with time, capable of physical feats like tossing grown adults across rooms like toys and crushing human heads with his bare hands. Derrida noted that, "One cannot control its [the revenant's] comings and goings because it begins by coming back,"[21] which aptly fits Michael. In *Resurrection*, he is discovered to have literally been haunting the Myers home by living in a makeshift space underneath the property. His ability to materialize quietly and quickly around camera frames, visually emphasized by the stark whiteness of his mask offsetting his appearance within otherwise dark rooms, gives him a poltergeist aesthetic. He is Death himself, literally disconnecting everyone.

What makes surveillance precariously dangerous for Black people, people of color, and members of other historically oppressed communities is when the surveillant group values white supremacist patriarchal capitalist standards that normalize social inequity, making it easy for vulnerable groups to be monitored in intentionally aggressive and intrusive manners. As David Lyon notes, surveillance is a mechanism for categorizing and sorting people based on areas of group differentiation that interest those with surveilling power and control over the management of information infrastructures. A danger with social sorting is that it affords for discriminatory practices that impact "visible minorities"[22] differently from the white status quo. In these instances, surveillance stops being an invisible, integrated part of one's everyday life—it is a disruption that can occur at any time based on regulated inequality and inequity. A person's data may be investigated closely simply because they can be categorically sorted into a specific group. Profiling based on race, ethnicity, culture, gender, sexual orientation, and other identity categories can lead to exclusion from spaces and opportunities—sometimes temporary, sometimes permanently (such as voting rights for individuals with prison records). The systematic nature of scrutiny caused by social sorting can lead to social injustices that are detrimental to one's survival ("access to healthcare, credit, insurance, social security, educational institutions, student loans and employment options"[23]) if not fatal (being murdered by individuals who claim "stand your ground" protection or similar defensive testimonies of feeling threatened). Everyday consciousness of surveillance can create "the fear of being seen, the exhaustion of watching and being watched, the degradation of being monitored and judged, always aware of the results of non-comformity: bullying, insults, exclusion, scorn, blows."[24]

Yet racialized struggles are denied credibility by an American society designed with white supremacist values; Black people are expected to "perform their innocence"[25] by accepting invasive, denigrating acts of transparency or else risk punitive actions that may have residually dire consequences. In *Under Surveillance: Being Watched in Modern America*, Randolph Lewis argues that surveillance can corner vulnerable populations into "producing the ideal face of a compliant, nonthreatening citizen," insisting that folks "modulate behavior in light of *how things might appear* rather than just being in the world without second thoughts. In short, it asks us to internalize an exhausting regime of predictability, to repress chaotic human urges and organic feelings, all to make sure the system doesn't misread us in a way that might cause problems."[26] This expectation of self-regulation appeases discriminating white ideologies of how society would prefer its citizens conduct themselves, promoted through scrutinizing, punitive threats and organized goals of conformity.

Resurrection presents Black representation through:

- Rudy Grimes (Sean Patrick Thomas): male on-screen participant (surveilled/performer)
- Nora Winston (Tyra Banks): female off-screen producer (surveillant)
- Freddie Harris (Busta Rhymes): male director both on and off-screen (surveillant) (figure 15.1)

Within the surveillance diagram of watching/watched, the job of *Dangertainment* team members Freddie and Nora is to evaluate the participants' performances and determine actionable steps needed to provoke stronger on-camera reactions. In one scene, as the participants explore the house, the pair sits in their director chairs at the multi-screened surveillance station staged in the garage. With wine-filled glasses, Freddie toasts, "For successfully . . . puttin' together something collectively so ingenious as a team and a duo, that we should definitely be able to secure a lot of food on the table for ourselves as long as everything goes as nicely as it's goin' right now."[27] This is a calm-before-the-storm celebration of Black success. And it may be read as progressive representation of two Black creatives in control of a white-majority horror production.

Yet the dangers of *Dangertainment* are its operations within capitalism, driven by an inherent white patriarchal framework of greed. Ruha Benjamin warns against the assumption that visible racial diversity in teams or organizations will automatically lead to equitable business operations, an issue that comes with "discriminatory design practices that grow out of the interplay of racism and capitalism."[28] The expectation should be that if whiteness is the categorial identity given preferential treatment, people of color may feel inclined to, or forced to, cater to racist values or else face consequences.

FIGURE 15.1 Nora (Tyra Banks, left) and Freddie (Busta Rhymes, right) explain that the selected participants will "explore America's worst nightmare" at Michael Myers's family home. Image by *Dimension Films*.

As a teacher, Benjamin gives the example, "The 'blandness' of Whiteness that some of my students brought up when discussing their names is treated by programmers as normal, universal, and appealing. The invisible power of Whiteness means that even a Black computer scientist running his own company who earnestly wants to encode a different voice into his app is still hemmed in by the desire of many people for White-sounding voices."[29] *Resurrection* does not give narrative space for how the *Dangertainment* team chose the official six participants—we as the film's audience are not privy to who else was in the candidate pool to guess how these specific students were selected. Furthermore, we are given no indication as to what *racially* or *ethnically diverse* candidates were rejected in the process. Instead, there being one Black contestant to five white(-presenting) ones suggests some questionable considerations about Freddie and Nora buying into the normalized expectation of visible profitable whiteness. In a 2020s world, diversity and equity initiatives would interrogate *Dangertainment*'s promotion strategy—where, when, and how they advertised the program opportunity; how they screened participants for on-screen entertainment purposes; and how biases may have prevented other cast possibilities.

In "The Politics of Greed," hooks deconstructs class issues along racial lines, considering the mechanisms deployed that render Black Americans conscious of, and targeted victims of, socioeconomic injustices. While struggling within systems that profit an economic stratification that positions white conservative values favorably, hooks argues that Black Americans can succumb to capitalism when *some* level of success seems attainable, though it is never offered with equity or equality with regards to:

the popular truism that "anyone can make it big in America." Multimass media has played the central role as the propagandistic voice promoting the notion that this culture remains a place of endless opportunity, where those on the bottom can reach the top. . . . Along with the revamped myth that everyone who worked hard could rise from the bottom of our nation's class hierarchy to the top was the insistence that the old notions of oppressor class and oppressed class were no longer meaningful, because when it came to the issue of material longing, the poor, working, and middle classes desired the same things that the rich desired, including the desire to exercise power over others. What better proof of this could there be than calling attention to the reality that individuals from marginal groups who had been left out of the spheres of class power entered these arenas and conducted themselves in the same manner as the established groups.[30]

The notion of historically excluded groups adopting the same attitudes, processes, and actions as the historically privileged runs parallel to *Dangertainment*'s actions. Freddie enjoys controlling the version of Michael's story that he and his team constructed. They repurpose the Myers's house from a site of tragedy to an exploited performative space.

And they do so by manipulating the surveilled. Freddie pushes back defensively, yet assertively, when his motivation (greed) is called into question by the participants' changing moral perspectives of the facade enveloping them. When Freddie gets caught by Rudy, Sara, and Jim while dressed as Michael Myers, Freddie tells them:

> You really have no idea of how nicely I worked things out. So that we all can receive somewhat of a robust back end when this shit is all over. Now, I don't know what you wanna do about your share, but please don't fuck it up for me. I want my money, a'ight? Now, if you don't mind, I'd like to go scare the shit out of some more of these motherfuckers, so I'm gonna get it crackin'. Yall do what the fuck yall gotta do."[31]

Morrison discusses an intersectional struggle for Black Americans to unpack a reclamation of nationality when it is coded in racism. She highlights "American means white, and Africanist people struggle to make the term applicable to themselves with ethnicity and hyphen after hyphen after hyphen."[32] Freddie's speech heralds the great capitalist objective: make money. And he will do whatever is needed to get his cut of the profit, including dressing up in a realistic costume to mimic diegetic cultural references to Michael Myers. In this sense, throughout the film, Freddie adopts Morrison's "hyphen after hyphen" attribution by being the business owner, director, casting mentor, publicity relations mediator, show host, and other duties as self-assigned (such as casted into other performative roles).

Freddie insists on his business knowledge of what his target audience wants. Says Freddie, "I'm only tryin' to give America a good show. . . . America don't like reality, first of all. Second of all, they think the shit is boring. You know what I mean? They want a little, a little razzle-dazzle. A little pizazz, a little thrill in their life, you know? And us being the ones that give it to 'em . . . I don't see nothin' wrong with that."[33] Freddie's actions align with hooks's deconstruction that "token marginal individuals who entered the ranks of ruling class privilege that they, like their mainstream counterparts, could be bought—could and would succumb to the corrupting temptations of greed. The way had been paved to bring to the masses the message that excess was acceptable. Greed was the order of the day, and to make a profit by any means necessary was merely to live out to the fullest degree the American work ethic."[34] Sara, Rudy, and Bill deride Freddie for his deception, a callout that seems both hypocritical (since they seem familiar with the concept of reality TV being a product of staging and production team interference) and a projection of "good" (read: white-coded) morality against Freddie that enforces a derogatory racialization onto his entertainment greed. Producing something novel can become a steppingstone toward other deals and financial payoffs. Freddie does specify he has planned for them all to be compensated when the show ends, sharing the wealth in a manner that does not quite fit the Americanized individualism; yet that distribution plan is ignored by the frustrated participants.

The act of shaming Freddie is complicated by the distinct vernacular differences within the scene, wherein the optics show the group confronting their Black male employer. While both sides use profanity in their dialogue, Freddie's speech is laced with an informal African American Vernacular English (AAVE) approach compared to earlier scenes when his professional performance caters to white-dominated audiences (i.e. to the news reporters during the pre-show preparation, an opportunity to boost event buzz; and at the meet-and-greet interview session, when it would behoove him and Nora to establish favorable impressions and solidify participatory commitments). Freddie postures power, yet code-switching moments reveal sides of Freddie that exude the cinematic gaze of racialized otherness. He is presented in contrast to Rudy, whose displays of educated, nonthreatening Black masculinity are comparatively coded as being more white status-quo-friendly (per his on-screen platonic friendship with Sara and Jen) than the more unpredictable nature of Freddie's bravado.

While it is unclear whether *Resurrection* director Rick Rosenthal intended on this critical interpretation of the entertainment industry, it is difficult to ignore that *Dangertainment*'s programming practices reinforce Hollywood applications of diversity exclusion regarding their hiring/casting practices. Diversity is only expressed through a division of binary gender selection, college major identifications, and cosmetic aesthetics: three men and three women were chosen (a typical "battle of the sexes" practice in reality TV casting), each person pursues a different academic focus, and each person has a different early 2000s fashion style. All six are seemingly heterosexual/heterosexual-presenting. When two Black leaders (with no other higher-ups identified) have the control to enact more inclusive casting, the optics present a normalization of patriarchal whiteness. Then again, to quote Benjamin and the cynicism that can occur with inauthentic hiring practices, "Why bother with broader structural changes in casting and media representation, when marketing gurus can make Black actors *appear* more visible than they really are in the actual film?"[35] On a meta-level, *Resurrection* is a film produced by white leadership (director, writer, producers), so its presentation filters through white Hollywood creative viewpoints. Even though the film features a Black-owned production company, Black cultural values or perspectives are not evident in their business operations. Nothing about Nora necessitates a performance by a Black female actor. The web show uplifts a predominantly white cast of young people. Their cameraperson is a white man. The other extras in the meet-and-greet scene, assumed *Dangertainment* staff, are also white. In other real-world creative hands—for example, if *Resurrection* was remade as a "Black horror" film rather than a "Blacks in horror" film[36]—this diegetic reality might have been addressed as part of the characters' arcs, highlighting on-screen visibility of the challenges of being entertainment creatives in a white-dominated industry (figure 15.2).

As producer, Nora technically runs the show. Even though their cameraperson, Charley, is a white man whose professional expertise is to set the options for the internet audience's gazes, Nora's Black authority directs his actions. This business relationship model is unusual within the horror genre. Rarely do we see media directors/producers as people of color; such roles are usually reserved for white men. As such, *Resurrection* provides a racialized surveillance gaze that operates outside of the usual white-dominant status quo. And because Nora's role sets her in the garage-turned-production studio, her gaze is the most consistent one reviewing the participants (compared to Freddie's occasional forays into the house), which could have suggested a departure from a "cinematic male gaze" in favor of a Black female gaze.

Nora Winston is a fairly neutral, one-dimensional character. Aside from the assertive employer admonishment she gives Charley during set-up, she speaks predominantly to Freddie with playful professionalism. Surveillance can employ a "gendered gaze, and the overvisibility of the feminine body by packaging it as a form of 'sexual feminine liberation.'"[37] Arguably, Nora's most memorable scene is when the plot requires her to be oblivious as Michael murders Charley with a camera tripod, prolonging the discovery of a real killer being on the premises. The cinematic camera cuts from the killing scene to a close-up of Nora's butt as she slowly dances from her surveillance station to the espresso maker. Charley's death is subsequently juxtaposed with Nora's casual-yet-seductive moves to an R&B song, a sequence that: establishes that *Dangertainment* is highly

FIGURE 15.2 Nora (Tyra Banks) radios camera operator Charley (Brad Sihvon) during his surveillance setup as she watches from the garage-based production studio. Image by *Dimension Films.*

unprepared for this surprise guest; reinforces Nora's Blackness with a genre-specific musical cue and her femininity with an eroticized cinematic gaze; and suggests Nora will not be a dependable, functional character during the broadcast.

Arguably, Nora's off-screen murder aligns with what hooks calls "cinematic racism" connected to the "violent erasure of black womanhood."[38] Nora's presence is completely effaced from the diegetic audience's perspective. As a creative producer, she has no logistical reason for being on-screen; her role is designed to be out-of-sight to control what the audience sees by scripting accordingly. Yet her death is taken completely offline and off-screen—the real audience does not even see what happens to her. We, along with Sarah, witness only the aftermath of her murder. In *Recreational Terror: Women and the Pleasures of Horror Film Viewing*, Isabel Cristina Pinedo applies feminist and cultural studies to analyze postmodern horror characteristics that appeal to female spectators. Pinedo identifies that there is pleasure in the tension between when postmodern horror allows for full, partial, and no spectatorship of the bodily violence that creates "the ruined body" or a "wet death"; she argues that "a partial vision negotiates the tension between the desire to see and dread at the prospect of seeing."[39] Compare Nora's and Charley's deaths. Charley's murder includes the "unclaimed POV shot," when "one or a series of shots is held long enough and framed in order to create the impression that someone is watching";[40] the impact emphasizes the "spectacle of the terrorized and ravaged victim" so that "the inability to see what is not shown heightens the power of the image to horrify."[41] Pinedo uses the original *Halloween* to describe when "a tracking shot . . . allows us to see some part of the monster's body from the monster's point of view but refrains from revealing the identity of the killer."[42] *Resurrection* breaks the obscurity by showing both Michael's actions and Charley's reactions. Yet Michael's weaponization of the tripod allows for jump-cut reclamations of monstrous first-person shots, forcing the film viewer to witness Charley's death from Michael's perspective.

Nora's death scene,[43] on the other hand, produces the "blocked vision"[44] aspect of horror filmmaking, in which the audience is denied full view of the spectacle. Instead, "the prominence of blind space in the horror film, what lurks outside the frame or unclearly within it, generates uncertainty about what one is seeing."[45] The discovery of Nora's body plays with "blind space" by forcing fixed perspectives until a last-minute reveal. At first, the filmic gaze watches Sara move through the garage in claustrophobic close-up shots. The filmic gaze shows the pool of blood and viscera covering the floor before Sara notices it only too late, slipping and falling hard. As the camera lingers on her dawning realization of being covered in blood, her literal gaze pans upward into the previous blind space; the filmic gaze cuts to Sara's first-person camera, revealing Nora hanging above her.

Simultaneously, one may interpret a lack in cultural sensitivity in having Nora, a Black woman, die by a white man's hands in what could be considered a modern lynching. Her death could have been reserved for one of the more plentiful white characters.[46] Furthermore, Nora's corpse makes a fragmented follow-up appearance. When Freddie attacks Michael with an electric cord, the shock entangles the slasher into dangling cables, revealing Nora's heeled boots swaying from the impact. Intentional or not, the casualness of Nora's death exemplifies the dangers of systemic practices involving devaluation and inattention paid to people of color, especially members of Black communities, victimized by white supremacist forces. If there is no clear-cut evidence of the violence happening, some are less likely to believe the testimonies, outcries, and protests of the historically attacked—not without surveillance evidence showing offenders doing the most against undeserving individuals. In Nora's case, her occupancy of the show producer role meant that no one was looking out for her. That lack of visibility made her an easy target, since any discovery of her body would come too late. Yet her absence speaks ironically (and morbidly) to the fact that, as a behind-the-scenes Black woman, no one missed her, unlike the white female bodies that were constantly under a visualized threat of violence (figure 15.3).

In white-produced art, one idea that Morrison poses is "the Africanist character as surrogate and enabler. In what ways does the imaginative encounter with Africanism enable white writers to think about themselves? What are the dynamics of Africanism's self-reflexive properties?"[47] Rudy represents the Black sacrificial horror trope to whiteness. He is the surrogate male protector and enabler for Sara and Jen in lieu of the physical presence of significant others/love interests who can fulfill these roles for either woman. Intentional or not, there is subtext to his navigation of predominantly white spaces and the way he contributes to such spaces in nonthreatening ways. In Rudy's introductory scene, he expresses excitement when Jen shares that all three of them have been cast in the show. When Sara admits her apprehension, Rudy tells her, "Listen, without me, you would die of boredom," only for Jen to correct him ("Us! Without *us* you would die of boredom").[48] Rudy is immediately framed as a friend, someone used to Jen's unabashed confidence and Sara's risk aversion. Arguably, there are no hints of interracial romantic chemistry between them. Rudy's focus on the culinary arts also renders him in a nontraditional academic path for Black men.

FIGURE 15.3 Culinary student Rudy (Sean Patrick Thomas) prepares vegetables before his friends arrive and share that they have all been cast in the *Dangertainment* program. Image by *Dimension Films*.

The details provided about Rudy unveil the gaps that his presence fills within the diegetic cast, which we can relate to storytelling evocations of color blindness and color consciousness. Morrison identifies a need to critique "the technical ways in which an Africanist character is used to limn out and enforce the invention and implications of whiteness. We need studies that analyze the strategic use of black characters to define the goals and enhance the qualities of white characters."[49] Similarly, hooks addresses a concern about how Black representation can be co-opted for non-Black-centered purposes, flagging that it is not uncommon for white appropriation to "make black culture and black life backdrop, scenery for narratives that essentially focus on white people."[50] In "Eating the Other: Desire and Resistance," hooks focuses on mass culture's enjoyment of racial difference when it can be treated through the objectified lens of commodification—profiting from difference as capitalistic effect. She explains that "Within commodity culture, ethnicity becomes spice, seasoning that can liven up the dull dish that is mainstream white culture"; furthermore, if you accept that racial and ethnic categorizations have "become commodified as resources for pleasure, the culture of specific groups, as well as the bodies of individuals, can be seen as constituting an alternative playground where members of dominating races, genders, sexual practices affirm their power."[51]

Of the Black characters, Rudy is the only one whose perspective is designed to be adoptable to the diegetic audience. He is a legitimate member of the *Dangertainment* talent, operating the personalized surveillance gear alongside his white castmates; his presence as a contestant prevents the casting from appearing racially exclusive. His culinary skills and observant, smart personality are leveraged by the *Resurrection* script to hint at the house's deceptive set-up. While in the Myers's kitchen, Rudy investigates a container of fennel, only to flag for Sara how "strange" it is that the spice "smells fresh."[52] In a later scene, while Sara applies her psychology class knowledge to interpret what they have found so far, an unconvinced Rudy tells Sara that "It's not right. It's too easy,"[53] presenting critical analysis of the situational context. After Freddie reveals himself in the Michael costume, clearly playing slasher to scare the participants and influence live stream engagement, Rudy is the first participant to confidently quit the show, which enables the already-skittish Sara to follow his lead. In a progressive manner (or with a liberal reading), Rudy is smart, cool, likable to his peers, brave when the occasion calls for it (capable of owning a leadership role, at least with his immediate friends), and selfless. In a critical manner, Rudy is the token representative[54] of the Black community for an invisible digital audience.

That visibility becomes Rudy's undoing. Symbolically, Rudy walks a fine line of racialized characterization and traditional horror blandness to provide what filmmakers assume audiences want—a high body count of kills, which requires having characters created for death. Unlike Nora's effaced murder, Rudy's participant identity causally affords his murder to be a spectacle, as he is skewered into the kitchen door by multiple knives. To reinforce Rudy's sacrificial foreshadowing, he intentionally offers himself in confrontation with Michael to bide Sara time to flee. His murder is captured on both his headset and the kitchen surveillance camera. Yet the diegetic party audience

FIGURE 15.4 At the pre-production meeting, Freddie (Busta Rhymes) demonstrates the body camera that will be worn during the livestream to simulate first-person perspective. Image by *Dimension Films.*

responds with initial dismissal to his murder, assuming they are watching a dramatic performance (figure 15.4).

In *Horror Noire: Blacks in American Horror Films from the 1890s to Present,* Dr. Robin R. Means Coleman concludes her survey of Black horror representation in film history with the 1990s on, identifying that "Like the horror genre as a whole, films featuring Blacks (though not necessarily written, directed, or produced by Blacks) are skewing to young people, purposefully hailing youth of all stripes of the hip-hop generation by saturating its horror with rappers and rap music through 'Black horror' films."[55] Busta Rhymes is an artist whose horror-film credit uses his stage name rather than his real name (Trevor George Smith Jr.), perhaps a reflection of individual preferences, but likely a choice rooted in capitalist gains (using the higher profile names that ordinary people recognize will increase promotional marketing opportunities). He is a hip-hop star who expanded his performative interests to include film. Benjamin notes that the hypervisibility of Black celebrities or actors cast in roles can be a feature of white supremacy, "mask[ing] the widespread disenfranchisement of Black communities."[56] A sudden boost in back-to-back Black male representation (with LL Cool J as Ronny the security guard in *Halloween H2o*) could efface the limited inclusion of Black representation across the *Halloween* franchise. This visibility reflects a marketing practice of cosmetic diversity to potentially draw in more audience members of color without authentically featuring those actors in the plot, or by having them portray supportive characters to the white protagonists. Likewise, that visibility makes money for the filmmakers/company.

Coleman also remarks on the tendency for Black participation to be cast in comedic relief roles in horror: "In the past, Blacks have been the source of 'the funny' in comedy-horror, putting on full display their incredible talents of being simultaneously petrified and hilarious. Unfortunately, the performances were at the expense of Blacks' humanity."[57] The characterization of Freddie Harris exemplifies this comedic relief relegation. As the participants find suspicious props around the house that were clearly planted by the production crew to spin their interpretation of Michael, in one famously ostentatious scene, a costumed Freddie slowly moves through the house only to encounter the real Michael Myers. Freddie's costume conveniently matches Michael's fit, and the filmic audience is treated to a visual doubling of slasher danger; however, Freddie breaks character to berate who he assumes is Charly behind the other mask. The mistaken identity scene creates some tension in the polar opposition presented by both Michaels: the fake Michael yells, curses, and moves with threatening gestures and actual physical contact as performative attempts to belittle or dominate; the real Michael remains eerily stoic, still, and silent (except for the audible sound of his breathing behind the mask). The comedic traces within Freddie's exaggerated masculine aggression diffuse tension, while the threat of Michael unexpectedly attacking Freddie during the tirade increases tension.

In the film's finale, Freddie spits profanity-laced one-liners at Michael in what could be interpreted as a performance of male dominance against another male threat, including: "Trick or treat, motherfucker," "Burn, motherfucker. BURN!" and "Hey Mikey! Happy Fuckin' Halloween!"[58] The use of expletives adds a racialized performance of masculinity evocative of Coleman's description of the hip-hop generation—directing foul language at antagonistic entities is a standard practice, functioning as criticism against institutions and advocates of racist, classist, misogynistic values inherent in white supremacy. The intentional use of disrespectful language expresses Freddie's anger toward the killer, and this justifiable anger translates into defensive actions to both physically disarm (via direct attacks) and mentally disarm (via psychological maneuvers, such as informally referring to the slasher by the youthful nickname "Mikey") to escape death. We might consider Freddie as a transitional characterization of Black representation from the pre-millennium into what would become oncoming horror films in which Black characters are treated as more than peripheral characters supporting white leads.

In an unusual twist to the slasher genre, which usually has a sole "Final Girl" survivor, *Resurrection* has two Final People. Carol Clover's identification of the Final Girl in the seminal *Men, Women, and Chainsaws: Gender in the Modern Horror Film*, a go-to study in slasher scholarship, is key to recognizing this quirk. She defines this character type as the survivor:

> who encounters the mutilated bodies of her friends and perceives the full extent of the preceding horror and of her own peril; who is chased, cornered, wounded; whom we see scream, stagger, fall, rise, and scream again. She is abject terror personified. . . . She alone looks death in the face, but she alone also finds the strength either to stay the killer long enough to be rescued (ending A) or to kill him herself (ending B). But in either case, from 1974 on, the survivor figure has been female.[59]

Clover refers to John Carpenter's belief that in his *Halloween* treatment of the Final Girl and slasher, they are linked by a "sexual repression," to which she adds, "It is also a shared masculinity, materialized in what comes next (and what Carpenter, perhaps significantly, fails to mention): the castration, literal or symbolic, of the killer at her hands. The Final Girl has not just manned herself; she specifically unmans an oppressor whose masculinity was in question to begin with."[60] In *Resurrection*, Sara fights Michael in the final act by matching his chef's knife with a chainsaw she finds in the garage-turned-production station. But her aggression backfires when she accidentally slices through production equipment cables, sparking an explosive fire that incapacitates her within a web of more cables. At the last moment, Freddie suddenly emerges and takes over the final battle, using a nearby shovel and production cords to electrocute Michael and bide him time to carry Sara out of the swiftly burning building. As such, *Resurrection* features both a white woman and a Black man inadvertently tag-teaming to disarm their overpowered white male oppressor. Clover's notion of a "shared masculinity" between survivor and slasher offers an opportunity to consider Freddie's actions as a reclamation of his Black masculinity against Michael's unchecked white masculinity, and as refutation of the white-coded capitalist venture that drove Freddie's motivation.

In her description of the typical slasher film resolution, Pinedo says, "After a protracted struggle, a resourceful female usually subdues the killer, sometimes kills him, and survives."[61] Pinedo observes that "The slasher film violates the taboo against women wielding violence to protect themselves by staging a scene in which she is forced to choose between killing and dying."[62] *Resurrection* offers a racialized reading of this sentiment. While Sara has her major moment to defend or die against Michael, Freddie gets the official opportunity for the killing move against the slasher. In an MTV interview, Sean Patrick Thomas (Rudy) tells Busta Rhymes, "You're a black hero in *Halloween* already."[63] In this way, *Resurrection* as a slasher film violates a taboo against Black people—especially Black men—wielding violence against whiteness by making it an acceptable and necessary choice (i.e. against the notorious mass murderer). This white supremacist taboo of striking back against whiteness exists within the real world, especially in the United States, and can extend to issues of colorism and anti-Black racism that exist globally.

Resurrection's mixed reception and questionable depictions of representation may continue to be argued, but it remains a pivotal transition point in the *Halloween* franchise and the slasher subgenre while preceding some of the surveillance horror themes and styles to come in the 2000s on. British miniseries *Dead Set* (2008) situates the zombie apocalypse during an eviction night filming of *Big Brother*, creating confusion and chaos among the reality contestants and production crew trapped in the studio. The importance of surveillance cameras (for celebrity culture and survival reconnaissance) and the use of the iconic TV title emphasize challenges in the entertainment industry, including the capitalist dissonance of prioritizing fame despite circumstantial danger, such as zombies. Various films employ found-footage aesthetics to immerse investigator characters (both professionals and amateurs) in spaces with dark histories or corrupted present-states. Spanish film *[•REC]* (2007) follows reporter Angela Vida (Manuela Velasco) and camera operator Pablo (Pablo Rosso) on a late-night assignment shadowing firefighters in Barcelona. Pablo records their horrific experiences inside a residential building wherein an abrupt government-sanctioned quarantine is designed to cover up a violence-inducing virus. (The 2008 American remake *Quarantine*, set in Los Angeles, closely replicates its predecessor; however, it casts Steve Harris as camera operator Scott Percival, effectively making a Black man the diegetic production perspective and voice of reason.) South Korean film *Gonjiam: Haunted Asylum* (2018) presents a vlogging crew's livestream investigation of the haunted Gonjiam Psychiatric Hospital as a means to bolster views for the horror web channel *Horror Times*. Goaded into action by channel owner Ha-joon's (Wi Ha-joon) fixation on viewership, the team ignores various warning signs, leading to their traumatic demises by violent spirits—deaths that are witnessed by the real audience through handheld and body camera footage. *Resurrection*'s combined paranormal reality elements and slasher relationships with spectatorship and violence run in tandem with evolutions in horror consumerism and both American and global considerations of (un)acceptable features within surveillance cultures. The focus on entertainment through self-aware surveillance, and the intricate ways that we voluntarily engage in acts of watching/letting ourselves be watched, morphed into creative avenues of producing our own stories.

Notes

1. "*Halloween: Resurrection,*" *Rotten Tomatoes*, accessed February 12, 2022, https://www.rottentomatoes.com/m/halloween_resurrection.
2. Carol Clover, "Her Body, Himself," in *Men, Women, and Chainsaws: Gender in the Modern Horror Film* (Princeton, NJ: Princeton University Press, 1992), 24.
3. bell hooks, "The Oppositional Gaze: Black Female Spectators," in *Black Looks: Race and Representation* (Boston: South End, Press, 1992), 115.
4. Ibid., 116.
5. Ibid.
6. "Real Contestants," *Halloween: Resurrection*, directed by Rick Rosenthal (2002; Los Angeles: Miramax, 2011), Apple iTunes, https://itunes.apple.com/us/movie/halloween-resurrection/id1520266988.
7. Karen Williams, "The Liveness of Ghosts: Haunting and Reality TV," in *Popular Ghosts: The Haunted Spaces of Everyday Culture*, ed. María del Pilar Blanco and Esther Peeren (New York: Continuum, 2010), 150.
8. Williams, "Liveness of Ghosts," 149–150.
9. Ibid., 150.
10. Ibid., 152.
11. Ibid., 154.
12. Ibid., 151.
13. Tiya Miles, *Tales from the Haunted South: Dark Tourism and Memories of Slavery from the Civil War Era* (Chapel Hill: University of North Carolina Press, 2015), 3.
14. Miles, *Tales from the Haunted South*, 2.
15. Rosenthal, "Real Contestants," 2002.
16. Toni Morrison, *Playing in the Dark: Whiteness and the Literary Imagination* (New York: Vintage Books, 1992), 33.

17. Tiffany A. Bryant, "Horrifying Whiteness: Slasher Conduct, Masculinity, and the Cultural Politics of *Halloween*," *Offscreen* 18, no. 8 (2014), https://offscreen.com/view/horrifying-whiteness.
18. Williams, "Liveness of Ghosts," 156.
19. Ibid., 160.
20. Alissa Burger, "*Ghost Hunters*: Simulated Participation in Televisual Hauntings," in *Popular Ghosts: The Haunted Spaces of Everyday Culture*, ed. María del Pilar Blanco and Esther Peeren (New York: Continuum, 2010), 163.
21. Burger, "*Ghost Hunters*," 163.
22. David Lyon, *The Culture of Surveillance: Watching as a Way of Life* (Cambridge, UK: Polity, 2018), 20.
23. Lyon, *Culture of Surveillance*, 107.
24. Randolph Lewis, *Under Surveillance: Being Watched in Modern America* (Austin: University of Texas Press, 2017), 46.
25. Lyon, *Culture of Surveillance*, 64.
26. Lewis, *Under Surveillance*, 16–17 (emphasis in original).
27. "You Watch," *Halloween: Resurrection*, directed by Rick Rosenthal (2002; Los Angeles: Miramax, 2011), Apple iTunes, https://itunes.apple.com/us/movie/halloween-resurrection/id1520266988.
28. Ruha Benjamin, *Race After Technology: Abolitionist Tools for the New Jim Code* (Cambridge, UK: Polity, 2019), 28.
29. Ibid., 29.
30. bell hooks, "The Politics of Greed," in *where we stand: class matters* (New York: Routledge, 2000), 66.
31. "This Is Not a Hoax," *Halloween: Resurrection*, directed by Rick Rosenthal (2002; Los Angeles: Miramax, 2011), Apple iTunes, https://itunes.apple.com/us/movie/halloween-resurrection/id1520266988.
32. Morrison, *Playing in the Dark*, 47.
33. Rosenthal, "This Is Not a Hoax," 2002.
34. hooks, "Politics of Greed," 66.
35. Benjamin, *Race After Technology*, 18 (emphasis in original).
36. Robin R. Means Coleman, *Horror Noire: Blacks in American Horror Films from the 1890s to Present* (New York: Routledge, 2011), 6.
37. Lyon, *Culture of Surveillance*, 132.
38. hooks, "Oppositional Gaze," 119.
39. Isabel Cristina Pinedo, *Recreational Terror: Women and the Pleasures of Horror Film Viewing* (Albany: State University of New York Press, 1997), 51.
40. Ibid.
41. Ibid., 52.
42. Ibid., 51.
43. The discovery of Nora's body parallels with the discovery of another murdered Black female character in the franchise, Nurse Virginia Alves (Gloria Gifford) in *Halloween II* (1981). Nurse Alves works the late shift at Haddonfield Memorial Hospital and takes care of wounded Laurie Strode (Jamie Lee Curtis). Like Nora, Nurse Alves's death occurs off-screen, and like Nora, Nurse Alves's corpse is discovered on a table by a young white person (Jimmy, a part-time orderly) who falls from the pooling of her blood.
44. Pinedo, *Recreational Terror*, 54.

45. Ibid., 53.
46. Most of the contestants are killed on spiked/sharp objects—by stabbing (Charley with the tripod, Bill with a knife), decapitation (Jen), impalement (Donna on the underground gate, Rudy against the kitchen door). Only Jim is killed differently, his head smashed by Michael's hands (a possible callback to previous films, such as Brady's death in the 1988 *Halloween 4: The Return of Michael Myers*).
47. Morrison, *Playing in the Dark*, 51.
48. "We're In!" *Halloween: Resurrection*, directed by Rick Rosenthal (2002; Los Angeles: Miramax, 2011), Apple iTunes, https://itunes.apple.com/us/movie/halloween-resurrection/id1520266988.
49. Morrison, *Playing in the Dark*, 52–53.
50. bell hooks, "Eating the Other: Desire and Resistance," in *Black Looks: Race and Representation* (Boston: South End, Press, 1992), 32.
51. Ibid., 21, 23.
52. "Let the DangerTainment Begin," *Halloween: Resurrection*, directed by Rick Rosenthal (2002; Los Angeles: Miramax, 2011), Apple iTunes, https://itunes.apple.com/us/movie/halloween-resurrection/id1520266988.
53. "You Watch."
54. Ironically, fictional Rudy's tokenism parallels with actor Sean Patrick Thomas's tendency to be typecast into token Black male friend roles during this time in his career. He performed roles in popular movies across different genres, making him a recognizable young actor in Hollywood in a similar vein to Gabrielle Union being cast regularly as a token Black female friend in the 1990s and 2000s: romantic comedy—*Can't Hardly Wait* (1998); young adult dramas—*Cruel Intentions* (1999) and *Save the Last Dance* (2001); and horror—*Dracula 2000* (2000).
55. Means Coleman, *Horror Noire*, 199–200.
56. Benjamin, *Race After Technology*, 25.
57. Means Coleman, *Horror Noire*, 214.
58. "He's Still Alive!" *Halloween: Resurrection*, directed by Rick Rosenthal (2002; Los Angeles: Miramax, 2011), Apple iTunes, https://itunes.apple.com/us/movie/halloween-resurrection/id1520266988.
59. Clover, "Her Body, Himself," 35.
60. Ibid., 49.
61. Pinedo, *Recreational Terror*, 72.
62. Ibid., 84.
63. Ryan J. Downey, "Busta Rhymes 'Flabbergasted' by *Halloween: Resurrection*," MTV.com, June 12, 2002, http://www.mtv.com/news/1455149/busta-rhymes-flabbergasted-by-halloween-resurrection/.

CHAPTER 16

"TIME . . . NEVER STOPS"

The Power of "Sonic Anachronism" in Misha Green's Lovecraft Country

RACHAL BURTON AND AYANNI C. H. COOPER

"NOW, LET ME HEAR SOMETHING THAT'LL WAKE ME UP": ON THE SOUND OF TIME

THE summer of 2020 marked a moment of great civil unrest in the United States and around the globe. Worldwide, the coronavirus pandemic spread into its first summer, sparking confusion, disagreement, and despair. Mass protests unfolded in the wake of the police killings of Breonna Taylor and George Floyd in Louisville, Kentucky, and Minneapolis, Minnesota, respectively, earlier that year. Donning protective facemasks, protesters gathered in the streets by the hundreds and thousands to demand that Black lives like Taylor's and Floyd's, as well as those of other countless Black folks murdered by the police and as a result of anti-Black violence, mattered. This was the stage onto which *Lovecraft Country* debuted.

On August 16, 2020, the Home Box Office (HBO) network released *Lovecraft Country*, a period horror–science fiction–fantasy drama mainly set in the mid-1950s. The show, created by Misha Green (*Underground*, *Heroes*, and *Sons of Anarchy*), adapts author Matt Ruff's novel of the same name published in 2016. *Lovecraft Country* primarily follows two main Black characters, Atticus "Tic" Freeman (played by Jonathan Majors) and Letitia "Leti" Lewis (played by Jurnee Smollett), as they attempt to decode secrets about Tic's ancestry and the shrouded, mysterious world of magic. The show also features various supporting characters, including Leti's older half-sister, Ruby Baptiste (played by Wunmi Mosaku); Tic's comic-loving younger cousin, Diana "Dee" Freeman (played by Jada Harris); and the enigmatic antagonist Christina Braithwhite (played by Abbey Lee). These characters populate a world filled with other villainous figures,

Lovecraftian monsters, and fictionalized versions of Black historical figures like Jackie Robinson and Emmett Till.

Though *Lovecraft Country*'s creative team could not have predicted the cultural landscape their show would debut in, a resonance nonetheless exists between the rallying cries of that summer and the narrative's arguments about race, history, time, and memory. Much of the show's main thesis centers the connectivity of Black American experience across time, as well as the legacies of trauma and resilience that extend from slavery into the future. See, for instance, the time- and space-spanning adventures of Dee's mother, Hippolyta (played by Aunjanue Ellis), in "I Am," or the harrowing "Rewind 1921," which drops Leti, Tic, and his father, Montrose (played by the late Michael K. Williams), in Tulsa on the eve of the infamous massacre. The show is no stranger to playing with both the collapsing and expanding of history and future potentialities. Central to our considerations, and a major part of what makes *Lovecraft Country* incredibly special, is how the musical directors, Laura Karpman and Raphael Saadiq, disrupt narrative temporalities by relishing in both seamless and jagged "sonic anachronisms," gesturing to the horror and potentiality of Black pasts, presents, and futures through sound.

Sound plays a crucial role in the horror film genre, frequently acting as the linchpin on which scenes are constructed and augmenting the horrific acts on display. In his chapter from *A Companion to Horror Film* (2014), scholar William Whittington specifically discusses sound designers' role in the genre and the implications of their aesthetic choices. He asserts that, "In regard to film music, contemporary horror films dislocate popular music standards, displacing them from their cultural context."[1] Taking Whittington's assertion into account, Karpman and Saadiq not only "displace" popular and contemporary music from their cultural (and historical) contexts in *Lovecraft Country*, they also do so regarding past genres, such as the mid- to late-nineteenth-century minstrel song, speeches by prominent Black political figures like James Baldwin, and the spoken-word poetry of Gil Scott-Heron, to name a few. Whittington also claims that, "Like an unreliable narrator, the soundtrack design cannot be trusted in a horror film."[2] This statement definitely applies to the way Karpman and Saadiq employ sound in *Lovecraft Country* when considering the (in)fidelity of sound and music in certain episodes to the time period in which those episodes take place. In this way, the musical directors use sonic anachronism to emphasize the oft-horror of Black life across time and space.

We define "sonic anachronism" as the use of music, voice-overs, and/or sound effects that call attention to the significant difference between the period in which the aural element was produced and that in which it is portrayed. Careful music directors can deploy this kind of anachronism to add layered meaning to the sequence being scored. Sonic anachronisms fall on a spectrum from seamless, in that the quality of difference is more subtle or less drastic, to jagged, in which the anachronistic quality draws immediate attention to its difference. For instance, *Bridgerton* (2021–) uses instrumental covers of modern pop songs by the Vitamin String Quartet in its ballroom scenes. This tactic may fly under the radar if a viewer does not recognize the adapted song, but intentionally intrudes upon the fantasy of the Regency period as soon as the connection is made, placing these instances toward the middle of the spectrum. Karpman and Saadiq pair the logics of horror soundtracks with the power of sonic anachronism from across the spectrum in scoring *Lovecraft Country*, crafting a complex soundscape that interacts with the show's visual elements.

For the purposes of our essay, we will discuss two specific episodes from *Lovecraft Country*. The first is "Sundown" (written by Green and directed by Yann Demange), which sets the tone for the rest of the season, as it is rife with various otherworldly creatures and features music from numerous eras. "Sundown" begins with a dream/nightmare sequence in which Tic is fighting a war against aliens and the famous Jackie Robinson saves him from a giant, tentacled—dare we say Lovecraftian?—monster. After a brief encounter with an extraterrestrial who descends to earth on a massive spaceship, Tic wakes up seated in the back of a segregated bus on the way to Chicago. After he reunites with his family, and Leti with her sister Ruby, Tic, Leti, and Uncle George (played by Courtney B. Vance) embark on a journey to the fictional Ardham, Massachusetts, to find Montrose, who is missing. They travel through the segregated Midwest and along the way encounter racist, white sheriffs who later transform into shoggoths, or vampiric monsters covered in eyes. By the end of the episode the group arrives ragged on the doorstep of the Ardham mansion, leaving viewers wanting to know more about the future adventures that await them.

"Jig-a-Bobo" (written by Green and Ihuoma Ofordire; directed by Green), comes late in the season, the eighth of ten episodes. It contains about four intertwining storylines centered on Tic, Leti, Ruby, Montrose, Christina, and Dee. From the onset, the creative team establishes that the episode will be weighty. "Jig-a-Bobo" opens on a massive crowd waiting to view Emmet Till at his open-casket funeral, the visuals often distorted to give audiences a sense of the oppressive summer heat. Dee, Tic, Leti, Ruby, and Montrose make their way in the crowd, covered in sweat and clearly uncomfortable. Audiences learned that Dee and Emmett were friends in a previous episode, and the creative team makes it abundantly clear that she is deeply disturbed by the funeral rites unfolding before her. In a press of panic, Dee leaves the crowd, and the others split up to look for her. By breaking the group into splinters, Green and Ofordire create opportunities for the characters to find themselves in a wide array of troubles. Tic and Leti find a guest in their house plucked from Tic's past in Korea; Ruby tries to find some solace in the arms and body of another(s); and they are all plagued by magic both within and outside their control.

Using these two episodes, we explore how, and to what effect, Karpman and Saadiq employ sonic anachronism. We've broken our analysis into three major sections organized by temporality. First, we look to *Lovecraft Country*'s future, that is, our present, and consider the ways Tierra Whack's "Clones" (2019) and Alice Smith's "I Put a Spell on You" (2015) interface with their respective scenes. Next, we examine the reverberations of overlaying excerpts from James Baldwin's debate with William F. Buckley–which took place only 10 years after the setting of *Lovecraft Country*–with scenes of segregation. Last, we direct our attention to the fraught legacy of minstrelsy and the manner in which Karpman and Saadiq transform a 175-year-old song into a beacon of horror.[3]

REACHING FOR THE FUTURE: THE IMPACT OF CONTEMPORARY SOUNDTRACK CHOICES

"Everybody talkin' like me now": The Use of Hip-Hop in Lovecraft Country's Inaugural Episode

One strategy the creators of *Lovecraft Country* employ, perhaps to attract younger viewers of a different era than when the show takes place, is incorporating more contemporary music such as rap and hip-hop, which in turn results in a sort of sonic anachronism. The first sonically anachronistic moment occurs in a transitional scene in Episode 1 ("Sundown"), when Tic walks from Uncle George's bookstore, through the streets of Chicago, to a bar named for Denmark Vesey in hopes of gaining information on the potential whereabouts of his father, Montrose. The sequence begins with a shallow-focus, close-up shot of Tic sitting in George's bookstore with an intense expression after a brief conversation with the latter about Montrose. At the same time, the introduction to "Clones," a song first released in 2019 by the Black, Philadelphia-born rap artist Tierra Whack, plays in the background. The subsequent lyrics put the song in conversation with themes related to the show (e.g. race and racism in the United States before, during, and after the mid-twentieth century) and hint at Blackness being in vogue, or the current popularity of rap and hip-hop music in the twenty-first century.

In "Clones," Whack suggests that Blackness is something that is often mimicked or imitated. Specifically, the lyrics heard during the scene are: "Everybody walkin' like me now / Everybody talkin' like me now / Heard I'm who they wanna be now."[4] One cannot help but think, then, of the cultural appropriation of Black music and speech, which has been discussed in a variety of contexts. Critics have, for instance, commented on white musicians like the Seattle-born Macklemore and Iggy Azalea, who is from Australia, as well as Latina performer Jennifer Lopez and Chinese-Korean actress Awkwafina, the latter two of whom are both from New York.[5] That these instances are but a few of many illustrates how, as philosopher Paul C. Taylor so well puts it, "The borrowing, exchange, and theft of cultural objects and practices across racial lines is, when it comes to black folk, typically fraught with ambivalence."[6] One reason for this ambivalence is because, although Black music is a popular art form, the reality of living as a Black person in American society can be one of horror, a nightmare.

Both the music and the images in the transitional scene also hint at the history of police violence against Black children in the United States. After the scene with Tic at Uncle George's bookstore, a cut to a medium close-up shot then shows a group of young Black children joyfully playing in the streets as a fire hydrant gushes water on a hot, summer day. In the same shot, a white police officer stands close by, somewhat inconspicuously, observing the young Black children (figure 16.1). As the cop walks up to one of the children, the camera quickly pans downward, then upward, and leftward to show

FIGURE 16.1 A white cop encroaches upon a group of Black children playing around a fire hydrant on a hot summer day in Chicago. From *Lovecraft Country* episode 1, "Sundown."

a young Black girl gleefully screaming when she is drenched by the fire hydrant. For a brief moment, the cop seemingly is out of the picture. The camera then cuts to a medium shot of Tic as he walks across the street and toward the children, still with a serious expression on his face. After a backward-moving tracking shot, the scene cuts to a long shot of the white cop turning off the fire hydrant and ending the children's fun. The scene symbolizes the reality of many Black children in the United States: that they are not regarded as children. Critical theorist Christina Sharpe powerfully sums up the predicament of Black children in the United States in her book *In the Wake: On Blackness and Being* (2016) when she describes it as "that violent arithmetic, in which blackness disrupts the figure of the child."[7] In other words, race precedes age as a requisite for state violence against Black children.[8]

In the same transitional sequence in which Green and Demange subtly allude to the nightmare of state-sanctioned anti-Blackness faced by Black youth, Karpman and Saadiq also employ contemporary rap music to draw young (and older) viewers' attention to historical allusions that highlight the significance of the Black protest tradition. A prime example is when Tic reaches his destination in the transitional sequence: Denmark Vesey's Bar. In this case, the nondiegetic "Clones" playing in the background grabs and holds spectators' attention just long enough to teach them, broadly speaking, a brief history lesson.

The lesson entails the revolutionary act organized by a formerly enslaved Black man named Denmark Vesey in 1822, when he and 34 other enslaved Black folks planned a slave revolt in Charleston, South Carolina. Historians Douglas R. Egerton and Robert L. Paquette provide a thorough account of events that led to Vesey's planned rebellion as well as those that took place thereafter. "Instead of abandoning his extended family," many of whom were enslaved, Eagerton and Paquette explain, Vesey, who was free,

> resolved to orchestrate a rebellion followed by a mass exodus from Charleston to Haiti, where rebellious slaves had declared formal independence from France in 1804 and where Haitian leaders, beginning with Alexandre Pétion (1770–1818), had been officially encouraging black migration from slaveholding areas to soil guaranteed free by Haiti's constitution.[9]

Vesey's plan eventually failed. Still, he was "a man whose reputation terrified many white Americans while inspiring perhaps as many black Americans."[10] Therefore, Karpman and Saadiq at this moment subvert the nightmare of being Black in an anti-Black society by employing nondiegetic music to prime viewers and to hold their attention to the television screen so that they notice a direct allusion to a revolutionary Black historical figure. In other words, Karpman and Saadiq's use of Whack's song along with mise-en-scène ultimately brings viewers' attention to the horror and potentiality of Black pasts, present, and futures.

"I put a spell on you, Because you're mine": Using Sonic Anachronism to Explore Relationships

In a later episode, Karpman and Saadiq employ sonic anachronism to different effect to explore the romance between Ruby and William/Christina, choosing modern interpretations of Screamin' Jay Hawkins's "I Put a Spell on You" (1956) as a theme for their sexual relationship. The characters have on-screen sex twice over the course of the series, first in episode 4 and again in "Jig-a-Bobo." The musical directors first use Marilyn Manson's 1997 version in episode 4, which evokes a similar brash, in-your-face energy to the original version. However, episode 8 features a cover by Alice Smith from the album "Nina Revisited . . . A Tribute to Nina Simone." Smith performs a more mournful interpretation described as "unforgettable" and "haunting" by an *NPR* review.[11] Through pairing this song with the larger narrative frame of the episode, the creative team exposes the depth and complication of Ruby and Christina's relationship, ultimately using "a melding of different time frames to produce new formations and understandings."[12]

By this point in the narrative, Ruby knows that Christina transforms into William occasionally to further her aims, though the original William died long ago.[13] This fact, while a surprise at first, does not deter Ruby from seeking comfort from Christina after leaving Emmett Till's funeral. Following a confrontation with a white neighbor that William defuses, the two go through the wrought-iron gate of the property with "I Put a Spell on You" (2015) playing in the background, carrying viewers into the next scene.

As the music plays, William runs a bath, undresses, and washes Ruby. The camera lingers on close-ups of their slow, intimate touches as visual representation of their internal desires. After leaning tenderly on one another, William kisses Ruby deeply, but she pulls away. Green cuts to Ruby's reflection in the mirror as she takes the transmogrification potion and dons the body of her white persona, Hillary. William undresses behind her as the potion takes hold. Green then cuts to Ruby and William, both wearing someone else's body, in the throes of sex. As Ruby climaxes, she begins the bloody and painful process of shedding her white skin. As she bursts forth from her false body, Alice Smith croons, "I love you. I love you. I love you," followed by vocalizations. Ruby's own moaning cuts hazily through the soundtrack, intermingling with Smith's voice, as the last of Hillary's visage slides from her face.

A clear connection exists between the song and magic usage. Both women inhabit bewitched bodies as they have sex; more literal lyrics for this sequence could perhaps be "I put a spell on myself." That acknowledged, Karpman and Saadiq purposefully enact Smith's "haunting" rendition to underscore the complex nature of Ruby and Christina's connection, recognizing a productive tension in both its interraciality[14] and queerness.

"Putting a spell" can, on one hand, conjure discourses with their roots in slavery concerning the sexual assault of Black women. In the essay "Seduction and the Ruses of Power," scholar Saidiya Hartman traces the routes taken to remove Black women from any legal protections against rape, in part through language of seduction and manipulation. "Rape," Hartman states, "disappeared through the intervention of seduction—the assertion of the slave woman's complicity and willful submission. . . . The sexual exploitation of the enslaved female, incredulously, served as evidence of her collusion with the master class . . . to be the mistress of her own subjugation."[15] Essentially, the master class codified into law that Black enslaved women bewitched their white enslavers with a spell of desire, legalizing their assaults through lies about lasciviousness and enthusiasm. Though far removed from assault, and wholly consensual, Ruby speaks to the anxieties around interracial relationships that stem from these fraught legacies in her claim that she transformed her body because, on the day of Till's funeral, she "didn't wanna be a Black woman fucking a white man."[16]

And yet, Ruby makes the decision to go to Christina, even in a moment when she feels she "should be on the south side with [her] people."[17] In this vein, Christina argues that Ruby "took that potion because [she] wanted to hide from the fact that even on today of all days, [she was] a woman who wanted what she wanted." Throughout this confrontation sequence, they stand close and their eyes flicker across each other's faces, highlighting both the emotional and sexual tension of the scene. The phrase "wanted what she wanted" takes on extra weight when we consider that Ruby understands that William and Christina are the same person. Though popular culture often contextualizes the 1950s "mostly in terms of repressive norms" related to gender and sexuality,[18] the "who" Ruby desires cannot be read as just a man or just an extension of heterosexual desire. Admittedly, Ruby and Christina only have sex on screen through William's body. Yet, we use "through" pointedly, as Christina asserts in this sequence that *she* is the one having sex with Ruby, not William.[19] In this sense, the transmogrification spell functions as a conduit for their queered desire. Through her dialogue and

FIGURE 16.2 A close-up, over-the-shoulder shot of Christina Braithwhite gazing intensely at Ruby Baptiste in *Lovecraft Country* episode 8, "Jig-A-Bobo."

actions in these two scenes, Christina asserts, "I put a spell on you[, me, us] / Because you're mine"[20] (figure 16.2).

While Christina and Ruby's relationship does not end well by any means—perhaps even disappointingly by some measures—Karpman and Saadiq's deployment of contemporary music provides another avenue to explore their multi-layered dynamic. Ultimately, "Clones" and "I Put a Spell on You" act as vehicles to connect our present day with *Lovecraft Country's*, pointing to relationships between our eras.

"GOOD RIDDANCE TO THE OLD JIM CROW": THE AMERICAN NIGHTMARE OF SEGREGATION

Part of Karpman and Saadiq's magic as the music directors stems from their ability to keep audiences on their toes by infusing audio decisions with multiple layers of meaning. The Midwest montage sequence from episode 1 provides a prime example, showcasing the horror of racial segregation for Black folks during the mid-twentieth century and connecting it to the present day. The sequence proceeds as the nondiegetic voice of prominent Black author and social critic James Baldwin plays in the background. The voice-over is excerpted from Baldwin's debate in 1965 with white conservative William F. Buckley at the Cambridge Union. That Baldwin's monologue is contemporaneous to the time of the show but also still relevant today highlights the legacy and lasting impacts of racial segregation on Black folks in American society.

In the Midwest montage sequence, two main scenes that take place at a burger stand and movie theater emphasize the horror of racial segregation. While these places may seem like sites in which "terror can hardly be discerned,"[21] in the episode they serve as locations that exhibit the horrors of anti-Black racism. Through the food stand and movie theater scenes, the creative team provides social commentary on the insidious history and nightmare of segregation in American society. In the sequence, Baldwin exists as a spectral figure, an omniscient narrator of both the past and present horrors of Black life in the United States.

To provide context, the Baldwin and Buckley debate originally took place during a seminal moment in history: 1965. Significant political gains were made that year, including the passage of the Voting Rights Act in the United States and later Race Relations Act in the United Kingdom. The former legislation provided protection for voters, especially Black folks who had been systematically disenfranchised since slavery and Reconstruction, while the latter was the first instance of legislation that addressed racial discrimination in the United Kingdom. Despite these gains, however, 1965 was also the year of massive Vietnam War protests and the assassination of Malcolm X, the latter of which occurred only 13 days after the Baldwin and Buckley debate. So, the question up for discussion at the Cambridge Union—"Is the American Dream at the expense of the Negro?"—in many ways got to the root of racial tension and antagonism in the United States at the time. Baldwin not only answers the debate question affirmatively and quite eloquently given his opponent's stance, but also demonstrates how the American Dream for white people is a nightmare for Black folks.

Buckley built part of his argument's foundation during the debate on attempts to reduce anti-Black racism to mere individual acts. That is, in his own work, Buckley often drew upon arguments made by people like sociologist Daniel Patrick Moynihan, who wrote the infamous *Moynihan Report*, which was also published in 1965, and blamed Black mothers instead of institutional racism (e.g. segregation) for social problems afflicting Black folks in midcentury American society. As historian Daniel Robert McClure aptly notes in his article on the Baldwin and Buckley debate, Buckley's reduction "of the racial problem in the U.S." from the institutional to individual level suggests anti-Blackness as "a problem for reform, not radical solution."[22] Relatedly, critical theorist Frank B. Wilderson III in his book on racial antagonism in American cinema also argues that film spectators in the United States often exhibit an impulse akin to reducing racism to individual acts, as opposed to understanding anti-Blackness as ingrained in the institutions of society. "Among spectators in the United States," Wilderson asserts, "there is a strong tendency to 'see' anything and everything in a film except race, to intuitively crowd out or simply forget any manifestation of structural antagonism by speaking about the plot at the lowest scale of abstraction."[23] Rather than allow spectators to fall into this colorblind mode of viewing, *Lovecraft Country* and, specifically, the Midwest montage sequence, calls for viewers to understand individual and institutional racism as two sides of the same coin, as the episode provides a sonic and visual glimpse of the nightmare that is the history and legacy of racial segregation in the United States.

As mentioned before, Baldwin's voice narrates aspects of the nightmare of segregation over a duration of a little more than two and a half minutes. The sequence begins with a high-angle, extreme long shot of Uncle George's car (given the moniker "Woody") being driven at dusk on a country road; however, Baldwin's voice precedes the image, thereby underscoring the significance of his speech to what will take place in the sequence. After briefly following Woody cruising in the early evening, the director cuts to a medium-long shot of a burger stand, the fluorescent lighting of which illuminates the otherwise dark night. A group of folks stand outside the restaurant, with some on the left in front of the window presumably waiting for their order, while others sit at an umbrellaed bench off the sidewalk. To the right of the frame is a smaller group of people, including Tic, Leti, and George, in similar positions: the former standing at the window placing their orders and the latter three sitting on a bench conversing (figure 16.3). As the camera slowly tracks and zooms forward, it becomes clear that the patrons are separated by race, with the white customers situated on the left and Black customers on the right side of the stand.[24]

Baldwin's assessment of the American Dream vis-à-vis racial inequality simultaneously overlaps with this first shot of the burger stand. Specifically, he says that he does not "disagree that the inequality suffered by the American Negro population of the United States has hindered the American Dream."[25] At the same moment that Baldwin completes his sentence, the shot shows a sign that reads "Colored" hanging above a Black man's head as he orders his food. The purpose of the sign in this scene is twofold:

FIGURE 16.3 George, Tic, and Leti sitting on a bench outside at a segregated burger stand in the Midwest montage sequence. From *Lovecraft Country* episode 1, "Sundown."

within the diegesis, or world of the film, it signifies that this side of the burger stand is the place where Black folks are to order and receive their food, which is deliberately separate from that of the white patrons. The sign also indicates, however, the making of Blackness and how segregation is a "race making institution."[26] In his article that draws a connection between the institutions of slavery, segregation, and mass incarceration, sociologist Loïc Wacquant deftly explains:

> Slavery, the Jim Crow system and the ghetto are "race making" institutions, which is to say that they do not simply process an ethnoracial division that would somehow exist outside of and independently from them. Rather, each *produces* (or co-produces) this division (anew) out of inherited demarcations and disparities of group power and inscribes it at every epoch in a distinctive constellation of material and symbolic forms.[27]

Taking Wacquant into account, the burger stand scene portrays Black subjection, given how segregation exists as part of the legacy of slavery. So, while segregation as a constituent part of American life may (have) be(en) a dream, perhaps, for white people, its historical relation to slavery renders it a nightmare for Black Americans.

In fact, segregation is a recurring nightmare both in the 1950s and '60s, as well as now, which the movie theater scene in the sequence makes clear. The scene occurs after another transitional shot of Woody going down the road at dusk. The camera then cuts to a sidewalk shot outside of what appears to be a segregated movie theater. A blue-and-red neon sign reads "Colored Entrance" as a Black woman in a light-blue dress tends to a young Black girl in a frilly, white dress. In the same shot, Leti walks out of the entrance door followed by George, then Tic. A long take shows the three main Black characters walking across the street to Woody, when Tic separates from the group to chat with a Black woman cradling her baby in one arm and holding flowers for sale in the other, as she stands in front of a grocery store. Tic admires the woman's baby, then buys a flower from her.

Though Baldwin's voice plays throughout the sequence, in the movie theater scene he continues his argument that a person's answer to the question up for debate depends on their worldview. He says that someone's answer "depends on assumptions, which we hold so deeply as to be scarcely aware of them."[28] Understood in tandem with the images playing out on-screen, Baldwin's claim sheds light on how segregation is often regarded as a thing of the past, which causes people today to "be scarcely aware" of the fact that it still exists. In their chapter on racial covenants and housing segregation, for example, legal scholars Carol M. Rose and Richard R. W. Brooks challenge post-racial ideas that segregation is no more. According to them, while "racially restrictive covenants have receded into a set of increasingly vague memories . . . they are a part of the past of housing segregation in the [United States], and their role as legal instruments undoubtedly helped to shape both physical patterns and social attitudes about segregation and integration . . . that to some degree persist today."[29] Moreover, while racially restrictive covenants, or deeds that explicitly restrict a property from being sold to Black people or other people of color, were rendered "unenforceable in court" after the 1948 *Shelley v. Kramer* decision and "flatly outlawed by the Fair Housing Act of 1968," the covenants continue(d) to periodically appear in deeds and "pop up to bite unwary celebrities or political figures," like the late conservative Justice William Rehnquist and then-Senator Joseph Biden in the 1980s.[30]

Relatedly, the end of the movie theater scene highlights the connection between race and class given the material consequences of segregation for Black folks. While many people believe that segregation in present-day American society is a "natural" phenomenon or are "scarcely aware" of it, it is not natural and has many unnatural and deleterious effects. Sociologist Elizabeth Korver-Glenn makes this key point in her book *Race Brokers: Housing Markets and Segregation in 21st Century Urban America* (2021). She notes, for instance, that many "housing market professionals [view] racial segregation as so ever-present as to seem 'natural.' "[31] She also makes the assertion that "racism, like racial segregation has become naturalized—so pervasive that it seems natural."[32] Taking into account how racial segregation and racism have come to be understood as natural phenomena, Korver-Glenn helps to show how Black folks are living in the nightmare of the afterlife of slavery. As she points out, "Racial segregation . . . is tied to ongoing wealth, educational, and health inequalities; intensified and more violent policing of Black and Latinx people; social isolation and lack of interracial contact; and sociopolitical conflict. In other words, racial segregation is one of the key mechanisms at the core of systemic American racial inequality."[33] So, while Baldwin's nondiegetic monologue during the Midwest montage sequence may be contemporaneous to the time of the show (i.e. 1950s/'60s), the points he makes in his debate with Buckley about the American Dream/Nightmare vis-à-vis Black folks are still ever so prescient today.

"LET ME IN": FINDING HORROR IN THE LEGACY OF MINSTRELSY

Continuing our navigation of *Lovecraft Country*'s sonic journey through time, we have arrived at "The Past." While most of the show's story unfolds in the past relative to our present, Karpman and Saadiq purposefully include music from eras that would be considered bygone even by 1950s standards. As we contend, this sonic anachronism exists in part to underscore the connected nature of Black experiences across time. Moreover, the creative team uses this connectivity to highlight elements of horror that linger in Black histories. In one of the most harrowing episodes of the series, "Jig-a-Bobo," Karpman and Saadiq reach back to the complicated history of American minstrelsy. Using the manic "Stop Dat Knocking at My Door" (1847), written by A. F. Winnemore and performed by Christy's Minstrels, the music team calls upon the complex, inextricable legacy of blackface minstrel performances to conjure horrific figures of the past into the present.

As a reminder, "Jig-a-Bobo" takes place on an oppressively hot day against the backdrop of Emmett Till's funeral. Overwhelmed by the sights, sounds, and smells of the humongous funeral crowd, Dee flees into the Chicago streets to collect herself. However, her reprieve is short-lived. Two cops familiar with the magic world corner Dee, and when they cannot gain any information about her mother, Hippolyta, they use the language of Adam and spit to place a curse on her. For the rest of the episode, Dee is pursued by Topsy (played by Kaelyn Gobert-Harris) and Bopsy (played by Bianca Brewton), two monstrous pickaninnies plucked from the minstrel history of *Uncle Tom's Cabin* (1852) and made flesh. Though Dee fights valiantly, her episode plotline ends with Topsy digging her claws into Dee's arm and enacting the officer's awful enchantment.

While it is tempting to dive right into the layered visual and sonic landscape of this episode, we must first establish some context on the episode's title, the link between the show's depiction of Topsy and pickaninny imagery, as well as a short gloss of minstrel shows, to have a rich discussion on Karpman and Saadiq's use of "Stop Dat Knocking at My Door" (from here on out "Stop Dat Knocking"). To start, "Jig-a-Bobo" draws immediate connection to "jigaboo," a "depreciative and offensive"[34] term for Black folks. The *Oxford English Dictionary* and *Merriam-Webster* both list the term's etymology as a portmanteau of "jig" and "bugaboo,"[35] though others have suggested origins in Bantu languages.[36] The episode title itself is a portmanteau, inserting Till's in-show nickname "Bobo" in place of "boo," linking both his death and the term's derogatory connotations to the episode's overall narrative.

Though not as common in our modern era, the use of a somewhat dated slur in the title speaks to Green and Ofordire's deployment of monsters based on stereotypes of Black children popularized through minstrel and other blackface performances. Minstrel shows hold a complicated place in American history, being both derided as insidiously racist while simultaneously being inextricable from our current media and cultural landscape. Cultural historian Eric Lott points to this intertwined nature in the introduction to *Love and Theft: Blackface Minstrelsy and the American Working Class*, stating that "[the] minstrel show has been ubiquitous, cultural common coin; it has been so central to the lives of North Americans that we are hardly aware of its extraordinary influence."[37] Arising in the 1830s and growing in prominence through the nineteenth century, popular performances often consisted of:

> four or five or sometimes more white male performers . . . made up with facial blacking of greasepaint or burnt cork and adorned in outrageously oversized and/or ragged "Negro" costumes. Armed with an array of instruments, usually banjo, fiddle, bone castanets, and tambourine, the performers would stage a tripartite show [consisting of] a random selection of songs interspersed with what passed for black wit and japery . . . , a group of novelty performances [and, finally] a narrative skit, usually set in the South, containing dancing, music, and burlesque.[38]

As Lott shows, musical numbers formed an integral part of the three-part performance, appearing interspersed from the beginning to the end of the show. These songs and performances attempted to replicate Black dialects, rhythms, and movements. Take, for example, a sampling of lyrics from "Stop Dat Knocking":

> She was the prettiest yaller Gal
> That eber I did see,
> She never would go walking,
> Wid any Colored man but me.[39]

Winnemore, marking specific pronunciation of words like "yaller" and "wid," aims to reflect Black accents and pronunciation. Just as we earlier gestured to the modern appropriation of Black speech, scholars have traced the continuing lineage of minstrel shows through to the present day, for instance in the skit-structure of *Saturday Night Live* (1975–) or in the endurance of certain children's jokes.[40] In "Jig-a-Bobo," Green and Ofordire bring the lingering legacy of minstrelsy front and center through Topsy, Bopsy, and their pursuit of Dee set to a minstrel song. Markedly, the episode calls attention to the connection between minstrel performances and Harriet Beecher Stowe's *Uncle Tom's Cabin* that codified the racist caricature of Black children known as the pickaninny.

Hiding in the bathroom after having an argument with Montrose, Dee turns on the radio and eyes a copy of *Uncle Tom's Cabin* resting on the bookshelf. The book's cover features an image of Eva—the very blond, very pale, and very sick "angel-child" at the core of the 1850s narrative—and Topsy, designed by Stowe to be Eva's "polarized dyad, . . . the 'cringing' black child who had been viciously beaten by her previous owners,"[41] standing near a mirror. Stowe arguably crafted one of the "most powerful antislavery or antiracist novels of the nineteenth century" in *Uncle Tom's Cabin*.[42] Interestingly, her depiction of Topsy was heavily inspired by minstrel performances, "which is visible in Topsy's comic violence and dancing of breakdowns."[43] However, as historian Robin Bernstein highlights in her award-winning *Racial Innocence: Performing American Childhood from Slavery to Civil Rights* (2011), the author envisioned Topsy as a tragic character worthy of protection and empathy: "Stowe combined that tradition of [minstrel] performance with a sophisticated argument that Topsy was an essentially innocent child who has been brutalized—hardened and made 'wicked'—by slavery."[44] While diametrically opposed to Eva's pure whiteness, she was still placed under the banner of childhood innocence. Unfortunately, as *Uncle Tom's Cabin*'s star rose as a stage play, the character's portrayal lost its nuance: "Topsy's stagers . . . cultivated the seeds of minstrelsy that Stowe had sowed in the character while exterminating the innocence that Stowe had insisted was Topsy's birthright."[45] In these performances we find the birth of the pickaninny.

Bernstein describes the pickaninny:

> an imagined, subhuman black juvenile who was typically depicted outdoors, merrily accepting (or even inviting) violence. . . . Characteristics of the pickaninny include dark or sometimes jet-black skin, exaggerated eyes and mouth, the action of gorging . . . , and the state of being threatened or attacked by animals . . . . Pickaninnies often

wear ragged clothes (which suggest parental neglect) and are sometimes partially or fully naked.[46]

While Bernstein insists that not every representation must include all of the above, she does reiterate that, regardless of depiction, "they never experience or express pain or sustain wounds."[47] Tolerance of and invulnerability to pain make the pickaninny, and thus remove from them an accepted undergirding of humanness. And audiences loved this nonhuman, punching-bag version of Topsy. According to Tavia Nyong'o,

> Topsy quickly became one of the most popular characters in the play, as necessary as Uncle Tom. Actors playing Topsy sometimes received top billing in mid-nineteenth century productions, and Topsy's song was a hot seller in sheet music. Rival productions of *Uncle Tom's Cabin* were soon advertising two Topsies—double the fun and fidelity to Stowe's novel be damned.[48]

Using this legacy of Topsy, her dehumanization, and her connection to musical performance, the creative team crafted their monstrous duo of Topsy/Bopsy and tied them to the musical motif of "Stop Dat Knocking."

Audiences first hear "Stop Dat Knocking" while Dee hides in the bathroom. As she's tying her Chuck Taylors, the upbeat jazz transforms into the minstrel song, moving from a genre cultivated by Black people to one meant to mimic them. Dee's gaze sweeps around the room until she stares at the cover of *Uncle Tom's Cabin*. The illustration of Topsy has also transformed, her face warped into a cruel, grinning mask, and her fingers elongated into claws. Judging by the broken glass and her grip on Eva's face, Topsy has slammed her cover companion into the glass, adding to her threatening aura. Meanwhile, the song's chorus plays: "Stop that knocking at my door. / (Let me in.) / Stop that knocking,"[49] complete with knocking sound effects. As the melody reaches its most frantic state—a group of voices chanting "Stop that knocking" four times and with a quarter note attached to each syllable—Dee flees out the bathroom window and back into the street. When Montrose finally enters the bathroom, both the book and the music have returned to normal.

From this moment in the bathroom on, Karpman and Saadiq use "Stop Dat Knocking" as a leitmotif for Topsy and Bopsy, often pairing "Let me in" with punctuated percussion of their own design and occasional distortion for dramatic effect. As scholar of music Philip Hayward states, their use of "Stop Dat Knocking" lines up with standard musical practices in horror, which look "to unnerve and shock the audience through use of atonalities . . . ostinati and various musical and/or sonic rumbles and booms (present in the form of either developed passages or short stingers) and, frequently, to create identification and engagement through use of leitmotifs."[50] Karpman and Saadiq insert the leitmotif in two additional, poignant moments: when Dee first sees Topsy and Bopsy on a train platform, and before she confronts the two police officers who hexed her. Interestingly, as opposed to the first instance, the musical directors chose to make the subsequent instances of "Stop Dat Knocking" nondiegetic. The song becomes a cue to the audience that the pickaninnies draw near, even if the song's absence leaves Dee unaware. By uniting "Stop Dat Knocking" with Topsy and Bopsy, the creators have horrors from the past figuratively and literally pursue Dee through Chicago and, through this pursuit, allude to the insidious and enduring aspects of these particular interpretations of Blackness.

In creating Topsy and Bopsy, the creative team drew on and mutated typical features of pickaninnies and minstrel performers, creating further resonance with their minstrel leitmotif. The two go about their goal of inflicting pain upon and torturing Dee as if it were a performance, dancing in a variety of styles that appear simultaneously childish, unsettling, modern, and timeless. Pulling on Bernstein's definition, they both "merrily" dispense violence and bounce back from any of Dee's attempts at defense with nary a scratch, that is, "they never experience or express pain or sustain wounds."[51] While the creative team eschewed blackface, Topsy and Bopsy have horrifically "exaggerated eyes and mouth[s],"[52] both red, to mark a further move into the nonhuman, and "outrageously oversized and/or ragged" clothing.[53] However, the creative team also designed Topsy and Bopsy to visually mirror Dee. All three appear around the same height and age. Moreover, Dee takes on "the state of being threatened or attacked,"[54] but by monsters rather than by animals. And, although her white funeral dress echoes Eva's on the cover of *Uncle Tom's Cabin*, and by extension a certain conceptualization of childhood,[55] she changes into a pair of black Chuck Taylors and a Chicago American Giants' hat[56] before she leaves. Both Topsy and Bopsy wear the same style of shoes in red and white. This paralleling creates connection between the characters and forces viewers to reckon with lingering impacts of the dehumanizing of Black children, as well as the legacy of violence against Black girls and women (figure 16.4).[57]

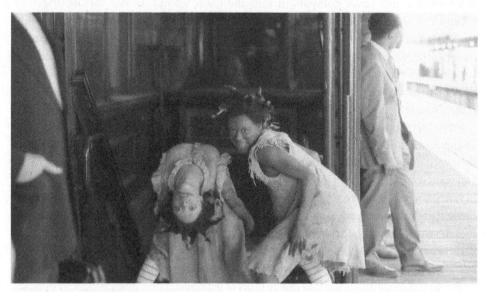

FIGURE 16.4 Topsy and Bopsy stand in the opening of the stairwell to an elevated train platform. Topsy bends over backward and Bopsy twists to look over her shoulder, both looking into the camera. From *Lovecraft Country* episode 8, "Jig-A-Bobo."

In particular, the conjunction of "Stop Dat Knocking" with the episode's other horror elements places a spotlight on misogynoir across time periods, in part through highlighting moments of access and permeability. Audiences first see Dee surrounded by bodies waiting to enter Till's viewing, pressed upon from all sides. The camera zooms into her face in a close-up, highlighting her clear discomfort as she looks around the crowd. The sheer number of people collapses her personal space and their various reactions to grief invade her senses. As such, she cannot process her own feelings and flees to a place with more physical/mental space. However, Dee's encounter with the two police officers stymies this processing with a sequence reminiscent of sexual assault. The creative team lean into what psychologist Kathryn M. Ryan calls the "real rape script," which "involves a sudden and physically violent attack on an unsuspecting woman, usually by a stranger. The woman is alone at the time of the attack. She may physically resist the rape or she may be too afraid to resist."[58] In the sequence, the police officers surround Dee, one with his body pressed against her. As she tries to run away, he trips her, then holds her against himself. The other spits in his hand, then presses the saliva to her forehead. The creative team deliberately depicts the saliva as sticky and viscous in order to recall semen.[59] The threat of sexual violence infuses the scene, from the officers' extremely close and threatening body positions to the gratuitous shots of bodily fluids. Moreover, this violation represents a connection to the long history of physical and sexual violence against Black girls and women.

The refrain of "Let me in" clearly conveys a demand for access, especially when linked to a creature of horror at the door. However, if we look at the lyrics not included in "Jig-A-Bobo" proper, we can draw an intriguing connection to the discussion of access to the bodies of Black women and children. The first verse of the song centers on Suzy, "de fairest in de town."[60] We learn that, before daybreak, a man named Sam has come to call on Suzy and has been knocking on her door. Suzy asks him to stop ("you better stop dat knocking"), while Sam demands entrance ("Let me in," "No I'll never stop that knocking").[61] Though the singers perform this exchange lightheartedly, access to a Black woman, despite her protests, forms the core of the revelry. When taken in conjunction with sequences like the above, the creative team calls attention to the way the imagery from the past continues to proliferate and have consequences across time.

"A WORLD WHERE I CAN NAME MYSELF ANYTHING": LOOKING TOWARD A FUTURE BEYOND

Overall, Karpman and Saadiq's incredible use of sound and music in *Lovecraft Country* works to highlight key issues facing Black people in American society. Some of these key issues include the cultural appropriation of Blackness without seriously addressing the reality of Black (non-)life in American society; how legacies from the past influence present and future conversations of queer and interracial sex/desire; the persistence of segregation; and the ways in which the history of minstrelsy speaks to various past and present forms of violence against Black folks, including Black children. In bringing attention to these issues, the music directors, show's creators, and production team challenge, more broadly, the horror of anti-Blackness pervading American society. Episodes like "Jig-a-Bobo" that address how American culture perpetuates anti-Blackness and misogynoir in songs like "Stop Dat Knockin'" also celebrate the words of activists like Naomi Wadler, an 11-year-old from Virginia who said, "never again for black girls, too"[62] during her speech at the March for Our Lives rally in Washington, D.C., on March 24, 2018.

Wadler, as a young Black girl in America, is much like Dee in *Lovecraft Country*. However, whereas Dee is continually haunted and harassed by America's racist past in the show, and whose calls for help are at times imperceptible to those around her, Wadler speaks loud and clear "to acknowledge and represent the African American girls whose stories don't make the front page of every national newspaper, whose stories don't lead on the evening news."[63] Like Wadler, *Lovecraft Country* "[re-]write[s] the narrative for this world"[64] in how it (re)mixes sound and music to coincide with images that speak not only to the history of Black subjection in the United States, but also to the history of the Black protest tradition, which is signified by allusions to Black figures like James Baldwin and Denmark Vesey in the "Sundown" episode. *Lovecraft Country* therefore calls for viewers to not forget the past while still looking forward. The show also demonstrates how Black music, including contemporary genres and musicians like rap artist Tierra Whack and R&B singer Alice Smith, alongside Black film, in this case Black horror, becomes part of the Black protest tradition that pushes for a future beyond racialized violence. In other words, *Lovecraft Country* conveys the power of sound and speculative fiction to radically imagine a Black future beyond pain and violence.

NOTES

1. William Whittington, "Horror Sound Design," in *A Companion to the Horror Film* (West Sussex, UK: John Wiley and Sons, 2014), 169.
2. Ibid., 177.
3. As a note, because our discussion largely focuses on the use of sound and two targeted episodes, we did not have space to explore the critiques leveled at other aspects or episodes of the series, for example the disappointing (and potentially triggering) depiction of a Two-Spirit Native character, allegations about on-set treatment, or larger concerns about the depictions of violence. Please see Wren Sanders, "Lovecraft Country Creator Apologizes for 'Failed' Attempt at Two-Spirit Representation," *Them*, October 13, 2020, https://www.them.us/story/lovecraft-country-failed-two-spirit-representation; James Hibberd, "James Andrew Miller on the Big Revelations in HBO Book 'Tinderbox,'" The Hollywood Reporter, November 17, 2021, https://www.hollywoodreporter.com/tv/tv-features/tinderbox-hbo-book-james-miller-interview-1235048630/; and Grégory Pierrot,

" 'Lovecraft Country': A Spell Gone Awry," Public Books, November 9, 2020, https://www.publicbooks.org/lovecraft-country-a-spell-gone-awry/, as starting points for each of these topics, respectively.

4. Tierra Whack, "Clones," Interscope Records, 2019.

5. For more on discussions concerning the aforementioned entertainers and cultural appropriation, see Paul C. Taylor's discussion of Macklemore in *Black Is Beautiful: A Philosophy of Black Aesthetics* (Hoboken, NJ: John Wiley and Sons, 2016); Brittney Cooper, "Iggy Azalea's Post-Racial Mess: America's Oldest Race Tale, Remixed," Salon, July 15, 2014, https://www.salon.com/2014/07/15/iggy_azaleas_post_racial_mess_americas_oldest_race_tale_remixed/; Veronica Wells, "Why Is J. Lo Calling Herself a Black Girl?," MadameNoire, October 19, 2020, https://madamenoire.com/1195310/j-lo-black-girl/; and Ernest Owens, "Awkwafina's Non-Apology for Using a Blaccent Is the Problem," TheGrio, February 7, 2022, https://thegrio.com/2022/02/07/awkwafinas-non-apology-for-using-a-blaccent-is-the-problem/.

6. Taylor, *Black Is Beautiful*, 184.

7. Christina Sharpe, *In the Wake: On Blackness and Being* (Durham, NC: Duke University Press, 2016), 97.

8. The Black nonchild, particularly vis-à-vis American media culture, will further be discussed later in the chapter.

9. Douglas R. Eagerton and Robert L. Paquette, *The Denmark Vesey Affair: A Documentary History* (Gainesville: University Press of Florida, 2017), xx.

10. Ibid., xix.

11. Salamishah Tillet, "Review: 'Nina Revisited . . . A Tribute To Nina Simone,'" *NPR Music*, NPR, July 6, 2015, accessed on February 11, 2022, https://www.npr.org/2015/07/06/419252433/first-listen-nina-revisited-a-tribute-to-nina-simone.

12. Heike Bauer and Matt Cook, "Introduction," in *Queer 1950s: Rethinking Sexuality in the Postwar Years*, ed. Heike Bauer and Matt Cook (London: Palgrave Macmillan, 2012), 7.

13. For the sake of clarity, we will refer to the character as "William" when she occupies that body and "Christina" when she is in her own. Also, while outside the purview of this essay, Christina's connection to and condescension of maleness and masculinity is definitely worthy of further analysis.

14. For instance, it is not lost on us that Karpman and Saadiq chose versions of "I Put a Spell on You" by both a Black woman and a white man.

15. Saidiya Hartman, "Seduction and the Ruses of Power," *Callaloo* 19, no. 2 (Spring 1996): 545.

16. *Lovecraft Country*, season 1, episode 8, "Jig-A-Bobo," directed by Misha Green, written by Misha Green and Ihuoma Ofordire, featuring Jurnee Smollett, Jonathan Majors, and Wunmi Mosaku, aired October 4, 2020, https://play.hbomax.com/page/urn:hbo:page:GXzYd2woID2eowgEAAAIq:type:episode?reentered=true&userProfileType=liteUserProfile.

17. Ibid.

18. Bauer and Cook, "Introduction," 2.

19. ". . . that's not what *I* saw when *I* was fucking you."; *Lovecraft Country*, "Jig-A-Bobo," emphasis added.

20. For further exploration of Christina and Ruby's relationship, please see Courtney Bryant, "Incarnational Power: The Queering of the Flesh and Redemption in Lovecraft Country" *Black Theology: An International Journal* 19, no. 3 (2021), 207–217.

21. Saidiya Hartman, *Scenes of Subjection: Terror, Slavery, and Self-Making in Nineteenth-Century America* (New York: Oxford University Press, 1997), 4.

22. Daniel Robert McClure, "Possessing History and American Innocence: James Baldwin, William F. Buckley, Jr., and the 1965 Cambridge Debate," *James Baldwin Review* 2 (2016): 62.

23. Frank B. Wilderson III, *Red, White & Black: Cinema and the Structure of U.S. Antagonisms* (Durham, NC: Duke University Press, 2010), 99.

24. It is important to note that the very next shot in this scene, preceded by a quick cut, is an image directly inspired by an untitled photograph taken by the late Gordon Parks. Another tableau shot appearing later in the Midwest montage sequence that we discuss more in detail and consists of a finely dressed Black woman and young Black girl standing under a "Colored Entrance" sign is also based on his "Department Store" photograph taken in Selma, Alabama. Both the untitled and "Department Store" photographs are from Parks's 1956 series titled "Segregation Story."

25. *Lovecraft Country*, season 1, episode 1, "Sundown," directed by Yann Demange, written by Misha Green, featuring Jurnee Smollett, Jonathan Majors, and Aunjanue Ellis, aired August 16, 2020, https://play.hbomax.com/page/urn:hbo:page:GXzYd2woID2eowgEAA AIq:type:episode?reentered=true&userProfileType=liteUserProfile.

26. Loïc Wacquant, "From Slavery to Mass Incarceration: Rethinking the 'Race Question' in the US," *New Left Review* 13, no. 13 (2002): 54.

27. Ibid.

28. *Lovecraft Country*, "Sundown."

29. Carol M. Rose and Richard R. W. Brooks, "Racial Covenants and Housing Segregation, Yesterday and Today," in *Race and Real Estate*, ed. Adrienne Brown and Valerie Smith (New York: Oxford University Press, 2015), 161.

30. Ibid.

31. Elizabeth Korver-Glenn, *Race Brokers: Housing Markets and Segregation in 21st Century Urban America* (New York: Oxford University Press, 2021), 2.

32. Ibid., 3.

33. Ibid.

34. "jigaboo, n.," *OED Online*, December 2021, Oxford University Press, accessed February 03, 2022, https://www.oed.com/view/Entry/101276?redirectedFrom=jigaboo.

35. Bugaboo—"An imaginary evil spirit or creature; a bogeyman," or "foolish or empty talk." ("bugaboo, n.," OED Online, December 2021, Oxford University Press, accessed February 03, 2022, https://www.oed.com/view/Entry/24357.)

36. Nikki Giovanni, *Honey, Hush!: An Anthology of African American Women's Humor* (New York: W.W. Norton, 1998), 430; Katherine Harris, "African Languages and Ebonics," *Africa Update* 4, no. 3 (Summer 1997), https://sites.ccsu.edu/afstudy/africaupdate/upd4-3.html#h2.

37. Eric Lott, *Love and Theft: Blackface Minstrelsy and the American Working Class* (Oxford: Oxford University Press, 2013), 5.

38. Ibid., 6.

39. A. F. Winnemore, *Stop Dat Knocking at My Door: As Sung with Great Applause by Christy's Minstrels* (Boston: G.P. Reed, 1847), 8.

40. Robin Bernstein, *Racial Innocence: Performing American Childhood from Slavery to Civil Rights* (New York: New York University Press, 2011), 18, 7.

41. Ibid., 20, 15.

42. Lott, *Love and Theft*, 34.

43. Bernstein, *Racial Innocence*, 15.

44. Ibid.

45. Ibid., 16.
46. Ibid., 34. Of note, Bernstein comments that "in the nineteenth century, the word was used pejoratively and in reference mainly to black children in the United States and Britain, but also to aboriginal children of the Americas, Australia, and New Zealand (in this case, the black-white dyad erases the specificity of nonblack children of color by absorbing them into blackness)."
47. Ibid.
48. Tavia Nyong'o, "Racial Kitsch and Black Performance," *The Yale Journal of Criticism* 1, no. 2 (Fall 2002): 376.
49. *Lovecraft Country*, "Jig-A-Bobo."
50. Philip Hayward, "Introduction: Scoring the Edge," in *Terror Tracks: Music, Sound and Horror Cinema*, ed. Philip Hayward (Sheffield, UK: Equinox Publishing Ltd., 2009), 10.
51. Bernstein, *Racial Innocence*, 34.
52. Ibid.
53. Lott, *Love and Theft*, 6.
54. Bernstein, *Racial Innocence*, 34.
55. In *Racial Innocence*, Bernstein discusses how childhood innocence became "raced white" in the nineteenth and early twentieth centuries, as well as how some elements of minstrelsy survive through children's popular culture (7–8). Green and Ofordire play with these ideas in Diana's storyline, showing a quick scene of three White girls jumping rope dressed in their Sunday best. They sing a jump-rope rhyme to the tune of "One, Two, Buckle My Shoe," but instead sing about "Topsy and her yellow eyes." Like Dee with her pursuers, the two groups of three girls visually echo one another and forefront the contrasted experience of childhood. The scene also echoes a similar sequence from *Nightmare on Elm Street*, where children jump rope and sing "One, two, Freddy's coming for you" to the same melody.
56. The Chicago American Giants was a Negro League baseball team.
57. Green and Ofordire also parallel Till, Topsy, and Bopsy. Earlier in the episode, Ruby remarks that Till "looked like a monster" due to the mutilation from his murder. Dehumanization and insidious ideas about resistance to pain propagated by figures like pickaninnies feed into racist ideologies like those of the men who killed Till.
58. Kathryn M. Ryan, "The Relationship between Rape Myths and Sexual Scripts: The Social Construction of Rape," *Sex Roles* 65, nos. 11–12 (December 2011): 776. Admittedly, Ryan criticizes the over-use of this script in media. However, it is important to acknowledge its referential power in "Jig-A-Bobo."
59. During this sequence, Dee also repeats "I can't breathe!" while held in a chokehold, calling to mind the murders of Eric Garner, George Floyd, and others, along with a rallying cry of the Black Lives Matter movement.
60. Winnemore, "Stop Dat Knocking At My Door," 2–3.
61. Ibid., 3–4.
62. Naomi Wadler, "I'm Here to Say Never Again for Black Girls Too," *CNN*, March 24, 2018, video, 3:34, https://www.youtube.com/watch?v=mfuaMRYPIVI.
63. Ibid.
64. Ibid.

CHAPTER 17

(RE)SUMMONING CANDYMAN FOR A "POST-RACIAL" ERA

Black Horror, Allegorical Adaptation, and the Traumatic Racial Violence of American Capitalism

BYRON B CRAIG AND STEPHEN E. RAHKO

IF one were to choose a word to describe the state of American race relations during the year 2020, one could do no worse than "reckoning." "Reckoning" entered America's racial vernacular in June 2020 as historic Black Lives Matter (BLM) protests swept across the nation decrying the country's shameful legacy of police brutality and structural racism. The protests prompted an unprecedented series of responses that included public statements of support from celebrities and professional athletes, as well as pledges from corporations, universities, and the professions to financially support racial justice initiatives, increase diversity hiring, and confront the legacy of racism in their institutions, products, and services. Social media sites were flooded with personal testimonials about racism and tips for would-be racial allies. Books about racism shot to the top of bestseller lists, and polls indicated growing support among self-identified white Americans for social reform. Yet, by 2021, the tide of public opinion dramatically turned into feverish moral panics over the 1619 Project and critical race theory.

The sweeping, yet predictable, change in public attitudes and sentiments toward Blackness between 2020 and 2021 illuminates the structural predicament of anti-Blackness in the United States. In this chapter, we offer an analysis of Nia DaCosta and Jordan Peele's remake of *Candyman*, which appeared during the fall of 2021 at the height of the moral panics over how American schools should teach the racial history of the United States. Drawing on horror scholarship that traces the relationship between the genre's rhetorical conventions and cultural trauma, theorists of Afro-pessimism, and postmodern theories of adaptation, we advance an Afro-pessimistic interpretation of *Candyman*. We understand DaCosta and Peele's adaptation as a response to current post-racial ideologies that allegorically critiques the legacy of slavery and race trauma hidden in the foundations of American society by the spatial and racial violence of American capitalism. DaCosta and Peele advance what we shall call an "allegorical adaptation" of *Candyman* that can be read as Afro-pessimistic, since it refuses to posit a narrative redress of the violence of American structural racism, for those who have summoned Candyman since his 1890 lynching only face death, be it by hook or by corporeal transmutation into the mystical and shadowy realm of horror that has haunted American liberal democracy since the failures of Reconstruction.

Candyman and the Politics of (Post)Race

Since its original release in 1992, the *Candyman* horror franchise has polarized scholars and critics. Some have defended Bernard Rose's film, arguing that Candyman is a complex figure that at once represents both a terrifying monster and a victim of anti-Black violence. Paul Wells, for example, has remarked that Candyman is "a metaphor about racist culture and the prevailing legacy of slavery, the monster—essentially a brutal avenger—is . . . morally ambivalent because of the apparent justice that motivates him."[1] Likewise, Jessica Baker Kee has claimed that Rose's use of uncanny doubling and mirroring destabilizes tropes of Black monstrosity within the film's visual iconography, and thus reveals the instability of representations of race and gender.[2]

Other critics, however, have persuasively argued that Rose's original film celebrates white womanhood while advancing racist tropes and narratives of abject Black masculinity and miscegenation.[3] Michael J. Boulin, moreover, argues that *Candyman* exemplifies a form of neoliberal racism that enables audiences to ideologically avoid questions of race by transforming it from a question of collective responsibility into a private matter marked by individual choice and judgment. For him, the film minimizes racism by falsely conflating "the oppression of inner-city African Americans with the oppression of [white] women."[4] Robin R. Means Coleman has argued that while *Candyman* does address everyday forms of racism that Blacks experience, it ultimately interrogates these matters "through the lens of Whiteness" in ways that ultimately reinforce historical stereotypes of Blackness and fears of racialized inner-city housing projects.[5] Candyman, contrary to the interpretations advanced by Wells and others, is not a brutal avenger motivated by justice; instead, as Means Coleman notes, "Candyman is not looking for revenge" so much as he is motivated to court Helen, the film's white protagonist, even at the expense of Black people who suffer from his violent wrath.[6] Accordingly, *Candyman* ultimately fulfills the racist trope of a "Black monster trying hard to seduce a White woman."[7]

We enter this debate and seek to respond to received scholarly commentary about the *Candyman* horror franchise by focusing on Nia DaCosta and Jordan Peele's 2021 adaptation, which takes place in the present, and now gentrified, Cabrini-Green neighborhood of Chicago. For us, the discursive and contextual discrepancies between Rose's original film from 1992 and DaCosta and Peele's 2021 adaptation signify both the aesthetic and political significance of Black horror's contribution to American public culture.

When we place Rose's *Candyman* within its historic context and in terms of the white directorial gaze that informs its narrative, we can understand it as a story of the unjust 1890 lynching of a Black man, Daniel Robitaille, which then presents that very victim as a supernatural Black monster. The American horror film, despite its cultural subversiveness, frequently relies on fears of an otherness that is drawn from and constitutive of the cultural scripts and *doxa* of the historical era in which a given film text circulates. Since most American horror films have been produced and directed by white artists, it should come as no surprise that racial difference has frequently been instrumentalized as a marker of fear and monstrosity in ways that symbolically affirm popular attitudes and assumptions about white superiority and supremacy. Indeed, since it is Black people who incur Candyman's violence, not whites, Rose's film discursively participates in the popular discourse of "black on black" inner-city crime. The racial tropes that killed Robitaille are the same that breed the myth of Candyman in the white imaginary, and this myth has taken many forms in America's shameful rhetorical tradition of anti-Blackness. It was evident in the moral panic over Willie Horton, the fear of "super predators" lurking in America's inner cities, and in officer Darren Wilson's public testimony after he killed Michael Brown, an unarmed Black teenager.[8]

Since the white directorial gaze on the Black body has been historically fraught with ethical and political risks for Black audiences, Means Coleman's distinction between "Blacks in horror films" and "Black horror films" is all the more necessary to guide scholars committed to the theorization and critique of racial representation. The categorical difference between these types of horror films is quite significant, for they can "variously position Blacks as the thing that horrifies, or as the victim or that which is horrified."[9] Black horror films draw from the rhetorical conventions of the genre to affectively craft fear, monstrosity, and shock, but also advance a narrative focus that emphasizes Black identity, experiences, history, and politics. The aesthetics of Black horror, moreover, are grounded in the intellectual and artistic movements constitutive of Black cultural traditions in music, style, comedy, literature, painting, photography, oratory, theater, performance, and, of course, film.[10] Black films are creatively led by Black directors, producers, writers, and performers who examine the *topoi* of horror through the lens of Black culture, and who are capable of addressing the "specific fantasy needs of the Black social imaginary."[11] In cultural and political terms, there is much at stake in the tradition of Black horror, especially since (white) America has proven time and again to be stubbornly reluctant to reckon with its history of racial violence against Blackness. "Because of the volatile nature of race," notes Carol E. Henderson, "African Americans have had to represent the brutality of their historical experiences in ways that amplify the literary, social, and oral replications of these themes expressed in America's collective memory."[12] Indeed, the horror genre has offered Black artists a range of rhetorical conventions for "flipping the script" as it were on not only the white norms that have informed the history of American cinema, but also on the very white power structure that underlies American liberal democracy.

The tradition of Black horror is even more culturally and politically significant now in our purportedly "post-racial" era. Grounded in an ideological investment in the normative value of "colorblindness," America's ideological commitment to a post-racial social imaginary has served as a basis for the symbolic retelling of American history in a way that has sought to vindicate its violent past of slavery and Jim Crow segregation while affirming the nation's mythic conviction in its own exceptionalism. The post-racial claim—that America has reached a moment in its history in which racial equality necessitates neither the law nor state policy—first emerged after the 1960s, only to become a dominant point of social and ideological consensus with the election of Barack Obama as president in 2008.[13] Indeed, for proponents of this claim, Obama's triumph proved that race no longer matters. The post-racial consensus posits that racial discrimination can no longer be declared systemic in a way that warrants the state to intervene and promotes the idea that race be disregarded as a category for government policy. Hence, criticisms regarding the racial disparities in healthcare, criminal justice, housing, wealth, access to education, and even voting are, in the parlance of our post-racial times, disingenuous expressions of "political correctness" or "playing the race card." Accordingly, policies seeking to correct the historical legacy of racial discrimination are said to perpetuate the race problem by creating a new class of victims through purported "reverse racism."[14]

The post-racial question is as much a statement about the capacities of liberal democracy as it is what Roderick A. Ferguson has called a "civilizational" discourse that posits "political, economic, and historiographical theses about US society in the post–civil rights moment."[15] Proclamations of the arrival of a post-racial society, in fact, also suggest that liberal democracy is more capable of producing both anti-racist outcomes and more racially just outcomes than radical alternatives that have made the end of capitalist exploitation a primary condition for racial justice. Instead, as many scholars have noted, the ideological narrative "post-race" obscures the persistence of structural racism and racial inequality while it simultaneously relegates the topic of race from a question of historically rooted economic and social disadvantage that we all have a collective responsibility to address as a condition of democratic cooperation and will-formation to a question of personal and individual initiative and preference. As Herman Gray notes, the "postracial disavowal of race as a social factor in the organization of society and the distribution of inequality is an example of the *continuing salience of race*. Indeed, in this play of race, race is the driving force in the moral panics about family decline, black criminality, and welfare dependency."[16]

Given the exigencies underlying our contemporary era of intensifying political uncertainty and violence, for us, the most important question is: What cultural and rhetorical resources do the conventions of Black horror arm artists with to critique America's historical legacy of anti-Black violence in an era when race is said to no longer matter? Film scholars have long held that the aesthetic conventions of cinematic horror can play a crucial cultural role in representing the traumatic horrors of history.[17] "To speak of history's horrors, or historical trauma," notes Adam Lowenstein, "is to recognize events as . . . wounds in the fabric of culture and history that bleed through conventional confines of time and space."[18]

Black horror is well suited to represent the trauma that has come to mark the horrors of the Black experience in America. *Black* trauma, as George Yancy describes, exists "within the context of a shared *symbolic* world, a world whose meanings are both explicit and implicit, whose meanings can impact us and undo us in violent and harrowing ways," and "one predicated upon a constitutive anti-Black ethos."[19] "Black bodies," Yancy continues, "share the trauma of trying *to be* in a world in which their existence is already negated, nullified; perhaps they are already dead, where existing within a White racist anti-Black world is like *waiting* one's turn to die, where the bell tolls for Black bodies in ways that leave White bodies unscathed, where Black bodies constitute a kind of 'unreality' from the incipiency of Black life."[20] But the horrors of the Black experience are not confined to space and time; indeed, the pain of Black trauma echoes from history to haunt the present, where the unsettled injustices and violence of the past manifest through microaggressions, the white gaze, chants that "All Lives Matter," police brutality, and Confederate monuments.

Scholars of horror have also long held that the rhetorical device of allegory can serve as an apt aesthetic strategy for representing trauma in cinematic terms. Etymologically, "allegory" derives from the Greek *allos* ("other") and -agorein ("to speak publicly") to mean "other speaking" or "speaks otherwise."[21] The Roman rhetorician Quintilian defined allegory as a device that "presents one thing in words and another in meaning," which, as Robert Hariman notes, is a rhetorical sleight of hand of "saying one thing and meaning another."[22] As a mode of figural presentation and composition, allegory paratactically organizes an assemblage of signs that, in their totality, direct an audience toward a common theme, meaning, or interpretation. Allegorical technique often makes use of double coding to convey dissent in repressive cultures and is well suited for critiquing the anti-Black ethos of a late-capitalist American culture marked by the fragmentation of historical narrative, meaning, and an endless reproduction of signs.

Lowenstein argues that allegory culturally functions as a critique of horror and trauma through what he calls the "allegorical moment," which he describes as "a shocking collision of film, spectator, and history where registers of bodily space and historical time are disrupted, confronted, and intertwined."[23] The horror film's assemblage of images, sounds, music, and narrative, when combined with the audience's emotional experience of terror, disgust, sympathy, or sadness, creates liminal affective space for the embodiment and interrogation of issues that characterize historical trauma diegetically within the textual strategies of the film. "The allegorical moment exists as a mode of confrontation," Lowenstein writes, "where representation's location between past and present, as well as between film, spectator, and history, demands to be recalibrated."[24]

Indeed, it is the political confrontation of allegory that makes DaCosta and Peele's 2021 adaptation of *Candyman* such a timely cinematic artifact of this era, and one that displays the cultural significance of Black horror in our troubled times. Through the eyes of DaCosta and Peele, *Candyman* becomes an Afro-pessimistic allegory of the traumatic violence and false promises Black Americans have endured since Reconstruction.

Over the past two decades, Afro-pessimism has emerged to become one of the most important, influential, and contentious meta-theories in the theoretical humanities. Coined by Saidiya Hartman and expounded on by Frank B. Wilderson III, Jared Sexton, and Christina Sharpe, Afro-pessimism maintains that the modern world was created by Black slavery. "The imaginary of the state and civil society is parasitic on the Middle Passage," writes Wilderson III, such that the genocidal violence foundational to the invention of "Black" "remains constant, paradigmatically, despite changes in its 'performance' over time—slave ship, Middle Passage, Slave estate, Jim Crow, the ghetto, and the prison-industrial complex."[25] Afro-pessimism both illuminates and interrogates the structural positionality of Blackness in modernity, which renders Blacks as the slave and metaphysical void against which all other subjects (be they workers, queer, trans, immigrant, feminist, or post-colonial in orientation) categorially become defined. Accordingly, Blackness comes to be constitutively and performatively bound in terms of the fundamental antagonism that paradigmatically divides it from all other sentient beings. Black suffering is distinct from that of all other claims to suffering, since its orientation and agency is fundamentally shaped not by "freedom" or self-determination as much as by the afterlife of slavery itself. Afro-pessimists reject narratives of progress in the face of ongoing suffering and anti-Black violence, and actively anticipate the destruction of the structures that enable them.[26]

Aesthetically, Afro-pessimists maintain a slew of theoretical conditions for judging the question of abstraction and representation. The meta-theory demands that any aesthetic representation signify Blackness in terms of its ontological negation without offering any hope for national redemption or progress.[27] Instead of progress, an Afro-pessimistic aesthetic outlines in visual, sonic, and narrative terms the grammar of suffering that underlies Blackness's constitutive antagonistic relation to the modern world, and observes and mediates its dispossession, condition of gratuitous violence, and ultimate "un/survival."[28] As Wilderson III puts it, "Can film tell the story of a sentient being whose story can be neither recognized nor incorporated into Human civil society?"[29]

Black horror is an ideal genre for advancing an Afro-pessimistic critique of our (post) racial order, and we seek to build on the work of other critics who have also made this claim.[30] We understand Black horror cinema as a rhetorical and aesthetic strategy for, as Sharp eloquently puts it, "encountering a past that is not past."[31] We will argue that DaCosta and Peele's adaptation of *Candyman* is Afro-pessimistic in aesthetic and political tone. By symbolizing the structural positionality of Blackness in the afterlife of slavery, DaCosta and Peele not only offer an allegorical rebuke of the hubris of the post-racial idea but raise skepticism about the prospect and possibility of racial progress for Black Americans. Indeed, DaCosta and Peele's adaptation exemplifies what we shall call an "allegorical adaptation"; that is, their film is not meant to faithfully repeat or rewrite the original 1992 text so much as summon its reappearance and recontextualization for a new era.[32] In the next section, we offer a close reading of specific scenes in the film

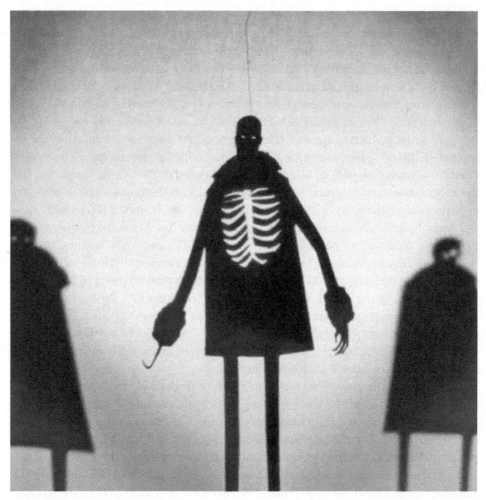

FIGURE 17.1 Candyman, 2021.

in order to highlight the rhetorical conventions and cultural trauma that underlies our Afro-pessimistic interpretation of *Candyman* (figure 17.1).

THE MORE THINGS CHANGE, THE MORE THEY STAY THE SAME

From the very beginning of their adaptation, DaCosta and Peele establish a tone, ethos, and narrative vision rooted in the Black gaze. In the opening scene of *Candyman*, we are introduced to a young William Burke as he reenacts an event familiar to the Black experience—the police arresting and violently assaulting an African American.

In this scene and throughout the film, DaCosta and Peele make use of puppetry to reenact flashbacks to the past that challenge the white rendition of the urban legend by emphasizing the horrors of being Black in America. William is central to this challenge, for he will serve as a narrative guide for the audience as it navigates both the genealogy of the figure Candyman and the history of anti-Black violence from the period of Reconstruction through the era of George Floyd and Breonna Taylor.

The shift in narrator offers a Black perspective that audiences have to this point been denied. In Rose's 1992 version of the film, the story is told through the protagonist Helen Lyle, a white anthropology student, and it is through her white gaze that we learn the story of Candyman and Cabrini-Green. In Rose's film, Black characters do not get a point of view to share, for they are only pitied or feared. Our new narrator, William, is a character who would have lived in Cabrini-Green in 1992 but was never given an opportunity to speak. In DaCosta and Peele's adaptation, the point of view will come not from an outsider, but from someone who has always lived in Cabrini-Green. The adaptation thus highlights the importance of Black horror and the way the racial gaze informs genres of cultural production.

Additionally, DaCosta and Peele's adaptation (re)centers the Black gaze by introducing a set of Black protagonists who propel the new narrative. Instead of following Helen, the story of *Candyman* is now led by Anthony, an artist, and his girlfriend, Brianna, a talented art scout and show designer at a Chicago-based art gallery. Anthony is not a new character, for we were first introduced to him in Rose's 1992 film when he was a baby. In that film, Helen fulfills the popular Hollywood trope of a white savior when she rescues him from a fire that Candyman engineers. However, as we learn the story of Candyman from the Black gaze, the racial narrative that marks the 1992 film—that of a heroic whiteness triumphing over the horrors of pathological urban violence—quickly falls apart. Instead, the Black narrative gaze emphasizes the horrors of Cabrini-Green, and the legend of Candyman, in terms of the violence of structural racism endemic to the history of American capitalism. DaCosta and Peele's adaptation makes this very clear through a series of scenes that describes the horrific and traumatic violence of Black dispossession through segregated redlining, racial violence, and neoliberal gentrification.

DaCosta and Peele emphasize this in a scene very early in the film, when Anthony and Brianna entertain her brother Troy Cartwright and his partner, Grady Greenberg, in their new loft, which sits where Cabrini-Green was once located. After arriving for dinner, Troy chides Brianna and Anthony's choice of residence and criticizes the couple by listing the problems with gentrification:

[Troy] You overpaid, Bri.
It's not just the inside that counts.
[Brianna] It's close to the gallery.
Yeah, it's very practical.
[Grady] Okay, what is wrong with it?
[Brianna] Nothing.

[Troy] As I told my sister many times, the neighborhood is haunted.
[Brianna] Troy, do not start with that.
[Troy] Sure, sure, sure, but why you choose a place that used to be called Smokey Hollow?
Then, Little Hell, then what is it? Combat Alley?
[Grady] What's it called now?
[Anthony] Cabrini-Green.
It was the projects.
It was affordable housing that had a particularly bad reputation.
[Grady] You would never know.
[Anthony] Because they tore it down and gentrified the shit out of it.
[Brianna] Translation: White people built the ghetto and then erased it when they realized they built the ghetto.
Oh, no offense.
[Grady] None taken.
[Troy] They took the opportunity to make it livable.
I could've got you a better conversion.
[Brianna] They kept telling people they were gonna make it better, moving 'em from place to place, but they were just tearing it down, so they could develop everything around it.
[Grady] Oh, like here.

Troy's critique of Brianna and Anthony's residence is important to the narrative of the film. The horrors of gentrification, racial violence, and the white gaze are apparent in this opening dialogue. It is Troy's association of gentrification with the Cabrini-Green urban legend Candyman that diegetically introduces the "monster" to Anthony and Brianna, but Troy's perspective also sets the stage for a new context for audiences to understand the racial meaning underlying the figure Candyman.

Aside from offering an early critique of the horrors underlying gentrification, Troy's rendition of the events from 1992 are also important, since he describes Helen Lyle as a monster-like figure rather than the heroine, as told in the original film. This move challenges audiences to reconsider what the *real* monstrosity underlying *Candyman* might be. Indeed, Troy's rendition of events is affirmed later in the film when Anthony encounters William while doing research on Cabrini-Green. The retelling of the urban legend from new Black perspectives raises doubts about the veracity of Helen's point of view from 1992 and establishes early on that audiences should suspend their judgment regarding the question of monstrosity until the residents of Cabrini-Green have had a chance to tell the urban legend on their terms.

CABRINI-GREEN: THEN AND NOW

After the dinner scene, the film follows Anthony and his bourgeoning fascination with Cabrini-Green. His fascination soon becomes a source of inspiration for his art, which enables DaCosta and Peele to draw rich allegorical links between gentrification, the complicity of white women, and the appropriation and commodification of Black culture. We begin to see this as the film takes us deeper into the cultural machinations of the art industry, which appropriate Blackness and Black culture for the pleasures of white and cosmopolitan audiences. Anthony, for example, is encouraged by Clive, an art dealer, to paint about Cabrini-Green, which prompts him to do research at the housing project. Anthony's research spurs an insatiable curiosity about Candyman, which leads him to encounter William in Cabrini-Green.

Anthony's first encounter with Cabrini-Green allows the audience to see what has come of the housing project. Gazing upon the remains of Cabrini-Green, the camera pans to images of older, dilapidated buildings to only see them plastered with modern advertising, including a lifestyle residence advertisement atop what appears to be a vacant building with a bulldozer behind it and a fenced-in area where a yoga studio will be located in the future (figure 17.2).

While taking pictures of some of the buildings in the neighborhood, a bee stings Anthony, which sets into motion his eventual transformation as the reappearance of the figure Candyman. More terrifying, however, is the moment he swats the bee away, killing it. After being stung, Anthony appears in an almost catatonic state that marks the beginning of his ultimate narrative arc: Anthony's transformation into this current version of Candyman. While in this state, the camera fixes on Anthony's gaze, which is fixated on the next image—the bee being violently swarmed upon by ants, dismembered, and taken away by what signifies a mob. Indeed, it is in this scene that Anthony comes to be cosmically linked to the violence of the past. It is on this land, of course, that the original Candyman, Daniel Robitaille, was gruesomely tortured and slain by a white mob with bees and fire (figure 17.3).

FIGURE 17.2 Candyman, 2021.

FIGURE 17.3 Candyman, 2021.

DaCosta and Peele use Anthony's first encounter with William as a means of commenting on the history of racial violence that underlies the American experiment. William's narration of the story of Candyman begins to reveal allegorically how anti-Blackness is representative of the violence perpetuated by the state on innocent Black bodies through violent policing tactics. Right before they meet, a police car goes by, and Anthony responds to the siren by reversing his motion almost ceremoniously and hiding out of their sight—part of the experience of being Black in America. William then describes how practices of policing in Cabrini-Green began to change as it became gentrified. William tells Anthony, "they almost never come around here back in the day, unless it was to take someone down. Actually, that was a long time ago. Now they can't seem to stay away. At night, they post up with the last of us who still live here. A police car on that side of the block. *Keeping us safe. While keeping us in.*" We use emphasis with the last two sentences, since William grows more irritated as he comes to the end of this comment. This scene establishes the history of police violence in the community and its corresponding trauma—we can hear the trauma in William's voice. It is the trauma of excessive state violence on Black bodies.

As William and Anthony walk to the laundromat where he works, William calls out the names of several Black victims of police violence in a jeremiad tone that underscores the casual indifference of the new white residents gentrifying the neighborhood. As they walk, William says, "Home sweet home. The more things change; the more things stay the same. Ask the White people around here about Girl X, Dantrell Davis ... blank stares. A White woman dies in the hood, and the story lives on forever." Anthony responds by saying, "it's a good story, I guess." William tells Anthony the story of Sherman Field's violent death at the hands of the police, in which his face was beaten beyond recognition in Cabrini-Green. As William tells the story, DaCosta and Peele's adaptation clearly emphasizes the empathy deficit underlying Black death that stems from the paradigmatic dehumanization of Blackness that the very category of white requires. William describes a long line of Black victims of police violence. The Afro-pessimism is quite evident, for William's narrative draws attention to the universal disposability of Blackness such that it is never granted the status of full subjectivity and humanity, for as Wilderson III has noted, "the Black is needed to mark the border of human subjectivity" that whiteness itself colonizes at the expense of the other.[33]

Indeed, it is through William's story about Sherman that the legacy and the future of Candyman turn into something quite unexpected. In the 1992 film, the figure of Candyman took the form of the original victim, Daniel Robitaille. In DaCosta and Peele's adaptation, however, we see Sherman as the image of Candyman. Candyman is not singular but in fact plural; it is a figure that at once reveals and is resurrected by the corpsing of Blackness. The Black subjects that assume the figure of Candyman are *not actually subjects*, rather, they are slaves in the afterlife of slavery. Daniel Robitaille, Sherman, and those who eventually become Candyman all desired subjectivity, and in fact were promised it by the legal and political discourses of modern human rights, only to discover that this was never in fact possible. William's Afro-pessimistic storytelling invites the audience to witness the legacy of trauma from racial violence and American capitalism. Because the film takes place in the present and now gentrified Cabrini-Green neighborhood, we can think about the shift of the gaze through the lenses of both spatiality and racial violence. It is also here, in Cabrini-Green, which is haunted by this violence and the failed promises of Reconstruction, where Anthony gradually begins his transformation into the latest resurrection of Candyman for a purportedly post-racial era (figure 17.4).

It is telling that much of the violence of DaCosta and Peele's adaptation occurs within the art world. Candyman's victims in this film include art gallery owners and art critics. Their focus on the role of art as an institution of structural racial violence emphasizes the way the industry itself contributes to the violence of gentrification, but also is a commentary on the symbolic role Western art curators and critics have played in articulating categorical distinctions between what is purportedly beautiful and what is ugly and uncivilized that underlies the Black/white paradigmatic binary. Indeed, it is at the art gallery where we meet several of Candyman's victims.

Anthony first comes face to face with Candyman (embodied as Sherman) while visiting art critic Finley Stephens after she summons him to come to her home for an interview. It is in this space where Anthony begins to have a glimpse of his actual transformation. But it is in his first interaction with Finley at the gallery as she examines his work that the white neoliberal vision of gentrification surfaces. Mirrors, which summon

FIGURE 17.4 Candyman, 2021.

Candyman, become important to the scene that takes place in the gallery. As Anthony attempts to explain his work to Finley, she offers a terse yet unsurprising response to his explanation of the art as it pertains to the gentrification-as-violence theme. Mirrors are used to reflect the images of a white woman and Black man found in the same place but separated through the mirrored images and spatiality of the gallery.

It is through Finley's commentary on gentrification, as well as Anthony's themes in the artwork, that the realized nightmare of how the city built the ghetto, trapped Black people in the ghetto, and then displaced them without ever acknowledging any guilt becomes a part of the visuality of the film. In the gallery, Anthony attempts to explain his work to Finley, which is a piece that recalls Sherman's violent death by the police and includes a mirror that beckons spectators to "say his name." Finley, however, dismisses his work, and the violence portrayed in the art. After he explains the artwork and finally insists that it speaks for itself, she disregards it and him, arguing that "It speaks alright. It's didactic knee jerk clichés about the ambiance of the violence of the gentrification and the fact remains that is your kind, the real pioneers of that cycle, you know." Anthony responds, saying "excuse me?" She offers, "Artists, artists descend upon the disenfranchised neighborhoods to find cheap rents so that they can dick around in their studios without the crushing burden of having a day job." As this scene plays out, Finley's and Anthony's images are reflected on the mirrored wall across from his work. The use of mirrored images establishes this point of view in this interaction and is a critical point for Finley's upcoming death. Importantly, it is only after the film's first two murders that happen later that same evening in the gallery that Finley becomes interested in his work, which suggests that the art industry is driven less by the timelessness of aesthetic reflection as much as it is by public and viral episodes of spectacle and scandal (figure 17.5).

Finley is a character that marks another important contrast between the original 1992 film and DaCosta and Peele's adaptation. If the gaze of whiteness permeated the 1992

FIGURE 17.5 Candyman, 2021.

film, to the exclusion of Black perspectives and Black voices, Finley serves as a voice of whiteness within the adaptation. First, at the gallery, Finley dismisses Black criticisms of gentrification as a kind of cliché, but when they meet at her apartment to further discuss his work, she begins blaming aspiring artists like him for gentrification. During their meeting, Finley appears steadfast in her dismissal of the problems of gentrification and white complicity in what has happened to Black neighborhoods. Anthony then reminds her that "it seemed like you didn't quite get it." Finley glibly responds, telling him she does get it, saying, "the whole gentrification, etc." Anthony snaps back, "artists gentrified the hood?" He asks her, "who do you think makes the hood? The city cuts off the community and waits for it to die. Then they invite developers in. And say 'hey, you artists, you young people, you White preferably only, please come to the hood, it's cheap. And if you stick it out for a couple years, we'll bring you a Whole Foods.' "

The exchange between Anthony and Finley on gentrification reveals the ways DaCosta and Peele's adaptation advances a critique of what Keeanga-Yamhatta Taylor has called "predatory inclusion."[34] Federal housing policy sanctioned the segregation of African Americans into deteriorating urban neighborhoods, only to starve these communities of resources necessary to access high-paying jobs and well-resourced public schools. Structural poverty and segregation allowed these communities to become overcrowded, which hastened their deterioration. But even after Jim Crow–era discriminatory policies were formally dismantled, the inertia of economic exploitation and residential segregation ensued, since the bifurcated racial housing market continued to add value to racially exclusive suburbs while enabling new racially predatory lending practices. During the postwar suburban boom, risk was a pretext for excluding potential Black homeowners; yet, by the 1970s, with the advent of new Federal Housing Administration (FHA)–insured home mortgages in Black neighborhoods, risk, or "subprime" mortgages, made Black buyers attractive, since it allowed lenders to charge higher interest rates and parlay Black foreclosures into profits as their homes were reintroduced to the housing market ad nauseum as Black communities gentrified.[35] If the racial discrimination of the Jim Crow era became the cause of the Great Migration, the racial machinations of predatory capitalism since the 1970s has caused what could be called a "gentri-migration"; that is, racial migration caused by predatory forms of financialization tied to gentrification. DaCosta and Peele's adaptation thus displays a rare form of cinematic critique of Black dispossession by the allegorical codes of the horror genre.

During his visit, Anthony invites Finley to summon Candyman in the form of Sherman. He knows Candyman is present in Finley's home and what is to come of her. When Candyman slaughters Finley, the violence symbolically avenges the brutality done to Black communities through predatory capitalism and to Black bodies through state violence. The violent figure of Candyman reverses the historical relationship between white colonizers and Black victims of oppression. The image of Finley's body, dressed in white and dragged across the large window of her downtown Chicago home, becomes a cathartic moment for Anthony, all of those who have been Candyman, and for the haunted Cabrini-Green and other low-income inner-city homes (figure 17.6).

The murder of Finley intensifies Anthony's fascination with the legend of Candyman and hastens his transformation. After coming face to face with Sherman Field for the second time at Finley's apartment, Anthony consults William in the laundromat. They have the following conversation in which William, like a griot, passes on the story to Anthony as he learns of the manifold resurrections of Candyman for the first time:

[Anthony] What is he?
[William] Candyman ain't a he. Candyman is the whole damned hive.
[Anthony] There are others?

FIGURE 17.6 Candyman, 2021.

William begins to tell the story of the hive that now shapes the remainder of the film's narrative and continues the transformation of Anthony into a part of the hive:

> [William] Samuel Evans. Run down during the White housing riots of the '50s. William Bell, lynched in the '20s. But the first one, where it all began, was in the 1890s. It's the story Helen found. The story of Daniel Robitaille.

As William tells the story of Candyman and the original victim of white mob violence, Daniel Robitaille, the camera pans across what appears to be Anthony's studio, where we see the paintings of what seem to be the different Black men who have been the victims of white mob violence.

William's narrative of racial violence displays DaCosta and Peele's skillful use of allegory. *Candyman* addresses a scope of victimization that encompasses forms of systemic violence inflicted by American institutions upon people of African descent. The world perceived by the characters undergoes an allegorical transposition to the nightmarish brutality lying hidden in the foundations of American liberal democracy. The past is in fact never past, since it is always a material force threatening to emerge in the present, which is underscored by William's narrative and his emphatic emphasis on the continuity of anti-Black violence through time. The resurrections of Candyman mirror the repetition of anti-Black violence, which suggests the helplessness of Blackness before the onslaught of history. This past is registered in literal historical references William makes to specific violent events in the history of Chicago as well as earlier references to specific victims of violence, such Girl X and Dantrell Davis, but this also registers in Anthony's art. The audience of the *Candyman* franchise is presented with a story ostensibly about an urban legend but is actually given an allegory about the hidden brutality of their own institutions and their participation in the nightmare of history (figure 17.7).

Moreover, DaCosta and Peele's adaptation explicitly associates the film with the cause of contemporary racial justice movements. We see this in a scene that takes place after Candyman's first two victims, Jerrica and Clive, are murdered in the art gallery. While Clive and Jerrica are murdered, Anthony is visited by a bee trapped in the mirror of his art studio. Later, as Anthony, Brianna, and Troy watch the report of the grisly murders, Anthony's name is mentioned as one of the artists whose work is displayed at the gallery where Clive's and Jerrica's bodies are found. As the camera concentrates on Anthony's face, we see him smiling as he says, "they said my name. They said my name." As the camera pans out, we see Brianna and Troy look perplexed at Anthony, with mouths agape as he celebrates his name being called. The phrase inversely alludes to the popular and well-known phrase "say her/his name" evoked during Black Lives Matter protests following the police murders of unarmed Black women and men.

The inversion of the phrase is significant beyond the reason that it celebrates the calling of his name. Inverting the phrase in this way suggests two things. First, saying of the name is a reference to summoning Candyman five times. Second, and perhaps more

FIGURE 17.7 Candyman, 2021.

important, voicing this phrase through a Black body that is normally the victim of such violence cathartically inverts its meaning such that the victim is empowered. In this case, the slogan is used to address the violence that was and is done to Black bodies and that are living within a white power structure that continuously violates and destroys them physically and emotionally.

"They Love What We Make; but Not Us"

As the film unfolds, we begin to see Candyman enact violence on the wealthy white dwellers of now gentrified Cabrini-Green. These violent episodes can be understood as a critique of the white appropriation of Black culture. A notable scene occurs in a girl's bathroom of what is likely Walter Payton College Preparatory High School, a highly rated school that became part of the gentrification of Cabrini-Green when it opened in 2000. The scene positions Candyman as a menacing and haunting figure who avenges the commodification of Black culture, acts of violence done on Black bodies, and base white narcissism.

In the bathroom, Candyman is summoned by a young white teenager, Haley Guilick. We are introduced to her earlier in the film when she attends the opening night of the exhibit where Anthony's work is displayed. At the gallery, Haley snaps a shot of Anthony's "Candyman" exhibit before leaving. As Haley views the exhibit at the art gallery, she seems mesmerized by the story and yet, we must wonder if she appreciates the full scale of his work. She does not open the mirror. She seems only engaged with the mirror and the caption attached to the mirror that says to "say his name." Beyond that, she seems voyeuristically indifferent, as if Black art were something for her to consume without reflection on the deeper meaning the art seeks to convey about the Black experience. Black culture and aesthetic expression appear to be just one on a spectrum of tastes for her to consume at her pleasure.

The bathroom scene only serves to confirm this, for she convinces her friends in the school bathroom to call Candyman's name five times. Notably, the two young students of color in this scene appear to be the only ones who survive, including a young Black student in the stall that Haley harasses. She pays no respect to the victims, as she seems to be interested only in the spectacle of the murders and their mythic association with the urban legend. Her act is one of indifference to the trauma left behind from the violence and the legacy of the space she inhabits. Haley's trespassing in the community is certainly indicative of the white appropriation of the land through gentrification, but she is also representative of the appropriation of Black culture. Haley takes the message of the artwork and appropriates it for her own use. The Black gaze of DaCosta and Peele offers incisive commentary on this matter when William so eloquently reminds us, "they love what we make, but not us" (figure 17.8).

Yet, of all the splendors of DaCosta and Peele's adaptation, from its cultural commentary on the state of race in America to its innovative use of puppetry for flashback, perhaps the most important and generous legacy it offers us is the memory of Cabrini-Green itself. Indeed, if one were to walk the streets of West Locust and North Hudson, as we did in May 2022, you would barely find a trace that the Cabrini-Green neighborhood ever existed. All that remains of the neighborhood lies behind fences ready to be bulldozed and destroyed, to become part of an upscale simulacrum of posh townhouses in Parkside of Old Town. It is a cultural space that Chicago would rather forget and erase from memory, no differently than the rest of America would rather erase the horrors of slavery and the violence it has visited on its African American citizens from all educational curricula (figure 17.9a, b, c).[36]

Scholars will continue to debate the meaning and iconography of the *Candyman* horror franchise for decades to come, but this much we know is certain: *Candyman* is a

FIGURE 17.8 Candyman, 2021.

unique artifact for posterity that reveals an inconvenient truth about the history of race that many Americans would prefer to forget. To be sure, we should take literally the advice Daniel Robitaille imparts to us when his resurrection is complete in the film's final scene: "tell everyone."

CONCLUSION

In this chapter, we have argued that DaCosta and Peele's adaptation of *Candyman* is Afro-pessimistic in aesthetic and political tone. We understand this adaptation as a response to current post-racial ideologies that allegorically critiques the legacy of slavery and race trauma hidden in the foundations of American society by the spatial and racial violence of American capitalism. By symbolizing the structural positionality of Blackness in the afterlife of slavery, DaCosta and Peele not only offer an allegorical rebuke of the hubris of the post-racial but raise skepticism about the prospect and possibility of racial progress for Black Americans, since the film refuses to posit a narrative redress of the violence of American structural racism. DaCosta and Peele's adaptation forces audiences to reconsider what monstrosity is and where it lies within this popular franchise, and given the ongoing violence that continues to be visited on Black bodies and the evolution of predatory capitalism, the film poses a darker and more unsettling question: Will *Candyman* ever end?

FIGURE 17.9 a, b, c Modern-day Cabrini Green. Photos by author.

NOTES

1. Paul Wells, *The Horror Genre: From Beelzebub to Blair Witch* (London: Wallflower, 2000), 107.

2. Jessica Baker Kee, "Black Masculinities and Postmodern Horror: Race, Gender, and Abjection," *Visual Culture & Gender* 10, no. 1 (2015): 51–53.

3. See Judith Halberstam, *Skin Shows: Gothic Horror and the Technology of Monsters* (Durham, NC: Duke University Press, 1995), 5; E. Ann Kaplan, *Looking for the Other: Feminism, Film, and the Imperial Gaze* (New York: Routledge, 1997), 122–131.

4. Michael J. Boulin, *Magical Thinking: Fantastic Film, and the Illusions of Neoliberalism* (New York: Palgrave Macmillan, 2016), 93.

5. Robin R. Means Coleman, *Horror Noire: Blacks in American Horror Films from the 1890s to Present* (New York: Routledge, 2011), 189.

6. Ibid.

7. Ibid.

8. Byron B Craig and Stephen E. Rahko, "Visual Profiling as Biopolitics; Or, Notes on Policing in Post-Racial #AmeriKKKa," *Cultural Studies⇔Critical Methodologies* 16, no. 3 (2016): 287–295.

9. Means Coleman, *Horror Noire*, 8.

10. Ibid., 7.

11. Harry M. Benshoff, "Blaxploitation Horror Films: Generic Reappropriation or Reinscription?" *Cinema Journal* 39, no. 2 (2000): 31.

12. Carol E. Henderson, "Allegories of the Undead: Rites and Rituals in Tales from the Hood," in *Folklore/Cinema: Popular Film as Vernacular Culture*, ed. Sharon R. Sherman and Mikel J. Koven (Salt Lake City: Utah State University Press, 2007), 166.

13. See Roopali Mukherjee, "Antiracism Limited: A Pre-History of Post-Race," *Cultural Studies* 30 (2016): 47–77; Catherine R. Squires, *The Post-Racial Mystique: Media and Race in the Twenty-First Century* (New York: New York University Press, 2014), 17–64.

14. Byron B Craig and Stephen E. Rahko, "From 'Say my Name' to 'Texas Bamma:' Transgressive *Topoi*, Oppositional Optics, and Sonic Subversion in Beyoncé's 'Formation,'" in *Beyoncé in the World: Making Meaning with Queen Bey in Troubled Times*, ed. Christina Baade and Kristin McGee (Middletown, CT: Wesleyan University Press, 2021), 262–263.

15. Roderick A. Ferguson, "On the Postracial Question," in *Racism: Postrace*, ed. Sarah Banet-Weiser, Roopali Mukherjee, and Herman Gray (New York: New York University Press, 2019), 73.

16. Herman Gray, "Race after Race," in *Racism: Postrace*, ed. Sarah Banet-Weiser, Roopali Mukherjee, and Herman Gray (New York: New York University Press, 2019), 31 (italics added).

17. See Adam Lowenstein, *Shocking Representation: Historical Trauma, National Cinema, and the Modern Horror Film* (New York: Columbia University Press, 2005); John Lutz, "From Domestic Nightmares to the Nightmare of History: Uncanny Eruptions of Violence in King's and Kubric's Versions of *The Shining*," in *The Philosophy of Horror*, ed. Thomas Fahy (Lexington: University Press of Kentucky, 2010), 161–178; Claire Sisco King, *Washed in Blood: Male Sacrifice, Trauma, and the Cinema* (New Brunswick, NJ: Rutgers University Press); Kendall R. Phillips, *A Place of Darkness: The Rhetoric of Horror in Early American Cinema* (Austin: University of Texas Press, 2018).

18. Lowenstein, *Shocking Representation*, 1.

19. George Yancy, "Black Embodied Wounds and the Traumatic Impact of the White Imaginary," in *Trauma and Transcendence: Suffering and the Limits of Theory*, ed. Eric Boynton and Peter Capretto (New York: Fordham University Press, 2018), 143.
20. Yancy, "Black Embodied Wounds," 150 (emphasis in original).
21. Lowenstein, *Shocking Representation*, 1–10.
22. Quintilian, *The Institutio Oratoria*. Translated by H. E. Butler, 4 vols. (Cambridge, MA: Harvard University Press, 1920–22), 8.6.44; Robert Hariman, "Allegory and Democratic Public Culture in the Postmodern Era," *Philosophy and Rhetoric* 35, no. 4 (2002): 268.
23. Lowenstein, *Shocking Representation*, 12.
24. Ibid.
25. Frank B. Wilderson III, *Red, White, & Black: Cinema and the Structure of U.S. Antagonisms* (Durham, NC: Duke University Press, 2010), 11, 75.
26. Frank B. Wilderson III, *Afropessimissm* (New York: Liveright, 2020), 14–15; Jared Sexton, "People of Color Blindness: Notes on the Afterlife of Slavery," *Social Text* 28, no. 2 (2010): 31–40; Saidiya Hartman, *Lose Your Mother: A Journey along the Atlantic Slave Route* (New York: Farrar, Straus, and Giroux, 2007).
27. Wilderson III, *Afropessimism*, 15.
28. Christina Sharp, *In the Wake: On Blackness and Being* (Durham, NC: Duke University Press, 2016), 14.
29. Wilderson III, *Red, White, & Black*, 96.
30. Ryan Poll, "Can One 'Get Out?' The Aesthetics of Afropessimism," *The Journal of the Midwest Modern Language Association* 51, no. 2 (2018): 69–102.
31. Sharp, *In the Wake*, 13.
32. Our theory of adaptation is heavily indebted to postmodernism. See Francesco Casetti, "Adaptation and Mis-Adaptation: Film, Literature, and Social Discourses, in *A Companion to Literature and Film*, ed. Robert Stam and Alessandra Raengo (New York: Wiley-Blackwell, 2004), 82–85.
33. Wilderson III, *Afropessimism*, 164.
34. Keeanga-Yamhatta Taylor, *Race for Profit: How Banks and the Real Estate Industry Undermined Black Homeownership* (Chapel Hill: University of North Carolina Press, 2019), 17.
35. Taylor, *Race for Profit*, 17–25.
36. Simon Romero, "Texas Pushes to Obscure the State's History of Slavery and Racism," *New York Times*, May 20, 2021, https://www.nytimes.com/2021/05/20/us/texas-history-1836-project.html.

Works Cited and Consulted

Aranke, Sampada, and Huey Copeland. "Afro-Pessimist Aesthetisc: An Open Question," *ASAP/Journal* 5, no. 2 (2020): 241–245.

Blake, Linnie. *The Wounds of Nations: Horror Cinema, Historical Trauma, and National Identity*. Manchester, UK: Manchester University Press, 2008.

Casetti, Francesco. "Adaptations and Mis-Adaptations: Film, Literature, and Social Discourses." In *A Companion to Literature and Film*, edited by Robert Stam and Alessandra Raengo. New York: Wiley-Blackwell, 2004.

Ferguson, Roderick A. "On the Postracial Question." In *Racism: Postrace*, edited by Sarah Banet-Weiser, Roopali Mukherjee, and Herman Gray. New York: New York University Press, 2019.

Gray, Herman. "Race after Race." In *Racism: Postrace*, edited by Sarah Banet-Weiser, Roopali Mukherjee, and Herman Gray. New York: New York University Press, 2019.

Kee, Jessica Baker. "Black Masculinities and Postmodern Horror: Race, Gender, and Abjection." *Visual Culture & Gender*, [S.l.] 10, (October 2015): 47–56. ISSN 1936-1912. <https://www.vcg.emitto.net/index.php/vcg/article/view/94>.

Lacy, Michael G., and Kent A. Ono, eds. *Critical Rhetorics of Race*. New York: New York University Press, 2011.

Lowenstein, Adam. *Shocking Representation: Historical Trauma, National Cinema, and the Modern Horror Film*. New York: Columbia University Press, 2005.

Lutz, John. "From Domestic Nightmares to the Nightmare of History: Uncanny Eruptions of Violence in King's and Kubric's Versions of *The Shining*." In *The Philosophy of Horror*, edited by Thomas Fahy. Lexington: University Press of Kentucky, 2010.

Marriott, David. *Haunted Life: Visual Culture and Black Modernity*. New Brunswick, NJ: Rutgers University Press, 2007.

Means Coleman, Robin R. *Horror Noire: Blacks in American Horror Films from the 1890s to Present*. London: Routledge, 2011.

Mukherjee, Roopali, Herman Gray, and Sarah Banet-Weiser, eds. *Racism Postrace*. Durham, NC: Duke University Press, 2019.

Phillips, Kendall R. *A Place of Darkness: The Rhetoric of Horror in Early American Cinema*. Austin: University of Texas Press, 2018.

Poll, Ryan. "Can One 'Get One?' The Aesthetics of Afro-Pessimissm." *The Journal of the Midwest Modern Language Association* 51, no. 2 (2018): 69–102.

Sexton, Jared. "People of Color Blindness: Notes on the Afterlife of Slavery." *Social Text* 28, no. 2 (2010): 31–56.

Sharpe, Christina. *In the Wake: On Blackness and Being*. Durham, NC: Duke University Press, 2016.

Sharrett, Christopher. "The Horror Film as Social Allegory (And How it Comes Undone)." In *A Companion to the Horror Film*, edited by Harry M. Benshoff. Hoboken, NJ: Wiley-Blackwell, 2014.

Sisco King, Claire. *Washed in Blood: Male Sacrifice, Trauma, and the Cinema*. New Brunswick, NJ: Rutgers University Press, 2011.

Squires, Catherine R. *The Postracial Mystique: Media and Race in the 21st Century*. New York: New York University Press, 2015.

Wells, Paul. *The Horror Genre: From Beelzebub to Blair Witch*. New York: Wallflower Press, 2001.

Wilderson III, Frank B. *Red, White, & Black: Cinema and the Structure of U.S. Antagonisms*. Durham, NC: Duke University Press, 2010.

Wilderson III, Frank B. "Close Up: Social Death and Narrative Aporia." *Black Camera* 7, no. 1 (2015): 134–149.

Wilderson III, Frank B. *Afropessimism*. New York: Liveright, 2020.

CHAPTER 18

THE ALLEGORY OF THE
TICKLE MONSTER

TESSA ADAMS

IN 2016, Black British director and writer Remi Weekes made the short horror film *Tickle Monster*, which premiered on the United Kingdom's Channel 4 *Fright Bites* series.[1] In *Tickle Monster*, aspiring Grime rap artist Elliot discovers that his girlfriend's (Natalie) room is haunted by the eponymous creature—a monster that tickles people and then quickly disappears. While only four minutes and fifteen seconds long, *Tickle Monster* includes strong critiques regarding race. In this chapter, I utilize a critical textual analysis and ideological analysis of Elliot, Natalie, and the Tickle Monster to argue that the short film is a response to oppression, microaggressions, and ideologies associated with the post-racial mythology. Further, I contend that the representation of the Tickle Monster serves as a reminder to audiences that while racism does not always present itself as overt, it is continuously covert and always on the attack. In other words, Weekes's short film is a reminder to "stay woke!"

This chapter begins by introducing director and writer Remi Weekes. I will discuss his motivation for creating *Tickle Monster* in addition to discussing aesthetic patterns in his work. As *Tickle Monster* is a short film, I bring in a discussion of Weekes's feature length film, 2020's *His House*, to further contextualize his directorial style. I then discuss critical race theory, its tenets, and how it relates to post-racialism and colorblind mythology. Lastly, I analyze *Tickle Monster*, illustrating how it responds to oppression, microaggressions, and ideologies associated with post-racialism and institutional racism.

REMI WEEKES'S *TICKLE MONSTER*

Prior to *Tickle Monster*, Remi Weekes directed the short films *Exhale* (2009) and *Metamorphosis* (2011) in addition to a host of commercials.[2] Other than a few comments focusing on stylistic and aesthetic choices, there is a dearth of press about *Tickle Monster*. Weekes's major feature length, *His House*, premiered at Sundance Film Festival followed by distribution to Netflix. In *His House*, refugee couple Bol (Sope Dirisu) and Rial Majur (Wunmi Mosaku) escape war-torn South Sudan by kidnapping a young girl, Nyagak (Malaika Wakoli-Abigaba) and pretending she is their child, which allows them to board a boat headed to the United Kingdom. Unfortunately, the boat capsizes, and many people, including Nyagak, perish.[3] Bol and Rial survive, and after being placed into their new home through probationary asylum, the couple learns that an evil spirit haunts their new residence.[4]

In a roundtable discussion of *His House*, Weekes explains that the film touches on a variety of subjects, including refugees, immigration, asylum, migration, and spirituality.[5] Additionally, *His House* also comments on assimilation, "a process of interpenetration and fusion in which persons and groups acquire the memories, sentiments, and attitudes of other persons or groups, and, by sharing their experience and history, are incorporated with them into a common cultural life," in the attempt to help audiences understand what it feels like to be a racial "other" or "the deviation from the norm."[6]

Moreover, Weekes related that his films reflect his personal experiences as a member of the African diaspora who had to assimilate in the United Kingdom. He notes that sometimes "others" never really feel accepted or like a permanent member of the United Kingdom and that a segment of members of othered populations feel they need to conform to the hegemonic culture. In contrast, others work to remain connected to their native cultures and proudly display this.

While I discuss the aforementioned themes in more depth later in this chapter, it is important to note that analyzing Remi Weekes's artistic works is of the utmost importance, as he is a Black man directing in a new era of horror sometimes referred to as "woke horror." While horror has always critiqued societal issues "by viewing and evaluating culture-centered films, often centered around race—and critically analyzing them,"[7] woke horror does this work from Black persons' perspectives. Examples of woke horror include *Get Out* (2017) (which is regarded as the "original" woke horror film), *The First Purge* (2018), *Us* (2019), and *Antebellum* (2020). Woke horror productions often feature predominantly Black casts and boast multiracial crews, attributes that categorize them as what Robin R. Means Coleman defines as Black horror films.[8] These movies differ from the abundance of mainstream horror films that have white directors, casts, crews, and feature Black characters in small, underdeveloped roles.[9] Conversely, Black horror films also present a diverse range of Blackness and challenge traditional stereotypes. In short, Black horror films center *Blackness*.

Woke horror and critical race theory (which I discuss in the next section) are especially effective means to analyze systemic racism, as many of their critiques come from writers and directors who have experienced racism. Weekes explains that his work derives from his feelings and experiences, further subscribing his films to Aymar Christian and Khadijah White's concept of organic representation. These scholars note that "meaningful representation emerges in writing, directing, and producing by filmmakers of color."[10] Thus, *Tickle Monster* and *His House* have degrees of authenticity, as they were created through a Black lens and, thereby, reflect Weekes's experiences as a Black man and member of the African diaspora. As a Black man critiquing assimilation, race, and masculinity, Weekes offers an oppositional gaze, a concept coined by bell hooks that essentially explains that his critical perspective is different from many mainstream filmic renderings of Blackness.[11]

CRITICAL RACE THEORY: THE UNITED STATES

Critical race theory (CRT) grew out of U.S. legal studies, particularly scholars Derrick Bell, Kimberlé Williams Crenshaw, Richard Delgado, Jean Stefancic, and Kendall Thomas, among others.[12] CRT asserts that racism is endemic in social systems and that society consists of oppressors and oppressed.[13] Tenets of the theory are used across disciplines, including education, political science, urban planning, religion, sociology, queer studies, and more.[14] While the core tenets can be worded in a variety of ways, they adhere to basic principles: (1) racism is a normal function of everyday life that is embedded in institutions and systems; (2) racism is supported through hegemony; (3) race is a social construction that has no bearing on biology or genetics; (4) as marginalized members of society, people of color deserve to have their voices heard; and (5) CRT should move beyond scholarship into social justice movements, activism, pedagogy, and other areas.[15]

CRT recognizes that racism exists at both the individual and systemic levels, and therefore, it highlights the consistent inequalities people of color face. A key component is that society inherently subscribes to whiteness and white supremacy.[16] Moreover, whiteness is the societal default to which everything else is compared, therefore making it inherently supreme in societies around the globe. Consequently, whiteness is often considered raceless and as an attribute that warrants full privilege.[17] Significantly, Jeremey Bohonos relates that "recognizing privilege can be difficult for those who possess it."[18] Generally, whiteness offers protections in the form of its invisibility and innocence for those who visually identify as white. An example of the protection that whiteness affords people manifests in media portrayals of Black women versus white women. Media have historically depicted Black women as animalistic, hypersexual, racialized, and exotic,[19] while portraying white women as innocent, civilized, and attractive.[20] Unfortunately, these mediated stereotypes are mapped onto individuals in real-world contexts and, as such, have real-world implications. Thus, Black people do not have the same protections due to race and gender stereotypes associated with their race and gender.

CRT has several subcomponents and related theories. One of its tenets notes that "individuals experience multiple intersecting identities," which is a subcomponent of Kimberlé Williams Crenshaw's intersectional theory.[21] Intersectional theory, or intersectionality, asserts that racism, sexism, and classism interconnect and consequently shape individuals' real-world experiences.[22] Although this theory originally focused on the experiences of Black women, scholars have expanded it to include members of other historically marginalized populations,[23] all of whom may experience discrimination at structural, political, and representational levels.[24]

CRITICAL RACE THEORY: THE UNITED KINGDOM

CRT was introduced into U.K. discourse in approximately 2003.[25] Like the theory's beginnings in the United States, it primarily surfaced in the United Kingdom's education sector. Although CRT emerged in the United States, in the United Kingdom, the basic tenets remain the same: racism is endemic in society and, as a result, divides society into oppressors and oppressed. Additionally, in the United Kingdom, CRT is also considered in areas such as education, political science, urban planning, religion, sociology, contemporary queer criticism studies, entertainment, and others.[26]

The first lead CRT paper was presented at the British Educational Research Association (BERA) Conference in 2003.[27] Three years later, on November 20, 2006, the first international CRT seminar took place in the United Kingdom at the Education and Social Research Institute at Manchester Metropolitan University.[28] Scholar Mike Cole notes that at the time of this conference, CRT had few supporters in the United Kingdom.[29] For instance, sociology scholar Carl Parson referred to it as "imported CRT."[30] A primary criticism of CRT in the United Kingdom is that the theory focuses on racial inequality at the expense of issues such as gender, sexuality, and class.[31] Other CRT detractors support "objective" notions of class and apply "subjectivity" to race, therefore asserting that the theory's tenets have a "personal" bent.[32]

Importantly, CRT opponents neglect intersectionality, or the idea that racism, sexism, and classism are interconnected and consequently shape individuals' experiences.[33] Further, some detractors perceive CRT as an attack on the white working class. Dennis Hayes, for instance, contends that CRT claims "if you are white you are racist . . . critical race theorists will dismiss my claim as absurd, but that is because they avoid saying what they really think."[34] Further, Cole takes issue with CRT because he believes it lumps all white people together and asserts that all white people have power and privilege on equal levels.[35] Moreover, Cole believes CRT attempts to teach the white working class that white culture is racist culture.[36] Hence, similar to in the United States, a segment of scholars and people in the United Kingdom have adopted CRT's core tenets while adamantly rejecting the theory.

CRITICAL RACE THEORY TODAY: THE UNITED STATES AND THE UNITED KINGDOM

As mentioned, CRT emerged from critical legal studies.[37] While scholars in many fields use the theory, prior to 2020, the mainstream did not give it much regard.[38] However, after former Minneapolis police officer Derek Chauvin publicly executed George Floyd by kneeling on the back of his neck for nearly nine minutes, CRT was thrust into mainstream discourses in both the United States and United Kingdom. After this avoidable injustice, people engaged in monumental calls to end systemic racism. During that time, scholars, politicians, and everyday citizens who understand CRT brought its tenets into public discourses to exemplify how Floyd's death (and similar injustices by extension) occurred in an allegedly post-racial society. CRT then moved into the mainstream as international news outlets, social media users, and others helped spread the theory around the globe.

POST-RACISM

The post-racial myth gained traction when Barack Hussein Obama secured the White House in 2008. His election was historic, given the fact that Obama was the first Black person ever elected as the president of the United States. Obama's election helped cement the idea that U.S. society had finally moved into an era when race no longer presented barriers to Black excellence. Post-racialism proponents incorrectly claimed that race no longer matters since a Black person held the highest position in the world. In essence, post-racialism is a social and political strategy that works to erase the "historical abomination" that is indeed racism and its enduring effects.[39]

While many people support its assertions, the historical record and contemporary events reveal it as a myth. In addition to Floyd's execution, a brief survey of racially motivated attacks on unarmed Black people since former-President Obama's election elucidate that post-racialism is a fallacy. As examples, in 2012, vigilante George Zimmerman stalked and murdered Trayvon Martin; Ferguson, Missouri, police officer Darren Wilson killed Michael Brown in 2014; and, in 2020, Louisville, Kentucky, police officers serving a no-knock warrant shot and killed Breonna Taylor while she was asleep in her bed. Additionally, the election of President Donald J. Trump, who continually used racist, sexist, classist, ableist, and xenophobic language while on the 2016 campaign trail, also reveals the U.S. post-racial narrative as a fallacy.

Unfortunately, U.K. police officers and security forces have also unjustly killed Black persons at alarming rates. For instance, in 2010, Jimmy Mubenga died after GS4 security officers restrained him to his chair on a flight out of the country.[40] The following year, acting on a tip that Mark Duggan was carrying a gun, police officers forced the minicab in which he was riding to a stop. Although Duggan leapt out and dropped the firearm in the grass, an officer immediately shot and killed the 29-year-old. In 2017, as police were arresting Darren Cumberbatch outside a Nuneaton hostel, they beat him with batons and excessively tasered him, killing him in the process.[41]

While these instances of blatant racism were overt, anti-Black discrimination can also be covert, processes that Eduardo Bonilla-Silva refers to as "new racism."[42] This form of racial discrimination is more insidious, because it operates in an inferential, hidden, and coded fashion. New racism manifests in the form of oppressive policies, microaggressions, and colorblind ideology. For instance, a school policy that prohibits Black students from wearing hairstyles unique to their cultures, like Afros, unfairly targets them. However, since it is a policy, it is protected under the law.

Microaggressions, "brief and commonplace daily verbal, behavioral, or environmental indignities, whether intentional or unintentional, that communicate hostile, derogatory, or negative racial slights and insults toward people of color" are common forms of anti-Black discrimination.[43] In regard to hair, microaggressions might involve asking a Black woman with long hair if it is real, as it potentially suggests that Black women must wear weaves to achieve Eurocentric beauty standards. Colorblind ideology absolves people who use microaggressions, because if societies are post-racial, its citizens do not see race, and therefore cannot be racist on either individual or institutional levels.[44] *Tickle Monster* critiques these insidious forms of racism.

BLACK BRITISH HISTORY

Among the most notable ways in which post-racialism manifests in the United Kingdom is via erasure. For instance, the absence of Black British history in U.K. educational systems is a topic that politicians, teachers, and others continually engage.[45] In fact, Black British history is often mentioned in the context of slavery, postwar immigration, and Black History Month.[46] There are three components that amplified Black British History in education: E. P. Thompson's book *The Making of the English Working-Class*, which explores the history of "lost, forgotten, or neglected people"; the continued growth of African Studies and African American Studies that emerged after the U.S. 1960s civil rights movement; and Black radicalism.[47]

The ever-present concern that CRT is anti-white has resulted in a lack of support for CRT in the United Kingdom. Additionally, the March 2021 Commission on Race and Ethnic Disparities report (known as the Sewell Report) regarding the current state of race relations in the United Kingdom is another contributing factor. According to the report, the United Kingdom is free of systemic racism in health systems, education, housing, and other institutions.[48] Dr. Sewell argues that disparities among people are not rooted in racism; rather, they are results of geography, culture, and poverty;[49] that "we no longer see a Britain where the system is deliberately rigged against ethnic minorities"; and that "too often 'racism" is the catchall explanation and can be simply implicitly accepted rather than explicitly examined."[50] Sewell also asserts that based on his years of experience studying race relations and racial inequality in the United Kingdom, institutional racism has not been a factor there for decades. The Sewell report received backlash and was regarded as a dangerous document that attempted to gaslight British people of color who experience racism daily. Scholar Leon Tikly explains that the Sewell report contributes to colorblind discourses by essentially asserting that people in the United Kingdom no longer see nor care about race.[51] Finally, since the report fails to acknowledge racism as a serious issue, it perpetuates white supremacy in education, and in other aspects of U.K. life as well.

TICKLE MONSTER: A SOCIAL-PROBLEM/ SOCIAL-THRILLER/HORROR FILM

Significantly, *Tickle Monster* is a social-problem/social-thriller/horror film of sorts. Vineet Kaul defines social-problem cinema as a set of films about issues such as racism, poverty, and education.[52] The social-thriller film is an offshoot of the social-problem film, as it also critiques social issues but with the addition of aspects of the thriller and/ or horror. Jordan Peele, who is credited with galvanizing the social-thriller movement, defines it as films where the monster is society.[53]

In this section, I engage in a critical textual analysis and ideological analysis concurrently. The critical textual analysis is at the forefront, while the ideological component is overarching. A critical textual analysis goes "beyond the manifest content of the media, [and] focuses on the underlying ideological and cultural assumptions of the text."[54] Ideological analyses delve beyond surface levels to uncover artifacts' deeper implications and meanings.[55] To conduct this analysis, I first watched *Tickle Monster* several times to become acquainted with characters, character traits, and plot to see what themes and patterns emerged. Next, I conducted a close reading of *Tickle Monster* while considering CRT, intersectionality, oppression, microaggressions, ideologies, post-racism, and related topics to help guide my analysis. Since *Tickle Monster* is a short film, I compared it to Weekes's 2020 film, *His House*, to provide context.

Director and writer Remi Weekes has distinct writing, directorial, and aesthetic styles. While some aesthetic choices in *Tickle Monster* carry over into *His House*, such as Weekes's penchant for showing dark doorways, including jump scares, and general haunted-house motifs, most of the director's style emerges from characters and themes. For example, *Tickle Monster*'s Elliot has much in common with *His House*'s main character, Bol. While they do not have as much in common, Natalie (*Tickle Monster*) is comparable to Rial (*His House*), and the Tickle Monster and the Apeth, or a night witch, share similar attributes. Consequently, the analyses focus heavily on these characters.

Tickle Monster is an allegory for the functioning of individual and institutional/systemic racism, and it responds to post-racial mythology by examining it in the text.

The film challenges the United Kingdom's CRT opponents by adequately outlining how individual and institutional racism works and by exposing audiences to CRT tenets when they otherwise may not be. Although it was released in 2016, *Tickle Monster* challenges and debunks Sewell's 2021 report contending that in the United Kingdom, systemic racism is no more.

Elliot

Tickle Monster opens with Elliot rapping, "Fuck feds, fuck court" and "I'ma shank him at his front door," lyrics that immediately construct him as a stereotypical rapper. He's a young, possibly violent, Black man. Elliot's violent rap style exemplifies Grime rap, an "electronic music, often with rap-style vocals, which emerged from London around the turn of the millennium, and which offers insights into the experiences of a section of, predominantly black, working-class urban youth."[56] Initially produced in inner-city housing projects, at raves, and at pirate radio stations, Grime is specific to London and centers neglected working-class Black urban youth's experiences. Weekes uses the musical form to establish Elliot as tough, an attribute the character further attempts to communicate with his demeanor and facial expressions as he raps. However, Weekes includes clues indicating that Elliot's demeanor may be a front. For instance, he looks quite young and unintimidating, and he's not a very good rapper.

Further, the set includes a heart-shaped wall that is visible in the background as Elliot is rapping. Interestingly, the wall art is made from rope, and if a person were to slightly adjust it, it would be reminiscent of a noose. The art is an interesting metaphor and a reminder that while on the surface it may appear that Elliot is dangerous and aggressive, he identifies with the oppressed.

Elliot consistently endures subtly racist attacks (tickles), which function as microaggressions of sorts. When the Tickle Monster initially tickles him, the glassy look in Elliot's eyes illustrates that he is nervous and frightened. After a few more aggressive tickle attacks, Elliot runs to his bed and tries to put on his pink sweater as a form of protection from the Tickle Monster. Like the wall art, the pink sweater seems to be a deliberate costume choice that once again symbolizes that Elliot is not the embodiment of societal stereotypes. Unfortunately, he struggles to put the pink sweater on, and sound effects create an aural illusion that the sweater is swallowing Elliot up. Eventually, he gets the sweater on, and then his girlfriend, Natalie, jumps onto his bed and tickles him. They both laugh, then suddenly, Natalie's laugh becomes ominous. Elliot hurriedly turns on the light and sees Natalie sitting on the bed, staring into the distance. Next, there is a shot of Elliot; the Tickle Monster, which is standing behind him, begins to viciously tickle him.

Because many of Elliot's actions do not align with his tough exterior, I argue that his persona is connected to assimilation. As mentioned, Remi Weekes said that some of his experiences with assimilation into the United Kingdom influenced *His House*.[57] Generally, assimilation "requires immigrants to lose their indentures and values from their countries of origin in order to adopt those of the dominant culture"; however, Elliot attempts to assimilate into the Grime music scene, and Black culture by extension.[58] In doing so, he adopts a segment of white peoples' stereotypical views of Black people. For instance, the stereotypes perpetuate fallacies that all Black men are tough and violent, attributes Elliot attempts to embody through his rap.[59]

In *His House*, Bol is comparable to Elliot in that he also attempts to assimilate. However, he tries to assimilate into the United Kingdom's dominant white culture. Bol avoids facing what he did in South Sudan to get to the United Kingdom. He and Rial are told that they need to prove themselves as worthy and well behaved enough to become citizens, and Bol sees assimilation as a way to achieve this. By attempting to assimilate without acknowledging his South Sudanese roots, Bol adopts colorblind ideology in the effort to seamlessly integrate into U.K. culture. For instance, in one scene, he walks past a pub, attracting the attention of a patron, who asks if he is "one of those refugees" before asking him to come inside.[60] Bol goes inside, and when a song familiar to the other patrons begins to play, they all sing along. Bol knows the song and excitedly sings with the others to fit in. In another scene, in which he shops for new clothing, Bol notices a poster of a happy and successful white family modeling casual clothing. Bol continually looks at the poster as he navigates the store, and eventually finds each article of clothing that the male model is wearing so that he may replicate his look. In an additional scene, Bol tells Rial to speak English, and when she expresses discomfort about eating with a fork, as it is not her norm, Bol tells her she will get used to it.

Importantly, if Bol is successful in his attempts to assimilate, he might gain "honorary whiteness," which is to be accepted as a minority who presents as white.[61] Bol's willingness and eagerness to assimilate speaks to the ways that white supremacy exerts its power and is central to social operations. Hence, Bol and Elliot are on opposite ends of the spectrum, as the latter tries to lean into his Blackness while the former works to erase his. That Elliot and Bol feel pressure to assimilate speaks to the CRT tenet that racism is a normal function of everyday life embedded in institutions and systems.[62]

Natalie

In *Tickle Monster*, Natalie is the voice of reason (somewhat), as it is she who cues Elliot in on what he is experiencing. As Elliot raps in the opening scene, Natalie is engrossed in her phone, and viewers can hear her using it. She looks up and, clearly unimpressed, smirks at Elliot as he struggles with his rap game. After being tickled twice, Elliot asks Natalie if she tickled him, to which she responds with a "no." Eerily nonchalant and continuing to look at her phone, she suggests that it may have been the Tickle Monster and tells Elliot that their room is haunted by the Tickle Monster that's hiding in the closet. It is extremely clear that Natalie is aware of what Elliot is experiencing, yet she does not really seem to care. If the Tickle Monster is a stand-in for racism, then Natalie functions as whiteness and microaggressions. She is racially ambiguous and, thus, has a level of protection from the Tickle Monster (read as racism). She acknowledges its existence, but essentially advises Elliot to brush it off, demonstrating that she does not understand that enduring microaggressions is comparable to, for lack of better words, death by a thousand tiny cuts.

Like Natalie, in *His House*, Rial serves as the voice of reason. She helps Bol understand that he is being haunted because of his past decisions and, subsequently, his Blackness. Bol must face what he did in South Sudan when he kidnapped young Nyagak, and consequently, he must face the fact that in his new environs, he is the "other." Similar to the way that Natalie helps Elliot understand the Tickle Monster, Rial consistently reminds Bol that they are being haunted by ghosts and spirits from the past because of his decisions. She recognizes that their actions will forever define their legacy, much like their racial/ethnic identities will always be visible markers that will prevent them from assimilating. Hence, they will overcome neither their previous mistakes nor their otherness.

Importantly, Rial faces her past and does not want to assimilate. She remains grounded in her culture and consistently reminds Bol to respect it. For instance, near the end of the film, Rial and Bol are both transported back to South Sudan prior to their arrival in the United Kingdom. While Bol is transported back to the moment where he kidnapped Nyagak, Rial is transported to a South Sudanese classroom, where she is surrounded with former friends. Rial receives a loving welcome from her friends, who welcome her back into her culture. This moment also foreshadows Rial killing the creature, Apeth, who is haunting them, because she is the one who possesses the cultural wisdom and belief to defeat it.

Tickle Monster

Although *Tickle Monster* is a short film named after a haunting creature, audiences see the eponymous character's full body only once. Otherwise, audiences only see the Tickle Monster's hands the three times it attacks. The first few times one hand is shown, and as the tickling becomes more aggressive, audiences see that it has five or six hands. Next, its full body is revealed, and the Tickle Monster has long greasy hair and an emaciated frame. While certainly monstrous, the Tickle Monster bears a striking resemblance to a white man, and therefore, it is consistently protected and gets away with racism (tickles).

Conversely, Weekes's portrayal of the Apeth does not appear to be symbolism for whiteness, as the creature is not tied to Bol and Rial's house, where they are under the institutionalization of whiteness through the asylum system. Instead, it is tied to the personal decisions they made prior to arriving in the United Kingdom. The Apeth is a spirit of revenge that forces people to confront their wrongdoings and themselves, and in that way, the Apeth is a reminder that people cannot run away from who they really are.

Based on its appearance, the Tickle Monster has the ultimate protection, a point evidenced by the way Elliot seems relieved, as if the tickles were only minor infractions, even though they are indicative of subtle racism. The Tickle Monster's attacks go unchallenged, and Elliot downplays them for most of the short film. Ideologically, *Tickle Monster* illustrates how contemporary racism sometimes operates covertly or is ignored, thus perpetuating the myth that society is post-racial. While *Tickle Monster* does not explain what happens after the monster is fully exposed, it is ultimately a reminder to "stay woke" to the ongoing facets of individual, social, and institutional racism.

Notes

1. *Tickle Monster*, directed by Remi Weekes (2016, United Kingdom: Fruit Tree Media). YouTube.
2. "Remi Weeks," Remi Weekes—Movies, Bio and Lists on MUBI, accessed October 12, 2022.
3. *His House*, directed by Remi Weekes (United Kingdom: Regency Enterprises, 2020).
4. "His House," IMBD, accessed January 5, 2022, https://www.imdb.com/title/tt8508734/?ref_=fn_al_tt_1.
5. Remi Weekes, "AAFCA Virtual Roundtable: His House Interview," The AAFC Channel, November 11, 2020, video, 30:23, https://www.youtube.com/watch?v=n-j5kpghfzw.
6. Robert E. Park and Ernest W. Burgess, *Introduction to the Science of Sociology* (Chicago: University of Chicago Press, 1921).
7. Janice D. Hamlet, *Films as Rhetorical Texts: Cultivating Discussion about Race, Racism, and Race Relations* (Lanham, MD: Lexington Books, 2020).
8. Robin Means Coleman, *Horror Noire: Blacks in American Horror Films from the 1890s to Present* (New York: Routledge, 2011).
9. Ibid.
10. Aymar Jean Christian and Khadijah Costley White, "Organic Representation as Cultural Reparation," *JCMS: Journal of Cinema and Media Studies* 60, no. 1 (2020): 143–147.
11. bell hooks, *Black Looks: Race and Representation* (Boston: South End Press, 1992).
12. Alison Cerezo et al., "Giving Voice: Utilizing Critical Race Theory to Facilitate Consciousness of Racial Identity for Latina/o College Students," *Journal for Social Action in Counseling & Psychology* 3, no. 5 (2014): 1–24.
13. Audrey P. Olmsted, "Words Are Acts: Critical Race Theory as a Rhetorical Construct," *Howard Journal of Communications* 9 (1998): 323–331, DOI: 10.1080/106461798246934.
14. Richard Delgado and Jean Stefanic, *Critical Race Theory: An Introduction* (New York: New York University Press, second edition, 2012).
15. Ibid.
16. George Lipsitz, *The Possessive Investment in Whiteness: How White People Profit from Identity Politics* (Philadelphia: Temple University Press, 2006).
17. P. C. Johnson, "Reflections on Critical White(ness) Studies," in *Whiteness: The Communication of Social Identity*, ed. T.K. Nakayama and J. N. Martin (Thousand Oaks, CA: SAGE, 1999), 1–9.
18. Jeremy W. Bohonos, "Including Critical Whiteness Studies in the Critical Human Resource Development Family: A Proposed Theoretical Framework," *Adult Education Quarterly* (American Association for Adult and Continuing Education) 69, no. 4 (2019): 315–337: DOI: 10.1177/0741713619858131.
19. Barbara Perry and Michael Sutton, "Seeing Red Over Black and White: Popular and Media Representations on Inter-racial Relationships as Precursors to Racial Violence," *Canadian Journal of Criminology & Criminal Justice* 48, no. 11 (2006): 887–904.

20. Diane Railton and Paul Watson, "Naughty Girls and Red-Blooded Women: Representation of Female Heterosexuality in Music Video," *Feminist Media Studies* 5, no. 1 (2005): 51–63.

21. Kimberlé Crenshaw, "Mapping the Margins: Intersectionality, Identity Politics, and Violence Against Women of Color," *Stanford Law Review* 43, no. 6 (1991): 1241–1299.

22. Ibid.

23. Devon Carbado, "Colorblind Intersectionality," *Signs: Journal of Women in Culture and Society* 38, no. 4 (2013): 811–845.

24. Crenshaw, "Mapping the Margins."

25. Mike Cole, "Critical Race Theory Comes to the UK: A Marxist Response," *Ethnicities* 9, no. 2 (2009): 246–269, DOI: 10.1177/1468796809103462.

26. Delgado and Stefanic, *Critical Race Theory*.

27. Paul Warmington, "Critical Race Theory in England: Impact and Opposition," *Identities* 27, no. 1 (2020): 20–37: DOI: doi.org/10.1080/1070289X.2019.1587907.

28. Cole, "Critical Race Theory Comes to the UK."

29. Ibid.

30. Warmington, "Critical Race Theory in England."

31. David Gillborn and Paul Warmington, "An Unwelcome Guest? The Legitimate and Radical Place of CRT in England," Paper presented to the American Educational Research Association Annual meeting, Chicago, Illinois, 2015.

32. Warmington, "Critical Race Theory in England."

33. Crenshaw, "Mapping the Margins."

34. D. Hayes, "Teaching Students to Think Racially," *Spiked*, https://www.spikedonline.com/newsite/article/13459%23.WhffbjGDPIU.

35. Cole, "Critical Race Theory Comes to the UK."

36. Ibid.

37. Cerezo et al., "Giving Voice."

38. "Americans Who Have Heard of Critical Race Theory Don't Like It," *The Economist*, last modified, June 17, 2021, https://www.economist.com/graphic-detail/2021/06/17/americans-who-have-heard-of-critical-race-theory-dont-like-it.

39. Kent A. Ono, "What Is This 'Post,' in Postracial, Postfeminist . . . (Fill in the Blank)?," *Journal of Communication Inquiry* 34, no. 3 (2010): 210–253, DOI: 10.1177/0196859910371375.

40. "Jimmy Mubenga," *The Guardian*, https://www.theguardian.com/uk/jimmy-mubenga.

41. "Met Officers Involved in Deaths of Black Men et to be Interviewed Under Caution," *The Guardian*, https://www.theguardian.com/uk-news/2022/oct/01/met-officers-deaths-of-black-men-chris-kaba-oladeji-omishore-not-interviewed-under-caution.

42. Eduardo Bonilla-Silva, *Racism Without Racists: Color-Blind Racism and the Persistence of Racial Inequality in America* (Landham, MD: Rowman & Littlefield, 2017).

43. Derald Wing Sue et al., "Racial Microaggressions in Everyday Life: Implications for Clinical Practice," *American Psychologist* 62, no. 4 (2007): 271–286, DOI: 10.1037/0003-066X.62.4.271.

44. Bonilla-Silva, *Racism Without Racists*.

45. Tony Sewell, "No Evidence of Institutional Racism in UK, Says Report Commissioned by Government," Channel 4 News, March 31, 2021, video, 4:38, https://www.youtube.com/watch?v=JAsEZuDgjS8.

46. David Dabydeen, John Gilmore, and Cecily Jones, *The Oxford Companion to Black British History* (Oxford: Oxford University Press, 2007).

47. Paul Gilroy, *The Black Atlantic: Modernity and Double Consciousness* (Norfolk, UK: Biddles, 1993).
48. Sewell, "No Evidence of Institutional Racism in UK."
49. Ibid.
50. Ibid.
51. Leon Tikly, "Racial Formation and Education: A Critical Analysis of the Sewell Report," *Ethnicities*, online first (2022), DOI:10.1177/14687968211061882.
52. Vineet Kaul, "Representation of Social Issues in Films," *Madhya Pradesh Journal of Social Sciences* (2014), https://www.thefreelibrary.com/Representation+of+social+issues+in+films.-a0436230259.
53. Dawn Keetley, *Jordan Peele's Get Out: Political Horror* (Columbus: Ohio State University Press, 2020).
54. Elfriede Fürsich, "In Defense of Textual Analysis: Restoring a Challenged Method for Journalism and Media Studies," *Journalism Studies* 10, no. 2 (2009): 238–252, DOI: 10.1080/14616700802374050.
55. Sonja K. Foss, *Rhetorical Criticism: Exploration and Practice* (Long Grove, IL: Waveland Press, 1996).
56. Ruth Adams, "Home Sweet Home, That's Where I Come From, Where I Got My Knowledge of the Road and the Flow From" (Kano, "Home Sweet Home"): Grime Music as an Expression of Identity in Postcolonial London," *Popular Music and Society* 42, no. 4 (2019): 438–455, DOI: 10.1080/03007766.2018.1471774.
57. Weekes, "AAFCA Virtual Roundtable."
58. San Juanita Garcia, "Bridging Critical Race Theory and Migration: Moving beyond Assimilation Theories," *Sociology Compass* 11, no. 6 (2017): E12484-N/a.
59. Tia C. M. Tyree, Carolyn M. Byerly, and Kerry-Ann Hamilton, "Representations of (New) Black Masculinity: A News-Making Case Study," *Journalism* 13 (2012): 467–482, DOI: 10.1177/1464884911421695.
60. Weekes, *His House*.
61. Pawan Dhingra, The Racialization of 'Honorary Whites': Asian Americans and New Conceptions of Race," last modified, October 30, 2018, https://www.brown.edu/academics/race-ethnicity/events/pawan-dhingra-%E2%80%9C-racialization-%E2%80%98honorary-whites%E2%80%99-asian-americans-and-new-conceptions-race%E2%80%9D.
62. Delgado and Stefanic, *Critical Race Theory*.

....

CHAPTER 19

FROM *TALES FROM THE HOOD* TO *CANDYMAN*

Teaching Trauma Studies with Black Horror Cinema

....

COLLEEN KARN

TEACHING trauma studies, especially in general education courses, can prove to be extremely difficult due to the topic and because materials are multidisciplinary and sensitive in nature. However, pairing the study of trauma with monster studies along with Black horror cinema can not only ground the course in cultural studies but also focus it on important social issues. Exploring fictional trauma narratives within the context of related historical and contemporary social issues allows students to learn about trauma in the safe space of analyzing fiction before moving into the more difficult discussions of injustices in our society. Moreover, using popular culture, specifically monster stories and the narratives of Black horror cinema, provides students an access point into the complex and important topic of trauma, which can then lead to the praxis of trauma-engaged practices that students can apply to their lives, majors, and future careers. Please note, this chapter discusses only one of many ways to teach trauma and Black horror cinema.

RELEVANCE AND PRAXIS OF TRAUMA STUDIES

....

Before helping students develop a more critical understanding of trauma by working with them to connect the concepts to monster studies and apply them to cultural texts, it is crucial to foster student buy-in. Discussing the relevance and possible praxis of trauma studies to their lives, fields of study, and future careers more easily allows students to find value in the topic and lessons. For trauma studies, in particular, the development and deployment of trauma-informed and trauma-engaged practices and policies in different fields along with their positive outcomes provides effective examples of relevance and praxis. One such example—trauma-engaged education—comes from public-school systems.

A modern and pragmatic approach to trauma comes from various public-school systems in the United States, including the Alaska Department of Education and Early Development (ADEED) and the Chicago Public Schools (CPS). CPS defines trauma as "our response to an event, series of events, or set of circumstances that is experienced by an individual as physically or emotionally harmful or life threatening. Specifically, a traumatic experience overwhelms our ability to cope and has lasting negative effects on our functioning and mental, physical, social, emotional, or spiritual well-being."[1] Due to the large percentage of students who have experienced trauma, whether as victims or witnesses of violence, abuse, or neglect or through living in communities with systemic oppression and an ever-present threat of violence, both the ADEE and the CPS have created and instituted trauma-engaged programs throughout their public schools. What is trauma-engaged, and why is it important? "Trauma-engaged" is the latest and most advanced phase of dealing with trauma outside the clinical setting. Trauma-engaged incorporates and steps beyond the initial phase of "trauma-aware"—understanding and awareness of trauma—and the secondary phase of "trauma-informed" to create a more proactive and activist phase of trauma-engaged. Trauma-informed, though proactive in creating policies and practices to reduce triggers, foster autonomy, and replace judgmental and disciplinary actions with kindness and assistance, mostly attempts to mitigate trauma-inducing situations and trauma-induced behaviors. Conversely, a trauma-engaged approach does not just try to prevent or handle trauma. Rather, such an approach tries to change communities by de-stigmatizing trauma, advocating for community-centered healing, and assisting individuals with their personal wellness. Another aspect of a trauma-engaged program involves self-awareness. Gretchen Schmelzer, a psychologist who specializes in trauma, explains that being trauma-engaged requires "healing from our own trauma" in order to "support the healing of others."[2] This progression from trauma-aware to trauma-informed to trauma-engaged can align with pedagogical goals to move from awareness to empathy to advocacy, and, therefore, provides an effective model for students.

The people for whom trauma-engaged programs are developed commonly are victims of insidious, systemic, and/or generational trauma, all of which are what Schmelzer calls "repeated trauma."[3] Trauma-engaged programs, such as the one employed by the CPS, research and acknowledge the causes and effects of the trauma the people in their community face in order to, as a community, de-stigmatize, heal from, and stop the continuation of trauma. CPS explores the many ways trauma can be "transmitted across generations. For example, in Chicago, this includes the impact of redlining in creating segregated neighborhoods, racialized hiring practices that widen racial wealth gaps, and multi-generational incarceration."[4] Additionally, CPS analyzes how social conditions and local context combine as factors in the "systemic role" of "perpetuating trauma." The CPS document offers the following example: "in Chicago, minoritized racial and ethnic groups are disproportionately affected by trauma through experiences like chronic microaggressions; structural racial discrimination in policing; and poor social conditions such as poverty, housing instability, and community violence."[5] All of this analytical work is done in an effort to create programming that openly discusses the truths about trauma. Trauma-engaged programs help those who experience trauma, especially systemic and insidious trauma, understand that they are not alone and that their experiences are not their fault but the fault of an inequitable society. These steps help to de-stigmatize trauma, which opens the door to greater advocacy for engaging it. The CPS's materials for creating trauma-engaged schools not only furnish a relevant example of praxis but also, due to their setting and social commentary, directly relate to two cultural texts—*Candyman* (1992) and *Candyman* (2021)—that will be analyzed later in this chapter.

Trauma Studies

When approaching trauma studies from a cultural studies perspective, there are two important aspects that should be the foundation of the course curriculum. First, the course should provide a multi-disciplinary understanding of the history and concepts of trauma studies. Second, the course needs to provide cultural texts that depict trauma in their narratives and provide a framework by which to analyze and discuss the texts through the lens of trauma studies. Neither of these tasks is simple, as trauma studies and the cultural texts that depict trauma are complicated and require a thoughtful and sensitive approach. For the purpose of the first task, I have broken down trauma studies into the following accessible models: (1) the singular experience model, (2) the feminist model, and (3) the decolonized model. However, before exploring the models, students need to understand some of the key concepts and terminology related to trauma.

Concepts and Terminology

Trauma Narratives

Trauma narratives encompass everything from the testimonies of trauma victims to fictional narratives of trauma. Testimonies are a specific type of trauma narrative in which the direct victims or witnesses of trauma recount the experiences that produced the trauma. Fictional trauma narratives are cultural texts that, through design, depict a fictional trauma, often for the purpose of social commentary.

Witnessing

Witnessing directly relates to trauma narratives, as narratives need to have an audience, a witness. Witnessing, though, goes beyond merely reading, listening to, or viewing a trauma narrative. For testimony as well as fictional narratives, the listener, or audience, must be careful not to lose themselves in the experience, because they need to process the narrative critically and not just emotionally. This is especially important when it is a fictional narrative created or employed for the purpose of spotlighting and challenging injustices.

Intergenerational Trauma

Intergenerational trauma is the passing of trauma from one generation to the next. Intergenerational trauma can happen for various reasons and at different levels. At an individual level, not confronting and dealing with one's trauma can cause the victim to act in ways that reproduce the trauma for themselves and for others. Often, the traumatized are unaware of experiences that caused them trauma and of the effect those experiences have had on them. Nicolas Abraham and Maria Torok called these unknown traumas *phantoms*.[6] In intergenerational transmission of trauma, or phantoms, the traumatized unknowingly pass their trauma on to their children by the way they behave, especially when their children are young. On a cultural or community level, systemic trauma can influence the way cultures and communities are constructed, including their values, preferences, fears, etc., that one generation receives from the prior.

Insidious and Systemic Trauma

Insidious trauma, by the nature of its name, is trauma that gradually builds up until the effects are felt. This type of trauma often occurs due to microaggressions and stressful living conditions. Systemic trauma, such as systemic racism, is a type of insidious trauma that occurs on a societal scale in the form of discrimination, oppression, and violence.

TRAUMA STUDIES MODELS

Singular Experience Model

The singular experience model of trauma is based in Freudian psychoanalysis and given form and direction by Cathy Caruth and the Yale School. The model focuses on a single traumatic experience, though this can be experienced over a period of time, that lies "outside the range of human experience."[7] In other words, the ordeal is extraordinary, such as a severe accident, natural disaster, kidnapping, or active military combat. The incident, in this model, is so extreme that the brain cannot, or will not, encode it in one's memory as it would other experiences. Another important aspect of the singular experience model is the telling and witnessing of memory narratives. Adhering to the tenets of psychoanalysis, this model purports that recounting the memory of the traumatic experience to someone—testifying—is a crucial step in recovering from the trauma. As previously discussed, witnesses must balance being empathetic and remaining critical in their thinking. Additionally, the audience must be prepared for the magnitude and ways in which the narrative will affect them.

Feminist Model

Feminist approaches to trauma expand the definition and types of traumas beyond those in the single experience model. The feminist model recognizes commonly occurring trauma, such as domestic abuse, as well as insidious and systemic trauma. Laura Brown, in "Not Outside the Range: One Feminist Perspective on Psychic Trauma," presents a feminist perspective on traumatic stress that troubles the singular experience model and the DSM-3-R definition of a traumatic event. DSM-3-R states that, for a diagnosis of post-traumatic stress disorder (PTSD), the traumatic event must be extraordinary; it must be "outside the range of human experience."[8] This qualifier contradicts the inclusion of battered women and sexually abused women and children, because those experiences are not outside the range of human experience. Brown also notes that, in the early 1990s, the experiences that qualify as traumatic and outside normal human experience in both psychiatric manuals and scholarship on trauma are based on the experiences of men.[9] In addition to not including female-focused events, the approved traumata also do not produce stigma for the victims. In contrast, women who survive rape or incest not only carry the stigma of the trauma but are often blamed for their victimization. This feminist approach to trauma can be helpful in thinking about the traumas experienced by other marginalized populations. For example, Black Americans, who suffer from systemic trauma, are often blamed for the violence they encounter due to racism. The feminist model also troubles the single experience model by exposing our society's perpetuation of trauma. The feminist model of trauma recognizes that the dominant population cannot and will not see the trauma they cause, except for the trauma of which the dominant population are the victims. The feminist model delivers a call to action for us to be change agents in our communities and professions.

Decolonized Model

The decolonized model focuses on postcolonial and systemic trauma caused by racist oppression. Additionally, the model and its theories "redress the marginalization of non-Western and minority traumas," "challenge the supposed universal validity of Western definitions of trauma," and "provide alternatives to dominant trauma aesthetics."[10] The concept of racial trauma needs to be included in this model as well, because a central reason for postcolonial trauma is racism. Though there currently is not a clinical definition or prescribed treatment for it, Wendy Ashley, a trauma psychotherapist, explains that one of the major problems with racial trauma is our society's reluctance to recognize it: "In psychological fields, there is no diagnostic criteria for that. There is nowhere where it is written that people can receive treatment for this kind of lived experience, so it's not validated."[11] It is precisely this lack of validation that allows the trauma to continue. This relates back to the issues in the feminist model regarding our society refusing to acknowledge certain types of traumas because it would then have to own the responsibility for causing it.

Monster Studies and Black Horror Cinema

Monster Studies

Monster studies is a framework that can be employed to approach the cultural texts used to teach trauma studies. Pairing monster studies and trauma studies works well because monsters represent our fears and anxieties; they are what torments us. Monsters can symbolically represent the trauma—cause, effect, or both—of a single person or an entire community. Using Jeffrey Jerome Cohen's seven monster theses for theoretical and analytical guidance gives students an accessible lens through which to view fictional trauma narratives. Particularly for monster trauma narratives and, as I will discuss shortly, Black horror cinema, the following theses should prove the most beneficial: Thesis I: "The Monster's Body Is a Cultural Body"; Thesis II: "The Monster Always Escapes"; Thesis IV: "The Monster Dwells at the Gates of Difference"; and Thesis VII: "The Monster Stands at the Threshold . . . of Becoming."[12] Thesis I postulates that a monster is created by a certain culture, at a certain time, for a certain reason. The monster's body is "pure culture," and is constructed by a culture for the sole purpose of conveying meaning; "the monster exists only to be read."[13] Thesis I will aid in the discussion of trauma caused by or feared by a particular culture and can be used in conjunction with any of the three trauma models. Thesis II purports that our need for monsters is the reason they never truly die, even if killed in a cultural text. The monster escapes permanent termination because we bring them back to life in new cultural texts. The re-animated version of the monster will be slightly different each time, because the culture that constructs it is different each time, which directly relates back to Thesis I. Thesis II will be important in discussions of intergenerational and systemic trauma and especially important with the decolonized model. Additionally, when analyzing narratives with sequels, remakes, or transmediations, Thesis II demands a discussion about why the trauma has not gone away and why the monster is needed in a new form. Thesis IV examines a deceptively simple idea. The monster is the other, because a culture has inscribed the difference of an othered population upon it. "Any kind of alterity can be inscribed across (constructed through) the monstrous body, but for the most part monstrous difference tends to be cultural, political, racial, economic, sexual."[14] Thus, this monster of difference can be used to treat othered populations as monsters. Additionally, cultures, when needed for sociopolitical ends, can inscribe additional difference onto an already defined monster-other. This continual revision of the monster of difference gives the monster power to threaten the culture that created it, because it becomes living proof that difference is "mutable rather than essential."[15] Thesis IV will be particularly relevant in discussions of systemic and racial trauma and with the decolonized model. Thesis VII examines how the monsters a culture has created come back and, like Frankenstein's monster, ask their creators why they were created.

> And when they come back, they bring just not a fuller knowledge of our place in history and the history of knowing our place, but they bear self-knowledge, *human* knowledge—and a discourse all the more sacred as it arises from the Outside. . . . These monsters ask us to reevaluate our cultural assumptions about race, gender, sexuality, our perception of difference, our tolerance toward its expression.[16]

I will give examples of using these analytical lenses later in my discussion of *Tales from the Hood*, *Candyman* (1992), and *Candyman* (2021).

Black Horror Cinema

Black horror cinema provides a uniquely effective genre of cultural texts for the study of trauma. To begin with, horror films almost always depict traumatic situations (Martin Moorehouse being beaten by police and killed),[17] characters experiencing traumatic situations and dealing with the trauma from them (Laurie Strode battling Michael Myers and living with fear and paranoia),[18] or characters living with trauma from situations prior to the present narrative (Brianna witnessing her father's suicide).[19] Horror also "is one of the most intrepid of entertainment forms in its scrutiny of our humanity and our social world."[20] Coupling the trauma in the narratives and the critical commentary of our culture and society positions horror films at an intersection that can bring awareness to the types, causes, and effects of trauma in our society. Using Black horror cinema can be even more impactful, because it can bring some understanding of and conversations about systemic, intergenerational, and racial trauma that affect Black Americans and have not been validated in our society. Black horror cinema "can say so much about society and about history and racism,"[21] and students need to engage with what Black horror cinema is saying. Caruth, in her discussion of trauma narratives, claims that the other, who tells the narrative, "commands us to awaken" and to bear witness to the trauma.[22] It is this awakening to traumatic experiences, especially systemic trauma, that Black horror cinema can accomplish.

Using fictional narratives, specifically Black horror narratives, to teach students about trauma allows for conversations about the trauma in the narrative, the experience of the students witnessing the narrative, and the ways in which the students can employ trauma-engaged practices as an answer to the narrative's call for action. Though teaching trauma can be accomplished with nonfictional narratives and testimonies, fictional narratives provide both distance (students feeling safer knowing the story is fictional) and direction (the story purposefully presenting the trauma in a way to teach a lesson). Darin Scott purports that horror films actually make it easier for the audience to be open to the lesson: "You can take a societal issue. You can be subtle with it, or you can be more direct, but when it's put in the realm of sci-fi or the supernatural a lot of times people will consider an idea that they would've put a wall up in front of if you had just come at them directly or even in a direct drama. And then we can slip in a little message about, as Rusty [Cundieff] says, the real monsters that people face in real life, the abusers."[23] Additionally, horror narratives traditionally and fundamentally teach lessons about humanity and society. Rick Worland claims that a "significant dimension of the horror tale is its affinity for the lesson, often metaphysical, implicitly social. Though we will never encounter such unnaturally powerful monsters in the real world, such stories serve as parables or convey a sharp message of warning."[24] Therefore, I posit, it is horror, as a genre, that will effectively depict such trauma, so we, as a society, are moved to action instead of placation.

The audience of a horror film willingly takes on the identity of a collective witness to the film's fictional yet representational trauma. Viewing the film, the witnessing audience "partakes of the struggle of the victim" and "feels the victim's victories, defeats and silences."[25] As discussed earlier, this witnessing needs to be done in a reflective and critical manner, as to foster empathy and understanding while still analyzing what message about trauma in our society the film is conveying. Helping students keep this critical focus can be accomplished through pre-film discussions and assigning students prompts they need to respond to regarding the film. When creating the prompts, be sure to include a variety of prompts, some that ensure the student is paying attention and some that direct them to view the film through the critical lens of trauma and monsters. They need to remember that the film is part of a lesson and not fully lose themselves in it.

When viewing horror films, the monsters are not always easy for students to identify. Students will often look for the obvious monster, much like the ones Worland describes: "The monster is often a liminal figure, an uncertain amalgam or transitional form between living and dead; human and animal; male and female. The most potent character in the genre, the paradox of the monster is that it incites our fear, compels our attention, and quite often courts our empathy and fascination, even though it remains the most remote from any possible reality."[26] Though Worland's definition of a monster works for many horror films, the definition proves to be limited, as some monsters are fully human and not transitional forms, such as the abusive stepfather, Carl, in *Tales from the Hood*. Additionally, the real monsters, according to the lesson of some narratives, are not characters at all but monstrous beliefs and behaviors of society, such as the judgement and hatred shown to Frankenstein's monster. Additionally, those monstrous beliefs and behaviors can also be represented by a monster, like Candyman, who represents the horrors of racism. Moreover, the monsters are not always the villains. Some contemporary horror films have sympathetic monsters or even monster protagonists to teach lessons, such as that being a monster is a matter of perspective or the detrimental effects of monstrous others. However, it is important for students to identify the monsters in horror narratives, because the monsters are the key to understanding the lessons.

Another issue students may have with horror films involves their reaction to horrific scenes of violence and destruction. Precautions should be taken so students are not themselves traumatized by the horror narratives. First, prepare the students for what they will be viewing by discussing the types of violence in the film and details of specific scenes—better to spoil a scene than traumatize students. These discussions will not only lessen the horror of watching those scenes due to the shock being alleviated by the prior discussion but also serve as trigger warnings for students who may need to skip certain scenes for their own mental health. Second, scrutinize the films you plan to use. Use horror films that have a message that makes the horror worth watching. Tananarive Due ponders how to create a horror film with a message: "You have to entertain first, teach second. Right? How do we walk that line; how do we walk that line of creating the dread you need, the violence you need in a horror project without literally traumatizing the audience you're trying to service?"[27] Choose horror films that are careful about balancing entertainment and social messages about horror without overwhelming the audience. Horror films can accomplish this through minimizing the visual depiction of violent and traumatic events by telling the story instead of showing it—the trope of telling the horrific origin story of a monster or urban legend around a campfire or at a party, having the violence happen off-screen, like Greek tragedies did, or having only shadow images of the violence visible. Due praises *Candyman* (2021) for its focus on dread instead of violence and gore: "The puppet show is a perfect example of a way to convey a scene that's supposed to be violent without showing the violence."[28] Similarly, *Candyman* (1992) describes the violence of Daniel Robitaille (though he had no name other than Candyman in the first film) being lynched, mutilated, tortured, and killed in a storytelling of the ordeal with audio of the event being played in the background. Additionally, the story is depicted in murals painted on the walls of Candyman's lair. Though there are scenes of violence in both of those films, the most violent and traumatizing story—that of Robitaille's murder—is never directly shown. Additionally, Nia DaCosta, in *Candyman* (2021), had most of the actual violence occur in shadow, shot from far away, or off-screen with the audio conveying the violence. These films work well when teaching trauma through horror.

As discussed previously, Black horror cinema provides narratives that speak about the trauma the Black community has historically faced and still faces, from the perspective of Black filmmakers. The continued racism and violence against Black Americans have created a "collective mourning" in Black communities and "is a great concern to experts and medical professionals who consider the intersectionality of racism and various forms of trauma impacting communities of color a serious public health crisis facing America."[29] These "various forms of trauma" include racial trauma, intergenerational trauma, and systemic trauma. Racial trauma is "built upon centuries of oppressive systems and racist practices that are deeply embedded within the fabric of the nation. Racial trauma is a unique form of identity-related trauma that people of color experience due to racism and discrimination, according to Dr. Steven Kniffley."[30] The collective trauma of the Black communities must be validated before it can be rectified. A step in this direction is teaching trauma by using Black horror narratives.

Before analyzing Black horror films with a trauma lens, students need to study the history[31] and unique features of Black horror cinema. First, students need to distinguish between Blacks-in-horror films and Black horror films. Robin R. Means Coleman clearly delineates the two. " 'Blacks-in-horror' films present Blacks and Blackness in the context of horror, even if the horror film is not wholly or substantially focused on either one. Nevertheless, these films possess a particular discursive power in their treatment of Blackness."[32] Examples of such films are *The Shining* (1980), *Night of the Living Dead* (1968), and *Candyman* (1992). "Black horror films are informed by many of the same indicators of horror films, such as disruption, monstrosities, and fear. However, Black horror films are often 'race' films. That is, they have an added narrative focus that calls attention to racial identity, in this case Blackness—Black culture, history, ideologies, experiences, politics, language, humor, aesthetics, style, music, and the like."[33] Examples of such films are *Tales from the Hood* (1995), *Get Out* (2017), and *Candyman* (2021). "Perhaps most interesting for both types of films is when and how they variously position Blacks as the thing that horrifies, or as the victim or that which is horrified."[34]

Coleman touches on the second aspect of Black horror films that raises questions students need to consider. What does it mean when Black horror films have Black monsters, Black victims, or both? What does the Black monster represent, and why are particular Black characters killed or spared? Additionally, Black horror films incorporate elements of African American Gothic narratives, such as "rethinking questions of victimization, agency, collective memory, and cultural trauma,"[35] themes of revenge and retribution, and an unwillingness "to guarantee a happy ending."[36]

TEACHING WITH BLACK HORROR

I will be discussing three Black horror films, *Tales from the Hood*, *Candyman* (1992), and *Candyman* (2021), and effective ways to use them to teach trauma studies. I suggest starting with *Tales from the Hood* because it breaks down into four short stories, which permits a narrower focus to help students become accustomed to analyzing film narratives. Then, students should be ready to move on to a more complex analysis of *Candyman* (1992) and *Candyman* (2021). Each of the Candyman films should be examined on their own and then in relation to each other through a comparison and contrast approach. Before beginning lessons on any of the films, be sure to provide a brief synopsis of scenes that are extremely violent or could be triggering for students, as discussed earlier. Students should be prepared to watch the films by having lessons on the materials covered in the beginning of the chapter, as well as providing them with handouts of the three trauma models, the definitions of terms and concepts, the monster theses, the main aspects of Black horror cinema, and guided notes (the chapter appendix on assignments) with prompts for them to respond to. Additionally, I recommend having students watch the films as homework and not in the classroom. This gives students the opportunity to pause, rewind, restart the film as much as necessary to take notes, write down quotes, etc. Additionally, some students will feel safer watching the films in their own homes or with people they trust.

Tales from the Hood

Tales from the Hood is an anthology horror film like *Tales from the Crypt*, *Tales of Terror*, *Tales from the Darkside*, *Creepshow*, and many other films, television series, and comics. There is either a narrator who, breaking the fourth wall, speaks directly to the audience and introduces the episodes, or there is a wraparound story in which a character begins to tell the short story and then it cuts from the wraparound to the story being told. *Tales from the Hood* is the latter, with Mr. Simms, a mortician, telling stories to three young men who have come to buy a stash of drugs Mr. Simms claims to have found. Though the wraparound is a wonderful story in itself and Clarence Williams III's performance as Mr. Simms is phenomenal, for the sake of teaching trauma studies, focusing on the four individual episodes proves more effective. Each of the four episodes—"Rogue Cop Revelation," "Boys Do Get Bruised," "KKK Comeuppance," and "Hard-Core Convert"— features a specific type of traumatic situation. Additionally, each of the episodes, though fictional and enhanced with monsters, the supernatural, and science fiction, are based on nonfictional people, events, and circumstances. Cundieff and Scott purposefully create the episodes to represent and to convey lessons about injustices and trauma. Through the horror in the episodes, the injustices are addressed, and the perpetrators punished. Rusty Cundieff comments on the film using the genre of horror, which historically vilified and monstrified Black people, to now atone for the injustices, "We've got to turn the tables and make the horror redemptive."[37] Ashlee Blackwell responds to the justice for Black people that takes place in the film: "This movie is kind of like helping us see justice happening when we're not seeing it happen outside of a movie screen or a movie theatre. There's cops being acquitted, and there's LA riots, and it just seems like things are so hopeless, but then you kind of like exercise retribution in a horror film for, you know, for justice, for racial justice." Though I advocate for teaching all of the episodes in the film and have provided guided notes and an assignment for them in the appendix, I will only use the last story, "Hard-Core Convert," as an example of how to analyze the situations, monsters, and Black horror cinema aspects of the film.

In the episode "Hard-Core Convert," Jerome, aka Crazy K, a young Black male gang member, is arrested by police after being shot in retaliation for killing a rival gang member. Crazy K is in prison when Dr. Cushing offers him the opportunity to be released if he completes rehabilitation therapy. Crazy K agrees and is taken to the dungeon of a creepy castle. The dungeon contains rows of small cages, reminiscent of those in an animal shelter. Guards throw Crazy K into a cage next to a white suprema- cist who thanks Crazy K for doing his work for him by killing other Black people. Later, Crazy K is taken to Dr. Cushing's laboratory for his treatment. Dr. Cushing attempts to re-program Crazy K to stop killing his own people. Crazy K is strapped down and force-fed a green liquid. He is subjected to an "optical sequence" that alternates be- tween images of Black gang violence and racist hatred, violence, and murder of Black people by the KKK and other white people, ultimately showing there is no dif- ference between the results. Then Dr. Cushing puts Crazy K into a sensory depriva- tion chamber. A strobe light comes on, and Crazy K is confronted by the people he has murdered. He shows no remorse and takes no responsibility for his actions. Dr. Cushing is unsuccessful.

Though it might seem, at first, as if the traumatic experience in the episode is that of Crazy K being tortured in order to try to cure him, the more prominent trauma is that of the Black community suffering from the fear and violence that gang activity and the lack of value for human life causes. To more effectively analyze the episode, it needs to be put into the context of monster culture. The episode clearly alludes to *Frankenstein* and its many transmediated film versions. The character of Dr. Cushing is named after actor Peter Cushing, who starred in nineteen Hammer horror films and performed as Victor Frankenstein in six of the seven Hammer Frankenstein films. If Dr. Cushing is the mad scientist, Victor Frankenstein, then Crazy K is the monster. Crazy K falls into the cate- gory of the human-made monster, not that he was physically put together by a human, like Frankenstein's monster was, but human-made in the sense that his society created him. One of the dilemmas in the *Frankenstein* narrative is that Frankenstein's creature acts monstrously only after being treated like a monster by society. However, he is intel- ligent enough to know that his actions, specifically killing innocent people, are wrong, and he is remorseful in the end. In "Hard-Core Convert," Dr. Cushing tries to unmake the monster society created by re-programming Crazy K to repent for his actions and see that he needs to stop the violence. After Crazy K has been confronted by the people he killed, the last being a little girl who was shot while playing in her room, he and Dr. Cushing have the following exchange:

"I don't owe no responsibilities for these motherfuckers."

"But you are responsible for the lives you've taken, for the dreams you've turned into nightmares."

"Nightmares? Motherfucker, what about my nightmare? What about the night- mare I lived in? What about the nightmare I lived in ever since I was born in this motherfucker? Who's responsible for that?"

"I don't know, Jerome. You tell me. Who is responsible? Your mother? Your father? Your teachers? The world? Who?"

"Yeah, that's right. All of them motherfuckers cause they created me. So now I'm a motherfucking nightmare."

"The nightmare ends when you say it does, Jerome. You've got to take responsibility to wake up. You've got to take responsibility to break this chain!"

"I've got one motherfucking responsibility in this world, and that's me."[38]

Unfortunately, Dr. Cushing fails in her efforts to rehabilitate Crazy K. However, Crazy K, as the monster of the story, does his job by conveying a clear message to the audience that the violence must stop. Rusty Cundieff discusses how the movie and specifically "Hard-Core Convert" made an impact on their audience, "We want to be entertaining, but we actually had some teaching moments. I've had gang members come up to me say that they rethought what they were doing because of the Crazy K episode."[39] Additionally, according to Darin Scott: "The more important thing to us about that story was just commenting on Black on Black violence, and the fact that we've spent three or four hundred years with being oppressed and being attacked; it's a good time to stop oppressing and attacking each other. I think that's why it's been inspirational to some people to be able to see the irony of the way they're living their lives."[40]

Cohen's monster Thesis I, "The Monster's Body Is a Cultural Body," helps to explain how and why Cundieff and Scott created the character of Crazy K to achieve their goals. Crazy K is not just a gang member; he represents all the young Black men who, due to their circumstances, turn to violence to protect themselves and then end up perpetuating the culture of oppression and violence. Both the causes and effects of that cyclical, intergenerational trauma are the fears and anxieties of the Black community, which is why Cundieff and Scott created Crazy K. However, please note that, though the filmmakers both present and discuss that violence against Black people at the hands of white supremacists has the same outcome—the oppression and death of Black people—as violence against Black people at the hands of Black gang members, those are not nec-essarily equivalent. Be prepared, if necessary, to discuss how audiences can resist what filmmakers present as "facts."

Candyman (1992)

Bernard Rose's 1992 horror film, Candyman, based on the Clive Barker short story "The Forbidden," offers a variety of traumatic situations for discussion. Many characters—Helen Lyle, Anne-Marie McCoy, Candyman, and the residents of Cabrini-Green—are affected by horrific circumstances. Since the film is a Blacks-in-horror film, it is not sur-prising that the main trauma we follow throughout the film is that of the white protag-onist, Helen Lyle. Though Helen endures a variety of traumas, such as being attacked, being framed for murder, losing control over her own life, etc., it is the betrayal and abandonment by her husband that leads to her becoming a vengeful entity after her death, as evidenced by the fact that it is Trevor she kills at the end of the film. After Helen is arrested and locked up in a psychiatric ward, Trevor gives up on helping her and has his student, with whom he has been cheating on Helen from the beginning of the film, move into his and Helen's home. When Helen escapes from the psychiatric ward, she makes her way back home and finds her replacement re-decorating the apartment. It may seem odd that Trevor cheating on her would cause the most trauma to Helen. However, "trauma can also take the form of interpersonal betrayal; recent research has indicated that betrayal is a more potent risk factor for posttraumatic stress disorder (PTSD) than is life threat. Betrayal traumas are especially likely to occur in relationships of care, trust, and dependency."[41] Though the film focuses on Helen's experiences, Candyman's trauma proves to be the most poignant in the narrative.

Candyman's lynching and murder takes place over a hundred years before the events in the film. The horror of the lynching is shown in the murals Candyman painted on the walls of his lair, not in actual scenes. This artistic representation allows for distancing. A similar concept is used in the 2021 film, when shadow puppets depict the brutal, racially motivated killings of several different Black men. In Bernard Rose's 1992 production, Phillip Purcell, a white professor, tells the story of Candyman through a white, yet somewhat sympathetic, lens:

> The legend first appeared in 1890. Candyman was the son of a slave. His father had amassed a fortune from designing a device for the mass producing of shoes after the Civil War. Candyman had been sent to the best schools and had grown up in polite society. He had a prodigious talent as an artist and was much sought after when it came to the documenting of one's wealth and position in society in a portrait. It was in this latter capacity he was hired by a rich landowner to capture his daughter's virginal beauty. Of course, they fell deeply in love, and she became pregnant. Poor Candyman. Her father executed a terrible revenge. He paid a pack of brutal hooligans to do the deed. They chased Candyman through the town to Cabrini Green, where they proceeded to saw off his right hand with a rusty blade, and no one came to his aid. But this was just the beginning of his ordeal. Nearby there was an apiary. Dozens of hives filled with hungry bees. They smashed the hives and stole the honeycomb and smeared it over his prone, naked body. Candyman was stung to death by the bees. They burned his body on a giant pyre, then scattered his ashes over Cabrini Green.

Candyman (who is never given a name in the film, though in later films his name is revealed to be Daniel Robitaille), due to the extreme nature of his death, becomes an immortal monster fueled by the hatred of racism who punishes those who doubt him. Isabel Cristina Pinedo succinctly explains Candyman: "The monster of *Candyman* is a product of white racism."[42] Moreover, Brigid Cherry purports that Candyman "elicits sympathy as a victim of racism."[43] Candyman in many ways is the antihero of the film, as audiences find him both sympathetic and entrancing. Discussing Black antiheroes, Worland claims that even though Blaxploitation horror films were mainly produced, written, and directed by white men, the films' antiheroes, such as Blacula, "remain highly sympathetic throughout."[44] Similar to the antiheros of the Blaxploitation horror films, Candyman, the Black monster in a Blacks-in-horror film, is a sympathetic character. Coleman expounds upon this to note that "Candyman is to be viewed as a tragic, wounded monster, perhaps *Frankenstein*-esque in that he was created, made by folks far more terrible than he is. However, the film strays from the monster-with-a-heart-of-gold theme by playing on fears of the big Black boogeyman coming in and taking away a White woman."[45] Ashlee Blackwell concurs with Coleman: "We have this movie that echoes what happened in *King Kong* in the '30s. There is this Black boogeyman, and he's in pursuit of this blonde, White woman."[46] Despite being a sympathetic character, Candyman also represents society's fear of Black men, which Cherry notes was the anxiety in the United States during the 1990s.[47] Candyman "is the personification of racism in the United States."[48] Looking at Candyman through the lens of Thesis I, "The Monster's Body Is a Cultural Body," Candyman, as the monster of the narrative, was created by Rose to both reflect white society's fear of Black men and comment on the injustice and horror of racism, which makes Candyman a complicated and complex character. This complexity is also seen in Candyman's trauma. Candyman's lynching and murder clearly classify as a singular event beyond the normal scope of human experience, and the extreme nature of this ordeal is the cause of his rebirth as a monster. However, it is the ongoing systemic trauma of racist oppression that sustains Candyman and gives him power—a theme that is even more prominent in DaCosta's 2021 production.

Candyman (2021)

Nia DaCosta's 2021 *Candyman* is a continuation of the story that began in Bernard Rose's 1992 *Candyman*, and it seemingly disregards the happenings in the two previous *Candyman* sequels, *Candyman: Farewell to the Flesh* (1995) and *Candyman: Day of the Dead* (1999). The film was written by DaCosta along with Jordan Peele and Win Rosenfeld. They wanted to tell the Candyman story from the Black perspective. In other words, they wanted to evolve it from being a Blacks-in-horror film to a Black horror film. This shift in perspective created a powerful vehicle for portraying, through fictional horror, the true horror of racist trauma in the United States. As in Rose's film, there are a variety of traumatic situations and multiple characters who experience trauma. Unlike Rose's film, DaCosta's film gives us two adults, Brianna and William, who were subjected to terrifying experiences as children. Brianna had lost her father to suicide, and William must cope with the murder of Sherman, a man mistakenly identified by police as the Candyman killer, and then the murder of his sister by Sherman's Candyman. How each of the characters is affected by and deals with their childhood proves fascinating and should be included in discussions with students. However, for the sake of being able to compare and contrast the films, I am going to once again focus on the trauma Candyman suffers in the film.

The opening credits signal to the audience, especially if they have seen *Candyman* (1992), that the perspective of the film has changed since that earlier film. A view of Chicago is seen from the point of view of someone on the street looking up, while in the 1992 film, the opening credits are shot from above, looking down on the streets. There is a shift from what is happening in the city being the subject of an observer looking down, to that of the people actually living there. Additionally, this new telling is from a Black perspective, which is made clear when a Black character who actually lives in Cabrini-Green, William Burke, tells the tale of Candyman to Anthony McCoy. McCoy asks Burke, "What is he?" To which Burke replies, "Candyman ain't a *he*. Candyman's the whole damn hive." McCoy asks, "There are others?" and Burke replies with the tale of Candyman that explains how he is a conglomeration of many Black men murdered due to racism and hatred:

> Samuel Evans, run down during the White housing riots of the '50s. William Bell, lynched in the '20s. But the first one, where it all began, was in the 1890s. It's a story Helen found. The story of Daniel Robitaille. (The visual shifts to shadow puppets acting out the story.) He'd made a living touring the country painting portraits for wealthy families, mostly white, and they loved him. But you know how it goes. They love what we make but not us. One day, he's commissioned to paint the daughter of a Chicago factory owner, who made his fortune in the stockyards. Well, Robitaille committed the ultimate sin of his time. They fell in love. They had an affair, she got pregnant. The girl tells her father, and, well, you know. He hires some men to hunt Robitaille down, told them to get creative. Chased him through here in the middle of the day. He collapses from exhaustion right near where the old tower in Chestnut used to be. They beat him; tortured him. They cut off his arm and jammed a meat hook in the stump. They smeared honeycomb from the nearby hives on his chest and let the bees sting him. A crowd started to form to watch the show. The big finale: they set him on fire, and he finally dies. But a story like that, a pain like that, lasts forever. That's Candyman.[49]

Burke's version of the legend, in contrast to Purcell's, introduces a Candyman who is not a single Black man who was tortured and murdered but a creature who embodies a multitude of Black men who have died at the hands of racist oppressors. This version of Candyman plainly moves from the single experience trauma model to the decolonized model, as he is a product of historical, systemic, racist trauma. Jordan Peele, one of the writers and producers of the film, explains that "Candyman is, in essence, it's an allegory for racism in America. We tried to bring out the connection with that fact that there's an epidemic of violence on Black people in the country. Candyman can't just be singular. He's a concept; he's a story; he's a boogeyman, and that means he applies across the boundaries of time. He's eternal."[50] As an allegory for racism and a mosaic of murdered Black men, this new rendition of Candyman requires not only a more contemporary and complex model of trauma but multiple and more complex monster theses.

Several of Cohen's monster theses apply to DaCosta's version of Candyman. Thesis I, "The Monster's Body Is a Cultural Body," can be used similarly to Rose's version. However, Thesis II, "The Monster Always Escapes," works well with this iteration of the Candyman monster precisely because DaCosta, Peele, and Rosenfeld brought him back to life because they needed him. DaCosta discusses Candyman's continued relevance and necessity: "The story of Candyman is so perennial, and that's part of the reason it's exciting to tell it at any time period. The cycles of violence and how history repeats itself and how we collectively grieve and process trauma which is through stories. It's a time to tell a story like Candyman which is kind of a big tragedy of the tale in the first place."[51] Moreover, Peele explains how the racial horror Candyman is born from mutates over time: "The very question of this eternal dance between monster and victim, the racial history of this county is at the center of this movie. There's a perpetualness to the story of racial horror in this country. It doesn't go away. It changes shape, and it changes form, and it's elusive, and it's sneaky, right?"[52] Just as the racial horror changes, so does the monster who embodies it. Even more interesting is how the latest Candyman troubles the society that first created him. Using Thesis IV, "The Monster Dwells at the Gates of Difference," helps to examine how Candyman, being alterable from his 1992 to his 2021 form, can recognize his mutability and use it to threaten the society that created him. Candyman in his latest form changes his narrative and function as a monster from terrorizer to champion of his people, as evidenced by the most recent rendition of Candyman only killing those who deserved to be punished for the atrocities of racism. Additionally, Thesis VII, "The Monster Stands at the Threshold . . . of Becoming," can be employed to discuss how this new Candyman overtly demands the attention of society and forces it to confront the horrors of racism.

In all the research I conducted for this chapter, the most moving moment comes at the end of the bonus feature, "*Candyman*: The Impact of Black Horror." Tony Todd is talking about what Candyman is: "It's a carrion cry. It's an eternal scream. It's a person that says 'I'm no longer going to take this, and I no longer care about the consequences. Callousness, lack of empathy, right is right and wrong is wrong.'"[53] Then Todd speaks from his heart and says, "I wish that Candyman didn't have to exist."[54] This statement is followed by Todd trying to say something more but being unable to due to being overwhelmed by emotion thinking about the continuing violence and trauma happening in Black communities. The approximately six seconds of Todd's sadness and anguish were more difficult to watch, for me, than the entirety of the film. Todd was testifying, and I was witnessing. I felt some measure of his pain, but I know I will never truly understand it. The most I can do is help students recognize the violence and injustices and try to be part of a trauma-engaged solution to help those who are traumatized and change our culture.

FINAL THOUGHTS

Teaching trauma studies, though rewarding for both the instructor and students, can be fraught with pitfalls and uncomfortable discussions. Do not let that dissuade you. Those difficult moments are teaching moments for the students and for you as an instructor, especially when you work through them together. Some additional Black horror narratives that would be effective for teaching trauma are *Get Out* (2017), *Halloween: Resurrection* (2002), *The Curse of La Llorona* (2019), *The Last Wave* (1977), and *Lovecraft*

Country (2020). Unfortunately, with the exception of the pedagogical materials provided by Langston League for *Candyman* and *Lovecraft Country*, scholarship and
materials for teaching Black horror films are practically nonexistent, despite entire
books being dedicated to the teaching of horror. However, there are some wonderful
resources about Black horror films, such as *Horror Noire: A History of Black American
Horror from the 1890s to Present*,[55] *The Black Guy Dies First: Black Horror from Fodder to
Oscar*,[56] *Jordan Peele's Get Out: Political Horror*,[57] *Pleading the Blood: Bill Gunn's Ganja
& Hess*,[58] "Blaxploitation Horror Films: Generic Reappropriation or Reinscription?",[59]
"Fear of a Blaxploitation Monster: Blackness as Generic Revision in AIP's *Blacula*,"[60]
and "The Blood of the Thing (Is the Truth of the Thing): Viral Pathologies and Uncanny
Ontologies in *Ganja and Hess*."[61] Teaching Black horror films, especially from a global
perspective, can continue to raise awareness of and inspire advocacy and action against
the real-life horrors acted upon Black bodies and Black cultures.

APPENDIX: ASSIGNMENTS

GUIDED NOTES: *TALES FROM THE HOOD*

For each of the four short stories, respond to the following prompts. Be thorough, provide specific examples from the stories, and use course material for support.

1. Describe each of the main characters. What is their function in the story?
   - "Rogue Cop Revelation" main characters: Martin Moorehouse, Clarence Smith,
     Newton (Clarence's partner), Strom (lead police officer), and Billy (Strom's
     partner)
   - "Boys Do Get Bruised" main characters: Walter Johnson, Mr. Garvey (Walter's
     Teacher), Sissy (Walter's Mother), and Carl (Walter's Stepfather)
   - "KKK Comeuppance" main characters: Duke Metger, Rhodie Willis, Eli (man
     who warns about the dolls), Miss Cobbs, and Doll
   - "Hard-Core Convert" main characters: Jerome Johns aka Crazy K, Dr. Cushing,
     and White Supremist (in cage next to Crazy K)
2. What type of monster(s) are in the story? Why and how are they monsters?
3. Which of Cohen's monster theses apply to the story? List each one and give a brief
   analysis of the story using each thesis listed.
4. Is this story Blacks-in-horror or Black horror? Explain and support.
5. Are Black characters the cause or victim of the horror, or both? What is the significance of this? What commentary is being made with these narrative choices?
   Explain and support.

6. List the traumatic situations in the story. For each of the situations respond to the following prompts:
   - Describe the traumatic situation.
   - What model(s) of trauma does it belong in? Why? Explain and support.
   - What are the causes of the trauma? Explain and support.
   - What are the effects of the trauma? Explain and support.
   - What role does the monster(s) play in the traumatic situation? What commentary is being made with the monster regarding the trauma? Explain and support.
   - What is the significance of the trauma narrative being in the genre of Black horror cinema? Explain and support.

ESSAY: *TALES FROM THE HOOD*

Type of Project

This project is a standard written essay.

Description of Project

Each of the four short stories depicts different types of trauma. Students will be assigned one of the four short stories to focus on for this paper. Discuss the trauma by addressing all the following prompts for your assigned story. The overarching concept for this essay can simply be what an audience can learn about trauma from the film. The purpose is to begin analyzing trauma narratives. Students will be put in groups with peers, at least one student who wrote on each of the four stories, to peer edit and discuss.

- What traumatic situations take place in the story? What types of traumas are depicted? Use the terms, concepts, and models of trauma to discuss this.
- What are the causes of the trauma? Be sure to discuss the individual perpetrators and societal and cultural causes.
- What are the effects of the trauma? Be sure to discuss the effects on the direct victims and on specific communities, societies, and cultures.
- What lesson about trauma and society can the audience learn from the story?

Specifications of Project

- Paper: minimum of 1,000 words, MLA, APA, or Chicago Style (12 pt. Times New Roman font)
- Project: equivalent of 1,000-word paper, MLA, APA, or Chicago Style

GROUP PROJECTS: *TALES FROM THE HOOD*

Type of Project

Group presentation using PowerPoint, Google Slides, or some other multimedia platform. The class will be split into four groups. Each group will be assigned one of the four episodes in the film.

Description of Project

Each of the four episodes, though fictional and enhanced with monsters, the supernatural, and science fiction, are based on nonfictional people, events, and circumstances. Using the focus points provided below for the episode, create a presentation about the nonfictional traumatic inspirations for the episode.

Focus Points for Each Episode

"Rogue Cop Revelation"

- Strom, according to Cundieff and Scott, is a representation of the deputy, Cecil Price, who was instrumental in getting three civil rights workers murdered by the KKK in Mississippi in 1964. Research that incident.
- Strom is named for Strom Thurman, a senator who opposed civil rights. Research Strom Thurman.
- How is the historical trauma of the civil rights area tied to and represented in the episode, even though the story in the episode takes place in the 1990s?

"Boys Do Get Bruised"

- Bullying is depicted in the episode. Research bullying.
- Domestic abuse is depicted in the episode. Research domestic abuse.
- Mr. Garvey recognizes that abuse is happening and tries to help Walter. Research the training, responsibilities, limitations, etc. of public school teachers when it comes to abused children.
- Research trauma-informed and trauma-engaged school practices.

"KKK Comeuppance"

- The character of Duke Metger is based on David Duke and Tom Metzger. Research Duke and Metzger.

- In the story, Duke Metger is a former KKK member. Research the KKK.
- The episode has a lot to do with testament and validation. The plantation house and the mural of Miss Cobbs with the dolls that contain the souls of the murdered slaves are a monument, a testament to not only the massacre of the slaves in that house but to the atrocities of slavery. Duke Metger, by living in the house and saying that after the election he is going to paint over the mural of Miss Cobbs and the dolls, threatens to erase and invalidate the history and truth of slavery and racism. Research real-life attempts to erase the history of slavery and racism. Research the need to remember injustices, inhumane treatment, and societal/cultural atrocities.

"Hard-Core Convert"

- The film clearly alludes to *Frankenstein*. The character of Dr. Cushing is named after actor Peter Cushing, who performed in 19 Hammer horror films. He performed as Victor Frankenstein in 6 of 7 of Hammer's Frankenstein films. One of the dilemmas in the *Frankenstein* narrative is that Frankenstein's creature (or monster, if you prefer) acts monstrously only after being treated like a monster by society. However, he is intelligent enough to know that it is wrong for him to kill people. However, he still makes the choice to kill. Crazy K can be compared to Frankenstein's creature. Discuss the difference between actions being understandable and being acceptable. Research when, legally, people are old enough to be held responsible for their actions, even if they are victims of trauma.
- Gang violence in Black communities is central to this episode. Research gang violence in Black communities. Be sure to research the historic and systemic causes.
- Living with the constant threat of violence can lead to suicide. Suicide is the third leading cause of death for young Black males in America. Research this.

Specifications of Project

- Sources must be cited in the material on the slides, and a reference slide must be provided at the end of the presentation.
- May use MLA, APA, or Chicago Style for documentation.
- Each group member must present an equal share of the presentation.
- Presentation must be 15–20 minutes in length.

TAKEAWAY REFLECTION: *TALES FROM THE HOOD*

Write a reflection (minimum of 250 words) on what you can take away from studying the film and doing the projects. Consider and write about the following:

- What did you learn?
- How can you use what you learned in your everyday life?
- How can you use what you learned in your academic endeavors?
- How can you use what you learned in your future career?

GUIDED NOTES: *CANDYMAN* (1992)

1. Describe each of the main characters. What is their function in the story?
   - Candyman
   - Helen Lyle
   - Bernadette Walsh
   - Trevor Lyle
   - Philip Purcell
   - Anne-Marie McCoy
   - Jake
2. What type of monster(s) are in the story? Why and how are they monsters?
3. Which of Cohen's monster theses apply to the story? List each one and give a brief analysis of the story using each thesis listed.
4. Is this story Blacks-in-horror or Black horror? Explain and support.
5. Are Black characters the cause or victim of the horror, or both? What is the significance of this? What commentary is being made with these narrative choices? Explain and support.
6. List the major traumatic situations in the film. Be sure to include Candyman's trauma, Helen's trauma from Candyman and from Trevor, Anne-Marie's trauma, and Jake's trauma. For each of the situations respond to the following prompts:
   - Describe the traumatic situation.
   - What model(s) of trauma does it belong in? Why? Explain and support.
   - What are the causes of the trauma? Explain and support.
   - What are the effects of the trauma? Explain and support.
   - What role does the monster(s) play in the traumatic situation? What commentary is being made with the monster regarding the trauma? Explain and support.
   - What is the significance of the trauma narrative being in the genre of Black horror cinema? Explain and support.
7. Pay attention to the opening credits. What do you see? What perspective is it from? (This will be important in the comparison and contrast with the 2021 film.)
8. Who tells the tale of Candyman? What is the significance of who tells it? How is the tale told; what is the attitude and tone?
9. When the tale of Candyman is told, what does the audience see and hear? Why might the tale be conveyed in this manner?
10. How is Cabrini-Green depicted in the film?

11. This film was written, directed, and produced by White filmmakers. What is the importance of this perspective when it comes to the story, message, and commentary about racism and trauma in the film?

GUIDED NOTES: *CANDYMAN* (2021)

1. Describe each of the main characters. What is their function in the story?
   - Anthony McCoy
   - Brianna Cartwright
   - William Burke
   - Troy Cartwright
   - Sherman Fields
   - Daniel Robitaille
   - Candyman (the conglomerate/amalgamation)
2. What type of monster(s) are in the story? Why and how are they monsters?
3. Which of Cohen's monster theses apply to the story? List each one and give a brief analysis of the story using each thesis listed.
4. Is this story Blacks-in-horror or Black horror? Explain and support.
5. Are Black characters the cause or victim of the horror, or both? What is the significance of this? What commentary is being made with these narrative choices? Explain and support.
6. List the major traumatic situations in the film. Be sure to include the trauma of the following characters: Anthony McCoy, Brianna Cartwright, William Burke, Sherman Fields, and Daniel Robitaille, and Candyman. For each of the situations respond to the following prompts:
   - Describe the traumatic situation.
   - What model(s) of trauma does it belong in? Why? Explain and support.
   - What are the causes of the trauma? Explain and support.
   - What are the effects of the trauma? Explain and support.
   - What role does the monster(s) play in the traumatic situation? What commentary is being made with the monster regarding the trauma? Explain and support.
   - What is the significance of the trauma narrative being in the genre of Black horror cinema? Explain and support.
7. Pay attention to the opening credits. What do you see? What perspective is it from? (This will be important in the comparison and contrast with the 1992 film.)
8. Who tells the tale of Candyman? What is the significance of who tells it? How is the tale told; what is the attitude and tone?
9. When the tale of Candyman is told, what does the audience see and hear? Why might the tale be conveyed in this manner?

10. Troy tells the tale of Helen Lyle. How does it differ from the events in the 1992 film? Why do you think the events in the tale told by Troy are different?
11. How is Cabrini-Green depicted in the film?
12. This film was written, directed, and produced by Black filmmakers. What is the importance of this perspective when it comes to the story, message, and commentary about racism and trauma in the film? How has the message and commentary about racism and trauma changed from the 1992 film to this one?

ANALYTICAL PROJECT: *CANDYMAN* FILMS

FROM "BE MY VICTIM" TO "SAY MY NAME": COMPARING AND CONTRASTING TALES OF TRAUMA

Type of Project

This project can be a standard written essay or a multimedia project (PowerPoint, Video, Paper with images and hyperlinks, Blog, etc.).
   If you choose the multimedia project:

- the thoroughness must match that of a written essay
- any audio narration must have a written transcript with citations
- the same source requirements as the paper must be met.

Description of Project

- Frame the comparison and contrast of the films with:
  o the 1992 film being a Blacks-in-horror film and the 2021 film being a Black horror film
  o the racism and trauma of the 1992 film being through a White lens and the 2021 film being through a Black lens
- Compare and contrast the traumas and journeys of Helen Lyle and Anthony McCoy
- Compare and contrast the depiction of Candyman, as a character, and his trauma in the two films—use the monster theses to assist you with this.
- Compare and contrast the types of traumas and the causes and effects of the trauma in the films.
- Compare and contrast the overarching messages of the films.

Specifications of Project

- Paper: minimum of 1,250 words, MLA, APA, or Chicago Style (12 pt. Times New Roman font)
- Project: equivalent of 1,250-word paper, MLA, APA, or Chicago Style
- Sources:
  - o *Must* use a minimum of four scholarly sources not provided to you for the course (find some on your own)
  - o May use, in addition to the four sources you find on your own, sources provided to you for the course
  - o *Must* use both *Candyman* films (1992 and 2021)
  - o May use bonus materials on the *Candyman* (1992 and 2021) DVD/BD
  - o May use *Horror Noire* documentary.

Takeaway Reflection: *Candyman*

Write a reflection (minimum of 500 words) on what you can take away from studying the Candyman films and doing the project. Consider and write about the following:

- What did you learn?
- How can you use what you learned in your everyday life?
- How can you use what you learned in your academic endeavors?
- How can you use what you learned in your future career?
- How can you be an advocate for people who experience trauma?
- How could you incorporate the concept of trauma-engaged in your community and in your future career?

Notes

1. Chicago Public Schools, *Chicago Public Schools' Healing-Centered Framework: Creating a Trauma-Engaged and Culturally-Responsive School District* (Chicago: Chicago Public Schools, 2021), 8. All subsequent citations will use the abbreviation CPS for Chicago Public Schools.
2. Gretchen Schmelzer, "Trauma Engaged Nation," February 11, 2021, http://gretchenschmel zer.com/blog-1/2021/2/11/trauma-engaged-nation.
3. Ibid.
4. CPS, *Healing-Centered Framework*, 11.
5. Ibid.
6. Maria Yassa, "Nicolas Abraham and Maria Torok—The Inner Crypt," *The Scandinavian Psychoanalytic Review* 25, no. 2 (September 2002): 83, https://doi.org/10.1080/01062 301.2002.10592734.

7. American Psychiatric Association, *American Psychiatric Association: Diagnostic and Statistical Manual of Mental Disorders*, 3rd ed., revised (Arlington, TX: American Psychiatric Publishing, 1987), 250.

8. Ibid.

9. Laura S. Brown, "Treating the Effects of Psychological Trauma," in *Psychologists' Desk Reference*, 3rd ed., ed. Gerald P. Koocher, John C. Norcross, and Beverly A. Greene (New York: Oxford University Press, 2013), 121.

10. Sonya Andermahr, "'Decolonizing Trauma Studies: Trauma and Postcolonialism'— Introduction." *Humanities* 4, no. 4 (2015): 501.

11. Coleman et al., "*Candyman*: The Impact of Black Horror." *Candyman*. Universal City, CA: Studio Distribution Services, 2021, Blu-ray Disc.

12. Jeffrey Jerome Cohen, "Monster Culture (Seven Theses)," in *Monster Theory: Reading Culture*, ed. Jeffrey Jerome Cohen (Minneapolis: University of Minnesota Press, 1996), 4–20.

13. Ibid., 4.

14. Ibid., 7.

15. Ibid., 12.

16. Ibid., 20 (emphasis in original).

17. "Rogue Cop Revelation," *Tales from the Hood*, directed by Rusty Cundieff (1995; Los Angeles: Shout Factory, 2017) collector's ed. Blu-ray Disc.

18. *Halloween* franchise. In *Halloween: Resurrection*, Laurie Strode is even hospitalized in a psychiatric hospital because her trauma led her to murder an innocent person she had mistaken for Michael Myers.

19. *Candyman*, 2021.

20. Robin R. Means Coleman, *Horror Noire: Blacks in American Horror Films from the 1890s to Present* (New York: Routledge, 2011), 13.

21. "*Candyman*: The Impact of Black Horror," produced by Ian Cooper, Jordan Peele, and Win Rosenfeld (Universal City, CA: Studio Distribution Services, 2021), BLU-RAY DISC. Tananarive Due, speaker.

22. Cathy Caruth, *Unclaimed Experience: Trauma Narrative, and History* (Baltimore, MD: Johns Hopkins University Press, 1996), 9.

23. "Welcome to Hell: The Making of Tales from the Hood," directed by Thommy Hutson (Los Angeles: Shout Factory, 2017), collector's ed., Blu-ray Disc.

24. Rick Worland, *The Horror Film: An Introduction* (Malden: Blackwell Publishing, 2007), 8.

25. Dori Laub, "Bearing Witness or the Viscissitudes of Listening," in *Testimony: Crises of Witnessing in Literature, Pschoanalysis and History*, ed. Shoshana Feldman and Dori Laub (New York: Routledge, 1992), 58.

26. Worland, *Horror Film*, 9.

27. "*Candyman*: The Impact of Black Horror."

28. Ibid.

29. Kat Stafford, "Black Americans Experiencing Collective Trauma, Grief," *Daily Herald*, April 18, 2021, par. 5, https://www.dailyherald.com/article/20210417/news/304179934.

30. Ibid., par. 6.

31. For the history of Black horror cinema, I recommend *Horror Noire: Blacks in American Horror Films from the 1890s to Present*, by Robin R. Means Coleman and the documentary based on the book, *Horror Noire: A History of Black Horror*, which is available on Shudder.

32. Means Coleman, *Horror Noire*, 6.

33. Ibid., 7.
34. Ibid., 8.
35. Maisha L. Wester, *African American Gothic: Screams from Shadowed Places* (New York: Palgrave Macmillan, 2012), 30.
36. Ibid., 27.
37. *Horror Noire: A History of Black Horror*, directed by Xavier Burgin, Shudder, 2019, https://www.amazon.com/Horror-Noire-History-Black/dp/Bo7NDQLVS7/ref=sr_1_1?crid=20G2LKK8GDLYP&keywords=horror+noire+a+history+of+black+horror&qid=1643836592&s=instant-video&sprefix=horror+noire+%2Cinstant-video%2C271&sr=1-1.
38. "Hard-Core Convert," *Tales from the Hood*, directed by Rusty Cundieff (1995; Los Angeles: Shout Factory, 2017) collector's ed. Blu-ray Disc.
39. "The Making of *Tales from the Hood*."
40. Ibid.
41. Brown, "Not Outside," 289.
42. Isabel Cristina Pinedo, *Recreational Terror: Women and the Pleasure of Horror Film Viewing* (New York: State University of New York Press, 1997), 128.
43. Brigid Cherry, *Horror*, Routledge Film Guidebooks (New York: Routledge, 2009), 181.
44. Worland, *Horror Film*, 97.
45. Means Coleman, *Horror Noire*, 189.
46. *Horror Noire: A History of Black Horror*.
47. Cherry, *Horror*, 170.
48. *Horror Noire: A History of Black Horror*.
49. *Candyman*, directed by Nia DaCosta (2021; Universal City, CA: Studio Distribution Services, 2021), Blu-ray Disc.
50. "Say My Name," produced by Ian Cooper, Jordan Peele, and Win Rosenfeld, *Candyman* (Universal City, CA: Studio Distribution Services, 2021), Blu-ray Disc.
51. Ibid.
52. Ibid.
53. "*Candyman*: The Impact of Black Horror."
54. Ibid.
55. Means Coleman, *Horror Noire*.
56. Robin R. Means Coleman and Mark H. Harris, *The Black Guy Dies First: Black Horror Cinema from Fodder to Oscar* (New York: Gallery/Saga Press, 2023).
57. Dawn Keetley, ed., *Jordan Peele's* Get Out: *Political Horror* (Columbus: Ohio State University Press, 2020).
58. Christopher Sieving, *Pleading the Blood: Bill Gunn's Ganja & Hess* (Bloomington: Indiana University Press, 2022).
59. Harry M. Benshoff, "Blaxploitation Horror Films: Generic Reappropriation or Reinscription?," *Cinema Journal* 39, no. 2 (Winter 2000): 31–50.
60. Novotny Lawrence, "Fear of a Blaxploitation Monster: Blackness as Generic Revision in AIP's *Blacula*," *Film International* 7, no. 3 (June 2009): 14–27, https://doi.org/10.1386/fiin.7.3.14.
61. Harrison M. J. Sherrod, "The Blood of the Thing (Is the Truth of the Thing): Viral Pathogens and Uncanny Ontologies in *Ganja and Hess*," in *Beyond Blaxploitation*, ed. Novotny Lawrence and Gerald R. Butters Jr. (Detroit: Wayne State University Press, 2016), 102–113.

Index

Figures are indicated by an italic *f* following the page number